BOOKS BY MALACHI MARTIN

The Scribal Character of the Dead Sea Scrolls
The Pilgrim (under the pseudonym Michael Serafian)
The Encounter
Three Popes and the Cardinal
Jesus Now
The New Castle
Hostage to the Devil
The Final Conclave
King of Kings (a novel)
The Decline and Fall of the Roman Church
There Is Still Love
Rich Church, Poor Church
Vatican (a novel)
The Jesuits

THE LINDEN PRESS
Simon and Schuster
New York 1987

THE

JESUITS

The Society of Jesus
and the Betrayal
of the
Roman Catholic Church

MALACHI MARTIN

Designed by Helen L. Granger/Levavi & Levavi
Manufactured in the United States of America

10 9 8 7 6 5 4 3 2 1

Library of Congress Cataloging-in-Publication Data
Martin, Malachi.
    The Jesuits.

    Includes index.
    1. Jesuits—History—20th century. 2. Jesuits—History. I. Title.
BX3706.2.M35 1987   271'.53   86-27941
ISBN: 0-671-54505-1

For Our Lady of Fatima

CONTENTS

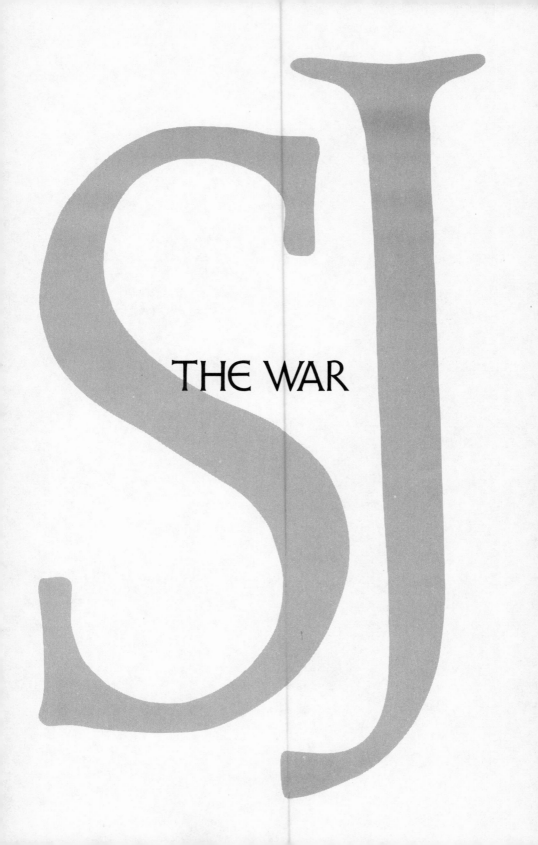

THE WAR

A state of war exists between the papacy and the Religious Order of the Jesuits—the Society of Jesus, to give the Order its official name. That war signals the most lethal change to take place within the ranks of the professional Roman clergy over the last thousand years. And, as with all important events in the Roman Catholic Church, it involves the interests, the lives, and the destinies of ordinary men and women in their millions.

As with so many wars in our time, however, the Jesuits did not *declare* theirs against the papacy. Indeed, though the first open skirmishes began in the 1960s, it took time for the effects of the war—even very profound effects—to become widely apparent. Because the leaders in the war were the Superiors of the Order, it was a simple matter to place men of like mind in charge of the organs of power and authority and communication throughout the organization. With that much accomplished, the vast bulk of Jesuits had precious little to say in the extraordinary decisions that followed.

In time, there were rumblings and warnings of what was happening. "A *coup d'état* is taking place," one Jesuit wrote, as he looked aghast at "the ease with which the dissolution of the established order [in the Society of Jesus] is being achieved."

By then, however, it was already the early seventies, the war had

already been underway for nearly a decade, and such alarms were
of little avail. In fact, given the strict obedience of Jesuits—a fabled
and time-tested element of the old structure that the new leaders
still found useful when dealing with dissenters from their strange
and unfamiliar policies—the rank and file of the Order were given
no alternative but to go along with the changes that, in the words
of another Jesuit, "wrenched the Society of Jesus from under us
and turned [it] into some monstrous entity under the guise of good
goals."

Still in all, one might be inclined to ask, suppose there is a
problem between the Roman papacy and Jesuits; how bad can it
be? Call it a war if you like. But, really, isn't it just another squabble in the Roman Catholic Church? In a world that finds itself
teetering on the perpetual brink of annihilation, and in which half
the population is starving to death while most of the other half is
pinned in the mud by one sort of injustice or another, how important can some dusty theological argument be? About as important,
perhaps, as how many angels can dance on the head of a pin!

The fact is, however, it is not a squabble about niceties, nor
even a theological falling-out between the papacy and Jesuits that
involves only scholars, clerics, and the faithful. As both papacy
and Jesuits know, the effects of their policies go far beyond the
confines of the Roman Catholic Church; even far beyond the
nearly one billion Catholic men and women around the world.
Almost everything that happens in this war bears directly and
immediately on the major dissensions that wrack every nation and
people in the world. It is involved in the very heart of the rivalry
between the United States and the Soviet Union, for example. It
bears right now on the fate in misery or happiness of 350 million
people in Latin America. It affects the deeply changing public
moral code and national consensus of the American people; the
imminent preponderance in human affairs of the People's Republic of China; the fragile persistence of a free Western Europe; the
security of Israel; the still rickety promise of a viable Black Africa
just aborning. All of these things, separate and unconnected as
they may seem, are not only interwoven with one another, but are
and will be profoundly influenced by the tides and outcome of the
global collision between the papacy and the Society of Jesus.

All wars are about power. In the war between the papacy and
the Society, power flows along the lines of two fundamental and
concrete issues. The first is *authority*: Who is in command of the
worldwide Roman Catholic Church? Who lays down the law as to

what Roman Catholics must believe and what sort of morals they must practice?

The second issue is *purpose*: What is the purpose of the Roman Catholic Church in this world?

For the papacy, the answers to both questions are clear and well-known. Authority to command and to teach descends through its hierarchic structure from Pope to bishops to priests to laity. And the sole purpose of the Church in this world is to make sure that each individual has the means of reaching the eternal life of God after death. It is an exclusively otherworldly purpose.

For many Jesuits, on the other hand, the Church's centralized authority, the command structure through which it is exercised, and its purpose are all unacceptable today. The traditional prerogatives of this Pope, John Paul II, or of any Pope, are objectionable.

In place of a hierarchic Church, they are aiming at a church composed of small and autonomous communities of people—"the people of God," as they are collectively known, or "the people's Church"—all loosely associated only by faith, but definitely not by one central and centralizing authority such as the papacy claims to be.

In place of the otherworldly purpose of the traditional Church, the Society of Jesus has substituted the here-and-now struggle for the liberation of one class of men and women in our society today: those millions who suffer from social, economic, and political injustice.

The way of speaking about that class struggle is an important and delicate matter for the Jesuits. The new mission of the Society —for it is nothing less than that—suddenly places them in actual and, in some instances, willing alliance with Marxists in their class struggle. The aim of both is to establish a sociopolitical system affecting the economies of nations by a thorough-going redistribution of earth's resources and goods; and, in the process, to alter the present governmental systems in vogue among nations.

It won't do, however, for the Society to come right out and say as much as a matter of corporate policy. That would be to lose the war before the troops are even thoroughly deployed. To cover the same reality, the expression current among Jesuits and others within the Church who are sympathetic to this new mission is a phrase torn from its original context in a document issued in 1968 by a Conference of Catholic Bishops held in Medellín, Colombia: "to exercise a preferential option for the poor and the oppressed."

None of this is to say that the Society of Jesus at any point became officially Marxist. It did not. Nevertheless, the brute fact is that many Jesuits wish to see a radical change in the democratic capitalism of the West, in favor of a socialism that seems inevitably to come up smelling just like totalitarian Communism. And the fact is as well that there is no lack of individual and influential Jesuits who regularly speak up for the new crusade.

A brief cameo of three Jesuits—a sociopolitical scientist, a devoted guerrilla, and a formidable theologian-teacher—will quickly sketch the wide and all-encompassing arc of the modern Jesuit endeavor to win this war.

The first, Arthur F. McGovern, S.J., is an outstanding and convinced apologist for the new Jesuit anticapitalism. In 1980, he published a book on the subject—*Marxism: An American Christian Perspective*—and he has made his mind clear on many occasions. Essentially, McGovern says that Marxism was and is a social critique, pure and simple. Marx just wanted to get us to think more clearly about the means of production, how people produce; and about the means of distribution, the people who own and control the means of production. In all this, Marxism cannot be written off as "untrue." It was Engels and Lenin who added the disgusting ingredients of "scientific materialism" and atheism. You have only to read the unpublished writings of the young Marx to become aware of "his more humanistic side."

Consequently, McGovern concludes, we must isolate Marx's social critique, which is "true," from those foreign elements. We can accept Marx's concept of class struggle, because there *is* a class struggle. This *does* mean revolution, but "revolution does not clearly mean violence . . . it means we have to have a new kind of society, definitely not democratic capitalism as we know it."

McGovern sees in Jesus, as portrayed in St. Luke's Gospel, a paragon of revolution. St. Luke's is "a social Gospel," he says, quoting Jesus in support of his cause: "I have come to preach the good news to the poor, to set the downtrodden free, to redeem captives."

"See," McGovern adds, "how many times Jesus speaks about poverty; identifies with poor people; criticizes people who lay burdens on the poor." Clearly, therefore, Jesus acknowledged the "class struggle" and endorsed the "revolution."

Consciously or unconsciously, like most modern Jesuits and many Catholic activists, McGovern has effectively laid aside fourteen hundred years of rich Catholic, authentically Christian interpretation of the Bible. He has reinterpreted the Gospel and the salvific mission of the Son of God in an economic sense, a this-worldly sense, a nonsupernatural sense, an un-Catholic sense. All the rest follows.

Because the "new kind of society" cannot be "democratic capitalism as we know it," the United States as the leader and most successful exponent of democratic capitalism comes center stage. Indeed, as early in the war as the 1960s, when Jesuits in the United States established a "Jesuit national leadership project," their Working Paper was explicit about their intention to change the fundamental structure of America from that of a capitalist democracy: "We as Jesuits must recognize that we participate in many sinful structures of American society. Hence we run the risk of sin unless we work to change that."

As one swallow does not make a summer, so one McGovern— or even one "Jesuit national leadership project"—does not make a war. Its stated policy aside, in every practical sense the Society of Jesus is committed corporately to this class struggle. Its message comes today from a thousand different sources among clergymen and theologians living in the countries of democratic capitalism. It is enshrined in a totally new theology—the "Theology of Liberation"—whose handbook was written by a Peruvian Jesuit, Father Gustavo Gutierrez, and whose Hall of Fame includes a remarkable number of prominent Latin American Jesuits such as Jon Sobrino, Juan Luis Segundo, and Fernando Cardenal. Those are not household names heard on the nightly news in the USA. They are, however, men of significant international influence for the Americas and for Europe.

Though the movement has been global since its inception, it was above all in Latin America that the strange alliance between Jesuits and Marxists gathered its first practical momentum. It was there that this new Jesuit mission, entailing as it does nothing less than the transformation of the sociopolitical face of the West, first entangled lives far more profoundly than McGovern and theoreticians like him anticipated. Quickly, scores of Jesuits began to work with the passion and zeal that has always been so typical of them, for the success of the Sandinocommunists in Nicaragua; and, when the Sandinistas took power, those same Jesuits entered crucial posts in the central government, and attracted others to join at various regional levels. In other Central American countries, meanwhile, Jesuits not only participated in guerrilla training of Marxist cadres, but some became guerrilla fighters themselves. Inspired by the idealism they saw in Liberation Theology, and encouraged by the independence inherent in the new idea of the Church as a group of autonomous communities, Jesuits found that all was permitted—even encouraged—as long as it furthered the concept of the new "people's Church."

Such men were the dream and ideal of the true Liberation Theologians. For they were the fighters, the cadres who took Liberation Theology from theory to what they called *praxis*—the implementation of the people's revolution for economic and political liberation. From that *praxis*, the Liberation Theologians insisted, from "below among the people," would come all true theology to replace the old theology once imposed autocratically "from above" by the hierarchy of the Roman Church.

The second name on that arc of the new Jesuit endeavor is James Francis Carney, S.J., a man who was the paragon of *praxis*—perhaps the most thoroughgoing if not the most famous or influential of all modern Jesuit Liberation theologians.

Carney was Chicago born and bred. He trained as a Jesuit in the Chicago Province; at the end of his Jesuit training, he volunteered for work in Central America, and was sent there in 1961. He was so taken by his stint there that he became a Honduran citizen. Over the years, Carney drank in Liberation Theology like rare wine. He became known as a champion of the poor and an acerbic, unrelenting, unmerciful critic of the governments and the established armies, particularly in Honduras. His name and activities were publicly associated with the jungle-based guerrillas. Even when a price was laid on his head by Honduran Army authorities, there was no move by Jesuit Superiors to curb Carney's guerrilla associations. Indeed, Carney was only one of several Jesuits in Honduras, Nicaragua, Guatemala, and Costa Rica who were all pursuing the same course with the blessing of their local and Roman Superiors.

Sitting happily in a ramshackle, dirt-floor *champa* in the Nicaraguan town of Limay where he had sought temporary refuge from the guerrilla warfare in Honduras, the forty-seven-year-old Jesuit priest finished writing his autobiography by candlelight. It was March 6, 1971. By that time, Carney already had behind him ten years of hardship and labor in Central America, and he had some twelve more years to live. "Padre Lupe," as his Indians called him affectionately (it was short for Guadalupe), told the world how he had derived the three mainstays or basic truths of Liberation Theology from the writings of fellow Jesuit Juan Luis Segundo. It makes for bleak, saddening reading.

Segundo's *Grace and the Human Condition* showed Carney that "everything is supernatural in this world." Segundo's *The*

Sacraments Today revealed to Padre Lupe that "humanity is evolving a more correct idea of God." And Segundo's *Evolution and Guilt* taught him that "the revolutionary dialectic has to overcome the sin of conservatism of the Church."

With the saddest of loves, Lupe had already written to his family in the United States to tell them what he was going to do. The letter is reproduced in his autobiography. He had to share the revolution with his beloved Honduran *campesinos* because, he wrote, "I can't stand living with you in your way of life." Capitalism, he said, in whose sins all Americans were immersed, was just as heinous an evil as Communism was supposed to be. Only armed revolution could eradicate "capitalism and transnational imperialism from Central America. . . . To be a Christian is to be a revolutionary.

"We Christian-Marxists will have to fight side-by-side in Central America with the Marxists who do not believe in God, in order to form a new socialist society . . . a pure Central American model."

Drunk on the ignorance-laden idealism of Liberation Theologians, this Jesuit came to the belief that "a Marxist is not dogmatic, but is dialectical. A Christian does not dogmatically condemn anyone, but respects the beliefs of others. A dogmatic anticommunist Christian is not a real Christian; and a dogmatic anti-Christian Marxist is not a real Marxist."

Having invested the hard reality of Marxism as it has been known historically with an airy magic based on no three-dimensional reality, Carney sketched for his family his "pure Central American model."

"Neither communist nor capitalist . . . ," the new socialism will be "a brotherhood and sisterhood of all humanity . . . and equally a classless society. . . ." Theologically speaking, "the universe of man is in dialectical evolution towards the Kingdom of God. . . ."

Even though everyone "respects the belief of others," Carney was able to be far more honest than McGovern in recognizing that ". . . dialectical means conflictive, advancing by a series of struggles between people of contradictory ideologies. . . ." In fact, Carney had become convinced that the very purpose of the dialectic of struggle was to overcome "the sin" of conservatism that is the peculiar sin of the Roman Catholic Church. God's very plan for the evolution of the world and of human society would unfold in conflict and armed revolution. The change thus brought about would be complete; it would be at one and the same time "a cultural-spiritual" change, and an "economic-social-political change" as well.

Carney ended his autobiography with a plea to all Christians: ". . . get rid of any unfair and un-Christian prejudices you have against armed revolution, socialism, Marxism, and communism. . . . There is no third way between being a Christian and being a revolutionary. . . ."

This was the ultimate plea for *praxis*.

Later that spring of 1971, with the agreement of his Superiors, Carney illegally crossed the border back into Honduras to share the hit-and-run life of a guerrilla commando. It was the beginning of twelve years of gun-toting *praxis* for the "dialectical conflict" he treasured as the key to the future of Catholicism.

In agreement with his Provincial Superior, Father Jerez, who was under some pressure by then from Rome and the Vatican, Father Carney finally resigned from the Jesuits. The understanding he had with Jerez and his Superiors was that he could rejoin the Society once the struggle was over. The Society, after all, was merely a convenience. In a world where everything was already supernatural, as Padre Lupe wrote that it was for him, there was no room for any hard-and-fast rules; no room for an infallibly authoritative Roman Church. There was no need for any Church to sanctify anything because all was supernatural and therefore holy already. The Church was just another part of humanity, on a par with humanity in relation to God, learning as humanity learns, moving with humanity toward the Utopia on earth.

"It pains me," Carney wrote, "but I want to be honest and not hurt the Jesuits by joining the guerrillas as a disobedient fugitive from the Society, forcing them to expel me." As others who came after him have shown, Carney needn't have worried about disobedience or expulsion. Still, if Father Lupe had not preserved the rudiments of his Roman Catholic faith, he had at least preserved his candor, and his ability to make a clear choice.

In September 1983, Carney's ninety-man commando unit was wiped out in a battle with the Honduran troops of his long-time enemy, General Gustavo Alvarez Martinez, whom he had often denounced in public. A few of his men who survived were captured and thrown into a rectangular pit in the jungle behind the Honduran military camp of *Nueva Palestina*. Was Carney one of those men? No one has ever been able to find out. Is he dead? In all likelihood. From exhaustion? At least from exhaustion. Was he interrogated? Probably. Tortured? Probably. Was he starved? Probably. Is he still alive and a prisoner somewhere in the jungle? That does not seem possible; but no definite news has ever been revealed.

That's the kind of war this is. It's not even remotely about the number of angels who can dance on the head of a pin. It's a war in which blood is spilled regularly and in great quantities. Priests like Carney are not rare exceptions. Surely, they don't all write testaments of their conversion to revolutionary violence for the world to read; and not all go so far as to live the life of commando fighters. But in the many and varied roles they do play in the world's purely political arena, men such as Father Carney, S.J., each and every one of them, are essential to the success of the Jesuits in their war against the papacy.

The fact of life for Jesuits now is that our bipolar world spins inexorably around Soviet Marxist-Leninism and Western-style capitalism. The only contest that seems to matter for the Society of Jesus in this last quarter of the twentieth century is the one between those two spheres of influence. And the fact is that though the Society itself is not officially Marxist, individual Jesuits who were and are self-proclaimed Marxists—for Padre Lupe was hardly alone even in that—are not for that reason expelled from the Society or censured or silenced. Rather, the greatest pains are taken to protect them from attack. So blatant has this element become that not long ago, when Pope John Paul II met an Indian Jesuit who, as he found, was not a Marxist, he exclaimed in surprise, "So you're not all Marxists!"

The war between the papacy and the Jesuits appears, then, to be political in nature. And in one sense it is. But to assume, as many Jesuits of the new mission do, that their war against the papacy begins and ends with the Marxist-capitalist contest for power and authority and domination in the world, would be to mistake the symptoms of rot in the Society for the more basic condition that allows those symptoms to progress and multiply. For while the war they have chosen to fight takes place on the plane of geopolitics, it is also and more fundamentally a war over the question of the very existence of Spirit as the basic dimension of the world of men and women. It is about the supernatural as the element that makes each of us human and that defines our existence and our world.

At this level, the new Jesuit concepts concerning authority in the Church, and the Church's purpose in the world, represent a turnabout of the profoundest nature. For the Society of Jesus, the ultimate authority for belief and morality is no longer in the

Roman Catholic Church with its papacy and its worldwide hierarchy, but in the "people of God." The results of that exchange are
that, to date, there is not one major dogma or one capital moral
law of Roman Catholicism that has not been both challenged and
denied by individual Jesuits, beginning with Jesuits of the highest
rank and the most honored stature.

They have been imitated and joined by myriad groups, both
Catholic and non-Catholic, with most diverse reasons for championing this new church, the "people of God," over the Roman
Catholic hierarchic Church. But it is they, the Jesuits, who blazed
the trail, and who have set the highest and the most consistent
examples in this changed attitude about the Roman Pontiff and
Rome's defined dogmas.

The theologian-teacher in this war—and the third name on that
arc of the new Jesuit endeavor—is the man accepted and celebrated as the greatest Jesuit theologian in one hundred years, Karl
Rahner, S.J. Rahner spent a lifetime of effort—carefully at first,
but more and more stridently as time went on—to change Catholic belief. While Rahner did not work in lonely fields, his stature,
his uncaring boldness, and his success mark him as the leader in
what can be aptly described as the wolf-pack of Catholic theologians who, since 1965, have lacerated and shredded not merely the
flanks but the very substance of Catholicism.

Rahner was as different from his fellow Jesuit James Carney as
cold is from heat. The contrast between the two men is the best
illustration of the old saying that an idea may light a blazing in-
ferno in the hearts of some men, but it explodes in the brains of
others. While Carney was an impulsive and passionate doer, Rahner was the musing, reflective, deadpan intellectual. Where Carney could write illogically but emotionally to justify his actions
in the eyes of his family, and then count on their love alone to
accept him as he was, Rahner wrote and lectured and conversed
with subtle logic and passionless mind to unlimber the dearest
held tenets of faith in the minds of his readers and listeners.

Carney railed at injustice, revolted against oppression, cried out
painfully over human misery. His ammunition and weapons were
not only bullets and guns, but his profound compassion, his wrath
at injustice, and his congenital refusal to make the slightest compromise. It was his heart in overwhelming agony that guided his
judgment.

Rahner, on the other hand, trained the heavy artillery of his
logic and his vast reputation as a theologian on the sacrosanct

authority of Popes. He chose the long-accepted, immemorial formulas of belief as his targets. He had other weapons than Carney did at his disposal: the keenest of minds, a truly encyclopedic knowledge, an ever-ready and acerbic humor, and an indomitable arrogance of intellect. "I will not suffer injustice," was Carney's cry. "I will not serve," was Rahner's.

At a critical and painful moment in the modern history of the papacy, Rahner refused point-blank to defend either Catholic teaching on contraception or the Pontiff who asked Jesuits as "Pope's Men" to help him in his desperation. It was the same with virtually all the other dogmas and rules of the Catholic Church which Rahner had sworn to uphold.

Yet his voice seemed so authentic that he was taken by many to be more authoritative than three successive Popes when it came to interpreting the moral teaching of the Catholic Church. Rahner himself went to great pains to fulfill this role of a modern prophet. As he traveled in Europe and the Americas dressed in his correct business suits, he was untiring in his biting and sarcastic criticism of the papacy and Roman authority.

In *Unity of the Churches: An Actual Possibility*, the last book he wrote before his death in 1984, Rahner gave the most telling and overt presentation ever made of the accepted new Jesuit attitude about the papacy and the defined dogmas of his Church. Working with a Jesuit colleague and coauthor, Heinrich Fries, and with the imprimatur of his Jesuit Superiors, Rahner made a sweeping and outrageously anti-Roman proposal. To achieve Christian unity, he said, it was necessary to drop all insistence on papal infallibility as a dogma, and to drop insistence as well on all other doctrines about the Roman Pontiff and Roman Catholicism that had been defined and proposed by Popes since the fourth century.

In effect, Rahner was proposing that the Catholic Church officially take the entire body of rules concerning faith and morals as developed and taught by his Church for sixteen centuries, and unhinge them from everyday life. Marriage, homosexuality, business ethics, human liberty, piety, every sphere of human existence, were all to be set adrift on the ever-changing tides of redefinition. But the dogmas of the Church would be the prime casualties. For what the Church has defined as basic and obligatory for Catholic belief would, in Rahner's plan, become optional. The integrity of Christ's person; the meaning and value of the Seven Sacraments; the existence of Heaven and Hell; the divine character of the authority of bishops; the truth of the Bible; the primacy and infallibility of the Pope; the character of priesthood; the Immaculate Conception and the Assumption of Mary, Christ's mother—all would be up for ecumenical grabs.

Over and above all of that, however, stood Rahner's principal targets, the roadblocks that stood in the way of everything else: the papal authority he wished dismantled and the hierarchic Roman Catholic Church he wished to see reduced to one more idiosyncratic expression of Christ's message. In other words, the practical authority and the spiritual purpose of the Church —always the real issues in the war between papacy and Jesuits—would be rejected and replaced by whatever authority and materialistic mission might be in vogue.

On the merely personal level, one must reasonably surmise a total failure of Catholic faith in Rahner. But it is less the condition of Rahner's soul that is at stake, than the practical influence he and many other like-minded theologians have on life as it is lived in our world.

To say that Rahner—and Fries as a secondary coauthor—was only expressing the antipapal sentiment that was very current among Catholic theologians by 1984 is not to tell the half of the ruin wreaked by him. Rahner, occupied in teaching theology at a prestigious Jesuit university for the major portion of his life, became over the years an icon of theological wisdom and good judgment for literally thousands who, in their turn, are now priests, professors, and writers with command and influence and renown of their own.

Admittedly, such work seems to many to take place in ivory towers. But such men as Karl Rahner have helped mightily to mold the thinking and the mores of priests and bishops who are now engaged at every level of worldly matters in every part of the globe. And once they become convinced, even on a purely personal plane, that the Rahners in the Church are right and that the papacy is wrong, there is no chance at all that the conflict can remain theoretical. Instead, it reaches into the deepest areas of thought and belief and feelings of millions who are dragged by the heart—and by the direct or indirect influence of theologians like Rahner— into a world where the nature, the meaning, and the most basic purpose of their lives as Christians are redefined in a purely rational and materialistic setting.

Without such a giant as Karl Rahner, one doubts if Liberation Theology would do much more than creak and teeter and collapse; or that a Francis Carney would have been so uncritical of the

writings of Juan Luis Segundo. Nevertheless, it must be said that
Rahner was not an inventor; nor were the men of his generation
who were his tintypes. Rahner did not himself initiate the huge
theological turnabout in the Society of Jesus or in the Roman
Church. His importance was not as innovator, but as faithful and
effective evangelist for a pernicious and destructive influence that
had already been spreading covertly within the Society of Jesus for
decades before he came on the scene. Whether lecturing in Europe
or ferrying over to the Americas, clad in his acquired prestige,
unassailable in his authoritativeness, presenting always the un-
beautiful face of the materialist, quick in any bout of infighting,
and bowing to no one, Rahner was the apt point man for Catholic
self-cannibalism. He taught several generations how to consume
their own faith with logic, skepticism, and disobedience.

So single-minded was his devotion to the antipapal and anti-
Catholic point of view that he became its incarnation, as one
might say. And yet so effective was he in maintaining his own
theological stature within the Society of Jesus that he gave that
point of view a new respectability, both inside and outside the
Society and the Church. No Jesuit Superior, either in his own
country or in Rome, ever curbed him. Having been flesh-and-blood
proof of the strange corruption that had set into the Society, Rahner died as he had lived, in an aura of honor among his colleagues
and Superiors.

For all their differences, the three men sketched here—the sociopolitical scientist, the devoted guerrilla, and the theologian-
teacher—typify inclusively the aberration of the Society.

Certainly, at this moment in time, the Society of Jesus is not
alone in the war against the papacy. It has been imitated and joined
by many groups—Catholic and non-Catholic, religious and secular
—each with its own reasons for championing the idea that a new
church, the "people of God," has replaced the old, hierarchic
Roman Catholic Church. But it was the Jesuits who blazed that
trail; it is they who have set the highest and most consistent examples of this changed attitude about the Roman Pontiff and
Rome's defined dogmas; and it is they who continue to labor at
the farthest reaches of what one can only call divine politics.

And so it was that the present Father General of the Society of
Jesus, Piet-Hans Kolvenbach, was able to face the Jesuits who
elected him as head of the Order in 1983—the year James Francis
Carney was gobbled up in a jungle battle; the year before Karl
Rahner went back to God—and promise with solemn confidence

that, among other things, his job would be to ensure their chosen Jesuit quest for justice, and not to be distracted by the "groaning complaints of popes."

*   *   *

When you speak about the Society of Jesus today being at war with the papacy, and even before you realize what a strange and distressing turnaround that is for a body of men whose prime claim to fame has been their achievements and reputation as "Pope's Men," you must not think that this Religious Order of Jesuits is just one more human organization. So many such organizations have their heyday, then decline, ossify, and eventually disappear.

The Society of Jesus was started in 1540 by an obscure Basque named Iñigo de Loyola, better known as Ignatius of Loyola. You cannot place Iñigo's Jesuits on a par with any other organization for the simple reason that no single organization we know of has yet rivaled the Jesuits in the immeasurable services they have rendered to the human family—over and above what they did on behalf of the papacy and the papacy's Roman Catholic Church.

Iñigo was a rare genius. If Leonardo Da Vinci, Iñigo's contemporary, had designed a machine right down to its nuts and bolts that had withstood every test of time and changing circumstance over a period of 425 years—and if only a dismantling of his original design had provoked that machine's collapse—it would not be a greater marvel than the Society Iñigo designed. For, as he built it —the mold of its Jesuitism, its functional structure, its devotion to the papacy, its character and goals—the Society has withstood every test of time and circumstance except one: the perversion of the rule, role, and spirit he assigned it. Otherwise, its quite extraordinary durability has been proven.

Not even Iñigo could have foreseen the quasi-miracle of his Society's organization, its meteoric and brilliant success, and its universal influence on the world of man, when he founded it. For the next 425 years the tens of thousands who joined Iñigo's Company established a record that in its own category stands unmatched in past or present history—a record both for services to the Roman Church and to human society at large.

Looking backward, a twentieth-century genius-like zealot, Lenin, misguided but admiring, swore at the end of his life that if he had had twelve men like one of those early Jesuits, his Communism would have swept the world.

Though few in number, the basic principles that Iñigo had set forth for his Company were powerful catalysts. Once his men harnessed their energies within his organization to the worldwide work of the Roman Church, they produced a unique phenomenon of human history. "Never," wrote the eighteenth-century German theorist Novalis, "never before in the course of the world's history had such a Society appeared. The old Roman Senate itself did not lay schemes for world domination with greater certainty of success. Never had the carrying out of a greater idea been considered with greater understanding. For all time, this Society will be an example to every society which feels an organic longing for infinite extension and eternal duration. . . ."

"The more universal your work," Iñigo had said, "the more divine it becomes." Within thirty years of his founding the Order, his Jesuits were working in every continent and at practically every form of apostolate and educational field. Within one hundred years, the Jesuits were a force to be reckoned with in practically any walk of life along which men seek and sometimes secure power and glory.

There was no continent Jesuits did not reach; no known language they did not speak and study, or, in scores of cases, develop; no culture they did not penetrate; no branch of learning and science they did not explore; no work in humanism, in the arts, in popular education they did not undertake and do better than anyone else; no form of death by violence they did not undergo— Jesuits were hanged, drawn, and quartered in London; disemboweled in Ethiopia; eaten alive by Iroquois Indians in Canada; poisoned in Germany; flayed to death in the Middle East; crucified in Thailand; starved to death in South America; beheaded in Japan; drowned in Madagascar; bestialized in the Soviet Union. In that first four hundred years, they gave the Church 38 canonized saints, 134 holy men already declared "Blessed" by the Roman Church, 36 already declared "Venerable," and 115 considered to have been "Servants of God."[1] Of these, 243 were martyrs; that is, they were put to death for their beliefs.

They lived among and adapted to Chinese mandarins, North American Indians, the brilliant royal courts of Europe, the Hindu Brahmans of India, the "hedgerow" schools of penal Ireland, the slave ships of the Ottomans, the Imams and Ulema of Islam, the decorum and learning of Oxford dons, and the multiform primitive societies of sub-Saharan Africa.

And, in the long catalog of insults and calumnies men have devised in order to revile their enemies, no name was bad enough to call the Jesuits because of that fearsome fixation they had from their first beginnings for another of Iñigo's principles: to be

"Pope's Men"; *the* Pope's men. Iñigo de Loyola, Thomas Carlyle wrote, was "the poison fountain from which all the rivers of bitterness that now submerged the world have flowed."

Such insults have been enshrined in the very languages of men. *Webster's Third New International Dictionary*, having given the basic meaning of *Jesuit* as a member of the Order, then supplies the negative meanings: "one given to intrigue or equivocation; a crafty person"; terms that are amplified by Dornseif's Dictionary into "two-faced, false, insidious, dissembling, perfidious . . . insincere, dishonorable, dishonest, untruthful." A French proverb states that "Whenever two Jesuits come together, the Devil always makes three." A Spanish proverb admonished people not "to trust a monk with your wife or a Jesuit with your money."

The perennial enemies of the papacy never could forgive Iñigo and his Jesuits as long as they were on the Pope's mission, fulfilling that sacred oath of obedience even unto disgrace and death. It was all according to Iñigo's express wish. "Let us hope," he once wrote, "that the Order may never be left untroubled by the hostility of the world for very long."

In truth, his wish was fulfilled, for his Jesuits *were* Pope's Men. Their first main targets: the new Protestant churches pullulating throughout Europe. Precisely, the vital issue at stake between the Catholic Church and the leaders of the Protestant revolt—Luther, Calvin, Henry VIII of England—was the authority of the Roman Pontiff and the preeminent primacy of his Roman Catholic Church.

The Jesuits carried the battle right into the territories of these papal enemies. They waged public controversies with kings, they debated in Protestant universities, they preached at crossroads and in marketplaces. They addressed municipal councils, they instructed Church Councils. They infiltrated hostile territories in disguise, and moved around underground. They were everywhere, showering their contemporaries with brilliance, with wit, with acerbity, with learning, with piety. Their constant theme: "The Bishop of Rome is successor to Peter the Apostle upon whom Christ founded his Church. . . . That Church is a hierarchy of bishops in communion with that Bishop in Rome. . . . Any other churchly institution is rank heresy, the child of Satan. . . ."

Everyone was aware of the Jesuits, in other words; and everyone knew the Jesuits were the single-minded champions of that authority and primacy.

While the Jesuit onslaught against the enemies of Rome was

mighty, their pervasive influence on Roman Catholicism itself has never been equalled. They had a monopoly in the education of Europe for over two hundred years, and numbered the famous and infamous in their worldwide alumni—Voltaire, Luis Buñuel, Fidel Castro, and Alfred Hitchcock included. Alone, they literally re-molded the teaching of Roman Catholic theology and philosophy so that it became clear and accessible once again, even to the new mentality of the dawning and turbulent age. They provided novel means for the practice of popular piety. They advanced the study of asceticism and mysticism and missiology. They provided fresh models for seminary training of priests. They spawned, by example and by the inspiration of their own Religious Rule, a whole new family of Religious Orders. They were the first body of Catholic Scholars who became preeminent in secular sciences—mathematics, physics, astronomy, archeology, linguistics, biology, chemistry, zoology, paleography, ethnography, genetics. The list of inventions and scientific discoveries by Jesuits had filled endless numbers of volumes in the most diverse fields—mechanical engineering, hydraulic power, airflight, oceanography, hypnosis, crystals, comparative linguistics, atomic theory, internal medicine, sunspots, hearing aids, alphabets for the deaf and dumb, cartography. The list from which these random samples are taken numbs the mind by its all-inclusive variety. Their manuals, textbooks, treatises, and studies were authoritative in every branch of Catholic and secular learning.

They were giants, but with one purpose: the defense and propagation of papal authority and papal teaching.

Nor were their amazing energies and talents confined to science. They made every field of art theirs as well. By 1773, they had 350 theaters in Europe, and Jesuit theatricals laid the first foundation for modern ballet. They founded the first theater on the North American continent—actually in Quebec—in 1640. They taught France how to make porcelain. They brought back to Europe the first acquaintance Western men got of Indian and Chinese culture. They translated the Sanskrit Vedas. Even the *chinoiseries* of the rococo period were derived from Jesuit Chinese publications. The umbrella, vanilla, rhubarb, camelia, and quinine were Jesuit innovations in Europe.

The exploits of Jesuits as Far Eastern explorers and missioners outdid anything even dreamed of by their contemporaries, and constitute a heroic tale that tastes of the almost magical. The names of Jesuits will be forever linked with places that for most of us are the stuff of fantasy—Kambaluc, Cathay, Sarkand, Shrinagar,

Tcho Lagram, Tcho Mapang, Manasarovar, Tashi-Ihumpo, Koko Nor, and the long-leaping name Chomolongmo (known to us as Mount Everest).

Less than one hundred years after the founding of the Society, Jesuits became the first Europeans to penetrate Tibet and then proceed on to China. Jesuit Father Matteo Ricci was the first person to prove that Marco Polo's Cathay was identical with China and not a different country. In 1626, Father Antonio Andrade and Brother Manuel Marquis opened the first Catholic Church in Tibet on the banks of the Sutlej River in the Kingdom of Guge at Tsaparang. Brother Benito de Goes lies buried at the northwest terminus of the Great Wall of China. The grave of Brother Manuel Marquis is 25,447/7,756 Kamet, capstone of the Zaskar Range overlooking the Mana pass in western Tibet where the good Brother died in 1647 after a long imprisonment at the frontier post.

Other Jesuits—Austrians and Belgians—were the first Europeans to reach Lhasa on October 8, 1661, and witnessed the construction of the Potala Palace for Dalai Lama Chenresik. Father Grueber, an Austrian, was the first to determine Lhasa's position accurately at 29 degrees 06 minutes north latitude. He and his companions were succeeded by a line of distinguished Jesuit Tibetologists who produced dictionaries, language studies, maps, geological studies, and theological treatises. Their graves, like those of Benito de Goes and Manuel Marquis, dot an area that was as remote and forbidding to their contemporaries as the other side of the moon still remains for us.

These men and their Religious colleagues elsewhere were not merely "the lonely and the brave" celebrated in a stage drama of the 1940s. They were not befuddled in mind between the dimensions of Religious Poverty and economic poverty as so many Jesuits have become in the final decades of this century. They were not aiming at some foggy, this-worldly goal such as the "integral liberation of the human individual." They were giants who, proportionately speaking, rivaled the later exploits of Scott and Perry at the Poles, Hilary on Mount Everest, and the first astronauts in space and on the moon. But more than that, they were Jesuit missionaries obedient to the voice of the Roman Pontiff, living and working and dying in fidelity to him, because he represented Peter the Apostle who represented the Christ they believed was Savior.

At the height of their efforts, two hundred years after their founding, the Jesuits had a formative and decisive hand in the education and science of practically every country in Europe and

Latin America. They had a part to play in every political alliance in Europe—an influential post with every government, an advisory capacity with every great man and each powerful woman. A Jesuit was the first Westerner to frequent the court of the Great Mogul. Another was the first to be declared an official Mandarin at the Beijing Emperor's palace. Oliver Cromwell, Philip II of Spain, Louis XIV of France, Catherine the Great, Cardinal Richelieu, Queen Cristina of Sweden, Mary Queen of Scots, Napoleon, Washington, Garibaldi, Mussolini, Chiang-Kai-Shek—the list of history's greats frequented by Jesuits stretches on for pages. They drafted treaties, negotiated peace pacts, mediated between warring armies, arranged royal marriages, went on hazardous rescue missions, lived where they were not welcome as underground agents of the Holy See. They passed as pig farmers in Ireland, *bazaaris* in Persia, businessmen in Prussia, clowns in England, merchant seamen in Indonesia, beggars in Calcutta, swamis in Bombay. There was nothing anywhere they would not undertake, as they said, "for the greater Glory of God," under obedience to the Roman Pope. They were in every European, African, Asian, and American country where the slightest burgeoning of Catholicism was possible. All their influence was wielded in pursuit of the papal will. To be a Jesuit was to be a papist in the strict sense of that once opprobrious term.

The worldwide power of the Jesuits became so great that the ordinary people of Rome invented a new title for the Jesuit Father General. "The Black Pope," they called him, comparing his global power and influence with that of the Pope himself; and distinguishing between the two only on the basis of the Pontiff's all-white robes as against the simple black cassock of the ordinary priest that Iñigo's successors wore in imitation of his example. That popular nickname was an exaggeration, of course. But the Romans were near enough to the center of things to know who wielded an impressive part of the real power residing on Vatican Hill.

As Iñigo had intended, that power of "the Black Pope" and his Company was harnessed to papal will, even unto the death of the Order itself. In 1773, when Pope Clement XIV decided—correctly or incorrectly—that a stark choice had to be made between the extinction of the papacy or the death of the Jesuit Order, he alone and by his own personal decision abolished the Society of Jesus. By an officially published document, he disbanded the 23,000 Jesuits altogether, and he put their Father General and his advisers into papal dungeons, even as he imposed exile and slow death on thousands of Jesuits who were stranded without help or support in dangerous parts of the world.

Pope Clement did not explain his decision to the Jesuits or anyone else. "The reasons [for this decision] We keep locked up in Our Own heart," he wrote. Nevertheless, the Jesuits obeyed, collaborating obediently in the death of their Order.

Forty-one years later, in 1814, Pope Pius VII decided the papacy needed the Company, so he resurrected them. The revivified Jesuits started off again, with renewed zeal for the papal will, and made a huge commitment of men and labor to ensure that the First Vatican Council in 1860 would decree that the infallible authority of the Pope was an article of faith and a divinely revealed dogma.

That effort was so trenchant and successful, and so odious to many, that it won for the postsuppression Jesuits a new epithet; they were "Ultra-Montanes"—people who backed that hateful Bishop who lived "beyond the mountains" (the Alps) down in Rome. The contempt in that abusive name is a clear pointer to what the Jesuits championed as vigorously as they always had: the old Roman Catholic belief that by divine decree the man who in himself carried all the authority of Christ in the Church was to be identified by a physical link with one geographical location on the face of this earth—the city of Rome. That man would always be the legal Bishop of Rome. And personal Vicar of Christ.

The fresh enemies of that belief lived mainly in France, Belgium, Holland, Germany, Austria, Switzerland, and England. They were bishops, priests, theologians, and philosophers. Speaking from their side of the Alps, they called themselves "Cis-Montanes" (people on "this side of the mountains," the northern side), and opposed the authority and primacy of the Roman Bishop.

That Roman Catholicism centered on the Roman Pope flourished and maintained itself in western Europe until the last quarter of the twentieth century was mainly due to these "Pope's men" —to their zeal, their devotion to that papal mission, their learning, and the evolution they instigated in the Roman Catholic mind. For into any area they touched, the Jesuits introduced a note of reason, of rational discourse, and they leavened it with a shining, muscular faith.

Simply put, they took the mentality of Catholics in the sixteenth century by storm. That mentality had all its moorings in a prescientific, prenaturalistic sphere. Over a space of four hundred years, with their own entombment in between, the Jesuits changed all that. By their educational methods, their researches, and their

intellectual intrepidity, they made it possible for Roman Catholics
to hold their own, as believing and faithful men and women, in
the ocean of new ideas and fresh technology that began in the
1770s and has never stopped since.

Periodically, in their more than four-hundred-year existence,
the Jesuits were expelled and banned from various countries—
France, Germany, Austria, England, Belgium, Mexico, Sweden,
Switzerland. So synonymous had the name of Jesuit become with
papal authority, that their expulsion was always a clear signal that
the government of that country was determined to eliminate the
authority and jurisdiction of the Roman Pope. And when brute
force was used against them, they went underground or packed
their bags and departed, to await the day they could return. They
always returned. Even when matters did not go as far as downright
expulsion, no one had any illusion as to what they represented—
the papacy—and often the Jesuit function for the papacy was
twisted by their enemies. In early nineteenth-century America,
Protestant opposition and hatred of Jesuits was pithily expressed:
"They [the Jesuits] will bring Rome to rule the Union."

That identification with and devotion to the papacy had been
the will and intent of Ignatius, their founder; and it was the condition on which the papacy had consented to bring the Society of
Jesus into existence. In life and death, the Jesuits indeed wrote
history as "Pope's Men"—whether it was Jesuit Father Peter
Claver wearing out his existence among South American slaves;
or Father Matteo Ricci becoming a genuine Mandarin at the Imperial Court of Beijing; or Father Peter Canisius, the Hammer of
the Heretics, reclaiming whole provinces and cities from Protestantism by his tireless, incessant traveling, preaching, and writing;
or Father Walter Ciszek languishing in the Soviet Gulag for seventeen years; or Father Jacquineau mediating between warring Japanese and Chinese over Hong Kong; or Father Augustin Bea
traveling clandestinely throughout the length and breadth of the
Soviet Union in Stalin's day to get an accurate picture of conditions for the Holy See; or Father Tacchi Venturi ferrying negotiations between Dictator Benito Mussolini and Pope Pius XII.

No matter who or where they were or what they did, inherent
in the mind of each Jesuit was that holy structure of Christ's
Church, anchored by Jesus on his personal Vicar, the Pope, and
held together by the hierarchy of bishops and priests, religious and
lay people in union with that personal Vicar of Christ. And no
matter the year or the century in which he worked, each Jesuit
knew that the Catholic Church he had vowed to serve under the

Pope was the same Church that had existed in the sixth century under Gregory the Great, in the eleventh century under Innocent IX, and in 1540 under Paul III.

Indeed, what held their will to their work over great distances of space and time was the fabled Jesuit attachment of obedience, consecrated by their special vow: that all and every work they undertook would be under papal obedience.

For the enemies of the Jesuits, meanwhile, it was that very service of and obedience to the papacy that was the Jesuit abomination. Their critics never ceased accusing the Jesuits of having distorted humanist philosophy. But French writer F. R. de Chateaubriand, himself no friend of the Society, was quite accurate in his judgment when he said that "the slight injury which philosophy thinks it has suffered from the Jesuits" is not worth remembering in view of "the immeasurable services which the Jesuits have rendered to human society."

The mind and the outlook evolved by the Jesuits reached its highest flowering in the first half of the twentieth century. As a result of their efforts, there took place a pseudo-Renaissance of social and cultural Catholicism, making it possible for Catholics to be scientists, technologists, psychologists, sociologists, political scientists, leaders, artists, scholars, holding their own even in the newest branches of knowledge, yet reconciling all of it with their rock-solid belief. Testimony to all of this lies in many things—in the poetry and literature of a G. K. Chesterton and a Paul Claudel; in the militant sociology of French, German, Belgian, and Italian Catholics between the two world wars; in the flowering missiology that transformed the mission fields of Asia and Africa; in the redoubtable school of apologetics in Europe and the United States; in the standardization of popular devotions and ecclesial regulation; in the vibrant Catholicism of the United States; and not least in the grudging but finally conceded respect, both from anti-Catholic and non-Catholic, that was evident for Catholicism in the world of the 1950s.

During the time of its greatest flowering, in the first half of the twentieth century, Jesuit numbers reached their apogee—about 36,038—of whom at least one-fifth were missionaries. Jesuit influence on papal policy was never before (or since) greater; and Jesuit prestige among Catholics and non-Catholics was never higher.

Yet, already some inner rot was corroding both Jesuits and the Catholic ecclesial body. Some hidden cancer planted decades before within these bodies had gone neutral, but not benign.

Occasional symptoms betrayed its presence—sometime revolts by Jesuit scholars on an individual basis; now and again, flagrant abuses in liturgy by individual groups; rarely but regularly, the confusion between spiritual activity and political advantage. But nothing that happened foretold the violent change that awaited the Church, the papacy, and the Jesuits in the 1960s.

In full view of that unparalleled achievement, it becomes fascinating to examine what sort of character the Society of Jesus developed during its centuries-long effort, and why or how in the twentieth century it changed from its original purpose. Not that this is the first time that one or another group in the Church has broken ranks and declared war on the papacy. But it is the first time that the Society of Jesus has turned on the papacy with the clear intent to undo the papacy's prerogatives, to dilute the hierarchic government of the Catholic Church, and to create a novel Church structure; and it is the first time that the Society of Jesus both corporately and in its individual members has undertaken a sociopolitical mission.

Iñigo founded his "Company of Jesus," as he originally called it, for one purpose: to be defender of the Church and the papacy. The Pope who brought the Order into official existence in the sixteenth century made that purpose the mission of the Society and the reason for its existence. As an institution, it has always been bound to the papacy. Its Professed members have always been bound to the Pope by a sacred oath of absolute obedience. For 425 years, they stood at the papacy's side, fought its battles, taught its doctrines, suffered its defeats, defended its positions, shared its power, were attacked by its enemies, and constantly promoted its interests all over the globe. They were regarded by many as they regarded themselves, as "Pope's Men"; and the many extraordinary privileges granted by Popes over the centuries were as badges of the trust the papacy placed in the Society.

Never, it can be said, did the Society of Jesus as a body veer from that mission until 1965. In that year, the Second Vatican Council ended the last of its four sessions; and Pedro de Arrupe y Gondra was elected to be the 27th Father General of the Jesuits. Under Arrupe's leadership, and in the heady expectation of change sparked by the Council itself, the new outlook—antipapal and sociopolitical in nature—that had been flourishing in a covert fashion for over a century was espoused by the Society as a corporate body.

The rapid and complete turnabout of the Society in its mission and in its reason for being was no accident or happenstance. It was a deliberate act, for which Arrupe as Father General provided inspiring, enthusiastic, and wily leadership.

Perceptions, however, especially in matters of great religious institutions, do not change easily or quickly. The reputation earned by the Society over hundreds of years was the best camouflage behind which to build the new and very different Society that has come into existence over the past twenty years. In effect, the past and glorious history of the Society has seemed to render present deeds invisible, and to make it possible for the new Jesuit leadership to present its new outlook to the world as the latest and finest expression of Ignatian spirituality and loyalty.

For the general mass of Catholics, clerical and lay alike, it was unthinkable that the Jesuits, of all people, would propagate a new idea of the Church; or that they would wage war with even one Pope, let alone three, by denigrating him, deceiving him, disobeying him, waiting for each to die in turn in the hope that the next Pope would leave them with a free hand.

Inevitably, the Jesuit war against the papacy has intensified during the pontificate of Karol Wojtyla as John Paul II. This charismatic, stubborn-minded man came to the papacy with his vivid experience of Marxists in Poland. Everything about him—but especially his aims, his policy, and his strategy as Pope—spoke of a sharp departure from everything that had been in vogue in Rome since the late 1950s.

From the moment of his election, it was clear that John Paul was opposed by many in the Vatican bureaucracy he inherited. What was less clear, even to seasoned Vatican observers, was that he was also deeply opposed, and his authority was to be violently challenged as a matter of policy, by the Society of Jesus.

Nothing John Paul has tried since he came to the Chair of Peter in 1978—and he has tried everything from persuasion to confrontation to direct intervention—has dissipated or even softened the resolute Jesuit stance against him. Thus far, the Jesuits have eluded the Pontiff's efforts to corral them; and their example is still being followed on an ever-wider scale.

But as the Society is learning, this Polish Pope is not another Paul VI. He refuses to throw up his hands in utter despair. On the contrary, he has just opened a new campaign in the war, this time on a battlefield of his own choosing.

As John Paul is learning, the Jesuits will be as clever and as witted in their answer to each new papal offensive as they have always been in everything they have done. In fact, it was the Jesuits, not the papacy, who fired the first salvo in the latest direct confrontation, in an effort to take the initiative away from the papacy and the Roman hierarchy.

Whatever the outcome of this latest campaign, and of others that are sure to follow, there can be no doubt that during our lifetime what the papacy stands for has become unacceptable to the Jesuits; and that what the Society of Jesus has lately come to stand for is inimical and therefore unacceptable to the papacy.

Yet, despite the fact that each now stands at the opposite pole from the other, there still' remain powerful similarities between the papacy and the Society—similarities that will mean the war between them will be lethal at a level and to a degree that few wars are.

The first and most powerful similarity is the ineradicable sense of divine mission that is the driving instinct in both papacy and Jesuits. Each of them claims to be acting solely for the worldwide commonweal of God's people, and for the exaltation of the Church Christ founded on Peter.

A second is that, as organizations of manpower and equipment, each has a grip on the levers of immense worldly power. Each applies its energies and resources to specific situations with particular, concrete, and defined ends in view, year in and year out.

Nevertheless—and this is yet a third similarity—amid the passion and seeming confusion that always accompany human activity, both papacy and Jesuits perform on a passionless and universal plane, with motives that do not permit the vulnerability of human feelings. Both grasp at the value of the present, passing moment. But both have hoary memories; both constantly measure their plans and actions against a template of the future they wish to see realized; and both assume that time is on their side. Plenty of time.

It is on this capital point of time that the inevitable outcome of all the battles can best be glimpsed. For in the Roman Catholic perspective—and in the perspective of classic Ignatian Jesuitism as well—there is another dimension, another condition of human existence, that overshadows this war between the papacy and the Society: Two cosmic powers—intelligent good and intelligent evil, personified in God and Lucifer—are locked in a life-and-death struggle for the allegiance of all human beings. That struggle becomes tangible—can be tracked and identified—only in the multiple details of complex human situations. But by the same token, everything tangible, each and every human situation, is colored by what is transhuman and eternal.

It is ultimately on that plane that the war between the papacy and the Society of Jesus is being fought. And on that plane, it is the papacy alone that has the divine promise of time.

On the plane we occupy as viewers of contemporary events, we are unable to foresee what seeds of good may sprout in what we must sum up as a disaster area. We are too near those events. We lack perspective—as well as foreknowledge. We see through the glass of history darkly. We cannot therefore know what changes could come about for the Society of Jesus, if all the present extremisms in the Jesuit Order were cut off—the obvious extremisms being the abandonment of basic Roman Catholic teaching, the replacement of it with sociopolitical solutions, and the inevitably consequent abandonment of the prime Jesuit vocation to be "Pope's Men." Such a reform of the Society and a new adhesion to its original charism seems, humanly speaking, unlikely when even a mild indictment of its latterday condition is reviewed.

THE INDICTMENT

PART I

1 | PAPAL OBJECTIONS

Every Pope worth his salt sets a dominant strategy for his papacy. He formulates many policies, pursues various particular aims: but all policies and each single aim are framed within the scope of that strategy.

The Society of Jesus was established by the papacy in 1540 as a very special "fighting unit" at the total and exclusive disposal of the Roman Pope—whoever he might be. From their beginnings, the Jesuits were conceived in a military mode. Soldiers of Christ, they were given only two purposes: to propagate the religious doctrine and the moral law of the Roman Catholic Church as proposed and taught by the Roman Pope, and to defend the rights and prerogatives of that same Roman Pope. Purely spiritual and supernatural purposes. And specifically Roman Catholic. Surprisingly enough, given this mandate of the Society, papal strategy itself has become the wedge of separation between Jesuits and papacy—indeed, the very arena where the lethal battle between the two is being fought.

Pius XII, Pope from 1939 to 1958, had found himself in a new world dominated by two rival superpowers, one of which—the USSR—he held in anathema. His postwar policy was one of intractable opposition to Soviet Marxism, and of support for "Western" civilization, centered in Europe and protected by the United States.

John XXIII, Pope from 1958 to 1963, was convinced that an "open windows, open fields" policy would induce others—including the Soviets—to refashion their own attitudes and policies. Pope John lowered as many barriers between the Church and the world—including the Soviet Union—as he could in his short, action-packed pontificate. He even went so far as to guarantee the USSR immunity from attacks by the Church, a stunning reversal of papal attitudes.

It was a huge gamble. And it could only work if an adequate amount of goodwill reigned among his opposite numbers.

The gamble failed. The great poignancy was that when he died, Pope John, peasant-realist that he was, knew that his openness had been seen as weakness, and had been taken advantage of by men of much smaller spirit.

Pope Paul VI, 1963–1978, blind to the deficiencies of John's policy, further refined it. The Holy See became nothing less than a plaintiff at the bar of Soviet power, pleading on diplomatic grounds for a hearing; instituting cautious conversations; practicing the week-kneed art of concessionary approaches—and even stooping to mean-spirited deception and betrayal of the admittedly difficult Primate of Hungary, Cardinal Mindszenty, in order to please the Soviets and their castrated Hungarian surrogate, Janos Kadar.[1]

In all of this, Paul VI, personally the gentlest of all modern Popes, unwittingly compromised his papal authority. His grand strategy for his Church was taken over and prostituted by others, reducing him to an impotence that scarred his last disease-ridden years until his death on August 6, 1978.

Still, it was Paul VI who, very late in the day of his papacy, realized that the original dual purpose of the Society of Jesus had been changed. Under his pontificate, an extensive critical dossier about the Society was compiled. It is enough for the moment to say of that dossier that its contents were damning. It was a portrait, in effect, of a Jesuit Order that, like a weathervane atop a roof, had been turned by a different wind. For Jesuits, the papacy no longer held primacy of position. The corporate aim of the Society was now to place itself and the Church at the disposal of a radical and purely sociopolitical change in the world, without reference to—indeed, in defiance of—papal strategy, policies, and aims.

In 1973, Paul VI, alarmed more than ever by the way the Society's members were behaving, tried to stop the onrush of events. He met with the head of the Order, Jesuit Father General Pedro Arrupe, several times. More than a few of those interviews be-

tween the two men were stormy. More than once, Paul wanted
Arrupe to resign. One way or the other, Arrupe survived all papal
attacks. Paul VI did insist that Arrupe convey to his Jesuits "Our
demand that the Jesuits remain loyal to the Pope." Arrupe and his
assistants in Rome at that time were intent on preparing for another international assembly of the Order, a General Congregation, as such an assembly is called. So he bought time, valuable
time. Paul, in his weakness, could find no alternative but to wait.

Paul did make one last but equally ineffective attempt to recall
the allegiance of the Society to the papacy during the ninety-six-
day international assembly of Jesuit leaders, the 32nd General
Congregation of 1974–1975. His effort met with total incompre-
hension and stubborn—some said even self-righteous—opposition
from the Order. Pope and Jesuits simply could not agree. The
Jesuits would not obey. Paul was too weak to force the issue
farther.

"When you have people [the Jesuits]," wrote Jesuit Father M.
Buckley about Paul's attitude to that 32nd General Congregation,
"who do not think they have made errors either in content or
procedure, and when they are suspected, resisted or reproved by
the very man they are attempting to serve . . . you have . . . a very
serious religious problem."

To say the least.

Cardinal Albino Luciani of Venice was elected to succeed Paul
VI on August 26, 1978. Even before he became Pope, he had apparently made up his mind unfavorably about the Society.

And apparently the Society had already made up its mind about
Pope John Paul I. No sooner had he been elected than the Jesuits
asserted themselves. Father Vincent O'Keefe, the most prominent
of the four General Assistants to Arrupe, and the one being
groomed to succeed Arrupe one day as Father General of the Order,
told a Dutch newspaper in an interview that the new Pope should
reconsider the Church's ban on abortion, homosexuality, and
priesthood for women. The interview was published.

Pope John Paul I was incensed. This was more than contempt.
It was an assertion that the Society of Jesus knew better than the
Pope what morals Catholics should practice. And it was an assertion that the Society had the authority to speak out; that is, it was
a direct appropriation of the authority that belonged exclusively
to the papacy.

John Paul I summoned Arrupe and demanded an explanation.
Arrupe humbly promised to look into the whole matter. But John
Paul could read the handwriting on the wall as clearly as any Pope.

On the basis of Paul VI's critical dossier, and with the help of a very experienced old Jesuit, Father Paolo Dezza, who had been Confessor to Pope Paul VI and now was John Paul I's confessor, the Pope composed a hard-hitting speech of warning. He planned to deliver it to the international assembly of Jesuit leaders and Father General Arrupe at another of their General Congregations to be held in Rome on September 30, 1978.

One of the striking features of his speech was John Paul I's repeated reference to doctrinal deviations on the part of Jesuits. "Let it not happen that the teachings and publications of Jesuits contain anything to cause confusion among the faithful." Doctrinal deviation was for him the most ominous symptom of Jesuit failure.

Veiled beneath the polished veneer of its graceful *romanità*, that speech contained a clear threat: the Society would return to its proper and assigned role, or the Pope would be forced to take action.

What action? From John Paul's memoranda and notes, it is clear that, unless a speedy reform of the Order proved feasible, he had in mind the effective liquidation of the Society of Jesus as it is today—perhaps to be reconstituted later in a more manageable form. John Paul I had received the petitions of many Jesuits, pleading with him to do just that.

The Pope never delivered that speech of warning. On the morning of September 29, after thirty-three days on the Throne of Peter, and one day before he was to address the Society's General Congregation, John Paul I was found dead in bed.

In the following days, Jesuit Father General Arrupe petitioned Cardinal Jean Villot, who as Vatican Secretary of State ruled the Holy See in the interim period between John Paul I's death and the election of his successor: Could the Jesuits have a copy of that speech?

After a discussion with the College of Cardinals who were helping him to prepare for the election of the next pope, the Cardinal prudently refused. Arrupe was told instead that in the opinion of Villot and the Council, "it was high time the Jesuits put their affairs in order."

For their part, Arrupe and the Jesuits decided to sit the time out and see who would become the next Pope. Time was the commodity they always sought to have.

More than either of his two immediate predecessors, Karol Wojtyla of Poland, elected as John Paul II on October 16, 1978, could not afford to hesitate in this matter of the Jesuits. John Paul

II's grand papal strategy embraced the First World of capitalism, the Second World of Soviet Communism, and the Third World of so-called underdeveloped and developing countries.

Wojtyla was extremely hard-headed in analyzing the character and limitations of papal strategy since 1945. In his view, Pius XII had guided the Church on the basis of a "siege" mentality, permitting papal strategy only clandestine movement within the Soviet empire, but providing no challenge to the continual erosion of the Church in that area. John XXIII's policy of "open fields" had been a failure. Paul VI's policy had consisted merely of a refinement of an already faulty and failed policy. By the time of Paul VI's death in 1978, his Secretariat of State had managed to work out protocol agreements with more than one member-government of the Soviet Socialist "fraternity," but none had been initialed, let alone signed and sealed into law. In any case, even had those protocols been ratified, it had already become clear enough that they would have made no difference to the status of Roman Catholics under Soviet rule.

In John Paul II's analysis, as long as the so-called First, Second, and Third Worlds were locked in the glacial chill of superpower rivalry unendingly fueled by the face-off between Marxist Leninism and rigid capitalism, there would not be the faintest hope in earthly terms that anything could be salvaged—that any battle would be won or any solution found for the dangerous dilemma of the nations. The situation would only disintegrate, slowly but inevitably, possibly levelling civilization as men have known it in the last quarter of the twentieth century, and reducing human history to a long, tortured sleepwalk until the end of the human night.

Wojtyla judged the time ripe for a completely different tack than Pius, John, or Paul had taken before him. His would be a "muscle" approach: Where Catholics constituted majorities or sizeable minorities in closed societies, there they should lay claim to the socio-political space that was rightfully theirs—make an assertion of their rights, in other words, on the basis that their very presence as Roman Catholics would be enough to make such self-assertion stick.

As Cardinal Archbishop of Krakow in Poland, Wojtyla had already sharpened his wits in devising a strategy whereby such Catholic majorities and minorities as he had in mind could lay claim to their rights; yet he had not run afoul of the totalitarian and unscrupulous military control characteristic of Communist governments.

John Paul's "muscle" approach did not rule out dialogue and discourse with the Soviets and their surrogates. On the contrary. But it would be of a totally different sort than John XXIII or Paul VI had carried on. And in fact, no world leader today has personally spoken to Soviet leaders as often and as directly as John Paul II, starting from the very beginning of his pontificate. He received the USSR's prestigious and many-lived Andrei Gromyko on January 24, 1979, barely more than three months after his papal election. That was but the first of eight personal meetings between this Pontiff and Gromyko between 1979 and 1985. His telephone conversations with Eastern Europe and the Soviet Union are the Pontiff's own business; let it merely be said that they take place. If you are a Slav of the Slavs, if you speak Russian in addition to two or three other eastern European languages, if you are Pope, and if you are Karol Wojtyla, the powerbrokers wish to speak to you.

It would be essential to John Paul II's "muscle" strategy that he provide and successfully impose a new world leadership, fueled exclusively and unimpeachably by moral and spiritual motives. In order to have even a hope of succeeding in so bold and so radical a strategy, John Paul II would have to demonstrate such leadership as he was proposing in two key areas: His supreme authority in doctrine and morality would have to be vindicated and reasserted within his worldwide Church; and a concrete example would have to be forthcoming of what such leadership could provide by way of solution to the international dilemma.

Hence the two most visible lines of John Paul's papal activity: his worldwide trips, and his careful guidance of the Solidarity movement in Poland. The appearance of his papal persona in all major countries and many minor ones would be the means of reestablishing that authority. And if the Solidarity movement achieved freedom of economic and cultural action under the aegis of Soviet Communism in Poland, then both Communists and capitalists would have a ready example to show that doctrinaire politics need not result in slavery or poverty or devastating militarism.

This was the dream. Hard-headed certainly, in strategy; but still, the dream. And it put this Pope immediately at loggerheads with the globally powerful Society of Jesus.

With the guidance and financial help of John Paul II, Poland's Primate, eighty-year-old Stefan Cardinal Wyszynski, was achieving progress in evolving an attitude in the Solidarity organization by which the Church and its people could escape the grip of Communism culturally and socially. The ethos of Solidarity was developed precisely to allow such cultural and social freedom, while leaving intact the political and military grip of Marxism. "Do not endanger the Marxists in the Communist Party of Poland, in the National Parliament, in its army or the security forces," was the watchword of Solidarity's founders. "Let them be. Let us claim freedom in the other areas."

At the same time, at the other side of the world, in the area that stretches from the southern borders of Texas down to the tip of South America, Jesuits and others were carrying on their own policy as creators and chief fomentors of a new outlook—"Liberation Theology," they called it in a typically effective bid for romantic appeal—based on Marxist revolutionary principles and aimed at establishing a Communist system of government. The contradiction between John Paul's Polish model and the "Liberation" model advocated ardently and openly by the Jesuits in Latin America could not have been more stark or bold-faced.

John Paul II, like John Paul I before him, was privy to the dossier on the Jesuits compiled under Paul VI. And he possessed as well the speech of reproval John Paul I had prepared but never delivered. In November of 1978, within a month after his election, the Pope sent John Paul I's speech to Father General Arrupe in the Gesù, as Jesuit international headquarters in Rome are called. The Pope meant the gesture as a benign warning: I make this speech my own, the gesture said. He received in return, as was to be expected, the Father General's due protestations of loyalty and obedience. But they were to prove to be only that—protestations.

On the evening of December 31, as a gesture of goodwill, the Pope went to the Jesuit Church of the Gesù, in order to honor the Society by his presence during their traditional year-end religious ceremonies of thanksgiving to God. John Paul let the Jesuits know beforehand that he wanted to see no Jesuit in civilian clothes. Nor did he. It was perhaps a small enough concession to the Pope, to whom each and all present had important and unique vows. But it was the only concession.

Even John Paul's retinue remarked on the polite coldness of the Jesuit notables gathered for the occasion. After the religious ceremonies, the Pope dined with the Jesuits in their refectory. He was pleasant in his remarks, one Jesuit present at the meal complained later, but "he gave us no hint about the future of the Society."

That complaint spoke volumes. The Jesuits had been able to ignore Paul VI and John Paul I. Why should they heed John Paul II? Jesuits would simply have to hold on and outlive this Pope, as they had the previous two.

Within two months of that year-end meeting between the Pope and his Jesuits, during February and March of 1979, Father General Arrupe called press conferences in Mexico and Rome at which he asserted blandly that there was no friction between the Holy Father and the Jesuits. Yes, Arrupe acknowledged to journalists at the International Press Office of the Holy See, he had received that speech of John Paul I, which John Paul II had made his own. Rumor had it, he went on, that "it had a pejorative sense and was a reprimand" for the changes made in the Society under Arrupe's fourteen-year leadership. But that was nonsense, Arrupe said. The Pope knew that "of course, the Society of Jesus had changed," he went on. "It could not do otherwise, seeing that the Church herself has changed." There was, in reality, no friction, he concluded.

His Holiness saw it otherwise: There was grave friction. What John Paul called "friction about fundamentals."

Jesuit theologians and writers in Europe and the Americas had been, and were still, writing and teaching about fundamental Catholic beliefs and laws in a way that opposed traditional papal teaching and the previous teaching of the Church as a whole— about papal authority; about the marriage of Marxism and Christianity; about sexual morality in all its aspects; about such sacred Catholic beliefs as the Mass as a sacrifice, the divinity of Jesus, the Immaculate Conception of the Virgin Mary, the existence of Hell, the priesthood. They were in fact redefining and recasting everything in Catholicism that Catholics have always considered worth living for and dying for—including the very nature and constitution of the Church that Christ founded.

Father General Arrupe continued to permit the publication of books that contradicted the entire gamut of traditional teachings, and to defend his men who wrote and taught in this vein. No papal appeal to Father Arrupe seemed ever to have any effect in the face of the Jesuit General's intricate and resourceful delaying action.

Arrupe would examine the situation, he promised the Holy Father. He already had inquiries in hand, he said. He would report back soonest. It was difficult to separate truth from vicious rumors. He would endeavor to clarify positions. Time was needed. His men were doing their best. Their views had been distorted. The accusations against his men were too vague. He needed names and details and dates and places. Father Arrupe would, in fact, do anything except get his men back into line as the Pope's men. As this Pope's men, in particular.

It was significant in John Paul's eyes that Father General Arrupe had allowed such a situation to arise at all. After all, reason dictates that if, as head of the Order, you allow one of your Jesuits to publish a book advocating a change in the Church's ban on homosexuality, you as General must regard it as an open question. Jesuit John J. McNeil was permitted by his American and Roman Superiors to publish such a book. If you repeatedly bless the work of another of your Jesuit men who openly votes in the United States Congress for financing abortion-on-demand, you as General must regard abortion, too, as somehow an open question. Together with American Jesuit Superiors, Arrupe repeatedly blessed the ten-year career in Congress of Father Robert F. Drinan, who did just that. "We reject the idea," said Arrupe, directly contradicting John Paul's explicit wish and command, "that Jesuits must systematically avoid all political involvement."

By summer's end 1979, it was clear to John Paul that Arrupe would do nothing to curb even those of his men who cast doubt on basic doctrines ranging from the divinity of Jesus to the infallibility of the Pope.

In September 1979, some dozen presidents of national and regional Jesuit Conferences were gathered in Rome for a meeting with Arrupe. Arrupe and his Jesuit aides thought it would be a good idea to have an audience with the Holy Father. Accordingly, Arrupe requested and was granted an audience for himself, his chief Jesuit counselors in Rome, and the dozen visiting presidents.

The audience took place in the Vatican on September 21. John Paul posed for photographs with individuals, made small talk after his formal address, presented gifts of rosaries to each one present. But there was no mistaking his message.

"You are causing confusion among the Christian people," the Pontiff complained in his message to the Jesuit leaders, "and anxieties to the Church and also personally to the Pope who is speaking to you." The Pope listed his complaints about the Jesuits, speaking about their "regrettable shortcomings" and their "doctrinal unorthodoxy," and requesting them to "return to full fidelity to the Supreme magisterium of the Church and the Roman Pontiff." He could not, he said, be more explicit or go much further in his forebearance with Jesuit deviations.

No longer could a screen be thrown up in the form of a complaint that the Pope "gave us no hint of the future of the Society." But there are other sorts of screens, and the men of the Society have ever been resourceful.

Arrupe sent a circular letter dated October 19 to all Major Superiors of the Society together with a photograph—a copy for each single community of Jesuits all over the world and, of course, destined for wide publication in the world media—showing himself as Father General kneeling before the Pope. His letter, he commanded, was to be read by each and every one of his 27,347 Jesuits.

John Paul II, he reminded his men, was the third Pope who had called them to attention. He quoted John Paul II's words in his September 21 speech, and demanded annual reports from all Superiors as to how they were observing John Paul's admonitions.

When all in the letter was said and done, however, both its tone and the framework were merely political. In effect, the General was saying, Jesuits had failed to observe the formal exterior conventions that normally satisfied papal demands and Roman bureaucratic conditions. His letter was in essence an invitation for Jesuits to consider how they were acting and come up with rationalizations and explanations that would conform to exterior norms and thus offset open papal criticisms.

Not once did Arrupe say bluntly: We have gone astray, we Jesuits. As Superior General, I now forbid this, recall that man, expel this other man, impose the following rules and reforms. Rather, the letter implied: We have political difficulties with this new Pope; help me politically.

Reaction to the letter—and therefore to John Paul's strictures—were of a kind with Arrupe's letter. Father Arrupe received what in essence he had asked for: commentaries from Jesuits in bulk quantities, some quite resentful, on the Pope's admonitions. As one intramural joke went, Arrupe was a victim of "fallout" from the "W [for Wojtyla] bomb."

While Arrupe's tactic in dealing with the situation bore its fruit in much paper, one Roman Cardinal remarked, "He should not have asked for a basketful of letters—which he got—but the bleeding heads of just about 5,000 Jesuits—the greatest offenders—all neatly arranged on wooden platters."

Be that as it may, there was no trace of the hoped-for change. No shift in corporate Jesuit behavior was in sight.

It was all becoming too much. By now, John Paul II was in a great historical hurry. The Solidarity movement was being readied for its first major public operation; as far as John Paul could find out from soundings in Warsaw and Moscow, Solidarity's planned future could come off. At the same time, the galling fact was that on the other side of the Atlantic, the Jesuits' adversary strategy was progressing just as rapidly, if not more so. Above all in Nicaragua.

Nicaragua was, in fact, fast developing into a public and dramatic test case between Pope and Jesuits. There the Pope's aims and those of the Jesuits were irreconcilable. Solidarity in Poland was developed precisely to loosen the effective grip of Marxism on the sociocultural life of the Polish people. In Nicaragua, the Jesuits aimed at establishing a Marxist system of government that would embrace the sociocultural and political and economic life of Nicaraguans. If John Paul could not control the Jesuits in Nicaragua, where the stakes on the table might, in essence, involve the success of his entire papal strategy, then he could simply not control them anywhere.

On the other hand, from the Jesuit point of view, if John Paul II could frustrate their explicit policy of political activism in favor of a Marxist regime—if their expenditure of men and energy in Nicaragua were brought to nothing by this Pope—then they would have failed in their corporate objectives. This Pope would proceed to move in on them elsewhere.

It was an adversarial situation from the beginning. Clearly, the matériel of war between Pope and Jesuits was in place.

2 | THE TESTING GROUND

L ong before John Paul II came upon the scene with his radically new papal strategy, Nicaragua had already been made, as if by formula, a test case for the global struggle gathering momentum between the papacy and the Society of Jesus.

Nicaragua is totally Roman Catholic in tradition and in practice. Geopolitically, it is of enormous importance because of its access to both the Atlantic and the Pacific, because of its potential to be virtually self-supporting economically, and not least because of its position at the center of the strategic Central American land bridge between North and South America. Add to those circumstances the extreme social and political oppression of the Somoza dynasty that had held Nicaragua in a vicelike grip since 1937. The mixture was explosive.

There was one point in modern times when another destiny might have been possible for Nicaragua. This was during the brief lifetime of Augusto César Sandino, the son of a dirt farmer who became a very successful revolutionary general. By 1926, while still in his twenties, he was strong enough militarily and expert enough in guerrilla tactics to elude capture by a force of 2000 U.S. Marines and by the Nicaraguan National Guard. His military prowess and leadership were so compelling that he forced President Franklin D. Roosevelt to establish the famous "Good Neighbor Policy." In 1933 the Marines were withdrawn, and a lawfully elected Nicaraguan president was inaugurated.

Sandino had potential greatness. For him, war was merely another way of pursuing diplomacy. Once diplomacy was possible, he laid down his guns and entered public life. There is very little doubt that in time he would have led his nation politically. His personal charisma, his intelligence, and his deep faith would have steered Nicaragua to a greatness all its own. Unfortunately, in 1934, he was assassinated at the age of thirty-seven by disgruntled members of the National Guard.

From that point on, it was only a matter of time before the ingredients present in Nicaragua boiled to the point of explosion. Nicaragua's population, primarily *mestizo*—a mix of Caucasian and non-Caucasian races—was bled both literally and figuratively by an utterly corrupt regime led first by the suave, cool-eyed dictator Anastasio Somoza, then by his son, Luis Somoza Debayle. Both Somozas were backed by the United States, and each was always ready to bolster his regime by the use of the remarkably brutal National Guard, a unit that would have given Hitler's elite corps a run for their money.

At the same time, however, the murder of Sandino had produced its own legacy. For, on his death, Sandino immediately became a mythical figure embodying Nicaraguan independence and resistance to the hated *"yanqui"* and the murderers the *yanqui* had trained. Nicaraguans began to form a romantic revolutionary ideal around his name. The nationalism of one of Latin America's greatest poets, Ruben Darío, and the writings of Salvador Mendieta—both Nicaraguans—fed that ideal. By the 1960s, an entire gallery of young, intelligent activists had gathered in the north-central provinces of Matagalpa and Jinotega. They called themselves Sandinistas, thereby assuming the mantle, the appeal, and the romanticism of the one man who still remained the champion and hero of the Nicaraguan people.

In that gallery of young, enthusiastic revolutionaries, a few stood out as prototypes of the revolutionary ideal. One of these certainly was Jesuit Father Fernando Cardenal. His brother Ernesto came on as a good runner-up for that distinction.

The Cardenals came from a well-to-do Nicaraguan family. Fernando entered the Jesuits; Ernesto joined the diocesan seminary of Managua. Although they both developed into thoroughgoing Marxists and dedicated Sandinistas, their courses differed. Ernesto, with some claim to being a poet, decided to try the life of a Trappist monk at Gethsemani Abbey in Kentucky, under the direction

of Thomas Merton. He loved Merton, but could not take the cloistered life, so he returned to Nicaragua and, styling himself a new
type of monk-in-action, moved to the main island of Solentiname
on Lake Nicaragua, where he proposed to establish his own monastic community. Ernesto had ambitions to be the Ruben Darío
of the Sandinista revolution; but politics and perhaps a genuine
lack of poetic genius has kept him from attaining this status.

Fernando was of a different caliber. Ruggedly handsome, serious
and humorous, fanciful and pragmatic by turns, quite intelligent,
a clever philosopher, a convincing speaker with a voice he could
modulate to suit the occasion, Fernando had little of his brother's
poetism; but he had a steely resolution masked in romantic—and
at times, when required, religious—language. And he had a genuine gift for diplomatic intricacies. Whether clad in blazer and gray
flannels as he talked on U.S. Jesuit campuses, or in Army fatigues
giving orders from his government office in Managua, or in a three-
piece business suit visiting Cardinal Casaroli in the Vatican Secretariat of State or negotiating with Castro in Cuba or with the
USSR representative in Panama, Cardenal was a man for all sea-
sons.

His Jesuit training merely sharpened an already acute intelligence. As the occasion required, he could mold his language. With
the Jesuit Father General, he knew what Jesuit terms to use. Dis-
cussing the assassination of Luis Somoza Debayle with the Nicaraguan Junta, he was at one in language, purpose, and words with
his colleagues. With the Sandinista cadres, he spoke as effectively
as any commissar of the people. In an assembly of bishops and
clergy, he could wrap the death and oppression of Marxism in
neotheological terms larded with traditional-sounding references
to the death and resurrection of Jesus.

He thus stood out among his Marxist Sandinista colleagues.
Daniel Ortega y Saavedra and Tomás Borge were doctrinaire Marx-
ists. Miguel D'Escoto was roly-poly in body and sly in manner.
Ernesto Cardenal was wildly romantic. But Fernando was the at-
tractively cool, calculating element—almost a caricature of the
Jesuit of fiction.

When Fernando, like his brother Ernesto, joined the Sandinistas,
he had the unmitigated support of his Major and Minor Superiors
in the Society of Jesus. Indeed, for the rank and file of Jesuits,
Cardenal became the paragon of what a twentieth-century Jesuit
should be: a man totally devoted to correcting the injustice perpetrated by rich capitalists on "Christ's poor." Here was a man, it

was said, who was the embodiment of the "Jesuit mission to the People of God."

In fact, it was specifically as a Jesuit that Fernando Cardenal became a close collaborator of prime importance to the Sandinista Marxists. For them, none of Cardenal's personal gifts and abilities, impressive though they were, equalled his identity as a priest and as a Jesuit. Jesuits had a far longer history in Nicaragua and a far deeper influence than any other group, including the government itself. Jesuit missionaries had been present in Nicaragua since the 1600s. Whatever intellectual life there was in Nicaragua was formed by the Jesuit schools, study centers, and university faculties. Jesuit personnel provided the longest unbroken chain of influence in every walk of life, at every level from the most neglected peasant village to the most powerful family dynasties. By the time the Sandinistas were ready to move in the 1960s, whatever national analysis was being performed of Nicaragua's potential was in the hands of the Jesuits. A man like Fernando Cardenal was absolutely essential to the revolution—was, in a very real sense, its fuel, its driving force, and its claim to legitimacy both among the people of Nicaragua and out in the wide world.

The Sandinista struggle against the Somozas began with an attack on the National Nicaraguan Guard at Pancasan, Matagalpa, in 1967. From the start, the Sandinista leadership—Fernando Cardenal included—made no bones about their identity as hard-line Marxists, or about their intention to seize the country by violent means and to stay in power. As early as 1969, Carlos Fonseca, the principal founder of the Sandinistas, published a political tract displaying hard-line Stalinist Marxism. The agreements and pacts the Sandinistas made during the 1960s with Soviet surrogate Fidel Castro in Cuba, and with direct representatives of the USSR, were ample testimony both to that intent and to the support gathering for it. Their agreements with Havana and Moscow concerned armaments and propaganda. They also entered into a pact with the Palestine Liberation Organization whereby the PLO would train Sandinistas in guerrilla tactics.

The overall arrangement was that Nicaragua, as a nation, would be completely assimilated into the Marxism of one party. There would be no Nicaraguan army, only a Sandinista army "politicized to an unprecedented degree." No Nicaraguan Television Network, only the Sandinista Television Network. The Sandinista leadership wanted the very soul of the Nicaraguan people, just as the Soviets had taken the soul of the Russian people. More than that, by the early seventies, at least seven years before their grab for power, the Sandinista leaders openly proclaimed their ultimate aim: to create a Marxist society in Nicaragua to serve as the womb from which Marxist revolution throughout Central America would be born. "Revolution throughout the Americas" was the slogan.

From their beginnings as a group, when they were nothing more than rag-tag guerrillas, bank robbers, and hit-and-run terrorists, the Sandinistas understood full well that they had no hope of installing a Marxist regime in 91.6 percent Roman Catholic Nicaragua unless they could enlist—in effect, inhale—the active cooperation of the Catholic clergy, together with suitably altered Church doctrine and Church structure. Mere passive connivance on the part of the clergy would not be enough. If the Sandinistas wanted the very soul of the people, they knew the road: Catholicism was inextricably bound up in the warp and woof of Nicaraguan culture, language, way of thinking, and outlook, and was integral to all the hope of the people.

Here, Fernando Cardenal, as priest and Jesuit, was a towering influence. For some time, certain Catholic theologians in Latin America—principally Jesuits of the post–World War II period—had been developing a new theology. They called it the Theology of Liberation, and based it on the theories of their European counterparts. It was an elaborate and carefully worked out system, but its core principle is very simple: The whole and only meaning of Christianity as a religion comes down to one achievement—the liberation of men and women, by armed and violent revolution if necessary, from the economic, social, and political slavery imposed on them by U.S. capitalism; this is to be followed by the establishment of "democratic socialism." In this "theological" system, the so-called "option" for the economically poor and the politically oppressed, originally described as a "preferential" option by Catholic bishops in Latin America at their conference in Medellín, Colombia, in 1968, became totally exclusive: There was one enemy—capitalist classes, middle and upper and lower, chiefly located in the United States. Only the "proletariat"—the "people"—was to be fomented by the imposition of Marxism.

Liberation Theology was the perfect blueprint for the Sandinistas. It incorporated the very aim of Marxist-Leninism. It presumed the classic Marxist "struggle of the masses" to be free from all capitalist domination. And above all, the Marxist baby was at last wrapped in the very swaddling clothes of ancient Catholic terminology. Words and phrases laden with meaning for the people were co-opted and turned upside down. The historical Jesus, for example, became an armed revolutionary. The mystical Christ became all the oppressed people, collectively. Mary the Virgin became the mother of all revolutionary heroes. The Eucharist became the bread freely made by liberated workers. Hell became the capitalist system. The American president, leader of the greatest capitalist country, became the Great Satan. Heaven became the earthly paradise of the workers from which capitalism is abolished. Justice became the uprooting of capitalist gains, which would be "returned" to the people, to the "mystical body" of Christ, the democratic socialists of Nicaragua. The Church became that mystical body, "the people," deciding its fate and determining how to worship, pray, and live, under the guidance of Marxist leaders.

It was a brilliant synthesis, ready-made and just waiting for the activists who would set about erecting a new sociopolitical structure on its basis, as a building rises from a blueprint.

The Nicaraguan people were the first guinea pigs on whom the theory was experimentally tried. And the priests who were charter members in the Sandinista leadership—Jesuit Fernando Cardenal, Ernesto Cardenal, Miguel D'Escoto Brockman of the Maryknoll Fathers, Jesuit Alvaro Arguello, Edgar Parrales of the Managua diocese—made the experiment doubly blessed and likely to succeed. If such men, duly ordained as priests, could successfully get this new "theological" message across—that the Sandinista revolution was really a religious matter sanctioned by legitimate Church spokesmen—they would have both the Catholic clergy and the people as allies in a Marxist-style revolution by armed violence.

Without a doubt, the plan had been carefully thought out and elaborated, based on a profound analysis of the Nicaraguan people and of its clergy. No doubt, too, the first connivers in the scheme were the priests themselves; there are even those in Managua today and among prominent Nicaraguan exiles in Panama, Honduras, and Miami, Florida, who point the finger at Fernando Cardenal as the prime architect of the scheme. But what evidence there is does suggest that he was not the only Jesuit involved.

In any case, the Sandinista undertaking was ever more brilliantly explained, refined, and dinned into the ears of seminarians, nuns, university students, and the popular mind by increasing numbers of their Jesuit, Franciscan, and Maryknoll teachers and lecturers throughout the schools of Central America. The seeding time was well spent in the view of ultimate Marxisation. The pathetic court testimony of the young Nicaraguan Edgard Lang Sacasa told the world as far back as 1977 that it had been his priest educators who had persuaded him and thousands like him to join the Sandinista guerrillas.

Hand in hand with this new Theology of Liberation went, of necessity, the establishment of a new and "pliant" Church structure to replace the old one. In the traditional Roman Catholic structure, knowledge about God, Christ, Christian salvation, personal morality, and human destiny derived from the hierarchic pastors of the Church—namely, the Pope and his bishops. They were the only authentic source of knowledge about the faith; apart from them, there was no accurate knowing possible about Christianity. Submission to them and acceptance of their teaching and laws were necessary for salvation.

It was precisely this structure, in which ultimate control is Rome's, that stood between the Sandinistas and the people. And it was precisely this structure that the earlier, European-based architect-theologians of Liberation Theology had criticized. This structure was, Liberation Theologians said, dictated by "a view from above" and "imposed from above" on the people "below."

Franciscan Liberation Theologian Leonardo Boff, teaching in a Brazilian seminary, put it in terms Fernando Cardenal and his clerical colleagues could champion: "There has been a historical process of expropriation of the means of production on the part of the clergy to the detriment of the Christian People." Boff was not talking about industry or commerce, but about theology and religious doctrine; the means of production—the "plant," as he called it—was the preaching of the Gospel.

According to the new theologians, "Roman" and therefore "alien" imposition of religious doctrine was the very reason social injustice and political oppression flourished in lands where this hierarchic Church flourished. In lands such as Latin American countries. In countries such as Nicaragua. On top of that, the argument went on, Christianity and specifically Catholicism was not merely alien in and of itself, but had always accompanied actual invasion by alien European cultures. *Alien*—that was the key word.

To counter that alien, imposed structure, the new theologians looked "from below." From the level of the people. From the perspective of oppression and injustice—because that, they said, was all they found "below" among the people. The task, in other words, was to impose the "preferential option" on all the people, rich and poor alike.

Immediately, as Fernando Cardenal and the other Sandinista

priests quickly realized, a new concept of "Church" was born. The ordinary body of believers, by revised definition, would become the very source of revelation. The faith of believers would "create" communities among those believers. Base Communities, they are called in Nicaragua and elsewhere in Latin America—*comuni-dades de base.* And those Communities taken together would form the new "Church," the "People's Church."

These Communities began to form years before the Nicaraguan revolution stormed onto the stage of geopolitics in 1979. Group-ings of laymen and laywomen would gather regularly to pray, to read the Bible, to sing hymns, to discuss their local concrete prob-lems in economics and politics; to choose not only their political leaders but their priests as well; and to determine not only the solutions to their secular problems, but how best to worship and what to believe.

It was a dream come true. A dream put into clear words by the same Father Boff: "The sacred power must be put back in the hands of the people." No teaching or directing authority would be allowed "from above," from the alien, hierarchic Church. In fact, the very symbols of that Church must be firmly rejected. Symbols and all else must only come "from below." From the people. From their Base Communities—nearly 1000 of them in Nicaragua alone, in time; and nearly 300,000 in Latin America at large. The idea of Base Communities spread to the United States, where they are sometimes called "Gatherings."

Fernando Cardenal, Ernesto Cardenal, Miguel D'Escoto Brock-man, Edgar Parrales, and Alvaro Arguello were the showcase priests of the Sandinistas, the intended and willing legitimizers of this new "People's Church" that would appropriate and redefine all the words of Catholicism, while it severed all papal influence from the Church in Nicaragua. The Catholicism of Nicaraguans was about to be "converted" to Marxism.

And they were effective, these Sandinista priests. As tens, and then scores, and finally hundreds of other priests, nuns, and reli-gious brothers up and down the country became inspired with this new zeal, the Base Communities slowly spread wide enough and sent their roots deep enough to make the Sandinistas the new hierarchs of Nicaraguan Society.

Up to a certain point in time, it is fair to assume that Pope Paul VI, in whose reign the most fervid phase of this activity took place, might have reversed it, or at least reined it in. Logically enough, however, Paul depended on the loyalty and theological soundness of Jesuit Superiors in Rome and Central America, not realizing early enough in the game that they were complaisant in the activity of their Nicaraguan Jesuit subjects.

By 1965, when advice and information prompted him to start his dossier on the Jesuits in earnest, Paul VI had his hands full with other problems. He felt, too, that he could still rely on the Superiors of the Society to manage their rank and file, as Popes had done for four hundred years. And indeed, those Superiors did tell Paul the truth about one aspect of Nicaragua—the fact that the Catholic bishops and the Jesuits and everybody who was any sort of a Christian in the country were united against the lethal dictatorship of Luis Somoza Debayle. But they did not tell him that the Sandinistas were aiming at a Marxist takeover.

It was only in 1973 and 1974 that Paul VI became truly alarmed about the Jesuits in general; but by that time his control over them had weakened. Nicaragua, meanwhile, continued to fester with revolution, killings, bombings, bank robberies, torture, and mutilation on all sides. In that theater of violence, strong Jesuit support and Paul VI's procrastination bought the Sandinistas precious time.

                              *   *   *

In the United States during these same years, with dictator Luis Somoza still unfettered in his brutal repression of the Nicaraguan population, the Sandinista influence and new religious fervor were already making inroads. Two political activists in the Democratic Party, Richard Shaull and Brady Tyson, together with some others, founded the North American Congress on Latin America (NACLA). Shaull put the aims of NACLA succinctly to the Catholic Inter-American Cooperation Sessions in St. Louis as early as 1968: "For an increasing number of Catholic young people there is only one hope: The organization of armed movements of national liberation with all the sacrifice and bloodshed that involves."

NACLA was far from the only group in the United States with this view. The following decade seemed to spawn organizations and groups like guppies, each of them a supporter of relaxed relations with Fidel Castro and with his affiliates throughout Latin America, and each of them with an active lobby working in Washington to make the Nicaraguan Sandinistas acceptable to U.S. lawmakers and their constituents. Chief among these organizations, apart from NACLA, were the Institute of Policy Studies (IPS) and its subsidiary, the Transnational Institute (TNI); the Washington Office on Latin America (WOLA); the U.S. Committee for Justice for Latin American Political Prisoners (USLA); and the Council of Hemispheric Affairs (COHA).

WOLA, which became by far the most outspoken of these lobbies in favor of the Nicaraguan Sandinistas, brought two of the
showcase priest-guerrillas to testify before U.S. Congressional
Committees. One of them was Fernando Cardenal's brother, Ernesto, who by now had become the poet-singer of the Sandinista
revolution and a professed Marxist. The other was Maryknoll
priest Miguel D'Escoto Brockman, less poetic but succinct: "We
back a new, non-capitalistic system for Nicaragua," he told the
American lawmakers.

The emergence of post-Vietnam, post-Watergate Washington
produced a veritable wonderland for these highly intelligent,
extraordinarily capable, and even romantically appealing activist-
ambassadors among the Sandinista leadership. It was the Washington of the Carter Administration. Left-wing Democratic views,
incarnated most visibly in politicians of the stripe of George
McGovern, Birch Bayh, Frank Church, Robert Drinan, and Edward
Kennedy, dominated the scene. Carter's men in the United Nations—notably Andrew Young and Brady Tyson—exerted influence over the administration so that none of Fidel Castro's
adventures, whether in Angola, Ethiopia, or Latin America, would
evoke an adversarial reaction. "Don't get panicky about the Cubans in Angola," Andrew Young counseled Carter.

One prime goal of President Carter became the conclusion of
the long-delayed Panama Treaties. The strongman of Panama was
Omar Torrijos, a personal friend and protector of the Sandinista
leaders and of Cuba's Fidel Castro, and a man with whom Carter,
in turn, professed personal friendship. Torrijos also advised Carter
to let things be in Nicaragua. Carter's ambition was to sign the
Panama Canal Treaty; Torrijos was an essential part of that ambition. Torrijos was listened to, even if Carter knew that Torrijos
was giving arms and sanctuary to the Sandinistas.

The targets of these able Sandinista spokesmen and ambassadors for Marxist revolution in theological clothing were not all
centered in Washington or even in the United States—and they
were certainly not all political. Wooed and won as champions and
defenders were scores of religious publications—newspapers, magazines, bulletins, releases—put out in the United States by the
Jesuits, the Maryknoll Missionaries, the Sisters of Loreto, the Sisters of St. Joseph of Peace, the Sisters of Notre Dame of Namur,
the Leadership Conference of Women Religious, the Conference of
Major Superiors of Men, and kindred organizations. In Ireland,
England, and Europe, Jesuit publications stoutly defended the
Nicaraguan revolution and the role of clerics in it.

Everywhere, Jesuit activists and supporters took up the cause. They were zealous, knowledgeable, capable, and effective, inspired, as one of them said, "with a sense of our mission as Jesuits to promote social justice and express our preferential option for the poor existentially." In the Nicaraguan context, all of this spelled support of "the people's Church," *la iglesia popular.*

By 1977, all this activity had brought the Sandinistas a very long way indeed. When Ernesto Cardenal was a guest that year of WOLA and the IPS in Washington, he spoke eloquently at the Latin American Round Table program organized by the IPS/TNI under the direction of Orlando Letelier who, researchers have concluded, was a Cuban agent. A simple review of some of the members of that Round Table is a review as well both of the support and the intentions of the Sandinistas. In addition to Letelier and his assistant, Roberta Salper, there were Cheddi Jagan, head of the pro-Soviet Communist party in Guyana; Julian Rizo, member of Castro's intelligence organization (DGI) and of the Cuban secret police, and Letelier's case officer; and James Petras and Richard Fagan, Americans known openly as favoring Cuban-style revolutions throughout Latin America. Truly, as Shaull of NACLA had said nine years before in 1968, "More and more in Latin America, the Christians and Marxists are not only having a dialogue but they are working together."

In mid-July of 1979, Nicaragua's fate was sealed. After a prolonged revolution in which 45,000 were wounded, 40,000 children were orphaned, and over 1,000,000 people were reduced to starvation, the Sandinistas marched in triumph into Managua on July 17, 1979. All opposition was quenched in Nicaragua by July 19. After forty-two years of rule, dictator Luis Somoza was ousted by the three factions of the Sandinista Front for National Liberation (FSNL), acting with the FPN (a broad opposition front) as well as with a coalition of youth organizations, radical left-wing parties, and worker groups.

The victory, when it came, was sweet consolation for Cuba's Castro, partly because the plans of assault had been drawn up under his guidance, and partly because the Marxist FSNL had come out on top when the dust settled; but perhaps most of all because it was Castro's only victory that year. Of the four guerrilla-terrorist groups clawing for power in the Latin America of the seventies thanks to Castro's arms and influence, the Uruguayan Tupamaros, the Argentinian Montaneros, and the Puerto Rican Socialists had all failed. Only the Sandinista group in Nicaragua was successful.

If Castro was consoled, so did Jimmy Carter appear to be so. The Carter Administration immediately contributed millions of American tax dollars to the Sandinista regime; and Carter posed with the attractive young Sandinista leader, Daniel Ortega y Saavedra, and two other members of his Junta in the Rose Garden of the White House.

Later that year, Somoza, his driver, and his bodyguard were cut down on a street in Asunción, Paraguay's capital, by a six-man Sandinista hit-squad using bazookas and machine guns. The twenty-five bullets that peppered Somoza's body freed the new regime from the haunting fear of his return. By February of 1980, some 2000 political enemies of the Sandinistas had been executed. Some 6000 more lay in prison. For the moment, all opposition to the Sandinistas ceased.

From its very first days in power, the Sandinista Junta included those same five loyal and useful priests in the new government at cabinet-level posts. Jesuit Fernando Cardenal; Jesuit Alvaro Arguello; Father Ernesto Cardenal; Maryknoll Father Miguel D'Escoto Brockman; and diocesan Father Edgar Parrales.

In the immediate aftermath of the July 1979 revolution, with the acquiescence of Pope John Paul II, who had been elected barely nine months before, the Nicaraguan bishops allowed Fernando Cardenal and the other Catholic priests serving in the government throughout the country to remain at their political posts "temporarily until the country recovered from the effects of the armed revolution." The bishops saw no great difficulty in this. Had they not themselves declared in June of 1979, on the very eve of Somoza's ouster, that "no one can deny the moral and legal legitimacy" of the Sandinista revolution? Indeed, they went much further in their famous pastoral letter of November 17, 1979, entitled *The Christian Commitment for a New Nicaragua.* There, they endorsed "Socialism" and "the class struggle" and spoke of the revolution as ushering in "a new society that is authentically Nicaraguan and not capitalist-dependent or totalitarian."

Their political naiveté and sociological unawareness shines through that letter in its every line. Of course we are for socialism, the bishops asserted stoutly, if socialism means giving pre-eminence to the interests of the majority of Nicaraguans . . . , a continual lessening of injustice . . . following the model of a nationally planned economy. . . ." They admitted "the dynamic reality of the class struggle that leads to a just transformation of structures . . ."; but, buttering their bread on the other side as well, they clearly opposed "class hatred" as contrary to "the Christian duty of being ruled by love."

Reading that letter, one might have been tempted to answer, "Tell it to the Hungarians, Your Graces; their churchmen collaborated in the 'Socialist' revolution, too. And so did Cuba's." Yet at that stage, even such an abrupt splash of cold water would have made no difference to the bishops of Nicaragua. After the fall of Somoza, a kind of euphoria about Marxism gripped the minds of many—bishops, Jesuits, Maryknoll missionary priests and nuns, diocesan priests, and layfolk. Nor were Catholics alone in this. Five Protestant pastors issued a statement in 1979 claiming that "Christians can honestly use Marxist analyses without ceasing to be Christians," and that "Marxists can experience faith in Jesus Christ without ceasing to be revolutionary."

Indeed, euphoria seemed to run as out of spigots, to flood the world. Poet-priest Ernesto Cardenal wrote in the April 1980 issue of *One World*, the organ of the World Council of Churches, "This is a revolution that carries a deep sign of Christian love. It is enough that you look at the faces of the young Sandinistas who carry weapons in our streets. In them there is no hatred, their look is clean, their eyes shine, and their hearts sing."

The Reverend Ian Murray, Chairman of the Scottish Catholic International Aid Fund (SCIAF), dutifully visited Nicaragua and looked at all those young faces. He gave the Sandinistas his "unqualified support" because "in Nicaragua it is almost as though an attempt has been made to implement the Beatitudes."

Father Carney, a Jesuit working among Guatemala's poorest, wrote ecstatically about "this wonderful, popular, Sandinista revolutionary process" and about "the intimate relationship between Sandinism, as it is lived today in Nicaragua, and Christianity"; and he spoke about his work "with the lay leaders and many good Christian revolutionary Delegates of the Word, most of whom belong to the Sandinista Militia."

This kind of "ecumenical" madness delighted the minds of the Jesuits and many others. It found lyrical, almost poetical expression in religious publications of the United States. And it produced a welcoming echo in as important a personage as Jesuit Father General Arrupe in Rome. His were warm, encouraging words to "our brothers in Nicaragua" who were "championing God's littlest ones."

Arrupe's men in Nicaragua, certain of the support of their highest Superior in the Order, ventured still further. "If anyone in Nicaragua is not willing to participate in the revolution," said

Jesuit Father Alvaro Arguello from his government post in Managua, "they are certainly not Christian. To be a Christian today, one must also be a revolutionary." The turnabout was complete.

Inevitably, both Nicaraguan bishops and Vatican officials lost all their illusions. By the end of 1980, the honeymoon was over. The Sandinista investment of military and civil life in Nicaragua with Cuban and East European trainers, guides, and supervisors, the known relationship with Moscow, and the overtly brutal tactics of the Sandinistas in removing all obstacles from their path—all this and more—forced them to lose their euphoria for the revolution.

Toward the close of 1980, at the insistence of John Paul II, the Nicaraguan bishops requested those priests in government over whom they had direct authority to exit from politics and government, and to return to clerical duties. They also petitioned the Jesuit and Maryknoll Superiors in Rome and Central America to recall Fernando Cardenal and the other Jesuits, as well as Miguel D'Escoto Brockman, over whom the bishops had no jurisdiction.

The best the bishops were able to evoke with their demand was a seesaw struggle in which all the weight seemed to pile on at the other end. The five cabinet-level priests, including the two Jesuits and their local Superiors, answered the bishops with vague assurances. Yes, in time they would leave the government, when no dislocation in the onward path of the Christian revolution of Nicaragua would be caused by their doing so.

Continual and repeated insistence, whether from the Pope's Roman officials or from the Nicaraguan bishops, could not budge the priests from their political appointments. Nor could John Paul get Jesuit Father General Arrupe in Rome to invoke religious obedience to have Fernando Cardenal resign, or persuade the Maryknoll Superior General to retire Father Miguel D'Escoto Brockman, Nicaragua's Machiavellian Foreign Minister.

Rather, it seemed, the line to be followed in preference to papal wishes and demands was the one struck in the July 1980 issue of the Maryknoll Mission magazine—an encomium of "priests taking up arms, and others espousing the cause of those who feel that only blood will redeem Central America."

From the start of this struggle with the Pope, Jesuit Fernando Cardenal was as pivotal as he had been in the wider Sandinista struggle itself. For his Superiors in his Order, for the rank and file of Jesuits, and for many non-Jesuits and laymen in Nicaragua, the United States, and Europe, Cardenal was seen as he has been for a long time by the Sandinistas: a model for every twentieth-century priest, a man totally devoted to correcting the injustice perpetrated by the rich, the capitalists, on Christ's poor.

The struggle that was developing with Rome was Cardenal's meat. He was more than up to the challenge. No heavy-handed blunderer like his brother, Ernesto, Fernando Cardenal was a clever, attractive persuasive "gentleman Marxist," a "communist of the salons," as the French described his genre. He could talk turkey with Fidel Castro on his own terms, and just as easily talk to the Vatican's powerful Secretary of State, Agostino Cardinal Casaroli—and in each case come away with what he wanted.

Not that Secretary of State Casaroli was unwilling to accept Fernando Cardenal's assurances of good faith. He had his own very real political and ideological reasons to show favor to the Sandinistas, and indeed to all Latin Americans who were bending their efforts to marry Marxism and Catholicism.

Casaroli had cut his diplomatic teeth in the Vatican Secretariat of State under Pius XII and John XXIII. He was one of the original architects of the *Ostpolitik*, the Vatican policy toward Eastern European Communist states and the USSR, which began even during World War II with an attempted rapprochement with Stalin's USSR. Casaroli together with the future Paul VI (then an archbishop) led the Vatican of Pope John XXIII to make a secret pact with the Moscow Politburo: the Roman Catholic Church authorities would not formally denounce the USSR, its atheism, or its Marxism. The preservation of that pact was Casaroli's prime rule of diplomatic behavior.

Consequently, Casaroli's first and most basic principle of foreign policy as Vatican Secretary of State was clear: neither by word or action to show any opinions condemnatory of the Soviet Union and the Marxist-Leninism on which it is built, or of the Soviet Union's client states and surrogates.

That the Sandinistas were protégés of the Soviet Union, and their leaders professed Marxists, was not lost on Casaroli. As early as July of 1979, immediately on the heels of Luis Somoza's ouster by the Sandinistas, Casaroli removed the Papal Nuncio in Managua—Monsignore Gabriel Montalvo, who had long been identified with Somoza—and replaced him with a young *chargé d'affaires*, the Reverend Pietro Sambi, who had spent three years in Cuba and expressly believed the Church should taken an active part in the revolution.

Casaroli's knowledge of Nicaraguan affairs, as of all geopolitical realities, went very deep. There is no way that he—or indeed, Father General Pedro Arrupe—would have been unaware of the secret pacts signed between the Sandinistas of Nicaragua and Moscow in 1980. Nor could they have been ignorant of the arrangements made between the Nicaraguan Junta and Cuba's Fidel Castro during Castro's visit to Managua in July of 1980. That visit was ostensibly to celebrate the first anniversary of the Sandinista revolution, but its more concrete results were the arrangements to cover such matters as the shipment of arms, the transfer of young Nicaraguans to Cuba for indoctrination, the appointment of Cuban commissars to oversee the purity of Marxist ideology in the Nicaraguan armed forces, and coordination with Marxist-trained guerrilla forces already operating in the neighboring Central American states of El Salvador and Guatemala.

Indeed, from the time of that Castro visit, the Junta in Nicaragua began its public and triumphant talk of "open revolution in all the countries of Central America."

If eloquent testimony of the Cardinal Secretary of State's support for the Junta—its priest members included—were needed, it came in April and again in October of 1980, when Casaroli received Father Ernesto Cardenal and members of the Sandinista Junta in the Vatican and expressed his "understanding of the revolutionary process in Nicaragua and its importance for the whole of Central and Latin America."

With the inspiration and support of such powerful Roman figures as the Secretary of State and the Jesuit General, Jesuits in and out of government in Nicaragua continued full-tilt their collaboration in the Nicaraguan revolution and in the Marxist-Leninist policies of the Junta to which they had by now so effectively and thoroughly wedded their revised Church doctrine.

John Paul II's frequent and openly stated objections notwithstanding, clerics multiplied rather than diminished in government posts in Nicaragua. Ernesto Cardenal remained the most powerful spearhead figure within Nicaragua for Liberation Theology, as the government's director of the Literacy Campaign. In 1983, in fact, he became Nicaragua's Minister of Education. Fernando Cardenal, meanwhile, was busy ensuring the support of the clergy in Latin America and North America. Jesuit Father Alvaro Arguello remained as State Delegate. Jesuit Fathers Ricardo Falla and Ignacio Anezola were active members of the Ministry of Planning. Fathers Antonio Valdivieso and Uriel Molina were advisers on foreign affairs. Father Xavier Gorostiaga, as chief economic adviser to the Junta and architect of the official *Plan '80* for economic reconstruction, was proud to say that "we are designing a new economy," and that "the former capitalist-dependent economy was under direct imperialist domination." The list of Jesuits alone engaged "in similar works of justice," as it was put by Father Peter Marchetti, director of the Land Reform Commission, would run to approximately two hundred.

The value of the Jesuits to the Junta came to be measured also in dollars and cents, as well as in theological, ideological, and political value. They proved to be worth many times their weight in capitalist dollars directly from United States sources. The Nicaraguan Evangelical Committee for Aid to the Development (CEPAD), staffed by Jesuits and other clerics, received $305,000 from the National Council of Churches in 1981 alone. Father Valdivieso began receiving grants from North America at his Managua Ecumenical Center (AVEC) in 1981; by 1983, such grants alone came to $176,000. Father Gorostiaga who, as director of the Nicaraguan Institute for Economic and Social Research (INIES), was busy "designing a new economy" to replace the ". . . capitalist-dependent . . . imperialist domination," obtained a grant of $30,000 from the United Methodists and the National Council of Churches in 1983.

The Central American Historical Institute (ICHA), established by the Jesuits in Managua, was able not only to kick in $36,000 received in 1983 from the World Council of Churches, but to establish a North American branch of ICHA in Georgetown University to help its mother organization promote the revolution.

On their own testimony and from their activities, it was clear that INIES, ICHA, CEPAD, and AVEC were not engaged in religious activity with these monies. In their words and those of their American benefactors, all of these organizations were "immersed in the revolution" (CEPAD's executive director), fomenting "the participation of Christians in the revolutionary process" (World Council of Churches speaking of AVEC), and "at the service of the organs of political decision-making which seek the social and political transformation of the region" (Father Gorostiaga on the purpose of INIES).

Richard Shaull of NACLA had been a prophet without peer in his 1968 declaration that Christians and Marxists in Latin America were not merely having a dialogue but were working together. By 1983, the North Americans were becoming happy co-laborers.

One can legitimately conclude that Fernando Cardenal was the most important priest holding office in Nicaragua. Other clerics, Jesuit and non-Jesuit, took him as their inspiration, and his words as their justification. His success in evading John Paul II's wishes and the demands of the Nicaraguan bishops that he and the other priests resign from the government was a shining beacon of success. In every respect, he remained a pivotal figure in the Sandinista Junta as it consolidated its strength in Nicaragua and its standing in the world panoply of "fraternal socialist democracies." And, without a shadow of a doubt, Fernando Cardenal could not have achieved any of this but for the full support he enjoyed from his local Jesuit community, his Superiors, his Rector and Provincial; and from his Roman Superiors, including the Father General, Pedro Arrupe himself.

*   *   *

From his vantage point in Rome, Pope John Paul II developed a clear perception of what was going on in Nicaragua. He had no objection to a spirit of self-sacrifice and cooperation for the national good, as when the Jesuits donated El Charcho, the largest milk-producing farm in Nicaragua, to the government.

What John Paul did object to was the patently political and ideological activity of the priests, and their bastardization of Catholicism, of its hierarchic structure and its doctrines. The Pontiff's dossier of information about the Sandinista government was fat with details. He knew, of course, that the supreme Nicaraguan leader, Daniel Ortega y Saavedra, together with his Junta colleagues and the members of the nine-man Directorate, was establishing a Marxist-Leninist regime in close collaboration with Cuba as Moscow's surrogate and puppet in the western hemisphere, and with Moscow itself. But his information told him much more. John Paul knew that all the priest members of the Junta gave their assent to the party-to-party agreement signed in 1980 between the Sandinistas and the Soviet Communist Party.

He knew of the constant presence in Nicaragua of "advisers" from the Soviet Union and the Soviet European satellites, and of experts in guerrilla warfare from the PLO, the Baader-Meinhof gang of Germany, the Red Brigades of Italy, and the Basque ETA from Spain. He knew that Muammar Quadaffi of Lybia deposited $100 million in the Nicaraguan Central Bank, and that the Sandinistas received 110 Soviet tanks.

He knew that, in imitation of the "Pax Priests" movement in his own Poland and of the "Patriotic Catholic Church" in Communist China, the intracabinet plan of the Junta—again formed with the collaboration of Cardenal and his priest-colleagues in government—was to edge the Catholic bishops out of all authority and from the country itself, and finally to declare the People's Church as the only "Catholic Church" permitted in the new Nicaragua.

He knew that to help achieve this aim, the Literacy Campaign directed by Ernesto Cardenal was being used to instill Marxist principles in all who were being taught to read; and that to help further this aim, the Jesuits in government and their religious Superiors, officially joined with the Sandinistas and their organization of Base Communities to condemn in acrid terms the Nicaraguan bishops' objections to moral violations by the government.

The Pope knew that Ernesto Cardenal in his role as Education Minister was responsible as well for sending Nicaraguan youths to Fidel Castro's Marxist training island (for Cuba, it is the *Isle of Youth;* for the rest of the world, it is the *Isle of Pines*) to join the 10,000 African students in the seventeen schools of indoctrination named after Marxist president Agostino Neto of Angola. He knew that the Sandinistas, on their arrival at the levers of power, executed over 1500 political prisoners and that over 3000 were still kept—and some tortured—in Sandinista prisons.

In sum, through accurate reports about these and many other activities, the Pope knew that his priests—Jesuits and others—in Nicaragua were in close and corporate collaboration with a regime that violated human rights and sought the aid of others whose history of such violation was consistent and gross. Indeed, these priests were at the very heart of the regime that not only broke the laws of the Catholic Church, but was bent upon the systematic destruction of the hierarchic Church and on the usurpation of its authority in order to produce a totalitarian state organized on Marxist-Leninist lines.

Beyond that, in Ortega's own words, it was the Junta's intent to do the same in all of Central America. "Wide open revolution for all Central America," Ortega frequently repeated, the nutshell statement of his program.

In April of 1980, at about the time his Secretary of State, Cardinal Casaroli, was receiving those visiting members of the Nicaraguan Junta and reassuring them of his understanding support, the Holy Father received a delegation of Nicaraguan bishops. It was at just about the same time that the bishops had begun to pull back in their support of the Sandinistas. John Paul made it clear that he already saw the danger, and expected his bishops to act accordingly. "An atheistic ideology cannot serve as an instrument for the promotion of social justice," the Pope warned their Graces significantly.

Speaking to priests and clergy in Kinshasa, Zaire, that May, the Pope offered the ideal of the true priest: "Leave political responsibility to those who are entrusted with it. The role that is expected of you [priests] is another, a magnificent one. You are leaders in another jurisdiction as priests of Christ."

Back in Rome, on May 12, he was more pithy in his language: "A priest should be a priest. Politics is the responsibility of laymen."

By the time John Paul made these statements, the diplomatic cable traffic of his Vatican Secretariat of State had for nearly a year been reporting the triumphant declarations of members of the Junta about open revolution in all the countries of Central America.

It began to be a puzzle for some, given the increasingly open disobedience of his priests for his commands, and the Pope's own insistence on a recall to order, that John Paul did not take direct and serious action. But the little-known fact is that not long after his travels in spring 1980, and scarcely two years into his papacy, John Paul did begin to move in on the Jesuits, who, alone of all priests in the Catholic Church, owed special fealty and obedience to the papacy. His action began as a reaction to a blast of disobedience remarkable for its blatancy and impertinence even in a Church that worldwide was flooded with acts of disobedience.

The matter in hand this time did not concern Nicaragua directly. Rather, it involved the prestigious French Jesuit review *Études*, edited by Father André Masse, which published a three-part series of articles written by Jesuit Father Joseph Moingt. The articles dealt with priestly ministry, the nature of priesthood, and priestly celibacy. Because of his early writings, Father Moingt's views on the same subjects had been made all too clear; on the occasion of those earlier articles, Jesuit General Arrupe had been told by the Roman Congregation for Doctrine (the CDF) that Moingt was not to publish his views again. Arrupe had agreed, but excused Moingt's advocation of a married priesthood on the curious basis of Moingt's assertion that the bishops of Laos and Cambodia had requested permission from Rome for their priests to marry.

Whatever Arrupe had conveyed of the CDF's disapproval was like so much water off a duck's back for editor Masse and writer Moingt. In direct violation of that order from CDF, and in a remarkable display both of the impudence of some Jesuits and of the puzzling refusal of Arrupe to obey his Pope, editor Masse proceeded to publish the articles in June, July, and October of 1980, just as the recalcitrance of the Nicaraguan priests was creating heightened problems for papal strategy.

The timing, however, was not the offense. Moingt had gone

much farther now than merely proposing a married priesthood. In the words of an official report, he had—to his own satisfaction—"demolished the [traditional] Catholic concept of priestly ministry."

As a direct result of the incident, the entire shambles of Jesuit decline over the previous fifteen years was reviewed by John Paul. It was brought home to him that he was not dealing with dangerous pockets of recalcitrant Jesuits, but that an increasingly organized attack was being mounted against him from within his Church, and that its perpetrators enjoyed total immunity with their religious Superiors.

Father General Arrupe was informed by the Pope that the Society of Jesus needed thorough reform in its theologians, in its writers, in its social activists, in its method of training Jesuit candidates, in its colleges, universities, and institutes of higher learning, in its missionary methods in Africa and Asia, in its parishes, and in its social apostolate. In fact, throughout, from top to bottom in the Society, reform and housecleaning were imperative. Father Arrupe's own usefulness as General was also represented as nearing zero-point.

Of course, Holy Father, was the essence of Arrupe's dutiful answer. But according to the Jesuit *Constitutions*, which several of His Holiness's predecessors on this blessed Throne of Peter had approved and confirmed many times over the centuries, such reform could only be carried out in a normal and juridically correct manner by a General Congregation of Jesuit leaders from all over the world gathered at the Gesù in Rome with their Father General —with the permission of the Holy Father, of course. The Father General and his colleagues would need at least a year—it usually took fifteen months—in order to prepare adequately for such an important General Congregation.

John Paul's answer was unhesitating: Convoke the General Congregation. And prepare for it well. The problem had to be solved. There was no further word at that moment about ending Arrupe's term as General.

As of April 1980—the same busy month in which the Sandinistas were visiting the Vatican Secretary of State, and the Nicaraguan bishops were visiting the Pontiff—Father General Arrupe notified all the Provinces of the Society throughout the world that a General Congregation would be held the following year, or, at the latest, in 1982. Preparation in the Provinces was to begin immediately.

Actually, at this stage of the struggle, Arrupe was near the end of his tether. He had run out of options for eluding papal efforts at controlling the Society. In large part, his Society appeared to be beyond recall to its due order, even by a Pope. Arrupe was the best placed man to recognize this. He had presided over the growing and now irreducible lump of resistance by Jesuits to John Paul II. Well-founded Vatican rumor had it that John Paul was going to remove him from the Generalate, as a start in the right direction. God alone knew what that direction was. Arrupe was tired.

In the course of a ten-minute meeting granted him in August of 1980, Arrupe inquired if the Holy Father wished him to resign his post as Jesuit general. No, was the Pope's brusque answer. John Paul did not say so in so many words, but he had made up his mind that he himself should keep the initiative in his hands rather than appoint a successor or caretaker to carry on independently in the General's place. Nor had the Pope any intention of letting Father General Arrupe escape so lightly from the mess he had created over his fifteen years at the helm of the Society. The Holy Father, Arrupe was informed, was not talking about the simple resignation of one man. What was at issue was the nature and function of the whole Society as the Pope's militia.

There were many possibilities. The status of the Society could be changed. The draft text of the Church's latest version of Canon Law was in its final stages; one small paragraph in it would suffice to deprive the Society of Jesus of all its privileges in the Church and of its special status in relation to the papacy. It could be reduced to the rank of an ordinary diocesan congregation governed locally by single bishops. There were still other and more drastic possibilities. It might be necessary to suppress the Society, at least for a time, and perhaps reconstitute it later according to its original principles; certain more traditional-minded Jesuits had in fact already petitioned Rome to do just that.

The unremittingly ominous tenor of this papal answer was not lost on Arrupe. But to be certain the matter was clear to the Jesuit, his allies in the Vatican Secretariat of State explained the fundamental cause of the Pope's dissatisfaction to the Father General: In the Holy Father's strategy, bent to cope with Marxism as *the* threat, the Jesuits were the greatest obstacle; and they were the greatest consolation of His Holiness's enemies. Like it or not, that was fact.

Ostensibly to clear his own record as General and to demonstrate that all Jesuits were alerted in the proper fashion, and so to repudiate any thought of official Jesuit approval for Marxism, in December of 1980 Father Arrupe composed, but—in the circumstances, curiously—delayed publishing a letter on the subject of Marxism which could be interpreted in an orthodox way.

By this time, John Paul II had become a giant striding across the international landscape. He was forever in the public eye. The atmosphere around him was ever more tense, ever crisis-ridden. With each month, his intentions and his actions became more significant to the rival planners in Washington and Moscow, as well as to grandiose financial centers. For in one sense, John Paul had seized power. He commanded public attention. He was skillfully evoking whatever respect or veneration or even sheer worldly interest still existed for his office as Pope.

Moscow nervously watched the growth of Poland's Solidarity movement and the decay of political Communism in that country. Washington nervously eyed Soviet military threats to inundate Poland as they had Czechoslovakia in 1968 and Hungary in 1956. Washington also fidgeted over the decay of the situation in Nicaragua and Central America.

International financial analysts and investors began to fear that a success of Solidarity would ruin the entire system of investment, lending, and industrial production built up in Soviet-dominated economies over twenty long years. The nonunion, strike-free, low-wage conditions of labor in those economies was a boon. A Solidarity that obtained freedom of action in the field of labor relations would eliminate that boon.

In 1980, Anatoly Adamshin, head of the Soviet Foreign Ministry that dealt with Italy, France, Turkey, and Greece, met with Pope John Paul II. "If the Church commits itself to stem the ardor of the Polish strikers within the limits acceptable to Moscow," Adamshin declared, "then Moscow in her turn would renounce the idea of invasion." Moscow might even be willing to go further. That "further" was the great carrot dangling in front of John Paul's eyes.

With that much assured, John Paul decided to move forward in his negotiations. His intricate efforts reached a climax in February 1981, when Adamshin paid him a second visit, this time heading a top-flight Soviet delegation. Again, the subject was Poland's Solidarity. Again, the subject was the format in which Moscow would allow Solidarity to flourish. The results were concrete: There could be Soviet acquiescence in the further progress of Solidarity, provided Solidarity's success would leave intact three elements—the Communist Party of Poland, the domination of Polish parliamentary life by Communists, and the Communist security forces (army and police). Solidarity should, in other words, confine itself to the fields of culture, religion, and labor relations. No politics.

No militarism. No sabotage. No links with American underground armaments supplies.

Adamshin assured John Paul that such a successful turn in Solidarity, curing the continual malaise in the Polish economy, would be of direct interest to his masters in Moscow. Above all, it would be of interest as an example to be followed in their other satellites—the "other fraternal socialist states"—where the closed market economy was always in trouble.

It would also seem, on good authority, that Adamshin indirectly warned John Paul: Success in the Solidarity movement would mean the end of a low-wage, no-strike, tax-free industrial work force. And would this not have a direct effect on the internationalization of manufactured goods that relied on such a work force, not only in Poland, but elsewhere in the fraternal socialist states? And would not this affect the pocketbooks of powerful interests? Adamshin was not talking merely about the effect for hard-line Stalinists in the USSR and elsewhere.

By April of 1981, John Paul II was straining all the deepest reserves of his strength and ingenuity in order to carry an awesome double burden:

On the one hand, he labored to hold the allegiance of the approximately 350 million Catholics in Latin America; to keep them from falling into the net of Marxism spread, as his information clearly convinced him, not only by Moscow's "normal" allies—Cuba, Sandinista Nicaragua, and the like—but by influential Jesuits, some cardinals, some bishops, and many priests and nuns.

On the other hand, he sustained and guided the Solidarity movement in Poland not merely by counsel, not merely by funds, but by direct intervention with the succession of floundering governments in Warsaw, and with the frightened men of the Politburo in Moscow already knee-deep in bloody trouble in Afghanistan.

On top of all this, by early 1981 Pope John Paul had managed to travel to twenty countries spread over five continents, preaching in twenty-three languages. His most recent trip, in February of that year, had been a grueling twelve-day marathon to Pakistan, the Philippines, Guam, Japan, and Alaska. Everywhere, his message was the same: This is Peter the Apostle in his 267th successor, the Vicar of Christ, announcing the need for holiness, and for justice for all men in the name of Jesus.

Viewed from any angle, the total activity of this Pope was colossal. It taxed his physical endurance and his mental powers beyond the limits of most men.

Jesuit Father General Pedro Arrupe, on the other hand, did not seem to be able even to complete the preparations for the General Congregation of his Jesuits. Nor did he seem able somehow to get Fernando Cardenal in order. Rather, Cardenal—like the Pope—toured widely. He made his abilities, his imposing presence, and his political and ideological viewpoints clear to North American audiences on his lecture tour—mainly around the circuit of Jesuit campuses. So appealing and publicized a Sandinista spokesman had he become, in spite of John Paul's repeated admonitions to Arrupe, that in 1981, while his Pope was constantly delivering a totally different message and working for a totally opposed goal, Fernando Cardenal was delighted to receive a nomination for the Nobel Peace Prize from 133 members of the British House of Parliament and the European Parliament combined.

Fernando Cardenal was not the only Jesuit Arrupe seemed unable to control. Nor were Nicaraguan Jesuits alone in their continuing organized, corporate disobedience. Jesuits in Latin America, North America, Europe—everywhere it sometimes seemed—were sniping with carefree abandon at John Paul's social teaching and religious doctrine. There were continual streams of complaints arriving at the papal office, all detailing the unorthodox opinions being taught by Jesuits in Europe and the United States. There were, in addition, revelations that certain circles of the international section of the Masonic Lodge in Europe and Latin America were actively organizing opposition to the Pontiff in Poland; that Vatican prelates—some twenty in all—were formal members of the Italian Lodge; and that once again Arrupe's Jesuits seemed involved with the Lodge circles opposed to the Pontiff. Paul VI had already in 1965 warned Arrupe and the Delegates to the 31st Jesuit General Congregation of the dangers in belonging to the Compact; it began to appear to John Paul that the warning had not been too wide of the mark.

Some of Pope John Paul's most trusted advisers began urging him to wait no longer for Arrupe to act. There was too much at stake to allow the runaway Jesuit leaders to continue pillaging papal strategy, papal authority, and this Pope's clearly stated orders. Tempted though the Holy Father may have been to follow that advice, the problem was then and still is that to do so could be like shooting himself in the foot. Very likely, given the prestige of the Jesuits and the widespread rebellion against the papacy, to take unilateral action against Arrupe and his Jesuits could provoke repercussions that could damage his own papal policies and perhaps damage the Church.

For one thing, precisely because of the blatant Marxist outlook and Moscow ties of the Jesuits in Nicaragua in particular, unless the forced withdrawal of the priests in the Nicaraguan government were neatly done, it might be taken as an overt violation of that secret pact formed nearly twenty years before between the Moscow politburo and the Vatican.

Furthermore, because the observance of that pact and all its implications was Agostino Cardinal Casaroli's guiding principle as Secretary of Vatican State, Casaroli might well resign his post at the Secretariat in open protest. In that case, John Paul would lose an important player in the "hot-and-cold" diplomacy, the "carrot-and-stick" policy, he practiced vis-à-vis the Soviets. Meanwhile, Vatican protocol would still leave Cardinal Casaroli with considerable influence and power and somewhat less constraint if he removed himself or were removed from his post.

And, in addition to all of that, at this still early stage of his pontificate, as he realized full well, John Paul did not know who in the Vatican Secretariat and the entire bureaucracy was really on his side, nor how many within the system had been "acquired" by Moscow directly or indirectly.

It was, in other words, the wrong time for any scarifying action that touched the Soviet Union. John Paul's plans for Solidarity in Poland were maturing. The Soviets knew of them, did not approve or disapprove of them, but were waiting to see the clear outlines of the game, the nature of the *quid pro quo* John Paul could and would offer.

There was yet one more element to add to the Pontiff's caution in acting against the Sandinista priests: Vatican protocol. Normally, a Pope would take advice from his chief councillors—mainly the cardinals who head all important Vatican ministries. John Paul was not at all sure he could rally a consensus for direct and peremptory action against the priests-in-government, or the Jesuits in particular.

The brutal fact of life for John Paul, as for any Pope who is not highly endowed with ruthlessness and skilled in Vatican moves, is that he cannot force his will on every powerful member of his Vatican administration. And the brutal fact is, too, that John Paul, like Popes before him, is constrained by far-reaching actions of his predecessors on the Throne of Peter.

Too slowly for some, then, but nevertheless surely, the confrontation between the Pope and a growing number of his clergy, always spearheaded by the Jesuits, simmered toward a boiling point. Within three years of John Paul II's election, and despite efforts to block it—efforts in which yet again Jesuits seemed to be implicated—the mind-shattering success of Poland's Solidarity was being played out moment by moment on one side of the world, while on the other side, the Sandinista thrust at international Marxist leadership in Central and South America was strengthening, and resisted all papal efforts to block Jesuits and other priests from legitimizing that thrust.

With all the weights on the scales, and as insane as such a thought would have been a scant forty years before, it began to seem not only that there really could be a war between the Pope and the Jesuits, but that it would be open and bloody. And not far off.

3 | WHITE POPE, BLACK POPE

I n some respects, the meeting that convened in the middle of spring 1981 bore the marks of thousands of board meetings going on at the same moment in every daylight country of the world. Beyond glass-paneled double doors, a conference between seven men was in progress. A folder bulging with reports lay in front of each man. At each man's elbow a full carafe of water topped with a glass was perched. Anyone happening to glance in might have said that the men gathered there were absorbed in the sort of hushed but free-wheeling discussion typical of board meetings everywhere.

But this was not the sort of meeting most people have ever witnessed, or even glimpsed through shut, glass-paneled doors. This conference room was on the third floor of the Palace of the Popes on Vatican Hill. The report folders were red damask and emblazoned in gold with the Tiara and Keys. Outside the door, a secretary and two Swiss Guards in traditional uniform were on duty to block all intruders. Seated at the conference table were the Pontiff of the Holy Roman Catholic Church and six of his most powerful cardinals, the movers and shakers of the Vatican, a cameo of its most formidable strength. And the subject of discussion between them was the life or death of the Society of Jesus: whether, in other words, the Order headed by Father General Pedro Arrupe should be allowed to go on as it was, or be reorganized and reset according to the often-repeated wishes of three Popes, or be officially done to death by the power and under the authority of Pope John Paul II.

In theory, the Pope did not have to meet with anyone to make a decision in this matter. In principle, he had the power. All the power. All other officials, including the six cardinals who flanked him at this meeting, were appointed by him. And, though he alone of all major officials in the Roman Catholic Church is elected, once that is accomplished, his power—the power of the papacy—descends to him directly from God.

As is always the case with power, however, theory and principle are one thing, and reality is another. Each Pope must be strong enough to take in hand the power conferred on him, and wield it. Any scrap of it that he does not take up is certain to be usurped and used by others.

By this early spring of 1981, for example, John Paul had already felt the effect firsthand of the enormous power that had accrued over centuries to the Father General of the Society of Jesus. So great is that power in Rome and in the world at large, and so widely is it recognized, that whoever holds the office of Jesuit General also holds the unofficial title of "the Black Pope." Black in this case is not meant to indicate a menace of any sort. It is simple recognition of the fact that, like any other Jesuit, the hugely powerful General of the Society always dresses in black clericals, in contrast to the traditional white robes of the hugely powerful Holy Father.[1]

Another example would be forthcoming in this very meeting; if they had their way, at least three of the six cardinals at this table with John Paul II were going to give their Pope a lesson in Roman power. *Romanità*, that particular brand of power is called. It is axiomatic that any Pope who hopes to succeed must be at least two things: iron-willed, and skilled in *romanità*.

Romanità rests upon one basic principle: *Cunctando regitur mundus*. If you can outwait all, you can rule all. The hallmark of *romanità* is understatement in action and in all forms of expression. It is, in a way, power in whispers. Essential to it are a sense of timing reamed with patience, a ruthlessness that excludes the hesitation of emotions, and an almost messianic conviction of ultimate success. Few are born with it. Most genuine "Romans" who flourish must learn it over time.

For all his strength of will, John Paul did not come to the papacy skilled in *romanità*. And time was the one commodity that neither the situation in Poland nor that in Nicaragua afforded him.

At the meeting that day, His Holiness sat in his white robes at the head of the table like a man whose husky and ebullient strength was barely caged, barely restrained from bursting forth. At age sixty-one, this first Polish Pope was a personality in powerful ascendancy, breathing enterprise, cloaked in a personal charisma, already a staple figure of the international news media. With the power of the papacy behind him, most would have said, what prelate of his Church could stand up to him?

Romanità or no, Karol Wojtyla is a canny man. Surely, looking at the six cardinals seated to his right and left, dressed in their blood-red regalia, he understood where each of them stood not only in this matter of the Society of Jesus, but in the matter of his entire papal strategy.

In the chair immediately to the Pope's right sat *"Dottrina"*— the cardinal charged with overseeing the purity of Roman Catholic doctrine throughout the vast and varied world of the Church. A smooth-faced Bavarian, wise and by no means simple, *Dottrina* was a professional theologian with all the confidence of the intellectual cleric. At fifty-five, he was totally white-haired, and was the youngest man present. John Paul knew that *Dottrina* would always give total support to the papal will.

And so, he knew, would *"Propaganda,"* the cardinal responsible for promoting Catholicism among the non-Christian peoples of Africa and Asia. *Propaganda* was a Brazilian of Italian extraction, older looking than his peers, and saintly. Some said of him that he was simple as a dove and not quite as wise as a serpent. That was probably because his cardinal colleagues never knew what to expect of him. Despite his directness and simplicity of style, *Propaganda* was known to lob grenades into discussions with disconcerting accuracy.

Pope John Paul's final ally in the conference room that day was *"Clero,"* the cardinal at the head of the Congregation, or office, in charge of all Catholic diocesan clerics.

Of the three remaining cardinals at the meeting, one would not necessarily stand against the Pope—but he would not necessarily stand with him either. *"Vescovi,"* the cardinal who supervises all Catholic bishops, was a master of *romanità*. Heavily joweled, cunning, young for all his sixty-eight years, *Vescovi* once came within a brace of being made Pope. He knew how to extract a price for his support. He might throw his weight on the Pope's side, if he had his way in other things.

"Religiosi," as the Vatican's supervisor of all Religious Orders of men and women, an Argentinian of Italian blood, was certain to

oppose John Paul. He was an intimate of men in high places who
disliked any Pope who rocked their boat, and of men in secret
places who desired no triumph for the papacy in general and
abhorred this Pope in particular. From his carefully groomed head
down to his immaculate white French cuffs fastened with taste-
fully expensive gold links, *Religiosi* gave the appearance of a man
devoted to an aseptic *toilette*.

The most powerful single man at that table, other than the
Pontiff himself, was *"Stato,"* Cardinal Secretary of State for the
Vatican. *Stato* was the Pope's opposite in everything. Where John
Paul was robust and athletic, *Stato* was a diminutive, hollow-
cheeked, bespectacled northern Italian who was so gaunt, the
nickname they used behind his back was "Skull." His pale skin
seemed almost bloodless, and its contrast with the redness of his
lips and ears made it appear as if, for all of his thirty-seven years
in Vatican diplomacy, he had been facing into a perpetual zero-
chill wind.

Alone of all his generation, *Stato* had achieved a certain intimacy with and access to the leaders in the USSR and in the Soviet
satellite countries. As with his physique, it might seem, so with
his Soviet ties: They were small and bloodless by the side of the
Soviet dealings this Slavic Pope had already made his own. But the
skilled use of *romanità* can transform tiny inroads into great advantages. And in any case, in *Stato*'s view, it was more likely that
the day of this Pope's reign was young. *Cunctando regitur mundus.*

Interestingly, this meeting had not been requested by the Pope,
but by one or two of the cardinals present, so that they might avail
themselves of what, in the delicate cadences of *romanità*, would
be called "clarifications" about the Pontiff's plans for the Jesuits.

And so it was that even as the White Pope opened the meeting
with a ten-minute statement of "clarification," the Black Pope,
Pedro Arrupe, seemed an effective presence, an invisible eighth
man at the table. That slightly built, hook-nosed, seventy-three-
year-old Basque was known personally to each of these seven men.
He was loved by none of them. He was valued by some as a most
useful ally, and detested by others as a most dangerous enemy. His
Holiness had learned to fear him.

In explaining his mind about the Society of Jesus, John Paul
centered his remarks mainly around the headings of fidelity to the
papacy and propagation of authentic Roman Catholic doctrine.

When the Pope had finished, *Religiosi* made his own views
clear. True to form, his point of view was at odds with the Pon-

tiff's. After all, what the Holy Father found as faults in the Jesuits could be found in many other Religious Orders of men and women —Franciscans, Carmelites, Dominicans, Maryknoll Fathers and Sisters, the Irish Columban Fathers, and so on. And the same faults could also be found in the bishops of Latin America and indeed throughout the entire Church.

To illustrate his second point, *Religiosi* cited two of the most obvious examples. The former Bishop of Cuernavaca, Mexico, Mendez Arceo, started his Sunday sermons with the clenched-fist salute of the Communist Internationale and shouted, *"Soy Marxista!* I am a Marxist!"* And their own Venerable Colleague Cardinal Evaristo Arns of São Paolo, Brazil, took every opportunity to scarify rigid capitalism and laud the idea of a redistribution of wealth in order to relieve endemic poverty. And what about those French bishops who insisted on placing the birthday of Karl Marx on the official Church liturgical calendar to be celebrated along with the birthdays and death days of the Church's saints and martyrs? And what about the way Canadian bishops made use of the Marxist analysis of the class struggle when they discussed the social question?

Religiosi was certain that his Venerable colleague, *Vescovi*, sitting beside him at the table, who was in charge of all the bishops, could verify what he was saying.

It might have seemed to *Religiosi* that *Vescovi* had not yet decided where his own advantage might lie in the discussion, but this was a mistaken reading of *Vescovi*.

Vescovi had his reasons for not helping *Religiosi*—good ones. After *Stato*, *Vescovi* could be reckoned to be the most powerful single cardinal in the Vatican Curia. In charge of the Congregation of Bishops, he could—if he wished—have a decisive hand in the appointment of bishops everywhere, except in mission lands. There, *Propaganda* had the important say. But *Vescovi* was also president of the Pontifical Commission for Latin America, a position from which he wielded enormous influence. It was well-known that *Vescovi* shared a double persuasion with John Paul: that Latin America must be saved from Marxism, and that there was little to distinguish between the out-and-out Marxists in Latin America and the bulk of Jesuit, Dominican, Franciscan, and Maryknoll priests and nuns. "What happens in Latin America," *Vescovi* had said over two years ago, "will humanly speaking determine the fate of the Church in the next century."

No, *Vescovi* would not take up *Religiosi*'s implied invitation. Most of these left-leaning bishops in Latin America had been appointed before *Vescovi* laid his hands on the controls of episcopal appointments. Now, *Vescovi* remained silent.

No matter. *Religiosi* was quite ready to defend the Jesuits as acting in complete obedience to the bishops of the Church, who were, as he did not need to remind those present, the successors to the Twelve Apostles. The Second Vatican Council had emphasized the role of the College of Bishops in governing the Church and guiding its people. The real problem, in *Religiosi*'s view, did not lie with the Jesuits. Nor with the bishops, who were out in the field ministering as apostles to their dioceses, grappling with on-the-spot problems. For *Religiosi*, the real problem lay in the gap between all 3567 members of the College of Bishops and the Holy See. *Religiosi* avoided any direct mention of John Paul II's person. But no one had any doubt as to his meaning.

In his analysis, *Religiosi* concluded, the government as well as the teaching authority of the Church should be normally and regularly shared between the Pontiff and the College of Bishops. Perhaps His Holiness would allow the meeting to turn to this, the real problem: the lack of cohesion—in fact, the dissension and disunity—that existed between the Holy See and the bishops. But in any case, the Jesuits should not be made scapegoats for others guilty of graver faults—graver because those others shouldered greater responsibility than the Jesuits in the Church Universal.

As frank as *Religiosi*'s position was, and as deeply antagonistic to the Pontiff's, it was all expressed in terms acceptable to *romanità*. No gestures. No wagging of fingers. No raising of the voice.

So, too, with the reaction of the other six. No emotion was betrayed by an uneasy stirring, a straightening in one's chair, a deep filling of one's lungs, a pursing of one's lips, a knitting of one's brow. At the most, an eye might be raised for a swift glance at the speaker, or at a friend or a foe.

And certainly there was no clamoring to be the next to speak. At such meetings as this, *romanità* is the chairman; and at this meeting, *romanità* pointed its invisible finger at *Dottrina*, the professional theologian sitting at the Pope's right hand in every way, including his position as overseer of purity in Catholic doctrine.

Dottrina wished to remind his Venerable Colleagues of the words of the Second Vatican Council in describing the College of Bishops. He quoted the document of the Vatican Council on the subject: The College of Bishops was "to be understood necessarily and always with its head who, in the College, keeps in its integrity his office as supreme pastor of the Church Universal and as Vicar of Christ."

In other words, *Dottrina* pressed the point, it was a false distinction to speak, as his Venerable Colleague had just done, of the College of Bishops as distinct and separate from the Roman Pontiff. Rather, without the Roman Pontiff, there was no College of Bishops. On the contrary, the only real distinction that could be made was between the Roman Pontiff alone, and the College of Bishops that necessarily included the Roman Pontiff. The Roman Pontiff could act alone. The College could not act without the Roman Pontiff. Therefore, any bishops at variance with the Roman Pontiff—and their Venerable Colleague had just assured them there were many—were at variance with the College of Bishops. *Dottrina* was sure that *Vescovi* would make it his business— because it was his duty after all—to ferret them out and bring them to order.

It was as lovely a parry and thrust in the game of *romanità* as had been seen in some time. But there was not a smile of victory or a frown of defeat as the point went home. And indeed, *Dottrina* was not yet finished.

As to the case of the Jesuits, he went on, it was qualitatively different from that of the bishops. The College of Bishops had been established by God. The Jesuits had been established by the Roman Pontiff. To him they owed their existence and their allegiance. They were now in a state of revolt, according to His Holiness. As a Pope had created them, so a Pope could regulate them, or, if need be, terminate them. And that regulation or termination of the Jesuits was the proper subject of this meeting.

Religiosi's challenge to His Holiness to let the meeting go off-track, veer away from the matter of the Jesuit problem, had been surgically amputated.

With almost no gap in the discussion, however, *Stato* took up the cudgels. His approach was much more indirect than *Religiosi*'s had been. *Stato* reminded his Venerable Colleagues that he had been with the present Holy Father at His Holiness's two meetings with the Soviet negotiator, Anatoly Adamshin, the most recent of which had been earlier this very year of 1981. His Holiness had given the Soviets a guarantee that no word or action, either by His Holiness or the Polish Hierarchy or Solidarity's leaders, would violate the Moscow-Vatican Pact of 1962.

Stato did not need to explain to his listeners that in the late spring of 1962, a certain Eugene Cardinal Tisserant had been dispatched by Pope John XXIII to meet with a Russian prelate, one Metropolitan Nikodim, representing the Soviet Politburo of Premier Nikita Khrushchev. Pope John ardently desired to know if the Soviet Government would allow two members of the Russian Orthodox Church to attend the Second Vatican Council set to open the following October. The meeting between Tisserant and Nikodim took place in the official residence of Paul Joseph Schmitt, then the bishop of Metz, France. There, Nikodim gave the Soviet answer. His government would agree, provided the Pope would guarantee two things: that his forthcoming Council would issue no condemnation of Soviet Communism or of Marxism, and that the Holy See would make it a rule for the future to abstain from all such official condemnation.

Nikodim got his guarantees. Matters were orchestrated after that for Pope John by Jesuit Cardinal Augustine Bea until the final agreement was concluded in Moscow, and was carried out in Rome, in that Vatican Council as well as in the policies of the Holy See for nearly two decades since.

Stato said he had but two questions to ask. The Vatican Council and two Popes since John XXIII had respected this guarantee. Would His Holiness also respect the guarantee? And would his Polish Hierarchy and Solidarity's leaders respect it?

The question *Stato* did not ask was so clear to everyone by now that he did not need to put it into words: How could John Paul II indict the Jesuits for their support of Marxist thinkers and Communist guerrillas in Latin America without explicitly condemning Soviet Marxism and its Communist surrogates? Without, in other words, violating not only the Metz Pact, but his own assurance to Adamshin that "Metz," as the little-known agreement was generally referred to, would be respected during his pontificate?

Stato's message, then, was clear. He knew as well as anyone that Jesuit wanderlust from Catholic teaching could be reproved in terms that would violate no pact or agreement. But he would protect the Jesuits. Would His Holiness fight about it? Or compromise?

Probably hoping for the latter choice, *Stato* went on to point out that Father General Arrupe had just published an article demonstrating that no Catholic, much less a Jesuit, could rely on the Marxist analysis of human society and history in order to decide which side to take in the "struggle of the classes." The Cardinal Secretary did not point out that Arrupe had waited over three months, from December 30, 1980, until April 4, to publish it; or that the timing seemed to indicate that Arrupe had been alerted to the issue that would be considered at this very private meeting.

Stato's defense of the Jesuits was over; what he proceeded to do next was to indicate both his willingness and his ability to carry this fight over the Society of Jesus directly into the arena of papal strategy. To raise the stakes, in other words.

Stato reminded all present that his position as His Holiness's Secretary of State required him to maintain cordial if unofficial relations with the governments of the USSR and the Eastern bloc. They were at best tenuous relations, true. But it was far better than the position of other governments in relation to the Soviet Socialist fraternity. In order to maintain those relations, he would have to distance himself from any statement of the Holy See that offended that fraternity. *Stato*'s warning, his threat of resignation and open opposition, was clear; and it was known to the others that for his own reasons, John Paul did not want to provoke a resignation or dismiss *Stato*.

Stato assured His Holiness and his Venerable Brothers that no one was essential in the vineyard of the Lord, and the ultimate decision was His Holiness's. However, *Stato* and his office had been singularly useful so far in His Holiness's guidance and fomenting of Solidarity—in *all* aspects of that difficult affair, political and material.

Men of the rank of those present knew *Stato*'s role in funneling Vatican Bank funds through neutral channels—Vatican-owned and foreign-owned holding companies, for example, and off-shore finance houses in which the Vatican held equity control—into the ever-emptying coffers of Solidarity. *Stato*'s position in the Vatican made him an ex-officio member of PECA, the Vatican's Prefecture of Economic Affairs. PECA makes all major decisions regarding the movement of Vatican funds. John Paul II, meanwhile, like most Popes, is not acquainted with the intricate network of off-shore finance houses and holding companies within the ramification of the Vatican Bank. Strictly speaking, *Stato* could veto any *sub-rosa* shifting of funds. And yet, if the Pontiff's present plans worked out, a great deal more money, not less, would be needed for Solidarity.

Stato had but one more comment to make. His cooperation with His Holiness this last year in the matter of funds had acquired an element of danger. The Italian government was continuing its investigation into the scandal that had erupted in the *Banco Ambrosiano* of Milan, sending shock waves throughout the international world of finance. For better or worse, the *Banco Ambrosiano* and its director, Roberto Calvi, who had been indicted in his bank's scandal, had been associated in that all-important clandestine supply of funds for Solidarity.

Of course, the Secretary was confident that all would be well for the reputation of the Holy See and the Holy Father's labors for his beloved Poland. No one could doubt his own devotion to the best interests of both the Holy See and the Holy Father. It was in this spirit that he had made his earlier comments about the Jesuits.

Even *romanità* had a difficult time digesting the hard stuff of political and financial threats that *Stato* had chosen to shove across the table at the Pontiff.

For *Propaganda*, with that engagingly simple directness of his, it apparently seemed time for a change. Time, he said disarmingly, to discuss something he could understand far better than the intricacies of East European politics or the relationship of Jesuits to Marxists. Time to discuss what was going on in that part of the Church confided to his care—the mission fields in Africa and Asia.

Propaganda had prepared a report ahead of time; a copy was in each of the red damask folders, and it had been read thoroughly by everyone before the meeting. That report, which he summarized briefly, set out in painful detail how far Jesuit missionaries working in India had gone in adulterating Christian belief. *Propaganda*'s summary only touched on the deformed meaning of priesthood, of baptism, of the Sacrament of the Eucharist, and of the primacy and authority of the Holy Father in the Church, according to what the Jesuits taught in India. He talked now of the dilution into unrecognizable forms of the basic Christian beliefs in immortality, Heaven and Hell, the value of prayer and mortification and penance, the meaning of the Mass and of salvation.

Propaganda was all the more devastating in his remarks because he appeared to have no personal ax to grind. He merely had a question: Why? Why had the Jesuits adulterated and deformed even the most central Christian beliefs? He was aware that the Jesuits themselves referred to "inculturation" and "indigenization." But the result was an organized and steadily progressive de-Christianization of what was once in India a flourishing Roman Catholic population of some three million.

Propaganda answered his own question in the same even tone in which he had asked it. The Jesuits in India had become what they had because they and their Roman Superiors had continued to follow the teachings of Jesuit Father Pierre Teilhard de Chardin. De Chardin had been the darling of Jesuit intellectuals, in fact, for almost forty years, despite the Holy See's 1960 condemnation of the man and his writings. Those writings, *Propaganda* reminded his Venerable Colleagues in the very words of the official condemnation, "swarm with ambiguities, indeed with grave errors, so as to offend against Catholic doctrine." Small wonder then, as far as *Propaganda* could see, if the Jesuits persisted in following the star of de Chardin, that they were at cross-purposes with the Church's welfare.

In sum, *Propaganda* agreed both with the 1960 condemnation of the Jesuit de Chardin, and with the Holy Father's indictment of the society as a whole in 1981.

It seemed at first as if *Clero* would confine his contribution to an amplification of *Propaganda*'s link between Teilhard de Chardin's work and present-day Jesuit activity. Why was it, he seemed merely to muse about the problem a bit further, that the Jesuit faculties of philosophy and theology at the Sèvres Centre in Paris were organizing a celebration for the coming June 13 to honor the centenary of de Chardin's birth? According to *Clero*'s information, they were doing so with the blessing of Pontifical Institutes in Rome and the approval of the Secretariat of State and of the Jesuit General.

Clero's suggestion was that all involved would do better to offer Masses for de Chardin's soul than to try to sort out his ambiguous thought, and to act on his vague and dangerous theories. His Holiness's suggestion was more pointed. The Pontiff was sure that *Stato* would communicate to Father Arrupe the Holy See's disapproval of the planned celebration.

Clero did have one or two other questions, as it turned out. There was the matter of a devastating report received in the Vatican a year and a half before, in October of 1979. Their Venerable Brother Cardinal Vincente Scherer of Porto Alegre, Brazil, had written at length about the Jesuit *Colegio Anchieta* in that same city. According to Scherer, Marxist textbooks were used in the classrooms, Marxist principles were inculcated into the students, the Sacraments of Confession and Communion were derided as anachronistic. What, *Clero* puzzled, had happened to that report? The Jesuit *Colegio* had gone along its merry way. Why hadn't Father General Arrupe corrected those grave errors?

And then, too, *Clero* continued to puzzle matters aloud, there was the strange case of Jesuit Father Caprile, who wrote in the official Jesuit magazine, *Civiltà Cattolica*, published in Rome. At issue for Caprile was the Roman Catholic prohibition, under pain of excommunication, against Catholic membership in the Lodge.

Excommunication was a dead letter, Caprile wrote in his article, and Lodge membership was open to any Catholic. That was a blatant undermining of the Pope's own decisions about morality. How was it that Caprile could publish in this vein at all, much less with such impunity and with his Father General's blessing?

Both of *Clero*'s "puzzlings" were aimed specifically at *Stato*. The alliance between the Cardinal Secretary and *Civiltà Cattolica* was a matter of record. And it was well-known that *Stato* had appropriated Cardinal Scherer's damning report and buried it in a dead file.

Dottrina found that moment an appropriate one to tie a few threads together. It was not only in Rome and Latin America and India that such strange things were happening, always with Jesuits at their center. There were pages of documentation in the red damask folders before their Eminences about Jesuits teaching and preaching and acting consistently in ways that not merely departed from, but contradicted, the doctrinal teaching of the Church, as well as the explicit views of His Holiness on the most vital issues.

He could, *Dottrina* offered, point in pages of those reports to a dozen names of prominent European Jesuits, over two dozen more American Jesuits, at least twenty-five from Latin America, another dozen or so each from India, Japan, the Philippines, Ireland, and England. Among all of them, as far as *Dottrina* could see, the only common threat was their insistence on the need to support the "class struggle." If that wasn't Marxism, then *Dottrina* did not understand the meaning of the term. And if such a widespread phenomenon did not have the official sanction both of Father General Arrupe and of the other Jesuit Superiors, then *Dottrina* did not understand the machinery of the Jesuit Order itself.

For his part, *Dottrina* concluded, the whole situation had already gone too far. The Holy Father should act decisively. Now.

Religiosi made a second effort to influence the outcome of the discussion in favor of the Jesuits. He was certain that there was a deep misunderstanding at work here. Father Arrupe had freely acknowledged that the Society of Jesus had changed since the Second Vatican Council. And he had also given a good reason for that change: The church herself had changed. Catholics since the Council had come to realize that the Church is "the people of God," not a hierarchical body. Pope Paul VI had made this new outlook on the Church—this new ecclesiology—his own. Theologians and bishops had enthusiastically adopted this new point of view. The Jesuits, like the bishops, were simply listening to the voice of "the people of God." Their enemies, of course, accused them of being Marxists; but in reality, they were champions of the new concept of "Church."

Religiosi realized, he assured the Holy Father, that in isolated areas of the Church such as Poland, this freshest of Catholic ideas of what the Church really was had not yet penetrated. But it would only be a matter of time. His Holiness had been an active participant in the Vatican Council; so had *Dottrina* and *Clero* and *Vescovi*. They had accepted this new concept of the Church. How, then, could the Jesuits be blamed for following through on the idea? Only their enemies, *Religiosi* repeated his earlier point for emphasis, would take the Jesuits' interest in "the people of God" as an acceptance of the Marxist "struggle of the social classes."

By invoking the Second Vatican Council yet again, *Religiosi* had put himself back in *Dottrina*'s arena of expertise.

Dottrina thanked his Venerable Brother for clarifying this key idea driving Father Arrupe's Society of Jesus. The difficulty was, however, that the Jesuits and many bishops had apparently forgotten what the Second Vatican Council had said about "the People of God"; namely, that this "People" were to be led and guided not by their own instincts or by the social theory of Marx or anyone else. They were to be led by the doctrine and moral law of the Roman Pontiff and of the bishops in communion with that Pontiff. The Jesuits had forgotten this, and something had to be done about so serious an omission.

It was *Stato* again who intervened in the duel between *Dottrina* and *Religiosi*. And again he reminded all present that he had raised the stakes in the matter of the decision to be made about the Jesuits.

Yes, the Secretary agreed, something had to be done about the situation. The *entire* situation. It was the entire situation of the Church His Holiness was trying to better by his apostolic travels and by his Polish experiment with Solidarity. Still, there was that matter of the Moscow-Vatican Pact of 1962. And perhaps it was best to point out that even that 1962 pact was merely a renewal of an earlier agreement between the Holy See and Moscow.

Stato was referring, he went on, to the conversations held in 1942, in the reign of Pope Pius XII. It was in that year that Vatican Monsignore Giovanni Battista Montini, who himself later succeeded to the papacy as Paul VI, talked directly with Joseph Stalin's representative. Those talks were aimed at dimming Pius XII's constant fulminations against the Soviet dictator and Marxism. *Stato* himself had been privy to those talks. He had also been privy to the conversations between Montini and the Italian Communist Party leader, Palmiro Togliatti, in 1944.

If any of his Venerable Colleagues at the table wished them, *Stato* offered to supply reports from the Allied Office of Strategic Services about the matter, beginning, as he recalled, with OSS Report JR-1022 of August 28, 1944. *Stato* has obviously checked his references in detail before coming to the meeting, apparently expecting exactly the opposition that had been organized against him.

Pope John Paul seemed sobered by *Stato*'s information. Had His Holiness, Pius XII, been aware of these conversations and agreements at the time, he wanted to know?

No, *Stato* admitted. But the fact remained that everyone has to deal with ugly realities. Subordinates sometimes have to act without the knowledge of their Superiors in order to aid their Superiors' aims. Now, of course knowledge of the 1942, 1944, and 1962 pacts between Moscow and the Vatican were internal matters to the Holy See. Just as His Holiness's private conversations and arrangements at the present moment with the American Administration were internal and private to His Holiness and the Holy See.

Just so, then, the efforts of the Jesuits were to cope with social and political realities. They should not be lampooned as Marxist. They were part of the ferment in the Church. And a very valuable part of it.

Indirectly, again, and without personal criticism of John Paul, *Stato* had made his point. In the eyes of many, dealing with the Americans was as bad as or worse than dealing with Soviet Marxists. Everyone does what he thinks best in the circumstances. Jesuits were dealing with situations where Communism was already rampant. Perhaps their methods were as acceptable as any.

Stato was quick to add, however, that abuses should be corrected. Certainly, Father Arrupe and the other Jesuit leaders would put their house in better order when they assembled in Rome for their next General Congregation. Intense preparations were already underway. By patient waiting, in *Stato*'s opinion, the whole matter could be regulated and set in order. The last thing needed, in fact, was further divisiveness and disruptions.

Stato had in effect repeated his offer of compromise and revived his threat.

Such a dual possibility, the perfect meat for *Vescovi*, finally enticed that cardinal into the discussion. His only motive was as goodwill worker. After all, the wholesale suppression of the Jesuits now would create a host of intolerable gaps in colleges, seminaries, missions, universities, institutes. Many bishops would be left with severe manpower problems. And it would victimize the many excellent Jesuits who faithfully carried on at lonely posts, and the many more who remained outstanding public defenders of Pope and Church. What His Holiness needed was a reform of the Jesuits. And surely, as *Stato* had said, it would be best to let matters pursue a constitutional course. Let the Jesuits assemble for their General Congregation. Once the leaders were gathered in Rome, His Holiness would have the juridical means to intervene, and to get them to legislate themselves into reform. If need be, Father Arrupe could be retired. As *Stato* had said, with patience, all could be put in order.

Dottrina was not satisfied by half with *Vescovi*'s mediation. Pope Paul VI, *Dottrina* pointed out, whose name had been invoked several times in this discussion to justify the Jesuits, had twice tried to reform the Jesuits by the very means *Vescovi* and *Stato* were suggesting. Twice those means had failed. The situation demanded a more significant action.

What, *Stato* wanted to know, would *Dottrina* consider "more significant action"?

Dottrina put his suggestion plainly: a two-step action. First, accept Father Arrupe's "resignation." Second, appoint a papal supervisor to oversee the preparation of a truly effective reform of the Jesuits at the coming General Congregation.

As is generally the case in such meetings, the point had been reached when all sides recognized that they could each do far worse than to accept partial victory. *Dottrina* had begun with a hope for total suppression of the Society. *Stato* had argued for *laissez-faire*. *Dottrina*'s suggested two-step action was a compromise for both. It was the most either of the adversaries could hope to come away with for the present.

Silence fell. Pope John Paul glanced briefly at each cardinal in turn. Each nodded assent. The Secretary of State was the only one at whom the Pope stared directly for any length of time.

His Holiness had only one remark as he finally stood to leave the conference room. "Well, it took my cardinals eight ballots to elect me Pope. So!"

No one knew what to make of the remark. Was it wry humor of some sort? Or a reference to the respect now due to his papal persona? Or a warning that he could garner enough support among the cardinals to bypass *Stato* and anyone else in the matter of Jesuits? For all their deliberations and all their *romanità*, this Pope who had, as he had once said, "come from a very far country," where he had been used to blunt blows of exchange with the Marxist dragon, managed to end the meeting on a disquieting note of uncertainty for his Cardinals of State.

Of one thing all were certain, however. Very soon, Father General Pedro Arrupe would have a blow-by-blow account of the meeting. He would know all that had been said. He would know that this Holy Father was neither a Paul VI whose weakness made him pliable, nor a John XXIII whose visionary hopes blinded him to the machinations of subordinates. He would know that, for the moment, a head-on attack on the Society had been temporarily blunted, not out of love for Arrupe or esteem for the Society, but because it suited the policies of the present Secretary of State and the personal ambitions of *Religiosi* and *Vescovi*.

Head-on attack or no, however, Arrupe, the Black Pope, was as much a realist as Wojtyla, the White Pope. It would only be a matter of time before the Holy Father would move in on the Society of Jesus, to reform it from top to bottom, or to terminate its existence, possibly forever. In either case, this time Arrupe, who clung doggedly to his persuasion that he and his Jesuits knew better than the Vicar he served what was good for God's Church, would have to go.

*   *   *

The Roman stage seemed set for a battle of titans. Unforeseeable and decisive events tumbled onto that stage, however, and danced a jig of ironies and tragedies.

On May 13, 1981, within three weeks of that private papal conference, John Paul II was struck by two bullets from the Browning semiautomatic pistol of paid hitman Mehmet Ali Agča. By mistake, as it was later explained, the Pontiff was rushed to the Roman hospital of Gemelli rather than to the special hospital unit organized solely for papal use. He was given blood from the public blood bank; the private supply kept in readiness was never used.

In rapid succession, Pope John Paul underwent two major operations and suffered the consequences of the transfusion of impure blood; he contracted a severe case of hepatitis. At the height of the Pontiff's crisis, on May 28, Cardinal Wyszynski of Warsaw died. Wyszynski was John Paul's closest friend, and had made his career.

When the Holy Father was shot, *Stato,* on a formal visit to the United States at the time, hurried back home to take control of the Holy See as Vatican Secretary of State. In those hectic, suspicion-laden days of May and June of 1981, there was no medical certainty that the Pontiff would pull through. It would, as it turned out, take the Holy Father the best part of six months to get back to anything like a full schedule. In hindsight, many are forced to the conclusion that there were those, including both *Stato* and Arrupe, who considered that John Paul's grip on papal affairs had been loosened once and for all. They did not expect him to recover, to get back into harness. That is the most obvious reading of *Stato*'s and Arrupe's behavior in the immediate aftermath of the May 13 shooting.

One of *Stato*'s first public acts on his return was a direct violation of John Paul's will expressed at the papal meeting: He sent a highly congratulatory message to Archbishop Paul Poupard, President of the *Secretariat for Non-Believers*, lauding the work and thought of Father Teilhard whose centenary the *Institut Catholique* of Paris was celebrating. *Stato*'s message praised "the amazing echo of his [de Chardin's] research, joined with the radiance of his thought," all of which "has left a durable mark on his age."

It was an enormous gaffe of disproportionate arrogance. And although *Stato* dated the message May 12—one day before John Paul was shot—clearly it was written and sent after the event.

Arrupe followed suit almost immediately with what seemed a calculated and feckless disregard for John Paul's opinions and bidding. He sent a message dated May 30, and went even farther than *Stato* in his praise of de Chardin.

In a separate matter entirely, Arrupe outdid *Stato* as well in what can only be termed his own arrogance of power. During the early days of John Paul's hospitalization and convalescence, *Vescovi*, as president of the Pontifical Commission for Latin America, presided over a meeting summoned to discuss Central American conditions. Obviously targeted were Church problems in Nicaragua and particularly the role of Jesuits and other priests in the Sandinista Marxist government; but, one way or another, Catholicism was in trouble in every country of Central America. What troubled *Vescovi* was what troubled John Paul II: The Religious Order priests in Central America were becoming social workers and political activists. This departure from apostolic activity was always cloaked in some innocent-sounding expression—"diversity of methodology," "inculturation," or whatever. In effect, however, the Religious in those countries were becoming the allies of any and every left-wing movement, socialist and Communist.

Arrupe was included as a participant in the meeting. If he had been wise and opened his eyes to the precipice along which he had been walking ever since John Paul had become Pope, he would have pleaded his excuses—illness or absence from Rome—and sent a harmless, minor Jesuit functionary merely to be present.

But Arrupe seemed personally determined to squash *Vescovi*'s initiative.

The Jesuit Father General placed conditions on his attending the meeting. He demanded to see the agenda beforehand. He insisted on calling expert witnesses who knew each of the six Central American countries. He argued (and won the argument) that the meeting should include many more participants—priests and nuns—from the Religious Orders, since Religious made up seventy percent of priests and "apostolic" workers in Central America.

Arrupe, as *Vescovi* knew, had been elected president of the Council of Major Superiors of Religious Orders and Congregations, one of his most potent and prestigious posts in Rome. Affectionately called "Don Pedro," he was looked up to as leader, inspirer, path-blazer, and protector. Furthermore, it was among Religious Orders and Congregations that the most fervid form of change and secularization still burned in the wake of Vatican II. The experts and witnesses that Arrupe called would all sing the same song: The Church is "adapting" by a new "diversity of methodology" to the ongoing culture of the Central American peoples.

At that meeting, *Vescovi* suffered a signal defeat and humiliation. "Diversity" was approved. The presence of Jesuits and other priests in the Sandinista government of Nicaragua was said to be a temporary and necessary fact. Blame for any real problems was laid at the door of capitalist and ecclesiastical (meaning Roman and papal) interference.

In bulling his way through to victory in that meeting, though, Arrupe himself had forgotten—or maybe he had never known—the Roman adage, *Cardinales amici deboles, inimici terribiles.* Cardinals make weak friends, but terrible enemies.

By the time John Paul II had recovered sufficient energy and his doctors allowed him some activity, toward the latter half of July 1981, the decision to remove Arrupe by hook or by crook had been made by the Jesuit's accumulated enemies in the Vatican Curia and in the Latin American Church. Almost certainly *Vescovi, Dottrina, Propaganda, Clero,* powerful Latin American churchmen such as Archbishop Alonzo Lopez Trujillo of Medellín, Colombia, and some older Jesuits of a conservative, anti-Arrupe bent were in on that decision. Arrupe had to go.

John Paul II acquiesced readily. In fact, when he learned how *Stato* and Arrupe had been behaving, the Pope's own reaction was visceral. As an added sting to his reaction, he decided not to inform *Religiosi* of his papal decision to remove Arrupe. This was tantamount to insult: *Religiosi* was the cardinal directly responsible for the behavior of all Religious priests and of Arrupe in particular. Since the shooting, John Paul had wanted nothing of that cardinal in his life.

Stato and Arrupe were the Pope's targets, however. Quickly, he hit *Stato* with a typically Roman punishment for his transgressions. The Press Office of the Holy See and the official Vatican newspaper, *L'Osservatore Romano*—both private stamping grounds of *Stato*'s—were forced by papal order to publish an official statement correcting *Stato*'s praise of de Chardin and repeating the condemnation of 1960. The put-down was public.

In terms of *romanità*, the papal action was also a public, if indirect, warning to Arrupe. But more direct action followed immediately. *Stato* was ordered to implement step one of the papal decisions about the Jesuits. He was to remove Arrupe from the office of Jesuit General.

Before *Stato* could obey that command, another twist in the jig of ironies was danced. Arrupe had been on a visit to the Philippines. Whether it was caused by the fatigue of that trip, or the shock of a private word from *Stato* about his impending forced retirement once he returned to Rome, or because of some other violent strain, or simply from some normal pathology of nature that can occur in a seventy-three-year-old man, Pedro Arrupe was stricken on August 7 with a brain hemorrhage, as he deplaned at Rome airport. The cerebral blood clot left him paralyzed on his right side, and unable to speak.

In accordance with the Jesuit *Constitutions*, in such a situation a Vicar-General of the Society temporarily takes over the duties of Father General. In this case, American Vincent O'Keefe, Father Arrupe's personal choice as his successor in the Generalate, and the same man who had provoked John Paul I's ire in 1978 by his free-wheeling proposals concerning Catholic morality during an interview with a Dutch newspaper, took the helm of the Society of Jesus. There was no doubt in anybody's mind on either side of this developing war that if Arrupe did not recover, the Jesuits would apply the proviso in their *Constitutions* that envisaged the total incapacitation of the Father General. Arrupe would resign; a General Congregation of the Order's leaders would be held in Rome; and O'Keefe would be elected Father General.

In view of the virtual certainty that Arrupe would not recover —from the beginning, the prognosis was unfavorable—O'Keefe and the other General Assistants of the Order made several attempts to rebuild some of the bridges Arrupe had so arrogantly burned. But try as they would, they could not get to John Paul, or to *Vescovi*, or even to Arrupe's one-time ally, *Stato*.

On September 5, Arrupe was released from Salvator Mundi hospital and was transported back to his bedroom in the Gesù. The Jesuit press officer, Jean-Claude Dietsch, S.J., told the media that Arrupe's recovery would take "a couple of months." But this was merely public relations policy, as was the wave of sanctimonious comment and anecdotal praise circulated around Rome and the Society of Jesus for "Don Pedro." Jesuit Superiors were trying to buy time.

By late September, it was clear that, although Arrupe was not going to die immediately, he would never recover normal health, never again govern the Society of Jesus.

And so there they were, the two titans, White Pope and Black Pope. John Paul, convalescing twenty miles from Rome in the papal villa at Castel Gandolfo, weakened by the shock of Agča's bullets; weakened further by the successive operations and by virulent hepatitis; in daily receipt of ever gloomier reports about the fate of his child of hope, Solidarity, up in his beloved Poland; deprived of Cardinal Wyszynski's counsel and moral support. And Pedro Arrupe, lying in his bed at Jesuit Roman headquarters immobilized by the stroke, seemingly aware of what was going on around him, but unable to speak coherently.

Arrupe's special Council of Assistants, unaware of what was coming, were busy searching for the best way to obtain papal permission to summon a General Congregation so that they could elect a new Father General. That they had no word of John Paul's decision was a triumph of confidentiality. For in the windy corridors of the Vatican where secrets blow continually around ears of the ever-listening, genuine secrecy is rare. But John Paul II was angry; he wanted no one to defuse his bombshell.

When it came, there was something both poignant and puzzling in the last major clash between those two titans. In the circumstances, and in Roman terms, perhaps the greater punishment was for *Stato*, who had foolishly and directly contravened John Paul's intentions at his weakest moment, and connived at Arrupe's obstreperousness. For John Paul chose to lob his bombshell on Arrupe and the Jesuits by the hand of *Stato* himself.

                          *   *   *

Early on October 5, the diminutive figure of the Secretary of State emerged through the Vatican's Bronze Doors. He walked the few hundred yards across St. Peter's Square to Number 5 Borgo Santo Spiritu and appeared unannounced at the front door of the

Jesuit house where Arrupe lay. He bore a papal message for the Father General.

He was admitted. He mounted the stairs, was shown to Arrupe's room, and walked over to his bedside. He stood over the paralyzed form of the old Basque and read the words of John Paul's letter. "I wanted to be able to work with you," John Paul had written, "in the preparation for the General Congregation . . . ," but the assassin's bullets on May 13 and Arrupe's stroke on August 7 had ended all that part of the plan. "So I have decided to appoint a personal delegate. . . ." Effectively, that letter removed Pedro Arrupe forever from the Generalate, and it moved O'Keefe from his post as Vicar-General of the Society—and from all hope of being elected General by a subsequent Congregation.

It was not John Paul's grip on power that was ended.

The Pontiff's personal delegate and temporary Superior of the Society was Paolo Dezza. Nearly eighty years old, nearly blind, an authority on higher education, a past master of *romanità*, a man who stored innumerable facts and figures in his memory, Dezza had won his spurs nearly forty years before, under Pope Pius XII. He had been confessor to Popes Paul VI and John Paul I. One of the old Roman "hands," Dezza almost certainly had been called in during the latter phases of the consultations between *Vescovi*, John Paul II, and the other Curial notables. "The Pope," one Jesuit remarked, "is demonstrating his divine powers by saying to Dezza: 'Lazarus! Come forth!' "

Dezza was indeed old and frail; but he had more skill in his repertoire, more steel in his *pianissimo* manner, than many thousands of younger men.

As Dezza's assistant, John Paul appointed a fifty-one-year-old Sard, Giuseppe Pittau. Pittau held a doctorate from Harvard in political science, and had been Arrupe's appointee as Provincial of Japan and president of Sophia University, Tokyo. John Paul had in fact met Pittau the previous February during his trip to Japan.

The elimination of Arrupe and O'Keefe, the appointment of "a personal delegate of the Holy Father to the Society of Jesus," and their uncertainty as to John Paul's next move produced panic among Jesuit Provincials in the United States, who had gone so far down the road where Arrupe had led. They addressed a feverish questionnaire to Dezza even before he officially took office. What was the status of the *Constitutions* of the Society? Suspended? Totally or in part? What now? What was the constitutionality of the Pope's action? Was it legal? What powers did Dezza have? Could he override Provincials? Replace them? Could he dismiss

Jesuits from the Society? Was the General Congregation to be put off indefinitely? When could they elect a new Father General?

On October 26, Dezza dispatched a long telex in reply. He reassured the American Jesuits about the *Constitutions*. The convocation of the General Congregation, however, had been put off "for the sake of better preparation."

On October 30, Dezza took formal charge of the Society; he presided at a concelebrated Mass and preached the homily in the Gesù. From the pulpit, he gave another and even more disturbing reason why the General Congregation had been put off by Pope John Paul: "The Holy Father thought it better to wait until the new code of Canon Law was promulgated."

That immediately raised still worse fears. In the new Church law, would the Society be stripped of its privileges? Perhaps placed under the jurisdiction of local bishops? Perhaps new laws would forbid Jesuits doing what they were doing? The panic increased. Dezza, however, remained imperturbable.[2]

John Paul's intervention in the government of the Society was gall and wormwood for *Stato* and for *Religiosi*; but for Arrupe's colleagues in that government, it was a moral outrage and devastation, a total and overwhelming surprise. "This," said one Jesuit lawyer, "is a breathtaking leap of total illogicality."

A majority of the Society's 26,622 members in 1981 had expected some such papal move to correct the disorders among them.[3] But for the "advanced thinkers" and the establishment of the Society worldwide, it was unthinkable that a majority would welcome the papal intervention. "There are probably only about eight percent of Jesuits in the world," a Roman-based Jesuit remarked, "who can put their hands on their hearts and say: 'Thank you, Pope John Paul.' " A Pope, this Pope, had dared intervene directly in the running of the Jesuits. It was now their role, their duty, to dig in for the duration.

The lamentable and revealing fact is that Jesuit leadership and the intellectual heavyweights screamed like members of an exclusive and autonomous club whose precious liberties were suddenly snatched away by a crude and illegal hand. The reaction spoke volumes about the deterioration of obedience in the Society. "After all, Popes are not immortal," was a frequent consolatory phrase used in those days.

As was inevitable in an organization like the Society, the establishment view prevailed in public. Over 5000 letters of protest from individual Jesuits all over the world poured into the Gesù, all condemning John Paul's action. In West Germany, eighteen Jesuits, including the theological heavyweight of his time, Karl Rahner, addressed a letter to John Paul II in which they declared they could not recognize "the finger of God in this administrative measure." They were "shocked at his distrust" of Father Arrupe. John Paul's attitude "is part of our experience that tells us that not even the highest authority in the church is preserved from error." Then came the threat of retaliation by revolt. "The Holy See is Superior of the Society only within the framework of the *Constitutions* approved by the Holy See. Therefore Your Holiness's interference puts our loyalty to Jesus Christ and the Church into fundamental question." In other words, if Your Holiness violates the *Constitutions*, we will feel free to disobey Your Holiness.

Of course, as another Roman Jesuit added, there was no question of any fault on Arrupe's part. "This latest move against the Jesuits involves the submission of [Cardinal] Baggio and [Cardinal] Lopez Trujillo to the multinational corporations and their Opus Dei friends."

There were, in fact, veritable rivers of Jesuit ink poured out upon acres of paper. Provincials, theology professors, and activists wrote to tell one another how "angry" they were over John Paul's appointment of the Dezza-Pittau team, and how they were "struggling" to overcome that anger. In Jesuit publications, editorials and still more letters savaged the Pope, the Vatican, the "institutional" Church, and the government and economic system of the United States and most of the free world. "This affair marks the papal repudiation of the liberal reading of Vatican II. . . . As they say out West, the Society is a burr under his saddle. . . . This attempt to hijack the Society. . . ." On and on the Jesuit commentaries went.

The Council of Major Superiors, of which Arrupe had been undisputed head and which was taken over by the Dominican Master General, Vincent De Couesnongle, planned to make its own forceful protest to the Vatican. If the Pope could pick off Arrupe, he could do the same to the head of any other Order.

When Dezza and Pittau sent a document to the full Society offering some initial and rather anodyne guidelines for what they called "renewal," the outcry again was deafening. The Superiors of the Chicago and Maryland Provinces of the Society expressed their anger in terms that left little to the imagination. One prominent Chicago Province Jesuit Superior, a man already known as fiercely antipapal and anti-"institutional" Church, derided the very thought of returning to the religiously strict formation of young Jesuits: "We can't go back to monasticism."

The most complimentary remark passed by Jesuits about old Father Dezza himself, meanwhile, was that he was old-fashioned. The mildest epithet used for him by his astounded colleagues was "the Cossack."

Through all the acerbic criticism and unrestrained objections to papal action ran an equally unrestrained demand that they who reacted so violently, and who so arrogantly criticized the Pope, should be held immune from all criticism in return. Those who paid no heed, Jesuit or non-Jesuit, to this imperious demand, and condemned the rebellious actions of establishment Jesuits, were at once surrounded, virtually drowned in a violent keening and then buried beneath complaints about the suppression of "democratic dissent" in the Church.

Stato, meanwhile, who had been around far longer and had weathered more storms than most Jesuits, knew enough to take a certain consolation even in this bitterest of situations. He felt that Dezza and Pittau, each for vastly different reasons, would diffuse the "difficulty" with Pope John Paul II without altering the *status quo* in any substantial way.

At first blush, the choice of Dezza seemed optimal from the papal viewpoint. His age, his association with Pius XII, his record as an observant Religious, his devotion to the Holy See, his role as confessor to Popes Paul VI and John Paul I, all this boded well. Pittau, meanwhile, was Dezza's own choice and reportedly a friend of John Paul since the Pope's visit to Japan. Unwittingly, however, John Paul had chosen two men who could not possibly bring themselves to do his will in the matter of the Society of Jesus.

At his ripe old age, Dezza was a loyal Jesuit to the marrow of his bones. And he was the incarnation of *romanità*. He had absorbed *romanità* as if through his pores, in fact. For him, the principal aim in an institution such as the Holy See, where the dominant reality is a "political" reality—papal power—was to observe the expected "rituals" and "forms" that gave *romanità* its safe facade. The correct words, the required statement of purpose, the official repetition of formulas about faith and morals—these were the stuff of reconciliation and peace. On the other hand, any and all visible signs of disagreement, rebellion, revolt, or independence were both unnecessary and downright stupid.

Jesuit loyalty coupled with total mastery of *romanità* is a powerful combination. In Dezza's analysis, there was nothing wrong with the Society as a whole. There couldn't be. Dezza could not even begin to think that a reform of morals and a change in the theological outlook of Jesuit Superiors and intellectuals could be necessary. If the Jesuits had found "difficulty" with His Holiness, it was because some jackass somewhere had violated the accepted formats, had sinned "politically," had failed to fathom and understand that for Rome, authority is power—as all genuine spiritual authority should well be. In short, someone had failed to understand the supreme "political" value of Jesuit relations with the Pope and with the outside world.

For Dezza, then, as for the general run of Jesuit Major Superiors, there was no real problem or difficulty in their Society about the doctrine of faith, their vow of obedience to the Pope or the moral teaching of the Church. The real undertaking for Dezza—for any mind that worked like Dezza's—was to present an appearance of cohesive unity such that the Society would be acceptable, would again enjoy its prestige and be able to continue on its way undisturbed any further by the "difficulty" John Paul II had created.

One became acceptable by observing the formats and conventions of *romanità*. One thus cut a *bella figura*. That is, one made "a fine impression" on the Holy See because one was in order; on the general public, because one occupied an honored place in the Vatican; and on Jesuits worldwide, because the Roman Superiors of the Order were on such a high Vatican footing. *Bella figura* all around—this was Dezza's aim and ideal.

Dezza's solution, in short, had everything to do with repairing relationships, and nothing to do with intra-Society abuses. *Romanità* specializes in the *bella figura*.

Pittau was of a different background than Dezza. He was not an Italian, but a Sard. He had reached his maturity not in Rome but as Provincial of Japan, where he had succeeded Pedro Arrupe in that post and then had worked under Arrupe's direction and inspiration for fifteen years. His Jesuitism was Arrupe's. And like Arrupe, he had now been called from the Provinces to Rome, that capital with whose power he had had to tussle from his distant post. But he, like Dezza, appreciated the value of Jesuit relations with the Pope and the world at large.

The Pope's objections, then, in the Dezza-Pittau mind, concerned the appearances of deviation from the Roman norm. Yes, Jesuits had perhaps been seen as egregiously deviant from the stock formularies Rome expects to see in written documents, in instructions from Superiors to subordinates, in the periodic repetition of sentiments of loyalty. But in this, they had merely—perhaps a little too ebulliently—been manifesting the spirit of the new Catholic Church born out of the Second Vatican Council of

1962 to 1965. It was "the spirit of Vatican II" that carried them to excess.

As for those Jesuits of a more traditionalist mind, those who had objected to the way the Society had developed, they simply shared with Pope John Paul a theology that predated the Second Vatican Council. Arrupe, Dezza, and Pittau, meanwhile, together with all major Superiors in the Society, marched to the beat of the new post-Council theology.

The task Dezza and Pittau faced, therefore, was a thoroughgoing attempt at restoring the *bella figura* of the Society of Jesus. The Holy Father would have to see instructions from Dezza and Pittau to all Jesuits emphasizing the traditional formularies of Rome. The Superiors of the Society would have to hold meetings, study groups, provincial assemblies, house discussions, and the like, to show their avid interest in the Pope's call to order. From each local Superior, the Roman Superiors would have to receive extensive and detailed reports on how everything was progressing. The dissent of the more traditionalist-minded members that threatened the visible unity of the Society must be muffled, isolated, removed from public view. If all else failed, because the appearance of unity was so essential to the Dezza-Pittau "reform," persistent dissenters would have to be quietly released from the Society.

Continuity was part and parcel of the "form" Dezza sought to demonstrate. Dezza insisted, in fact, on "continuity with Arrupe" and his leadership. He carried out his papal assignment with the advice and help of those men whom Arrupe had located in positions of authority and under whose directions the Society had deteriorated. It was less than surprising for *Stato* and others who understood *romanità* and the Dezza mind that the papal Supervisor did not in any way touch the Jesuit administrators who had been responsible for the political and theological state of affairs that had evoked anger from three Popes, and had provoked John Paul's direct intervention into the governance of the Society.

There was no demand under Dezza and Pittau, any more than there had been under Arrupe, for obedience from Jesuits to specific Church teachings—about papal infallibility, abortion, homosexuality, divorce, Marxism. They did insist, however, rather more than Arrupe had done, that the more extreme dissenters from Catholic doctrine in the Society mute their voices until the Society would once more be allowed to pick its own Superior-General, thus closing the door on the unfortunate incident of direct papal intervention.

In the meantime, Dezza began a very discreet but carefully directed search for a suitable candidate as the next Father General. Someone already established in his own right, successful in his particular career, reliable in virtue, intelligent about *romanità* and Popes and cardinals. Someone impeccable religiously. Someone capable by character and Jesuitism of steering the Society through the foreseeably difficult years of this Polish Pope.

Cunctando regitur mundus.

4 | PAPAL HUMILIATION

J ohn Paul II's recovery seemed painfully slow. The year 1981 had been devastating not only to his health, but to the heart of his papal strategy. With the Pope felled by bullets and then weakened by hepatitis, and with the death of Cardinal Wyszynski, his close friend and indispensably reliable ally in the development of Solidarity as a showcase, Solidarity had been effectively stopped in its plan of overt, public development. There was nothing for it but retrenchment, regrouping, and a return to a largely underground existence.

At the same time, the stakes in Latin America, the second major focal point of John Paul's "muscle" strategy, had been raised considerably. American intelligence had ascertained in 1980 that the Sandinistas were using their funds, including the liberal quantities of United States aid that had been begun under President Carter, to funnel arms to Marxist guerrillas in neighboring El Salvador. In 1981, U.S. Secretary of State Alexander Haig had bluntly characterized Nicaragua as first on a Soviet "hit list" of Latin American countries destined for Soviet domination. That same year, American aid was halted. But by early 1982, aerial and ground reconnaissance demonstrated beyond doubt that major military construction was under way in Nicaragua, carried on with Cuban and Soviet money, supplies, manpower, and technology. Simultaneously, the revelation that CIA-backed anti-Sandinista guerrillas were operating both in Nicaragua and out of neighboring Honduras frightened the Sandinistas and evoked howls of protest from Church-related newspapers and periodicals in the United States, Canada, and Europe.

For all the players in the global geopolitical game of nations, Nicaragua had clearly become the bellwether of the western hemisphere. In the eyes of Cuba's dictator, Fidel Castro, in the eyes of the watchful men of the Reagan Administration in Washington, and from the viewpoint of the men who plotted the course for Moscow's Politburo, as Nicaragua went, so would go all Central American countries, and eventually some in South America as well.

Geopolitically, Pope John Paul II agreed with that assessment. But for him, the fight was for the very survival of Roman Catholicism in the southern hemisphere, where almost one-half of all Roman Catholics live. And, in his eyes, the true opposition in that fight was filled with the most dangerous rebels in the Church since Martin Luther's revolt in the sixteenth century.

On that one point, the Roman Catholic Pontiff and the Marxist Junta of Nicaragua saw eye-to-eye. The central source of popular strength for the Sandinista revolution was the steady development of Base Communities grounded in and sustained by the "People's Church." The only ones who could confer some legitimacy on that venture were the Roman Catholic priest-politicians of the Sandinista Party. Their loyal collaboration behind Jesuit Fernando Cardenal as the show-piece activist had proved vital to the maintenance of the onward momentum in the establishment of a Marxist regime acceptable to the Nicaraguan people. All in all, it was the most intelligent attack on the very soul of Catholicism that had ever been mounted; and it bid fair to rid the hemisphere, and ultimately the world, of any effective Roman Catholic presence.

So reliant had the Junta become on this clerical support to achieve its aims that it stopped at nothing to silence any churchmen who opposed the "People's Church" concept, and the establishment of its politically indispensable Base Communities. It was not uncommon for the Junta to take a page of two from Gestapo tactics, as when they fabricated evidence of sexual immorality on the part of dissident Father Bismark Carballo, or when they sent a squad of toughs to rough up no less a figure than Managua's Archbishop Miguel Obando y Bravo, who had become unrelenting, if he remained unsuccessful, in his call for the resignation of all priests from government posts.

Such tactics seem not to have brought so much as a blush to the cheeks of Fernando Cardenal, or to those of his poet-brother Ernesto, or of Alvaro Arguello, or of any of the other government priests. In 1982, when local Church authorities in Nicaragua slapped an ecclesiastical censure on the Junta's priests, forbidding them to say Mass or hear confessions or perform any priestly duties, Fernando Cardenal's reply was imperturbable: "We are free men," he declared; they could not be forced to resign.

The censure was to a certain degree pointless, in any case; already many of the priest-politicians had given up any practice of such specifically priestly duties as Mass and confessions. Nevertheless, a swarm of protest against the censure swept through the Sandinista press and radio and into the media in the United States and Europe, not least in sympathetic religious publications.

It would seem that Pope John Paul was still hopeful that he could rectify what in his view had gone awry in the Jesuit Order, and that the Society itself in that case would bring back under control not only such men as Fernando Cardenal and Alvaro Arguello in Nicaragua, but the enormous cadre of so-called "Pope's Men" around the globe who had set their faces so resolutely against this Pope, and indeed against the very concept of papacy in the Catholic Church.

In any case, early in 1982 the temporary Jesuit Superior-General, Paolo Dezza, was meeting with the Provincial Superiors from all over the world at Villa Cavaletti, a Jesuit house outside Rome in the Alban hills. The four General Assistants—Vincent O'Keefe, Horacio de la Costa, Parmananda Divarkar, Cecil McGarry—suggested to Dezza that it would be a good idea to ask for an audience with the Pope at this point, on behalf of the Provincial Superiors of the Society who were assembled in Villa Cavaletti.

It was a current view among the Assistants—one ably voiced in particular by O'Keefe—that the main difficulty about John Paul II was his background. Before he came down to Rome as Pope, Karol Wojtyla had been a bishop, successful and effective, true, but still limited to one diocese, Krakow, in Poland. In the traditional style of bishops of the old school, and particularly of bishops in Poland, Archbishop Wojtyla had been accustomed to the instant obedience of his priests and nuns at a mere snap of his fingers. As Pope, in O'Keefe's opinion, Wojtyla still behaved with that bishop's mentality. Wojtyla needed to realize that the Church Universal was not just a larger version of the traditional and submissive Polish diocese, and that "poping" was not the same as "bishoping." Any chance, therefore, to open the Polish Pope's eyes should be grasped.

The audience was set for February 27, 1981, in the Vatican. That morning before the audience, Pedro Arrupe, who had recovered enough to move slowly with help, and the Provincials concelebrated Mass in the Church of the Gesù. Arrupe's homily during the Mass, read by another, was replete with all the appropriate buzzwords and formularies with which Arrupe had strewn his fifteen-year path of opposition to papal behests and divergence from papal doctrine. Arrupe praised "the full and filial obedience" with which Jesuits had accepted the Holy Father's intervention in the government of the Society, and he exhorted his fellow Jesuits to obey not only by doing what the Pope said, but by doing it "with joy."

When the Mass was over, the group walked across St. Peter's Square to the Vatican and assembled at the time appointed for the Pope's arrival. They were kept waiting for an hour while John Paul held a conversation with French President François Mitterrand.

When John Paul arrived, he greeted Arrupe most graciously, addressing him as "Carissimo Padre Generale!" John Paul read an eighteen-page address that began in Italian, switched to French, then to English, and ended in Spanish.

In many respects John Paul wore velvet gloves; but from the point of view of the Society's leadership, things did not go too well.

The implications of his address were both threatening and reproachful, and were obviously intended for all 26,622 members of the Order. Three-quarters of the speech (the Italian, French, and English sections) told the Pontiff's audience plainly what they should and should not be and do, as well as the Pope's own intentions and wishes for them. He was clear that " . . . There is no room for deviation . . ." and that, "Since the Roman Pontiff is a bishop and head of the hierarchy, Jesuits are to be obedient to bishops as to the Pope, head of all bishops."

As to the Jesuit vocation itself, the Pope had a great deal to say. "The ways of the religious-minded do not follow the calculations of men. They do not use as parameters the cult of power, riches, or politics. . . ." The only Jesuits the Pope would tolerate were those who hewed to the traditions from which the Society had not previously wavered for over four hundred years. "Your proper activity is not in the temporal realm, nor in that one which is the field of laymen and which must be left to them." Stick to the

various forms of traditional apostolate, he told them. And traditional Jesuit rules. In the Society, do not shorten the period of
training.

Those Jesuit traditions they must preserve were devotion to the
papacy, and propagation of Roman Catholic beliefs as championed
by the papacy. "St. Ignatius was, in all instances, obedient to the
Throne of Peter. . . . Superiors should not abdicate their duty to
exercise authority, and to administer sanctions against rebellious
members. . . ."

John Paul then drew a picture in succinct words of what the
classical Jesuit character used to be. If anyone listening to him still
knew what Ignatius had founded as an Order, the Pope's words
must have pierced them like a sword of bitter regret for the glory
that once was the Society's and for the ideal Jesuits had created.
"Bishops and priests," John Paul said, "used to look on the Society
as an authentic and hence a sure point of reference to which one
could turn in order to find certainty of doctrine, lucid and reliable
moral judgment, and authentic nourishment for the interior life."

The Pope paused to glance up, meaning and appeal and hope
glinting in his eyes, a sort of physical gesture to underline what he
was about to say. The Society, John Paul said, could again achieve
that Ignatian ideal, but only by "loyal fidelity to the magisterium
of the Church, and in particular of the Roman Pontiff to which
you are duty-bound."

In the last quarter of his speech, given in Spanish, John Paul
finally declared himself in favor of allowing the Jesuit Delegates
to assemble—after due preparation—in order to elect a new Father
General. The mechanism of preparation could start in 1982.

The entire meeting, including papal speech and formalities,
took about seventy-five minutes. Just about sixty-five of those
minutes were wasted effort. The last portion of John Paul's speech
—that papal go-ahead for them to convoke the 33rd General Congregation of the Society—was all most of the Pontiff's audience
wanted to hear. They would be allowed to elect their own Jesuit
General. Things could get back to normal. The Provincials and the
Roman Superiors filed back across St. Peter's Square to the Gesù,
satisfaction regnant among them. Their obdurate, patient wait had
paid off.

How long Pope John Paul maintained his hopeful attitude that
the Society of Jesus would at last return to those traditions he had
held up to them is not quite certain. What is certain is that everything he said in reference to religious and spiritual matters was
interpreted by Dezza, by his assistant Pittau, by the General Assis-

tants, and by the Provincial Superiors in the light of that very special political outlook of theirs. That outlook told them that what the Holy Father was *really* saying to them was rainbow bright: "I had to act in a somewhat frightening manner by removing Pedro Arrupe and Vincent O'Keefe. But now that we have got together, things are all right."

There was still, in other words, no recognition and, despite the very plain speech of the Pontiff, perhaps no consciousness on the part of the Jesuits who listened to him that day that John Paul II was talking about serious flaws in the Society; no idea that the Pontiff was saying, as gently as he could: "You are wrong. Seriously gone wrong. You must correct your course." Quite the contrary, in fact. What seemed to bother many of the Provincial Superiors listening to him was that John Paul seemed to imply they would have to obey the home bishops. "Does this mean we have to obey conservative bishops?" one Provincial complained in the privacy of the Gesù.

The best answer to the question was probably given to a newsman who good-naturedly asked one of the Jesuit General Assistants if "you people have finally surrendered to the Pope?" The answer came with a smile: "Don't you believe it!"

Once the Provincial Delegates were back in their Jesuit houses around the world, the official line was that in his papal and peculiarly Polish and "episcopal" way, John Paul had "apologized" and "made amends" for his extraordinarily "un-Churchmanlike" action in removing Arrupe so unceremoniously.

Jesuit Father Gerald Sheehan, an American who resided in Rome and counseled Roman Superiors about American Jesuits, went so far as to state blandly that John Paul recognized he had been misinformed by the enemies of the Society, and that he now realized how wrong his information had been. The Jesuits need be angry with the Holy Father no longer.

"We have been happy to come here," one Provincial commented to a newsman, "and listen to the Pope. Now we will return home and remain silent for a time, avoiding any spectacular gestures or publications or criticisms of the Pope. Later on, we will elect the Father General of our choice. And nothing will change."

The mind-set revealed in those remarks and others like them set the stage so that the openly traditionalist-minded and orthodox Jesuits who had been fighting against the changes in the Society could now be blamed for the "misinformation." Meanwhile, Superiors now knew how to avoid provoking further papal outbursts. The order of the day was to be: "Steady as you go, but with a little more 'political sensitivity' than we practiced under Arrupe." The Society itself had been exonerated.

One of the General Assistants had put it all pithily, as the group emerged from the audience with John Paul. Asked what he thought, he said with a satisfied grin: *"Acqua passata."* All the troubles and all the words they had just heard were "water under the bridge," gone by forever.

It was no wonder, then, that Fernando Cardenal and the other Jesuits and priests who followed his lead in Nicaragua saw no need to budge from their positions.

*   *   *

However John Paul's hopes for the Society of Jesus may have waned or waxed after that February 27 meeting, clearly the Pope was not prepared to sit back and wait, or to abstain from more direct action in the vital country of Nicaragua. With Solidarity lost to him, he could not afford to do so, if the "muscle" strategy of his papacy was to have any foothold.

In a letter to the Nicaraguan bishops dated June 29, John Paul denounced the "People's Church" in harsh and pointed terms. This church "born of the people," he quoted its clerical founders in Nicaragua, was a new invention that was both "absurd" and of "perilous character." Only with difficulty, John Paul went on, could it avoid being infiltrated by "strangely ideological connotations along the line of a certain political radicalization, for accomplishing determined aims. . . ."

The Sandinista leaders and their clerical colleagues understood clearly what that line of "political radicalizaton" represented in the Pope's mind. The Junta's decision therefore was to suppress the letter, to allow it no publicity.

For once, however, the Nicaraguan bishops were able to trip the Junta up by blatant manipulation of its own propaganda machine. Once the letter was public, the Junta's fall-back position was a storm of well-organized criticism of the papal letter on the government radio, and in Jesuit publications in Nicaragua and the United States: "Rome" was interfering unduly in the political affairs of the sovereign state of Nicaragua. This Pope was going against the teaching of the Second Vatican Council, which "renamed" the Roman Catholic Church "the People of God." This Pope was going against the statements of the American bishops at Puebla, Mexico, in 1979, where the very title *iglesia popular* was used. This Pope had aligned Vatican policy with the policy of the Reagan Administration as it fomented terrorist *contras* on Nicaraguan soil. This

Pope forbade his priests to politick, and yet here he was un-ashamedly politicking.

The worst and most threatening implications were publicly read into the Pope's letter by the Junta; and, side-by-side with the Junta, the Jesuit Superiors of Nicaragua made it publicly clear that they disassociated themselves totally from the spirit and the state-ments of John Paul's letter.

Under direct pressure from the Pontiff, for whom the clerical rejection of his letter was not acceptable, temporary Superior Gen-eral Paolo Dezza wrote to Jesuit Father Fernando Cardenal, order-ing him in the name of his vow of obedience to withdraw from his government post.

It was a measure of how far obedience in the Society had dete-riorated that Cardenal's answer was a formal request to Superior General Dezza that he put his reasons for such an order in writing so that Cardenal could reflect on them. It was a measure of how far the Society's structure and mandate had deteriorated not only that the Superior General's answer, dated January 12, 1983, was written at all, but that it was a mirror of weakness and vacillation. Dezza's tone in that letter was that of a man asking a favor of a stubborn colleague and equal. Cardenal's work with the Sandinis-tas was beyond reproach, Dezza wrote, and there were no reasons for asking Cardenal to resign beyond the fact that this Pope kept insisting that he and other priests retire from government and politics. The message, in sum, was clear: If it weren't for this Pope, we would leave you be, Father Fernando.

If Dezza had assumed that Fernando Cardenal was one to respect the demands of his precious *romanità*, and to fit his actions if not their substance to some format Dezza could manage in Rome, the old man was quickly and rudely disabused. Cardenal commented publicly and with lucid clarity on Dezza's letter of "explanation." "There weren't any reasons" (for asking him to step down out of government), Cardenal summed it up. "It was just an order from the Pope."

Cardenal did not obey. Nor did his Jesuit Superiors, either in Nicaragua or in Rome, insist.

For all of the Pope's continued attention to the Jesuit problem, John Paul did not place his full reliance on them, or on any other formal structure within his Church. Before he had been shot, be-fore Wyszynski had died and Solidarity had failed, the Pope had traveled to twenty countries. Not only in Poland now, where he had dealt with Marxists from the very cradle of Marxism, but also in the most diverse and even hostile places, he had spoken over the heads of State and Church authorities alike; he had spoken directly to the people. And he had been heard. Not only that; he had changed things. In spite of the cold, formal respect of the Mexican government, he had given a vogue to religion in public that the government didn't want to see. In spite of Freemasons in France and Marxists in Benin, he had successfully created a respect for the papacy. He could, he was convinced, do those same things in Nicaragua, in spite of Daniel Ortega and his Junta, and in spite of the obdurate Fernando Cardenal and his fellow priests in government.

While the efforts of Church authorities to retire the priest-politicians in Nicaragua from government droned fruitlessly on through 1982, John Paul's papal office began detailed arrangements for the Pontiff's fourth trip to Latin America in less than four years. It was to be a gruelling eight-day tour of Central America. The Holy Father would have his headquarters at the Apostolic Nunciature in Costa Rica, but he would visit the six other nations of the area—Nicaragua, Panama, El Salvador, Guatemala, and Belize—as well as the island dictatorship of Haiti.

Nicaragua, however, was the Pope's chief target area, with its budding, deeply political and heretical "People's Church," its activist clergy, its recalcitrant Jesuits, and its thoroughgoing Marxist Junta pulling strings that, in reality, had simply been stretched to reach their hands.

Arrangements—or negotiations in this case, perhaps, as between hostile nations—for the papal visit to Nicaragua were conducted between the Pontiff's personal representative in Managua, Monsignore Andrea Cordero Lanza de Montezemolo, and the head of Nicaragua's Junta, Daniel Ortega y Saavedra. From the beginning, those negotiations were difficult. John Paul had several conditions he wanted met before he would agree to an actual date for his visit to Managua. And Ortega and the Junta were almost intractable in their opposition to those conditions.

Some of those conditions concerned the public Mass that would be celebrated by the Pope in Nicaragua, as during each of the papal stops. It was an immemorial Catholic practice and, in this case, a specific papal condition, that a crucifix be placed over the altar for Mass. In addition, the backdrop for the altar could not be a revolutionary mural—that is, one depicting violence. The absence of a crucifix at Masses and its replacement by just such revolutionary murals had become standard practice in the new "People's Church."

A more significant condition from the Junta's point of view concerned those priests and other Religious who worked for the Sandinista government. At work in Nicaragua's government by that time there were some 300 priests, including literally scores of Jesuits, and 750 men and women Religious—250 of them "missionaries" from Spain and the United States. At least 20 acted as advisers to the Junta, and 200 more functioned as the Junta's organizers in the fields of health, communications, and local government throughout Ohio-sized Nicaragua with its 2.2 million people.

John Paul, however, set his sights on the five priests—including the two Jesuits, Fernando Cardenal and Alvaro Arguello—who held cabinet positions in the Nicaraguan government. "They must resign [and return to proper priestly activity], or I will not come," the Pope told Ortega through Montezemolo.

In the end, the Junta made it a hard choice for John Paul. Fernando Cardenal saw no purpose, and only harm, to Nicaragua's "Christian revolution" in a papal visit. "We are not Poles," Cardenal said at one point in the preparations. "This Polish Pope wishes to make another Poland out of our beloved Nicaragua." The Pontiff's challenge was thrown back at him in reverse terms: Either he renounce his proposed visit to Nicaragua—the clear preference of the Junta—or he abandon what the Junta characterized as his "dictatorial" demands.

Though in the end he had to make do with only one of his conditions—the backdrop for his Mass would not be a revolutionary mural—John Paul chose to go. The arrangements were concluded. His entire Central American trip would last from March 2 to March 9, 1983. He would spend March 4 in Nicaragua.

It was John Paul's misfortune that, long before his arrival in Nicaragua, his intentions and his planned and written speeches were all betrayed in detail to the Sandinista rulers by those in Rome's multilayered bureaucracy—including some in the Pope's own Secretariat of State—who were against this Polish Pope, or who were not against the Marxist-Leninist revolution in progress in this key country of the volatile Central American isthmus.

As a consequence of such thorough and continuing intelligence, the Sandinistas were able to plan with punctilious detail for the day-long papal stay. For all their bravado in the face-off with the Pope's personal representative, they saw John Paul and the power of the papacy which he personified as an immediate and even mortal threat to all they had built up so painstakingly over twelve hard, laborious years. More than ever, their Marxist dream rested on the platform of Base Communities spawned out of the "People's Church." It was precisely the aim of John Paul's trip to Nicaragua to attack the "People's Church" and to cut that platform of Base Communities from beneath their feet, or at least leave it in an irreparably weakened condition.

While the Junta knew John Paul's intentions as well as the texts of his written speeches, it is doubtful John Paul realized the full intentions of the Junta, for his intelligence about the Junta's preparations had been tampered with. It was to be a theater of organized and deliberate desecration both of John Paul's papal persona and of the sacrosanct Sacrifice of the Mass. It was to be a set piece of institutionalized disrespect and opposition not equalled for a very long time, even in countries dominated by sizeable blocs of anti-Catholic or less-than-sympathetic populations, or in officially Marxist countries. And all of it was to be orchestrated to the last detail—to the last wire stretched to the farthest microphone—for the international television, radio, and print media that were always part and parcel of every papal trip.

That Fernando Cardenal and the other activist priests of any rank at all were implicated in such elaborate plans, there can be no serious doubt. That they chose not to create an unwanted public image for themselves became obvious by their absence from the coming desecrations set to begin at the moment of John Paul's arrival on Nicaraguan soil.

*   *   *

From the very moment the Pontiff's Alitalia DC-10 glided into its approach over Managua's César Augusto Sandino Airport that March 4 morning, the cameras glinting in the sunlight below began their busy whirring. They followed the touchdown and hovered their focus on the airliner until it stopped near the waiting dignitaries of the Sandinista regime and the carefully selected crowd of onlookers—the Sandinista claque. They zoomed in on the door of the plane then, until at last it opened and Pope John Paul stepped into its frame, his robes gleaming white as he emerged from the interior darkness.

The Pope descended to the tarmac and knelt to kiss the ground in that gesture that had become so familiar to hundreds of millions of people around the world. From that moment on, everything was in the hands of the Junta.

Daniel Ortega, as leader and spokesman for the Sandinista government, welcomed His Holiness with a twenty-five-minute abusive tirade against the United States, in utter delight that the Pontiff's arrival, covered here as everywhere by the world press, gave Ortega his first truly international platform. John Paul listened, chin cupped in one hand, head bowed, his eyes on the ground. He had heard all this before from Polish Communist Commissars and village Marxists.

John Paul's moment finally came to speak in reply to Ortega's bellicose and deliberately discourteous "welcoming" speech. The Pontiff's prepared remarks in praise of Managua's Archbishop Obando y Bravo were greeted with perfectly timed hoots of derision from the organized and well-marshaled Sandinista claque. His words denouncing the "People's Church" as "a grave deviation from the will and salvation of Jesus Christ" were all but drowned out from first to last by loud and continuing shouts and catcalls.

The Sandinista leaders had reason for deep satisfaction; here, at least, this Pole would not be able to speak over their heads to the people; he would not have a voice in deciding the fate of Nicaragua.

John Paul concluded his prepared arrival speech with pain and anger in his voice. He passed down the receiving line, shaking hands perfunctorily with Junta members and National Directorate Commanders. Certain Cabinet members were conspicuous by their absence. The Foreign Minister, Maryknoll Father Miguel D'Escoto, found it more convenient to be in New Delhi. The OAS Ambassador, Father Edgar Parrales, and the State Delegate, Jesuit Father Alvaro Arguello, were each at home watching the indignities on television. Jesuit Father Fernando Cardenal was also absent. His brother, Father Ernesto Cardenal, was the lone ranking government priest in attendance, a bespectacled figure whose rustic white cotton shirt, baggy blue trousers, and black beret were uncomfortably out of sync with his shiny black shoes.

Of all those gathered to welcome the Holy Father to this overwhelmingly Catholic country, Ernesto Cardenal alone dropped to one knee as the Pope pointedly stopped in front of him. He removed his beret and put out his hand to take the Pope's and kiss his ring. But John Paul did not extend his hand. Instead, he wagged an admonitory finger at Ernesto. "You must regularize your situation!" the Pontiff spoke in a clear voice, and then repeated his words for emphasis. "You must regularize your situation!" Cardenal's only reply was to stare back, smiling at His Holiness.

John Paul passed down the remainder of the receiving line, and departed for the first portion of his planned itinerary in Nicaragua, a visit to the city of León, some forty miles to the northwest of Managua.

The reception at Sandino Airport was but a thin and reedy over-

ture to the full symphony of humiliation that had been orchestrated for John Paul, to be performed before the world at the climax
of his papal visit. The public Mass that was the centerpiece of John
Paul's visit was to be celebrated that evening in the spacious *Plaza
of July 19,* named for the day in 1979 when the Somoza dictatorship had been smashed and the Marxist Junta of the Sandinistas
had taken power.

*   *   *

The setting sun splashed its red-gold rays on an unforgettable
scene as John Paul II entered the Plaza clad in full pontifical robes,
papal miter on his head, papal staff held upright in his hand.

The crowd jammed into the Plaza, officially estimated at
600,000, was all neatly sorted out and massed in prearranged blocs.
One end of the packed Plaza was spanned by an enormous backdrop of revolutionary billboards depicting the heroes of the Sandinista revolution. Facing the billboards on the opposite side of the
Plaza, a long wooden platform with a railing had been constructed.
An altar—a simple, long table draped for the occasion with linen
—had been placed on the platform. On either side of the platform,
facing the crowds, were two official viewing stands where the
three-man Junta and the nine-man National Directorate waited,
all twelve clad in olive green army fatigues.

In the places closest to the makeshift platform and its flanking
reviewing stands, the Junta had arranged special blocs of supporters provided with megaphones and a microphone pick-up. Everywhere—on buildings surrounding the Plaza, on the billboards, in
the hands of the crowds, around the platform and the altar itself—
were red and black Sandinista flags. Here and there a yellow and
white Vatican flag popped up, and there was a smattering of blue
and white Nicaraguan flags.

Tauntingly, Ortega and his colleagues had ordered hung as backdrop to the altar a mural depicting in enormous proportions the
faces of Carlos Fonseca Amador, hero-martyr of the Sandinista
revolution, and Augusto César Sandino, the man in whose name
the Sandinistas had made their revolution.

There was no crucifix above the altar. That immemorial Catholic practice had been forbidden by the young rulers of Nicaragua.
In its place had been stretched yet another long banner, this one
emblazoned with man-sized lettering: *"John Paul is here. Thanks
to God and the Revolution!"*

As always when such a mass of people is gathered together,
there was never a moment of silence. Massed crowds, unless they
are silenced by something extraordinary—a spellbinding orator, a

dazzling spectacle—emit a continuous rumble and jumble of sounds. That evening the Plaza echoed with that same rumble-jumble, punctuated with nicely timed bursts of cheering and occasional singing and chanting. John Paul began his Mass tranquilly; he was used to the behavior of crowds.

When the moment came for him to deliver his prepared homily —a vigorous onslaught on the People's Church—he appeared surprised that even the microphone that had been set up for him could not overcome the well-rehearsed and beautifully timed cacophony that now rose from the crowds, an ear-splitting litany of rhythmic, revolutionary slogans.

The claques started even before the homily began, in fact. When John Paul strained to make his deep voice resound over the competition, the litany of the crowd became thunderously loud and as regular as heartbeats:

"Power to the People!"

"National Directorate, give us your orders!"

"Speak to us of the poor!"

Progressively, John Paul could barely be heard. His sympathizers tried to protest, to make their support for him heard, but they had been located as far as possible from the platform, and had neither megaphones nor microphones. John Paul could be seen, his hand slicing the air trenchantly in violent gestures; but he could not be heard over the incessant clanging of the Sandinista slogans.

"We want a united Church on the side of the poor!"

"There is no contradiction between Christianity and revolution!"

John Paul's face became livid with indignation as he realized what was happening: He was being trapped and nullified in a well of noise. In anger and desperation, he finally shouted, *"Silencio!"*

In the well-orchestrated symphony-of-the-claques, the Pope's command was but a signal to increase the tempo of slogans.

"Silencio!" John Paul shouted a second time. A new crescendo of slogans engulfed him. A third time: *"Silencio!"* the word accompanied now by a staying gesture of his hand.

An unimaginably loud chorus of "Power to the People! Christ lives in the People's Church!" overwhelmed his efforts. The crowd was beyond his control.

Angered, John Paul shouted a taunt into his microphone, his fury-filled glance shooting over at the Junta in their reviewing stand: "Miskito Power!"

The taunt hit home. The Miskito Indians were in dire opposition to the Sandinistas, and the Junta had been doing its utmost to liquidate them. The response was instantaneous. The nine military Commanders of the National Directorate and the Junta raised their clenched fists to urge the blocs of slogan-chanters to even greater efforts. Simultaneously, government technicians connected the microphones of the claques surrounding the platform to the main loudspeaker system over which John Paul had been trying to make himself heard. That done, and to swell still further the sound already drowning out the Pope, they threw a switch to cut in a prerecorded taping of crowds chanting Sandinista slogans.

Finally the thumping cascade of amplified shouts defeated John Paul. He did not finish his homily. But even that was not enough for the Junta. The slogans continued through the entire Sacrifice of the Mass, drowning even its most sacred moment, the Consecration, in cries of "Power to the People!" and "It is possible to be Marxist and Christian!" and "Speak to us about the injustice of capitalism!"

Yet still the humiliation was not complete. When John Paul and his entourage took their seats in the Alitalia DC-10 at Managua's airport that night and the pilot notified the control tower that he was ready for takeoff, the Junta ordered the papal plane to be kept waiting an extra ten minutes on the ground. It was their final gesture to underline who was really in control here.

When at last the humiliation had been played to its last note, the government radio insisted to the Nicaraguan people that the Pope should apologize for his behavior. "The indignation and spontaneous protests of our people were natural in the face of the indifference of the Pope," one broadcast explained. "This Pope is a Pope of the West, the Pope of Imperialism," a member of the Sandinista Directorate grumbled. "The Pope is trying to convert Nicaragua into another Poland," Interior Minister Tomás Borge accused. "He is trying to make the Church commit suicide," added a Maryknoll missioner piously.

As was so often the case, it was left to Father Fernando Cardenal to give the briefest, clearest summary of the Junta's position as well as its justification for its degradation of the Pope, the papacy, and the Catholic Mass: "The Pope's speech," Cardenal commented, "was a declaration of war."

5 | SUMMARY DISOBEDIENCE

L ove them or hate them, for 425 of their 443 years as an Order, the Jesuits were in their own eyes as well as virtually everyone else's the torchbearers of Church attitudes regarding both Pope and papacy. In normal times, had any Jesuit been involved even more remotely than Fernando Cardenal in a humiliation a fraction of the one heaped upon John Paul II in Nicaragua on March 4, 1983, that Jesuit would have found himself out of the Society and shunned by its members literally within hours.

Even in less normal times, as in the fifteen years of Pedro Arrupe's Generalate, there would have been at least a theater of shock and loyalty, a show of concern, a barrage of assurances that the matter would be looked into, coupled with the unending explanations and delays in corrective measures.

The reaction in the Society to the news of John Paul's humiliation in Nicaragua that spring of 1983, however, seems to have been one of a kind both among Superiors and the majority of leaders in the Order: John Paul II had stuck his head into the lion's den and had got more or less what he was asking for. The hope now among many Jesuits was that this Pope might have learned his lesson, emerged from his "Polish ghetto bishop" mentality, and realized how complicated the big, bad world really was. This Pope had decided to take over the governance of the Society by the highhanded action of deposing Arrupe and O'Keefe. Very well. Now he knew better. It was felt that John Paul would draw in his horns, retire and lick his wounds.

That attitude was reinforced by the absence of any strong reaction on the part of John Paul II's Secretary of State, Agostino Cardinal Casaroli, who was content to utter some acceptable platitudes about the need for all sides to cool down.

With such a weak response from the papal office itself, the Jesuits felt not the slightest pressure to call Cardenal and the other Jesuits involved in the papal humiliation to order. A "wait-and-see" attitude set in. But in many eyes, John Paul had lost an important battle. The Sandinista humiliation prepared the way for copycat aggressiveness against the Pope in the years to come.[1]

In one clearly defined sense, that "wait-and-see" attitude was only made possible by John Paul himself. By an unheard-of exercise of papal authority, he had dismissed one Father General, Arrupe, and had placed two hand-picked men of his choice at the head of the Jesuit Order. Had the Pontiff pressed his two appointees after his return from Nicaragua, both men would have had to bend to John Paul's will, however distasteful, even to the point of starting a total reform of the Society. Given precise and unequivocal orders—"Expel all Jesuits in the Nicaraguan government!" "Recall all Central American Superiors!" "Replace them with men who can obey!"—there is little doubt that Dezza and Pittau would have done as they were told. Indeed, such specific action, such unabashed exercise of papal strength, would have been read in *romanità*'s terms as a warning: Do as I say this time, as extreme as the action is, or there will be far worse in store—the dissolution of the Order.

To the consternation of many, however, though John Paul had taken the first step of removing Arrupe and his chosen successor, Vincent O'Keefe, he failed to take the second, despite the fact that the Nicaraguan fiasco had given him far more reason than ever. Instead, he let things remain in the hands of Dezza and Pittau.

There were reams of speculation about the causes of the Pope's inaction, but no certain answers. Had the Holy Father given up? Was he warned by his Cardinal Secretary of State, Casaroli, that he had gone far enough? Did he flinch from further action because of across-the-board threats by whole blocs of Jesuits that they would exit en masse from the Society?

Casaroli, did, indeed, attempt to exercise a restraining hand with John Paul. Whole blocs of Jesuits did threaten to walk. Still, given John Paul's character, it seems more likely that the Polish Pope made only one mistake: He trusted Dezza and Pittau to do his bidding. His original orders to Dezza had been clear and pressing: Change and reform the Order now. Not tomorrow. Not next year. Now. He presumed good faith and good Jesuitism on Dezza's part. He trusted Pittau. They knew his mind. He presumed that Dezza, as one of the oldest Roman hands among the Jesuits, a man who had served both the papacy and the Order well for four decades, would not only know what must be done in detail, but would find the means to accomplish it with the least amount of lasting damage. It was perhaps even logical for the Pontiff to assume that under Dezza's skilled direction, Pittau, with his own long experience in the field and his association with Arrupe, would make the perfect partner in leading the Society of Jesus out of its morass of secularization, disobedience, and disaffection from the papacy.

In the papal mind, moreover, the experience in Nicaragua should have demonstrated to Dezza and Pittau far more than the Pope's mere verbal insistence could, the urgent need for reform. The Pope himself had never seen the depth of the problem as clearly as he did in Nicaragua. Even in Communist countries—in Poland and Hungary as examples—all the mighty threats of armed Marxist troops had never been able to get the people to shout for hours, as the Nicaraguans had done, against their Church or their Pope. Surely, after the Sandinista government's singular performance in Managua, no further urging by John Paul would be needed.

The Pope's judgment concerning Dezza and Pittau turned out to be dead wrong.

Dezza read the whole matter differently. If the Pope didn't give him specific orders, then the Pope was not being papal. He was not fully exercising his power. When John Paul I was alive and he made a specific request to Dezza concerning the composition of the address he wished to give to Arrupe and his Jesuits in 1978, Dezza complied; he knew what the Pope wanted. Few Jesuits ever knew that Dezza's hand had molded the speech which John Paul I never gave, but which John Paul II had made his own.

Now, in 1982, the lack of specificity in John Paul II's demands meant, according to *romanità*, that there was some power loose in the area, and whatever hand picked up such unused power could run with it. It was up to Dezza to decide what to do.

In this case, actually, Dezza didn't exactly run with the power; he skillfully tucked it away—held it in reserve, as one might say —for the moment when the Jesuit Order would be allowed to resume its own governance. It was to that end—the return of the Society to its proper "form"—that Dezza bent his own efforts.

Certainly, John Paul had a great deal more on his plate to deal with than the Jesuits. There was the continuing ache of Poland. There were struggles completely internal to the Vatican—about the New Law code of the Church Universal; about the liturgy of the Mass; about the policy of missionaries in Asian and African cultures; about the continuing deterioration of the Church in the United States. As crowded as the Pope's agenda was, the direct challenge to Church structure and authority flung in the face of his papacy in Nicaragua would certainly have put the Jesuit matter high on his list of priorities if it had not been for his trust in Dezza.

By the time Dezza's waiting game became obvious—his silence and inaction over the Nicaraguan desecration and his business-as-usual preparation for the General Congregation were clear indications—members of the papal administration were advising John Paul II not to intervene in a direct disciplining and punishment of the Society. It was like a repetition of the warning *Religiosi* had given the Pope in the secret State Council meeting two years before. Only now the warning was a full-blooded chorus, and the problem had worsened greatly: What ailed the Society of Jesus, ailed large segments of the Pope's Church. All the major Religious Orders were affected now, together with a frighteningly large number of bishops, theologians, and priests, not to speak of activist lay Catholics and nuns.

John Paul understood the warnings very well. More accurately than any man alive, he understood the precarious hold of the traditional hierarchic Church over its people. He knew that the secularism animating the Jesuits was as widespread as antipapalism; that one fed off the other; and that both were widely fostered by men as different as Holland's sophisticated Dominican theologian Edward Schillebeeckx, Brazil's abrasive Archbishop Helder y Camara, Germany's subtly vicious Karl Rahner, S.J., Ireland's busybody Bishop Casey of Galway, and the United States' "honest-John" but ever dissident Richard McBrien.

It was no surprise to John Paul when Schillebeeckx addressed a Dutch antipapal rally, or that he proclaimed there—infallibly as it would seem—that the Church's hierarchical structure is not God's will and that infallibility in the Pope "is from the Roman Catholic viewpoint a clear heresy."

A statement of Monsignor George Higgins of the United States appeared to be more innocuous only because his style is naturally bland and inoffensive: "Active, intelligent and truly informed par-

ticipation in the liturgy is the primary means of developing a social conscience and special consciousness among Catholics—
other things being equal, a congregation steeped in the Church's
liturgical life will be more socially conscious and better prepared
to make sound moral judgments in economic and political life
than one that is not."

In the Pope's view and in the entire history of the Church from
the time of the Apostles themselves, liturgy has always meant
something totally different; it has meant participation by individuals in the Sacraments of the Church. Sacraments are not social-
consciousness raisers or group organizers, and they do not prepare
one to make sound judgments in political life.

Higgins's statement was important precisely because it mirrored the spread in the clergy itself of a concept of "liturgy" di-
vorced from Sacraments and oriented instead to the social,
political, and economic warfare of the day among nations.
It reflected, in fact, the secularization of divine functions of exactly the sort provided by the Sandinista model; it mirrored the
Sandinista-Marxist switch of "communal" Catholicism for personal faith and judgment; and though not snappy in its style, the
statement was a fair summary of the latest form of the heresy,
called Modernism, condemned by Popes since the last century.

Secularization of the divine had already gone very far, even to
the bald statement by one expert in such a publication as the
Journal of the Liturgical Conference, redefining the central Sacrament itself: "Christians have not always recognized the political
aspect of the Eucharist. Yet the Eucharist is a political act. . . ."

It was yet another hard choice for John Paul, but even some of
his personal and most trusted advisers were telling him by summer of 1983 that the rot had spread so far beyond the Jesuits that
to single that Order out for its infidelity to the papacy and papal
prerogatives, and for its secularization of the purpose of religion,
would provoke a storm that would be difficult to ride out. It could
harden opposition to an extreme from which there would be no
return, no easement.

In the view of those advisers, the Pope had only two options if
he was to lay the ax directly at the root of the Church's troubles.
He could either summon another Roman Catholic Ecumenical
Council in the Vatican—Vatican Council III—or he must rally his
bishops from around the world to his side in a synod, and with
them issue a thoroughgoing corrective to the abuse and misuse of
the much-vaunted but critically weak statements of Vatican
Council II that had met in Rome from 1962 to 1965. It was, after

all, the Pontiff's advisers reminded him repeatedly, "the spirit of Vatican II" that was continually invoked to justify any and all corruption of traditional Roman Catholic faith and morals, not only in Nicaragua, but in the United States, in Europe, and virtually everywhere.

However compelling John Paul's reasons for inaction in the matter of Jesuit reform, in the opinion of many, his fateful decision to allow the Society to resume its own governance was also a fatal one. In the view of such observers, the truth seemed to be that the Pope had given up in this particular struggle, and the whole Church would pay the piper. All too soon, such opinions proved prophetic.

When at long last the 33rd General Congregation of the Society of Jesus, composed of 220 Delegates, did meet in Rome in September of 1983, its first order of business was a charade. It "accepted" Father Pedro Arrupe's "resignation." In the Jesuit annals, there would be no official acknowledgment of the extraordinary exercise of papal authority by which Arrupe had been removed from his post. Just as a prior Congregation had chosen him in 1965, now this Congregation claimed to be acting "sovereignly" in "releasing" him from his job. It was not only a self-consoling gesture; it was a juridical slap on the papal wrist.

The Congregation's second order of business was to choose Arrupe's successor. In one ballot on September 13, the Delegates elected Piet-Hans Kolvenbach, a Dutchman, scholar and specialist in Near Eastern Catholic rites, long-time resident of Beirut, Lebanon, and since 1981 Rector of the Jesuit-run Pontifical Oriental Institute in Rome. Tall, heavy-framed, with a full head of graying hair, a severe face, Woody Allen look-alike spectacles over large eyes that seldom smiled even if his mouth did, an ample white beard surmounted by a black mustache, Kolvenbach's character had been already noted. He was *furbo*, the Romans commented, using a word that meant both cunning and sly. He was a man of very few words—"the Church has been drowned in words lately," Kolvenbach reportedly commented on the deluge of speeches, addresses, and sermons that started flowing from the papacy once John Paul II was elected in 1978. When Kolvenbach did speak, it was said, he went for the jugular, to use a popular phrase.

Kolvenbach's hasty election was a remarkable thing in itself. The Jesuits had had ample time since Arrupe's dismissal in October of 1981—the year Kolvenbach was summoned to Rome—to prepare the candidacy of a suitable man for the day they would be allowed elect a Father General, but it was rather unique in the history of the Society for a Congregation to elect a new General in but one ballot. Normally, it takes several just to sort the true candidates from those who have no realistic chance of success. Nobody observing the situation in the volatile years and months leading up to that September day had any doubts that Kolvenbach's candidacy and his election were the result of a long, well-thought-out process into which the General Assistants had put their best efforts.

Nor had such observers any doubt that Kolvenbach's Generalate would be a continuation of the "Arrupe spirit" at the helm of the Order. The Jesuit leaders had made a "defensive" choice. They had no intention of changing their course of neo-Modernism. They had no intention of finding themselves in the embarrassing position of the Dominican Religious Order who, around the time of the Jesuit election of their Father General, were themselves gathered in Rome to elect their own General—Master-General, the Dominicans call their Major Superior. An Irish Dominican, Father Albert Nolan, received a vast majority of votes. Nolan, however, an ardent foe of apartheid in South Africa and already a noted activist, had no intention of putting his head "into the lion's mouth," as one Dominican colleague remarked. He knew what had happened to Jesuit Arrupe at the hands of John Paul II. The Dominican assembly of leaders were forced to choose another Master-General, another Irishman, Damian Byrne. The Jesuits in fixing on Kolvenbach were sure they ran no risk of his refusing or of his not hewing to strict Arrupism.

Kolvenbach left the Jesuit Delegates who had elected him in no uneasy doubt about his Arrupism. The first words he addressed to them as 28th General of the Society of Jesus must have been nectar for their minds.

Right from the start, Kolvenbach was reassuring in a ponderous sort of a way. "I assume the office [of General]," he told the Delegates, "with great trust in the Society." The remainder of his approximately thirty-line speech was a development of that theme. The Lord did not require of Jesuits that they wallow in dark and gloomy thoughts about the weaknesses and deficiencies of the Society. No Jesuit should feel he could be pushed around. By anyone. Neither the criticisms made by Pope Paul VI nor those made by Pope John Paul II have changed Jesuits or reversed the very welcome change Jesuits had undergone since the late sixties—he meant, he said, their heightened sensitivity to the needs of justice and their increased concern for the plight of the poor and the oppressed.

The dismissal of Father Arrupe by the Pope had not been a very wise move, Kolvenbach declared. For, in great part, today the life of the Society is directed by the spirituality and apostolic zeal that Father Arrupe developed for the Society. The whole spiritual and apostolic slant that the Lord had given Jesuits in the Society had come through Father Arrupe. The Society would not abandon the Arrupe tradition.

On the contrary, the core and essence of Jesuit activity had been and would still be directed against injustice in the world. This was and is the mission of Jesuits today.

This policy of the Society has not sat well with some people, he said. There are even some Jesuits who see this new mission of the Society of Jesus as a definite and dangerous deviation from the Ignatian spirit. But many other Jesuits do not agree.

Nor has this new mission sat well with Popes. But he, Kolvenbach, had lived in the middle of that injustice before he came to Rome in 1981: He had lived in Beirut. *"Io ero là,"* he said trenchantly. "I was there." And from that firsthand experience of the grave injustice Jesuits are fighting, he had come away freed from any illusions. "I am not bound either to the Romans [the Holy See], or to the United States, or to the French, or to the Latin Americans," he stated stolidly as a simple matter of fact. "So, now, we must see what we can do!"

We must, he continued, answer the cries of men suffering injustice with a language and with provisions that suit their language and their life conditions. Thus we can "best serve God, Church, the Vicar of Christ, Pope John Paul II"—the words came out of him in staccato fashion—"but we will serve the Church and the Pope only if, by serving them, we can be of service to men."

For, he continued, our responsibility is to the Divine Majesty. He wanted his Jesuits to have "a dimension of interior liberty" that put that Divine Majesty in the prime place, and all else on earth—he almost added "including the church and the papacy"—in second place. The Divine Majesty was their only "paragon" of how to behave.

The Gospels told them to be vigilant, not to grow tired, like the Foolish Virgins tiring in their wait for the Bridegroom's arrival. Some Jesuits, Kolvenbach admitted, seemed to be growing tired of being vigilant. But all had to be vigilant and not allow themselves to be worn down by fear. Christ said, he reminded them, that he who wanted to save his life must be ready to lose it. The opposite was also true: He who concentrated only on saving his life would be bound to lose it. Perhaps, indeed, the General Congregation and the Society would be forced to lose its life, if Jesuits were not willing "to go to the wall" for the Decrees and the principles already laid out, and if what they do is not pleasing to the Divine Majesty.

The present opportunity of fighting injustice must not be lost. Jesuits must "discover" the Society all over again. Jesuits, since the removal of Father Arrupe, had behaved themselves a little more carefully. But no one of them was disposed to change his convictions about the modern mission of the Society. To abandon that, to abandon the fight against injustice, would be to abandon Christ's humanity.

Of course, there would be objections and criticisms from various quarters that Jesuits were indulging in politics. Actually, Kolvenbach said, the number of Jesuits directly engaged in political activity is quite small. But great was the number of Jesuits who indirectly but powerfully influenced politics through their involvement in labor unions, peasant organizations, social movements and causes. Some Jesuits became socialists. Some became Marxists. All of this produced "groaning complaints" from Popes. But the Society was still disposed to forge ahead in this manner with its mission of justice and its preferential option for the poor, without paying much attention to the "groaning complaints of Popes."

His job as Father General was to ensure that Jesuits not be distracted by papal groans from carrying out their mission among men.

When Kolvenbach had finished, it was small wonder that in the subsequent days of GC33, the Delegates went on to reassert the goals and values of Arrupism all over again. Of course, from the Decrees of this Congregation, and from the transcript of Father General Kolvenbach's address to the Delegates, John Paul II could see clearly that nothing in the Society had changed. His subsequent dealings with the new Father General confirmed that.

For the remainder of 1983 and into the spring of 1984, the new Father General was the recipient of insistent requests from Church authorities in Managua and Rome to remove Fernando Cardenal either from his political Cabinet post in the Sandinista government or from the Jesuit Order. And for all that time, the new Father General continued the same circular motion of polite evasions, toleration of indirect refusals by Cardenal himself and by his local Jesuit Superiors in Managua, and tacit acquiescence in public protests and objections to Rome's interference from the Sandinistas broadcast in the international media.

The situation between the Jesuits on the one hand, and the Nicaraguan bishops and Rome on the other, came to a new boiling point in the spring of 1984. The Nicaraguan bishops issued an Easter pastoral letter in which they repeated Pope John Paul's words excoriating *la iglesia popular* and the Base Communities. The letter blasted all clerics and nuns who were neglecting their spiritual vocations in favor of building up "the People's Church" as part of the Sandinista infrastructure, and it demanded a return to ecclesiastical normalcy. In bald terms, the bishops accused "a small sector of the Church" of having betrayed the apostolic structure of Christ's Church "in order to foment Marxist-Leninism."

The knife cut very close to the Jesuit bone, and the reaction was as devastating as it was predictable. The Jesuit Provincial of all Central American countries, together with a group of Nicaraguan Jesuits and ably assisted by Father Fernando Cardenal, replied with a detailed and bitterly scathing critique of the bishops' pastoral letter. The reply insisted that the People's Church *was* Christ's Church. It summarily rejected all episcopal claims to control that Church.

In addition to everything else that letter was, it was a painful measure of the immunity the Jesuits felt they enjoyed by now from John Paul II's authority. They had, after all, evaded even direct papal intrusion into the Order itself. They now had their own chosen General.

At the same time, the Sandinista government increased its harassment of the Nicaraguan bishops, and of priests, nuns, and layfolk who supported the bishops. So aggressive did the harassment become that it provoked the Archbishop of Managua, Obando y Bravo, to comment publicly, "The Sandinista regime is now more brutal and repressive than the Somoza people were in their day."

As if to show their teeth against any move to deprive them of their priest-colleagues in government, the Junta decided on a brutally clear move against the bishops and Rome. On July 9, 1984, armed government officers and officials arrived at the residences of ten priests who had been loyal to the bishops, arrested them, and transported them unceremoniously to Managua's airport. Father Santiago Anitua, S.J., one of the few Nicaraguan Jesuits loyal to the papacy and the traditional Church, was picked up in the same manner from where he worked and brought straight to the airport. All eleven were deported on the spot for the crime of hindering the formation of *la iglesia popular*.

A worse fate awaited others. Father Amado Pena was arrested and indicted for plotting the armed overthrow of the Junta. The evidence presented against him consisted of dynamite and arms planted on him when his car was stopped at the roadside, while he was out answering a sick call that turned out to be a hoax.[2] Another priest, a fifty-five-year-old Nicaraguan, Father Bayardo Santa Eliz Felaya, was tied to a post outside his own parish church along with four of his parishioners, doused with gasoline, and set ablaze. Miraculously, he lived to tell his story to the American press in Washington, D.C., "in order to bear witness against the Sandinista rulers."

Just in case such actions left any lingering doubt as to the position of the priests in government, Father Edgar Parrales, Sandinista Welfare Minister, stepped forward to make things plain to all. "Now is not the moment for us to return to the cloister," Parrales said categorically, "to be locked up and waiting for the saint, the beggar, and the First Communion."

Repression and torture aside, the official Jesuit critique of the bishops' pastoral letter was at least a tactical error; it put in John Paul's hands a concrete reason for exerting renewed pressure on Jesuit Father General Kolvenbach to make a final decision about Fernando Cardenal as the standard-bearer of Jesuit recalcitrance, and about the other Jesuits in government in Nicaragua.

In July 1984, Father General Kolvenbach, under this new pressure from Pope John Paul, dutifully sent a special envoy to Nicaragua to inquire firsthand into the affair of the bold Jesuit critique of the bishops' letter. The envoy found out that things were as bad as John Paul had told Kolvenbach. There was no way to lessen the severity of the politicking and the Marxism of Fernando Cardenal and the other Jesuits in government.

John Paul II therefore insisted that Fernando Cardenal and the other priests holding government cabinet positions resign either from the government or the Order by August 31.

Kolvenbach, prompted by his own advisers and Cardenal's friends, persuaded John Paul not to insist on that date, but to wait until after the Nicaraguan elections in the autumn, "so as not unduly to disturb matters."

Yet again, by agreeing to a seemingly reasonable and seemingly cooperative request for a delay, the Pontiff allowed the initiative to be removed from his own hands. Kolvenbach did telex Fernando Cardenal in August, urging him to resign his post, saying that Cardenal "cannot be permitted to carry on a [ministerial] assignment because of its incompatibility with your status as a Jesuit." But the results were predictable.

Cardenal's reply was a public and pompous redeclaration of independence from his Church and his Superior General: "The achievement of my Jesuit vocation is only to be had in my commitment to the revolution." He sent an urgent request to his Father General for a face-to-face meeting in the United States, where Kolvenbach had scheduled a visit for the coming autumn.

In the intervening time, an opportunity arose for Kolvenbach to make clear where he himself stood in the struggle between John Paul II on the one side, and Fernando Cardenal with his Liberation Theology colleagues throughout Latin America on the other. The occasion was a document issued under John Paul's authority by Joseph Cardinal Ratzinger, head of the Vatican's powerful Congregation for the Doctrine of Faith (CDF), the Roman Ministry charged with overseeing the purity of Catholic teaching. The CDF document criticized Liberation Theology and its practitioners for their adoption of the Marxist analysis of history, and for their insistence on the "class struggle" and the proletarian revolution as integral parts of genuine Christianity. Between the lines of the document, despite *Stato*'s prior warnings, was the implicit rejection of Soviet Marxism-Leninism.

In response, Father General Kolvenbach did something the likes of which no Jesuit Father General before him had ever done. Under his official title, he issued a critique of the Vatican document, accusing it of being too negative, and expressing confidence that a more balanced treatment of Liberation Theology would be issued by Ratzinger's CDF in the future. The teachings of Liberation Theology, Kolvenbach wrote, must be "recognized as possible and necessary."

In issuing so direct and open a rebuttal of Ratzinger's official document, Kolvenbach was not only testing his own strength and the weakness of John Paul; he was redoubling Fernando Cardenal's assumption of immunity from John Paul II's authority demonstrated the previous spring. And he was acting with sure knowledge that he had at least two powerful allies against Cardinal Ratzinger and Pope John Paul.

Indeed, the Jesuits' principal ally in Rome, Cardinal Secretary of State Agostino Casaroli, swung into action at around the same time. There would, the Secretary said, be another and better composed statement on the subject soon. In the meantime, he said, flinging his threatened bombshell in the face of Pope John Paul, he as Secretary of State would have to place a distance between himself and Ratzinger's document.

In a subsequent speech, the Secretary of State went out of his way to praise John Paul's predecessor, Pope Paul VI, as the papal champion and ideal of dialogue with countries of the so-called real socialism.

Casaroli had an eye on his friends at the other side of the Iron Curtain who had excoriated the Ratzinger document as "the disgrace of our time." The Secretary wished to tell those friends that he was in total disagreement with John Paul's policy toward the USSR and its satellites. As he had told the Pontiff, he intended to nurture and protect his lines of communication with Moscow and its eastern European satellites; that meant tender treatment of Marxism and its modern womb, the Soviet Union. In Casaroli's eyes, the greatest misfortune would be for him to become *persona non grata* in such quarters.

Father General Kolvenbach's second muscular ally in this matter was the Archbishop of Lima, Peru, Cardinal Juan Landázuri Ricketts. Landázuri had been Archbishop of Lima for thirty-two years, and he enjoyed a truly enormous prestige not only in Lima and all of Latin America, but in Rome. In addition, he was a personal friend and admirer of the very man, Jesuit Father Gustavo Gutierrez, who had published the basic manual of Liberation Theology in the seventies.

At what seemed the most opportune time from Kolvenbach's vantage point, Landázuri descended on Rome that autumn with an entourage of his Peruvian bishops in tow. In protracted interviews with John Paul and Cardinal Ratzinger, he was able to shield Jesuit Gutierrez from condemnation or censure.

The strategy was pointed: True, Gutierrez did not hold a cabinet post in Peru; but he did analyze "theology" in the light of the Marxist theory of class struggle; he did head the *Las Casas* study group which belonged to the *Izquierda Unida* (IU), Peru's equivalent of the Sandinista coalition. If John Paul could not censure a man like Gutierrez, the reasoning ran, his hand would be weakened when he tried to deal with other Jesuits allied with Marxists in other countries.

Cardenal himself, meanwhile, remained very active in the fray. In conversations and correspondence throughout the autumn of 1984, Fernando fought desperately to stay on in his government post, and to provide his Father General with adequate reasons for refusing to give in to John Paul's demand that he retire from politics or be "retired" from the Jesuit Order. Even as late as October 21, when he had his hoped-for face-to-face meeting with Kolvenbach in New York, he seemed to have real hope that he could keep both Jesuit collar and cabinet minister's portfolio. Cardenal emerged from that meeting with his Father General telling his friends, "A solution has been found."

But it was not so. Despite the open support of Casaroli and Landázuri and others besides, Father General Kolvenbach's hands were tied. John Paul II was insistent that Fernando Cardenal resign from his government post or be dismissed from his Order, and that the same demand would apply to all other priest-politicians in Nicaragua. All chose dismissal. It remained only to issue the formal documents.

On December 4, Fernando Cardenal received an official notice from his Father General telling him that he was being dismissed from the Society, and encouraging him "to take thought regarding some other path of life in which he can serve God with greater tranquility."

Simultaneously, and for the second time in his short tenure, Kolvenbach took a step unprecedented in Jesuit annals. He wrote an official letter to all Major Jesuit Superiors around the world "explaining" Cardenal's departure, and recognizing Cardenal's "conflict of conscience." Because Cardenal's insistent argument all along had been that only by staying at his government post could he help the poor, Kolvenbach expressed the hope that no one among the Jesuits would conclude from Cardenal's decision that to help the poor, one had to cease being a Jesuit.

What Kolvenbach did not include in his letter of explanation to the Society was any mention of the will of the Holy Father. He did not detail or even address himself to the deep conflict about Church structure and Church authority in Nicaragua. Nor did he invoke the issue of Jesuit obedience—his own, Cardenal's, and the whole Society's—to the Pope. Instead, it appeared that one good charade to disguise Pedro Arrupe's dismissal deserved another to disguise Fernando Cardenal's.

In effect, Kolvenbach's letter said, Cardenal's decision to leave was his own, and he made it because there was a troublesome Canon Law of the Church, #285, that forbids priests to occupy government posts without special permission from the Holy See. The Holy See, which was to say the Holy Father, had refused to make an exception of Father Fernando Cardenal. There was no "dismissal," properly speaking, merely a mutual agreement that Cardenal could only follow his conscience outside the Society of Jesus. Indeed, Cardenal's own reaction to his dismissal—"They are not punishing me for my sins but for what I experience as God's call to me"—was vindicated by Kolvenbach's letter.

When the official notification of Cardenal's departure was issued by Jesuit headquarters in Rome on December 11, official and unofficial Jesuit commentary and reaction predictably followed the model and the spirit of the Father General's brash and unprecedented letter to Superiors about the whole affair.

Father Johannes Gerhartz, Secretary-General of the Society, agreed fully that the "dismissal" of Cardenal was not a penal act, a punishment, wasn't *really* a dismissal. Nor did it laicize Cardenal; he was still a priest in good standing, but subject now to the authority of Archbishop Obando y Bravo of Managua rather than to the Superiors of the Society. Nor, Gerhartz went on incredibly, was there any pressure from the "Vatican" (the accepted code word for John Paul) on the Father General to request Cardenal's "departure."

Joseph McHugh, S.J., Jesuit Secretary for Communication and Information in Washington, D.C., made a bow in the direction of the truth, but only a very oblique one. McHugh acknowledged that "Cardenal was allowed to leave" because there were "strong political realities at work here." He later clarified those "realities" with the term "organizational," a reference to papal pressure on the Society. Cardenal's leaving, McHugh went on to observe, "was a very sad thing" and had created "a sense of regret" among his fellow Jesuits who retained "a feeling of family loyalty" to Cardenal.

Vatican Radio, which is run by Jesuits for the Holy See and comes directly within the sphere of influence of Cardinal Secretary of State Casaroli, was even more lavish and personally tender in its treatment of Cardenal. Fernando, Vatican Radio announced, referring to him almost affectionately by his first name, had departed "in an atmosphere of mutual esteem and respect on the part of all those involved; but obviously, for Fernando and for many other Jesuits, it was a painful affair."

Letters written to the media by Jesuits in Europe and the Americas stressed to the point of defiance that Cardenal could not be denied access to his Jesuit Community at Bosques de Altamira in Managua. "It may mean," one conceded grudgingly "that Fernando has to live in a tent at the bottom of the garden."

In any event, Cardenal's Jesuit colleagues in Central America took no warning from his shipwreck. In the words of Valentin Menendez, S.J., Jesuit Provincial for all of Central America, "Our goal is to try to accompany the Nicaraguan people along its difficult path and in its great hopes, from our position as Jesuit Religious in the Church."

So deeply effective was the charade and so widespread and consistent were its fruits, that unless one chooses to accuse at least some Jesuits working far from Rome of propagating untruths about the case, the best face one can paint is one of ignorance among Jesuits at large about Cardenal. That is the best one can assume for such comments as American Jesuit Tennant C. Wright's, made in June 1985, that "although the Pope and the Cardinal of Managua have asked priests in government to resign, they have not insisted upon the resignation." At such an extreme, though, it seems almost pointless to worry whether it is a man's veracity or his ignorance that should be questioned.

Fernando Cardenal, perhaps having read the handwriting on the wall sooner than he was willing to admit, had composed a statement quite a time before he received his official notice of dismissal on December 4. "A Letter to My Friends," he called the statement; he sent it out at the height of the reaction to his case.

In spite of his "unjust dismissal," Cardenal said in his letter, his conscience grasped "as if in a global intuition that my commitment to the cause of the poor in Nicaragua comes from God. . . . I would commit a grave sin before God if I abandoned, in the present circumstances, my priestly option for the poor." On the other hand, "the Holy See in the case of Nicaragua appears to be imprisoned by conceptions in the political sphere that it has received from the traumatic experiences of Eastern European conflicts. . . ." The disrespectful innuendo about John Paul, though muted by comparison to the humiliation during the Pope's visit nearly two years before, was clear.

Cardenal expressed deep gratitude to all his fellow Jesuits and Superiors, implying clearly what does appear to be true, namely that all who mattered in the Society of Jesus, including Father General Kolvenbach, would have wished him to continue his work at his government post and as a Jesuit. "The one who has categorically refused . . . has been Pope John Paul II." That sentence alone is replete with un-Catholic insolence. Later, Cardenal added a further demeaning remark. "There is a coincidence between the policies of President Reagan toward Nicaragua and the policies of the Vatican toward Nicaragua." The word *Vatican* on Cardenal's lips is his belatedly discreet expression for John Paul II.

Still not content, Cardenal was more scathing in an interview he gave on December 14, 1984. "We are not Poles," he said. "The Vatican is incapable of recognizing anything new unless it comes from Europe. . . . I recognize the fact that the Pope applied pressure to have me dismissed from the Society. I continue to feel I am a

Jesuit . . . so that one day I will be received into the Society once again."

Though in an official sense the case of Fernando Cardenal was over, Father General Kolvenbach again made clear his now famous "preferential option for the poor and oppressed." In doing so, he clarified as well his own doubts and lack of conviction concerning the Sacraments and the most basic beliefs of the Catholic Church.

When we receive the Eucharist, Father General said in a speech in Caracas, Venezuela, about a month after Cardenal's dismissal, we enter "into solidarity with His [Christ's] brothers and especially with His preferred brothers, the poor. . . ."

In Church teaching, neither poverty nor riches confer union and solidarity with Christ. Only the grace of Christ himself effects that. Grace is open to all, not exclusively or even "especially" to the poor. To say otherwise would be, as religious scholar Kolvenbach doubtless knew, a heresy condemned at least twice by the Church. To say that one cannot partake of the Eucharist "without struggling against poverty through personal sacrifice, selling one's goods and seeking solidarity with the victims of misery," is more than simply bad theology; it is theology at the service of economics, and overshadowed by prejudice against capitalism as a way of life. It is, finally, a doctrine condemned by the Roman Church as far back as the fifteenth century.

Whatever his formal training and scholarship might have told him, Father General Kolvenbach was frank in that Caracas speech about a great doubt and unresolved dilemma in his own mind as a Jesuit. "It is easy," he acknowledged, "to throw oneself into a class struggle on the one hand, or to take refuge in the disincarnate spirituality of poverty. . . . It is difficult, and we are just beginning to understand how . . . to maintain the two demands." Prior generations of Jesuits had had admirable ways of satisfying both obligations. Kolvenbach's try at a formulation of the modern ideal was a model of obscurity: ". . . the integral liberation of the human which is the City of God within us."

Kolvenbach appears to have been aware of how different the "preferential option for the poor" was as the shining Jesuit ideal, when compared to the Ignatian ideal that had remained solid and virtually unchanged in the Society of Jesus until 1965. In a letter dated March 3, 1985, to all Jesuits, Kolvenbach continued to struggle with that difference. He noted that the Society's "preferential option for the poor" had caused conflicts among the Jesuits (a rare if oblique admission that not all Jesuits by far had fallen into the

Society's official line) and with local Church and government officials. We do not know, he remarked, "all the concrete consequences of this [preferential option] for the Pastoral ministry."

Such a struggle is difficult to understand unless one presumes, as many observers have come to do, that Kolvenbach, like so many Jesuits, had ceased to realize what his vow of obedience—and obedience itself as a virtue—meant.

However tortured the reactions were to Fernando Cardenal's dismissal from the Order after five long years of struggle, the outcome did not spell victory for Pope John Paul II. Barely two months after Kolvenbach's Caracas speech, John Paul was reminded how bitter the fruit of delay and indecision can be, and how far the nettle of Modernism championed by the Jesuits had spread. The reminder did not come from the Jesuits this time, but from the order of Friars Minor, popularly known as Franciscans, who assembled in Assisi in May of 1985 to elect a new Minister General, the Franciscan equivalent of the Jesuit Father General.

John Paul was aware of a move in the assembly to elect California's Father John Vaughn to head the Order. Vaughn was widely known as a progressive who favored Base Communities, "collaboration with Marxists," progressive "liturgical" celebrations, and the entire gamut of Modernist theological ideas that Popes have continually condemned as irreconcilable with traditional Roman Catholicism. Pope John Paul sent his personal representative, Archbishop Vincenzo Fagiolo, to block Vaughn's election.

The effort was as great a disaster for John Paul as the Jesuit General Congregation of September 1983 had been. Fagiolo was isolated and treated as an interfering outsider. Vaughn was elected as Minister General by 117 votes out of 135; that is, with 87 percent of the votes cast. The Friars issued a bulletin in effect telling John Paul they would not abandon the practices they had adopted: "It is too late for us to turn back. As Franciscans, we cannot start all over again. We are not going out in search of our identity. . . ."

The Franciscans and Vaughn then proceeded to embellish their answer exactly as the Jesuits had, performing the very same theological sleight-of-hand. They unabashedly adopted Liberation Theology, complete with its "preferential option for the poor," an "anticonsumerism" stance by which anticapitalism was meant, and the choice of a "nonhierarchic" church structure, all of this masked in optimal and optimistic language about "the African Conference."[3] The ultimate trick, performed with the aid of a bland ecclesiastical version of disinformation, was to declare that this Franciscan "identity"—which had never crossed the minds of Franciscans since they were formed in the fourteenth century— had always been theirs, "the fruit of centuries of history, doctrine, traditions, and of commitment to the world."

In an official letter to the Pope, Vaughn and the outgoing Minister General, Onorio Pontoglio, patronized His Holiness by the same liberal use of consecrated phrases that had been perfected over the past twenty years by the Jesuits: ". . . fidelity to the Order's traditional values of fraternity and evangelical poverty . . . a unanimous desire for . . . absolute fidelity to the Gospel which constitutes our identity and the reason for the existence of the Franciscan family."

Later in the summer of 1985, the Franciscan leaders received a Working Paper prepared by the Order's Justice and Peace Office. "The attitude of the Church to Marxism has changed from a mere condemnation to a critical dialogue. . . . Christians with a clear awareness of the risks have come to appreciate that there are differences within Marxism. . . . Many of them [Christians] have long been dissatisfied with the evils of capitalism."

John Paul II now had no way of responding. He was reaping the whirlwind of his inaction in the matter of the reform of the Jesuits. The innate un-Catholic and Protestantized savor of that sentiment —"fidelity to the Gospel which constitutes our identity and the reason for the existence of the Franciscan family"—rejecting as it did at least implicitly any acceptance of Church teaching and authority, was allowed its freedom, unchallenged. There was no rejection of Vaughn's letter or the sentiments of the Assembly. There was no assertion that the Holy See, and only the Holy See, was the reason and the cause of Franciscan existence and identity, as it was of every Catholic Religious Order.

Perhaps there was some faint hope among John Paul's supporters that his forcing of the Jesuits' hand in the case of Fernando Cardenal, as belated as it was, might yet ignite a sort of "backfire" that would eventually halt the blaze of secularized religion. To date, there is no sign that any such hope was justified.

The information that now reaches Father General Kolvenbach by diplomatic pouch and by word of mouth from Jesuits visiting Nicaragua, would give any man pause. Perhaps they make him reflect on the official Jesuit attitude to "Father Fernando." For Cardenal and the other political priests have stayed on within the hierarchy of terror, the Sandinista *nomenklatura*, enjoying all the perquisites of power and privilege of a Marxist elite. They live in homes expropriated from the ousted middle class, in comfortable

Managua suburbs such as Las Collinas. They shop at specially designated hard-currency and "dollar" stores, where there is no "preferential option for the poor." They dine at luxury restaurants restricted to Party officials, and lunch in their government offices on the daily loads, delivered by official vans, of ham, lobster, and other delicacies unobtainable elsewhere in Sandinista Nicaragua. They relax in reserved box seats at the baseball stadium, enjoy unlimited supplies of gasoline and water that are rationed to the people, and vacation in the mansions of the Somoza dynasty, suitably rebaptized by the Sandinistas as "protocol houses." They travel around their native Nicaragua with personal bodyguards of Cubans and East Germans who are armed with Soviet automatics, ostensibly to be pointed at potential assailants but presumably equally effective even against an activist priest who might waver in his enthusiasm for politics of the Sandinista brand.

With such incentives to fuel their "theological" ardor, Fernando Cardenal and his brother priests tour other Latin American countries organizing revolution, and jet at Soviet expense on diplomatic missions to the United States, the Middle East, and Europe.

Those missions are hardly less effective now than they were before the priest-politicians were removed from their Orders and diocesan appointments. The president of the National Conference of Catholic Bishops in the United States, Bishop James Malone of Youngstown, Ohio, sent warm words to Father Miguel D'Escoto, late of the Maryknoll Order and still Sandinista Foreign Minister: "Your record of distinguished, dedicated ministry is a source of enormous pride to us bishops today. I hope you know . . . that the bishops of the United States are in solid support of your work."

Vatican diplomatic documents continue day by day to record how, in Washington, the organizations nurtured so carefully by the Sandinistas over the years are nurtured still. WOLA, NACLA, IPS, TNI, USLA, COHA, all continue battering lawmakers to refuse military aid to the Contras, the new guerrillas of Nicaragua, some 4000 in number, who prepare their packets of explosives, train their cadres, and plan their operations against a repressive government just as the Sandinistas once did.

Los Muchachos, the Contras are called by the men and women who gather at night in darkened houses and curse the Junta and its activist priests and nuns, just as they once cursed the Somoza regime. They can only do that when the Sandinista patrols and "inspectors" are not present. Only then can they pray to the Virgin of Guadalupe for *Los Muchachos*, as they once prayed for the Sandinistas.

Scores of publications put out by Religious Orders keep up the same barrage as WOLA, NACLA, and such groups; the Franciscans are far from the only Order to follow the Jesuit model. By now, in fact, it is all a vast, well-coordinated, well-financed, and single-minded operation; a web in which the likes of Fernando Cardenal have become small if symbolically important strands.

Meanwhile, John Paul takes no comfort from the news bulletins sent by his Central American representatives recounting in detail how the "Sandinocommunist" system, championed so well for so long by Jesuit Superiors and advanced thinkers, goes on apace. Some reports concern the nationwide network of Sandinista Defense Committees, modeled on the Cuban design, operating in every neighborhood. Others report on the control groups set up for professionals and women and blue collar workers. There is even the Association of Sandinista Children. There are official accounts of groups of Sandinista bully-boys, which in a bit of minor blasphemy the regime calls *"divinas turbas,"* "divine mobs," who continue to intimidate Nicaraguans who come to vote in elections. The regime has eyes and ears everywhere, in fact—on the streets, in the workplace, in the schools, in the kitchen and the bedroom.

In the countryside, the regime can operate with even greater freedom than in the cities. Government death squads continue to liquidate Miskito Indians and other dissidents with the same impunity as when John Paul turned to Daniel Ortega at the papal Mass in 1983 and shouted at him, "Miskito Power!" By the Vatican's count, nearly 30,000 Miskito, Sumee, and Rama Indians who have not been killed have been forced to leave their farms and all their possessions, and watch everything be blown up behind them. Another 50,000 Nicaraguan peasants have been similarly evacuated from northern zones. Everywhere young farm boys are conscripted into military training. Government officers burn down houses and destroy the livestock of peasants who resist collectivization.

The trade-off for such brutal and rigid central control is anything but a "preferential option for the poor." Instead, Nicaragua's once vital cotton, sugar, and beef production has collapsed. Naked children, stomachs distended from hunger, search for food in streets and fields alike. Bank accounts are confiscated. Ration cards for the purchase of beans are distributed to villagers according to the "loyalty" of each; but even ration cards cannot make up for the 71 percent decline in real wages since 1979. And they can do nothing to revive Nicaragua's *cordoba,* one of the most worthless currencies in the world; or keep Nicaragua from defaulting on its long-overdue interest payments to the International Monetary Fund.

Presumably, however, there is no cause for discouragement in all this for Fernando Cardenal, who had worried in *A Letter to My Friends* that he might commit a grave sin before God if he abandoned his priestly option for the poor. Rather, there is no reason to suppose that he was not a part of the three-day Sandinista tribute of mourning for the death of Konstantin V. Chernenko of the Soviet Union in March of 1985. Chernenko was a "great statesman and untiring fighter for the cause of world peace and solidarity," the Sandinista network declared.

By that time, 50,000 refugees from Sandinista terrorism were crowded into Honduras; "Little Moscow" was taking shape in Central America; and Pope John Paul had bitter reason to reflect on the judgment passed on men like Fernando Cardenal and his priest colleagues by the greatest atheist of the twentieth century —Vladimir Ilyich Ulyanov. "If a priest comes to cooperate with us in our work," Lenin wrote, "we can accept him into the ranks of Social Democracy. For the contradictions between the spirit and principles of our program, and the religious convictions of the priest could, in these circumstances, be regarded as a matter in which the priest contradicts himself. . . ."

THE SOCIETY OF JESUS

PART II

6 | IÑIGO DE LOYOLA

I t is probably not possible to appraise Pedro Arrupe's vision of how the Society of Jesus and the Roman Church should answer the challenge of our day without some understanding of at least three things: Ignatius of Loyola himself; his vision of how the same Church in his day should answer essentially the same challenge Arrupe faced; and what sort of Society Ignatius constructed in order to make the same fateful transition as confronted Arrupe.

It is a curious fact that Iñigo Lopez de Oñaz y Loyola, commonly known now as Ignatius of Loyola, and Pedro de Arrupe y Gondra, known most often among his Jesuits simply as Pedro, are the only two Basques to have been elected to the supreme post of Father General in the 446-year history of the Society of Jesus.

It takes on a touch of irony, then, that in the sixteenth century the first Basque built the most efficient and effective organization ever placed at the disposal of the papacy for its own defense and for its propagation of the otherworldly, supernatural teachings of Roman Catholicism; while in the twentieth century, the second Basque bent all his efforts to switch the organization from the seemingly sinking fortunes of that papacy, and to fasten it—together with the entire Church—to the apparently imminent creation of a this-worldly, here-and-now, utterly new human society.

There is another curious fact about these two Basque Jesuits, and it is far more important than their common homeland. The challenge thrown at the Roman Church Loyola knew nearly five hundred years ago was identical with the challenge to the Church Arrupe and the rest of us know. Loyola's sixteenth century was every bit as much a turbulent "threshold" time as ours is. The mind and outlook of Loyola's world was as suddenly and as abruptly and as deeply swept out of its thousand-year-old medieval habitat as our world has been swept out of its nineteenth-century, colonial state into the post–World War II, atomic and electronic age. The floodgates of newness then were the high Renaissance, the discovery of the Americas, the onslaught of the Protestant revolt, the rise of capitalism, the birth of our Western scientific technology. The waters that swept through those gates deluged the men and women of his time.

The irresistible floodtides of newness that carry our present generations across another threshold are multiple: the new genetics affecting the foundations of our human society, new methods of mass warfare and industrial slaughter of millions, instantaneous global communications, international financial and economic interdependence, man's entry into outer space whose borders recede infinitely into the unknown.

The challenge to the Roman Church at the violent crossing of the threshold of Loyola's time was as stark and as clear and as inescapable as it is in our own; it was in fact the very same challenge: How could the Roman Church adapt itself to the new era and yet not forsake the essentials of its beliefs and its morality?

The curiosity is not that the challenges of Loyola's time and ours are parallel, but that the reaction by Arrupe and the Jesuit establishment to the challenge in our day has in every way been the opposite of Loyola's.

The life of Iñigo de Loyola is seemingly a simple one to tell. It exhibits no spectacular gesture or earth-shaking elements, nothing our trained educators would point to as early "signs of genius." Perhaps in a way the marvel for our minds should be that Iñigo alone devised an organization as important in the fortunes not only of the Church, but of the wide world, as the Society of Jesus proved itself to be.

Most disarming for our curiosity about this man is the apparently easy way we can compartmentalize his sixty-five years. There was a first period of twenty-nine years during which he grew up and sowed his wild oats; there was a second period of repentance that lasted eight years; then a twelve-year period of study and preparation; and, finally, the fifteen years it took him to establish his Society of Jesus.

In retrospect, and superficially, it was a prosaic pattern. He never stirred outside Europe except for one short visit to Jerusalem, and he had little or nothing to do directly with great men of his time. Yet in long-range influence, influence that literally molded our world of the twentieth century, Iñigo surpasses even the greatest of his contemporaries—Charles V of Spain, Henry VIII of England, Ivan the Terrible of Russia, Luther, Calvin, Suleiman the Magnificent. For what he constructed is still in place, still functioning, and still considered so important that entire regimes, revolutionary and otherwise, tie their fortunes to its influence.

Iñigo de Loyola was born in 1491, the youngest of five sisters and eight brothers. As with another great contemporary of his, Christopher Columbus, we know neither the day nor the month of his birth at *Casa Torre,* Tower House, the home of the Loyolas that stood in the Iraurgi Valley between two little towns, Azpeitia and Azcoitia, in the Basque province of Guipúzcoa in northern Spain.

The Loyolas, knights and warriors by profession, were landed gentry in reduced circumstances. Iñigo's mother, Doña María Saenz, died when he was still an infant; she and her husband, Don Beltrán, had been married twenty-five years at Iñigo's birth. Iñigo was baptized at St. Sebastian's Church in Azpeitia. He was nursed by a nearby farm woman, María Garin, and reared by Magdalena de Aráoz, wife of his elder brother, Martin García.

His earliest memories were of *Casa Torre,* set among fruit trees and fields carpeted with flowers; and of María Garin's husband, a smith, roasting Azpeitia chestnuts over the fire in his forge, and telling endless stories about the great events taking place in the wide world outside their beloved Guipúzcoa.

Those great events would quickly usher in a new world that would invest all of Europe. For the Garins, for the Loyolas, for all Basques, the onetime isolation and self-sufficiency of Guipúzcoa was over by the time Iñigo was born. As we today can see in hindsight, those events made inevitable the emergence of the new era in which Iñigo would become one of the greats.

The first of the events Iñigo learned about in this pleasant, storybook fashion had taken place some forty years before he was born. The fall of Constantinople to the Ottoman Turks in 1453 was fit stuff for storytelling, for it led to the destruction of one half —some would say the more valuable half—of Christian civilization. Constantinople had not only been the capital of the 1000-year-old Byzantine empire; it was Europe's only living link with the ancient Greek world, and the sole custodian of one invaluable expression of Christian tradition.

The most profound effect of Constantinople's fall was on Europe's Christian civilization. Some valuable parts of Byzantine civilization were carried to Europe by those who escaped the Ottoman conquest. One prime result, then, was the flooding into the minds of Europeans of vast treasures in literature, in the fine as well as the decorative arts, in philosophy, engineering, architecture, theology, and science, all of which Constantinople had preserved and developed during its long reign. The small beginnings of the Renaissance manifested during the early part of the fifteenth century now received an infusion of vigor and inspiration which made possible the flood of the high Renaissance.

Much of what had preceded Christianity in Rome and Greece became available to what had been the closed medieval world of the late 1400s. Men's imaginations and ambitions, their natural curiosity about this world, and their instinct for progress were stronger than the ancient bonds by which they had been held in a sort of cultural isolation. Suddenly, within Iñigo's lifetime, no longer would the world be seen as the physical focal point of the cosmos. Instead, astoundingly, it was seen as heliotropic, as just one more planet circling the sun.

That rearranged cosmos cocked a beckoning finger. Roman Christianity in the first 1000 years of its history had enclosed Europeans in an exclusive self-contained house of their own, off limits to anyone or to any ideas that came from the outside, and dominated by the central idea of God's eternity. Now there arose in Europe a drumming, beating insistence, a steady clamor for greater freedom, for experimentation, for risk-taking, as men realized the richness and breadth of the pre-Christian mind. Under the impulse of this new infusion, Europeans were about to go forth from that house forever and enter the convulsions of the world at large. They were about to head out of parochial history into history itself and, in Robert Penn Warren's impressive image, "into the awful responsibility of Time."

Within thirty years of Iñigo's birth, the Church authorities in Europe became aware that they were failing to communicate with this new mentality; that they were in fact losing the allegiance of millions because they no longer could speak intelligibly to them, no longer understood what moved them, what inspired them, and could not respond to the attacks of the Reformers in Germany and

England. The new spirit abroad among men bid fair to change everything. If the Gospel and religion of Rome were going to be communicated successfully to this fresh mind—the postmedieval and Renaissance mind—a totally new method of explanation was needed.

Until this moment, the Basque province of Guipúzcoa and the small town of Azpeitia into which Iñigo was born had remained, like so many other provincial places in Europe, completely locked away by itself. Bounded on the north by the Bay of Biscay and the Pyrenees, backed to the south by the Aralar and Aritz mountain ramparts, secure in its 771 square miles, with San Sebastián as its largest town, Guipúzcoa and its Basques felt that Vascongadas—Basque country—was all that was important. It was a small country, true enough; indeed, in many ways it was the typical small country. But the Basques who inhabited it were never small-minded. They seemed to understand the wide world outside and around them with a breadth of vision at once perceptive but standoffish—more because they were quite self-sufficient than from any parochial fear of the unknown. There was enough poetry and beauty for them in their country's oak and chestnut forests and along its limestone scarps. There was sufficient variety in the trellis patterns of valley and sierra and meadow formed by the Bidassoa, the Urumea, the Urola, and the Aria rivers flowing down to the sea. There was sufficient law and order in the traditional *fueros,* the Basque law codes, to make life secure. And magical town names like Mondragon, Rentería, Vergara, Roncesvalles (where Basques had cut Charlemagne's rearguard to pieces in the year 778 A.D.) never allowed Basques to forget their own uninterrupted history of independence and self-contentment.

By the time Iñigo was born, Guipúzcoa, together with every other isolated pocket of medieval culture, was opening up to the new era.

The second great event influencing Iñigo was summed up for him in a word that had an almost mystical connotation for him and his contemporaries: *Kingdom.* Some 750 years before the birth of Iñigo, Spain had been invaded by Muslims. *Moros,* the Spaniards called them, because they came from what was then called Mauretania, which then comprised parts of modern Morocco and Algeria.

The long struggle to evict the Moors from Spain lasted six hundred years. Whole families like the Loyolas reckoned their own history in terms of battles fought by their members, of decorations won for valor, of tragic deaths in combat. How many stories must Iñigo have heard from María Garin and her husband, and from his brothers and his father, about those glorious battles.

For Spaniards, the Kingdom and its fate was their whole world. By 1481, only the southern city and fortress of Granada remained in Moorish hands. The rest of Spain was united under the banner of Their Most Catholic Majesties, Ferdinand of Aragón and Isabella of Castile. The Most Catholic Kingdom would not be safe and integral until the last "infidel" power center of Granada had been scoured clean of the Muslim overlord. The safety and integrity of the Kingdom was on everybody's mind in a country where generation after generation went on fighting and dying for it.

The enemy, the Moor, was seen as squat and small in stature, dark-faced, death-dealing, cunning, deceptive, cowardly, lodged in his rocky fastnesses, threatening war and pillage and slavery.

The Most Catholic King was pictured as tall, bright-faced, noble, and lustrous, as he called all his subjects to fight for the Kingdom and thus enter with him into the glory of victory.

Iñigo's father Don Beltrán and three of his sons answered that call.

For the Moor, however, Granada was much more than a military toehold in continental Europe. Granada was a sacred foretaste and an incarnation of Paradise.

Paradise, which Muslims believed Allah allowed faithful Muslims to enter after death—especially after a death suffered for the sake of Islam—would supply all that the arid, burning sands and steppe of the desert had always denied them and their Arabian ancestors: green, luxuriant vegetation; meadows carpeted with unimaginably beautiful flowers; clean, clear, fresh, ever-leaping fountains; cooling breezes; balmy shade beneath kindly palm trees; plentiful food; sweet pleasures with beautiful women; slaves galore to attend to their every whim and wish; no cold nights or boiling hot days, but perpetual lightsomeness, instead; and the undisturbed strains of desert music played by angels on heavenly lyres.

But chiefest among all paradisiacal blessings was that one commodity the desert as desert must always lack: water. Water, like air, is necessary to life itself. According to the sacred Muslim law, the *Sharia*, you needed water to wash before praying; and you had to observe the *Sharia*, had to pray, at least five times a day. Otherwise, you would not reach Paradise after death. This was the very reason, in fact, that Muslims called their sacred law *Sharia*; literally, *Sharia* means "the road to a watering-place," and thus "the path to Paradise."

Now Granada supplied all that the after-death Paradise promised Pious Believers. It lay in the lap of the Sierra Nevada, in
Andalusia, the southern fertile region of Spain. It was sump-
tuously built and decorated on and around two hills between
which ran the sweet-flowing Derra river. Around the city, the
Moors had built mosques and dwellings to rise up fittingly in
shaded groves that yielded citrons, pomegranates, figs, apples,
dates, oranges. All about them lay nourishing vineyards, vegetable
gardens, grassland meadows. And above them, the sun was benign
in the azure sky.

For the Moor, Granada was Paradise on earth, or the nearest
thing to it. It was no wonder, then, that they guarded the periphery
of its province with fortified towns and villages, and watchtowers
manned by Moorish Knights ever at the ready with their bristling
scimitars.

The lilting desert music wafted undisturbed around Granada's
Eden until the knights and legions of Their Catholic Majesties
finally cordoned it all off in battle after battle, massacre after massacre, and narrowed Granada down to its central fortifications.

It took a final ten years of bloody warfare involving Spaniards
from all over the Kingdom—three of Iñigo's brothers died fighting
in what was a sacred war for the Kingdom—before Boabdil, the
last Moorish king, surnamed in history by his own people as El
Zogaybi, the Unlucky One, decided to capitulate. He signed away
his beloved Granada on November 25, 1491, the 897th year of the
Muslim Hegira. By the following January 6, he had departed with
a safe-conduct pass, together with his royal family and his royal
retinue of servants.

The leave-taking from that earthly Paradise was heartrending,
and later inspired much pathos and poetry. Before the royal retinue
passed out of sight of Granada, it stopped by the river Xenil. The
departing Muslims wanted one last look at the red towers of the
Alhambra and their once impregnable fortress of Alcazaba. At that
very moment, they saw the flag of the Sacred Christian Crusade
with its glittering silver cross flutter from the great Watchtower,
the Torre de la Vela. They heard the victors' shouts of their pa-
tron's name, Saint James of Compostella, echo from the Court of
Lions in the Alhambra: "Santiago! Santiago!"

Iñigo was a mere babe in arms the day Boabdil and his family
gave that long last look at their beloved Granada. When he grew a
little older and could understand, his family must have repeated
to him the last words of sighing regret that floated in a loud wail
back to the ears of the victorious Christians in the Court of Lions:

"Ay de mi! Granada!" the Muslims cried as they turned away. "Woe is me! Granada!" Later still, Iñigo would have been shown that spot near the Xenil which Spaniards then and since have called *el último suspiro del Moro.* The last sigh of the Moor. The safety of the Kingdom, its pride and beauty, was tied to such places by folklore and religious fervor as well as by love of Spain.

Iñigo was not quite two years old when the third great influential event in his life took place. Early on March 15, 1493, after eight months of hazardous sea-voyaging, the fifty-foot sailing ship *Niña* entered the Spanish port of Los Palos carrying a weary but triumphant Christopher Columbus back from his epoch-making discovery of the New World. Her sister ship, *Pinta*, followed in a few hours. Columbus's flagship, the *Santa María*, had gone down off Hispaniola, the island today divided between Haiti and Santo Domingo.

Columbus's news was mind-boggling and electrifying for Spaniards and subsequently for all Europeans. Now, they realized, millions of other human beings existed—had existed for hundreds of years already—across the ocean in vast new lands full of unimaginable riches. All of it was Spain's by right of first discovery, so Spaniards thought. Overnight, the kingdom had become an empire. All had to be secured by conquest. All had to be civilized by conversion to Christianity.

It is difficult for us to imagine the sudden expansion of mind and outlook this discovery forced on the men and women of Iñigo's day, unless we compare it to our own speculations about extraterrestrial life. His generation was the first to grow up with the beginnings of genuinely global outlook. The whole earth now became their inheritance and the playground of their endeavors.

The event had personal significance for Iñigo. When Columbus sailed off on his second voyage to this marvelous New World in 1493, one of Iñigo's brothers, Martin García, the husband of Magdalena de Aráoz, sailed off with him. Surely, Magdalena relieved her loneliness by telling the two-year-old Iñigo fabulous tales of the New World. The stories about how the Sacred Crusade had won the Kingdom's safety against the Moor, how this knight or that soldier had faithfully served His Most Catholic Majesty, leader of God's armies, were now expanded to include the empire and the whole world.

The idea of service in the Kingdom was only emphasized and further refined by Iñigo's early career as boy and youth. At age sixteen, about the time his father, Don Beltrán, died, he was made a page boy at the royal summer residence of Arevalo. He was to spend the next ten years of his life in the pomp and formalism of court life and aristocratic ways.

It was just about then that the Queen of Spain, Germaine de Foix—a fifteen-year-old French princess whom the fifty-two-year-old King Ferdinand of Aragón had married after his first wife, Isabella of Castile, died—began to frequent Arevalo. Germaine, saucy, fat, a heavy drinker, played on the fact that she was the niece of the King of France. She turned the royal court upside down.

Iñigo, the page, was assigned to serve the new Spanish Queen goblets of wine at table, to light her way with candles through the castle's corridors, to carry the long train of her mantle. In other words, to serve her.

With everyone else, Iñigo was overwhelmed by this Germaine de Foix—by her French finery in silken raiment, linen caps, scented bed sheets, magnificent costumes, perfumes and cosmetics, by her royal manners, and the wild gaiety she installed in a court previously dominated by Isabella, who had frowned on all such things as ungodly and un-Christian. To serve this woman who replaced the dour and serious Isabella was, in fact, to serve grandeur and glory. In Iñigo's mind, to serve was to love. To love was to serve. Iñigo's first love was Germaine de Foix.

Automatically, at a certain age, he was inducted into the ranks of young knights and equerries at the Spanish royal court. From then until he was twenty-six, life would have been an endless round of martial exercises with sword, pistol, and lance; a life of hunting, dancing, wenching, flirtations, duels, feasting, drinking, brawling; and, finally, falling desperately in love with one particular lady "of no ordinary rank," as he later wrote in his autobiography, "rather a countess or a duchess; but of a nobility much higher than all of these."

Iñigo probably aimed at marriage, and service either to the ravishing Germaine de Foix, by then the widow of Ferdinand, or to the Princess Royal, Catherine, daughter of Queen Joanna of Spain. It was a characteristic of his: Never be satisfied with second-best.

Iñigo had become a 5-foot-1-inch, dark-eyed, bearded knight, armed with dagger, sword, and pistol, clothed in tight-fitting hose and soft leather cordoba high boots and a suit of gaudy colors. His abundant, bright blond hair flowed down from his red velvet cap, out of which a jaunty gray feather waved.

His education was limited. He knew no Latin, spoke a little

French *patois*. He spoke Basque and Castilian Spanish, could read well, and could write to the extent of signing his name and laboriously composing military dispatches or love letters.

His character was badly formed. He was one of the "young Turks" of his day whose youth, glorious times, and national pride egged them on. He lacked moral scruple in his conduct to the degree that eventually the law, in the shape of the *Corregidor*, the correctional judge, in Azpeitia caught up with him in his escapades. After "atrocious crimes carried out during the night [of the 1515 Carnival in Azpeitia] with premeditation and involving ambush and treachery," the police arrested Iñigo with his priest-brother, Pedro Lopez, who was also involved.

Bold, defiant, lying through his teeth, blaming others, described as "the criminal," as "disgraceful in his dress, worse in his conduct," Iñigo got himself transferred to the bishop's prison in nearby Pamplona, and finally wangled a slap on the wrist and dismissal of his case from a judge who tells us in his still extant report that "Iñigo de Loyola was cunning, violent, and vindictive." The unbendable iron of his will was noted: Iñigo de Loyola was defiant to the point of death when his honor or interest was involved. Once he had made up his mind, nothing could shake his determination or put him off the pursuit.

In 1517, at age twenty-six, he was still desirous of finding glory in the service of the Kingdom, and so of giving expression to his yet unclaimed unconditional obedience—as well as winning his lady's hand. He joined the army of the Viceroy of Navarre, the Duke de Najera. Six years later, he found himself defending an impossible position in the citadel of the town of Pamplona against an overwhelming French army. On May 20, 1521, a French cannonball passed between his legs, shattering his right and wounding his left. The fight was over.

French army surgeons set the bones of his right leg so clumsily that when Iñigo reached home, his own doctors had to break and reset them all over again. But still the bones knitted incorrectly, leaving an ugly protuberance. If it remained, he would not be able to wear the fashionable military boot, nor would he be able to dance or bow gracefully. Fine physical grace was part of a true knight's accoutrements.

At his behest, the doctors sawed off the protuberance; but then, they found, he walked with a limp. So they strapped him on a surgical rack where he lay motionless for weeks on end, suffering excruciating pain, all in a vain hope that the leg could be stretched back to its normal length.

Iñigo underwent all four of these operations without anesthetic and without a murmur or sign of protest "beyond the clenching of his fists." Later, he described it all pithily as "butchery." But his motivation was clear. How could he win the heart of his lady love if he cut a miserable figure? How could he excel in fighting for and serving in the Kingdom?

As often happened in Iñigo's life, however, one door shut and another started to open. During the long weeks of convalescence in the summer and autumn of 1521, as he read the lives of saints to pass the time, he underwent what is known in the language of religious experience as a profound conversion. In Catholic theology and belief, Iñigo was the recipient of divine grace—special, supernatural communications of strength in will, enlightenment in mind, and orientation of spirit. It was an initial purification. As soon as he was well enough, early in the New Year of 1522, he left *Casa Torre* of Loyola forever to find a new life.

He spent the best part of the next six years, from 1522 to 1528, cultivating the life of the spirit that had opened itself to him—doing dreadful physical penances for his sins, practicing contemplation of divine mysteries, performing works of charity, and codifying in writing his new outlook on life in a short book that has always been known as *Spiritual Exercises.*

Rare has been the spiritual devotee who suffered such wracking pains of spirit as did Iñigo in those years, paralleled by such sublime communications from the God he now worshiped and the Christ in whose salvation he now believed. But rarer still was Iñigo's peculiar ability to monitor minutely and exactly, during his inner pilgrimage, the various moods and motions that forever kept altering the atmosphere and tension of his psycho-physical being.

Buffeted by depression now, exalted by free-flowing happiness then, suddenly afflicted with growing doubts about God, about Christ, about the Church, about his sanity, about everything, he carefully sought to dissect the changing texture of his inner being. For he firmly believed that what affected and altered his psycho-physical condition was meant by some agent-spirit—of God or of Lucifer—to affect and alter his soul, to cripple or to encourage his will, to darken or to illumine his mind.

Out of this minute and unsparing self-observation, Iñigo fashioned a set of rules by which one could discern what action was taking place in one's spirit, and test who was the agent-spirit acting on one's soul. Side-by-side with these practical rules, he assembled a series of meditations, contemplations, and considerations.

The process was agonizing. There were moments when it did look as if the inner conflict would be too much for his sanity. At least on one occasion, in the depths of his misery, he was definitely tempted to commit suicide by throwing himself over a precipice. But by the spiritual means he had already devised and by heroic self-discipline in applying those means to himself, he recognized this inclination in time as the suggestion of the one whom Jesus had described as "murderer from the beginning."

Out of this crucible of trial, self-examination, and anguished yearning for peace and light there emerged in Iñigo de Loyola that balance of spirit and matter, of mind and body, of mystical contemplation and pragmatic action that has ever since been recognized as typically and specifically "Ignatian," as distinct from the spirituality of, say, St. Benedict or St. Dominic or St. John of the Cross and St. Teresa of Ávila.

Iñigo desired nothing more ardently then to meet the Risen Christ in person in his glorified body, and to venerate each of Christ's wounds—in his hands, his feet, his side, to kiss those wounds and to adore them, to cover them with his love and adoration expressed by his lips and his eyes and his hands. He had discovered that secret of Christian mysticism that makes it totally different from the disembodied—almost anti-body—mysticism of the Buddhist; a secret which in our time has eluded the minds and experience of far more illustrious men, humanly speaking, such as Aldous Huxley, Teilhard de Chardin, and Thomas Merton.

Automatically, the promise of Christ was fulfilled: "Who sees me, sees the Father." Through the very humanity of Christ, Iñigo was introduced into the bodiless, eternal being of the Trinity—apparently ascending, like Paul of Tarsus in his out-of-body ecstasy, to the "Third Heaven," to participate in the most hidden secrets of divinity for which human language has no words. God the Father, the Son, the Holy Spirit, as Three and as One, admitted Iñigo to an intimacy that few mortals every approach while alive on this earth.

This characteristic of genuine Christian piety—ascension to a bodiless spirit, God, through the humanity of a real man, Jesus—is a stumbling block for the non-Christian mind. But it is the touchstone by which you can find out what is authentically Christian or non-Christian in the turmoil of religion today.

When he had gone through all this travail of spirit and achieved the balance that would always mark the Ignatian way—balance between spirit and matter, between contemplation of the divine mysteries and implementation of their meaning in concrete actions—he had also finished putting together his book of *Spiritual Exercises*. He was ready now to test in action his ideals of service in the Kingdom. His basic categories of judgment remained from the earlier part of his life: love of the leader, service in the Kingdom, war against the Enemy across the recently opened-out battlefield of the world, the absolute necessity of total education, love expressed in unconditional service. But in his conversion, these ancient categories of his were filled out with totally different ideals and dimensions.

Iñigo himself described minutely how he now saw everything. The Enemy was that "murderer from the beginning," Lucifer, "the chief of all the enemies [who] summons innumerable demons and scatters them throughout the whole world to bind men with chains [of sin]." The Kingdom was "the whole surface of the earth inhabited by so many different peoples. . . . The Three Divine Persons [of the Trinity] look down upon the whole expanse or circuit of the earth filled with human beings . . . some white . . . some black . . . some at peace . . . some at war, some weeping, some laughing, some well, some sick, some coming into the world, some dying. . . ."

The summons of Their Most Catholic Majesties he heard no longer. It was Christ, the Supreme Leader, who was calling him now, and " . . . how much more worthy of consideration is Christ Our Lord, the Eternal King, before whom is assembled the whole world."

The dominating question for Iñigo now concerned loving service of his new leader, Christ. How could he serve? And where? Alone? If not, then with whom? How was he to know what service God required of him?

In 1523, in a quest for answers, he made a pilgrimage to Jerusalem. When he returned, he had made up his mind: He decided that the first step would be to become a priest. For this, he needed to study.

He began his studies in Spain, at the age of thirty-three or thirty-four; but in 1527 he made his way to the largest and most renowned university of his day, in Paris. It was here he chose to be called Ignatius: Enrollment at the Sorbonne was written in Latin, and Ignatius was the closest Latin equivalent to the Basque Iñigo.

Paris University was one of approximately forty universities in Europe of the time. It housed 40,000 students in fifty colleges. It was a center of learning as well as a hotbed of revolutionary ideas and advanced theology. Loyola's choice to go there was both a wise and a fateful decision. He moved from the comparatively sheltered intellectual life of Alcalá, Barcelona, and Salamanca, where he had started his studies; he was thrown headlong into the ferment that was Paris of the time. There, it can be said, he came up against the new mind of the Renaissance men for the first time. This was the mind slowly being alienated from the medieval world, as it became more and more exclusively oriented toward new concepts of man, of society, and of the cosmos.

Most of those who saw Ignatius every day in the narrow "Dog's Alley" between the Colleges of Montaigue (where he was studying ordinary grammar) and of St. Barbara (where he studied theology) could not have recognized the former hidalgo. He was now bone-thin, an oldish looking man who wore a long black robe and a tangled and unkempt beard.

Both previously in Spain and here again at Paris, he came under suspicion of heresy and was examined by the Inquisition. He was always cleared, but did spend some time in prison. He was, of course, perennially short of money; three years running, he paid visits to Bruges, Antwerp, and London, where he successfully solicited funds from rich Spanish merchants.

By the time he finished his studies and left Paris in April of 1535 as a Master of Arts, Ignatius had gathered a basic group of seven devoted companions around him and he was ready intellectually as well as spiritually to set foot on the path of his loving service of Christ. He became a priest in 1537.

From this point on, in the assessment of Iñigo's development, no rational analysis is possible of the whys and wherefores of his decisions. You can list his most obvious qualities: that iron resolve of will noted by the correctional judge years before, and a great resourcefulness which the same judge had seen as cunning. There was too that almost frightening driving power of his thought that he had cut through and tamed the dreadful spiritual trials he had endured, and resulted in *Spiritual Exercises*.

You can go on to make lists of what he decided before and during his years of study; and you can describe what he did. You can even tie all of that to his previous experiences and lessons in a purely sequential way. If you are a believer, you can refer to the uncreated light which the Holy Spirit does communicate to a docile candidate—and Iñigo was precisely that.

Still, after all that, you cannot explain in what today would pass muster as a rational manner, the tie between Ignatius's previous experiences and the new set of decisions he now took. He could have become a hermit, or joined an enclosed monastery, or gone back to the life of a knight, or sought a learned career in academia or in the Church. Instead, he veered off in a totally unexpected direction. In the end, one must perhaps be content to say what many have said about him: With very few parallels in history, Iñigo had as natural gift a piercing insight into the very foundations of human nature, both in individuals and in society. This determined his course of action.

By 1535, Iñigo's vision of the world around him was quite defined and definitive: There was, universally, a war in progress. It was not to be confounded with local wars—as, say, the Turks who under Sultan Suleiman the Magnificent had reached the walls of Belgrade in 1521, or the Spanish imperial army that had sacked Rome and the Vatican in 1527. It was not even the war being waged against the Lutherans, the Calvinists, and others who had revolted against the authority and teaching of the Roman Pope. Nor was it the war being waged by a few zealous and compassionate souls against the endemic poverty, disease, and injustice that characterized the social conditions of the masses of people throughout Europe of his day.

The war Iñigo saw was the war against Lucifer, chief of the fallen angels, who roamed the human environment seeking to destroy—whether by the homicide of war, by the destruction of religious culture, or by the degradation of poverty, injustice, and suffering—the image of God and the grace of Christ in the souls of men and women everywhere. As Lucifer's war against Christ and his grace and salvation was universal, so the war against Lucifer and his followers had to be correspondingly universal.

Iñigo, therefore, had a basic operating principle: *Quo universalius, eo divinius.* The more universal your operation is, the more divine it is.

An immediate consequence of this principle was that his could not be a one-man apostolate. Ever since his religious conversion in 1521, he had acted alone. Now, if he were to perform signal services in this warfare, if he were to be as divine as possible in his effectiveness, he would have to act corporately, would need a team of like-minded men working for the same goals as he, but all over the world.

Before he left Paris in 1535, Iñigo had already assembled that basic group of seven men around him. But he could not now be satisfied with a loose association in friendship or commonality of ideals. Nor was he content with merely a religious conversion and reform of their lives. Some perception—call it instinctual, if you must—told him: You must subjugate and transform each man's intellect, religious beliefs, perceptions of himself and the world,

and all his desires. You must do this in accordance with your own
ideas of Christ's Kingdom and the warfare he is waging for that
Kingdom. Only in this way will these men give the needed, loving
service.

Furthermore, as the war Iñigo had engaged to fight now was
exclusively a war over possession of souls, the spirit of each man
and woman in the world was the prize. The only weapon guaranteed by Christ to be effective in that war was the supernatural
grace Christ alone could and did dispense exclusively through his
living personal representative on earth: the Pope in Rome. Iñigo
therefore had a second basic principle: to work directly for and
under that Roman Pope. The more precise and closer one's bond
with the Pope, he reasoned, the closer would be one's bond with
the leader, Christ, and the more effective one's actions in this
universal, perpetual warfare.

Iñigo was always looking to that "more." His ambition as cour-
tier, as knight, as believer, had always been to excel above all
others in whatever he undertook. Second place never interested
him. His aim was not to promote the great glory of God, but as he
said, "the *greater* glory of God."

With these principles clear and sharp in his mind, Iñigo put each
of his seven early companions through the rigorous regimen of his
Spiritual Exercises, for that book was and always remained his
chief instrument of spiritual training, as it did for those who came
after him. Each man emerged from that weeks-long regimen as a
spiritual fighter completely won over to warfare, desirous of corporate unity under Iñigo's leadership, and as an utterly obedient
servant of the Pope.

The last facet of the enterprise to be considered was the way to
guarantee the effectiveness of his new corporate body of men engaged in the warfare all over the world. How could he unite and
coagulate a body of men that might number in the hundreds, living
and working in all parts of the world at multifarious jobs? How
could he make individual men separated by hundreds or thousands
of miles, with communication between them difficult at best, into
a uniform and exactly functioning organization? That "uniformity" in Loyola's mind concerned uniformity with the wishes and
intents of the Pope; and "exact function" meant the exact performance of the Pope's instructions in the spirit of Christ. How to
guarantee all that under the dissipating circumstances, great distances, and the time needed to communicate over such distances?

Iñigo wisely initiated a common discussion of this problem
with his basic group of seven: "Would it or would it not be more

advantageous for our purpose to be so joined and bound together in one body that no physical distance, no matter how great, would separate us?" This was the question they debated together.

Under his leadership, the unanimous decision of the whole group cohered perfectly with Iñigo's own solution: absolute obedience. The resolve was that they as a body would place themselves at the Pope's disposal for any mission in any part of the world, in any and all conditions, at any time, no matter how short or unwelcome the notice.

The main principle, then, was unconditional obedience to whosoever was Pope, as to Christ himself. Obedience as unresisting and as disposable, in Iñigo's words, "as an old man's walking stick, or as a cadaver"; these were the dramatic images he used to convey as clearly as could humanly be done his meaning of absolute obedience.

This unique papal orientation was, in fact, the "mission" of the Society in its broadest and fullest and most practical sense.

Iñigo drew up in written form this proposal of corporate unity of their new institute in absolute obedience to the Pope, and called it the *Formula of the Institute,* or First Sketch of the Institution he and his companions wished to establish. This *Formula* outlined the fundamental structure of the organization, and authorized the drawing up of detailed laws and statutes. In time, these would be written by Iñigo, and they would be called the *Constitutions* of the Jesuit Order.

For the moment, however, the only remaining task was to get papal approval for this *Formula.* Only with such approval could they become a Catholic Religious Order.

In the third paragraph of the *Formula,* Iñigo set forth the mind and attitude he envisioned for—indeed demanded of—the Jesuit. It is a description both friends and enemies of the Jesuits would readily have acknowledged as an accurate picture of the Jesuit the wide world knew until the sixties and seventies of this century:

> All who make the profession in this Society should understand at the time, and furthermore keep in mind as long as they live, that this entire Society and the individual members who make their profession in it are campaigning for God under faithful obedience to His Holiness Pope Paul III and his successors in the Roman Pontificate. The Gospel does indeed teach us, and we know from the orthodox faith and firmly hold, that all of Christ's faithful are subject to the Roman Pontiff as their head and as the Vicar of Jesus Christ. But we have judged nevertheless that the following procedure will

be supremely profitable to each of us and to any others who will pronounce the same profession in the future, for the sake of our greater devotion in obedience to the Apostolic See, of greater abnegation of our own wills, and of surer direction from the Holy Spirit. In addition to that ordinary bond of the three vows, we are to be obliged by a special vow to carry out whatever the present and future Roman Pontiffs may order which pertains to the progress of souls and the propagation of the faith; and to go without subterfuge or excuse, as far as in us lies, to whatsoever provinces they may choose to send us.

Obedience to the Pope—in fact, nothing less than a special vow obliging Jesuits to do what the Pope wished in any region of the world—so a Jesuit was summarized from the beginning. And so was born what can be rightly called Jesuitism, the complete subjugation of all a man is, thinks, feels, and does to a practical ideal achievable in the world around him, in absolute obedience and submission to the mind and decisions of the Roman Pope, the Vicar of Christ.

The most precious cameo in the faithful Jesuit memory is full of fact and devout wish. It shows you a Pope sitting on a high-back chair and surrounded by eleven kneeling men: Iñigo and his ten companions come to obtain the Pope's blessing for their "Company." In that time and that setting, the faces of those eleven men were strangely new. Each face was ascetically thin, yet it wore nothing of the traditional "monkish" or "clerical" look. These men were, in our modern expression, "streetwise." They knew what was going on in the wide world around them.

It was the morning of September 27, 1540, in a private reception hall of the Palace of the Popes on Vatican Hill, Rome. The Pope was Paul III, a Farnese of the noble Farnesi and a genuine Roman; seventy-three years old; six years on the Throne of Peter. He was lean, of medium height, with a bright complexion, small black vivacious eyes, a long aquiline nose, the gloomy forehead of the intellectual, and a full gray beard. On his head, the papal *camauro*, a red cap. A bright scarlet tippet, the papal *mozetta*, covered his shoulders, and from beneath it peered the fine satin papal garment. His voice was low-toned and his cadence slow. With one long, thin hand he held out a document he had just signed.

Iñigo de Loyola, hook-nosed, gaunt-faced, diminutive, and nearly bald-headed, rose and went forward to take the document from the Pope's hand. Like the other ten, he was wearing a clean, threadbare, black cassock. His right leg was deformed; he walked with a limp. He bowed on one knee, kissed the papal ring, and took the document from the Pope's hand. No one could foresee it then, but by approving that document—*The Formula of the Institute*, in which Iñigo had described the organization he wished to place at the disposal of the papacy—Pope Paul III was launching the most efficient and the most loyal organization the Roman Catholic Church has ever spawned in all its near-2000-year history. The document was in Latin and like all such Roman documents was named by the first three words, *Regimini Militantis Ecclesiae*, The Church Militant. It established the Society of Jesus, and authorized Iñigo to make an initial recruitment of up to sixty new members.

For twenty years now, since 1520, Paul III's entire Catholic world had been falling down around his ears in a roaring conflagration. The Protestant revolt in Germany and England had rapidly eaten its way into France, Holland, Belgium, Austria, Switzerland, and Czechoslovakia, and had infected every other country. It had shattered the once universally accepted papal authority; successfully attacked basic Catholic notions about priesthood, Eucharist, Sacraments, grace, episcopal office; emptied thousands of convents and monasteries; liquidated the unity of Catholic belief; converted whole nations to the new faith; and inspired both political and military alliances aimed at the physical destruction of Paul III's papacy.

Paul III's efforts to stem the tide against him and to reassert the faith had been hampered by a broad, noisome swathe of clerical corruption enfolding all ranks of the Church, from obscure nuns in Moravian convents right up to the papal household in Rome, a corruption so pervasive and taken for granted that it provoked the just wrath and hate of reform-minded Catholics, and the outright revolt of thousands.

As spiritual and moral weapons to defend himself and his papacy, Paul III had only leftovers from medieval times. Anciently founded religious Orders with antiquated rules of dress and activity, animated with a restrictive spirit, fused with a mentality opaque to the meaning of the cataclysmic events around them, hidebound by traditions, unskilled in the rough-and-tumble of controversy in the streets and the marketplace. Cumbersome papal procedures. Unwieldy papal bureaucracies. Out-of-date methods of preaching. Books of doctrine expressed in concepts inaccessible to the ordinary mind, in a Latin not understood by the popular ear, and in little-understood Latin formulas ill-adapted to current problems. Entrenched vested interests bent only on self-perpetuation.

None of these weapons was directly adaptable or properly useful against the new and terrible threat to the papacy and Roman Catholicism. The universal fire continued to devour the old Catholic heartlands.

Enter this Basque named Iñigo, or Ignatius, the diminutive little man with the limp, together with his ten companions.

"Holy Father," we can accurately paraphrase their hardheaded proposal to a beleaguered Paul III, "the papacy and the Roman Catholic Church are in mortal trouble. Needed is a modern weapon to fight this totally new warfare. Give us, as a group of companions, a new charter like no other charter given before to a Religious Order of men. Free us from strict monastic life, its rules, its formal clothes, its traditional methods. Make us independent of all local authorities and directly responsible to Your Holiness only. Set us up as a special group of Pope's men, his soldiers. With a new purpose: serving under Your Holiness, the Roman Pontiff, to defend and propagate the Faith. And let us bind ourselves in a new manner to Your Holiness and to all Your Holiness's successors in the papacy. Allow us to take a special vow of absolute obedience on our sacred oath directly to Your Holiness, to the effect that without demur or protest we will go anywhere at any time at any cost to life and comfort in order to do anything Your Holiness deems necessary for the defense and propagation of the faith."

"The hand of God is at work here!" Paul reportedly replied. It was, after all, exactly what he needed. So, formally and with his papal signature, the Pope approved of the new "Company," as Iñigo called himself and his ten companions. In fact, he called it the Company of Jesus. The name passed through the Latin *Societas Jesu* and came out the other end as the Society of Jesus, or—a derisive nickname soon given them by their enemies—the Jesuits.

By 1542, Iñigo was established in the first Jesuit house in Rome, an old stone building on the Borgo Santo Spirito. Within a short time, he was able to build a residence in which he had three small, low-ceilinged rooms at his disposal. Across the street from the house, there was a small chapel dedicated to Santa Maria della Strada. In this setting, in the center of Rome and within a stone's throw of the Apostolic Palace where the Pope lived, Iñigo was to live and work and die and be buried.

Iñigo was now fifty-one years old, in very fragile health, but with a capacity for work that was ferocious. He slept very little. His days passed in two occupations: writing the *Constitutions* and administering the burgeoning affairs of the expanding Society of Jesus by a voluminous correspondence—in those last fourteen years of his life, he wrote and dictated more than seven thousand letters, all of them signed by him. He was the recipient of extraordinary mystical graces, and practiced a type of spiritual contemplation than which no higher has been recorded in the history of spirituality. At the same time, he was immersed in concrete details, practical decisions. Contemplation and action seemed to mesh perfectly in his being, so that one can only marvel at the accuracy of judgment that perfect meshing produced.

We know sufficient detail about his intense work during that last period of his life—nothing came easy to Iñigo; he literally toiled and sweated over each detail—so that his method of devising the *Constitutions* of his Society becomes very clear to us.

Basically, it was a simple process, but it required a giant spirit to perform it successfully and not to end up in dreadful, self-deluding narcissism and choking parochialism. He analyzed minutely his own reactions to events in the world around him that affected his own era profoundly. Then he formulated the kernel truth of those reactions in a nonpersonal way, discarding what was particular and transient, elevating those reactions onto a universal plane so that as principles of action they became applicable by other men —his followers and members of his Society, all over the community of nations in radically diverse cultures and vastly different eras. He thus created one of the most efficient organizational systems of any sort that the world has ever seen.

But all this he accomplished only because he was willing to pay the human cost in terms of his own self-discipline and self-abnegation. In order to arrrive at universally valid ideas and principles of action, he had literally and without mercy dissected his own reactions to the events of his contemporary world, abandoning what was purely subjective, ego-seeking, parochial. That cold impersonal analysis exacted its own toll from him, as did the soul-wearying patience with delays of clerical bureaucracy and the wayward passions of ecclesiastical power brokers in the Rome of the Popes.

On top of his daily labor over the *Constitutions*, there were the demands on him at his post as leader and ultimate decision-maker in the young Society that very rapidly attained a global reach. Necessarily, Iñigo had to make decisions in view of international conditions of his day. The dominant political factors not only dictated his policy lines; they evoked political reactions from him when religion was involved. For example, unless the turmoil in Germany was pacified, Europe would not be in peace, Iñigo declared; his German envoy, Peter Canisius, accordingly received his instructions as to what he, Canisius, as a Jesuit, could do in that pacification.

Another example: Christian Europe's existence and its communications with the New World and the Far East were threatened by Islam. Emperor Charles V, the most powerful Christian ruler in Iñigo's day, was told by Iñigo that he should draft a naval fleet into the eastern Mediterranean.

Iñigo's concentration of men and resources in India, Japan, China, Ethiopia, the Congo, and Brazil was practical and deliberate, and found its justification exclusively in his realization that, for the first time in its history, the Roman Church had an almost exclusive chance of becoming truly universal.

His attention, therefore, was directed to questions transcending individuals, and to interests tied to vast spaces of land and to whole peoples. Caring for an organization engaged in such activities is not the same as caring for an individual. The impersonal was often in competition with the personal; as often, it was the impersonal good of the whole Society that had to win over the personal. This is always the crux in organizations and institutions.

By 1551, he had finished a first draft of the *Constitutions*,[1] and in 1552 a quorum of Jesuits assembled by him in Rome gave preliminary approval to that draft as an experimental model. It was put into effect immediately. He would continue to incorporate new elements into that draft until his death in 1556.[2]

This entire process of founding and administering his Society and always keeping his eye on the larger picture of the Church Universal had an inevitable effect on Iñigo, gradually producing a change quite evident to his close companions in Rome.

As he grew older, those around him remarked on the quiet, almost expressionless mask his face assumed through all the grueling day-to-day rounds of letters to be dictated, consultations with his advisers, documents to be composed, hard-and-fast decisions to be made about the disposal of Jesuit members for this mission, that work, the other assignment. Decisions, always decisions, and practically always made with papal policy, local politics, the logistics of travel and communication to be held as conditioners—these filled his days.

The effect of it all on him became increasingly obvious. For some years before his death, his companions had the impression that the face and voice and look they had known as Iñigo's had somehow gone into covert. Sensing that their father—so they called him—would die one day soon, they arranged for one of the well-known portrait painters of the time, Giambattista Moroni, to do a likeness of Iñigo in oils.

Iñigo would not approve, of that his companions were certain. So they smuggled Moroni into the house. In order to paint his subject, the artist peered through a half-open door at Iñigo asleep in his room during siesta hours. Moroni, whose protraits are famous and today hang in the museums and galleries of Detroit, Minneapolis, Cleveland, Chicago, San Francisco, Washington, D.C., London, Paris, and elsewhere, tore up five attempts to paint Iñigo, and gave up. "God does not wish this man to be painted," were Moroni's parting words.

For all the change in him, Iñigo did not become an iceberg of unapproachable coldness, nor an imperious and reserved automaton, impervious to emotions. Quite the opposite, in fact. And the love and veneration of his companions increased.

When someone came and told him one day that an avowed enemy of the Society, Cardinal Gian Pietro Carafa, had been elected as Pope Paul IV, Iñigo was visibly shaken. "His face changed and, as I knew a little later," one of his biographers and intimates tells us, "his bones shook. He got up without saying a word and went into the chapel to pray." In the end, Paul IV proved to be not so inimical. He found as Pope what his ambitions and worldliness as a Carafa had not allowed him see: Iñigo and his Jesuits were a Heaven-sent gift to the papacy.

Nor did Iñigo ever lose the touch of personal intimacy with those around him. From words written about him by men who knew him well, one can see his eyes light up with understanding; his lips could part in a luminous smile of sheer pleasure; but above all his expression never lost that deep reflection of inner light which each of his entourage vied with the others to see every day.

They were, each one of Iñigo's companions, witnesses to his genius and participants in the awesomeness of holiness's presence that accompanied him everywhere. Some used to find him sitting on the house roof at night looking at the silent stars, tears flowing down his face. Others were present when he said Mass, and were overwhelmed by his reverence in handling the Host and the Chalice. Others still listened to him counseling the wayward and the headstrong, and knew it was the closest they would get to hearing the tones and spirit of Jesus echoing in a human voice. "I will yield to no creature on the face of God's earth," he told one recalcitrant member of his Company, "in my love for you."

One of Iñigo's men persuaded him to dictate the bare details of an autobiography. He began in 1553, but worked at it only in dribs and drabs. He did reveal some tantalizing details of how God favored his soul with tastes of the mysteries of divine being—about the inner love of the Three Divine Persons, which flooded his being during his stay at the Spanish Shrine of Manresa and on the banks of the Cardoner river in 1522; about the persons of Jesus and his mother, Mary, and about Iñigo's own future service of them as he came to understand it in the wayside shrine of La Storta, fifteen miles from Rome, in 1527; about the nature of Jesuitism as a form of personal service of Jesus through the Pope as he refined it over that fourteen-year period while he was composing the *Constitutions* and guiding his Company of servants.

And yet, his language in describing all this was so sparse that it merely creates a hunger in you that you know will never be satisfied, at least on this side of eternity. Like his early companions, you will never know the texture of his living ecstasy or the fiber of his intentions.

One surmises that Iñigo had his own reasons for being reticent —one practical reason, at least. His men were to be activists— "contemplatives in action" is the consecrated phrase. He did not wish to set as the highlight example of Jesuit spirituality the highest form of mystical prayer. Not everyone could practice that and still, like him, lead a fully active life. The inherent attraction of mystical contemplation and absorption in God can paralyze and do away with all desire and inclination to have anything to do with the material world.

Whatever changes did take place in him over the years, Iñigo remained simple to the end; he liked everyone to call him Iñigo. He did not mind being twitted, as when one young protegé of his, Pedro Ribadineira, who later distinguished himself as a thoroughgoing Jesuit, would follow behind him imitating his limp. Iñigo enjoyed it, keeping a straight face as part of his role in the joke.

He never lost his sense of humor or his feeling for others. Once, at a low point in their finances, the cook placed a meager dinner of hard-boiled eggs together with toothpicks on the table, remarking wryly that the toothpicks might come in useful. Iñigo found the remark hilariously funny in the circumstances. When there was plenty of food, on the other hand, he liked to invite some already well-padded member of the Order to the table; it gave him satisfaction to see the man eat well.

He ate little himself and, on principle, drank very little wine; but he could joke about his diet. During a particularly painful attack of what seemed to be gastroenteritis, the cook offered him some wine. Iñigo quickwittedly quoted a phrase of St. Paul's, *modicum vinum non nocet* (a little wine does not hurt), but laughingly changed the word for wine (*vinum*) to *venenum* (poison).

But with all that, the erosion of self went on for Iñigo. Indeed, the real source of change in his appearance was the ever-increasing emptying out of all consideration and regard for himself. His death, when it came, was of a piece with that.

The work around Iñigo's office on Thursday, July 30, 1557, was intense because on Friday the mail would leave for Spain. Already, Jesuits were working in Spain, Portugal, Japan, and the New World. The mail had to catch the Royal Mail Ships sailing from Spain and Portugal for those distant parts of the world.

For three days, Iñigo had been suffering intensely from a gall-bladder attack. But he got through the day's work. In the middle of composing a very difficult letter that Thursday afternoon, however, a rush of saliva produced a peculiarly bitter taste in his mouth. He knew what it meant.

Intimating to his secretary, Father Polanco, that he was near death, Iñigo asked him to hasten across St. Peter's Square to the Pope and get His Holiness's blessing.

The secretary, not believing him, stupidly put him off, alleging the pile of work to be done, promising to get the blessing on the morrow, Friday.

"I would prefer you got it today," Iñigo answered, "but do what you think best."

The mail was dispatched on time.

Shortly before dawn on Friday, July 31, Iñigo cried out in prayer. He often prayed out loud during sleep, however, so no one paid any mind.

By the time the infirmarian assigned to look after Iñigo checked his condition at daybreak, he saw immediately that the sick man was in his last agony. Polanco, in tears, rushed off to get the papal blessing. He brought it back too late. Neither papal blessing nor the Sacred Oil of Extreme Unction was to be Iñigo's while he was still alive and conscious.

His leave-taking from his companions and from the world was witnessed only by two Jesuits. The hiddenness of the person who was Iñigo was complete. When the wide world came to know of him, it would be as Ignatius of Loyola. Nine out of ten ordinary people and three out of five Jesuits would not even know his original name.

After his death on that Friday, his surviving companions tried again—several times, in fact—to have a likeness of Iñigo made. They called in the famous artist Jacopino del Conte, a former penitent of Iñigo's. An unknown member of the community had a death mask made from the cadaver; and from that death mask Alonzo Sánchez Coello, court painter of King Philip II of Spain, tried to reproduce a portrait of Iñigo. But neither del Conte nor Coello succeeded where Moroni had failed years before. All those who had known Iñigo intimately for so long examined the attempts. "No," they said, "that is not our father." They swore that neither of those efforts nor the death mask itself were even remotely like Iñigo in life; that none of them caught his tense air of untiring energy and infinite resolution. We miss, they complained, the peace and calm that shrouded his aristocratic features.

The traditional paintings of Iñigo are, according to those who knew him, "fictitious." It was as if his wish to be the unrecognizable, the depersonalized—if possible, the unknown—architect of his Company was fulfilled by a loving Lord Jesus who values humility and self-effacement in his creatures more than any other human accomplishment.

On the evening of Saturday, August 1, Iñigo's remains were buried in the little chapel of Santa Maria della Strada, opposite the house he had occupied during the last sixteen years of his life. By 1587, the chapel was replaced by the famous Jesuit Church of the Gesù, and his remains were interred there. Barely seventy years after his death, he was canonized as a saint by Pope Gregory XV.

The price of Iñigo's enormous success was high merely in human terms. Already before his death in 1556, Jesuits in Rome alone numbered about 150; the Order possessed over one hundred houses in twelve different regions of the world. Iñigo had founded thirty-five colleges for the higher education of youth. Jesuits worked in places as widely separate as Japan and Brazil, were penetrating countries as opaque to sixteenth century minds as Ethiopia, and were accepted at all major Church assemblies as authentic voices of the Roman Catholic Pope's doctrine and authority.

The future of his Society was guaranteed as surely as that of any other existing Church institution. Iñigo had had the ability to pick the right man for the right work at the right time and send him to the right place. He sent a stolid Dutchman, Pieter de Houndt, better known by the Latin form of his name, Peter Canisius, to Germany in 1550 with two lone companions. When Canisius died in 1597, he left behind him 1110 Jesuits in that area and a row of Jesuit colleges in Austria, Germany, and Hungary, and had reclaimed whole provinces from Protestantism. Emperors, kings, and governments yet to be born had to contend with what Canisius wrought decades and centuries before they were on the scene.

Ultimately and intimately, however, it was Iñigo down in his little stone house in Rome who was the cause of that, as he was of the singular success of the Society of Jesus around the world and down the centuries.

Whatever be the achievements of Jesuits, and whatever be the changes and adaptations the Society of Jesus chooses to make in the passage of the centuries and the succession of new eras in human development, you will be able to discern the real value of those achievements, changes, and adaptations by using one norm and only one norm. This is the conformity of the Jesuits—as Order and as individuals—to the prime papalism of Iñigo as expressed in that *Formula of the Institute.*

The day that war exists between the papacy and the Jesuit Order, that day you can be sure the members of the Society have renounced the peculiarly Ignatian mold and taken a path that Ignatius and the Church never assigned to Jesuits.

7 | THE IGNATIAN MOLD

When Iñigo de Loyola received his mandate from Paul III and settled down in his Roman house with his first companions, the world he knew was stunningly like our own in many ways. If any of us today were to walk the same streets he walked and talked with the people he knew, we would probably feel rather at home in the volatile mix of frontier mentality and fear of war and annihilation. Iñigo's solution for the problems that world presented was already clear in his mind, however; and that solution was stunningly different from any then on the scene, and from any that Jesuits have devised and implemented during the past twenty years of this century. It is precisely in that difference that the key to the fabled success of Ignatian Jesuitism—the Ignatian mold of the Society and of each individual member—is most clearly to be seen.

If it were possible for some latter-day investigative reporter to produce one of those on-the-spot documentaries about the world Iñigo faced between 1521 and 1556, he would trundle his television cameras and microphones to any number of world centers and take account of a whole series of mind-bending revolutions. In Spain, France, Holland, Belgium, England, Germany, and Italy, he would record on-the-spot interviews with the bright-eyed, rambunctious, omnicurious, romantically inclined New Man of the European Renaissance for whom every question was wide open.

Everywhere, he would record wonderment and expectation. Above all, he would record the enterprising sense men had of totally new undertakings and discoveries that seized and sometimes bedeviled the generation to which Iñigo belonged.

"What's going on?" In one form or another that would be the question our reporter would ask every place he went. And it is not hard to imagine the answers he would receive.

In the Alcalá and Salamanca and Barcelona of Iñigo's Spain, he wouldn't hear about multiple Venus probes, of course, or plans for mining operations on the moon or scientific advancements in microbiology and genetics. But to his "What's going on?" he would uncover our same sense of discovery and expectation of huge change: "Why, haven't you heard? We've discovered an alien world beyond our western seas! It's teeming with resources that will change our lives forever, and with creatures we didn't know existed. Why, it's the overnight creation of a whole new empire! It's mind-boggling!"

In Paris, where Iñigo had studied, and in the theological faculties elsewhere in France, Holland, England, and Belgium, the talk wouldn't be of Liberation Theology, as it is in our day, or of women's rights in the Church, or of the People of God as the last and only reliable source of eternal salvation. But there would be close religious and theological equivalents: "Why, haven't you heard? A German monk, Martin Luther, and the English King, Henry VIII, have challenged Rome! They say they want to free us from Romish superstition, liberate our minds from slavery to false doctrines fabricated by the Latinate mind. They say we will convert the world now that we know that the Church and the Pope have no mandate from Christ, and no doctrine to teach us except what's in the Bible. It's mind-boggling!"

Similarly, in the Genoa and Venice of Iñigo's day, "What's going on?" wouldn't bring talk of Soviet missiles poised in Eastern Europe, threatening nuclear destruction to the West, or of NATO as the "West's" defense against the "East." But the geopolitical fear wasn't that much different: "Why! Haven't you heard about the Turks? Our whole Christian world could be wiped out by the Ottoman Sultan and his Christian-hating Turks from Constantinople. What's going on is nothing less than the war for Christianity's survival—the life or death of the Christian heartland. It's mind-boggling!"

If our reporter should frequent, as Iñigo had done, the salons and houses of the very rich—the aristocrats, the higher clergy, and the privileged classes—we would hear what Iñigo had heard. He would come up full tilt against the rampant individualism fanned into lustrous flame by the rediscovery of Graeco-Roman literature and civilization. He would recognize and sympathize with the Renaissance fashion of "humanizing" all things. And as a twentieth-century man, he would feel very much at home.

Such phrases as "creative growth toward integration" and "Christ the Revolutionary Freedom Fighter" weren't on the scene in those days. And there were no arguments about the social benefits of legalized abortion and euthanasia.

But there was a lot of talk about a Jesus refashioned à la Grecque into a beautiful Apollo or a wise Plato. About God the Father addressed as Father Zeus; and Heaven as the Elysian Fields; and angels and saints as godlets, nymphs, and dryads; and Hell as Hades governed by the infernal hound dog Cerberus. "Why!" anyone might respond to the reporter's question: "Haven't you heard? The whole of life is, after all, just what the ancient Greeks said it was—a play of whimsical and fortuitous events. It all comes down to nothing more than the clash of temporal princes. The Pope included. It's mind-boggling! Man has finally realized that what matters is who comes out on top in the clash of empires—the English, the French, the Spanish, the Venetians, the Austrians, the Germans. And if you want to know what goodness means, it means being rich. Evil means being poor. Poverty is the essence of evil."

When our reporter had done all his interviews, when the tapes had all been edited and the script finished, his wrap-up of man's quest to conquer and tame his cosmos would not deal with such things as the International Monetary Fund, global communications, the Olympic Games, the growing consensus on international finance and trade, or the economic exploitation of outer space. What he would distil as the outstanding attitudes, though, would surely strike a familiar and even sympathetic chord in our ears: "What this reporter found is the still-living truth given to us by the ancient Greek philosopher Pythagoras. Man is, after all, the measure of all things. This reporter saw it in the new theology. I saw it, too, in the tense international situation between the 'East' and the 'West'—slowly, painfully, Christian and Turk are trying to find a way to live and let live. But above all, I saw it in the wonderful twin adventures of the new science sprouting in Paris, Cambridge, Bologna, and Göttingen; and in the discoveries of utterly new alien lands. Man is just beginning to measure himself against vast new horizons through voyagers in the Orient, in Africa, in the New World. Even to measure himself against the stars in the sky through the new astronomers. Renaissance man's world is no longer earth-centered. Man is setting out on his own at last, to know and master his cosmos. All of it!"

In a very real sense, by the time Iñigo de Loyola began the detailed work of forming his Society of Jesus, he had already asked that same question. "What's going on?" He had already seen and heard everything our imaginary reporter would have seen and heard. He understood both the fascination of his contemporaries with the powerful adventures, discoveries and new freedoms; and the very mixed feelings that come with all of that.

What interested him, however, was not a mere reportorial description of new happenings and new reactions to them. His mind was not transfixed by science or new discoveries. He did not see a new theology of humanism leading to a new age of man on the horizon. Nor was he proccupied by the never-ending war between his Christian world and the Turkish Empire.

While most people were just preparing to measure themselves against the widening backdrop of newness, Iñigo was already thinking in universalist terms, and about the condition of man's entire cosmos.

For him, everything traced back to the single element common throughout the vast sea of change; the single element that, in its essence, never changed: the cosmic war between God and Lucifer. Just as it had in every age before his, that war was still being waged everywhere and daily. It permeated every event, every element of turmoil, of expansion. And it concerned just one thing: the eternal salvation of each human being.

Through the sacrificial death and resurrection of Christ, and by the founding of the Roman Catholic Church, God had made it possible for each man and woman to make godly choices in life, and by those choices to attain Heaven after death. In that cosmic and constant war, Christ was the leader of God's campaign; and Christ's personal, visible representative among men was the Roman Pope. Lucifer's aim in the war—the aim of Satan as adversary—was to ensure that as many human beings as possible missed that eternal after-life goal.

Unless you admit that this cosmic warfare was all that really mattered for Iñigo, that it was far more important and real than the Christian-Turk war, you have no chance of understanding how Iñigo succeeded in his venture. He read not only his contemporary history but also what he knew of the past and what he planned for the future in the light of that paradigm. That war was what was really going on, what really mattered. And it was his understanding of that war that gave him his hardy independence from the prevailing, piecemeal reactions of his generation to the earth-shaking changes in their world. In turn, it was that independence of mind that enabled him to fashion his Ignatian mold for his Order and for its individual members.

Not that his view of the warfare itself was innovative. His idea of the battle between God and Lucifer as the supreme reality in human life was the very old and authentically Christian teaching according to which each individual human being is the cherished objective of those two agents external to him: God and Lucifer. Fundamental to Iñigo's spirituality was the dogmatic belief that, while alive in this world, no one can escape the constant attentions of both God and Lucifer.

Old as that belief was, however, it was being swamped in a single generation by the new fascination men and women found in the here and now; in an ever more exciting temporal life; in the rush to fit into that life, to adapt to it and change with it; and above all, in the new humanistic cry of the Renaissance that "Man is the measure of all things."

For Iñigo, the very cry pointed to a shift in the current campaign of the constant war. It was Lucifer's latest ploy, his modern version of "I will not serve."

Ignatius saw his Roman Catholic Church and its papacy as an object of pathos in this sudden new phase of the war. There had been no time in the abrupt blossoming of the new world of the Renaissance for Church and papacy to develop apt and specific instruments for coping with problems that had never beset them before.

Sure enough, the Church did already possess a marvelous panoply of Religious Orders. But not one of them had been formed or trained even to understand, much less to deal with, the tasks that now presented themselves so urgently. One famous Religious Order in Iñigo's day, for example, had as its constitutional purpose the freeing of hostages held in slavery by the "Infidel." Another, the Dominicans, was primarily a teaching and preaching Order. The Franciscans professionally were supposed to celebrate the glory and the joy of poverty as a sign of Christ's love for all men and his intent to save them from the snares of worldly attachments. Other Orders, such as the Benedictines and the Carmelites and the Carthusians, had been formed to live a life at least partially removed from truck with the busy world of man, and to occupy themselves in singing the praises of God, in private prayer, and thus in perfecting their own inner spirits. More than one famous

Order was founded as a defense corps for the Holy Places of Christendom in Jerusalem and elsewhere. Still other Orders had been founded for nursing, for hospital work, and for what Christians have always called the works of mercy—care of the dying, the indigent, orphans, the hungry; organization of halfway houses for prostitutes, leper colonies, night shelters.

The point for Iñigo, however, was that every Roman Religious Order was constitutionally specified for just one particular objective. The members of each developed skills only for its specific purpose. In addition, all the members of an Order were ordinarily supposed to live and work and die in particular houses and communities, their lives regulated by specific rules detailed in *Constitutions*. And although the *Constitutions* of each Order were examined and approved by papal authority, once that had been accomplished not even a Pope could or would normally violate an Order's way of life by requiring its members to act outside that Order's specified tasks.

As far as Iñigo could see—which turned out to be farther than anyone else of his time—that left both Church and Pope locked away in a genuinely medieval structure of rigid Religious Orders at the very moment when the most painful characteristic of the warfare was the bewildering variety of new problems thrown into the fight.

Armed with the courage to think as no one had done before him —always a dangerous thing to do—and with an astounding versatility in that thinking, what Iñigo proposed was as truly revolutionary as anything in the world revolution around him. He reasoned that such a dense array of different problems facing the Church called for an unheard-of new corps of volunteers who would set out professionally to fight on Christ's side. They would have to be trained not for one task, but for hundreds. And they could not be confined to one house or community, but must be willing to go wherever the fight would take them. Sometimes sedentary living would still be required; Iñigo himself never left Rome once Paul III had approved his plan. Just as often, however, a fast-moving strategy would be the key to success. Their "specialty," in other words, would be the ability to tackle any job expertly, right away, once the vital interest of the Church were involved.

Paramount, however, was not the versatility or the mobility of the Order, but its single-minded purpose, its one and only reason for existence: to be an elite fighting unit on the side of Christ— and therefore on the side of Christ's representative, the Pope—in the war between Christ and Lucifer. That *Romanism*, as it came sometimes to be called, would therefore be the first preeminent hallmark of the Jesuit mold, a Romanism that would mean something different for Jesuits than for any other Religious Order. The others, too, were subject to the authority of the Roman Pope, after all—were Romanist in that sense. But by the same token, those various Rules of theirs determined what any Pope could and would normally ask of them. Their Romanism had limits.

Iñigo's Romanism was total. He wanted to answer the one new requirement of the papacy, namely, its urgent need to be able to call on cadres of religiously trained and religiously devoted men, and to be able, at the shortest notice, to throw them against virtually any problem that faced the papacy anywhere at any time.

That meant a special juridical bond, never conceived of before, between papacy and Jesuits that would entitle any Pope to dispose them in any way he judged best, where and when he chose. Before all else, and when all was said and done, Jesuits would be "Pope's Men," Romanist in their very souls.

The second essential of the Ignatian mold was implied by the first. If the very purpose of the Order was to be what today we would call the papal Rapid Deployment Force, then its members must be not only religiously trained and religiously devoted men; they must, as well, be trained in a whole gamut of other things, new branches of knowledge, new sectors of activity. They must stand as a ready supply of variegated talent, honed and refined to the level of the best the world had to offer. The second essential of the Ignatian mold, then, was its *polyvalency*. Jesuits would be Religious priests. But they would also be anything and everything else required by papal needs—chemists, biologists, zoologists, linguists, explorers, high-school teachers, university professors, geographers, astronomers, mathematicians, preachers, diplomats, confessors, intelligence agents, couriers, philosophers, theologians, public relations experts, popular writers, social communications specialists, artists, Indian swamis, Chinese mandarins, farmers, architects, even army commanders.

The third essential of the Jesuit mold was demanded by the first two. If the whole world around Iñigo was being drawn away from Christ and his Church by means of all the newness and innovation and this-worldliness of human affairs, what was to keep the same situation from corrupting his Jesuits? How could they do everything that was being done in the world and still remain genuinely Romanist, genuinely Pope's men?

The answer to that question was supplied by the strict asceticism Iñigo summed up pithily in four Latin words that gave his order its motto and monogram: *Ad Majorem Dei Gloriam.* A.M.D.G. For the greater glory of God.

His intent was simple: Whatever his Jesuits did, they would do with a Christianizing and ultimately a Romanizing intent. Of course, they would be as good as their secular counterparts—and better if possible—in science, learning social skills, and all the rest. Iñigo always aimed at being first. But whatever his Jesuits would achieve would be for a spiritual reason, with papal interest in mind.

In setting out the Jesuit asceticism, Iñigo drew on the thousand-year-old tradition of his Church. Still, even here he was innovative. He applied the principles of that ancient Christian asceticism in new ways, so that they would work in the entirely New World climate.

Iñigo had already been through the hard process of close and painful scrutiny of every facet of his inner self during the years when he had reformed his life and then had begun guiding the spiritual lives of his first companions. He had learned that in the warfare God and Lucifer wage for the individual soul, there takes place a kind of cosmic propaganda campaign for new recruits. While God can, in that campaign, communicate by immaterial, supernatural, totally spiritual means, he generally speaks through events. In terms of the individual, God can and does introduce images through sense data—through external events, words and actions in the world around each person.

Lucifer, meanwhile, can act only through that natural order. He is creature, not creator. He is preternatural, but not supernatural. Like all creatures without supernatural grace, he exists and moves and has his being completely and definitively outside the super-natural, which is God's exclusive domain. Lucifer's mode of impact, therefore, is entirely through sense data—through events, words, actions. Those are the means he uses to supply the ideas and the images and the motives he would like to see as the individual's interior intimates, the regulators of his decisions and actions.

The power of the individual in all this is crucial. His is the power to make a choice; the power that resides in his every act of will; the power to accept or reject any or all of what is offered. In fact, as in any propaganda campaign in any war, so with the cosmic campaign in the cosmic war: It is essential to find out where the data is coming from and what it really means, so that choices and decisions can be made.

Translated into the terms of Iñigo's ascetic mold for his Jesuits, the cosmic propaganda effort meant that each individual member would have to learn to *analyze* the data of his inner activity of which he was conscious. Whatever basic forms you deliberately allowed and nourished in your inner theater of consciousness, Ignatius said, would inevitably become the regulators of your decisions and therefore of your exterior actions. Practically speaking, therefore, Iñigo's task was to develop a process by which each individual would achieve a knowing perception of what kind of spirit—the good spirit of God, or the evil spirit of Lucifer—was acting on him, motivating him, driving him. That process Iñigo called "discernment of spirits."

Perception and analysis weren't ends in themselves, however. The real point of the exercise lay in the fact that Iñigo's Jesuits would be committed to a febrile course of exterior activity throughout the world. The *regulation* by each Jesuit of his own inner activity would be all-important. The ascetic way proper to the Society of Jesus, therefore, would give each member the means to *control* what entered his consciousness through his senses and his imagination, so that he could remain Romanist and activist. So that he could do whatever he did "for the greater glory of God."

It was to this end that every Jesuit's basic, ascetic training was aimed. Each member of the Society was to be formed and trained in very specific ways. Iñigo developed minute rules—the *Rules of Modesty,* for example, and rules for prayers, as well as scores of other instructions. Every Jesuit novice needed to have, and to learn to use, silence—a time of apartness from the apanache of the busy, active world outside him. He needed order in his living habits, and discipline in the way he spent those hours of silence and solitude, as well as his hours of activity.

By themselves, however, such elements had been perennially acknowledged in the Christian ascetic tradition as essential preconditions for spiritual formation and progress. To eliminate them —as has been done in many parts of the Jesuit Order that are vital training phases of the young men—would have been to fly in the face of one of the solidest traditions of that very Church Universal Iñigo set out to serve, defend, and propagate.

What was new about this asceticism, in addition to the rigorous self-analysis that became second nature to every Jesuit, was the cool, rational detachment it seemed to give to Jesuits, much as it had to Iñigo. It was a trait everyone noticed. In the heated battles they entered almost immediately as the Society sprang into active existence and contention, Jesuits were frequently admired for that cool detachment. Just as frequently, however, their adversaries pointed precisely to that quality as evidence of calculated cunning.

The criticism had a measure of accuracy; for the Jesuits out-talked, outargued, outwrote, and outmaneuvered the most formidable adversaries in every field; and yet they remained stubborn in the singular purpose for which they had each chosen to enter their Order.

Given the medieval mentality of his contemporary Churchmen, Iñigo's "invention," the Society of Jesus, leaps out as a stroke of daring genius. Neither the total Romanism nor the polyvalency of the Jesuit mold had a precise precedent nor a proven track record. And however rigorous and painful his ascetic way, there was no proof it would stand against the onslaught of humanism. The whole venture could have been disaster. In hindsight, his success was so phenomenal that it rates Iñigo among the few authentic innovators in the history of human organization. He had no predecessors; but he had many subsequent imitators.

It must have been downright disconcerting, in fact, for those who thought they had outclassed those hidebound, superstitious Roman Catholics at last. Suddenly there appeared men who had mastered the new knowledge. Men who could talk the newspeak of that day, but who remained totally at the beck and call of the Roman Pontiff. Men for whom man was not for a moment the measure of all things; Christ was.

Like Iñigo, no Jesuit had the slightest interest in developing his talents and powers for his own sake. Like Iñigo, Jesuits rejected out of hand the Renaissance preoccupation with the grandeur of the self. All of their information in the Ignatian mold, so meticulous and rigorous and full of attention to detail, remained always directed to just two things: the warfare between God and Lucifer for each individual, and the Pope's need of devoted servants.

And so it remained for over four hundred years. In fact, apart from that cool eye it gave to Jesuits, the most tantalizing fruit of the precious Ignatian mold was always the hardy independence that Iñigo first won for himself, and then systematized for his companions and followers. In all of the succeeding waves of fads and innovation to which the world has been so feverishly seeking to adapt since Iñigo's day, not one concession was made in the essentials of Jesuitism until the Ignatian mold itself was smashed by the ones who knew and understood it best: the Jesuits themselves.

Down all those centuries of the Society's fabulous and fascinating successes, it was inevitable that outsiders—commentators both favorable and unfavorable—would scan and analyze Ignatius's *Constitutions* again and again in an effort to lay bare what René Fülöp-Miller called "the power and secret" of the Jesuits. They assumed that those *Constitutions* are themselves the essence of the Order Iñigo founded.

Iñigo made clear that such an assumption was wrong. "What would you do," he was asked once after the long labor of writing, testing, revising, and honing the *Constitutions* was done, "if the Pope abolished the Society, wiped out the *Constitutions*, liquidated everything you've built?"

"It would take me a quarter of an hour in the Presence of the Blessed Sacrament," Iñigo answered, "to get back my peace of mind. Then I'd start all over again." He would, in other words, still have his ideal of how Christ and the Pope should be served. He always talked about an inner illumination that pointed the way. For him, it was not a question of studying history, or the psychology of his contemporaries. It was a question of divine inspiration rigorously tested in the crucible of hard reality to produce the Ignatian mold—the "power and secret" that made the Jesuits great.

There is no use claiming or pretending, however, that an answer like that can satisfy today's more sophisticated experts; and for the first time since Iñigo's time, no Jesuits are out there even making the argument.

No psychologist, for example, would be likely to discern—or admit it, if he did—an inner illumination or a divine inspiration in Iñigo. He would not understand reality as Iñigo regarded reality. The whole idea of the uncreated light of the Holy Spirit promised by Christ to his followers—a central idea that animated Iñigo—would be unacceptable as an outmoded superstition.

And as to a universal warfare of God-made-man against a Fallen Archangel for the spiritual salvation of souls—well, we have drugs for people who talk like that nowadays. Professionally, psychologists cannot hold that it is the diabolic light of that Fallen Archangel, Christ's adversary in the warfare, that enables such men as Lenin and Stalin and Hitler to spellbind and enslave the minds and spirits of millions. What makes for such men and their regimes, today's scholars explain, is not their choice between images, ideas, and motives that are "good," and those that are "evil," but a plethora of aberrant sociopolitical systems installed on earth, and the sick or twisted minds of those leaders.

Coming down to the nub of it then, a cosmic war such as Iñigo understood it, and certainly any talk of "discernment of spirits" or of controlling what enters the consciousness, would be symptoms of something far less flattering than sainthood or genius.

In spite of those "negative" elements, though—those "superstitions"—it has apparently seemed a shame to many that such an extraordinary power of practical analysis as Iñigo possessed should be lost altogether. After all, Iñigo did live in another day. Particularly in the light of the way the Society of Jesus has gone in the past twenty years, perhaps it would be fair (it is certainly inevitable) for the secular historian and the secular psychologist and the rest of the secular analysts to take another look, a "truly objective" look this time, at those *Constitutions* of Iñigo's. Perhaps it's time to ask again if Iñigo's principles should not be every bit as effective without the supernatural element that was so basic to him, and that was the very heart and center of the Jesuit mold he created.

The answer to that question lies in history itself. Iñigo's ideal of Jesuitism, so striking and so powerful, has always excited not just curiosity, admiration, and disdain, but an odd array of would-be imitators. Most of them wanted to get at that mysterious secret of Jesuit success locked away so cleverly somewhere in those *Constitutions* and in the *Spiritual Exercises*. The idea was to squeeze those pages of meticulous rules and procedures like sponges; to free them from the divine plan Iñigo saw as the cause of his success and of his Society's influence as a shaper of history. What would be left was bound to be the key to Jesuitical, if not Jesuit, excellence.

Reichsführer Heinrich Himmler, Adolf Hitler's closest collaborator in the Nazi regime of Germany, did something like that. He made it his business to assemble an extensive library about the Jesuit Order. He even dreamed at one stage of training his elite Waffen SS combat troops along Jesuit lines; went so far as to send the principal officers to Wewelsburg Castle in Westphalia, where he proposed they undergo a form of Iñigo's *Spiritual Exercises*—adapted, however, to a mad blend of the new Nordic cult of Wodin, Siegfried, the Holy Grail, and the Teutonic Knights of old. What he coveted was not the spiritual devotion, but that inner subjugation of will and intellect that Iñigo had produced in his Jesuits. The plan never succeeded, but even Adolf Hitler knew of it and joked about Himmler as "our very own Ignatius Loyola."

Curiously enough, given latter-day developments, the nearest historical parallel to the Jesuitism of Iñigo de Loyola is to be found in the Leninism of Vladimir Ilyich Ulyanov who, under the adopted pseudonym of Lenin, founded the Soviet Communist Party and there imposed the cancer of Marxism on the peoples of what we now call the USSR.

Both Loyola and Lenin, when compared to other great men, came from nowhere, as the phrase goes. Neither was born with a silver spoon in his mouth. Neither inherited a name already great in politics or literature or art. Neither had armies or bureaucracies at his disposal. Each literally created both his succcess and the means to that success. Each of them conceived an idea; rationalized that idea with uncompromising, merciless logic; of himself fashioned the means of implementing that idea; and then carried that idea out programmatically with unheard-of tenacity of will. Neither would or could be deflected from his goal. As a result, each of these two men revolutionized the feelings, thoughts, behavior, and destiny of hundreds of millions of ordinary people.

There is more in common, then, between the supreme Roman Catholic zealot of the sixteenth century and the supreme atheist of the twentieth century than their almost identical, below-medium height, their piercing eyes, their powerful foreheads, the strikingly apt connotations of their first names (Vladimir is usually interpreted as "owner of the world"—precisely what Lenin aimed at; and Iñigo or Ignatius signifies "defender"—Iñigo's chosen role was exactly that).

Where both innovators, Loyola and Lenin, coincided most significantly, however, was in their clear perception of the only means by which history can be deliberately made, and human destinies can be materially altered. Gold or pleasure won't do the trick; not for long, at any rate. Lenin knew as well as Loyola that it is not blind economic forces or weight of numbers or even access to power that enables men to make history. Only an ideal does that. An ideal by which the wills of individuals are won. An ideal for which people are convinced it is worth fighting and sacrificing everything—even life itself. It is men under the complete control and all-abiding influence of such an ideal accepted without reserve. Men, in other words, whose ordinary self-interest is transformed by an ideology into an all-absorbing devotion shot through with a high romanticism.

What Loyola and Lenin both understood, then, was that you must reach out by means of alluring images to possess the minds and imaginations of individuals; for it is through their minds that you grip and control their wills. With that tight union of wills at your disposal, history is yours for the making.

Even in the basic lines of the organization each man founded—

Lenin with his Communist Party; Iñigo with his Society—the similarities are so obvious that one is tempted to accuse the self-made twentieth-century Dictator of all the Russias with having plagiarized the sixteenth-century Saint.

In his famous pamphlet of 1901, *What Is to Be Done?*, Lenin outlined briefly what he thought was necessary for the total victory of Communism: a single party of professional revolutionaries, all totally under absolute obedience to the orders of the Central Committee of the Communist Party, and all bound together by a military discipline. A single organization; absolute obedience to a central authority; military discipline. These too had been the organizational elements Iñigo had adapted so brilliantly to a Religious Order, centuries before. "With such cadres," Lenin remarked, "one could turn the whole of Russia upside down"; and, he might have added, the entire world.

At that point, of course, the two men part company. Lenin's ideal—the "stateless paradise of the workers"—was not only wholly materialistic, but carried within itself its own contradiction. His utopia was to be achieved through various painful stages —notably through "the dictatorship of the people"—until the state would have "withered away," leaving only the proletariat in its total freedom and happiness. Or so Lenin promised.

The contradiction in Lenin's ideal was that it demanded renunciation of all material rewards for the people, but at the same time it plunged them into gross material conditions. And that has proved to be Leninism's downfall. It has crippled and confined the economic potential of the Soviet Union's totalitarian regime. It has forced Mao Tse-tung's hardheaded successors to head up capitalism's road. But the prime lesson Lenin's children are learning the hard way is clear: Men are finally not made happy except by what lifts them above the material conditions of human existence.

Loyola's ideal was exactly that. That was its promise. So it was he who best formulated that basic perception of how to engage men in making history. Programmatically, he best achieved that goal. First, by training his companions so they could achieve the desired unification of many wills, each and all locked into a super-human spiritual ideal. Then by providing them with a corporate blueprint, and sending them out on a conquest of their contemporaries' minds and wills.

Iñigo could easily have fallen into the trap that Lenin did not escape. He realized that, because the minds of men had virtually been assaulted and vastly changed by the revolution that was the Renaissance, the Roman Church was no longer able to speak to her people as she had for hundreds of years. Language, vision, thought—everything essential to communication, in fact—had changed, as it were, in a blink of history's eye.

His realization was an exact parallel of Lenin's at the beginning of the twentieth century. The old regime of the Europe Lenin knew was in its death throes. A regime built on hereditary titles, landed power, imperial ambitions, and social class superiority could by his time no longer speak to or satisfy the ordinary people. Something had awakened them from their submissive slumber.

Both men, therefore, stood at watersheds of profound change in human society. Lenin analyzed the change as sociopolitical, and seized the moment on those terms only.

Iñigo, however, while he perceived the change as sociocultural —already a more universal analysis than Lenin's, therefore—was convinced that the change was also and more tellingly a new phase in Christ's war with Lucifer.

Like it or not, that divine plan Iñigo saw so intimately and clearly saved him from the trap of mere "adaptation." Omit that as the overarching explanation and the real cause of Iñigo's success and of his Society's influence as a shaper of history, and there remains no other satisfactory explanation of Jesuit achievement. Omit that, and the best Iñigo might have accomplished would have been a sort of Leninism of his day. He would have "adapted to the situation." His men might have been the best at heightening and effecting the sociocultural change already hurtling along, but they certainly would not have transformed it. The ideal would have been the greater Renaissance man, not the greater glory of God. The conquistador, the *Prince* of Niccolò Machiavelli, the all-powerful Doge of Venice, would not have outdone Ignatius, but they would all have been playing the same game. Iñigo's ideal, in other words, would have been materialistic. And that materialism would have choked him and his proposals. His followers would have drowned in materialistic efforts. Eventually, too, his original aim—to propagate the supernatural mission of his Pope and his Church—would have been bastardized.

What sets Iñigo apart from Lenin and other such "geniuses," was that he refused to adapt in any sense that we understand that word. In his mind, to adapt oneself to the modernity of his or any time did not mean allowing that modernity to dictate how you behaved, what you thought, what your goals should be. Quite the opposite, in fact. To adapt was to choose, for supernatural reasons, a role and an activity that transformed modernity and its conditions—that made them into something they had not been, and could not, of themselves alone, become.

If you followed Iñigo, in other words, you were not only spiritually oriented; you were a hardheaded and practical realist. You did not become what modernity demanded in the vain delusion that once you had aped modernity's models, you could somehow play turnabout and transform those models into the ones you had left behind.

That, however, as Iñigo seemed to understand with prescient clarity, is the especially subtle trap awaiting the student of religion —Jesuit and non-Jesuit—in the exhortation of psychologist and social engineer to "adapt." It is very easy to be persuaded—as many Jesuits of Pedro Arrupe's day appear to have been—to understand "adaptation" not in the Ignatian sense, but in that modern sense of adjusting yourself to fit in, to "go with the flow," as the "flower children" of the sixties and seventies were so fond of saying.

One surmises that Iñigo avoided that trap because, while a Lenin or a Hitler or a Stalin or a Mussolini was motivated by pride, fear, or worldly ambition, Iñigo was drawn by love. By now, even the promise of Leninism, the most powerful of the twentieth-century sociopolitical "adaptations," has proven itself in the cold history of entire populations to have been a quasi-satanic delusion, a transformation of nations into a series of hells from which whole generations have failed to find an exit. Stone walls and steel traps were Lenin's means to the end for which he demanded absolute obedience and conformity.

The promise of Jesuitism, meanwhile, has held for as long as Jesuits themselves have been faithful to Iñigo's principles, for as long as the Ignatian mold was mirrored in their interpretation of his *Constitutions*, and for as long as they have honored the faith that underlay all the words of Iñigo. Whatever failure Jesuits have met in this century has its origins in the same false step that Lenin took. As of the seventies, the Order adopted a sociopolitical policy of adaptation that carried the same inherent contradiction that ensured the ultimate failure of Leninism.

8 | THE COMPANY OF IGNATIUS

T he functional structure of Iñigo's company is the miracle achievement in Iñigo's transformation of his sixteenth-century contemporaries from men who thought of "man as the measure of all things" into men devoted to an all-encompassing God and Savior.

Those contemporaries of his were marinated in the fantastic newness of life in their time, with all its golden possibilities. Their whole reaction was to leave behind the old forms of thought and models of behavior, the old ways of living, even the old places where they had lived and the old truths by which they had lived there—all they had inherited from their medieval forefathers.

Face to face with that mentality, Iñigo drew up the blueprints for his Company of Jesus on a model even more ancient than medieval times, namely the basic principle of Christianity itself: subordination. The subordination of the cosmos and all in it— from lifeless stones and earth up through plants, animals, and humans, angels and archangels, within a hierarchic principle of being —to the Trinity of Father, Son, and Holy Spirit. There is no democracy in this hierarchy, no communal aim of equals; only inferiors and superiors. There is no self-perfecting individualism; no personal integration. There is a hierarchy of ordered parts; there are individuals destined each one of them to complement each other; there is integration of each part in the whole in so far as each part is subordinate. For, to be a part of this system is to be subordinate. The only equality permitted was subordination. All was subordinate. Within that hierarchic system of being and existence, every object had its place. The Creator of all has arranged all in a certain agreement and order.

This was what God originally revealed to the Children of Israel through his prophets. This was what Christ revealed in its fullness. This is the foundation of all Christian anthropology, as distinct from and opposed to nineteenth-century Darwinism, genetic and social and political. No human development, no matter how new, and no modernity—whether that of the Renaissance or that of the atomic, technotronic age—can displace that system.

Iñigo destined his Society to reproduce in its working existence that hierarchic principle whereby "the lower submits to the higher," and where all elements were bound together in recognition of higher authority and therefore in readiness to obey. He intended the members of his Order to be bound together by a mystical union of hearts and wills in voluntary subordination, subjects to Superiors, Superiors to the Father General, the Father General to the whole Society, the whole Society to the Pope, the Pope to Christ, whose earthly representative he is.

Iñigo's Company was therefore extremely simple in structure— so simple that its enemies were always persuaded there was much more to Jesuitism than met the eye in the outward and actual framework of the Society.

It was a pyramid of authority. At its apex, he placed one man, who went by the name of General or Father General. The title was not taken from the military code. This official had authority over the general structure and governance of the whole Society. He had no obligation to follow any advice, or seek the consent of any other Jesuit when giving orders. He was the *general* "superior," as distinct from all other "superiors" in the organization, who were local and in charge of particular sections. He alone of all Superiors attained his position by election; all other Superiors were appointed by his choice or at least with his approval; and, once elected General, he remained at this post until death unless very grave reasons commended an ouster. His authority was absolute over the whole Society and its various parts and members. He could dismiss anybody from the Order, and no formal trial or similar process was necessary. Iñigo was unanimously elected in April of 1541 as the first Father General of the Society.

The body of the Society was composed of four categories, or grades as they are called in the Society; members were distinguished as a general rule by the degree of their access to the important positions of government and direction of the Society's manpower and resources. In practice, that meant their proximity to or distance from the General on the pyramid of authority and power.

First, in this regard, was the category or grade of Professed Priests. Jesuits in this category had successfully passed rigorous scholastic tests as well as proofs of their religious quality; had taken three solemn vows of poverty, chastity, and obedience (vows common to all Catholic Religious Orders); and had taken a special vow of obedience to the Pope. While all Jesuits were bound to obey the Pope, the Professed bound themselves by that fourth and special vow. Only these Professed had access to the highest office of General and the most immediate posts beneath the Generalate. And only they could participate in the election of a General.

The demands on the Professed by Iñigo were difficult. In principle, Professed could only be Jesuits "selected for their spirit and learning, thoroughly and lengthily tested, and known with edification and satisfaction to all after various proofs of virtue and abnegation of themselves." This, indeed, was a high ideal.

Even among the Professed, there were to be distinctions of function and therefore of power. Thus, a Professed Jesuit in charge of all Jesuits in Colombia, South America, was not as near to the Father General as the Professed Father in Rome who was the Father General's assistant for all South American countries including Colombia.

The Professed Fathers staffed the teaching faculties of philosophy and theology, headed the Jesuit houses of training for Jesuit candidates and the local offices of the Order throughout the world. According to Ignatius's original plan, the Professed would live in houses that had no fixed revenues, no endowment regularly yielding funds. The practice of poverty by the Professed was to be as perfect as possible.

The second category or grade below the General was composed of priests who took simple, not solemn, vows; and they took no special fourth vow to the Pope. They were traditionally called Spiritual Coadjutors, for in Ignatius's concept, they aided and seconded the work of the Professed. In Ignatius's eyes, the members of this class would engage primarily in the priestly ministry to people and supervise the material organization of Jesuit houses.

The third grade or category in the Jesuit pyramid was that of Lay Brothers; these never became priests, but took the three simple vows and were charged with the manual labor in Jesuit houses—

cooking, cleaning, farming, laundry, wardrobe, shopping, repairing, maintenance, taking care of the sick and enfeebled.

The fourth category was that of the young Jesuit trainees, generally called Scholastics because their preparation was through the various "schools"—humanities, philosophy, theology, science—of learning. At the end of their scholasticate, they were ordained priests and, depending on how they had fared during their training, they joined the ranks of the Professed or of the Spiritual Coadjutors. They were then put to work.

When Iñigo died in 1556, there were forty Professed Fathers out of a total number of 1000 Jesuits.

Iñigo designed only one element in his Society as superior to the Father General in whom he had invested such wide-sweeping powers. This was the General Congregation: an international assembly of Jesuits, Professed Fathers all of them, chosen from the body of the members, and meeting in Rome with the Major Superiors of the Society. The General Congregation is the supreme legislative body of the Society, responsible only to the Pope, not to the Father General. Indeed, it can depose a Father General for just reasons. It elects every new Father General; and he is bound by the General Congregation's decrees. In fact, normally, his administration should consist in administering the Decrees agreed upon by the General Congregation in voting that may be by secret or open ballot. In spite of the legislative superiority of the General Congregation, usually the Congregations give very extensive powers to the Father General. Nevertheless, as the Congregation goes, so goes the whole Society.

In accepting candidates for a position in his Society, and in making sure that once accepted they would acquire the mind and spirit of the Society, Iñigo relied chiefly on the religious efficacy of his book, *Spiritual Exercises.* Candidates, once they were allowed to enter as trainees, were put through the *Exercises* for a period of time varying between eight and thirty days. It was then that they were made to understand the specific call of a Jesuit by meditating on the foundational Ignatian ideas of the Kingdom, the divine Leader, the Enemy Archangel, and the Warfare, as well as Jesuit ideals of obedience to Superiors and to the Pope.

Some commentators, having examined the *Exercises* and the Novitiate process as Ignatius set it up, have been thoroughly anachronistic, describing the entire process in terms of that modern horror, brainwashing. But, an attentive analysis of the process displays as its fundamental principle Ignatius's central doctrine about the supreme importance of the human will. Whatever he used by way of physical images, metaphors, symbols—even physical postures at prayer—all of it had one purpose: to attract the choice of that free human will.

In the Novitiate, there was no direct assault on the brain, or mind. Rather, Novitiate training was directly aimed at dissecting what has classically been known as the will of the candidate into its component parts, examining those parts, eliminating what was undesirable, purifying what was adaptable and useful, and cementing it all with the ideology of the Kingdom and the Leader and of supreme obedience.

Having gone through the *Exercises* to the satisfaction of the supervising Jesuit, provided he were still of a mind to become a member of the Order, the candidate became a Novice. All candidates then did the same Novitiate, spending two years in basic training. Each learned to pray, to discipline himself, to obey commands. He became acquainted with the world of the spirit and the details of Jesuit spirituality. All the while, his faults and general character were studied. At the end, all successful Novices took three simple vows of Poverty, Chastity, and Obedience. Some became Lay Brothers; others went on as Scholastics for further training as Professed or Spiritual Coadjutors; at the end of that training, they took Final Vows. The Professed among them added that fourth special vow.

The manpower of the Society was organized into "Provinces." At the death of Iñigo in 1556, there were twelve: Andalusia, Aragón, Brazil, Castile, Ethiopia, France, Lower Germany, Upper Germany, the Indies, Italy, Portugal, Sicily. Creation of a Province in a particular locality depended on the number of Jesuits working there, and the extent and importance of the work to be done.

Usually, several Provinces were grouped together on the basis of common cultural identity or geographical contiguity, and called an Assistancy. Thus, the Andalusia and Castile provinces belonged to the Spanish Assistancy. In time, as the Provinces multiplied, man power increased, and the Society was called on for one mission or another, there would be an English Assistancy, a French Assistancy, an American Assistancy, and so forth.

From the beginning, Iñigo had insisted that his Society differ from all Religious Orders that had hitherto been sanctioned by the papacy. His members were not obliged to sing the Divine Office together in choir, for example; they had no distinctive clothes as the older Orders, such as the Benedictines, Carmelites, and Dominicans, were obliged to wear. Nor were there any common bodily penances.

The governance of houses and Provinces was also distinctive. It was not in the hands of a "General Chapter" of Order Members elected by the votes of their Religious brothers. Instead, individual Superiors along the chain of command made the main decisions. Loyola's aim was to free his men from such obligations to an assembly, so that their mobility—Superiors to be able to command of their own initiative, and members to obey one man—for work on behalf of the Church to be at its maximum.

He also refused to have what many older Orders had: a corresponding Order of female Jesuits, on the model of Dominican nuns, Benedictine nuns, Carmelite nuns, Franciscan nuns. One of the more lightsome episodes in early Jesuit history involved the temporary admission by Iñigo of five women—they were the only women in 480 years to become members of the Jesuit order—to the profession of vows. Isabel Roser of Barcelona, one of Ignatius's first patronesses, forced his hand by persuading Pope Paul III to allow her and three female companions to take solemn vows of obedience in the Society in 1545. This good and saintly woman had helped Ignatius in his most difficult years; it was impossible not to satisfy, at least by a gesture, her desire to be part of what she had helped to found, once the Pope had consented. After much botheration and a public court case, all three were released from their vows by the Pope in 1546. In 1555, under extreme pressure from the Royal Court, Iñigo admitted Queen Juana of Castile, daughter of King Ferdinand of Aragón and Isabella of Castile, to the profession of simple vows in the Society. Known as Juana la Loca (Joanna the Madwoman) because of a perceived emotional instability in her, she likewise was released from those vows in a short time. Ignatius had made those exceptions for special reasons, but accurately calculated that none of these women finally would fit into his Society.

The main types of work undertaken by Jesuits were preaching the Gospel in non-Christian lands, education of youth, priestly ministries, writing, research, and special missions confided to them by the Pope. The houses in a Province were usually of six kinds: residences (for scholars, for writers, for local Superiors, for retired and sick members, or for Jesuits engaged in outside work); houses of studies (for young Jesuits); a novitiate (where applicants for entry into the Society in that Province were examined and prepared for entry). In addition, there were schools and colleges devoted to the education of lay people, and houses of Spiritual Retreat where lay people came for spiritual advice and devotional purposes.

The chain of command from each house, no matter how small or remote, all the way up to the Father General, was clearly ordered. Each house had a Father Superior. Over the Superiors of all houses in a Province, there was a Father Provincial. Over all the Provincials of an Assistancy, there was an Assistant who normally lived in Rome at the central Jesuit residence with the Father General. The powers and limitations on the powers of each Superior were clearly delineated. In turn, each Superior had a group of Consultors, advisory in character but whose consent was necessary in making certain decisions. A house Superior drew his Consultors from his subjects in the house; a Provincial from the Province; an Assistant from his Assistancy; and the General had his Assistants, besides others he might wish to employ.

Within each house of the Jesuits, there were a series of Minor Superior posts: One Minor Superior would be in charge of house finances; another, called the Spiritual Father, would remain at the disposal of the community for spiritual advice and direction; other Superiors would be prefect of the library, prefect of studies, and prefect of health; if necessary, there would be one supervising the farm. All these intrahouse Minor Superiors derived their authority through the Father Superior of the house.

In a Province or an entire Assistancy, when called for, there would be the "procurators," men designated to oversee particular needs of the Province or Assistancy.

From the General in Rome, there would come at certain times Visitors, appointees sent to examine how a Province or an Assistancy was doing spiritually, financially, scholastically, socially, or politically.

The ramification of Major and Minor Superiors in the Society was complex but never unwieldly. There were no redundant elements. Each functionary, no matter his grade, served in the working coagulation of the worldwide body.

Obedience and wise command by Superiors was greatly facilitated by what Iñigo called the "account of conscience." In essence, this was a private and confidential interview between Superior and subject—between, say, the Father Rector of a house and one of the members of the house; between the Father Provincial and a member of his Province; between a novice and his immediate Superior, the Novice Master; between the Father General and any member of the Society.

Ignatius did not require the "account of conscience" to be the same as a confession, although confessional secrecy could be invoked by anyone. He intended that the subject would speak frankly about his weaknesses and strengths, his hopes and wishes, and his practice of religious virtue; that the Superior, listening and talking with him, would be in the most informed position to decide what the subject could best do in the Society so that his Jesuit character would be developed in the service of the Church specific to the Society.

The "account of conscience" was designed by Ignatius to be the acme expression of the father-son relationship that he desired should exist between Jesuit Superior and Jesuit subject. It was a frankly paternal system he had in mind. It was his means of ensuring that the prime coagulant of his Society, obedience, would be exercised by the subject and used by the Superior with the maximum possible compassion on the Superior's part and the greatest contentment on the subject's part. Neither mere obedience of execution nor obedience of the will, but obedience of the understanding should be attained.

The "account of conscience" also made for a highly personal mode of government. For the Superior as such was to be approached and treated and obeyed as Christ. The regulation of a Jesuit's normal life was, to use the modern expression, one-on-one. No Jesuit had to face a "chapter" or assembly of his brothers, as in the older Orders, to answer for his actions and hear decisions about his fate. The individualism of the single Jesuit in his duties, his rights, his personal development, his career, was thus fomented. The corporate unity of such members was ensured by the systematic obedience that fomented that individualism. Thus was achieved the intimacy and characteristic in-Society life of the Jesuit.

The internal government and unity of mind and action within the Society was carried on by a regular, approved, and systematic practice of report-writing: Minor Superiors to Major Superiors; Provincial Superiors to Roman Assistants; the Assistants to the Father General; the Father General to the whole Society; the Provincials to their individual Province members. The reports concerned the merits and demerits of Order members, the conduct and progress of this or that project, the financial and spiritual condition of this or that section of the Society, or a work entrusted to the Society.

From the time of Iñigo himself, a lively flow of communication was also encouraged between individual Jesuits, for this helped what he called "the bond of wills, which is the mutual love and charity they [Jesuits] have for one another . . . by getting information and news from each other and . . ." much intercommunication on a par with "their following one same doctrine and by their being uniform in everything as far as possible."

Having laid out the mere structure Iñigo devised for his Society, however, it is evident that, as effective as it was, it was not enough to unify or coagulate all the parts into a true whole—an Ignatian whole. What did that—what united all the many Jesuits, divided as they were into four categories of Professed Fathers, Spiritual Coadjutors, Lay Brothers, and Scholastics; and distributed among many parts of the world and among many functions throughout the structure of the pryamid—were the twin bonds of authority and obedience.

These were really two aspects of the same thing. Obedience was central, together with the subordination it necessitated. Every Jesuit was subordinate to somebody.

"Individual Superiors," Ignatius wrote, "should have much authority over the subjects, and the General over the Superiors; and on the other hand, the Society much authority over the General." In that way, "all may have full power for good," and yet be under a certain control.

As to the vow of obedience, it "unites individuals with their Superiors, and the local Superiors among themselves and with the Provincials, and both the local Superiors and Provincials with the General." Thus, the "subordination of some to others is diligently preserved."

In Ignatius's eyes, his Society was to be distinguished by the quality of its members' obedience. "The other religious leaders may surpass us in fastings, all-night vigils of prayer, and other austerities in food and clothing. Our members must excel in true and perfect obedience, in the voluntary renunciation of private judgment."

This fundamental principle of Jesuit obedience was a difficult one to implement. In fact, Ignatius found it necessary to codify in a special document exactly what he meant by Jesuit Obedience. In 1553, prompted by serious difficulties among the Portuguese Jesuits, several of whom he had had to dismiss, Ignatius wrote his *Letter on Obedience;* in it, he is crystal-clear on what he calls "true obedience."

Every Superior was to be obeyed as the representative of Christ. Obeying this representative, you were obeying Christ; you were doing the will of Christ.

Your obedience could be one of three kinds. The lowest grade is "obedience in performance: You do what you are told, even though you may disagree with the whole idea, think the Superior is a fool,

or think you know what he should have told you to do. You obey;
but unwillingly. Ignatius's judgment on this grade of obedience:
"very imperfect."

There is a second grade of obedience. You may still think the
Superior is a fool and that you know what he should have commanded, but out of obedience to Christ, you decide that you will
willingly do what he says. The point here is that you are so intent
on pleasing Christ, that your obedience is transformed from unwilling to willing. In effect, you choose to wish the same as your
Superior. "At this stage," Ignatius comments, "there is already joy
in obedience."

There is yet one more, the highest grade of obedience. You do
not merely do what you are told without showing any overt opposition. Nor do you merely choose to will as your Superior wills, to
do willingly what he commands. Now you agree mentally with
your superior; you have obedience of the *intellect.* Uncondition-
ally, you think like your Superior. You submit your judgment to
that of your Superior "so far as only the surrendered will can sway
the intellect." This highest form is what Ignatius calls "blind obedience . . . the voluntary renunciation of private judgment."

The grades of obedience, obviously, are ranged according to the
degree one's will is engaged in that obedience—according, in other
words, to one's "willingness." Ignatius penned in a few short lines
his ideal of the obedient Jesuit:

> Altogether, I must not desire to belong to myself, but to my
> creator and to his representative. I must let myself be led and moved
> as a lump of wax lets itself be kneaded. I must be as a dead man's
> corpse without will or judgment; as a little crucifix which lets itself
> be moved without difficulty from one place to another; as a staff in
> the hand of an old man, to be placed where he wishes and where he
> can best make use of me. Thus, I must always be ready to hand, so
> that the Order may use me and apply me in the way that to him
> seems good. . . .

The phrase "as a dead man's corpse," in Latin *perinde ac cadaver,* gave rise to the phrase "corpselike obedience"; and,
wrongly interpreted, was used to deride, even vilify Jesuit obedience. It takes discernment to understand what Ignatius meant; and
what he meant was in itself revolutionary.

Up to his time, the vow of obedience in Religious Orders (as
well as the other two vows of poverty and chastity) were designed

to help the members of those Orders to achieve personal holiness and, ultimately, eternal salvation.

Jesuit obedience was intended primarily to fashion a closely knit and utterly disciplined body out of men widely separated around the world; men who were directed by plans and strategies devised by coordinated and interlocking groups of Superiors; men whose work was aimed primarily at the world around them.

The passivity and corpselike character of that obedience, the malleability of the wax, the adaptability of the old man's staff, and the helplessness of the little crucifix—all those were images that referred to one process only: the choice of objective and the means to reach that objective.

As Jesuits have proved beyond all cavil, Ignatian obedience has never affected the resourcefulness, the perennial activism, the ingenuity, the extensive use of personal accomplishments and gifts by members of the Order.

Indeed, Jesuit obedience, over time, became an almost fabled characteristic of members of the Order. Their friends and admirers praised it. Enemies parodied it, complaining that Jesuits were obliged by their vow of obedience to do anything the Superior commanded—assassinate a leader, blow up a building, steal, corrupt, lie, commit suicide. But this is sheer calumny. Ignatius explicitly excludes from obedience anything that smells remotely of sin. So also does the general law of Catholic morality.

It has always been this apparently glaring contrast between the "corpselike" obedience of men arranged in pyramidal tiers on the one hand, and on the other, their resourcefulness, ingenuity, and other individual gifts so evident in their activism that has puzzled the Society's enemies. There was nothing to see, they said. "Nothing," as the nineteenth-century French rationalist and self-styled atheist Edgar Quinet complained in exasperation, "but provincials, rectors, examiners, consultors, admonitors, procurators, prefects of spiritual things, prefects of health, prefects of the library, prefects of the refectory, attendants and stewards." How then could such an anodyne organization be so formidable an enemy for Rome's enemies, so valuable an asset for the papacy?

That entire pyramidal structure built on "corpselike obedience" must, it was concluded, be a front either for a lethal and power-hungry but hidden elite, plotting behind this banal facade to take over the liberties and assets of all free men, or for what one Protestant writer called "secret magic arts by which the Jesuits on certain days bring strange things to pass. . . ."

"Show me among all these the Christian soul!" Quinet complained. And though Quinet and many like him down the centuries would not see it, the real secret of Ignatius's Jesuits was precisely the Christian soul; its honing and refinement in every member of the Order. Though all the regulations were spelled out by Ignatius in the *Constitutions* and his other writings, it is only when you understand those regulations in the light of the divine and spiritual dimension of the classical Ignatian mold that you can even begin to understand Jesuitism: that peculiar combination of highly developed individualism in each member, coordinated within the framework of the organization's cohesion around the Superiors; cohesion made up of Jesuit obedience. Rigid inner discipline fathered internal unity. Individual freedom blessed by obedience gave that tremendous momentum which has never yet been equalled by another organization.

Many, including early Jesuits, have used military metaphors to describe the nature and mode of operation that Ignatius designed for his Society. The pyramidal chain of command, the division of Jesuits into grades, the idea of Jesuit obedience, these elements are reproduced certainly in military groups. The very name Ignatius used to designate his group, *Compañia de Jesus*, seemed to many to be derived from army structure.

Yet, in the mind of Ignatius it is certain that his idea of what the Society of Jesus and his Jesuits would be was modeled directly on what Catholic theology and philosophy have traditionally given as the divinely revealed condition of all created things— subordination within a foreordained order. Sin and Lucifer had violated that order of created things. The great enterprise of Christ was to restore that order. The term *Compañia*, which undoubtedly had a military usage behind it, was nevertheless meant in his mind to underline the fact that he and his associates were rather *compañeros*, companions, in such a great enterprise; and that, through their subordination, they were directly linked with Christ.

Once any one of the subordinating links was severed—either within the Society or between the Society and Christ's representative, the Roman Pontiff—the very nature of the Society of Jesus would be changed.

9 | THE CHARACTER OF THE SOCIETY

O nce Ignatius had died (on July 31, 1556), the force of his personality and the example of his presence disappeared with him. Now that he was gone, those of his original companions who survived him together with the more recent members found it necessary to formalize and regulate the life of each individual Jesuit with rules and prescribed practices. What Ignatius had maintained as *esprit de corps* had now to be ensured by other means. He had left his followers the written *Constitutions*, but these of themselves provided merely a juridical structure. The spirit of Ignatius had to be nourished so that the character of a Jesuit as Ignatius intended it to be should develop and flower.

How the companions arrived at a regularized way of life and a formulated outlook designed to perpetuate the Ignatian character of the Society can be seen over a period of time after his death. They achieved this through common decisions enacted into law, thus providing the framework of training and life-style by which each member of the Society would attain, foment, and perfect their religious companionship. Some of these rules and laws—for instance, a fixed span of time each day for obligatory prayer— Ignatius had once considered but refused to adopt. In all frankness, Ignatius never quite realized the impact he personally had. His very existence, even a letter of his, was usually more than sufficient to keep his Jesuits in line and enthusiastic. Certain standards of holiness and zeal had depended on the personal impact of Ignatius in life. His surviving companions found it necessary for the well-being of the Society to adopt what Ignatius had rejected.

By 1581, within twenty-five years of Ignatius's death, several new rules regulated the religious life-style of the then 5000 members of the Society. Every day, each member was obliged by rule to make one hour of private prayer ("meditation"). He attended only two types of community activity: meals in common, and the "Litanies" (or prayers to the Saints) at the end of the day.

By then also, the training of new recruits had been refined. Before, these novices had been trained in ordinary Jesuit residences. Now, a separate establishment, the novitiate, was set up, for in the first fifty years of the Society, recruitment only increased with each year, and problems of space arose correspondingly. In the beginning, the training period for new recruits varied; but later in the Society's history, the normal length of training for a Jesuit (except for those who entered already ordained) was fixed at seventeen years.

The golden age of Jesuitism began with the election of a 37-year-old Italian, Claudio Acquaviva, as Father General, in 1581. Over a period of thirty-four years in that position, Acquaviva put the finishing touches to the classical character of the Jesuits.

Besides being a first-class administrator, Acquaviva had that "undauntedness" praised so highly by Renaissance writers. In anyone not endowed with Acquaviva's gifts it would have been fecklessness, a stupid disregard for the forces he faced. But he was by nature a man of great personal power. His mind was, as a rule, more comprehensive than that of anyone he had to deal with, whether it was Pope or emperor or bishop. Told that the Pope, Gregory XIII, was surprised that he, the new Father General, was so young in age ("He's not yet forty") and so short a time in religious life (Acquaviva had been a Jesuit for only fourteen years), Acquaviva reportedly said, for the Pope's benefit, that he knew this was a flaw but he promised to work at remedying it "even while I am sleeping." You have to be very sure of yourself to send an answer like that back to the Supreme Pontiff.

His Jesuit colleagues recognized his power, and, even when gathered in General Congregation, followed his leadership. The same Congregation that elected him General also decreed that in normal circumstances, it was the General who would explain what was meant by the text of the *Constitutions*. This was surely a vote of confidence in Acquaviva.

During a span of thirty-four years, through the reign of eight Supreme Pontiffs, not all of them friendly to the Society, Acquaviva tightened the bonds of obedience and internal cohesion throughout the Order. He instituted a system of regular reports sent in by all Superiors to the General's office, reports about individual members, about their performance and deficiencies, and about the Society's undertakings. He further specified the character of the Jesuit by organizing a uniform curriculum of studies both for Jesuits in training and for schools and colleges where Jesuits taught others.[1]

By 1594, another idea of Acquaviva's was adopted as society law: St. Thomas Aquinas and Aristotle were to be the chief sources for Jesuit theology and philosophy. The aim of Jesuit education was to show how the data of science and inquiries into nature could be harmonized with the data of faith; full scope was to be given to positive inquiry. At the same time, Acquaviva caused the Jesuit character to be hammered out in greater and greater detail by promoting the use of Ignatius's *Spiritual Exercises* for non-Jesuits (clergy and laity). This effort in turn caused the Jesuits to become more proficient in Jesuitism, more knowledgeable about it. An entire tradition of in-Society devotional and piety practices resulted.

Acquaviva's tight rule and administrative strictness proved the truth of Ignatius's original perception: If you succeeded in truly coagulating thousands of men in their hearts and wills, if you provided them with discipline and training and perceptive directives for the place and type of their work, then there were few limits on what you could achieve. When he became Father General, his office was already provided with assistants who did all the spade work, leaving him free to take care of the larger issues. His success was phenomenal. In his time, membership in the Society went from a little over 5000 in 1581 to more than 13,000 in 1615. Between 1600 and 1615 alone, there was an increase of 5000. Jesuits worked all over Europe, in some African countries, and in the Middle East; they expanded to the Philippines, Indonesia, and Indochina; they had extensive missions in Canada, Paraguay, and Japan. Over all, they had 370 schools and colleges, 33 provinces, 120 Jesuit residences, and 550 communities.

There is another reason for Jesuits to look back on the age of Acquaviva as the Golden Age. Their most well-known saints: Robert Bellarmine, Peter Canisius, Aloysius Gonzaga, Peter Claver, Alfonzo Rodríguez; their preeminent scholars: Francisco Suarez, Molina, Lessius, Francisco de Toledo; their renowned spiritual writers: Alvarez De Paz, Luis de la Puente, Antoine le Gaudier; all flourished in those years. Those names may not be household names today, but they once were.

In systematic obedience, in the formularies that fashioned the Jesuit character, in the Jesuit idea of reconciling religious faith with science, in the development of molds for popular piety as well as in direct and submissive service of the Holy See, Claudio Acquaviva can be said to tower above every other one of the twenty-seven Fathers General who have governed the Society since the death of Ignatius in 1556. He was in a certain sense the second founder of Jesuitism.

With time, every country in Europe and the Americas felt the Jesuit influence as a staple in the outlook and parlance of their leaders and their people. Through the character of the Society envisioned by Ignatius and solidified by Acquaviva, Jesuits as individuals and the Society as an institution acquired a fixed identity in the eyes of the populations they served. With that slow, steady, uniform rhythm of training; with their never discontinued traditions of scholarship, zeal in teaching, molding of character by tried means, general orthodoxy of belief, and regularity of practices and life-styles, Jesuits not only formed priests and theologians, they formed and guided spiritually (and sometimes politically) princes and kings, king's wives and mistresses, political leaders of every rank, and, of course, bishops and Popes.

This character shone through the various roles Jesuits played, the diverse "coats" they wore: the Jesuit Teacher, the Jesuit Confessor, the Jesuit Professor, the Jesuit Preacher, the Jesuit Scientist, the Jesuit Theologian, the Jesuit Humanist, the Jesuit Missionary, the Jesuit Preacher, the Jesuit Writer, the Jesuit Emissary, the Jesuit Spiritual Guide and Director.[2] But despite the multiplicity of roles played and "coats" worn, the central quality of Jesuit character was specified by one particular trait: devotion to the person of Jesus—to the Jesus of Nazareth and of history, who lived, died, rose alive again from the dead; who now lives on forever as savior and God for all men; and who is represented on earth by one living man, the Bishop of Rome, the Pope of the Catholic Church.

This central quality of the Jesuit character derived directly from the personal spirituality and teaching of Ignatius.

Each Jesuit joined the Society under the conviction that he personally had been called by Jesus to become one of Jesus's associates; literally, to become one of the companions of Jesus. Hence, the Company of Jesus. And hence the strictly individualistic Jesuit note: The call was to me personally; and my response was to this person, Jesus. I said yes to Jesus. On the strength of that yes, I was admitted to his company and to the company of those already closely associated with him in his time-bound, space-bound campaign as savior. Those close associates were principally the Virgin Mary, the angels, the saints, and after them, my companions in the Society.

Everything about the Society was meant to further that call, and at the same time to differentiate it from other calls. From the call, say, of ordinary Christians to work out their salvation at ordinary human occupations; from the call of the monk or the nun to live in an enclosed monastery or convent; from the call of "a born-again Christian" in the twentieth century. It also differed from the call felt by many nowadays—including some Jesuits—who profess a belief only in what they call "the Jesus of faith," and declare that we are forever cut off from "the Jesus of History" and "of Nazareth." Ignatius and the whole of Jesuit tradition would have treated such a profession for what it is: a semantic wile to trivialize that person, Jesus.

This devotion was to that person. I had guaranteed communication with him.

The Jesus to whom I as a Jesuit responded with my personal affirmation and commitment could be heard and obeyed personally through hierarchies of Superiors, each speaking according to his own individual mandate with the voice and authority of that Jesus to whom I had responded. The first and highest Superior was Jesus's sole Vicar on earth, the Pope. The second ranking Superior was the whole Society incarnate in all the other conpanions, and vocal in the Society's General Congregation, whose decisions were final and binding on all Jesuits.

Then came the lower hierarchies of Superiors: the Father General of the whole society; the Father Provincial of my particular Province of the Society; the Father Rector of the house to which I was assigned; and each Minor Superior within that house, from the man assigned to give me carfare, to the Lay Brother in charge of my laundry. "I may be here merely to dole out sausages for your breakfast and penances at your dinner," said one irate Father Minister to an uppity Scholastic, "but, by God, you'll take both sausages and penances as from the hand of Christ!" In his annoyance, the Father Minister was ludicrously but accurately summing up the ultimate and specific character of a Jesuit.[3]

That ultimate specification of my being a Jesuit—my vowed devotion to the person, Jesus, and my association with his companions—introduced me to Jesuitism. To get as far as that, the mandate of Jesuitism told me, I had first to be called by, and find, Jesus in the Society.

The second mandate of Jesuitism told me that, together with those companions, I had to acquire as thoroughly as possible the most up-to-date, state-of-the-art means suited to my talents by which to convert the world, all the world around us, to the same posture of personal devotion for Jesus. I, like the other companions of Jesus, wanted all men and women to give Him this subjugation and tribute of their minds and their hearts and their wills—this glory that was both personal to Him, and public about Him. Nothing second-best or secondhand would do. Partial results were not enough; merely good results were not good enough. In Jesuitism, as the philosopher said, the best is the enemy of the good. Results had to be better than good; the glory for Jesus had to be greater than the ordinary glory with which men satisfy themselves and their vanity—and, indeed, greater than the glory others concede to Jesus. His *greater* glory was what I wanted as Jesuit, just as Father Ignatius taught us.

In the multiple and complicated machinery of this highly organized and concentrated group of men, in other words, the character of the Society was a corporate expression of the individual character of Iñigo, the one-time hidalgo converted by the grace of Jesus into Ignatius the Saint. For all the years he labored in those three rooms in the stone house opposite the Chapel of Maria della Strada in Rome, those powerful words burned in his mind and his will: "For the greater glory of God." Never before or after Ignatius does one come across the founder of an organization who so successfully incarnated his own personal character both in a group of men drawn from scores of different nations over a changing and changeful era of civilization, and in each member of that diverse and heterogeneous group.

Like that man they called "our father," each Jesuit strove and was urged on all his life to deepen his personal relationship with the living Jesus; to ascend by prayer and devotion interwoven with hard, unremitting work, so as to arrive at a burning love of him whom Jesuit poet Gerard Manley Hopkins hailed as "hero of Calvary . . . Christ, King, Head . . . Jesu, heart's delight, Jesu, maid's son . . . Christ of the Father compassionate. . . ."

Like Iñigo's in his mortal days, that love was highly personal. It was Jesus, the divine person in human flesh, who was to be loved. Each Jesuit would desire to kiss each one of Jesus's five sacred wounds in adoration; to console his heart of God-man; to atone personally for the insults and the rejections he and his love underwent at the hands of unbelieving, unfaithful men and women; to be identified completely with him as the savior of the world.

For this, it would not be sufficient merely to observe his law and behave like an obedient creature of God. That was the barest minimum condition of creaturehood. Regarding the vow of holy poverty, for example, it would not be good enough for me as a Jesuit merely to be indifferent and neutral in my feelings about the power and pleasures and possessions of this world to the point of not caring whether I have them or not. A Buddhist monk, a Hindu swami, a Muslim Sufi, many others too could and do attain such indifference. My Jesuit hope, as Hopkins wrote, "holds to Christ the mind's own mirror out / to take His lovely likeness more and more."[4] Ideally, for total identification with my loving Lord Jesus, I as a Jesuit would want to be exactly like he was. As a Jesuit, I would prefer—and, if given the option, would concretely choose—to be covered with opprobrium; to be blamed without having done anything to deserve the blame; to be rated as worthless and as a fool, as a nothing, in the eyes of the world, for one reason only: It was under this guise that my Lord Jesus saved me and all the men and women of the world from eternal damnation. "Despised and rejected . . . emptied out . . . ," was the way St. Paul expressed the ideal. Merely to be like him—that was my only motive. Why? Because I love him. Because he was like that. Love always makes you yearn to be like the one you love.

Even to be like him was not enough, however. As Jesuit, I wanted to nourish an ever-growing desire to find him everywhere.

> I kiss my hand
> To the stars, lonely, asunder
> Starlight, wafting him out of it . . .
> Kiss my hand to the dappled-with-damson west.
> Since, tho' he is under the world's splendor and wonder,
> His mystery must be instressed, stressed
> For I greet him the days I meet him,
> And bless when I understand.[5]

These were not lovely but isolated words, either for the Jesuit who wrote them, or for any Jesuit. They expressed the very core of his life no matter what his talents or his work. Each companion in the Society was burning and busy to find every trace of God and God's handiwork throughout the cosmos where he, God the Workman, the *deus faber* of the medieval mystics, was ever at work creating, preserving in existence, renewing. Like Ignatius, I as Jesuit wanted to ascend to a love of Jesus as God the Workman. It was not enough for me to be grateful for His gifts to me personally and to my world. Of course, I saw God at work in all things— vivifying, beautifying, freshening, and quickening human beings and all of nature into life-nourishing cycles. Throughout, I thus saw *God in all things.*

But more than that, I strove with my spirit and my whole being to arrive at the summit of love where I could see *all things in God;* see them rather as manifestations of His power and beauty, as rays of light descending from the sun, as streams of water leaping from the spring well. Nothing in creation would escape this viewpoint —the fearful symmetry of the tiger, the ridiculous curl to a piglet's tail, perfumes, colors, tastes, the audible silence settled on mountaintops, the patterns traced by a dancer, the cries of children at play, the songs of birds, the toils of the least insects.

Seeing all things in God, with their being and their beauty, the scales would fall away from my flesh-bound eyes. Quietly, unresistingly, coherently all would be absorbed in Him, for me; and the dust and ashes of their mortality and of my own mortality would be consumed in the stainless luster of His eternal existence and beauty.

If even that were the whole of it, however, I would still not be a Jesuit. I might, in fact, be a perfect Carthusian monk, harboring my personal and living association with Jesus in my solitude. But as a Jesuit I must, as Ignatius intended, be an activist sustained by contemplation—a contemplative dedicated to action. Because Ignatius presumed that every Jesuit would have this perpetual preoccupation with finding God in all things, he refused to prescribe a determined length of time each day to be spent in prayer. His Jesuits would be in constant day-long prayer, he said. He did require each one to pause twice a day, at midday and in the evening, in order to examine his conscience. He required each and all to tackle quite palpable and concrete objectives in their work: to be dedicated activists, doers, and at the same time to keep the inner eye steady, never allowing it to waver from the blissful solitude of that contemplation.

When all of this was fitted together in my daily life as a Jesuit, I would increasingly see that the same Jesus, as human and divine, divinizes and sanctifies all of life for his own ineffable glory. With all that was good in my cosmos, I would be absorbed in God through love of that glory.

As a consequence, the theme of each Jesuit's life was dedication to Christ's glory and a surrender of himself according to the favorite prayer of Ignatius:

> Take, Lord, and receive
> All my liberty, my memory, my intellect,
> And all my will—
> All that I have and possess.
> You gave all that to me.
> To you, Lord, I return it.
> All is yours.
> Dispose of it according to your will.
> Give me your love and grace.
> Those will be enough for me.

It was the very good fortune of the Society and its Jesuits that quite early in their long history, this Jesus-oriented character of Jesuit spirituality and outlook should receive a literally heaven-sent confirmation—in fact, it amounted to a heaven-commanded commission to the Jesuits. Only the infallible authority of the Catholic Church could guarantee the authenticity of that commission.

It came through a nun of the Visitation Order. Her name was Sister Margaret Mary Alacoque. At her convent of Paray-le-Monial, France, she was the recipient of special divine revelations that began about the year 1670. Hers is one of the relatively rare cases in the history of the Church when the teaching authority of Rome has confirmed the authenticity of revelations made to a single person.

The revelations centered around the love Jesus has for men and women, and the neglect with which that love was treated in return. In the revelations, as the symbol of that love, the physical heart of Jesus was always shown to the nun. Furthermore, in the revelations, God asked her to spread a particular devotion to Jesus under that symbol so that the faithful by their piety would make reparation for the neglect and ingratitude of the generality.

In one of those events that are more than mere chance, a young thirty-four-year-old Jesuit, Claude La Colombière, was posted as chaplain to Paray-le-Monial in 1675. He remained only eighteen months there, but in that time the nun communicated her revelations to him, and he had confirming revelations of his own. In the six years that remained to him before he died at the age of forty-one in 1681, he successfully conveyed the divine wishes to his

Superiors, and through them to the Roman authorities. Rome accepted the nun's revelations and Claude La Colombière's witness, and instituted an annual feast day for the Church Universal, with a special Mass and Liturgy of prayers for the use of priests on that day.

From these simple actions on the part of two obscure people,[6] there flowed a devotion and a fresh aspect of theological thinking about the person of Jesus and his loving redemption of men and women from the lethal effects of sin. From the moment that Rome accepted the authenticity of Alacoque's revelations in the late seventeenth century,[7] the Jesuits officially and enthusiastically accepted the commission to spread this devotion. No image was to take such a hold on the piety and devotion of the ordinary faithful as that which came everywhere to be called the Sacred Heart of Jesus; and no other single ascetic devotion came to be recognized as so typically Jesuit as devotion to that Sacred Heart, the perfect symbol of the Jesuit ideal in personal holiness.

The deliberate cultivation of this specifically Jesuit note—personal devotion to Jesus, especially under the image of his Sacred Heart—in the members of the Order, as they spread out all over the world and worked at the most diverse jobs with different talents, techniques and results, explains what many have noted with curiosity about Jesuits in the past: the high degree of individualism rampant among them and, at the same time, that strangely winsome and impressive commonality shrouding them as a group.

The key that unlocks the puzzle of this common identity throughout so much diversity was that specific note: the personal call to each of them by Jesus to serve to the very best of his personal abilities. And to do so within the ranks of companions each of whom had the same specific, dedicating call; and each of whom obeyed it through the gentle (and, at times, not so gentle) voices sounding down to him through the hierarchies of Major and Minor Superiors. From God's mouth to every Jesuit's ear. All were good soldiers of Christ, as St. Paul wrote. No matter where they were or what they were doing or how they functioned, all were companions in the Company of Jesus; and thus, all were participants in Jesus's glory.

This was so for the government adviser, for the papal emissary, and for the parish priest in the Andes mountains. It was true for the patient high school or college teacher, the resident pastor in a Dublin or a Bombay slum, the research scientist in an atomic laboratory. And this was true for every one of the "front-liners," the "toughies," those sitting it out alone in Katmandu as mute, isolated witnesses to Christ, or sharing the haphazard lives of refugees in a Thailand border camp.

Not all Jesuits were of equal rank in the service of Jesus's glory, at least in the eyes of men. But the knowledge of God's glory in all, and the coagulation of obedience held each one to his place, contented, active.

No matter what calumnies and slanders were uttered about them, no matter what failures individual Jesuits became for one reason or another, the reputation of the Society and the Jesuit character held firm. Even the anticlerical and, for most of his life, agnostic Voltaire had to admit it. The Jesuits who educated him at Clermont College "devoted every hour of the day to our education or to the fulfillment of their strict vows. As evidence, I appeal to the testimony of thousands who, like myself, were educated by them." Being educated by the Jesuits at Balley College, wrote poet and statesman Alphonse Lamartine, "I there learned what can be made of human beings, not by compulsion, but by encouragement. . . . They [the Jesuits] made religion and duty attractive, and inspired us with the love of God . . . they began by making me happy—they would soon have made me good. . . ." It was left to that master of diplomacy, Talleyrand, to sum up what both friend and foe appreciated about the Jesuits. "Whether you agree with them or not, everyone finds in the Jesuits that precious note of reason. They are reasonably severe, reasonably lax, reasonably moral, reasonably inimical, reasonable even in their devotion to the papacy. Always, that note of reason. *Toujours cette note de raison.*"

It is historically certain that in the first three hundred years of the Society's life story, the Jesuit ideal in character was genuinely developed and lived by thousands of Jesuits. We are speaking here of the genuineness of Jesuit obedience to the Pope, and the genuineness of the Jesuit ambition to resemble Jesus in all things, especially in the humiliations, wrongful accusations, gross miscarriage of justice, and misunderstandings that Jesus willingly underwent as an integral part of his sufferings in order to redeem mankind from sin and its consequence.

Two momentous events in particular convince one of this genuineness. The first event concerned Jesuit penetration of China in the seventeenth and eighteenth centuries. The second was the abolition of the Society by a Pope. Throughout, it is the Jesuit reaction of obedience and Christlike perseverance in humility and hope that are most striking. The Jesuits who bore the shock of those two events were heroes by anyone's definition.

By the late 1600s, Jesuit missionaries to China had made great progress toward converting the emperor of China together with powerful mandarins and nobles. They also had created a multi-million-member Church.

The Jesuit thrust into China with an enormous expenditure of men, equipment, and time was a deliberate move based on their assessment of the geopolitical forces dominant in the Far East. The Middle Kingdom, as China was called, set the pace of culture and power for Japan, South-East Asia, Indonesia, and Tibet. Respect for the Middle Kingdom in its culture and imperial power was so great, and already the "overseas Chinese" population throughout the Far East was so valued economically, that a conversion of Peking's imperial court and its subject peoples was bound to have a ripple effect throughout the area. Francis Xavier, the first Jesuit missionary in Japan, had understood this from his Japanese converts; but he died waiting for the opportunity to enter the Middle Kingdom. China was the prize. It remains the prize today.

One of the adaptations that the Jesuits made in the course of their efforts in China concerned the Chinese ceremonies or rites honoring the Emperor, Confucius, and one's forefathers. Previous missionaries had condemned these as pagan and irreconcilable with Christianity. The Jesuits thought otherwise. They maintained the rites in question were misunderstood by Westerners who did not understand the Chinese language accurately. The Jesuits analyzed the composition and meaning of every Chinese ideogram used by the Chinese to put in writing what they meant by "veneration" and "rites." The adversaries of the Jesuits never seem even to have understood the argument.

Still, the Jesuits fought on. From a study of the spoken and the written language they proved, they said, that these rites in no way venerated either the Emperor or Confucius or one's forefathers as divinities, but merely as the Emperor, as Confucius the Sage, and as one's forefathers! The Chinese would never accept Christianity if these rites were forbidden. Moreover, the Jesuits argued, if this element could be absorbed into Christianity, the whole of China would follow the Emperor into the Church.

For over fifty years, the controversy raged, with good and zealous, as well as egotistical and ignorant, men on both sides of the fence. Jesuit activity in Rome in favor of the rites was only equalled by counterplots and bureaucratic cabals against them in the papal court. Eventually, Pope Clement XI banned the rites in 1704 and 1715, as did Pope Benedict XIV in 1742.

The immediate and long-range result was the loss of that magnificent opportunity to open China up to national conversion to

Catholicism—and with it the whole Far East was lost to the Church. Bloody persecutions broke out and the Catholic Chinese population was decimated. Once the papal decisions were given, however, the Jesuits obeyed, some with mere obedience of execution, most with obedience of the will, some certainly with obedience of the understanding. Frequently, this obedience cost many their lives.

The papal decision was wrong, as it proved. Almost two centuries later, in 1939, Pope Pius XII authorized a Roman decree permitting Catholics to take part in those same rites. What was permissible in 1939 should have been declared permissible in 1704. But the "substantial" of obedience to the Pope was the deciding factor for the Jesuits. Obedience brought them no worldly gain—their enemies, at this taste of Jesuit blood, were only whetting their appetites for the kill which was to come later in the century. But for Jesuits it did ensure that "substantial." This was, in the final analysis, all that mattered: that the Society be true to its character, obedient to the Pope, patient when wrongly and unjustly blamed. Therefore, Christlike.

The second event that tested the Jesuit character was the formal suppression of the Society of Jesus by an official act of one Pope, Clement XIV. In the hindsight of history, today's historian has little difficulty in detaching the salient facts of the event from what still remains puzzling and problematic.

There is no doubt in anyone's mind that the impulse and determination to wipe the Society of Jesus off the face of the earth forever had very strong support and advocacy among powerful members of the papal court in Rome; but nevertheless, the immediate and irresistible anti-Jesuit thrust came directly and principally and, as it turned out, successfully from the nonclerical, lay enemies of the Jesuits.

The frontline attackers were the members of the royal Bourbon family—all Roman Catholics—who occupied the thrones of Spain, Portugal, France, Naples, and Sicily. The Halsburg throne of Austria went along with the Bourbons because of a fear of being excluded from royal marriage partners. The best such partners were Bourbons or Bourbon dependents. We may find it hard in our world of two huge superpowers, the USA and the USSR, to imagine that far-off world of the 1700s. But the fulcrum of world wealth and power and culture lay within that ancient heartland of Christian Europe—precisely those areas dominated by "the family of the brothers Bourbon."

It is likewise historically certain that the "family" had made the

"Compact," as it was called: an agreement between them to act in unison on matters that affected them all. For some reason, the existence of the Society of Jesus affected them all, they maintained, adversely. They had to get rid of the Society. The economic or financial gains to "the family" from a wholesale suppression of the Society were negligible. Likewise, there was no substantial political gain from such a suppression. We are left with the desired triumph of some ideology as the motivating factor behind "the family's" determination to undo the Jesuits.

The reason for the lethal resolve of these enemies is puzzling, unless we admit as reason the existence of some deep enmity against the Roman Catholic Church and its chief defender and bulwark at that time—the Society of Jesus. The enmity could only be ideological.

The last element in what still remains a historical puzzle is provided by European Freemasonry in the context of the European Enlightenment of the 1700s. In those days, the most powerful statesmen necessarily belonged to the Lodge. It is certain that the chief advisers to the Bourbon princes were ardent members of the Lodge. The Marquis de Pombal, royal adviser in Portugal; the Count de Aranda, occupying the same position in Spain; Minister de Tillot and the Duc de Choiseul in France; Prince von Kaunitz and Gerard von Swieten at the Habsburg court of Maria Theresa of Austria. These are names that no longer mean anything to us moderns, but they were and still are held in honor on Masonic membership lists. Each one of those men held a position of trust and confidentiality in government, and each one avowedly desired the death of the Society. They saw in the Jesuits "the sworn enemies of Freemasonry," the "most cunning enemies of tolerance," and "the worst corruptors of freedom." Hatred of the Jesuits was intense and, as far as words go, noble: "I know the pains they [the Jesuits] have taken," Choiseul wrote to Joseph of Austria, "to spread darkness over the surface of the earth, and to dominate and confuse Europe from Cape Finisterre to the North Sea."

The greatest note of pathos in those last years of the pre-Suppression Society is struck by Jesuits themselves: Clearly, from letters and documents of the time, you know they knew who was endeavoring to kill them off.

There is no doubt that the papacy saw in European Freemasonry a mortal enemy, and for very good reason. By 1735, if not earlier, the main European Lodges were avowedly enemies of papal centralized jurisdiction and Roman Catholic dogmatic teaching. The general aims of the Lodge as such from the second two-thirds of the eighteenth century onward were founded on several premises unacceptable to Catholicism: Jesus was not God; there was no heaven or hell; there was no Trinity of divine Persons—just the Great Architect of the Cosmos, he being part of that cosmos; human beings were perfectible during their lives on this earth. What ruined human culture and perverted civilization was the claimed authority of the Roman Church.

This transformation of Freemasonry from being originally a Christian association of believers into a body of men resolutely opposed to the ancient faith of Europe was chiefly effected by the new onrush of scientific discoveries. In this "Century of Lights," men concluded that human intelligence was infallible, that revelation was no longer needed, that only uninhibited human inquiry and research were necessary for human happiness.

An entire galaxy of brilliant thinkers and skillful writers arose voicing this new attitude—La Mettrie, Diderot, d'Alembert, Montesquieu, Helvetius, la Chalotais, Voltaire, Baron d'Holbach. The Enlightenment now swept through socialite salons, royal meetings, political caucuses, and university assemblies. The Roman Church, the Roman Pope, and the Society of Jesus were branded from the beginning as the three big obstacles to the precious Enlightenment.

For this reason, Clement XII (1730–1740) condemned Freemasonry as incompatible with Catholicism and penalized with excommunication all Catholics who joined the Lodges. That condemnation has been upheld repeatedly by Rome up to as recently as early spring of 1984. It would be ridiculous for anyone to deny that the Masonic zeal of those in close contact with the Bourbon princes as advisers did not aim at crippling the papacy by removing the papacy's strongest weapon, the Society of Jesus.

The ideological reason, therefore, for getting rid of the Jesuits was present. There is no need to suppose that a formal plot was hatched and conspirators vowed secretly to undo the Society of Jesus. All those leaders of the Enlightenment were members of the Lodge, as well as prominent members of the Establishment in its political, financial, literary, and social circles. Whether they gathered in the Paris Lodge called "At the Nine Sisters" or the Madrid Lodge called "Crossed Swords," or at state dinners or financial meetings, all were of one mind as "Brothers of the Pyramid." Brother Pombal, Brother Choiseul, Brother Kaunitz all sent messages to one another and to the other brothers about the need to tackle the papacy through the Jesuits.

The Jesuits were too aware of what was going on not to smell their approaching death in the high winds that had already started blowing against their Institute. That the Jesuits of this time were conscious of the lethal danger that faced them is clear from the official declaration of their leaders, made when they met in Rome between May 9 and June 18, 1758: "If, God permitting it because of his hidden designs which we could do nothing else but adore, we are to become the butt of adversity, the Lord will not abandon those who remain attached and united to him; and as long as the Society is able to go to him with an open soul and a sincere heart, no other source of strength will be necessary for it."

You can hear through those words the voice of the old Society of Jesus echoing the basic themes of Jesuitism: submission and obedience; the acceptance of blame and disgrace; the personal relationship between the Society and God.

Pombal in Portugal started the roll of destruction. Between 1759 and 1761, all Jesuits in Portugal and its overseas dominions were arrested, transported by royal navy ships, and deposited on the shores of the papal states in Italy. All Jesuit property—houses, churches, colleges—was confiscated.

It was now France's turn. One grave error of tactical judgment on the part of the Jesuits gave their watchful enemies there the chance they had been looking for—the handling of the LaValette case.

Father LaValette was Superior of the Jesuit mission on the island of Martinique. To secure the financing he needed for the mission, LaValette had used commercial credit in order to undertake extensive trading enterprises. In so doing, LaValette broke the explicit rules of the Society. As late as 1751, Jesuit Superiors had reiterated the prohibition against Jesuits' engaging in any business as principals or partners. Ignatius himself had laid down such a prohibition.

The day came when he could not pay the credit companies, in particular one trading firm at Marseilles whose damages against him amounted to two and a half million francs. The French Provincial Superior and the Father General, Lorenzo Ricci, refused to pay LaValette's debts, claiming he had violated the Society's rules and therefore that the Society was not liable.

It was a mistaken tactic. The firm took the Society to court claiming it was responsible. The court ruled in favor of the plaintiff firm. The Jesuits appealed, as was their right, to the French *Parlement*.

That was the second grave error. The *Parlement* not only ruled against the Society in the LaValette case; it recommended and decided on August 6, 1762, that the Society should be expelled from France as incompatible with the welfare of the State. Obviously, more than the LaValette debt weighted that decision. The consent of King Louis XV was obtained—chiefly, it is said, because his mistress, Madame Marquise de Pompadour, had been refused Holy Communion by King Louis XI's Jesuit confessor, Father Perusseau, and she never forgot that slight to her honor. It was Pompadour who overcame Louis's scruples about signing the decree. *Parlement*'s decree became law. The Jesuits closed all their schools, houses, and churches. Some of them remained clandestinely in France. Others went into exile.

Barely six years later, in one single night between April 2 and April 3 of 1767, all houses, colleges, residences, and churches belonging to the Jesuits throughout Spain and the Spanish dominions in America were invaded by royal Spanish troops. About 6000 Jesuits were arrested, packed like herrings into the holds of Spanish men-of-war, and transported to the papal states in Italy, where they were unceremoniously dumped on the shores whether alive, dying, or already dead. The entire Spanish operation, which required over fourteen months' planning, was a triumph of bureaucratic secrecy and military precision.

Shortly afterward, the Bourbon kingdoms of Naples and Parma followed suit, and, still later, Austria. All expelled the Jesuits, and confiscated their possessions. It remained now only to have the Society liquidated by the papacy.

When a papal conclave of cardinals assembled in 1769 to elect a new Pope, "the family" of Bourbons made it clear that they would accept as Pope only someone who would guarantee to liquidate the Jesuits. Cardinal Lorenzo Ganganelli gave his assurances on this point to the ambassadors from the Royal Courts of their Majesties. He was elected as Pope Clement XIV.

Direct pressure was now brought on Pope Clement XIV to fulfill the promise he had made as a condition for receiving the support of the Bourbon princes in his election. He finally consented, closing the Society's seminary in Rome in 1772, then all Jesuit houses and churches in the papal states, and finally issuing a papal document entitled *Dominus ac Redemptor* on July 21, 1773, that completely suppressed the Society of Jesus. "The Society of Jesus is no longer in the position to produce those rich fruits and remarkable advantages for the sake of which it was instituted. . . ." It is "quite impossible to maintain a true and lasting peace within the Church as long as this Order exists. . . . We hereby suppress the Society of Jesus. . . ."

There could have been no question about obeying the papal edict. Mere obedience of execution was imposed by force of arms. But Jesuits did practice obedience of the will. They accepted, true even in this extreme to the character of their Society, the suppression; they did not pretend still to be an Order of men called the Society of Jesus. The Jesuits in Europe who were disbanded now grouped themselves into newly named nuclei—the Society of the Sacred Heart of Jesus, the Fathers of the Faith, the Society of the Faith of Jesus, and such. The ex-Jesuits of Spain and Portugal had their own groupings.

Two rulers, Catherine of Russia and Frederick of Prussia, refused to promulgate the Pope's decree. Legally, therefore, and canonically, the Order was not suppressed in either territory. The Jesuits there gathered together and formed a nucleus, and elected a temporary Vicar-General, Lithuanian Father Stanislaw Czerniewicz. When Pope Clement XIV died one year after suppressing the Society,[8] Czerniewicz wrote to his successor, Pius VI, asking His Holiness what he should do.

Pius VI was enigmatic but strangely encouraging, saying to Czerniewicz that he hoped "the result of your prayers, as I foresee and you desire, may be a happy one." It was a clear reference to a near-future restoration of the Society.

The Jesuits in Russia held five interim Congregations between 1782 and 1805. Each time they elected a new Vicar-General, he was authorized by the Congregation to act as Superior until the Society of Jesus was "universally restored." The restoration was not long in coming. In 1801, Pius VII made the then Vicar-General, Lithuanian Franciszek Kareu, into Father General of the Jesuits. Under the next General-in-exile, Polish Tadeusz Brzozowski, two official Provinces, Russia and Italy, were created. Finally, on August 7, 1814, Pope Pius VII formally restored the Society of Jesus in the universal Church. Father Tadeusz Brzozowski was the Father General; as he himself could not leave Russian territory, he was represented in Rome by a Vicar-General, Mariano Petrucci.

What followed over the next fifty years was a near-resurrection of the Society as it once was. All the elements of the presuppression Society were once more introduced: the Ignatian *Constitutions*; the set of common rules; the use of formal novitiates and separate training houses for the Scholastics; the practice and use of the *Spiritual Exercises*; the official backing for that principal Jesuit devotion and piety, the Sacred Heart of Jesus; the use of a refurbished form of the old *Ratio Studiorum*. Jesuit colleges and universities were opened. Membership in the Society rose smoothly from some hundreds in 1814, to a couple of thousand by 1830, to over 5200 in 1850, to nearly 12,000 by 1880.

The traditional character of the Society was set once again, as it were, in concrete by the Father General who governed between 1853 and 1887, Belgian Pieter Beckx. Beckx regarded one action of his as the highlight and focal point of his thirty-one years of governance of the Society. On June 9, 1872, he solemnly consecrated the whole Society as a body to the Sacred Heart of Jesus. This gave a fresh impetus to the classical Jesuit character with its note of personal attachment to Jesus. Throughout the Provinces, Jesuits started a series of organizations for lay people dedicated to this Jesuit devotion; there was a continual stream of studies on the subject. Beckx and succeeding Generals into the twentieth century kept emphasizing the centrality of this devotion for Jesuits. Long after he had resigned for health reasons—he did so in 1884, but lived for another eight years, to the ripe old age of ninety-seven— Beckx recalled that day of consecration in the Church of the Gesù in Rome.

With the renewal of this precious Jesuit character, there inevitably came an emphasis on Roman Catholic orthodoxy of doctrine. That, together with fidelity to the Pope, was the chief concern of Superiors. The most important lesson learned at the suppression was that without solid footholds in the Holy See, no amount of faithful service could save the Society from trouble. The Bourbons had been the Society's enemies, and the Freemasons. But some of its bitterest enemies had been among secular-minded Roman bureaucrats; and, after all, it was a Pope who had actually decided the Society was a danger to the papacy and the Holy See itself.

Orthodoxy, therefore, was the key to a greater security. Not merely the classical orthodoxy of St. Thomas Aquinas, but the developed orthodoxy of papal Romanism. Everything that could be done officially and by Superiors was done to this end. The theology and philosophy of St. Thomas was proclaimed as the official teaching of the Society. But above all, the watchword throughout all the Society was a reemphasis on the Society as the docile and efficient instrument of the papacy and the Holy See.

Members of the Society were to be the outstanding "ultramontanes." This should be their hallmark and glory as individuals, and as a group. This thoroughgoing Romanism put the finishing touches to the restored character of the Society.

The circumstances of the nineteenth century were tailor-made to allow the final emphasis, the ultimate grace note, of Romanism to be added to the Society's character. It was in 1869 that the First Vatican Council defined the infallibility of the Pope and brought out in the sharpest relief as a datum of faith that the Vicar of Christ on earth was to be perpetually identified by association with a single geographical place—Rome. Thoroughgoing Romanism included this "Roman fact," as it was called, allied to the infallibility of the Pope and the Pope's primacy—superiority— over every other bishop as well as over all the bishops together. Of this Roman hierarchic structure the Jesuits became the champions.

The most formidable enemies this emphasized Romanism faced in the nineteenth century were theologians and philosophers who called themselves Modernists. At heart, their fundamental principle was the perpetual need to modernize the Church and the Church's message. Otherwise, how could the Church be understood and accepted? A bridge was needed, they said, between the age-old Gospel and the ever-changing mind and culture of men and women. That idea was not in itself alien either to Church or to Jesuits. But Modernists drove a coach-and-four across that fragile bridge. Adaptation, in their mouths and under their pens, meant renunciation of basic doctrines. It meant that the Church could deny in one age what it had affirmed in a previous age as essential dogma. It meant, in sum, that there was no permanent datum of faith, no dogma, no fixed belief. For the data of science could and should be allowed to dictate what men and women should believe. Modernism was and still is the total harnessing of religious belief and practice to the cultural modes and vagaries of civilization in any given epoch.

It was a familiar arrow pointed straight at the heart of Romanism and the hierarchic Church. For the Modernist, the Church of Christ was no permanently established hierarchic institution centered on the Bishop of Rome as Supreme Pastor. That Church really was a much more "spiritual" thing, an assemblage of individual communities of believers in whom the spirit of Christ continually evolved fresh and new forms of worship, belief, and morality. Modernism and Catholicism could not possibly live in the same religious house. The papalist mind of Roman Jesuit Superiors, therefore, would not tolerate the slightest Modernist deviation that could be plainly detected in their Jesuits. Even the merest detectable whiff of Modernism in a Jesuit professor or writer was sufficient to guarantee his removal.

You must stress the word *detectable*, however; because, while this severe official stand on Modernism was preserved until the middle of the twentieth century, the Modernist mind among Jesuits and churchmen didn't die. It merely made itself undetectable. It went underground and developed methods and stratagems for its self-perpetuation.

For, around this time, in view of the rising importance of the "social question," the growing impact of Marxistic Communism, and the huge leap of the natural sciences, the Society decided to specialize its young men in the new branches of knowledge such as physics, chemistry, paleontology, anthropology, physiology, Assyriology, Oriental religions, Egyptology, sociology, and biology. Insensibly, there started emerging throughout the society a never-vocalized but quite well-knit brotherhood of highly trained academic specialists. They rarely if ever voiced their true feelings and ideas; but they found it increasingly difficult to reconcile the data of their scientific and scholarly training with the traditional doctrines and morality propounded by the Roman Catholic Church and officially defended by the Society. In their work, they consorted with non-Jesuit, non-Catholic scholars engaged in studies similar to theirs, read their results, and developed an understanding for their point of view, which almost without exception was anti-Catholic and theologically Modernist.

Two branches of secular science had an especially deep impact on Jesuit theological scholarship: archeological, linguistic, and historical research into the Near East, the cradle of Christianity; and modern researches into anthropology and paleontology. The latent Modernist mind dictated that a reconciliation should be sought between the data of these sciences and traditional data of the Christian Revelation. *Reconciliation* was the magic word, the Open-Sesame formula. Of course, it was a fatal error of procedural judgment. For *reconciliation* meant "interpreting" the data of Revelation so as to leave the data of science intact. Those data, after all, had been "proven" scientifically.

It never struck and has yet never entered the Modernist mind that the only sure procedure was to search in the treasurehouse of Christian tradition for what the Revelation of Christ had to say about those "proven" data. Thus, Modernism never conceived of a Christian anthropology, a Christian sociology. Modernists end up seeking the meaning of Revelation in those "proven" data of science, not realizing that *proven* as a working term in science often means "taken as hypothesis" until a new set of empirical data disprove what was previously "proven." Revelation's data are not of this nature.

While the Modernist current flowed silently and steadily onward to meet its day of destiny, an official facade was preserved and fomented both in the Roman Catholic Church and in the Society of Jesus. There was thus one last and rather long period of apparent uniformity and of external growth in membership of the Society and the Church.

It was during the twenty-seven-year Generalate of Father Wlo-dzimierz Ledóchowski (1915–1944) that the traditional character of the Society received the firmest stamp and clearest definition since the Generalate of Claudio Acquaviva in the sixteenth and seventeenth centuries. One might even say that Ledóchowski was a man of as much personal power as Claudio Acquaviva had been. Like Acquaviva, Ledóchowski insisted on fidelity to the structure of Jesuit obedience, was an almost merciless disciplinarian, and maintained a stream of instructions flowing out to the whole Society about every detail of Jesuit life and Ignatian ideals. He knew exactly what Jesuits should be according to the Society's *Constitutions* and traditions; and under the strong hands of two quite authoritarian Popes, Pius XI and Pius XII, he reestablished the close ties that had once linked papacy and Jesuit Generalate. Ledóchowski, in fact, gave renewed meaning to that old Roman nickname of the Jesuit Father General, "the Black Pope." Just as Pius XII can be described as the last of the great Roman Popes, so Ledóchowski can be called the last of the great Roman Generals of the Jesuits.

There seemed, indeed, during those years of Ledóchowski, Pope Pius XI, and Pius XII, no real limit to what both Jesuitism and overall Roman Catholicism could achieve. Even—especially, we should say—in the afterglow of Ledóchowski's long reign and into the Generalate of his successor, Belgian Jean-Baptiste Janssens, the magic power of momentum seemed to continue. The same General Congregation, or meeting of Jesuit leaders, that elected Janssens in 1946 also formally consecrated the Society to the Immaculate Heart of Mary—a devotion that sprang up as a parallel to the central Catholic devotion to the Sacred Heart of Jesus. That Congregation also affirmed its adhesion to the dogma of the Assumption of the Virgin Mary, as Pope Pius XII was to define it four years later. Mary, in Catholic belief, died, but her body never underwent the corruption of the grave. Instead, it was "assumed," taken up into the transforming glory of her divine son. The womb that conceived God as man, the breasts that fed him, the hands that held him, the body that labored for him should never be desecrated by the worms and the rats.

The traditional Jesuit character with its precious dual relationship to Jesus and to his Vicar, the Pope, seemed never to have been so vibrant, never so flourishing. It all culminated in that last era of Roman Catholic spiritual and religious prosperity of the immediate post—World War II period.

It was a time, too, when American Catholicism in particular seemed to come of age. While recruitment was going up and up and up worldwide, both in the Society and in other Religious Orders, Jesuit membership grew from 17,000 around 1917, to more than 35,000 in 1964, and more than 36,000 in 1965. American Roman Catholics went from 17 million in 1917, to 37 million by 1945, to 47 million by 1954. Along with their numbers, the prestige and power of Roman Catholics in America increased enormously. Even that indigenous American bigotry—anti-Catholicism—took a severe beating. Roman Catholics could attain the White House. Their Legion of Decency could affect the film industry. Their municipal and state vote was courted. As Will Herberg wrote, the population of the United States was now to be broken down into "Catholic, Protestant, and Jews." Herberg did add in "and some others"; but in that group he did not include Modernists, Catholic and Protestant or Jewish. They were not yet a "fact" in the American self-consciousness.

Nor was Modernism a fact in the general consciousness of the Jesuits during the fifties and sixties. No one seemed to notice that a strange, radical change was taking place in Jesuitism. Nevertheless, that specific note on the part of individual Jesuits of personal attachment to Jesus was being undermined silently, unobtrusively. One of the Society's greatest Father Generals emphasized that specific note in a warning fashion.

"We can measure the extent to which we are faithful to the call of Our Lord Jesus to his Society," Father General Ledóchowski wrote in one of his letters to the whole Society, "by the importance that devotion to the Sacred Heart of Jesus holds in each one of us and in the Society as a Religious Order."

Without here delving into the causes that did away with that importance of devotion to the Sacred Heart of Jesus as the centerpiece of the Jesuit character, we can get a very poignant idea of how profoundly that classical character of the Jesuit had changed at the beginning of the seventies, by reading the words of Father General Pedro Arrupe in 1972.

As that year was the centenary of Father General Beckx's consecration of the whole Society to the Sacred Heart of Jesus, Arrupe planned a centenary celebration. But when he broached the subject by word of mouth and in letters with the other Superiors and leading Jesuits in Rome and elsewhere, he found—as surely he must already have realized at least dimly—that Jesuits on the whole and in their majority had simply lost interest in devotion to the Sacred Heart of Jesus. Some regarded it as childish, primitive, unsophisticated, repellant, unworthy of a modern mind. Some found it even gross and sensuous. Some others had decided that the modern mind could not accept such a devotion, though they themselves saw some merit in it for very simple people—little children, peasants, and such. Still others alleged theological difficulties. Few saw any connection between this devotion and the Ignatian character of the Jesuits. In sum, Arrupe could not find a commonly shared persuasion any longer among his Jesuits that the Society had a divine commission from Christ through Saint Margaret Mary Alacoque and the Holy See to propagate this devotion.

Nonetheless, Arrupe went ahead with his plans. His letter to the whole Society about the centenary celebrations would make the angels weep.

Arrupe began by admitting that "conflicting opinons [are] found in the Society today regarding this devotion." He spoke of the "indifference" of some, the "subconscious aversion" of others, the "distaste, even repugnance" of still others, concerning this devotion. Some, he added, "prefer to maintain a respectful silence and await developments." His letter, therefore, consisted of an endeavor to solve "the ascetic, pastoral, and apostolic problems which the devotion to the Sacred Heart presents today," although he found it "difficult to treat of." He did not say why he found it difficult.

The letter, in digest, recommended that Jesuits develop "a broad understanding" of the devotion, that they put aside "one-sided exaggerations or purely emotional reactions," and in effect allow every Jesuit to do as he pleased.

In sum, devotion to the Sacred Heart of Jesus as an official devotion of the Society was as dead as a doornail. But Arrupe, in his own words, felt a "personal obligation" to speak out on the subject. He might have added that the then Pope, Paul VI, had sent the Society a letter in May 1965, fully seven years before, precisely alerting Arrupe to the need to revivify this devotion in the Society. For even then, in the Church at large as well as in the Society, this devotion was suffering the same fate as other practices of piety during the sixties.

One persistent trait of Pedro Arrupe's is revealed in his communications with Jesuits about devotion to the Sacred Heart: the apparent deference he always paid to the likes and dislikes, antipathies and deviations of the men placed in his charge as Jesuit General. His letters and instructions about almost everything were merely invitations to think as he did. He never seemed able to command, as every General before him had done. He had power, but was unwilling to take it in hand, to use it in order to correct deviations either from Roman orthodoxy or from what was traditionally Jesuit.

It was a fatal flaw in his character and a summary mistake in wielding Jesuit authority. In all such cases, Arrupe bowed to the majoritarian opinion. He carried this defect to the point of religious suicide when any issue arose involving the highest ranking Superior in the Society, the General Congregation of Jesuit leaders that meets periodically in Rome. I say to "the point of suicide," because during Arrupe's Generalate, the General Congregation did just that to the classical Jesuitism of the Society; and Arrupe, in line with the mood of his letter about devotion to the Sacred Heart of Jesus, declared himself as merely a servant of that highest ranking Superior in that self-destructive course of action adopted by the General Congregation.

10 | THE HIGHEST RANKING SUPERIOR

T
he world that has witnessed the ups and downs of Jesuitism for the last four and a half centuries has never, until
recently, been aware of the capital role played by the
General Congregations of the Society of Jesus—the formal gatherings of Jesuit Superiors from all the Provinces of the world in
Rome with the Jesuit Father General and his Assistants and aides.
General Congregations take place relatively infrequently—there
have been only 33 in 445 years.[1] But when any General Congregation is in Session it is, by Ignatius's own design, superior to every
individual Jesuit in the Society, including the Father General.

Only in this era of mass media and instant communication has
it become even vaguely apparent to the world at large that a General Congregation of the Society of Jesus can have a mind of its
own, distinct from the minds of many individual Jesuits, and from
the mind of the reigning Pope. Yet even with mass media to look
over its shoulder, the workings of any General Congregation are
guarded from close public scrutiny—indeed from any scrutiny at
all.

In drawing up the *Constitutions* of his Society, Ignatius devoted
seven full chapters to the General Congregation: its composition,
its manner and mode of meeting, its method of decision-making,
its full legislative powers. He never described the General Congregation as a Superior. Superiors, in his mind, were all men. But the

powers he conferred on the General Congregation ranked it above all the men who were Superiors in his Society. Only the Pope outranked the General Congregation in authority.

When it is time to summon a General Congregation—when a new Father General must be elected or some change has to be made that requires advice from all quarters of the Society, for example—the Father General or Vicar-General of the society asks permission from the Pope for the assembly. Once permission is granted, preparations begin.

Well in advance of the start of a Congregation, proposals—they are called *postulata*—are requested by the Roman Superiors from the various Provinces, Missions, and Vice-Provinces of the Society. The Father General and his staff in Rome are charged with sifting all proposals. The *postulata* reflect the mind of the Society at large and provide the materials for discussion and decision and formal Decree at the actual Congregation.

A major part of the preparation consists of putting order into the *postulata*—there is always overlapping and repetition; and there are sometimes what appear to be very minor, even footling issues, impractical or pointless *postulata*. At GC1, held after Ignatius's death, the Delegates solemnly debated the question of wearing a beard. Although now this issue may appear as inconsequential as the issue of flat tombstones versus upright tombstones for war veterans decided by a voice vote in the U.S. House of Representatives on May 20, 1985, it had a point: Should Jesuits imitate Ignatius, who had worn a beard all his life? They decided against the proposal.

One of the most important reasons to call for a General Congregation is to elect a new Father General. If a Congregation is convened for that purpose, much of the preassembly preparation consists of collecting data, *informationes*, about possible candidates. As with the cardinal-electors who choose one of their own number to be Pope at a papal conclave, and who enter each conclave with certain *papabili*, "popable" ones, clearly in mind, so it is the custom among higher Superiors in the Society to have ready a restricted list of possible candidates for the post of Father General. This list is a matter of the greatest confidentiality. It is indicative of the freedom exercised by the Delegates that only two Fathers General—Ignatius himself in 1541, and the twelfth Father General, Belgian Charles de Noyelle, in 1682—were elected by a unanimous vote.

The Jesuits who assemble in Rome with the Father General for the General Congregation are elected as Delegates by their fellow Jesuits in their own home Provinces. Until quite recently, they had to be Professed Jesuits (men who in addition to the three vows of poverty, celibacy, and obedience, have taken the fourth vow of special obedience to the Pope). Originally, only Provinces had a right to elect and send Delegates. Missions and Vice-Provinces acquired that right only in 1946 at GC29.

On assembling for the General Congregation, the Delegates hear from the Father General about the condition of the Society, its successes, its failures, its difficulties; and they survey the *postulata.* By voting—everything in a General Congregation is decided by vote—they select certain procedures in order to facilitate their discussions. They might create commissions, subcommissions, or special study groups, each one delegated to prepare the materials for common discussions, take note of actual discussions, produce new enlarged proposals, and finally produce the final text of the Decrees on which the Congregation will vote definitively. Only in GC30 was the voting performed by means of an "electric" board displayed to all the Delegates, as each one used a "yes" or "no" button to register his vote.

Soon after the Congregation ends, all the Decrees that have been adopted by vote are published as the *Acta* of that particular Congregation.

What form should discussion take between the Delegates once they are assembled in General Congregation? Fortunately, the mind of Ignatius is known in this matter. The model for him had been provided by the first lengthy debate he and his initial eight companions carried on among themselves in the spring and early summer of 1538, as they prepared to present their project for the formation of the Society to Pope Paul III. They lived together in an abandoned house near the Ponte Sisto in Rome, and in those months of solitude and prayer they hammered out between them the "platform" or basic principles of the Society.

They were all very different characters, and at first their debates about the "platform" were disorderly—"democratic," in that sense—and somewhat romanticizing. It quickly became obvious to them that they must decide on a discipline. First, they established a list of questions they should answer about their intentions and aspirations. "Throughout the day," as some of them described it later in writing, "we were accustomed to ponder and meditate on these [questions] and to prayerfully search into them." At night, they told each other what they had thought about the ques-

tions, and each viewpoint was discussed. When they felt a particular issue had been talked out, they held a vote. A simple majority
of votes was sufficient to warrant a common decision.

No doubt about it: This method of discussion was "democratic"
in more senses than one. Each man could speak his mind. Nobody
was regarded as having a primacy of opinion that excluded some
or all others. Voting in common and deciding by a simple majority
were also "democratic" modes of behavior. A simple reading of
how those early debates went convinces one that their exchange
of views was utterly frank, sometimes quite emphatic, but never
heated.

Still, when you have said that, you have covered the extent to
which their debates were democratic in any sense that fits our
modern usage of the term. For it is one thing to use "democratic"
means of discussion and decision-making when the participants
belong to a secular democracy, a system where government in
principle and, as far as possible, in practice is for, of, and by the
people themselves or by their freely elected representatives. So
functions the republican democracy of the United States of
America.

It is quite another thing for men to use the same "democratic"
means of discussion and decision-making in order to serve better
within a strictly "monarchic" system, a system built for the propagation of religious truth and constructed around a pyramid of
power in which absolute power is concentrated at the apex; and in
which all other exercises of power in the system are derived by
permission, not by right, from that apex. For, in such a system, the
concentration of power means that a certain ideology governs the
use of that power.

This was the position of those nine men, Ignatius and his eight
companions, as it is the position of the Delegates to a General
Congregation of the Society. Their free-wheeling discussions and
decision-making by simple majority vote may be democratic. But
all discussions—indeed, the very subjects discussed and the conclusions permitted—are strictly regulated not by "democratic"
opinion, but by the norms laid down at that monarchic apex.

Put in its simplest terms, participants in a secular republican
democracy can discuss freely and vote freely on the very nature of
their democracy and on its basic laws. In a monarchic system that
serves as the channel of divine things, the participants cannot do
so. They can only discuss and decide how better to serve their
system. The system is sacrosanct.

Like those companions in their early debates, therefore, the Delegates to a General Congregation enter discussions and vote on final decisions from an unalterable and unquestioned point of view, a group mentality that permits no individual variation. Jesuitism provides that mentality.

In that part of the *Constitutions* where he was describing the General Congregation, Ignatius confined his directives to the dry bones of procedural rules, the exterior conventions to be observed so that a Congregation could be said to have acted legally. Nowhere in his treatment of the General Congregation did he need to touch on the mentality, the attitude of mind that should characterize the Delegates when they were engaged in the ongoing discussions and business proper to the Congregation. He presumed that they—in their vast majority Professed Fathers of the Society and distinguished by that special fourth vow to the Pope—would have as the major premise of their activity what he had explained elsewhere in detail as the permanent mentality and outlook of his "typical Professed Father of the Society." He presumed the Ignatian mold.

His statement in the *Formula of the Institute* is clear; and he took it to be sufficient:

> All who make profession in this Society should understand at the time, and furthermore keep in mind as long as they live, that this entire Society and the individual members who make their profession in it are campaigning for God under faithful obedience to His Holiness, Pope Paul III, and his successors in the Roman pontificate. . . . We are to be obliged by a special vow to carry out whatever the present and future Roman Pontiffs may order that pertains to the progress of souls and the propagation of the faith. . . .

The function of the Pope as the ultimate Superior of the Society, of all it does and of all its aspirations, could not be clearer. Ignatius wished his followers to be, in one sense, fanatically devoted to what he repeatedly called "the true Spouse of Christ Our Lord, our holy Mother, the hierarchical Church." He insisted that Jesuit devotion be so extreme to this "hierarchical Church" that "what seems to be white, I will believe to be black if the hierarchical Church so defines." That hierarchy in his mind was composed of the Roman Pope at the head of the Roman Catholic bishops of the Church.

This, therefore, would seem to be the mentality with which the official body of the Society, the General Congregation, would carry on its deliberations and arrive at its decisions and decrees. This was the "mission" of Iñigo's Society. There is no hint in Ignatius's writings that he could foresee the day when the General Congregation, speaking and legislating for the whole Society, would veer away resolutely from the dictates of that overall Jesuit mission.

Doubtless, Ignatius instituted the Congregation as an element to balance the absolute power of the Father General and the extensive powers of lower Superiors. He also set it up because he felt sure that, in a general assembly of his followers, there would be less likely a danger of personal idiosyncrasies and minority tactics taking over the direction of his Society.

As his institution worked out in practice, however, the element of the General Congregation also provided his Jesuits—and incidentally the papacy—with a stumbling block. Rome and its papacy normally proceed along juridical lines. The papacy, therefore, does not deal with a Jesuit Father General as an individual. The papacy must deal with the Society whose official stance is vocalized by the General Congregation. The Father General is elected and instructed by the General Congregation, and is its personal representative. He remains answerable all his life as General to each Congregation. The General cannot, strictly speaking, make any Congregation do anything—even obey the Pope, much less obey himself.

The Society, in other words, for the Roman mind, is a legal entity. Only that legal entity can speak for Jesuits; and it speaks through the Congregation or the General.

In Ignatian theory, of course, the Pope is the ultimate Superior of the Society. He should have coercive means to exercise his authority as Superior, if coercion is needed. Coercion by juridical means would be quite feasible, if a Pope were dealing with a group of men who do not carry much weight in the Church Universal. But when a Pope has to deal with the Society of Jesus, he is faced with the most powerful and resourceful organization that the papacy has ever spawned within the Roman Catholic Church.

Coercion of such a powerful body can become a two-edged sword. In fact, attempts by Popes and papal offices to coerce the Society's General Congregation and, through it, the Society itself, have proven to be a downright hazardous occupation. Historical examples seem to show it is also a fruitless task; for, no doubt about it, wrangling between Popes and General Congregations has been a recurrent factor in the history of the Society, and the papacy has come off second-best more than once.

The worst crises between the two before Clement XIV suppressed the Society in 1773 nearly always concerned a wish or a decision of the Pope which the General Congregation, as the "mind and voice" of the Society, did not think it should accept.

These sorts of problems surfaced in full at the very first General Congregation in 1558. Pope Paul IV informed the assembled Delegates that, contrary to what Ignatius had laid down in the *Constitutions*, this General Congregation (GC1) should adopt a three-year span for each Generalate, instead of the life span prescribed by Ignatius; and that Jesuits should, like all the older Orders, sing the Divine Office in choir. The Congregation remonstrated with the Pope. Paul IV still maintained his commands. The Jesuits obeyed until Paul IV died one year later; then they reverted to the letter of the *Constitutions*, with the consent of the succeeding Pope.

A later Pope, Sixtus V, informed Jesuit Father General Claudio Acquaviva in 1590 that he disapproved of the views that Jesuit theologians had taken on certain points of doctrine. From the facts, it is clear Sixtus was being arbitrary and even mean-spirited. It is equally clear that Acquaviva exercised neither obedience of the mind, nor of the will, nor of execution. He simply threatened Sixtus in a letter: "If Your Holiness should inflict such a humiliation on the Order [by imposing those theological views of his], then there is no way I can guarantee that ten thousand Jesuits will not pick up their pens to attack this decree in a manner that is certain to prove detrimental to the prestige of the Holy See."

Acquaviva was making no idle threat. Sixtus knew it and drew in his horns. If Sixtus had gone ahead and imposed his views, Acquaviva would have written a formal and subtly worded instruction to the whole Society informing every Jesuit of the Pope's decision, asking prayers for strength to obey the Pope's order, and requiring Jesuit conformity to the Pope's views. The deluge would then have taken place.

Again in 1590 the same Pope, Sixtus V, decided to change the name "Society of Jesus" to "Ignatine Order." To use the name of Jesus in the title of a mere Religious Order, said Sixtus and many others, was "offensive" to pious ears. "Every time you name this Society," one Cardinal grumbled, "you have to doff your hat or bow your head."

Claudio Acquaviva remonstrated with Sixtus, pointing out that in Jesuit eyes the very name of the Society belonged to the "substantials" of the Society. Neither he nor a General Congregation of Jesuits could change the name.

Sixtus maintained his decision, and ordered his own papal officials to draw up a decree changing the name accordingly.

In the coercive circumstances, Acquaviva did the only thing left to him: He organized a nine-day flow of prayers by the young Jesuit novices to ask God's grace for himself and the whole Society so that they submit to the Pope's distasteful command. Sixtus died on the ninth day. His successor, Urban, dropped the whole idea.

In that set-to with one Pope, Aquaviva was making an all-important point about disputes in general with the papacy and the Holy See. Neither he nor the General Congregation were legally empowered to touch those "substantials."

Nevertheless, Acquaviva also made another point—concerning obedience. He was prepared to accept the change of name had Sixtus lived long enough to impose it.

Acquaviva had implemented what Ignatius in all his severely drawn-up rules about obedience had prescribed: the right and duty of the subject—whether the subject was an individual Jesuit or the whole Society—to remonstrate with the Superior, be he house Superior, Provincial, the Father General, or the Pope. Remonstration was official, so to speak, and consisted of explaining why the subject thought he could not obey the order given or, at least, not obey it in the precise way the Superior wished him to obey it. The subject's objections might be purely and simply prudential: He might feel it unwise to carry out such an order; or it might be based on a vivid apprehension of ill-consequences flowing from an execution of the order given—failure of the effort, say, or undue strain on the subject.

The overall and explicit proviso Ignatius included in his instructions was that no Superior could validly order the subject to do something that was sinful, or to do something lawful in a sinful way, or to do something lawful in a lawful way but for a sinful motive. In any one of those cases, the subject was absolved from obedience.

Outside of those cases, however, the subject was obliged—"in virtue of holy obedience," as the phrase ran—to obey the order at least by executing it, hopefully willingly, ideally from a newly acquired conviction in his mind that the order was the best thing to accomplish. Rebellion and refusal to obey under the set circumstances was not included in Ignatius's book of rules. Once you obeyed, you could do your best to get the Superior to revoke the order.

Ignatius himself had given a prime example of this during his own lifetime. When Pope Paul III imposed on Ignatius the obligation to accept five pious women into the Society, he obeyed, received them, and tried to live with this jarring arrangement. It proved a practical impossibility. Then he worked at effecting the departure of the five women with the same Pope's consent. The whole exercise cost him dearly, but he succeeded.

Until recently, one finds that in all the wrangles between papacy and Jesuits, that Ignatian rule of obedience was observed with variations. Occasionally, one comes across what seems a piece of naked arrogance, as when Acquaviva threatened to bury Sixtus V beneath that pile of ten thousand theological treatises attacking Sixtus's theology. But Sixtus was one of the most arrogant Popes ever to succeed St. Peter in Rome. From time to time Jesuits have resorted to ruses—intercession by powerful churchmen and important secular personages, for instance—when they felt the papacy was ordering something unwise. Again, Ignatius himself had done this. But never until the recent history of the Society of Jesus has there been a moment when papacy and Jesuits differed violently about the nature of the Church, about the privileges and powers of the Roman Pontiff, or about basic Roman Catholic rules of morality. In such cases, Ignatius provided no elbow room for "remonstrance," nor for backsliding once the papacy upheld its position and maintained the order it had given.

In that mentality of the Society's founder, to give a cogent example, if the General Congregation were to take up a position contrary to that occupied and vindicated by the papacy concerning such fundamental matters as papal powers, basic Catholic doctrine, or rules of morality, then the General Congregation as the ranking Superior would be operating outside the monarchic system by which it is mandated to deliberate and decide on issues at all, and outside the system on whose well-being depends not only the particular mission being contested, but the Society's own very existence.

In such circumstances, which were not even imagined by Ignatius, the General Congregation would become as much of a genuine stumbling block for rank-and-file Jesuits as for the papacy. Obedience is the coagulant of the Society; obedience and union of hearts within the Society, all of them with the Roman Pontiff.

At the same time, and given the rigid tradition of obedience and the sheer impossibility of one individual—or even of several individuals—resisting the voiced Decrees and opinions of the General Congregation, it is safe to say that there is no practical way for such individuals successfully to resist the will of the General Congregation. The "phalanx" instinct of higher Superiors—themselves under obedience to the Father General, and with him under strict obedience to the General Congregation—plus the sheer jur-

idical impossibility of fostering a contrary point of view once debate is resolved by majority vote, would lead a dissenting member
either to fall silent and into line or to leave the Society.

Theoretically, in fact, such a violent difference about Roman
Catholic fundamentals could not arise between the papacy and the
Society. Only as long as the Delegates to the Congregation were
faithful to their overall mission as Jesuits—docile instruments to
defend the papacy and to propagate Roman Catholic doctrine as
propounded authoritatively by the Roman Pontiff—could the
Congregation function admirably in the way Ignatius planned.

When you follow the varying postures of the Society as mirrored
in the transactions of the General Congregations from GC1 in
1558 right down to GC30 in 1957,[2] you will find that each Congregation, composed of different men in different epochs, seems to be
speaking with the same mind as all its predecessors. They constantly reflected the Ignatian ideal of service to the papacy and
propagation of Roman Catholic doctrine as proposed by the Popes.
Whatever changes and adaptations they made in Ignatius's original
Institute, these were truly calculated to preserve and enhance
what Ignatius had called the "substantials" of the Institute, given
the concrete circumstances of a certain age.

You also find that the recurring General Congregations faithfully mirrored the condition of the Society. The legislation was
aimed at easing newly found problems. The Congregations also
served to protect the rank and file of the Society from the personal
aberrations and idiosyncrasies of individual Fathers General.

When the Society was saddled with a Father General, Spain's
Tirso Gonsalez de Santalla, who favored a very strict, "Calvinis-
tic" approach to morality and was energetic (to say the least) in
forwarding his own views, no Jesuit disobeyed the Father General.
Nevertheless, the General Congregation and Jesuits all over the
world refused to go along with the Father General's personalistic
religious attitude that somehow or other did not rhyme with Ignatian spirituality and pastoral practice.

The General Congregation constantly proved itself a reliable
bellwether about coming difficulties. At the onset of what has
been called the Enlightenment in the 1700s, GC16 again returned
to the affirmation of Thomistic philosophy as essential for Jesuit
thinking and education. When it insisted on the use of Aristotle's
Physics, that was not an effort to oppose the new physics aborning
in the Western world; Jesuits themselves were prominently engaged in the new physics. Their insistence seemed to fly in the
face of contemporary wisdom which held, among other things,

that anything as medieval as Thomism was a strict no-no for "modern" minds. But, what the Congregation was pointing to in Aristotelian physics was its metaphysical underlay about divine causality and the need for a First Mover in the created cosmos of man; and what it liked about Thomism was its rational approach to divine things. Jesuits were opposed not to the methodical approach of "Science," but to the rising tide of agnosticism in that age of discoveries in the physical world. Their spirituality and supernatural ideals were their best bulwarks. Thomism and Aristotelianism provided a solid mental framework.

That Ignatian spirituality built around the two devotions—to Jesus as the Lord and to the Pope as his Vicar on earth—was one of the "substantials of the Institute." Another was the practice of poverty; and a third was the entire concept of Jesuit obedience. As the storm clouds gathered around the Society from 1750 onward, we find the two General Congregations of those years filled with decrees and recommendations aimed at preserving orthodox Roman Catholic doctrine, nourishing the Ignatian ideal of service to the papacy, and bolstering the personal spiritual life of individual Jesuits. That Jesuit character persevered throughout. Even after its forty-one years of suppression from 1773 to 1814, the Society swung back into action on all fronts, still firm in the Jesuit mold envisioned by Ignatius.

You can trace very clearly throughout the General Congregations of the next 150 years (GC20–30) a steady effort to reassert in the world the full bloom of that Ignatian character of the Society as a whole and of its members. After an initial ten years (1820–1830) with Father General Luigi Fortis—a member of the pre-suppression Society—there followed two strong Fathers General, Jan Roothaan and Peter Beckx, who between them governed the Society for fifty-eight years. Those were years of continuity and solid purpose.

When Pope Pius IX launched two major documents against Modernism, the Society enthusiastically adopted both as charters of its thought and action. In GC23, 25, and 26, the formal decrees of the members left no doubt on this matter. But for the first time, and as far back as GC23 in 1853, another voice—still faint, if already insistent—made itself briefly heard. A new source of rot and corrosion of classical Jesuitism had apparently lodged in the bosom of the Society by this time.

This voice was what one Delegate later described as the "Yes-but" mentality manifested by certain Delegates at GC23. Modernists did fall into errors, yes indeed, these Delegates admitted. But, they also argued, the Modernists were trying to reach the truth. Behind their error lay some truth. Wouldn't it be better to dialogue with them and so establish close relations with them? This Modernism, after all, was a very common mentality among non-Catholic Christians, among many Protestants, in the Western world. They may be bad philosophers and erring theologians, but they had the magnificent data of science at their fingertips.

This "Yes-but" voice was drowned out in the General Congregation's reaffirmation of the papacy's uncompromising stand against Modernism. Modernism was like the Black Death and required not merely total quarantine, but the merciless cutting down of anyone so infected. Lock, stock, and barrel, Modernists were to be drummed out of the Church—and out of the Society, if by some misfortune some Jesuits turned Modernist.

No one at GC23, 25, and 26 could have guessed that in the next century Modernism would be running through all the arteries of the Church and of the Society. Yet the Delegates to the next three General Congregations, GC27–29, found no obvious reason to emphasize either the danger of Modernism or the possibility that some internal rot was eating away at the vitals of Ignatius's Society.

On the contrary, after the end of World War II, a renewed vigor and growth was noticeable. A kind of Golden Age for the Society seemed to have dawned. Judged in the light of their numbers, in the importance of posts in the Vatican held by Jesuits, in the extension of their educational and missionary work, the future seemed cloudless.

Yet, right in the middle of what did genuinely seem a new Golden Age—or, at least, the beginning of one—a strange event took place. The voice of Pope Pius XII was raised querulously, complaining about dangers to Jesuitism; about abuses in the Society; about the ultimate sin for any Jesuit, revolt against obedience. It seemed such an anomaly at the time, that the ordinary rank-and-file Jesuit dismissed it as an aberration on the part of Pope Pius XII. The disturbing event took place in 1957, as the 185 Delegates of GC30 were summoned to assemble for their deliberations in September–November.

Certain customs had grown up, in ways no one now remembers, around the preparations for any General Congregation. In addition to approaching the Holy Father to ask His Holiness's permission to assemble the Congregation, the Jesuit General would also ask for the Holy Father to address the assembled Delegates, and would offer the Holy Father the collaboration of one or two Jesuit writers to help His Holiness in the composition and editing of the papal address.

When Father General Janssens acted accordingly, Pope Pius XII answered affirmatively to the first two requests: Yes, the Fathers could assemble in Congregation; and, Yes, the Holy Father would address them. But, no, His Holiness said, he did not need any collaboration from Jesuits designated by the Father General.

There was a touch of irony—evident to a few—in the actual way events took place in this Congregation. Father General Janssens first read a rather detailed account of the Society, treating of Provinces, houses, increase in membership, the practice of religious discipline, common difficulties encountered in religious life and possible remedies. He detailed those areas where the Society was succeeding and where it was undergoing either outright persecution or the next worse thing. He called for a frank exchange of views and great freedom of discussion.

His whole performance was paternal, encouraging, up-beat, and low-toned. None of the Delegates expected inspiring words from Father Janssens. They knew their Father General. It was not his talent to arouse high spirits or great enthusiasm. His was the quiet manner of a professional religious person. But, to everyone's ears, it was a creditable performance delivered in the vocabulary and mental formulas that were habitual for in-Society communication. All was well: that was the message. *And:* we must try harder. For the greater glory of God.

On September 10, Pius received Father General Janssens and the 185 Delegates in private audience at the Vatican. The eighty-one-year-old Pope had slightly over one year to live and the wracking illnesses that had continuously plagued him since 1950 had taken a heavy toll of a physique that had never been robust. Physically and spiritually, the impression of the ethereal he always had given was now etched in bold relief.

In contrast to his physical fragility, however, Pope Pius's address was tough and hard, a sharply worded catechism of what the Jesuits should be and, by direct implication—sometimes, in the address, by explicit statement—what they unfortunately were not, in the Holy Father's eyes.

From the first words of his address in Latin, His Holiness adopted the tone of a father warning his children what they should do, what they should be like; and what they should not do, what they should not be like. He followed a very exact arrangement of subjects; obviously for him, these were subjects about which Jesuits had not been observant, but negligent or even wayward. That was the implication.

The order in which Pius touched on these subjects indicated their relative importance in his mind. The Pontiff's tone was severe, at times quite peremptory. And as always with Pius, he seemed to be speaking with his eyes fixed on some celestial vision.

Chief among the things Jesuits had to watch over and improve was doctrinal orthodoxy, agreement with the teaching authority of the Church and the Roman Pontiff. The Society in its Superiors, Pius went on, beginning with the General Congregation, would have to labor in order to ensure that Jesuits held and taught correct doctrine and morality. Certainly, two-thirds of the 185 Delegates to this General Congregation would never have thought a reproach could be uttered to the Society now under this heading.

Immediately on the heels of orthodoxy, Pius brought up the question of obedience, in which Ignatius wished his sons to excel. The Pontiff wanted a faithful obedience from them; obedience to this Holy See, obedience to their Rules and *Constitutions* and traditions, obedience to intermediate Superiors. A second surprise for the Delegates. Hitherto in the eleven years of Janssens' Generalate, nobody in the Society had really complained of a failure in obedience by Jesuits.

Deficiency in religious discipline came next. It was not sufficient, Pius said, to decry Jesuit discipline and the repetitive character of its method as too formalistic and therefore unsuited to the modern person. His implication was clear: Some Jesuits want to relax the rules of Ignatius. Human nature, Pius went on, had not changed since Ignatius's time. Now the basis of all religious discipline was genuine humility and self-denial. Humility to acknowledge one's faults and dependence; self-denial to curb one's pride and vanity, to perform the Ignatian exercises of prayer and self-examination and penance. Jesuit life should resemble the life of Jesus in "carrying the cross" of labor, obscurity, and obedience, because only thus would Jesuits be apt instruments in the hand of God acting through the Church and through Superiors.

The practice of poverty in the Society also left a lot to be desired, the Pope intimated. There was too much vacation traveling, and too many vacations spent outside Jesuit houses. There was too much accumulation of possessions in the shape of equipment allegedly necessary for apostolic work; and there also was too much indulgence in abuses such as the use of tobacco. Pius was at his most peremptory on this seemingly small point. His Latin was curt: *Auferatur hic abusus de medio vestrum*, Let this abuse be wiped out from your midst. Thus, you will give good example to others.

The Delegates from Holland and those who knew the Jesuit houses in Holland listened with glazed eyes to this particular admonition. Smoking was so widespread and accepted in the Dutch province that you could smoke anywhere in their Jesuit houses except in chapel. For the Dutch, the Pope might as well have ordered them to stop breathing twenty-three out of every twenty-four hours.

Pius went on imperturbably. In all of your religious life, he told them, remember the Gospel ideal of poverty; and remember, too, that you have fallen natures due to Original Sin, and therefore are prone to deviation from the rule of goodness.

Pius's final point was his most important. The Society of Jesus, he said, had a monarchic form of government. This was one of the "substantials" of the Ignatian Institute. If Jesuits were not faithful to this "substantial," if they behaved in any other way, the Society as the Church and numerous Pontiffs in the past approved of it would cease to be.

What sank home to many during and after this astounding papal audience was not that Pius had spoken in such an admonitory fashion; the Delegates had half expected that. The more stilling realization was that the Society of Jesus outlined by him in his address as desirable, did not to a very large degree correspond to the Society as the Delegates knew it to be, either in their home Provinces, or in its Roman center. It was the first time that many Delegates had been forced to realize how wide a gap had opened between the Ignatian ideal of the Jesuit character and the actual practice among Jesuits.

What was particularly addling for some was the thought that no word had ever been changed in the rules of the Society, or in the way Jesuits described their work, and the Society itself to themselves and others. Yet the meaning that they gave to those words as they lived them differed considerably from the meaning Pius gave them. The traditional formularies of the Society had become hollow on Jesuit lips.

For most of the Delegates, however, the reaction was denial: Pius was speaking about unreality. Yet, not one Delegate present was unaware that at least in the major Jesuit theological schools, Jesuit professors shaved as close as possible—if not over—Roman rules of orthodoxy. In France and Germany, professors had one set of notes to show the Roman authorities as the substance of their lectures, and another set of notes for actual use in class. There was "double bookkeeping" at work in a wholesale manner.

The Delegates understood that on Pius's lips correctness and orthodoxy of theology and philosophy meant adhesion to Roman norms. But already for many Jesuits, Rome together with its Pope and his Vatican bureaucracy seemed to be anchored in a mentality that no longer existed outside the church at large. Pius had spoken to a hard new fact. There was something alien for Jesuits about Rome and Romanism.

Indeed, even such essentials of Jesuit life as the practice of religious discipline in daily spiritual exercises, the practice of one hour's prayer, and the examination of conscience were in a fluid state. Many Superiors no longer made any real attempt to enforce the rules that held Jesuits to residence in Jesuit houses, and once someone was specializing in a scientific subject, he could be exempt from other rules as well, such as those concerning the practice of poverty and community life.

Principally, however, it was when Pius was lecturing them about religious obedience, and adhesion to the will of the Pope and to the doctrine he pronounced, that the Delegates sensed the deepest qualitative difference between Pius's ideal of a Jesuit and the way Jesuits were developing in the Provinces. That was principally why "the monarchic form of government" Pius had described as the Society's struck a bizarre note. Of course, the Superior was the Superior; but very few of the Delegates would willingly have used the term "monarchic" to describe their idea of the government proper either to Church or Society. Pius seemed to be propounding a view of religious life, of religious obedience, and of "papalism" that was out of date, and that for one reason or another no longer found an echo in Jesuit lives as the Delegates knew them.

The long and the short of it seemed to be that by this fall season of 1957, the character of a Jesuit and the character of the Society as outlined in the Pope's address appeared unpalatable, undigestible in today's world. Pontiff and Jesuits differed in what they thought Jesuitism should be. Most did not know why this should be so; all still were Jesuits, and all wished to remain so. Nevertheless, the mood of the Delegates at the end of the address ranged from somber to mildly indignant.

Willy-nilly, the address of Pius XII was voted into the records of GC30 by the Delegates. But the mood of the Congregation had changed. Many had come to Rome with ideas and proposals that they now felt they could not expose frankly in democratic freedom. There is no trace in the published records of GC30 of any inclination on the part of the Delegates to ask the rather profound question: Why did the Holy Father make that type of address to them?

Unofficially, many did inquire who—and if Jesuits, which ones —had collaborated with Pius in putting the address together. Pius had three main Jesuit collaborators, all Germans, at that time. Blame of a kind was showered on them in private, as alternative scapegoats: and other older Jesuits were also blamed—men of the status of Paolo Dezza, a long-time collaborator of the Pope's.

In the end, though, no one was blamed specifically. It was felt that the Society had been treated rather rudely, its intentions misinterpreted, and that Pius had spoken from an aery-fairy optic to men who were plunged in the stuff and matter of a changing world where "monarchic" modes and "medieval" pieties had no place.

One virtue the Society still retained was Jesuit patience. There would be a new Pope eventually. There would be other General Congregations. Things would be better.

Here, the prime personage to fault, if anyone should be faulted, was Father General Janssens. True, he was *ex officio* the servant of the Congregation. But his position as General thrust on him the moral obligation of leadership. Ideally, Father Janssens should have turned the situation around and led the Delegates to consider in detail and in concrete ways what the Pope had said about the condition of men throughout the Society. But Father Janssens was essentially a man of the due forms and formulas that bureaucrats regard as their proper mode of discharging their duties. Besides, he was a timid man, a man never at home speaking Italian. Never comfortable in Rome. He never could adapt to *romanità*. Instead, he took refuge in a very formal way of thinking and talking and dealing with problems, which took the place of powerful leadership. There was no inspiration forthcoming from him.

GC30 ended without any earth-shaking decisions or new directives of an innovative kind. Ardor had been dampened; freedom of speech had been hobbled—this was the general feeling. Pius's Rome and Vatican were not hospitable places for Jesuits.

The only light note—but with a gently antipapal twist—was struck in the aftermath of GC30, and was provided by the Pope's condemnation of the use of tobacco. According to time-honored custom, the Father General wrote a letter to the whole Society about the General Congregation and the Holy Father's address. The Holy Father's wishes, in the matter of tobacco as in other things, were to be implemented. The General expected all the Provincials to inform him as to the implementation. Local Superiors—Provincials, mainly—had to take some concrete steps by way of a letter to all the members of their Province that would give bureaucratic satisfaction to Roman authorities that the Jesuits had taken the Pope's admonitions seriously.

Different Provincials made different provisions; some even made it a condition of entry into the Society that a candidate promise not to smoke, or if he already was a smoker, that he renounce smoking. The Dutch Provincial wrote a letter to his subjects which was polycopied and passed from hand-to-hand through virtually the whole Society as a classic. Smokers were divided into different classes: the obdurate smokers, the perpetual smokers, the beginner smokers, and so on. Prescriptions were given to deal with each class. The old and obdurate ones could be left alone; they had a nasty habit but were too old to change; they were incorrigible. The middle-aged Jesuits had the problem of middle-age to contend with. The "young" men . . . and so it went. In the end, the men of the Dutch Province of the Society went on smoking their way through life into eternity, as they had always done.

There can never again be a Congregation of the kind GC30 was, and for a very good reason that can be perceived only in hindsight. A small majority, but still a majority, of Delegates to GC30 were already very progressivist in their views and their practices. What paralyzed the Delegates at that GC30 was the sudden realization that this Pope, Pius XII—though reputedly a close friend of high-ranking Jesuits and severely dependent upon Jesuits for intimate services rendered to him personally[3]—had turned sour on them, accusing them in practical terms of betraying their vocation as Jesuits. What cowed the Delegates to GC30 was not the fact of this Pope's disapproval, however, but that they could neither accept it nor find any way around it.

Pius was known to be authoritarian and to brook no recalcitrance; and he apparently was amply informed about the inner turmoil of recalcitrance in the Society.[4] That was one inhibiting factor. Another was the fact that the already developed recalcitrance in the Society of the fifties had as yet achieved no legitimate outlet. Officially, it did not exist. It had no voice. The rather sullen and uncooperative reaction of GC30 to the Pontiff's catechism was about all that Congregation could manage in those circumstances.

GC30 ended in November of 1957. Pius was dead and his successor, John XXIII, elected within less than a year. Dutch Jesuits were quick to point out that the new Pope still smoked cigarettes. The Americans noted his love of travel. The French described him pungently as *une bonne fourchette*—the new Pope wielded no mean fork at table.

The progressivist faction in the Society, however, noted John's liberalism. From their point of view, the entire situation had turned around. The new Pope, the progressivists reasoned—a non-Roman, a man known to be nonauthoritarian—could provide the egress they needed from an underground existence.

Their expectations were amply fulfilled. Within three months of his election to the Throne of Peter, "the Good Pope John" had announced the Second Vatican Council. What followed, both prior to the opening of that Council in 1962 and during its four years of existence, resembled nothing more closely than an assault of hurricanes on the City of the Popes. The next time Jesuit Delegates met—for GC31 in 1965, eight years after GC30—the hurricanes of change had swept through all. A different spirit reigned among the Delegates; a very different Father General was in charge; a very different atmosphere filled the Rome of the Popes; and Jesuitism had already received a new mold.

11 | HURRICANES IN THE CITY

P ut yourself in the position of a born-and-bred city dweller setting out for work on the route you have used every morning for the last twenty or thirty years. Up one long avenue, then around a certain corner and down another avenue that seems never to have changed. That's it. You've done it hundreds of times, five days a week, for who knows how many weeks, year after year. It is a morning like all the other mornings, in a city that is exactly like it always has been for you yesterday and last month and as far back as you care to remember.

So you travel scarcely noting the landmarks and all the things you know so well and that tell you you're at home here—the pavements, side-street crossings, traffic lights, trees, lampposts, shops, buildings; the rising and falling rhythm of cars, buses, trucks; the newsstands, the usual man panhandling at his permanent spot, the medley of sounds from voices and machines, the smells in the air, even the usual variants in the weather; the crowds of businessmen, officeworkers, hardhats, householders walking their dogs, messengers, tourists, shoppers, loungers and loiterers.

All is so expected, so predictable, so reassuring, that no matter what the noise, or what the jagged movement of street things, in a certain sense, all of it ensures your peace of mind. Around that well-known corner, it will be the same as it always was. This is what you assume unconsciously. Rightly, too, for certain things don't change. Life is built on that premise, especially life's insignificant actions—like walking to work.

But picture yourself turning that corner and being suddenly seized from behind by a blasting high wind that seemingly comes from nowhere and in its hurricane passage shatters buildings, leveling some of them, throwing people about, littering pavements, uprooting trees and traffic lights, transforming the very skies above your head with a twilight color, and bending the clear-vision straightness of the avenue into corkscrew twists, as it carries you off willy-nilly with everyone and everything else in dizzying directions. This is a change so total, so abrupt, so irresistible in fact, that you no longer know where you are, where you're going, what is happening.

Before you have time even to reckon that you can't get your bearings, another high wind interlacing with the first comes screaming incoherently around your ears and, to your further panic, seems to affect most people around you with a sort of ecstatic joy, so that they throw themselves unresistingly into the rushing streams of those two winds that now carry everyone, yourself included, out of sight of all the old familiar landmarks. So eerie is the effect of the second blast that even in all this violence and turmoil, the most disorienting thing of all for you is the strange euphoria of expectation and of joyous confidence that seems to grip most of the people who are being tossed about as you and they are hustled forward on an unknown and uncharted journey.

A bizarre element of this disturbing euphoria is the way that people begin to talk, whether among themselves or to God. They seem in an instant to have learned a new language, to be thinking about everything with pop-up, prefab concepts. "Don't worship vertically! Worship horizontally!" "Whatever helps creative growth toward integration!" "Facilitators are needed!" "How are you performing interpersonally?" And, as if that were not disorienting enough, an almost manic tone pitched just this side of hysteria weaves its way from time to time into the vast confusion as men and women, claiming the Holy Spirit's gift of tongues, begin to jabber nonsense-sounds. "Ik bedam dam boolah"—or something to that effect—a Roman Catholic cardinal is heard saying ecstatically, ensuring confusion at the highest place. Glorious confusion. Euphoric confusion.

For a moment, you are tempted to fall in with it all as into a magical, fictional world. But wild questions assault you, and no consoling answers follow. Why was there no warning? Where were these winds moments before they struck? Were they in covert all along? Up above the clouds, perhaps, or hovering somewhere out beyond the streets and buildings? Or have they come from utterly alien and distant regions? Why is everyone so euphorically confident about the future, even while being carried away on the backs of these winds? Is their joyous leap forward into darkness illuminated by longings and informed by their instinct for the divine? Whence their new concepts? Their new language?

Whatever the answers, you know you cannot go back to the way things were before. Nobody will ever be able to go back home again to the old familiar places. Things will never again be the same in your home city.

Perhaps it is that stark realization that suddenly makes one thing seem sure and clear in your mind: Wherever they came from, those two violent hurricanes—the one tumbling all that was familiar to you, the other blowing that strange euphoria through people's minds—were no ordinary storms.

Such a scenario, wild and surreal as it seems, is barely enough to convey the completeness and the suddenness of the change, and the strange euphoria, that overpowered Roman Catholics—and, surprisingly, Jesuits along with them—in the 1960s. For an entire traditional way of religious life and practice was seemingly killed off just that suddenly, without warning. A centuries-old mentality was flushed out in a hurricane of change. In one sense, a certain world of thought, feeling, attitude, ceased to exist—the old Catholic world centered on the authority of the Roman Pontiff; the cast-iron "either-or" of Catholic dogma and morality; the frequentation of Mass, Confession, Holy Communion; the Rosary and the various pieties and devotions of parish life; the militancy of the Roman Catholic laity in defense of traditional Catholic values. That entire world was swept away, as it were, overnight.

When the violence of the winds had passed and the new day dawned, people looked about and found that suddenly the universal Latin of the Mass was gone. Stranger still: The Roman Mass itself was gone. In its place, there was a new rite that resembled the old immemorial Mass as a lean-to shanty resembles a Palladian mansion. The new rite was said in a babel of languages, each one saying different things. Things that sounded un-Catholic. That only God the Father was God, for example; and that the new rite was a "community supper," not an enactment of Christ's death on the Cross; and that priests were no longer priests of sacrifice, but ministers at table serving guests at a common meal of fellowship.

True, the Pope who presided over such enormities of doctrinal aberration, Paul VI, tried to backtrack somewhat in the direction of the one and only Roman Mass. But it was too late. The un-Catholic character of that new rite persisted.

The devastation of those hurricane winds had not stopped there. Churches and chapels, convents and monasteries had been denuded of statues. Altars of sacrifice had been removed or at least abandoned, and four-legged tables were planted in front of the people instead, as for a pleasant meal. Tabernacles were removed along with the fixed belief about Christ's Sacrifice as the essence of the Mass. Vestments were modified or laid aside completely. Communion rails were removed. The faithful were told not to kneel any longer when receiving Holy Communion, but to stand like free men and women, and to take the Bread of Communion and the Cup of the Grape of Fellowship in their own democratic hands. In many churches, members of the Congregation were immediately expelled for "public disturbance of worship" if they dared to genuflect, or worse still, to kneel, for Holy Communion in the new rite. Police were called in to eject the worst offenders, those who refused to cooperate and refused to leave.

Outside the churches and chapels, Roman missals, Mass cards, prayerbooks, crucifixes, altar cloths, Mass vestments, Communion rails, even pulpits, statues, and kneelers as well as Stations of the Cross were either consigned to bonfires and city dumps or sold off at public auctions where interior designers picked them up at bargain prices and launched an "ecclesiastical look" in the decoration of high-rise apartments and the elegant homes of suburbia. A carved oak altar made such an unusual "vanity" table.

Reaction to all this was not only immediate; it was turbulent and sustained. But do not think for one minute it was a reaction of horror, of disquiet, of insistence that the barbarity stop, that things sacred and sacrosanct be restored. Quite the contrary.

Attendance at Mass immediately declined, and within ten years was down by 30 percent in the United States, 60 percent in France and Holland, 50 percent in Italy, 20 percent in England and Wales. Within another ten years, 85 percent of all Catholics in France, Spain, Italy, and Holland never went to Mass. Seminary populations plummeted. In Holland, 2000 priests and 5000 Religious brothers and nuns abandoned their ministries. There is today, 1986, on an average one newly ordained priest per year in that country, where before there had been a mean average of ten. Similar declines were registered elsewhere. In the twelve years 1965–1977, some twelve to fourteen thousand priests worldwide asked to be relieved of their duties, or they simply left. Sixty thousand nuns left their convents between 1966 and 1983. The Catholic Church had never suffered such devastating losses in such a short time.

Very many teaching nuns simply doffed their religious habits, quickly acquired lay clothes, cosmetics, and jewelry, said good-bye to the local bishops who had hitherto been their major superiors, declared themselves now constituted as ordinary, decent, straightforward American educators, and carried on their teaching careers. The number of confessions, communions, confirmations declined worldwide every year, from an average 60 percent of practicing Catholics in 1965 to a figure somewhere between 25 percent–30 percent in 1983. Conversions to Catholicism were cut by two-thirds.

Those who remained—lay and clerical—were not satisfied with the attempted abolition of the traditional Roman Mass, with the overall changes of Catholic ritual and worship, and with newly exercised freedom to cast doubt on all dogmas. It wasn't enough. A clamor arose in favor of the use of contraceptives, of legalizing homosexual relations, of making abortion optional, of premarital sexual activity under certain conditions, of divorce and remarriage within the Church, of a married clergy, of women's ordination, of a quick patchwork union with Protestant churches, of Communist revolution as a means not only of solving endemic poverty but of defining faith itself.

A new form of blasphemy and sacrilege came into vogue. For homosexual Catholics, the "disciple whom Jesus loved" took on new meaning. Hadn't that beloved disciple "rested on Jesus's bosom" at the Last Supper? Man-love-for-man was thereby consecrated, wasn't it? Lavender-robed homosexual priests said Mass in the new rite for their homosexual congregations.

And if this could be so for homosexual males, what about woman-love-for-woman? Only Catholic women of the sixties generation were clever enough to perceive themselves as victims of ecclesiastical sexism; for them, a day of reckoning with the age-old sexist-minded Church had come at last. There now arose Womanchurch—one of those eerie, new pop-up words which meant meetings of women in private apartments where She (God the Mother) was worshiped and thanked for having sent her Child

(Jesus) by the fertilizing power of the Holy Spirit (Herself the primo-primordial Woman).

Backing up this motley array of changes and changers and changelings, there came marching in a whole phalanx of feisty "experts." Theologians, philosophers, liturgical experts, "facilitators," "socio-religious coordinators," lay ministers (male and female), "praxis directors"—whatever their pop-up titles, all were looking for two things: converts to the new theology, and a fight with the battered and retreating traditionalists. A flood of publications—books, magazine articles, new magazines, bulletins, newsletters, plans, programs, and outlines—inundated the popular Catholic market.[1] The "experts" questioned and "reinterpreted" every dogma and belief traditionally and universally held by Catholics. Everything, in fact, and especially all the hard things in Roman Catholic belief—penance, chastity, fasting, obedience, submission—was subjected to violent, overnight change.

At another level, meanwhile, throughout seminaries and Catholic colleges and universities a more subtle but still obvious weeding-out went on. Older, traditional-minded men were retired early or simply retired themselves in disgust.[2] They were replaced only with devotees of "the Renewal" (the word was always capitalized in those early days). Seminarians were dismissed if they found the newness abhorrent.

To heighten the twilight color of this storm-blown scene, there came the second storm, the blast of euphoria. There arose among those who were left the brave if not always convincing idea that the future of Catholicism, so abruptly reduced in its practice and in its numbers, was now somehow brighter than ever before. What seemed a shambles was really a vast pentecostal renewal under way; the real Church of Christ was about to emerge in all its beauty and truth.

These hopes—all hope—now centered on the community. "The People of God" was now distinct and separate from the old, still-boned hierarchy of Pope, bishops, priests, and nuns in the tight coagulation of Roman discipline. More than that, this People of God—all together, as well as in each little gathering of believers—was now said to be the real Church, the real source of revelation, the only legitimizer of morality, the sole source of what to believe. In matters of faith, morals, dogma, and religious practice, Rome, Georgia, had the same authority as the Rome of the Popes. Central authority was vanishing as a matter of practical Catholic fact.

As one looked about in the early days of the storm to get one's bearings, no one person and no one group seemed responsible for the birth of this euphoric conviction. But it ran like wildfire through the churches, loosening the bonds between laity and clergy, between nuns and ecclesiastical superiors, between priests and bishops, between bishops and Popes.

An immediate consequence was the insistent demand for democratization to replace central authority and bring a new and much needed order throughout the length and breadth of the Church. Priests organized themselves into leagues and associations and senates and unions on a national and regional basis. Nuns did likewise.[3] The laity, men and women separately, followed suit. All issued graphic statements of their rights and demands. All demanded that democratic methods be used not only in governing the Roman Church, but even in "deciding" what was to be believed. A whole new activist bureaucracy sprang up overnight, peopled by careerists who launched ever newer and headier activities.

Throughout all this vast transformation that joyous, Micawber-like conviction of great success around the corner of history never diminished. And that feverish conviction was what seemed to produce the euphoria. At times it produced what now, in retrospect, looks like a circus full of inconsequential clowns making antic fun of the dignity, the standing, the power, and the grace on which they still relied, if only for theatrical effect. A whole gamut of completely new careers opened up for clerics who had no interest in hearing confessions, baptizing babies, seeking out sinners, and saying Mass.

With surprising speed, the contemporary scene took on a ludicrous, comic aspect that seemed to beg for exploitation in slapstick films and by nightclub entertainers. Priests with lovebeads strung around their necks lobbied their bishops, strumming guitars and singing "To Dream the Impossible Dream." Nuns wearing makeup, jewelry, and fashionable clothes sipped cocktails at their annual "conventions" in hotel lounges. Bishops embossed their pastoral letters with the Hammer and Sickle instead of the usual symbols of the Cross and the Church. Theologians did figurative somersaults over the dome of St. Peter's Basilica in their efforts to leap beyond any and all Roman rules of morality and belief. One American archbishop blandly mounted the pulpit to ask his congregation to congratulate and pray for his auxiliary bishop who on the morrow would leave the episcopacy in order to marry. An American bishop, who later became a cardinal, organized "cookie committees" in all the parishes of his dioceses to bake cakes and muffins for use as Communion bread in the new rite that replaced the Roman Mass. A Mexican archbishop regularly began his Sunday sermons with clenched fist raised in salute and the defiant cry of the Communist Internationale, "*Soy Marxista;* I am a Marxist," on his lips.

The circus atmosphere was hardly lost on the public at large. For the first time in the history of the American film and television industry, the Catholic priest, the Catholic nun, the Catholic seminarian, Catholic rituals, became fair game for gratuitous laughs and for lurid drama. Like the Anglican parson in the England of Noel Coward and the Jewish *rebbe* in the Europe of the twenties and thirties, those once untouchable Roman Catholic personages—nun, priest, bishop, Pope, seminarian—now slipped into place in the world's bill of entertainment fare.

Still the euphoria persisted. Somehow, all of this, too, was read as part of the promise of a golden future for Catholicism.

The substance of both the euphoria and the confusion were never more literally pictured than by two Roman artists, Ettore de Conciliis—surely a name with a touch of historical irony—and Rosso Falciano. In the last days of the Second Vatican Council, commissioned to decorate the walls of a new church in Rome dedicated to St. Francis of Assisi, Conciliis and Falciano painted one swirling montage of faces in profile. It was as though a senseless hurly-burly of portraits had been whirled into place on those same high winds, fast rising by then to their full hurricane force. Pope John XXIII, Communist dictator Fidel Castro, professed atheist Bertrand Russell, Italian Communist Party leader Palmiro Togliatti, excommunicated actress Sophia Loren, Chairman Alexei Kosygin of the Soviet Council of Ministers, left-wing Mayor Giorgio La Pira of Florence, Communist dictator Mao Tse-tung of China, and, for whatever reason, Jacqueline Bouvier Kennedy.

Neither de Conciliis nor Falciano was Communist. But they were persuaded that, with Vatican II, all was changed. Nobody was wrong; everyone was right. Like the Church, St. Francis, the *poverello* of Assisi, could embrace everyone. For now the impossible had happened. The Roman Catholic Church had become human; and therefore nothing human could be seen as alien to it. Renewal was the way, the truth, and the life of Roman Catholicism. And its message was borne on the wings of its own delusion: If the hierarchic Church could change, could adapt to the humanity of the Renewal, then the Golden Age of Christianity would dawn.

Reality, Jean-Paul Sartre remarked once, is a bucket of icy water. It leaves you breathless, unable to speak. So sudden and overpowering were those two hurricanes, that articulate expressions of surprise or shock seemed impossible for the general run of men and women—witnesses and participants alike. The change was a real change. The euphoria was a real euphoria. Nobody questioned the genuineness of either. Their reality surpassed any fiction or pretence, in terms of strangeness or incongruity or inventiveness. But while there were individuals and pockets of people here and there who cried out some equivalent of "Wait a minute! What's happening? Why are we changing everything?", it was as though no one could hear them over the din of the twin storms raging through Catholicism.

As in our surreal scenario, in time such questions began to be taken up by greater numbers. Where had those hurricanes come from? Why the euphoria? Whence the new concepts and the new language? Even Pope Paul VI, in whose reign the devastating change and the ungovernable euphoria reached hurricane force, considered those questions, as well he might have. By then, however, His Holiness's reflection was of ultimate causes: "The Smoke of Satan has entered the Sanctuary and enveloped the Altar."

Then as now, most people, whether enthusiastic or condemnatory of the change, seemed to think it was all the direct result of Pope John XXIII's Second Vatican Council, which had assembled over 2500 Roman Catholic bishops in Rome for four separate Sessions between 1962 and 1965. But Vatican II, like every Council, left a clear record in its documents. And nothing is more certain than the fact that that Council reiterated what the two previous Ecumenical Councils had proclaimed, especially concerning the primacy and infallibility of the Pope, the hierarchic character of the Roman Church, and the unique character of the priesthood. As to the Roman Mass, the Council decreed that it, too, was to be preserved. All the essentials were to remain unchanged and sacrosanct. Only certain minor Mass prayers were allowed to be said in the vernacular. The traditional devotions of the Church were emphasized.

No matter how you turn it, in other words, the documents of the Second Vatican Council did not even suggest, much less authorize, the hurricane of changes; nor did they either create or justify the euphoria—the curious expectation of instant newness in everything—that seemed to convince men and women that to destroy the very vestiges of Catholicism would be to introduce Catholicism's Golden Age.

It was not the documents of Vatican II that authorized bishops to do the very opposite of what Rome prescribed in the matter of Communion-in-the-hand; in the matter of women readers at Mass; in the matter of altar girls replacing altar boys and of girls and women distributing Holy Communion; in the matters of contraception and homosexual unions. Vatican II documents did not give theologians carte blanche to interpret or deny dogmas of faith as they saw fit. Vatican II was conservative in its statements and traditional in its theology and morality. The Council did not recommend homosexual rights, or dancers in leotards leaping about the sanctuary, or bishops saying Mass in tennis shorts, or the abolition of strict enclosure for Contemplative Orders, or the use of Thomas' English Muffins as Eucharistic Bread.

Clearly, the impulse for change and innovation, the euphoria itself, and the almost infantile persuasion that renewal consisted of jettisoning age-old, sacred practices and rejecting the authoritative voice of Rome must all have been the result of another process.

What was that process?

The question is seen in more acute profile when you look at the effect of the hurricanes of change and euphoria on the Society of Jesus. Jesuits are not ordinary Catholics; they are of exceptional quality among high-caliber minds. And their Society is no mere parochial group, but an international organization based in Rome. To cap all those exceptional qualifications, by the 1960s the Jesuits had what may surely be called a hoary, centuries-tested corporate instinct for Church, for papacy, for Catholicism's essential bones of morality and dogma.

And they had their magnificent record. When some or all of the bishops and clergy in France, in Belgium, in Germany, in Austria, in Holland, in England, in the United States, decided at various times in the previous four centuries to oppose the teaching of the Roman Pope, the Jesuits never once deserted the Pope. When local governments, in vendettas against Rome, tried to set up "national" churches as opposed to the Church Universal governed from Rome, the Jesuits never deflected from their vow of obedience and fidelity to the papacy. No torture, no threat of prison, of exile, of death; no blandishments of power, of money, of privilege; not even the suppression of their Society for unjust reasons and by the Roman Pope himself; nothing, in other words, had ever brought the Society to the point of breaking from its vowed submission to and service of the papacy.

If even the Jesuits, then, were changed by these hurricanes—and they were—what can account for that? If they were infected with the euphoria—and they were—how did that happen? Hard-nosed, telltale facts might have been taken as warnings by men such as the Jesuits. They were after all accustomed to monitoring the horizon for history's red flags of coming danger. How could they have missed the out-of-pattern suddenness with which their own membership and recruitment began to drop? In 1914, there were 17,000 Jesuits worldwide. In 1965, there were 36,038. The continuing pattern should have been of growth—especially if there was a general renewal of the kind touted by Jesuits and non-Jesuits alike.

Instead, in 1966, that steady growth reversed itself; membership sank to 35,929. A loss of 109 men in one year was abnormal—was in fact the first substantial decline in fifty-four years. Jesuit Superiors, attuned to far more subtle and far more distant trouble signs, should have sat bolt upright and asked: Why now? They should have asked themselves the same question with increasing apprehensiveness right through to the end of the decade, for in a mere five years the Society suddenly lost over 6000 men. Why?

The pathetic fact is that some of the Jesuit Superiors did ask that question; and that they answered it by saying that the Society needed to abdicate its vowed relationship with the papacy and to change the very nature of Jesuitism. The Society needed the Renewal that was reducing the Church to visible shambles before their eyes. As a Jesuit answer, it was a species of self-destructive insanity.

Surely the Jesuits were affected by the general euphoria of that hurricane time, for the general characteristic of that euphoria was confident and unquestioning abandonment of what had always been sacred and valuable and considered essential. Any such characteristic had been alien not only to the Society of Jesus since its inception, but to the essence—the very reason for existence—of Jesuitism.

In fact, if you explain satisfactorily why the Jesuits—the Society of Jesus as a corporate body—went the way they did, you will have gone a long way to finding some answers for those questions provoked by the apparent suddenness of change and the wild-eyed euphoria throughout the Roman Catholic Church from 1965 onward.

Between 1965 and 1975, the Order held two General Congregations, GC31 and GC32. By the end of GC32 in March 1975, the Society officially and at the hands of its highest ranking Superior —the General Congregation—had undergone a complete transformation from the classical Ignatian ideal to a new Jesuitism. By the end of the decade, the Society in its new form was in full-tilt opposition to the occupant of St. Peter's Throne, after having run a severe gauntlet with that Pope's two predecessors. Virtual war between papacy and Jesuits had been declared.

One cannot rationally suppose that the Delegates to GC31 and GC32 just suddenly, without warning, underwent a sea-change of such a complete kind, and about two such fundamental issues as the nature of the Catholic Church and the meaning of salvation. Nor can one rationally suppose that a 400-year tradition was laid aside either painlessly or spontaneously.

No. That transformation must have been a long time in the making. Over one hundred years before the 1960s, in point of fact, a new and revolutionary current had entered the arteries of the Roman Catholic body, affecting particularly the intelligentsia of the Society of Jesus. That current was characterized by a wish to have freedom from control, freedom to experiment, to adapt to modernity, to exit from Roman Catholic exclusiveness and join the greater mass of men and women. In a word: *Liberation*.

Although that revolutionary current took many twists and turns, it had been quickly recognized by the Popes of the nineteenth century for what it was—a direct, murderous stab at the living heart of Roman Catholicism. Popes denounced it. The Society officially condemned it, even fought against it. But all efforts to get rid of that danger succeeded only in driving it underground.

The current was still flowing silently and in covert at the beginning of the twentieth century.

It reared its head openly for a moment in the immediate post–World War II years, but that authoritarian figure of Pius XII again drove it back. As early as 1946, he denounced it in an encyclical letter.[4] In spite of that, the current enjoyed some exposure to public light at GC29 in 1946 and GC30 in 1957. But it retired almost immediately into its covert position. The timing was off, apparently. But, by then, it was already a question of just that: *timing.*

The originators of that current of "liberation"—one prominent Jesuit in a fit of prophetic zeal once called them "the Liberators" —had done their work well. "From beyond their obscure tombs, they will reach for victory," that same Jesuit remarked about them. Indeed, Pedro Arrupe and his generation of Jesuits—leaders in Catholicism, all—who joyously plunged into the new Jesuitism of the sixties and seventies, were made possible by those Liberators who had come before.

THE LIBERATORS

PART III

12 | THE WINSOME DOCTRINE

Almost exactly one hundred years ago, Western culture in Europe and the United States underwent its one and only radical religious change since the fourth century, when Roman Emperor Constantine proclaimed Christianity to be the religion of the Empire, and this culture was born. That change, apparent among Europeans and Americans by the 1880s, was an utterly new thing: unbelief in God as an acceptable option.

Whether we like it or not, we of the late twentieth century take that option for granted as part and parcel of our culture. For someone to remark that he or she does not believe in God will normally cause no uplifting of eyebrows, beyond a certain surprise that anyone might take the trouble to bring it up at all. For unbelief has become an accepted and viable alternative nowadays.

To be sure, there have nearly always been professed—even professional—agnostics, atheists, unbelievers, and those whom Cotton Mather robustly lumped together in his grab bag of "every sort of backslider and son of Satan." But such people were always regarded as eccentric; certainly they were never acceptable as constituent and normal elements of the culture.

Rather, one steadily held given in Western culture was that a superhuman power named God with a capital G was somehow responsible for the cosmos and all in it. People might differ in their explanations of that given, but it was not permissible—more, it was unthinkable—to deny God's existence.

In the last quarter of the nineteenth century, unbelief "assumed its present status as a fully available option in American culture"[1] and in its European counterpart. It did not drive out belief. It did not dampen the ardor of religious revivals. It was merely that the "continuing absence of a conviction that any such superhuman power [as God] exists"[2] became then and remains today a perfectly acceptable attitude to religion, on a par with belief itself.

As James Turner shows in his book *Without God, Without Creed*, this change had been in preparation for at least two centuries. But his analysis demonstrates a point that is more important when it comes to thinking about those sudden twin hurricanes of the 1960s: The change did not come about as a direct "victory" of purely secular zeal over religious belief. It was not the rise of science, or the secularization of education and politics, or widespread industrialization, or the emergence of Communism and Marxism that forced unbelief on our culture as an acceptable option.

This radical change was directly due to the reaction of religious leaders themselves to modernity. Faced with the efficiency of reason applied to everything—to industrializing man's life; to critical inquiry into man's origins; to exact examination of the nature of the world; to the progressively improving technology in medicine, food-producing, and social science—religious thinkers fell into lockstep. They labored to include God comfortably in all these new modes of thinking and living. Science, technology, and the practical arts were taken as manifestations of man's religious zeal and as preparing for an imminent millennium on earth. "Religious leaders committed religion *functionally* to making the world better in human terms, and *intellectually* to modes of knowing God that were fitted only for understanding the world."[3]

In making those new commitments, religious leaders stepped out of the trenches. While the world was rushing to adapt to its new wisdom, churchmen failed to perform the one task that has always been the hallmark of great religious thinkers: to leaven, to modify, and to give transcendent meaning to the bare facts of life in the visible world. They failed, in other words, to train the supernatural light of their belief onto the new revolutionary wisdoms that flooded the minds of men in the nineteenth century.

Instead, they adapted. They consented to think and reason about God and religious truth according to the new rules by which modern secularism was making its rather impressive progress. In a word, they surrendered to modernity. "God," declared Gilbert Burnet, Bishop of Sarum, "is a progressing Providence."

By 1875, one orator at the University of Wisconsin could declare in public that "Social Science is the Healer, the life-thrilled Messianic Healer of the human race. It is the herald on the misty mountain top proclaiming through all this burdened earth that the Kingdom of Man is at hand." Unbelief was in. It was perfectly respectable. Not to believe was as much a right as to believe. To act on this unbelief in the various sectors of life—marriage, education, politics, social questions, psychology, sexuality—became a purely secular matter, a part of civil rights.

The new religious attitude of unbelief had attractions that were all its own, especially for intellectuals. Such people were, after all, the cream of the crop, the brains, the leading spirits. They weren't simply modern for their day. They *were* modernity. They set the pace. These were no second-rate minds. Some of them were the leading thinkers in their world, and their specialities—science, Biblical lore, the arts, history—were held in high honor.

There were still more reasons to be attracted willy-nilly by the new attitude of unbelievers. This new and revolutionary breed of men seemed so human in their understanding and so divine in their instinct! They were claimedly nonsectarian and democratic in their spirit of toleration—where a Protestant and a Catholic would be at each other's throats, the unbeliever could be friends with both, taking no side. He made no claim to decide on hotly debated religious issues. His claim instead was to be above them. His attitude seemed so broadminded and apparently so unprejudiced, so seemingly sweet and tractable, so winsome and peace-loving, so simpatico, that for many, indeed, it appeared to be the most genuine and noblest of attitudes a believing Christian could adopt. Even when a Lord Burleigh exclaimed, as he once did, that "Any man over fifty who believes in God must be a jackass," one could put this down to sheer annoyance at the unmeltable pettiness of lesser spirits and narrower minds. His lordship didn't really mind if you felt like believing in God.

Still and all, the new outlook could hardly have enjoyed its solid vogue—limited though it was for a time—among cultured people if it weren't for an obscure Hindu monk about whom most modern adherents of the winsome doctrine know nothing. In a brief, comet-like ascendency into fame, however, Swami Vivekananda[4] made their future roseate when he participated in the World's Parliament of Religions in 1893 in Chicago. Beturbaned and robed in orange and crimson, bearded, large-eyed, with an exotic accent and a hypnotic stare, the Swami spoke about the oneness of existence, the divinity of the human soul, the harmony of all religions, and the oneness of God.

Still, it was not so much what the Swami said; it was the way he made it fit so remarkably well with the journey of science and humanism toward a new idea of material perfection. "Man is not traveling from error to truth," Vivekananda declared to the newly receptive Western mind, "but climbing from truth to truth, from truth that is lower to truth that is higher. . . . The worm of today is the God of tomorrow. . . ."

The Swami from Calcutta took the academicians and high society by storm. He was lionized in Boston and New York and Philadelphia; he was honored by the philosophers and theologians of Harvard and Chicago. Wherever he went, in fact, he left an indelible tint in the bloodstream of academic thinkers among whom the winsome doctrine had already taken hold.[5] For he supplied the notion that what mattered was not religion in general or any religion in particular, but spirit. To be spiritual; that was the key. "If one religion be true," he said, "then all the others must be true. . . . Art, science, and religion are but three different ways of expressing single truth. . . . Everything ascends to the spiritual. . . ." Importantly for thinkers engaged in recodifying the world, the Swami supplied a vocabulary to express that spirituality. But most important of all, he consecrated the individual's own life as the only thing that mattered: "Who can help you to the Infinite? Even the hand that comes to you through the darkness will have to be your own."

The Swami succeeded where Christian leaders had failed. He provided the new cult of unbelief with an overarching, unifying, and completely acceptable mind-set.[6] That it was religious in the pagan sense of that word was unimportant. Its appeal was that it harped on the dignity of man, the privileged power of his reason; and it placed total trust only in human nature, so that if each person were free of all tinkering and tampering by organized religion, he could achieve his own happiness. Each one was on his or her own: ". . . the hand that comes to you through the darkness," as the Swami said, "will have to be your own."

The new unbelief had found a way to emphasize what brought people together, not what separated them. Now it could tell men and women what they could become, were destined to become, not what they shouldn't become. Some of its champions distinguished themselves in solving cruel problems: Some of the earliest Abolitionists, the earliest fighters for Black Civil Rights, those who fought against cruelty to animals and to children, and those against child-labor and slum landlords were beacons of encouragement for the new outlook.

As citizens, the new unbelievers were above reproach—amiable, industrious, generous, paying their taxes on time, maintaining good relations with their neighbors, fighting for their country when it was threatened by an enemy. When they died—they preferred to call death their "transition"—all they required by way of memorial service was that one of the living do another living person some kindness in their memory. For memory of them was all that survived. Otherwise, they had entered nothingness.

They were, all in all, totally civilized, as one would say nowadays. Believing Christians would patronizingly, but still admiringly, call them "obviously enlightened heathens." The new breed didn't like that term *heathen*, however, nor *atheist;* the negative connotations were too negative and too obvious. And in any case, the truth of the matter in their minds was that they were spiritual. For they claimed to be moved by the spirit of morality and its conscience, which urged them to do the best they could for other human beings. They supported all the moral good that formal religions both professed and performed, and they propagated friendship, love, reconciliation, and peace. That they also affirmed their lack of faith—as a formal profession—was a small enough difference as far as they could see.

We humans, they might comment wryly, have always desired more than we lack. And, in reality, what does it matter that we are godless? We tolerate all religious beliefs; we accept none of them. Hadn't the Swami put it best? "If one religion be true, then all the others also must be true."

Thus, the new religion of unbelief had acquired an ethos or mind-set and a vocabulary by the turn of the century. There were and have been and still are hundreds of thousands of men and women in the United States alone who at heart are unbelievers. They will, as good citizens, observe the amenities of public and civil and family life, belong to this church group or that; they would never dream of attacking formal religious belief. But at heart they have adopted unbelief.

Because of the new attitude, unbelief, championed our humanness, it could be described as a humanism—but definitely not the same humanism that had emerged in the European Renaissance three centuries previously.

"Man is the measure of all things," the Renaissance humanist had declared proudly as he lifted his head to talk to God.

"We humans have our rightful place in the long, still-unfolding drama, the biological adventure that is cosmic development," said the nineteenth-century unbeliever, looking up from his microscope. "From the worm up to man! Come! Join in!"

The new humanism underlined our privilege of being human together in a purely material cosmos. It championed human membership in that cosmos as something inherent in cosmic history, a happenstance that dated from remote beginnings in the primeval "soup" of lifeless chemicals on an ancient morning, all the way to the erect posture of *Homo sapiens,* and down to the scientist, the scholar at work on fossils and atoms, and his more practical-minded colleagues, the new social engineers. We are "brothers of the boulders, sisters of the stars," in the words of one latter-day scientist.

Everything about the new unbelief was different from the past. In its heyday during the nineteenth and three-quarters of the twentieth centuries, the new unbelievers and those who understood them called the new attitude or outlook "being modern" or "modernist." Modernism became the normal mode of thinking congenial to the unbelievers of Western nations. The Modernist mind foresees all sorts of "goodies" for mankind, and quite a spectacular development, if people will only consent to change.

The one obstacle to that sustained and spectacular development Modernism promised was a certain stubborn resistance to change, a certain fixity of religious belief, the clinging by many to ancient dogmas. Of course, any organized religion presented such an obstacle. But, for the new race of unbelievers and Modernists, the Christian churches and in particular the Roman Catholic Church were the prime creators of the obstacle.

No church, however, had had the history of the Catholic Church in this matter, because for hundreds of years Rome actually fed, regulated, and controlled all intellectual and artistic development in Europe and Latin America. By the end of the nineteenth century, Catholic clerical regulation of learning, research, and inquiry had had a long history marked by bitter experiences of ecclesiastical control over human destinies.

The new breed of unbelievers automatically had a deep antipathy for that control by churchmen. It had retarded man's development, they said. It offended man's dignity. Clerics themselves spoiled the natural unity of men by their churlish divisiveness, and their quarrels over abstract ideas and propositions and dogmas —formulated by other men long dead and moldering in dust— impeded modernity. Worst of all, clerics forbade change. They allowed no adaptation. If that clericalism and ecclesiastical control could be liquidated, men would be free to develop and meet the challenges of a new world.

The attitude, this increasingly militant, anticlerical unbelief, stood for what has come to be called secular humanism.

Unbelief, of itself, could not unseat popular belief and attachment to traditional religion among the masses of ordinary people. The very language it spoke was unintelligible to the ordinary mind. Of its very nature it was a development that suited the sophisticated minds of the learned, the well-educated.

For churchmen, on the other hand, as well as for other religious leaders and thinkers, theologians and social scientists, the new attitude represented a cup of fresh, sparkling water held out to them in what had become for many a tiring, wearisome, repetitious desert. There was, in fact, a noticeable lassitude, an uninventiveness, a sameness and monotony, to be found in the thought of Roman Catholic thinkers of the early nineteenth century. The dominant trait was a siege mentality. Historical events—the French Revolution; the Napoleonic wars; the rise of such great Protestant powers as the British, German, and Dutch empires, and the American Union; the rabid anticlericalism rampant in Europe —reduced Catholic intellectual activity to the spasmic reactions of retort, refutation, repetition.

Adding a taste of gall to this barren monotony was the obvious progress of science, and the substantial social betterment achieved by people who were either unbelievers or at least dead set against Rome, Romanism, and the intellectual tradition of Rome.

A great desire to join in the success, to participate in the "new age," to be colleagues of those who were pushing the frontiers of human knowledge far beyond all conceivable limits, began to play on the intelligentsia of the Church. Surely, they concluded, the Church must also evolve and therefore change. They too (in the Swami's words) were "climbing up from truth to truth that is higher."

Not surprisingly, the one visible and known organization that perceived clearly what harm this Modernism could wreak on its very soul was the Roman Catholic Church. For if Modernism were accepted, the backbone of Roman Catholicism would be broken, and before long its body would be an eviscerated ruin.

Roman Catholicism was built on fixed dogma and belief, and was tied irrevocably to the tradition that the personal representative of God on earth lived in a small but distinct enclave on the banks of the Tiber in Rome, Italy. From there, he authoritatively claimed fixed truths about belief and morality. There was a whole gamut of such traditional teachings dealing with every aspect of human life from before the womb to after the tomb and beyond, into God's eternity. Such traditions could not be changed without altering Catholicism completely.

Already in the 1840s, Italian philosopher Vincenzo Gioberti stated flatly that "the Church will have to reconcile herself with the spirit of the age . . . and with modern times. . . ." Otherwise, he said, the Church would perish. Within thirty years of Gioberti's death in 1852, leading Catholic scholars in France and Italy had succumbed to the power and charm of the new outlook. The continual progress of science, a new cast to the studies of Biblical scholars, the huge vogue of Darwinian evolution, were beginning to have their effect. Supernatural revelation and knowledge, wrote Monsignor d'Hulst, Rector of the *Institut Catholique* in Paris, must not only look reasonable; it must *be* "reasonable, if it were to enter the mainstream."

In practice, of course, this and other statements like it meant that if a conflict of ideas arose between Church teaching and science, the Church should modify or do away with her teaching.

Instead, however, the Roman Catholic Church attacked Modernism directly and by name as a heretical belief on a par with such major heresies of prior ages as Arianism and Pelagianism back in the third and fourth centuries. It pilloried the main principle of Modernism, that all of religion changes, must change, with all of culture according as men make progress and become better in their humanness. The Church of Rome forbade anyone even tinged with Modernism to occupy a teaching post in its seminaries and universities. Church authorities hounded any such people out of all positions of influence. It imposed a solemn oath of abjuration of Modernism on all its theologians. Publicly and officially, Modernism had no chance of resisting the papal attack within the confines of the Church.

Nevertheless, covert though it was, Modernism made its inroads in the Church. For the intellectual, for the culturally sophisticated, there remained that winsome attraction of the unbeliever —as well as his modernity. The Modernist mind was that of hundreds who helped mightily in bettering man's lot. He originated socially beneficial legislation. Modernists championed the underdog. They displayed none of the hate that was rife between differing religions. They claimed no infallibility. Surely, it was argued by Catholic theologians, there must be some truth in a lot of what the Modernists proposed?

We know of scores of Roman Catholic thinkers and theologians who felt that their Church's ban on Modernism was ill-conceived, myopic, the product of an archaic mentality and medieval superstition, a reaction of fear. Most of them were punished. Most of them submitted—some genuinely, others as a matter of form—in order to survive and await a better day. They went underground.

We also have on record what the attitude was in the Society of Jesus on the issue of Modernism around this time. At GC23, which met in Rome from September 16 to October 23, 1883, the Delegates gave unqualified support to the papal condemnation of Modernism. They instructed the then Father General, Anton Anderledy of Switzerland, "that by every means he take care to keep this plague out of the Society."

Clearly, however, the record shows that the attractiveness of the new attitude of unbelief, this Modernism, had made itself felt in the Society. Some Delegates to GC23 argued that the Church existed to save men, not to condemn errors. The unbelieving Modernists, they argued, were trying to do good. Would it not be better to adopt a more sympathetic and understanding attitude to these Modernists? How else could modern man of the 1880s be led "suavely and sweetly" to consider Christ and his salvation?

Of course, those voices advocating what they called a "positive" approach were drowned out by the overwhelming majority of Delegates. The papacy had spoken. The matter was decided. But the sound of those voices would be heard louder, clearer, and far more dominantly just one hundred years later. The same argument for a sympathetic approach would be used to exclude fidelity to the will and decision of the papacy.

A result of the propapal attitude of that time was certainly that in the formal training of Jesuits and in their published works, there was no advocacy of Modernism. But it can be said just as certainly that around this time a Modernist trend of thought entered the intellectual tradition of the Roman Catholic Church and the Society of Jesus.

Modernism was never, during that intervening period—the first fifty years of the twentieth century—professed overtly or openly taught. Indeed, no official Church body was more zealous in promoting papal extirpation of Modernism than the Higher Superiors of the Society up to the middle of the twentieth century. Still, a Modernist mind existed as the "upper ceiling of thought" beneath which many Catholic scholars, Jesuits included, faithfully taught the traditional doctrines of Rome. Many also joined the underground of crypto-Modernists. There was always the possibility that one day circumstances would permit that covert mind to pierce beyond that ceiling, and to experiment in the "blue yonder," if only "the old Church" would yield to common sense and crumble in its defensive siege mentality.

That dream was not always a passive thing. The more prominent and active of these crypto-Modernist Catholic theologians and thinkers vented their efforts to hasten the arrival of that longed-for day. A veritable brotherhood arose between them. They exchanged private copies of their speculations and theories, met at international "scientific" Catholic congresses, held private discussions, promoted each other's pupils and books, and corresponded at length with each other. Their attitude was well summed up by one of their more brilliant members, the famed French historian Monseigneur Louis Marie Olivier Duchesne.[7]

In a consoling and advisory letter to one of the brotherhood, Pierre Hébert, headmaster at the influential Paris *École Fénelon*, Duchesne told Hébert to act cautiously, attempt no "reform" of the "medievalist" teachings of the Roman Church, because the "only outcome of such attempts would be to get oneself thrown out of the window. . . ." No, Duchesne went on, Hébert "should teach what the Church teaches. But leave the explanation to make its way privately. . . ." Then he expressed the secretly nurtured hope of the brotherhood: "It may be that despite all appearances, the old ecclesiastical edifice is going one day to tumble down. . . . Should this happen, no one will blame us for having supported the old building for as long as possible." The abiding cynicism of Duchesne's words is clear.

When one recalls Duchesne's reputation and standing as a Roman Catholic scholar, and the enormous influence he wielded through his learned writings both on theologians and theology professors of his own time, and on successive generations of seminarians—the future priests and bishops of his Church—one begins to realize that the new outbreak of Modernism in the sixties of this century was no accident, no mere coincidence. It had been long and carefully seeded by hidden operatives like Duchesne.

Even after a second and fiercer onslaught on Modernists and their Modernism by Pope Pius X in the first ten years of the twentieth century, the underground continued on. A group of young French Jesuits calling themselves *La Pensée* (Thought) flourished in the twenties; they met privately in their free time in order to discuss the more advanced thinkers in the Society. One effort by their Jesuit Superiors to disband them in 1930 failed. Through the years of World War II and into the late forties, "they never ceased advancing in their notions of Christ and of Christianity," as Father Teilhard de Chardin, one of their prominent members, recalled later.

By the middle of the 1940s, strange rumors started to reach the sensitive ears of Pope Pius XII about de facto acceptance within pockets of the Church of new theories about creation; about denials of Church teaching about Original Sin, the divinity of Jesus, the primacy and infallibility of the Pope. Pius issued two encyclicals—*Mediator Dei* and *Humani Generis*—attacking errors that, in the eyes of the open, above-ground, everyday, public Church, were nowhere to be found. He condemned those who would gravely change the ceremonial of Roman Catholic Liturgy ("they would remove the Tabernacle from the altar"), and those who would let the hypotheses of scientists concerning the origin of man determine what Catholics should believe. He reasserted all the basic traditional Church doctrines.

Not until much later did it become clear that his targets were theologians and thinkers in seminaries who in private were not only experimenting with the new notions, but were privately communicating these notions to their students. *La Pensée* was under papal attack.

"The members of *La Pensée* will cling to their positions . . . ," de Chardin prophesied (with the same willfulness that would later become a hallmark of his fellow Jesuits), "and ultimately they will prevail. For they alone are truly active and capable of communicating their thought since they alone have adapted to the new method. . . ."[8]

Because French Jesuit seminaries were considered to be hotbeds of budding Modernism, in 1948 Jesuit Father General Janssens sent a stalwart conservative, Belgian Jesuit Edouard Dhanis, to visit the seminaries and houses of studies in that country. On completing his visitation, Dhanis recommended the dismissal of several professors and the removal of certain books from the seminary libraries. But, apparently, his efforts were to no purpose. *La Pensée*, in one form or another, behaved as Teilhard de Chardin had prophesied. Consequently, at an international assembly of Jesuits in 1950, Janssens delivered a sharply worded rebuke to the errant intellectuals of the Society. They were lax, he said, in their interpretation of Church doctrine, and they had shown themselves unenthusiastic for the defense of the Pope's encyclical letters that directly addressed the relationship of science and Church teaching about the origins of the human race.

Although five more professors were "resigned" from their posts in France, for members of the brotherhood it was now clearly a waiting game; and what they awaited was the demise of the authoritarian Pope, Pius XII, and the arrival of a more tolerant regime in the Church. In the meantime, similar convulsions began in the Order of the Dominicans. Their Father General had to reprove two prominent theologians, Marie-Dominique Chenu and Yves Congar, because they were too unorthodox for doctrinal safety in their thinking and teaching.

There is no way, no rational way, to explain the apparently overnight conversion to a Modernist stance of the Society of Jesus in its thinkers, Superiors, and principal activists in the sixties of this century unless you accept that really it was not an overnight thing, and realize that a Modernist current had entered the Society's intellectual tradition all the way back in the last decades of the nineteenth century, and that it had lived underground among the members of the "brotherhood" in clandestine groups such as La Pensée, waiting for its day of destiny in the sunlight. In its long, covert preparation, Modernism within the Church and in the Society of Jesus had simply matured; had developed a point of view among the intelligentsia of Church and Society; and now it needed only freedom of action to demonstrate its relevance and acceptability.

That the "brotherhood" labored in covert during those early years with precisely this end in view, there can be little reasonable doubt. Among the many clear signposts that point to this fact, three are so vital that they demand notice. Each one is stronger than the last in the context of classical Jesuitism.

There was, first, the example of Jesuit George Tyrrell, who was finally condemned by Rome and dismissed from the Society because of his Modernist views. Tyrrell was overcome by the "helpfulness" of Modernists compared to the hard, do-or-die, either-for-me-or-against-me attitude of papacy and Church. Above all, the new experts in Bible studies convinced him that Roman Catholic belief was founded on a mythical, not an accurate, reading of the Bible. All in all, those views, or at least many of them, are held by Jesuits today. The correspondence between the two points of view—Jesuit Tyrrell's and modern Jesuits'—is very often chillingly close.

Another signpost of Modernism's effective progress during its covert existence was the still stranger case of Jesuit Father Pierre Teilhard de Chardin. Teilhard was enthralled by what scientists were claiming to establish about prehistory—that enormously long period when our present cosmos was in geophysical gestation.

For him, the hypothesis of evolution proposed by Darwin was a proven fact. He proceeded to adapt Roman Catholicism to that "fact." He elaborated a whole new theory about Catholicism and Christianity. The strangeness of his case lies in the fact that Jesuits, whose undoubted intellectual powers could have made mincemeat of Teilhard's work, instead took him as their front-runner in philosophical and theological matters that concerned their Catholic faith vitally; and that today, above all, he holds an honored position in the Jesuit Hall of Fame, as well as an ascendancy over the Jesuit mind.

The third, and the strangest, of these most significant signposts of Modernism's early, covert hold on the Society was provided by what we know nowadays as Liberation Theology. Properly speaking, Liberation Theology was a Jesuit creation; and it has dominated the practical decisions of the Society's last three General Congregations. With the emergence of Liberation Theology and its concrete applications to the visible world of poverty in Latin America and the teaching of theology all over the Church Universal, the hitherto covert stream of Modernism in the Society gushed forth in full force from its subterranean channels and flowed far and wide in the bright sunlight. Its long-awaited day of destiny had arrived.

13 | GEORGE TYRRELL, S.J.

G eorge Tyrrell was born in Ireland of English parents in 1861. After converting from the Anglican Church to Roman Catholicism in 1879, he entered the Society of Jesus in England one year later. Once his Jesuit formation was finished, he taught philosophy to young Jesuits-in-training at the Jesuit Stonyhurst College for two years, from 1894 to 1896. There never was any doubt about his religious zeal, and no fault was found with his practice of normal Jesuit asceticism. He was, moreover, a man who formed deep and lasting friendships, and aroused a personal devotion to himself in those he counseled and helped spiritually.

Early in his teaching career, however, doubts arose about his judgment in intellectual matters; and in spite of his conversion, which was sincere, and his Jesuit training, which was thirteen years long, he sometimes gave the impression that he had never really grasped the underpinnings of Catholic belief. Whatever it was that was not quite well-adjusted, both he and his Superiors decided he would do better in a more actively apostolic setting. So he moved to London and lived at the Farm Street Jesuit residence as one of the Jesuit priests attached to the adjoining church.

By the time he moved to London, he had already become enamored of the outlook professed by the European Modernists of his day. He was disenchanted with the official policies of his Jesuit

Superiors concerning Modernism, with the quiescence of his fellow Jesuits as a group, and with the policies of the papacy and the Roman hierarchy of his time. In the glory of Victorian England and the *Pax Britannica*, what Tyrrell took to be the siege mentality of Rome seemed so unworthy of man, so uselessly backward. The First Vatican Council, which ended in 1870, had declared that the infallibility of the Pope was a revealed dogma to be believed on faith by all Catholics. This was totally unacceptable to Modernists. Even before that, Pope Pius IX had issued two lacerating documents against Modernism, reiterating all the old—and for Tyrrell, cliché-ridden—doctrines and "medievalisms" of the old Church. All of this added up to defensive authoritarianism in Tyrrell's mind.

During his own student days, Tyrrell had been very impressed with the results of the "higher criticism" leveled at the Bible, and with the promise of science to open up the universe. "The Modernist," he wrote later, "demands absolute freedom for science in the widest sense of that term." He refused to allow "theology to be tied down to any stereotyped statements, but only to the religious experiences of which certain statements are the spontaneous self-chosen expressions." The fixed dogmas of Rome were his target.

For some time, his real thought and outlook escaped any acrid notice or condemnation. He does seem to have had an agenda all his own, its principle being that in a series of publications he would unobtrusively introduce the substance of his ideas for reforming Catholicism and bringing it up to date—for "modernizing it." Thus, the irony and weaving style of his first five books covered over his full meaning. An article of his on Hell written in 1899 did provoke sharp criticisms from his Jesuit censors, but no profound criticism of where he was going intellectually.

For some time, then, his thought and outlook escaped any condemnation. Catholics of the time, including English Jesuits, were not of themselves likely to find most of what Tyrrell said and wrote objectionable—but just peculiar. He was, after all, trying to help modern-minded people to believe. Rome, so distant from England, seemed wrapped up in its own formalism.

Inevitably, however, one of Tyrrell's writings came in for heavy censorship by his Jesuit Superiors in Italy as being extremely dangerous and steering close to heresy. He was warned. Undaunted, he began to publish and circulate his writings privately, sometimes using a pseudonym. Finally, in 1906, his position came to a head. Tyrrell was asked by the Father General to retract his views formally. He refused and was therefore dismissed from the Society. He retired to a private residence at Starrington.

Because he was denied access to the Sacraments, he assumed he had been excommunicated from the Church. But, publicly at least, no formal bill of excommunication was issued against him. His former Jesuit Superiors wished to avoid the public scandal of a Jesuit in open revolt against the Pope. Moreover, although some English Jesuits and bishops were thought to be in secret sympathy with his views, Jesuits and bishops alike feared Rome's anger; the tendency on both sides therefore was to cover the affair up as quietly as possible. What no one said out loud was that Tyrrell in refusing to retract his Modernist views had incurred automatic excommunication; he had deliberately left the Roman Catholic Church. He could not be given the Sacraments of the Church.

One of Tyrrell's Modernist friends, French priest Henri Brémond, wrote him pooh-poohing the excommunication as "a little Roman formality" of no eternal significance. This probably was Tyrrell's own point of view. For him, for Brémond, and for all the Modernists, Rome no longer mattered. The Church for them was something other than the Roman Catholic hierarchic institution, something with new laws and a totally different structure.

Tyrrell, therefore, kept on publishing and lecturing and giving spiritual counsel undauntedly right up to his early and unexpected death in 1909, at the age of forty-eight. Among his last spoken words—he was unable to talk in the last few days before he died on July 15—was a firm refusal to retract his Modernist views, which by then were widely known.

The local bishop where Tyrrell died refused his body Christian burial in a Catholic cemetery, just as he had refused to allow the dying man to receive the Last Rites of the Church. To accept him or his mortal remains officially with formal Catholic Rites would have been a clear signal that a total revolt against Rome, its bishops, and its promulgated doctrine made no difference; that you could be a Modernist and still be regarded as a member of the Church in good standing. This was precisely the point that Tyrrell had hoped to make, and that the Modernists aimed at inculcating: that the day of Rome's primacy and leadership in the Church was over.

In spite of the bishop's ban, however, some priests who were friends and associates of Tyrrell's did administer the Last Rites to the dying man, and did pray over his grave.

The reason for his dismissal by the Jesuits, as for the bishop's refusal of Last Rites and of Christian burial, was, therefore, Tyrrell's stark refusal to retract his Modernist views. Tyrrell was indeed what he proudly called himself: a Modernist. For all of that, however, he was not uncritical, and could even be quite sardonic in poking fun at his more nebulous fellow Modernists. Having listened to the frothy Baron Friedrich von Hügel for a whole evening, he said that for von Hügel "nothing is true, but the sum total of nothings is sublime!" For all of his short life, Tyrrell remained in close touch with his Modernist colleagues in France and Italy and England; he was fully committed to the cause.

What makes Tyrrell's case most relevant in any assessment of a large number of Jesuits today—as well as an equally large number of theologians and bishops—is the uncanny resemblance between their views and Tyrrell's views, between their attitude to papacy and Church hierarchy and Tyrrell's attitude. The striking and vital difference is that today there are so many Tyrrells still held in good standing—that, unlike Tyrrell himself, they are still at their teaching posts in seminaries and universities; still retained in the Society of Jesus; still heading their episcopal sees. In other words, while Tyrrell in retrospect cuts the sorry and pathetic figure of a man (to quote a Slav proverb) who tried "to turn back the Danube River with a fork," whatever rot made him a pariah then has today a firmer and more widespread hold in the Society of Jesus and in the Roman Catholic Church. The credit for that lies to an appreciable degree at his own door.

All of Tyrrell's difficulties and his ultimate lapse into grave heresy centered around that keystone element of the Roman Catholic Church: the hierarchy and teaching authority of Pope and bishop and, ultimately, of priest. As the Church is structured and functions, this hierarchy delivers dogmas and other formulations of belief to the people for their loyal adhesion. Theologians can research and speculate on the data of faith. They can inquire into new avenues of thought. But only this triad—Pope, bishop, and priest—form the *teaching Church*. The people, theologians included, form the *believing Church*.

The adhesion of the believing Church to the doctrine delivered uniquely and authoritatively by the teaching Church is and has always been considered the crux of being a good Catholic, a member of the True Church.

Tyrrell argued against both the structure and function of the hierarchical Church. What that Church produced, he said in essence, was merely "an engineered unity" that had nothing to do with real spiritual unity. It was nothing more than a product of medievalism. Medievalism, he said, always holds on to the same outworn ideas and institutions. Modernism, on the other hand, "slides with the lines" of human development. Tyrrell presented himself unabashedly as antimedievalist and Modernist.

He was painstakingly explicit, and went back to basics. "Religion," he said, "is shown to be the spontaneous result of irrepressible needs of man's spirit which finds satisfaction in the inward and emotional experience of God within us." For the Spirit of God is in us all. The human spirit awakens to self-consciousness and recognizes its kinship with that Spirit which is striving to express itself in the historical process of science, morality, and religion.

Christ did not teach dogmas, ideas, or theories, Tyrrell maintained. The central inspiring theme of his preaching was his own near-future return in glory as the Son of Man to judge the whole world. But in that, according to Tyrrell, Christ miscalculated. The wait turned out to be a long one. In the meantime, Christ served to recall man to "inwardness" and the true "vitality of religion." Contrary to Church teaching, Jesus made no provision for an institution like the papacy, nor did he believe in or know the future.

What did happen then? That is, if the Church was not instituted by Christ, how was it created and what was its true nature and function?

For Tyrrell, the answer was that the same Spirit that created Christ, created the Church as a passing phase in the ongoing religious process. When the real inspiration of Christ's preaching died out with the death of the last of the twelve Apostles who had known Christ in the flesh, there arose a number of loosely federated communities of believers—what today would be called Base Communities, *communidades de base*—living a strictly democratic life and endowed with authority directly from the Spirit to teach what should be believed. Gradually, the present "highly centralized ecclesiastical empire" of the Catholic Church was imposed by human wile and ambition. Authority to teach was erroneously displaced from the communities of believers to this "ecclesiastical empire" of Pope and bishops and priests.

The argument is a lethal one for the Catholic faith and, if accepted, leads directly to a perfect expression of Modernism: The gift and the truth of faith—what is called the deposit of faith—was confided originally to the people. Fundamentally, the "Church" (that federation of communities) is democratic; and the only norm of faith is the democratic consensus of the people. That is to say: The "people," and not the Pope, is the Vicar of Christ. Neither Pope nor bishops channel the Word of God to the people.

The people have the Word already. The collective religious life of the people is the ultimate criterion of truth.

As a consequence, "what makes a Catholic is not this or that abstract theory of the Roman Church but a belief in the historical Catholic Community as the living outgrowth of the apostolic mission." Faith in the world thus becomes more fundamental than faith in the Church; for the world—humanity—is by revised definition the fuller and all-inclusive revelation of God.

Furthermore, as each age comes and goes, men invent formulas that reflect only one stage in the growth of the spirit in humanity. With another age, new formulas must be invented. Belief itself, therefore, changes. That is the true religious process. No intellectual truth, no dogma, has been given to us by God for our permanent assent. We have been given merely "a way of life," the highest life of the soul. Any and all formulas or dogmas of churchmen have no more authority for individuals than the formulas of scientists about anthropology or atoms or history. They all change, because they all progress, as humanity progresses.

What then about the Roman Catholic Church? Well, it was an experiment. And, to give it its due, at one dangerous stage for God's revelation in the early days, it was a necessary thing in order to keep memories of Christ alive. But those days were over, Tyrrell said. Humanity had progressed. Ideally today, the Pope and the bishops should merely formulate the feelings and beliefs of the faithful. The Pope, properly speaking, should be the publicly accepted and final exponent of the people's feelings and faith. But, all in all, the ecclesiastical experiment known as the Roman hierarchic Church had outlived its usefulness. It now represented " a perversion and stultification of a system that once promised such great things for the good of humanity."

Put simply, it was time to move on. In all its charity, the Modernist hope was that the Church would cease to claim divine origin and immutable doctrines and fixed government by Pope and bishops. If only she were to offer her spiritual services to civilization, then the Church too could reenter the religious process of humanity, and thus help toward the ultimate goal.

What goal? The "Catholic ideal of an international and universal religion inspired by the idea of democracy as the original constitution of the church." The Roman Catholic ecclesiastically-run Church must conform to the iron laws of the religious process leading inexorably to this goal.

A hard fact had to be faced in all this, Tyrrell admitted: The

Roman Catholic Church might have to die "in order that it may live again in a greater and a grander form." Why? Because, Modernist charity aside, there was no earthly hope that the ecclesiastical authorities would change their medievalist doctrines in the light of modernity—in the light of man's new discoveries in religion, in anthropology, in psychology, in physical science, in medicine. The Roman Church must therefore perish like every other abortive attempt to discover a universal religion as catholic as science. For science represented the ideal universality: It was the possession of all men.

Tyrrell, like all Modernists, believed in the possibility of a synthesis between the essential truth of his religion and the essential truths of modernity. For the Modernist, Catholicism can and must be reconciled with the results of historical criticism. Tyrrell therefore demanded guarantees for the liberty of individual Christians against encroachment by dogma-spouting ecclesiastics. He protested against the centralization of government by the papacy and the bishops, who deprived the people of their share in Church government.

The parallels are already clear between George Tyrrell's nineteenth-century Modernist theology and the present-day theology of such a man as, say, Fernando Cardenal, who has declared his true mission to be the political liberation of the oppressed. As a Jesuit, his priesthood meant nothing else. Neither the Pope in Rome nor the local bishops of Nicaragua had any importance in his optic. But the parallels between Cardenal and Tyrrell do not end with a few points of contention with the Church. Tyrrell left nothing untouched or unchanged.

Tyrrell must have been exposed to all the training, piety, and devotion of a man formed in the Society of Jesus in the late nineteenth century. Yet, clearly, from his explicit statements, he had abandoned the basic concept of Ignatian spirituality and the driving motives of Jesuit zeal: the Kingdom of Christ, the Leader, at war with the archenemy of Human Salvation; and Jesuit obedience to Christ's Vicar on earth, the Pope. To read Tyrrell's books is to understand that nothing of all that entered the warp and woof of his thought and belief. In fact, some time before his open rupture with the Jesuits and with Rome, he admitted that the Society of Jesus and all it stood for had become like so much "dust and ashes" in his mouth. The breakdown in his attachment to the Ignatian ideal could not have been more plain. The rest followed.

It is certain that Tyrrell did not believe that Jesus was God-made-man. He did not believe either in the resurrection of the body or in the existence of Hell or of Heaven. Nowhere in his eleven major books can you find that the Mass was for Tyrrell the Sacrifice of Christ on Calvary. In fact, Christ does not appear as a living Savior dying on the cross to effect the Salvation of the world. Christ's personal love for all men and women does not appear. Instead, Jesus is diminished to pygmy size. "We cannot frame our minds to that of a first century Jewish Carpenter," he wrote.

Small wonder, perhaps, that there is a lack throughout Tyrrell's writings of any sign of that devotion to the person of Jesus that was central to Jesuit spirituality, piety, mission, and zeal. And small wonder, too, that there is a similar lack of devotion to the Virgin Mary or to the saints. Small wonder—except that the absence of such devotion was both remarkable and symptomatic in a man educated and formed in the Society of Jesus in the late nineteenth century.

If Tyrrell was merely neglectful of the Virgin and the saints, he was downright vituperative and contemptuous when it came to the Pope, the Vatican bureaucracy, and the bishops. He was not merely criticizing obvious faults; faithful Catholics do that much all the time. Rather, he denied outright the infallibility of the Pope, the teaching authority of the hierarchy, the divine inspiration of the Bible, the existence of the Devil, and a whole gamut of other defined dogmas of the Roman Church. For Tyrrell, the papacy and the bishops had about as much to do with the Church and true religion as the academic faculty of All Souls College of Oxford University had to do with pig farming in Uganda. He could not abide the hierarchic Church as an idea or as a reality.

Tyrrell's mind was wholly and exclusively concentrated on the here and now. His voice was the authentic echo not of the Jesuitism he ostensibly chose, but of the unbelief that was born just about the time Tyrrell was born. For him, belief in Christ entailed no faith in Christ as "a teacher and in his doctrine, but [merely] an apprehension of his personality as revealing itself within us."

The true Catholic, according to Tyrrell, "believes in humanity; he believes in the world. To deny that God is the primary author of all intellectual, aesthetic, moral, social, and political progress seems to the Modernist mind the most subtle and dangerous form of atheism." In one sweep of his pen, Tyrrell had thus embraced at least implicitly several major and ancient heresies long since considered refuted and condemned by his Church.

No matter, however. For Tyrrell maintained that there was no point in defending the Roman Catholic Church as the one true Church. A more glorious option was open to mankind. "To feel the relation of fraternity between the various members of the religious family . . ."—Tyrrell had Christian as well as non-Christian religions in mind—". . . is to be a Catholic"; for "Modernism acknowledges among the religions of the world a certain unity in variety."

At the same time, however, there was "no organic unity between the various forms of religion as though they all complemented each other." For, in the final analysis, true religion was nothing more than "an adjustment of our conduct to a transcendent world." Whatever that meant, all forms of religion must conform to it or perish. Indeed, all beliefs and credal formulas of all religions were seen by Tyrrell as passing adaptations, and all were destined to disappear as man progressed from higher plane to higher plane. There was no "warfare" for the "Kingdom," but merely a "development of the Spirit of holiness" throughout humanity as it passed through its various stages. Swami Vivekananda could not have said it better.

Many prominent theologians and bishops in today's Church should be able to recognize in George Tyrrell a true ancestor of theirs. Enthusiasts of Liberation Theology such as Jesuit Father Gustavo Gutierrez and Juan Luis Segundo are following Tyrrell's lead in their insistence that theology must not come "from above" —from the hierarchical Church—but "from below"—from "the people of God."

Similarly, the vaunted "new" idea of Base Communities as the authentic unit of believers, and as the only trustworthy source of belief and revelation, is nothing more than a resurrection of Tyrrell's proposal precisely that the true "church" was formed by a gaggle of such communities.

Indeed, just about every major Church figure who throws obloquy on the teaching authority of Rome today need seek no further than Tyrrell for his exemplar. Teaching with an impunity denied to Tyrrell, such honored men as Karl Rahner, Hans Küng, Charles Curran, Leonardo Boff, Jon Sobrino, Edward Schillebeeckx—to name but a handful of self-established Church authorities and luminaries—claim, as Tyrrell did, that the spirit of God reveals itself in individuals and in local groups, and that those individuals and groups therefore have their own authority. They need pay no heed to Rome's voice.

Tyrrell set the Modernist model not only for teaching authority and authenticity of belief, but for religious mission. Tyrrell's total abandonment of the Ignatian ideal of warfare carried out for the sake of Christ's Kingdom will be recognized by Fernando Cardenal and his compatriots, and by every other Jesuit who has substituted a sociopolitical ideal—usually the Socialist/Marxist ideal—for that ideal of Ignatian spirituality.

Tyrrell's influence does not stop with structure and mission in the Church. Necessarily, the basic nature and function of priesthood in the Catholic Church comes into question.

In Catholic doctrine, priesthood is a Sacrament given through the Church to an individual. To receive the Sacrament of priestly Ordination, to become a priest, means that personally and individually the recipient's soul is forever qualified and added to. Another dimension is added to it by God's grace. It is a dimension of power exactly corresponding in its own limited, created fashion to the dimension of power that belonged to the human soul of Jesus as the savior God-man and as high priest of salvation.

That forever irremovable dimension of power has two principal areas of activity: The priest can offer the Sacrifice of the Mass as a reenactment of Jesus's sacrifice of his human life on Calvary, and the priest can forgive other men for their sins. Besides these two areas, there are others also—preaching the good news of the Gospel, spiritually advising others, dominating evil spirits, theological perception, moral judgment, and so forth.

A priest is fundamentally, essentially, and unchangeably a sacrificing, absolving, preaching member of the Church whose authority and whose priesthood come to him from God through the summons of the Apostles—the bishops of the Church of whom the Pope is head and supreme guarantor of every priest's authenticity.

In the Modernist doctrine as propounded by Tyrrell, all that Catholic doctrine is thrown out the window of human intervention. Neither the divinity of Jesus nor the sacrifice of his physical self for men's Salvation has any place in the ultimate stage of religious truth of Modernism.

What does take place in priesthood according to the Modernist mind—Tyrrell's and all the other Tyrrells who have flourished since and are flourishing in our day—is expressed as accurately as could be in a namesake of George Tyrrell, George Wilson, S.J., an American whose writings have had a wide impact, and reflect the mentality of an entire generation of Jesuit theologians.

For Jesuit Wilson, "the 'Church' is not, in the first instance, a world institution but rather a local acculturated sacramental reality. 'Local Church' is not in the first instance an administrative unit of a larger organization [in which the focus might therefore quite easily rest on the bishop], but rather [is] the life of the whole gathered people, with all its unique ethos, lived out initially in significant communities where people experience the reality of reconciliation/salvation; the family and the parish, and secondarily that local church we call diocese."

Though he is far from poetic, it is clear that in the tangle of sociology and anthropology that went into the making of Wilson's "new theology" of the "Church," teaching authority rests with the people, not in the Roman Catholic Church's bishops and Pope. That much is unadulterated Tyrrell.

Where Wilson makes his contribution, standing on Tyrrell's shoulders so to speak, is in putting into so many words the meaning of all that for the priesthood.

"Priesthood," Wilson explains, "is not in the first instance a personal gift bestowed on an isolated individual but a corporate gift given to a body of persons for the upbuilding of these local churches."

Immediately, Wilson has solved a Modernist dilemma. If you do away with the priesthood, you haven't a prayer of holding together anything even resembling an organized church such as the Catholic Church has always claimed to be. But if you've already done away with Jesus as God, and therefore have done away with his sacramental gifts bestowed upon individual priests, thus allowing them to stand in his place—to offer his forgiveness and his Sacrifice—well, the embarrassing problem obviously is what to *do* about the priesthood.

The answer is as simple as it is devastating. Priesthood is no longer given to an individual; it is given to, or perhaps resides in, a community. And its purpose is no longer sacrifice and absolution; it is the social "upbuilding" of the community. But then, of course, you have a problem about sins. What happens to them? Are they "evolved" away, out of existence? Or do you state there is only "social sin," but no really "personal" sins? Neither Wilson nor Tyrrell have any solution.

There is yet another striking note of similarity between the case of George Tyrrell and his descendants, the Modernists of our time: the note of fundamental and dangerous contradiction in the way they cling to the skirts of the Church they scorn. To the end of his days, Tyrrell grieved because he was not allowed to stay on in the Roman Catholic Church. He retained a fierce attachment to that Church—understood of course in his sense—and a fierce desire to aid in its transition from medievalism to Modernism.

Side by side with his deep Modernist persuasion, surely aware but apparently heedless of the contradiction, he insisted that the

Catholic Church of Rome "has on the whole preserved the message of Christ more faithfully than any other . . . and in it you can find the germ of that future universal religion for which we all look." So much so that "if Rome dies, the other churches may order their coffins."

For Tyrrell, then, every other church was "the work of the devil, a snare, an imposture, a spurious evolution." And "whatever Jesus was, he wasn't a liberal Protestant."

In line with such sentiments, Tyrrell's most vociferous condemnation of Martin Luther and John Calvin and the other Protestant reformers of the sixteenth century was that they should not have revolted, but should have stayed in the Church and worked for its change from within, as he yearned to do.

How Tyrrell would have envied such twentieth-century Modernists as Hans Küng, and all those many others who wish to be known as Roman Catholics, but who use that position to eviscerate and transform Catholicism. Indeed, today Tyrrell's case history is probably most notable for the fact that he was expelled at all from the Society of Jesus and excluded from the Sacraments of the Church. For, in our time, the Modernist spirit of George Tyrrell reigns supreme. Up and down the national hierarchies, and at large among Jesuits, Carmelites, Dominicans, Maryknoll priests and nuns, as well as among some two dozen other Religious Orders and Congregations, the Modernist point of view is openly declared and put into daily practice. Superiors—both Religious and episcopal—make no attempt to get rid of the Modernists in their midst. No one of the last three Popes has been strong enough or threatening enough to force the hands of those tolerant Superiors; and one is forced to suspect that those Superiors themselves share the Modernist mind and outlook.

Without a doubt, were Tyrrell alive today, he would not be beyond the pale, but would be flourishing in a professor's chair at a Jesuit university or seminary.

But such was not his fate. Once he went public, he became a threat to friend as well as foe. His Jesuit Superiors were afraid of what the strong Pope of that time, Pius X, would do if the Society of Jesus sanctioned Tyrrell as he was going. He died, therefore, in his regrets.

If you visit his grave today, you will see the headstone just as he himself sketched it before he died: the Host and Chalice at the top; beneath, his dates and the words "A priest of the Catholic Church"—the position he desired so much.

Host and chalice; priesthood and Church. No matter, he seemed to say, that these can no longer be accepted as the practical instruments Jesus provided to see his servants into the place of God's eternal glory. He could still cherish them as dearly beloved cultural artifacts identifying George Tyrrell, S.J., as belonging to one phase in the long development of "the spirit in man."

14 | PIERRE TEILHARD DE CHARDIN, S.J.

Without a knowledge of Pierre Teilhard de Chardin, S.J., it would be very difficult for any non-Jesuit to understand the kind of change through which the Society of Jesus has passed, the almost perfected mode of recalcitrance to all and any papal wish that the Society has learned to practice, the utter sincerity of this attitude, and the distance that now separates the Jesuit outlook both from the original Ignatian ideal and the common faith of the Roman Catholic Church.

Teilhard, as he was familiarly called, was born in France twenty years after George Tyrrell, in May 1881. At eighteen, he became a Jesuit trainee. At thirty, he was ordained a priest. His special studies concentrated on paleontology and biology. Trapped in Peking by the outbreak of World War II, he returned again to France after the war ended and spent some years there, but from 1951 until his death in April 1955 at the age of seventy-four, he lived in New York.

Over his lifetime, he achieved status and notoriety in scientific circles because of his wide knowledge and his original theories that enlaced biological evolution with religion. But his greatest stature was reached when he became almost an oracle and icon of what a twentieth-century Jesuit should be.

Perhaps it helped that Teilhard was tall, aristocratic in his bearing, distinguished in appearance, quick-witted, with an intensity of tone. He never lacked for devoted friends who put their houses at his disposal and aided him in his "exile," as he referred to the later years of his life spent in the United States. He was French to the core and a formidable adversary in an argument. He never lost the common touch—once, at a New York dinner party, he was offered what he ecstatically described as "a foie gras directly imported from Perigord and good enough to make one weep."

No doubt about it, he was fired by a messianism that sometimes shone in the dark intensity of his stare, and at all times attracted and commanded respect. Consciously, he identified with the sixteenth-century astronomer Galileo Galilei, making his own the mythical phrase attributed to Galileo. "The Earth turns!" Teilhard would exclaim,[1] giving to those words the meaning of evolutionary change. "We are dying today," he stated, "from the fact of not having anyone who knows how to lay down his life for the Truth." Like General de Gaulle, he would sometimes refer to himself in the third person, as when he praised one of his own uncles "as one of the most Teilhardian and the most intelligent" of all his relatives. There was an arrogance in his attitude that never repelled people, for it was an expression of his utter surety.

Still, it was not so much his remarkable personal attributes that conferred his stature of oracle and icon upon him, but a play of circumstances. In a sense, it was his destiny, given all the factors at work.

There was, in the first fifty years of twentieth-century Jesuit history, a role in search of a hero, an enterprise in need of a pioneer. A hero and a pioneer for Jesuits had to display certain characteristics: high intellectualism, stature with powerful secular figures, a definite touch of poetry and mysticism, a streak of persecution by men of lesser stature, a spirit of independence from Rome and of revolution for the sake of principle, and worldly-wise associations that gave him "class" and a certain degree of "star" quality—internationalism.

Pierre Teilhard de Chardin displayed all those characteristics to an eminent degree, and he had one more supreme advantage that consecrated him as icon. He sensed in himself and his contemporaries a certain ennui, a boredom with the status quo. The atmosphere of that time was full of the persuasion that human history had just turned a definitive corner, and that a brave new world awaited men and women.

In the immediate aftermath of World War II, physics and technology took great strides and pushed back ancient horizons of knowledge in every field. World power was now conditioned by physics—the A-Bomb and shortly the H-bomb. Crick and Watson revolutionized genetics by revealing the structure of DNA. Discoveries of prehistoric "man"—mainly the work of the Leakey family in Africa—excited the popular imagination. Teilhard's genius, for genius it was, lay in his being able to inject that new age with a new philosophy and a new excitement, and with a deeply appealing romanticism. So potent was he as figurehead and icon for the "winsome doctrine" of "all things new and renewed," that it can be said that Jesuit thought—especially among those Delegates who attended GC31–33—had been impregnated with his outlook long before those General Congregations assembled.

Teilhard's best known though not his most effective claim to his leadership role rested primarily on his very progressive theory of evolution. Teilhard's thought and language can be extremely complicated and obscure.[2] In order to convey his ideas, he made up a whole series of new terms. A brief account of his theory is necessary, but it must omit many of his refinements and details.

Roman Catholics had always held that the emergence of *Homo sapiens* was the direct result of a separate act of creation by God, as outlined in the Garden of Eden account in the book of Genesis. For man, in Catholic doctrine, has a spiritual and immortal soul which could not "evolve" in any acceptable sense from material forms, even from "higher animals." This is still the teaching of the Roman Catholic Church. When Roman Catholic scholars who had accepted Evolution as fact tried to reconcile official doctrine with Evolution, they assumed that God the Creator intervened at a certain moment in the evolutionary process and infused a spiritual and immortal soul into an already highly developed "higher animal."

It was a fragile supposition about a supposition, and Teilhard threw sardonic obloquy on Cardinal Ruffini of Palermo, who mentioned it as a possible way of reconciling Evolution and divine creation of the human soul. "The Cardinal is still convinced that Evolution implies that God breathed a soul into an ape," he commented acidly. "It is irreconcilable with what we know from biology that our human species should be descended from a pair." The image of pure spiritual Godhead bending over some hairy, comatose ape in a primeval jungle was just what Teilhard wished to evoke in order to ridicule Ruffini.

Teilhard's theory bypassed the difficulty. His starting point was Darwinian Evolution—he always "personalized" the word with a capital letter—which he took to be fact, not theory. The cosmos and all in it developed from inert, lifeless beginnings through suc-

cessive stages of development and over a duration of billions of
years. At a certain moment, men—*Homo sapiens*—appeared.
Human history had begun.

Essentially, however, Teilhard used that Darwinian starting
point as a catapult by redefining Evolution—and also by introduc-
ing that new vocabulary of his own invention. The human species,
he said, emerged from matter because of the innate connection of
matter and spirit—"there's no such thing as pure matter or pure
spirit, for us," he wrote. Consciousness was "present" the moment
anything existed and was composed of two parts. True religion, he
said, had started back at the moment that basic consciousness was
"present."[3]

Once individual men and women appeared on the scene in several disparate groups all over globe, there started a long last stage
of development toward a total unity of all individuals in the
"Omega Point" of history. We are still in the middle of that development. Once complete unity has been achieved, Christ—who
will be the Omega Point—will appear; man will then be more
than man, will be what Teilhard called Ultra-Human; the cosmos
will be transformed; and the glory of it all will be established.

Obviously, such a theory imposes either the abandonment or
the complete transformation of all the basic doctrines of Roman
Catholicism. Creation, Original Sin, the divinity of Jesus, redemption by Jesus's death on the cross of Calvary, the Church, the
forgiveness of sins, the Sacrifice of the Mass, priesthood, papal
infallibility, Hell, Heaven, supernatural grace—even the existence
and the freedom of God—all must be reformulated, and perhaps
abandoned in large part.

Teilhard's writings were censored heavily by Roman Superiors;
more than one of his books never saw the light of day during his
lifetime. It is a tribute to his mental agility, his cunning, and the
power of his ideas that he finally was left alone by his Superiors
and allowed to carry on his scholarly activities until he died.

Most of his fellow Jesuits, and in fact most of those who read
the mellifluous, complex, sometimes poetic prose Teilhard
churned out in books, magazine articles, and lectures, never quite
grasped his theory of Evolution.

He himself preferred the terms Cosmogenesis and Anthropo-
genesis. His self-made vocabulary was dizzying—amorization,
hominization, Christogenesis, Christification, Pleromization, ex-
centration, biogenesis, are examples of a far longer litany. Teilhard
often hesitated in defining precisely what his hybrid terms meant.
Still, his followers could excuse that; they felt they could usually

grasp the general lines of thought along which he marshaled his ideas into theories. So sure were many of his devotees of that feeling that they adopted those general lines of Teilhardism and applied them to their own concrete situations.

The most dominant of those lines was Teilhard's assertion that a new humanity was emerging as inexorably and as surely as night follows day. For, after all, this was a continuing Cosmogenesis-Anthropogenesis, wasn't it? Here at least was an honest-to-goodness scientist, and a Jesuit to boot, giving an acceptable "basis" for what poor, pathetic George Tyrrell had been trying to say all along but never quite got out: All the old things—thought-molds, mores, dogmas—had to go, had to change.

A second dominant line of Teilhard's thought was the slow and equally inexorable unification of all the diverse human beings up, up, up, through all kinds of bloody struggles, until they reached the Omega Point of perfect unity. Unification and equalization were the strong overtones here.

Teilhard more than once applied this line of reasoning to the sociopolitical situation of his day. His alienation from capitalism and his orientation to "the people" was quite manifest. Evolution for him implied evolution also in the distribution of goods, an equalization of property that capitalism made impossible. "Human society has been more and more caught up in a yearning for true justice . . . a liberation from the bonds [of poverty and dependence brought on by capitalism] in which too many people are still held," he wrote.

Like evolution itself, this sociopolitical dimension of his thinking was not theory but fact for Teilhard. In the aftermath of World War II, for example, both the Jesuit and Dominican Religious Orders had allowed some of their members to become worker-priests. These men ate and slept, lived and worked in the very same conditions as the ordinary workman. If their fellow workers joined Communist cells, they joined. If their fellow workers rioted in the streets or demonstrated in front of a government building, the worker-priests did too.

In time, these associations and activities led to so many casualties and defections that both Jesuit and Dominican Superiors were forced to recall their priests from this work. *Forced* is the proper word, for it is virtually certain that they would not have voluntarily retired. Nor would their Superiors have withdrawn them, had it not been for the reports sent to Rome by the Apostolic Nuncio in Paris, Archbishop Angelo Roncalli, the future Pope John XXIII, in which he indicated laconically that all in all, the Church had not gained one soul through this extensive output of manpower, but that the Communist and Socialist parties had benefitted enormously from the worker-priests, and so had several French women, who had acquired husbands.

Roman authorities called in the Jesuit Superiors and imposed on them an official recall of their men. Even then, however, about half the worker-priests refused to obey the recall order, and opted for membership in the Communist Party instead. Most of them had ceased by then to say Mass or exercise any priestly duties. They quit the priesthood.

Teilhard's reaction to all this was as sure and unequivocal as the man himself. He was distressed at Rome's intervention: "Under the circumstances, and in a capitalist world, how does one remain a Christian?" he asked. "Priest-workers find in the face of a humane Marxism not only justice but hope and a feeling for the Earth which is stronger than 'evangelical humanity.' " For Teilhard, Marxism presented no real difficulty. "The Christian God on high," he wrote, "and the Marxist God of Progress are reconciled in Christ." Little wonder that Teilhard de Chardin is the only Roman Catholic author whose works are on public display with those of Marx and Lenin in Moscow's Hall of Atheism.

The third and most ominous line of de Chardin's thought concerned the essential structural element of Christianity that all genuine Modernists—Tyrrell and Teilhard are no exceptions—must have as their chief target: its hierarchy of bishops united with the Pope as their head. The Three Persons of the Trinity constitute the supreme hierarchy. The Pope and his bishops constitute a second major hierarchy. The General of the Society of Jesus and its Superiors, Major and Minor, constitute a third hierarchy. Within God's Heaven, there are hierarchies of angels, and within Satan's Hell, hierarchies of fallen angels. Within the social body, there is the hierarchy of family. Hierarchy is an essential note of Roman Catholicism.

There was no way, from the point of view of pure reasoning, that any of these hierarchies could survive in strict Teilhardism. The most notable casualty was Jesus.

"I have come, not to destroy, but to fulfill the law," Jesus asserted. Teilhard literally and, for pious ears, blasphemously interpreted that as: "I have come not to destroy, but to fulfill Evolution." In other words, as Teilhard's theory went on to express, according as men and women in the Church become conscious of Evolution's perpetual forward movement—here we have another of Teilhard's brain-knocking word inventions: "physical-

biological-mental convergence"—their consciousness "irresistibly entails a total rebirth of mystical theology and Faith on every
level." Or, put in the simplest possible terms, Jesus and the Christian belief in his Incarnation in the womb of the Virgin Mary some
nineteen hundred and eighty-six years ago became a problem. For,
in the Teilhardian sense, Jesus has not yet been really incarnated
—only at the Omega Point will that take place; and even then it
is not Jesus of Nazareth we are talking about, but Christ "the
essential Mover of a Hominization leading on to an Ultra-Hominization [or man become greater than man]."

Teilhard called that event Pan-Christicism. The only problem,
Teilhard said, was "how to insert the mystery of the Incarnation
into the moving history of humanity." This was coded language
expressing one other giant problem: How reconcile all this theoriz-
ing with the data of Catholic faith?

The last dominant line of his thought was saturated in poetry
and a special mysticism that generated in Teilhard a strange and
new romantic excitement, side by side with a certain type of disregard for the individual.

From his correspondence, it is clear that Teilhard was not overly
shocked by bloodshed, regarded violence as a necessary concomi-
tant of Evolution, and seemed to have enjoyed war—what he saw
of it.[4] Death, bloody or otherwise, was what he called a "muta-
tion." Despite this trait, Teilhard was described fatuously by
American theologian David Tracy as "a poet of science—a rare
cultural type." But Teilhard himself stated that "it would be more
to my purpose to be a shadow of Wagner than a shadow of Darwin." The Götterdämerung of the Alemanni was more tasteful to
him than the uneventful "evolution of the species."

The consequence of Teilhard's preference in myths was clear.
To follow and accept Teilhard's reasoning meant an expectation of
some great, quasi-apocalyptic development built into nature as
part of the way things in nature reach their appointed purpose in
an imminent new era that was just around the corner. The acceptance of such invented romanticism—Teilhard had a lyrical pen,
to be sure—meant a rejection of the fundamental Christian belief
that all blood-letting, all savagery, all rampant animality, the dog-
eat-dog law of the jungle, the automatic war between animal and
man (and between man and man, as well) together with all destructive elements in the cosmos—earthquakes, floods, hurricanes, disease, poison, and death itself preceded by the miseries of aging—
that entire mass of suffering was due to one primordial offense
against God by the founders of the human race. The Original Sin

of Adam and Eve had no place in Teilhard's poetic, romantic apocalypse.

On this point of "nature's nature," Teilhard was quite pagan. When he saw the famous cyclotrons at the University of California's Berkeley campus, he was filled "not with terror but with peace and joy" at these tremendous "wombs of change." It was apparently not the specter of Doomsday he saw there, but the possibility that Doomsday would be the womb of the Omega Point.

While he awaited romantic cataclysm, everything that bore the mark of change, however small, was fascinating and enchanting for Teilhard. On one occasion, for example, a certain Miss Lattimer of East London, England, caught by chance a unique fish—the *Crossopterygian* (now surnamed *Lattimeria*)—that fascinated all paleontologists. "Shown to me by Miss Lattimer herself," Teilhard wrote delightedly, "an extraordinary spectacle! An enormous ganoid more than two meters long, with lobed fins!" He could wax just as eloquently about everything from the movement of subatomic particles to the architecture of ice crystals after an ice storm in eastern China. There was an eerie, chilling, not quite flesh-and-blood note in some of his delights. "Teilhard," remarked one of his early companions, "has very cold blood."

Admittedly, there was in Teilhard's writings an infectious, almost jaunty optimism. Always and everywhere he spoke and behaved as the visionary with a rock-solid sureness about the future. But, for all of that, there is not one line of his that indulges the same infectious enthusiasm for celebrating the Sacrifice of the Mass; for making reparation to the Sacred Heart of Jesus; for defending the rights of the papacy; for shriving sinners of their sins; for teaching children their catechism; or for consoling the oppressed. All of him was wrapped up in his version of the "winsome doctrine," in the impersonal glory that would come to every man with the arrival of the "Ultra-Human."

So impersonal did his belief become, and so typically sure of himself was he, that over time a certain bitterness and censoriousness came out in him toward anyone who clung to what he saw as the old, outworn dogmas and pieties of traditional Catholicism. He recounted in a 1952 letter how he went to hear Archbishop Fulton Sheen preach at St. Patrick's Cathedral in New York City. "One of Sheen's strengths," he dryly remarked, "was being able to live and see a religion without mysteries, save those of theology." Teilhard, who loved the mysteries of nature, concluded sardonically: "For him [Sheen] all is revealed."

On another occasion, visiting a new convent for cloistered Benedictine nuns in Connecticut, he noted that a traditional grille had been installed to separate the cloistered nuns from the world outside. "Alas! Alas!" he murmured, and thought it worth retailing in a letter how idiotic he thought the whole idea of the cloistered life had become at this stage of Evolution.

One Christmas, the spirit of festivity in New York evoked his disgust. The problem for Teilhard evidently was not the commerciality, however.

" . . . I do my best to put myself in the Christmas spirit," but all of it "makes me gag," the "state of excitement," the "touching mutual goodwill," all the fuss in this New York that was "so sophisticated" and so "childlike."

There was nothing of gentleness, of compassion, of fair-mindedness, of sensitive perception in Teilhard.

In the light of all this, how does one assess Teilhard de Chardin as a Roman Catholic and as a Jesuit? This man's influence on Jesuit thinking and on Catholic theologians as well as on the thought processes of Christians in general has been and still is colossal. Fortunately, we have Teilhard's own testimony on these important headings—the impact he hoped to have on his Church and on the Society of Jesus.[5]

Concerning the Roman Catholic Church—its papacy, its hierarchy, its doctrinal formulations, its piety, its place in the human cosmos—Teilhard was summarily and completely disillusioned. At the present moment in human history, he said, "no religion explicitly and officially offers us the God we need." The problem the Church had, he said, was that "she continues to live in a universe in which the rest of us do not." For she, "the Keeper of the Flame of modern monotheism, refuses to give the world the God it waits for." This Church "accuses the world of growing tepid, while it is really they the leaders who are letting the God of the Gospels . . . grow cold in their hands." Her celibate clergy appeared to the world to be "false brothers" of humanity, "halfbrothers" who reproached humanity with sins. The Church gave no real life to its adherents.

As a consequence, when Mao Tse-tung and his Communists overwhelmed China in 1949 and, with it, the Catholic Church of three million souls, Teilhard was able to pronounce a cool-eyed I-told-you-so judgment: "It is not because of their Catholicism that the faithful Chinese are better able to face the Marxism of Mao Tse-tung." Indeed, in the final analysis, "the Church will not again take up her conquering stride," until she sets out "to re-examine the relationship between Christ and a universe grown fantastically immense and organic."

The change demanded of the Church by Teilhard was total. The traditional idea of the Supernatural (a "monstrous idea," he said) was to be replaced by his own scientific theory that humanity as a whole was arriving at a point of total self-consciousness. The central question for religion was now the relationship of Christ to the material cosmos, about which the Church was silent. God must be seen as one who, by nature and in order to remain himself, must become the God of Evolution. God was not free to create or not create the cosmos. To be God, he had to. For Teilhard believed not in Nietzsche's "God who is dead" and not in the immutable God of the Church, but in "a God who changes."

As with the concept of God, so everything else in the Church must be rethought, according to Teilhard. She must ally herself with science, because "this would help clear away the obstacles that hinder the Church from knowing her own truth." Unless the Church invited mankind to develop its human powers by means of science, "she will not regain mankind's interest." She therefore needed to undertake "a complete rethinking of old values and institutions so that spirit could be liberated"; and she needed to abandon "juridicism, moralism, and all things artificial in order to live in the very function of the call to love by God who so elevates our energies."

Church theology must be completely revamped—everything from the meaning of the Sign of the Cross (not suffering and death tranformed into eternal life and glory, but Evolution's triumph) to priesthood (a function of being truly human). Indeed, "savants are priests," and scientific "research is prayer (perhaps the highest kind of prayer)." All men are priests, really, he said. Priesthood is not essentially the offering of Mass and the forgiveness of sin; it consists of being still more human.

Teilhard derided the Catholic idea of sexual continence, poking fun at "the colonies of virgins" and "the currents of continence in marriage." God's order to Adam and Eve "to increase and multiply" no longer applied. We should now use eugenics to aim at the optimum in birth, not the maximum in reproduction. For "tomorrow it will be devices of this kind [mechanical means invented by science] which will be employed to control life or the new biology." In the meantime, Teilhard declared, we have "the absolute right to try everything to the end—even in the matter of human biology" (sexuality, euthanasia, conception in vitro, homosexuality).

It seems extraordinary that Jesuits, who were becoming so devoted to the idea of fighting sociopolitical oppression, were not horrified by the specters such an idea raised, particularly after Hitler's human experimentation for the very same purpose. But the zeal and the euphoria of the time carried the day in Teilhard's favor.

Teilhard himself, meanwhile, was thrown off course by nothing. He had an answer for everything in his Church. He had no objection in 1950, for example, to Pope Pius XII's defining the dogma of the Virgin Mary's bodily Assumption into Heaven. The definition of the Assumption as Dogma was inopportune for Teilhard and for many, as it could not but repel the minds of the scientific world; all the "Marial" celebrations of the Roman Church, as he called them—"promenading a statue of [Our Lady of] Fatima across the Continents," "Marial" congresses, "emotional rallies," and other such Roman practices—these were his expressions of displeasure at the manifestations of Catholic devotion to Mary.

But the definition of this Dogma was not a significant problem for Teilhard. He simply redefined the Dogma to suit his own mind. The Pope's definition, he corrected His Holiness, had nothing to do with the Virgin being the mother of Christ. Provided that we look on such an assertion as merely "a biopsychological necessity" to offset the excessive "masculinity of Jehovah" in the Old Testament, it was a dogma that could be accommodated.

All in all, it seems fair and sensible enough on the evidence to say that there emerged in Teilhard a certain insensitivity to traditional pieties and personal devotion to Jesus which could only have been made possible by a collapse of genuine belief. One more small incident is shocking for the fecklessness he displayed. A certain Jesuit, Father Doncoeur, a member of the ever-persistent "brotherhood," gathered some other Jesuit members and lay people in a private house to celebrate Easter in 1951. Instead of the regulation Host made of unleavened bread, Doncoeur and his companions "consecrated" a flat bread-cake, a *galette*. Then each one broke off a piece of the *galette* over a cup of wine. This was their Paschal renewal Mass. In terms of traditional Catholic theology, this "Mass" would be viewed as not merely heretical; it would be condemned as an act of pagan idolatry, and a sacrilege. When Teilhard heard about it, there was no sign of disgust or horror. Sacrilege had lost all meaning for him. His reaction was a chuckle of amusement. His mind was on more serious matters.

What truly mattered now, Teilhard said, was that "a new humanity is being born by the natural force of events, which cries out toward and for a new God." The "real problem" now was "to find a fuel, an excitant, and finally a God," for Evolution. Teilhard literally defined that missing "fuel" into existence.

"An updated humanism," he declared, "a neo-humanism is therefore a necessity" which will be "exciting hearts and minds and inspiring mankind." For this "human adventure," we will have "the Divine Motor" of Evolution "which sustains the thirst for life." Thus at last, "a Science of Man, less ridiculous than the one which burdens us at this moment [Church teaching] will emerge."

With a divine Motor in place, and the fuel of neo-humanism to keep it purring along, Teilhard had no difficulty in defining the task of the Church. This was: to teach a new faith, "faith in the promise of technology, faith in humanity's final self-surpassing destiny," as "the human biological group rises towards a final goal."

No faith should be placed any longer in the supernatural, but only in what Teilhard called "the ultra-human"; in "ultra-hominization"; in man becoming more than man by his own innate drives. The rule was: "where man is most himself, there God must be." The maturing of the human world would be, in great part, "the fruit of man's own efforts." For "the day will come when Man will recognize that for him science is not an accessory occupation but the essential form of action."

One cannot but be impressed by Teilhard's prayer to his new god, humanity, which he addressed as "Jerusalem."

> Jerusalem, lift up your head. Look at the immense crowd of those who build and those who seek. All over the world men are toiling —in laboratories, in studies, in deserts, in factories, in the vast social crucible. The ferment that is taking place by their instrumentality in art and science and thought is happening for your sake. Open, then, your arms and your heart, like Christ your Lord, and welcome the waters, the Flood and the sap of humanity.[6]

When you examine Teilhard's personal piety and practice of religious belief, you are finally forced to conclude that even as far back as his early years of training as a Jesuit, he had lost his Roman Catholic faith. He continued as a Jesuit and a member of the Church partly out of inertia, perhaps; but partly, too, for strategic reasons—the same strategic reasons that George Tyrrell had for fiercely clinging to the skirts of Rome.

For part of his life, Teilhard had a very close Jesuit friend, Father Auguste Valensin. Valensin was a spiritual adviser, a philosopher, a very cultivated man, and more learned than most of his contemporaries. Over an early period of Teilhard's life, the two friends indulged in frequent conversations. By 1951, however, Teilhard discovered that Valensin thought Teilhard's "evolutionist adventure" was quite unattractive. Teilhard, for his part, described Valensin as a man "of quasi-infantine faith" and, because Valensin would not accept his "evolutionist adventure," a man of "complete intellectual skepticism."

Teilhard's subsequent remarks are frighteningly revealing about his own loss of faith. "If I were he [Valensin]," he said, "I would have given up believing a long time ago. . . . A God who is not the Energy of Cosmogenesis (this is the fundamental thing I believe), and a Catholicism which refuses to accept its place as a phylum of nature in which the highest kind of discovery of God can be made, is meaningless to me." Quite obviously, Teilhard had stopped believing as a Catholic. "I can no longer conceive of a religion that does not magnify and intensify our vision of creation. . . . I have not been able to find a form of expression of the God whom I adore interiorly, a God in whom the Christ of Evolution, the Personal and the Universal, are all joined."

Instead, Teilhard derived his inspiration and his intuitions as well as his drive not from an Ignatian or a priestly calling, but because

> I have looked so long at nature, and loved her face so much that I can read her heart, it is my dear, profound conviction—a conviction as sweet as it is tenacious, the humblest but the deepest of my certitudes. . . . Life does not go off on any road at all. Neither does it misjudge its End. . . . It shows us by what route will come all those who are neither liars nor false gods; it shows us toward what point on the horizon we must steer if we are to see the Light arise and fill the sky.[7]

Writing as early as 1928 to a friend, he already sounded the lyrical note he came to reserve for "nature." I have sought, he said, "to promote a certain taste, a certain perception of the beauty, the pathos, and the unity of being." Had Swami Vivekananda lived to read those words, they might have brought tears of joy even to his eyes.[8]

About his Jesuitism and his Jesuit vocation, Teilhard was less romantic; he was, in fact, a stark realist. "I find," he wrote, "I can't but realize again (and even more profoundly) the size of the abyss which separates my religious vision of the World and the vision in the *Exercises* of Ignatius (seen in the mold into which church people in high places still think that we can fit!). . . ."

However, he remarked with visionary foresight, it might just be possible to take those *Spiritual Exercises* of St. Ignatius and "transpose them into terms of a universe in Genesis where we must make room for the Ultra-Human. . . . Men today, whom circumstances have driven out of the framework of imagination that Theology has built, all are seeking a new God—One who is simultaneously 'Personal' and 'Ultra-Humanizing.' " (This last term emphasizes opposition to the "Supernatural" of the Theologians, which Teilhard called fictional.) "It is to the understanding of the Ultra-Christian God that I am irrevocably determined to devote the last years of my life."

Teilhard had started his publishing career in earnest with the publication of *The Divine Milieu* in 1927. From the beginning, there were sharp criticisms from the then Father General Wlodzimierz Ledóchowski. Teilhard had published two more books before he was told that, as things stood, the Order did not wish him to publish any more books or articles. When he returned to Paris from China after World War II ended, he found himself deprived of any forum for broadcasting his views. The new Father General, Jean-Baptiste Janssens, did not lift the ban that Father Ledóchowski had ordered.

Teilhard chafed under those restrictions. His French Superiors were also restive; they did not share the misgivings of the Roman Superiors. Everyone concerned knew that Teilhard's unpublished essays—his "clandestines," as he called them—were being handed around from person to person. He finally initiated a correspondence with Father Janssens about the questioned orthodoxy of his views, and the problem of how to exercise his talents in the circumstances.

Father Janssens had to contend with the then Pope, Pius XII; and Teilhard's pet subjects, evolution and anthropology, were precisely what was exercising that Pope's vigilance. Indeed, he was preparing an encyclical letter to the Church Universal about just those matters. Janssens pointed out to Teilhard that there was no way that the Vatican of Pius XII would give him (Teilhard) a free hand to publish and lecture. He was not to disseminate his views; they were suspect.

Europe, in fact, both men concluded, was not the ideal place for Teilhard. The United States finally became the ultimate choice; Teilhard could join research teams there and pursue his researches. But he was not to publish or give public lectures or teach young Jesuits.

Could Your Reverence not change some of your more controversial opinions, Janssens asked plaintively in one letter, at least as far as the words go? Holding on to these and explicitly doing so could result in a worse tragedy. . . . Both men were thinking of a possibly necessary dismissal of Teilhard from the Society. And both men shied away from this alternative—Janssens because of the revolt brewing in Jesuit ranks, Teilhard because he felt the Society and the Church needed him.

Writing to Father General Janssens in his own defense on October 12, 1951, Teilhard gave that poor, harassed Superior a stark choice:

> I think you must resign yourself to accepting me just as I am, even with the congenital quality (or weakness) because of which, from my earliest childhood, my spiritual life has always been completely dominated by a sort of profound "feeling" for the organic reality of the world . . . a precise and overwhelming sense of the general convergence of the universe upon itself. This is the basic psychological situation from which everything I do and am derives. It is a trait that I can no more change than I can change my age or the color of my eyes.
>
> . . . I feel it necessary to insist on my ever stronger commitment to . . . the unique value of Man in the path of the rise of Life; the axial position of Catholicism in the convergent bundle of human activities; and, at last, the essential consummating function assumed by the Risen Christ at the center and summit of creation. . . . I fully recognize that Rome may have its reasons for believing that in its present form my vision of Christianity is premature or incomplete. . . . Despite certain appearances, I am determined to remain "a child of obedience." . . . I cannot leave off exploring this path privately. But . . . I am no longer occupied with the propagation of my ideas, only with deepening them within myself. . . .

Teilhard's letter was only half frank, and was merely meant to provide his Superior with a document for the records that said he had submitted to "holy obedience." Writing to a friend, he was much more honest and self-revealing: "To tell you the truth, I'm quite aware I'm not as innocent as all that. But how can I stop

what I'm doing without failing in my duties before God and man?
. . . I'm quite aware that all the heretics have said this. . . ."

As to his word to Janssens that he would no longer be occupied
with the propagation of his ideas, that, too, seemed to be more
fable than fact; for on another occasion he wrote about his appointment to the prestigious *Institut de France* as "a platform from
which I can launch my projectiles . . . and [which] will protect me
against certain attacks."

Janssens, too, was aware that all heretics invoked obedience to
duty before God and man, no doubt. But Teilhard was more than
he could handle. Many prominent Jesuits, Superiors among them,
sympathized with his views. Janssens's letter in reply to Teilhard's
appeal was one of "reconciliation." Henceforward, Teilhard was
left untroubled by disciplinary efforts of Jesuit Superiors. He was
not required even to live in a Jesuit residence.

Consciously, and despite the amazing freedom with which he
spoke and published, Teilhard thought of himself as belonging to
the "brotherhood" for whom "thinking freely in the Church these
days means going underground. Come to think of it, that's what
I've been doing for thirty years. . . ." He joined in the Jesuit version
of the Soviet *samizdat,* or underground publication system; spoke
freely about "my clandestines" (his clandestine writings that were
circulated from hand to hand); and was overjoyed when he was
attacked in a 1950 monograph—"but none of my last clandestines
are cited in it." The authorities had been fooled.

Despite his rather romantic image of himself as an exile for the
sake of the truth, a fugitive in the intellectual underground, when
the occasion arose, he did not hesitate to proselytize even among
his fellow Jesuits. "We priests, we Jesuits," he proclaimed at nothing less than an international meeting of Jesuits at Versailles in
1947, "we must believe in research because research pursued with
faith is the very terrain fit for the growth of the humano-Christian
mystique that can create unanimity [among men]." Research, he
said—and on Teilhard's lips that meant specifically scientific research—was destined to become "the essentially human act and
the most direct form of Christification and adoration."

Of course, such a statement—like the main principles of Teilhard's thought—was irreconcilable with traditional Jesuitism and
with the Catholicism Jesuits were sworn to defend. "But they [the
Liberators] have already come and are here," he remarked once,
the implication being that their arrival was also their defense and
justification. "They will free the Church from what holds her back
. . . from beyond their tombs, they will reach for victory."

In that statement, at least, Teilhard was prophetic. In a true sense, he himself would reach for victory from beyond his tomb. Teilhard died quite unexpectedly on Easter Sunday, April 10, 1955, in the house of some friends in Purchase, New York. His obsequies were performed at the Jesuit Church of St. Ignatius on Park Avenue in New York City. His body was clothed for burial in priestly vestments. When his coffin was lowered into the ground of a Poughkeepsie, New York, cemetery, the earth was still frozen from the hard, long winter.

Death was one of only two problems Teilhard had failed to address even to his own satisfaction in his brave theology of change and evolution. Indeed, only in the presence of death did that confident optimism and surety that was the personal mark of this man seem to fade. "Now what does he 'see'? I wonder," Teilhard wrote after the death of a friend; "And when will my turn come?" On the occasion of another friend's death: "What shall I 'see' ?" That he put the word "see" in quotes showed no persuasion that he would see Jesus and the Father and the Saints. It was the sentiment of the deeply committed agnostic for whose lack of faith ordinary words are not sufficient.

Dying and death for him, he had said, were just the means of becoming one with the universe.

> The world I live in becomes divine. Yet these flames do not consume me, nor do these waters dissolve me for . . . the pan-Christian, I am finding, places union at the terms of arduous differentiation. I shall become the Other only by being absolutely my own self. I shall attain the Spirit only by releasing completely and exhaustively all the powers of matter. . . . I recognize that, in following the example of the incarnate God revealed to me by my Catholic faith, I can be saved only by becoming one with the universe.

Within the traditional perspective of Catholicism's clear views of what happens to every human being after death, one wonders what sort of shock Teilhard experienced when on that Easter day at last he "saw" the God of his eternal tomorrow, the God-man who by dying had not become "part of the universe" but remained its sovereign Lord.

*   *   *

Five years after Teilhard's death, in 1960, Roman authorities under the direction of Pope John XXIII issued a document warning both Jesuits and Catholics in general that Teilhard's ideas were extremely dangerous for the Catholic faith. It was tantamount to a condemnation. By that time, however, his name and theories were bathed in a vogue that could not be breached by mere ecclesiastical documents. Teilhard's thinking had become part of the thinking of the intellectual leadership of the Society of Jesus.

Their only difficulty with Teilhardism had to do with the second problem Teilhard had failed to develop adequately when he was alive. He presented no tangible objective in the here-and-now for his poetry and "scientific" proposals. Despite Teilhard's defense of the priest-workers more than two decades before, he had not really indicated any space in which his romanticism of evolution could be tried out.

This lack was rapidly filled by a fresh Jesuit initiative that began around the time of Teilhard's death. As Teilhard had filled the gap of scientific underpinnings for the new theology of George Tyrrell, S.J., so Liberation Theology—championed largely by Latin American Jesuits—provided a tangible objective for the new theories of Pierre Teilhard de Chardin, S.J.: the liquidation of capitalist and transnational (which is to say, American) economic imperialism. And those same Jesuits provided as well a real space in which to experiment with the installation and nourishment of the "new Humanity": every country in Latin America and the Third World.

15 | LIBERATION THEOLOGY

L ooking at the Society of Jesus from the outside, at the time of Teilhard de Chardin's death in 1955, anyone would surely have been struck by the signs of its flourishing vigor, from its still-growing membership to its ever-spreading influence in the wide world.

On the inside, however, the brute fact was that the Jesuit "sense of mission"—that remarkable and even explosive Ignatian mix of contemplative in action that had made of the Society the Rapid Deployment Force of the Church—could not much longer be satisfied within traditional molds.

Thomism, the official system of theology and philosophy of the Roman Catholic Church, was already for the minds of many—Jesuits and non-Jesuits—a system as barren, as dead, and as desiccated as the lunar crater of Copernicus. Tyrrell and Teilhard had been punished in part for saying the Church should jettison all that old baggage of medieval Scholastic philosophy. But long before they arrived on the scene—since the seventeenth-century Reformation, in fact—the Church's enemies had turned her stubborn use of Thomism into an insulting reproach against her.

By the 1950s, the dissatisfactions and the expectations of the once discreet and covert "brotherhood of the underground" had spread far and wide. Given the long tradition of close contact and correspondence among Jesuits, and the fact that Tyrrell and Teilhard, two of the "brotherhood's" most recent and important modern figures, were themselves Jesuits, there was perhaps no way that the Society could have escaped a chafing conviction that things had to change.

With such a mind-set as background, the only real difficulty for Jesuits with the theoretic poetry and airy prophecies of geniuses like Teilhard was that they still left everything tantalizingly up in the air. Theories and speculations were well and good; they formed a fascinating cloud of brilliant hues enveloping their heads, holding their hearts. But they shed no light as to how all the fine ideas could be concretely implemented. They just weren't practical.

On the other hand, the attraction of these speculations and theories was that they had gained a certain foothold in the farther—if tarnished—edges of respectability. It was not that humanism or Modernism of any stripe was accepted by the Church; it was not. It was more a question of its own tenaciousness. By now, humanism in one form or another had a long and well-established tradition that reached back beyond Tyrrell to the eighteenth century—to liberal Catholicism in France associated with names that every Jesuit knew, such as Robert de Lamennais, Marc Sagnier, Emmanuel Mounier. The huge importance of Tyrrell was precisely that he refused to remain underground; he insisted on surfacing. Whatever it cost him personally—and that sacrifice had a certain romantic appeal of its own in the Jesuit tradition—he was the first humanist in the Roman Catholic Church to go public and to refuse to be silenced.

The attraction of Teilhard de Chardin was another matter, and his importance was of another sort. For many Jesuits, he came in a sense to be seen as the new Ignatius, the man they had been waiting for during this threshold time that was so like Loyola's. For like Ignatius, Teilhard found a whole new way to talk to the world. Like Ignatius, he gave a whole new mind to Jesuits and to the intellectual leaders of his time.

Teilhard had completed his most important seminal work in the 1920s. Within thirty years, during his own lifetime, Jesuits in seminaries all over the world were using his vocabulary, arcane as it was, and his theories, obscure and difficult as they were, to explain everything.

What's more, Teilhard, unlike Tyrrell, had been able to remain in the Society of Jesus and had not been denied the Sacraments of the Church. The attempts by Jesuit Father General Janssens to bring him to heel were no secret; that those attempts failed crowned Teilhard's work with a tacit victory humanism had never before achieved in its long and mostly covert struggle with the hierarchic Church of Rome.

In the wake of Teilhard's stunning work of the 1920s and in the quasi-respectable tradition of French Liberal Catholicism, along came another Frenchman in the 1930s—Catholic philosopher Jacques Maritain. Maritain wrote one of the most influential books in the lengthening annals of humanism. *Integral Humanism*, he called that book; and in it he codified the humanist summons of the "brotherhood" to the Roman Catholic Church to identify itself with the revolutionary aspirations of the struggling masses of mankind.

For Maritain, the cry of the French Revolution—*Liberty! Equality! Fraternity!*—was "the erruption of Christian thought in the political order." The political Left, for Maritain, represented all that was historically most significant. In fact, Maritain adopted a sort of theology of history, as one might call it, built on Marxist philosophy: Religious truth was to be found exclusively in the masses of the people.

Although many years later Maritain retracted the challenge of *Integral Humanism*, at the time he was quickly taken up and openly imitated even within the Church hierarchy. In fact, no less a figure than Archbishop Giovanni Battista Montini—the future Pope Paul VI, who was to come to such grief in his confrontations with the Jesuits—graciously wrote the preface for the Italian edition of *Integral Humanism*. Montini remained an ardent admirer of Maritain's all his life, a fact that would one day have consequences far beyond the Society of Jesus.

Standing on the shoulders of the great humanist innovators, lesser men had their own effect. There was, for example, Dominican Father Chenu, somewhat younger than Teilhard and a student of his, who later taught his own students that the visible and apparently irresistible progress of socialism was developing "a community of mankind that becomes the very substance of the growth of the community of God's grace in Christ."

Another Dominican, Father Congar, a contemporary of Teilhard, did his Dominican brother Chenu one better. For Congar, Christianity could not Christianize mankind—the collectivity of the world's people—without becoming the people's political ally. For him, every step of temporal progress in the secular world, every people who liberated itself from domination by the right wing or by capitalists, represented a step in the development of the Kingdom of God. The Church must become the universal sacrament of the new cosmic salvation being ushered into man's world, not by supernatural grace, but by man's material struggles to better his economic and social position.

There is not the slightest doubt that the hidden current of Modernism, flowing underground since the eighteenth century and broadening steadily into the nineteenth century until George Tyrrell forced a geyser-like outlet for it, went a very long way to leaven spirits and prepare expectant minds for change. Human change. Rapid change. Deep change. But the Modernism of the integral humanists created a growing hunger it could not yet find a way to satisfy. As the authoritarian pontificate of Pius XII (1939–1958) drew toward its end, and after twenty-nine years under their own iron-handed Father General Wlodzimierz Ledóchowski (1915–1944) and the equally authoritarian rule of Pius's predecessor, Pius XI (1922–1939), restlessness in the Society became almost palpable. The problem Teilhard failed to address, the problem of a practical objective and a practical arena in which to pursue it, was like a terrible itch that no one had learned to ease.

There were hopeful experiments and trial runs at a new mission, even under Pius XII. The worker-priest project of the post–World War II years was one. There were occasional symposia and dialogues with Marxists. But none of that met the need.

For the need was: no longer to be different and apart from the great world outside, no longer to be a separate elite. The need was: to integrate with humanity, to be an active and effective part of man's struggle to be himself. And the need was: for a catalyst that would make this possible.

Suddenly, as it seemed, and accompanied by no spectacular or dazzling event, as unobtrusively as a snowflake falls, Latin America hove into sight. It had been there all along, of course. But only in the early sixties was it perceived in all its pitiful nakedness, its tearful resentment, its paining protest and heart-stirring plea that, at last, someone had to care, someone had to relieve the endemic misery of over 300 million men, women, and children.

All at once, Latin America was a meteor scattering light, filling minds and hearts at last with that magic fluid called "mission." Above all, it revealed close at hand the one thing that all the Modernist theories and conjectures of secular humanism had been lacking: a real occasion for *praxis*—a concrete way to catch up with the world; to convert the world; to be part of the world. "Mission" was now pragmatically possible.

The voices that answered that plea—and that defined the new mission—were at first local and disparate. But they soon gathered into a loud chorus and coalesced into what has come to be called

Liberation Theology. Almost before it had a name, however, it spread like fire, setting alight the minds of many, first of all in Latin America, but quickly then rushing through Asia, India, South Korea, Taiwan, and sub-Saharan Africa. It had invaded theological seminaries in the United States and Europe by the early 1970s. Very soon, even political lobbies joined the chorus in contented harmony.

There is a common persuasion that Liberation Theology began in 1973 with the publication of a book called *A Theology of Liberation* by a Peruvian Jesuit Father Gustavo Gutierrez. There is a certain romantic appeal in this idea, especially since it would place yet another Jesuit in the pantheon of liberators alongside Tyrrell and Teilhard—a third Jesuit to carry high the flame of secular humanism.

Those who are less romantic, however, or who know the history of Liberation Theology a little better, may point out that Gutierrez's work was inspired by a 1968 Conference of Latin American bishops at Medellín, near Bogotá, in Colombia, where the delegates highlighted the plight of the poor, and the need to remedy their awful conditions.

In any case, whatever the details, the common belief—even among many Liberation Theologians—is that Liberation Theology is by nature and origin and purpose a product of the Latin American situation. Indeed, one can understand the need for such an idea; how else would Fernando Cardenal and his brother priests-in-politics in Latin America be able to heap scorn with such popular effect on "alien" Rome and its "alien" Pope and on the "European" Church of the papacy?

Nevertheless, it is far more accurate to say that Latin America provided the living laboratory for trying out the various theories and formulas that gathered under the name of Liberation Theology; that Liberation Theology's inspiration, its primary formulation, and its chief champions were all Europeans[1]; and finally that its most zealous propagandists were North Americans, particuarly Jesuits and the Maryknoll Religious. It was the Maryknoll Congregation, in fact, that started Orbis Books, the main publishing source for the spate of sympathetic and biased books on the subject.

Essentially, Liberation Theology is the answer to that summons to the Church codified so many years before by Maritain—to identify itself with the revolutionary hopes of the masses. The difference, perhaps, insofar as there is one, is that while Maritain adopted a theology of history built on a misapprehension of Marxist philosphy, Liberation Theologians adopted a theology of politics built on Soviet tactics. In essence, the propagators of Liberation Theology took the current of theological thought developed in Europe and applied it to the very concrete situation in Latin America. Suddenly, theological and philosophical theory became pragmatic proposals and actual programs for changing the face of all social and political institutions in Latin America.

*   *   *

The appeal of Liberation Theology was commanding for Jesuits. Its attraction lay in the multiheaded promises it made.

A first promise was to free the Catholic mind from the outworn past and theological leftovers. Liberation Theology turned its back on the entire scope of Scholastic Theology, including what was sound in Maritain. It did not base its reasoning on papal teaching, or on the ancient theological tradition of the Church, or on the Decrees of the Church's Ecumenical Councils.

In fact, Liberation Theology refused to start where Councils and Popes had always started: with God as Supreme Being, as Creator, as Redeemer, as Founder of the Church, as the One Who had placed among men a Vicar who was called the Pope, as Ultimate Rewarder of the Good and Punisher of the Evil.

Rather, Liberation Theology's basic assumption was "the people," sometimes indeed "the people of God." "The people" were the source of spiritual revelation and religious authority. What mattered in theology was how "the people" fared here and now, in the social, political, and economic realities of the evolving material world. The "experience of the people was the womb of theology," was the consecrated phrase.

At one stroke, therefore, Liberation Theology unburdened prepared and restless minds from an entire panoply of ancient concepts, dogmas, and mental processes governed by the fixed rules of Thomistic reasoning, and from the directives of the authoritative voice of Rome. Theologians were freed from the ancient formulary strictures and the how-many-angels-can-dance-on-the-head-of-a-pin mentality. In fact, Liberation Theology was no theology in the Roman Catholic sense of the word. It was not primarily about God, about God's law, about God's redemption, about God's promises. Liberation Theology was interested in God as revealed today through the oppressed people. In God for himself, practically speaking, no genuine Liberation Theology was interested.

The second promise of Liberation Theology was even more exciting than freedom from Rome's theology. It was the promise of the longed-for participation in the New Humanity; in the new world emerging all around men in this twentieth-century threshold of a new era. It was the promise of evolution with the evolving conditions of men and women; of fundamental change with the fundamentally changing society of man. It was the Modernists—Tyrrell, Teilhard, Duchesne, and all the others—brought at last into the practical world of visible achievement.

Both of these promises—freedom from Rome's outworn theology and participation with "the people of God" in the enterprise of social evolution and revolution—were encased in the term *liberation*.

It was not lost on Gutierrez and his sympathizers and champions that "liberation" itself was a traditional Catholic term; or that its Catholic meaning had always been a freeing from those moral deficiencies that prevented an individual from pleasing God and attaining eternal life. Primarily, according to traditional Catholic teaching, Christ effected this liberation by his sufferings and death and resurrection. Traditionally, in other words, liberation is a spiritual liberation of individuals, groups, nations, races, and all human beings, so that all will be eligible for eternal life with God after death.

The liberation of the new theology, on the other hand, was specifically a freeing from political oppression, economic want, and misery here on earth. More specifically still, it was freeing from political domination by the capitalism of the United States.

In the eyes of Liberation Theologians, the endemic want and misery of Latin America, together with its political domination by strong-arm leaders and monopolistic oligarchies, were directly the fault of capitalism. American capitalism. The most specific, immediate, and practical aim of Liberation Theology, therefore—the very core of its "mission"—became the liberation of Latin Americans from oppression by *yanqui* transnational, capitalistic domination.

Even before Jesuit Gutierrez wrote *A Theology of Liberation*, this new "theological" idea of liberation was based on the analysis Karl Marx had made of the socioeconomic and political situation of what he called "the world proletariat." Marx's concern was for labor with its value and its rights. The masses—the proletariat—possessed nothing but the value of their labor, and were forced to work under the control of, and on the materials owned by, the capitalist elite, the few. For Marx, the historic task of the proletariat was to struggle against the capitalists and to liberate the people from their oppression.

The "mission" of Liberation Theology, in other words, was Marx's "class struggle." The battle that Liberation Theology told its devotees to fight and to win was not the Ignatian battle of Christ's followers against the Enemy, but the battle of a worldwide class of men and women against the toils and traps of capitalism. As a Liberation Theologian, your "preferential option for the poor" engaged you as champion of this struggling class. As a Liberation Theologian, your nearest, your most organized, and your most widely spread allies were Communists and Marxists. "The humane face of Marxism," as Teilhard de Chardin had said, promised you "hope of victory." The association of Liberation Theology with Marxists introduced you at once into the one supreme political issue at stake in our world today: the unending rivalry between the United States and the USSR. Liberation Theology was theology gone geopolitical.

For the religious mind already leavened by the doctrine of integral humanism, it was the perfect situation. What could these continual upheavals involving the masses of the poor in Third World countries and capitalist entrepreneurs mean, except that a New Humanity was endeavoring to emerge in the evolutionary process toward the Omega Point of perfection? Liberation Theology placed you in the thick of all that! What better, what wider, what humanistically holier movement to join?

A new age was at hand, just as Tyrrell and Teilhard had always said. But official Roman Catholic theology—Thomism and all that—proposed no *praxis*, no practical way of solving socioeconomic problems. There was no practical "mission" specific to "the Latin American reality" in all that ancient theology, the new theologians said. Whatever concepts and words they used had to be dictated by that "Latin American reality."

Because "the people" was the source of the new "theology," and because "the people" authorized religious beliefs and consecrated actions, what function remained any longer for an "alien" hierarchy of bishops and their subordinate priests, with their allegiance to someone who lived in Italy? What function remained for an "alien pope"? Certainly not to tell you the good and the bad of what you do. Certainly not to tell you about what Christ wants. "The people" know what Christ wants, what they must believe, what they must do. Theology now consisted in watching and listening to "the people."

Along the road in the development of Liberation Theology, a certain sleight-of-hand had taken place. *Disinformation* is the current polite word for the process.

Teilhard de Chardin knew he was not talking about anything remotely similar to traditional church doctrine; that was in part why he had to invent his complex and idiosyncratic vocabulary. Gutierrez and the other Liberation Theologians, unlike Teilhard, found it far more effective and appealing to co-opt traditional Roman Catholic vocabulary, but to give all the terms a new anti-Roman and simultaneously anticapitalist meaning.

The "preferential option for the poor," for example, as Gutierrez and the others explained it, was based on Christ's own preference for the poor, his preference for the working class versus the rich. After all, Christ *did* excoriate the rich. And he *was* poor—"the Son of Man has nowhere to lay his head, while even the birds of the air have nests and the foxes have their lairs." And wasn't it easier for a camel to slip through the tiny eye of a needle than for a rich man—a capitalist—to get into Heaven? And remember Lazarus, the disease-ridden hobo of Christ's own parable of salvation? And Dives, the fat capitalist of the same parable? Which of those two finally rested in the bosom of Abraham, and which was tortured on the tip of Hell's flame?

The appealing and even convincing sleight-of-hand here consisted of giving the Biblical term *poor* the same meaning as Marx and Marxists had given to the term *proletariat.* But this was as valid as saying that what Julius Ceasar meant when he talked about *ballista* was the same as our meaning when we speak of a modern ballistic missile.

Christ never singled out the proletariat with a preferential option in their favor. Christ acted on no sociological theory about the economic inequality and the political opposition between classes. He aimed at no armed revolution, no political liberation. He had no more preferential option for the poor to the positive exclusion—forcible or otherwise—of the well-off, than he had a preferential option for little children to the exclusion of adults.

Christ's option was for godliness and piety and innocence and humility and fidelity to God's law, wherever he found it—in poor man or rich; in little child or old man; in his rich friends like Nicodemus, Joseph of Arimathea, Lazarus and his two sisters, Mary and Martha; in his poor friends like Zacchaeus, Bartimaeus, the blind beggar, or any one of his twelve Apostles.

For Christ was a savior of sinners, not a secular leader. It was not poverty or riches that made or makes you desirable in Christ's eyes. It was what you *did* in your poverty or your riches—what sort of morality you practiced, what beliefs you nourished.

In reality, Liberation Theology is a quicker-than-the-eye trans-

formation of a spiritual warfare into a sociopolitical struggle; and
—if need be—into an armed revolutionary warfare against capitalism.

It is a transformation hinted at by Teilhard in his theory of man
endeavoring to evolve to the Omega Point by achieving complete
"hominization" so that he could pass over into the "Ultra-
Human." Indeed, Liberation Theologians were the ones who finally succeeded in giving all those airy concepts of Teilhard de
Chardin a practical meaning.

But that would have been little use among the ordinary masses
of believers, had the new "theologians" not succeeded also in
transposing the meaning of all the key terms used to convey the
basic truths and teachings of traditional Roman Catholicism. In
their writings, you can see the quick, skillful way in which this
was done.

The Church became "the people of God," not the hierarchic
Church of Rome. *Sin* is not primarily personal; it is social and
almost exclusively the injustice and oppressions due to capitalism.
Mary the Virgin is the mother of a revolutionary Jesus—indeed of
all revolutionaries seeking to overthrow capitalism. *The Kingdom
of God* is the socialist state from which capitalist oppression has
been eliminated. *Priesthood* is either the service given by an individual (the *priest*) who builds up socialism, or it is the "people of
God" as it worships according to its likes. The list of such adopted
Catholic expressions is as long as you like. For each and every
Catholic term about piety, belief, asceticism, and theology is
taken over by Liberation Theologians.

The refinement of such co-opted terms permits grinning twists
and ugly distortions of Roman Catholicism, as when the Marxist
Junta of Nicaragua calls its mobs of armed bully-boys *"las turbas
divinas,"* the divine mobs.

Ultimately, however, such use of Roman Catholic vocabulary,
laden as it is with deep attraction for the faithful, provided an
otherwise unattainable legitimacy for a this-worldly blueprint of
the future. Cleverly used, the new "theological" lexicon not only
justifies but mandates the use of any means—including armed
violence, torture, violation of human rights, deceptions, and deep
alliances with professedly atheistic and antireligious forces such
as the USSR and Castro's Cuba—in order to achieve the "evolution" of Marxism and its promise of material success.

Without the developed current of Modernist thought behind
them, and the models of such Jesuits as Tyrrell and, above all,
Teilhard, it is doubtful that Jesuits would have been won so easily,

if at all, by those twin promises of Liberation Theology—freedom from the little Caesars of Rome with their abstract formulas, juridical rulings, and traditional hierarchy; and freedom to join in changing the fundamental structure of man's society.

However, once Jesuits admitted the attitude that all prior theology was only speculation, and useless speculation at that, as far as Latin America was concerned, all need to study Thomism and traditional Scholastic Theology and philosophy in Jesuit seminaries ceased. An immediate consequence was that budding priests and theologians in the Society of Jesus were put at two removes from the teaching, language, tradition, and pieties of the Church.

First, all the traditional textbooks, manuals, doctrinal treatises, and other instruments of the "old theology" were judged to be out of date, and were to be jettisoned. Standard textbooks about moral rules and problems as well as recognized authorities on the theology of the Church and on Biblical matters, all were abandoned, indeed sometimes were thrown out or burned.

Second, because "the people" was not the "source" of "theology," Jesuits began to step back from the traditional hierarchy of the Church. Vow or no, what could loyalty to the papacy and its prerogatives possibly mean any longer? As Jesuit Fernando Cardenal put it, his priesthood would have lost its meaning if he did not resist the commands of the Pope and stay on as member of Nicaragua's Marxist Junta.

The rise and development of Liberation Theology, and the extraordinarily sympathetic response of the clergy—and notably of the Jesuits—has presented the Roman Catholic Church with a painful and costly loss not only in the so-called Third World of undeveloped countries, but in the First World of developed countries as well.

The genius of Ignatius of Loyola was that in tackling the firebrand of humanism of his day, he devised a way for his Church to cope with the new situations that had arisen in his world of the sixteenth century. In so doing, he gave up nothing of Catholic Sacraments or theology or loyalty to Rome. He just presented it all in a new way, thus solving the dilemma of the Church.

But the latter-day conversion of Jesuits—indeed of the Society of Jesus—to Liberation Theology means that Rome has lost the services of the one organization that should have provided it with a solution to the Catholic Church's problem in Third World countries.

The loss and the dilemma of the Church can be partially but aptly illustrated by the situation in the little country of Guyana.

Formerly the British Crown Colony known as British Guiana, this equatorial lowland of 83,000 square miles with a population of 900,000 is perched on the northeast shoulder of South America. In May of 1966, Forbes Burnham took this tiny country to independence under its new name, Guyana. By 1985, every sector of government was in sharp decline. The population and the economy suffered from government monopolies, brain-drain, fraud and corruption in high places, and social disturbances. The totalitarian methods of the Burnham government and the presence of Cuban and East European "advisers" produced widespread stagnation, discontent, and want. Many died of starvation in a country where wages were generally less than three dollars a day, where a loaf of bread cost six dollars, and where there was nearly a total lack of essential medical services. But in this country where the people suffer from political oppression and social deprivation, we do not hear from Liberation Theologians. Guyana is not held up as an example of a people needing "liberation." Why?

That Liberation Theologians have chosen not to apply their answers in Guyana is explained by two simple facts: First, Burnham's government is already a Marxist government. And, second, the problems that bedevil Guyana also bedevil Nicaragua, where Liberation Theology with its Marxist base, its priestly contingent of collaborators, and its ideological "mission" of class struggle is a manifest failure by all economic and political standards, while by theological, religious, and moral standards, it is a disaster.

On the other hand, there has been a virulent opposition to Burnham in the mainline churches of Guyana, which is religiously primarily an Anglican nation. The Roman Catholic diocese of Georgetown, the capital, had about 104,000 members as of 1985, distributed among twenty-five parishes and served by fifty priests. Eight of these priests were diocesan; the remaining forty-two were members of Religious Orders. There were also forty-three Sisters, six Religious Brothers, and two seminarians. The Vicar-General for the diocese was a Jesuit, Father Andrew Morrison, a native Guyanan. Morrison published a newspaper called *The Catholic Standard.*

As the country's economy declined and government oppression rose, Morrison felt he was faced with a classic choice. He could avoid reporting what the other media, through fear, would not report. Or he could provide *The Catholic Standard* as the national conduit for an accurate picture of the havoc being inflicted on the economy of Guyana by Burnham's totalitarian government. Morrison chose the second option—"the role we have been forced to play," as he himself commented.

The Catholic Standard therefore became the opposition paper in the classic political sense. It dealt in economic and political affairs—the $10 million flour mill that stands idle; the production of ground vegetables; dairy farming; wage controls; the job market; election rigging; government corruption. This opposition stance is a brave one; it has already cost the life of Morrison's Jesuit colleague, Father Bernard Darke, who was stabbed to death in the street by members of a strange cultic group that calls itself "The House of Israel" and that backs Forbes Burnham. The stance is also a patently political one—one among many that Liberation Theologians can point to, in order to justify their own political involvements.

Still, realistically, what else could the Georgetown diocese and its Vicar-General, Morrison, have done, except become the opposition? Preach doctrine? Counsel patience? Baptize, absolve from sin, prepare for death—and only that?

The Roman Catholic Church has no ready answer to such a dilemma; and neither the Jesuits nor anyone else in the Roman Church is leading the way to find the answer. The Jesuit answer is invariably a political one. If *The Catholic Standard* does not speak out, no one will. But, by default, that leaves the diocese of Georgetown and its Vicar-General Morrison hip-deep in politics.

That even well-intentioned priests find themselves irresistibly drawn into politics is not the whole dilemma, however. That is hardly a situation without a precedent.[2]

The fact of the matter is that while the Roman Catholic Church does not and could not claim to possess a ready-made Roman Catholic solution to economic and political situations in the Third World, Liberation Theology does. And it does so by masquerading as Roman Catholic; and by parading a group of influential theologians who are still perceived to be Roman Catholic; and by borrowing both the good name of the Church and the appealing terminology and liturgy and authority of Church doctrine for sociopolitical purposes.

The tactics of Liberation Theologians thus have a huge appeal for the believing Catholic laity, and at the same time they spawn a useful and acrimonious state of affairs throughout the Church, thus leading hundreds of bishops, priests, Religious, and laity to clamor for political "mission" on the part of the Church and for churchmen's support of socialist and Marxist solutions.

Thus the twin horns of the dilemma on which the Catholic Church is being impaled, particularly in Third World countries.

The Church has no economic and political solution for the struggle between capitalism and Marxism. True, the Church propounds a social teaching as part of its evangelization; but the solution of the capitalism-Marxism struggle is a question of economic forces and political power that calls for prudential judgments in the practical order. The Church is guaranteed no wisdom, much less infallibility, in making such judgments.

That is one horn of the dilemma.

The other horn is provided by Liberation Theologians. Despite two lengthy and official documents on Liberation theology issued by the Vatican Congregation for the Doctrine of the Faith and bearing Pope John Paul II's approbation and approval,[3] the Vatican has not successfully convinced people that Liberation Theology is an impostor siphoning off the Church's manpower, credibility and good name, and finally its continued existence.

The only escape route, it was always said by Jesuit dialecticians, from a dilemma is to find a third way between the two horns, as it were. Pope John Paul II has been trying to do exactly that, but so far he has not succeeded. If the Jesuits of the twentieth century were to repeat the success story of Iñigo de Loyola and his Company in the sixteenth century, they would have found that third way of escape from the dilemma and of solution for the central problem. But, as all the evidence indicates, the Jesuit solution lies along the path of choosing between capitalism and Marxism, of siding with the revolutionary Marxist forces—politically and, if necessary, militarily.

Today's Jesuits have no solution for their own consequent decadence or for the Church's continual losses in Third World countries. Jesuit genius—the primordial charisma of Iñigo and his Companions—has made no contribution that is acceptable. They have adopted Liberation Theology, which is bleeding the Church of its vital power and desiccating the spirit of the supernatural.

The Jesuits have thus been impaled on both horns of the dilemma. As Cardinal Ratzinger, Prefect of the Vatican Congregation for the Doctrine of the Faith, remarked in the CDF *Instruction* on Liberation Theology of 1984, revolutionaries very frequently have no answers to the problems created by their revolution.

*   *   *

Even with its well-laid-down lines of propaganda and the connivance of friends occupying high places in the Church and in secular governments, including that of the United States, however, Liberation Theology would have had no real chance of success, and the Jesuits would have had no justification for its wholesale adoption by the Superiors of the Society, had the Second Vatican Council not taken place.

A skillful use of certain ambiguous assertions of that Council together with a totally erroneous misquoting of the Vatican Council's assertions about fundamental Catholic beliefs has enabled the propagators of Liberation Theology to claim that Council's sanction for policies that are surely liquidating the true faith of Catholics and handing over all power to Catholicism's ardent enemies. This is the service rendered by Iñigo's Company to the Catholic Church of the late twentieth century. The Society has used the Council to justify its 180-degree turn from its mission as a team of papal defenders and as propagators of the official Roman Catholic doctrine, into an organization bent on altering the face of traditional Roman Catholicism and, inevitably, the political complexion of many nations.

16 | THE SECOND VATICAN COUNCIL

O n January 25, 1959, within three months of the death of Pius XII, his successor on Peter's Throne, Pope John XXIII, announced the startling news that he would convoke an Ecumenical Council (the twenty-first) of the Roman Catholic Church. It would be called a "Vatican" Council, because it was called to meet in the Pope's Vatican City. It would be called the "Second," because once before, in the previous century, a Council had been held there. All Catholic bishops would be expected to attend this Second Vatican Council.

John's stated purpose in summoning the Council was to present the beliefs of Roman Catholicism in an updated form so that they would be more intelligible than ever to modern man. He also hoped that with such an updating, the contemporary world of men would feel attracted to the Catholic faith, especially now that the Roman Church was adopting a conciliatory stand.

"At all times," John said in his announcement, "the Church has resisted errors. Often she has condemned them, sometimes with great severity. Today, however, the Spouse of Christ prefers the medicine of compassion rather than the arms of severity. She believes that the needs of today are more appropriately met by a full explanation of the power of her doctrine than by condemnation."

Hence, he went on, his Council would be pastoral rather than dogmatic. There would be no anathemas, no condemnations, just an opening out to the world, a modernization of the Church's appearance, "leaving the substance of the ancient doctrine intact . . ."

In the light of experience, many have thought that these words and ideas of "the good Pope John" went back to his early days as the young priest and theology professor, Angelo Roncalli, when there was, to say the least of it, a certain ambiguity in his own ideas which led some to suspect he had unwitting leanings toward Modernism. His career as a Roman professor had been cut short because of those suspicions. Notwithstanding the fact that, as Papal Nuncio in the Paris of the forties, it was he who had sounded the first serious alarm concerning the work of Teilhard de Chardin, John never quite understood the quick and subtle poison that Modernism was.

Still, the possibility that his Council might be used in an attempt to propagate false doctrines and opinions did not escape the cautious, suspicious peasant of Bergamo who had had that brush with doctrinal catastrophe early in his career. To those near him, he did mention his fears that his Council would be invaded by false doctrines. But they persuaded the Pope that, as he said himself later, such Modernist doctrines "are so obviously in contradiction to the right principles and have borne such appalling fruit that today men spontaneously reject such false doctrines."

That is the voice of Angelo Roncalli. But the sentiments were those of the churchmen who were closest to John XXIII in the Council years; and particularly they are the sentiments of the cardinal whom John XXIII called "the first fruit of Our Pontificate," Giovanni Battista Montini, who would in a few short years succeed John to the papacy as Pope Paul VI.

Montini was not being duplistic. Totally unrealistic trust and belief in the essential reasonableness and goodness of man was a principle of that mind Montini had acquired from his French mentor, Jacques Maritain. In fact, the principle was originally developed by Jean Jacques Rousseau in the eighteenth century, with his almost Teilhardian portrait of "the noble savage" untouched in his goodness by a corrupt and corrupting Christianity, and his belief in the power of man to achieve his own ideals by his own reason and nature.

Both for himself and as John's adviser, Montini's view of the Church was that she should become a role player in the "universal fraternity" of man. She should be the "big sister," the "inspirer" of good and nice things. She should win the sympathy of her "little brother," the world of man, by ceasing to be intransigent and authoritarian and separate. She must make religion acceptable. She must be practical, not dogmatic. You couldn't call an Ecumenical Council "practical," however. Call it "pastoral," therefore.

The Council which was convened on October 11, 1962, met in Rome for four separate months-long sessions, spread over a period of four years. By the time Session I was over, John already knew with his peasant's realism that "the substance of the ancient doctrine" of his Church, which he had believed would be protected, was under severe attack from within the Council itself; and he knew he would not live to defend it. Before the second session was convened, Pope John XXIII was dead.

Guided both by his sentimental principles and by advisers of his own who were perhaps less sentimental, Paul VI led Vatican II through the three remaining sessions. If Paul was sincere—and he was—he was also profoundly ignorant and philosophically of the shallowest understanding. On the other hand, most of the bishops had come to the Council with a quiescent, conservative mentality little leavened by theological study and reflection. By the middle of the Council, however, there had been developed in them a consensus in favor of opening all except the essentials to change and adaptation.

This leavening of the bishops' outlook was mainly accomplished not in obedience to John's original intentions or because they understood the vision that had led John to call the Council, but by the influence of the 280 theological experts, or Council *periti*, as they were called. These were, in the main, professors of theology in various Catholic seminaries; over three-quarters of them came from Europe and North America. An individual bishop chose one, two, sometimes three theologians he knew and took them to Rome as his theology advisers. The purpose of these *periti* was to supplement the bishops' lack of knowledge in theology. Inevitably, of course, they formed the bishops' opinions.

In addition, the *periti* represented their bishops in the various committees, subcommittees, and commissions which prepared drafts of the various documents that were discussed by the bishops during the actual sittings of the Council. The *periti* also took part in the continuously sustained informal discussions outside the Council; they gave series of lectures; they composed position papers. They had, in effect, enormous influence on the final votes cast by the bishops.

The *periti*, therefore, were the perfect agents for change. Traditionally, they were cast in the role of "elbow-men," the ones who sat next to the elbow of bishop or cardinal during Council discussions and ensured that the great man in question understood the theological issues at stake and answered to them correctly. During the Second Vatican Council, they had a ubiquitous, all-pervasive influence. There seems to be unanimity among students of the Council that those *periti* of Vatican II were, in the main, of a liberal-progressive frame of mind.

One can now add, in hindsight, that many of the more influential *periti*—men such as Hans Küng and Edward Schillebeeckx—were Modernist in the fullest sense of that word. Clearly, both types of *periti* were determined to promote a more loosely governed Church, a relaxation of traditional Catholic exclusiveness, and a more ambiguous interpretation of basic Catholic doctrines —in particular those safeguarding the prerogatives of the Roman Pope and the nature of the Church. It is equally clear that the "brotherhood" of Modernists among Jesuits and others was, for the first time in its history, able to climb above ground and advocate—sometimes subtly by ambiguous language, sometimes openly—the outlook that had up to then flowed silently and secretly.

Some day, some historian of Second Vatican Council affairs will have access to all the relevant documents—the correspondence between the *periti*, the private position papers drawn up, the policy outlines—and establish beyond doubt that the Council of John XXIII was the object of a concerted, and, as it turned out, a successful attack by the Modernist leaders among Roman Catholics. For now, this remains a tantalizing presumption justified by what evidence we have, but not proven beyond a shadow of doubt.

As the Council was conducted under Paul VI's overall direction, not only the *periti* but just about every element of Council machinery—the formal debates, the procedure of committees to draft and revise Council texts, the open resistance to Vatican officials, the backing and filling of cabals, the vote-counting, the strong North American presence—was used to suggest ever more insistently that now finally the Church of Rome had become a parliamentary democracy; that parliamentary democracy was synonymous with Catholic theological truth and Christian virtue; that the old "pre-Vatican" Church government was out forever; and that a new progressive government was in. In this manner were sown the seeds of revolt among the bishops themselves. Only in the eighties would the harvest from that seeding begin to be reaped, when bishops everywhere have begun literally to proclaim doctrine and redefine dogma without even a nod toward Rome.

The Modernist aim within the Council was not, however, to

achieve ascendancy, increased power, or independence for the bishops. The idea was to win over a majority of bishops to the idea that the Church should be "a changing Church," because the culture of the world around the Church was a changing culture; to convince the bishops in essence—through no one put the case publicly in so many words—that Teilhard's evolutionary view should be their guiding star.

To give the bishops their due—and even in the face of their effective "re-education" by the *periti*—the Council staunchly repeated what the Church had always taught about the essentials of faith. It was magnificent in its fidelity to Roman Catholic tradition. However, in all else, it achieved a degree of ambiguity and slobbery comprehensiveness throughout the thought and texts of its sixteen documents that has since proven to be calamitous.[1]

Modernists, and particularly those who adopted the principles of Liberation Theology, have capitalized on that ambiguity with consummate skill. Though many and varied have been the uses made of, and the abuses inflicted upon, these documents and the mind of the Council bishops who voted them as approved, the Liberation Theologians have concentrated in particular on three themes to be found in the Council documents: the definition of the Church; the meaning of "the people of God"; and the role and function of bishops in the Church. By means of these three themes —and the frequent use of truncated texts and quotations—the new theologians have been able to justify three radical departures from normative Roman Catholicism.

Concerning the first theme, the bishops in Council were clear and insistent on what they meant by the Church. It is, they said, "one complex reality which coalesces from a divine and a human element." There is the visible "society structure with hierarchical organs" (the human); and there is the Mystical Body of Christ, composed of all those who are "made one with the unity of the Father, the Son, and the Holy Spirit" (the divine). The Council was repetitive and firm: These two elements—the visible assembly, and the spiritual community—do not constitute two separate realities. They are one and coextensive.

Furthermore, the Council added, the visible assembly—the human element of the indivisible Church—*subsists* in the Roman Catholic Church "which is governed by the successor of Peter and by the bishops in communion with him." The texts of the Council discussions make it clear that the bishops deliberately used the Latin word *"subsistit"* to affirm as strongly as possible that there is only one Church of Christ, and it is *concretely* the Roman Cath-

THE SECOND VATICAN COUNCIL

olic Church. Elsewhere, in the same context, the Council document asserts the complete identification of the Church Christ
founded with the Roman Catholic Church. The meaning of *subsistit* is unequivocally basic and simple; it means "exists," "is to
be found." This Latin term is not the equivalent of the English
word *subsists*, which has acquired three or four meanings not part
of the Latin term from which the English term is derived.

Either the Modernist Liberation Theologians were bad Latinists
or they assumed everyone else was. They pounced upon that word
subsistit and gave it a modern meaning more congenial to their
purposes. The Council, the new theologians insisted, did not use
a word such as *"is,"* which in their opinion would mean "is perfectly identified with." The Council used a word, the *periti* said in
a subtle mistranslation, that means "to subsist." Now that, they
went on to compound their translation error with dogmatic error,
can only be a recognition by the Council that, while substantially
the Church is to be found within the Roman Catholic *tradition*,
other equally authentic and true parts of Christ's Church are to be
found *outside* that tradition—cheek by jowl with it, perhaps, but
certainly outside it.

In the words of one Modernist-minded Franciscan, Alan
Schreck, "the phrase [sic] 'subsists in' which means 'is rooted in'
or 'dwells within but is not limited to' was carefully chosen. It
means that the one true Church of Jesus Christ is found within
the Catholic Church but is not limited to it. The bishops pur-
posely did not say that the Church of Jesus Christ is the Catholic
Church."[2]

Either Schreck is in need of a remedial course in Latin and in
the reading of Council documents or, like the Queen of Hearts in
Alice in Wonderland, he is content to redefine everything as he
wishes. Either way you look at it, the results of his error are grim;
ignorance and redefinition are the stuff of theological nonsense.
For the effect of this Modernist interpretation was to decrease, if
not eliminate, the need to belong to the Roman Catholic Church.
It removed the need for anyone to submit to the Roman Pontiff
even in matters of faith and morals, or to remain within a Church
dominated by the hierarchy of bishops, for neither Pope nor
bishops would possess anything of exclusive value you could not
find elsewhere.

Once this interpretation of the meaning of *Church* is in place
and widely accepted, it is ready and convenient for use as part of
"the spirit of Vatican II." It becomes justification "by Vatican II"
for disobedience to the Pope's wishes; for doctrinal deviations

from papal teaching; for belonging to other churches; and for a host of other changes that may become useful as "evolution" continues.

The Liberation Theologian moves quickly on to the second theme of the Council documents in order to bolster his claim of independence from papal wishes and teachings—the theme of "the people of God." In this instance, he is perhaps on slightly firmer ground for, no doubt about it, the phrase *the people of God* is a term used frequently in Council texts to refer to the Church. It occurs no fewer than eighty times as a description of the Church, whereas, *the Kingdom of God* is used only eighteen times to describe the Church. Nevertheless, here again, a redefinition of the bishops' meaning comes into play.

The Council was quite clear about what it intended by the use of "the people of God." All men, the Council said, are called to belong to "the people of God"; but only those who are "fully incorporated in the society of the Church, who accept her entire system . . . and are united with her as part of her visible structure and through her with Christ who rules through the Supreme Pontiff and the bishops" actually belong to and are members of "the people of God." Furthermore, according to the Council, "the bonds which bind men to the Church in a visible way are profession of faith, the Sacraments, and ecclesiastical government and communion."

In spite of this clear statement, Liberation Theologians have seized on the expression *the people of God,* and have been enormously successful in giving it a meaning loaded with acrimony against the traditional, hierarchic Church. The new theologians emphasized what the Council also said about the faith and the charisms of the ordinary faithful; they then attached to the term *the people of God* a sociological meaning roughly equivalent to *proletariat* as used in Marxist analysis. Quicker than a wink, they were able to proclaim the autonomy and independence of this new "people of God" from the Pope and the Church hierarchy. With their very own faith and charisms proclaimed by the Council itself, "the people of God" was said to be autonomous in religious belief, in moral practice, and in sociopolitical life.

At once, another element of the much-invoked "spirit of Vatican II" clicks into place. The rise of Base Communities—*comunidades de base,* to give them their Latin American name—rests on this wholesale reinterpretation of "the people of God."

A summarily weak but activist theologian falls into this trap very easily. Such a man, for example, is Archbishop Rembert

Weakland of Milwaukee, Wisconsin, activist in liberal and progressive political causes and chairman of the drafting committee for the first draft of the U.S. bishops' ill-fated economic pastoral letter of 1984, which says in part: "The U.S. Conference [of Bishops] believes that the hierarchy must listen to what the spirit is saying to the whole Church. . . . Discernment, not just innovation or self-reliance, becomes a part of the teaching process."

Weakland is not alone, nor is he without precedent. A prominent churchman of the stature of Cardinal König of Vienna became almost foolishly confused on this subject in 1976: "The old distinctions between the teaching Church and the listening Church, between the Church that commands and the Church that obeys, have ceased to exist," he was quoted as saying. "Priests and laity form but one organic unity."

One can be sure that Archbishop Weakland will grace the See of Milwaukee until his retirement, and that Cardinal König has had an informative conversation with Pope John Paul II since his election in 1978. Nevertheless, such inaccurate theological pronunciamentos as these have given encouragement to the Liberation Theologians, who are by now thoroughly convinced that the Second Vatican Council did teach that "the people" are the real Church, and that the Roman Catholic hierarchic structure is an outworn relic of an age that has been bypassed by time, by cultural change, and by "the spirit of Vatican II."

The third Council theme of special interest to Liberation Theologians was the role and function of the bishops in the Church; and yet once again, the Council was clear, as it repeated the Church's traditional doctrine. The bishops of the Church, the Council text stated, are "successors of the Apostles in their role as teachers and pastors." But "they have no authority unless united with the Roman Pontiff, Peter's successor." He, the Pope, has "full, supreme, and universal power over the whole Church, a power he can always exercise unhindered." The bishops, meanwhile, "have supreme and full authority over the Universal Church" only when they are "together with the Supreme Pontiff, and never apart from him."

In spite of that clarity, the persuasion has been spread by the new theologians—not a few of them bishops and cardinals—that this Second Vatican Ecumenical Council had finally "liberated" bishops from "papal totalitarianism"; and that the bishops were now their own masters who could decide about faith and morals without consulting, or bending to the will and doctrine of, the Roman Pontiff.

While it may come as a shock to those bishops who have taken the bait, the intent of Liberation Theology's novel interpretation of this theme was not to enhance the status of the bishops. Far from it. The goal was and remains to unlimber and dismantle the centralized, hierarchic government of the Roman Church, and thus reduce the power and influence of the Roman Pope to nil.

While the results of these tendencies—fomented over time in large part by skillful use of the loose and ambiguous wording imposed on the official Council texts, as well as by the interpretation imposed on the Council's whole purpose—were not all at once obvious in themselves, a new image of the Church was steadily created. It was a mirage, really, that danced in front of the eyes of millions and began to dictate Jesuit thinking and Jesuit policy. It is hard to exaggerate the excitement, the sense of a vast new enterprise, that the mere existence and functioning of the Second Vatican Council evoked. The phrase "the spirit of Vatican II" came to be used as a password and a formula to authenticate any and every change desired.

In the middle of Session III of Vatican II, on October 2, 1964, the Jesuit Father General, seventy-five-year-old Jean-Baptiste Janssens, was incapacitated by a violent stroke from which obviously he would not recover. The eighteen years of his generalate had been fruitful in a statistical sense. When Janssens was elected in 1946, membership in the Society of Jesus had been 28,000; when he was stricken in 1964, it stood at 36,000.

A man more sinned against than sinning, Janssens had seen his share of trouble. He had demonstrated enormous personal courage, self-control, and resourcefulness when he tangled with Hitler's Gestapo in his native land, occupied wartime Belgium. He had also shown himself to be a man of great meekness and personal sanctity.

During most of his eighteen years as Father General, Janssens had managed to put a damper on the covert Modernism and the innovative revolution in doctrine and moral theology that seemed to be spreading through the ranks of the Society's intellectuals. An acquaintance of all the great names in the Church of his day, a close student of *romanità*, a realist behind the smooth manner he had always cultivated, Jean-Baptiste Janssens surely merited a special accolade for having perdured so long under pressure; at least he surely deserved better than the treatment he received.

In June of 1964, the liberal Dutch newspaper *Die Nieuwe Linie*, which counted three Jesuits among its editorial staff, had discussed openly the moral licitness of birth control, questioned the need for clerical celibacy, and thrown doubt on the sacrosanct Catholic doctrine of Transubstantiation—the Sacrament of the Eucharist as the actual body and blood of Jesus. In the subsequent uproar and dispute with Roman authorities, Janssens ordered the three Jesuit staff members of the newspaper under holy obedience to quit their posts. One obeyed; two ignored the command.

The traditionalists among Paul VI's curial bureaucracy weighed in with dire proposals both about Janssens and the Society of Jesus. Things got so bad that one story (apparently true) had it that when the second-in-command at the Holy Office was asked what he would like to see done, in reply he quoted the words of Salome's mother from the Gospel: *"Da mihi caput Joannis Baptistae in disco.* I want the head of Jean-Baptiste [Janssens] on a plate." Clearly, relations between the Jesuits and Paul VI's Vatican were becoming strained.

Still, severe as it was, the *Nieuwe Linie* dispute was only one of many brushfires that were breaking out and burning away at Janssens's feet. His Jesuits were prominent as *periti* in the progressive minority that was making such huge inroads on the initially conservative mentality of most Council bishops. Abroad, Jesuit publications were already beginning to barrage the Catholic mind with progressive proposals and plans.

His age and his weakness made the gathering clouds on the Jesuit horizon far too much for Janssens to handle effectively. His Vicar-General, Canadian John Swain, who had helped Janssens in governing the Society for the last eight years of his Generalate, seemed unable to be effective either.

Three days after Janssen's stroke, and twenty minutes before he died on October 5, Pope Paul came to visit him. When, on October 6, Paul said Mass for Janssens's soul and sent a formal telegram of condolence to Jesuit headquarters, one wonders if he understood that with Janssens, the *ancien régime* of the Society of Jesus had also died. Had he not been the man he was, one might imagine Janssens whispering in his immaculate French, as his last words of commendation to his surviving colleagues, the prophetic words of Madame Pompadour: *"Après nous, le déluge.* After we have gone will come the deluge."

Almost immediately on Janssens's death, Vicar-General Swain called for a General Congregation of the Society—the thirty-first in the Order's history—to elect the twenty-seventh Jesuit Father General, and to attend to other current affairs of the Society. It is a measure of the "hurricane" quality of the time that no one sensed that GC31 would make the Society Janssens had led a memory of the past, to be cherished only by older Jesuits who had served in the days before the deluge of "renewalism."

Though the particulars took time to emerge clearly, all the now-well-worn Modernist traits are discernible in hindsight in the mirage known as "the spirit of Vatican II." Suddenly the Church could be seen as essentially a fraternal communion of local churches and groups of believers devoted to "the Christ-man," "the Christ for others," the Christ who was the friend and defender of the proletarian poor, the Christ who, in liberating the poor, was to be seen as a real, live, weapons-toting revolutionary, whether in the jungles of Central America or the cities of South America or the capitalist cities throughout the world. The Catholic Church with its rulers—Popes and bishops alike—was ripe to be cast in the role of a leftover phase from an ancient time. Its collusion with capitalist powers, its exploitation of superstition, its false claims to be the one and the only true, Catholic, and Apostolic Church—none of this, it came to be said, would be enough to save the Church from extinction.

An undeveloped sense of that emerging mentality, that "spirit of Vatican II," had already begun to catch on quite a time before the Second Vatican Council ended in December of 1965. That "spirit" aroused the first great organized response among the Delegates to the Jesuits' 31st General Congregation, which convened with Pope Paul VI's blessing on May 6, 1965.

It remains a puzzling fact that even as late as 1967, when he had had time to review the Council and, presumably, recognize the Modernist trend among theologians, bishops, and Jesuits, Pope Paul blindly and foolishly did away with a universal rule that imposed on all theologians a solemn oath to combat Modernism. Who persuaded the Pope to do this? Then again, as late as 1969, when already the first ragged edges of the coming shambles in his Church and in the Jesuits were becoming painfully apparent, Paul VI could still refer breathlessly to the "wave of serenity and optimism" spreading through his Church.[3]

Those are the words of a man so befuddled on essentials that in the same year, 1969, he was preparing a document which would omit all reference to the immemorial sacrificial character of the Roman Mass; and change the function of the priest as offerer of Christ's sacrifice to that of a minister at a communal "memorial meal," complete with a table and bread of fellowship.

With reason has it been said of Paul VI that the first seven years of his reign were his "mad years" and the last eight were his "agony years." When "the spirit of Vatican II" took vigorous hold during the last eight years of his pontificate, even Montini's liberal mind was not prepared for the onslaught of change that billowed over his Church.

The extent of the damage produced in the Church by the hurricane mentality let loose after 1965 can be gauged a mere twenty years later. Pope John Paul II now presides over a Church organization that is in shambles, a rebellious and decadent clergy, an ignorant and recalcitrant body of bishops, and a confused and divided assembly of believers. The Roman Catholic Church, which used to present itself as the One, Holy, Catholic, and Apostolic Church, appears now as a pluralistic, permissive, ecumenical, and evolutionary ecclesial group.

The blame for the opening to such deterioration must perhaps be laid primarily at the door of those close to John XXIII, who persuaded him that "men today spontaneously reject such false doctrines." At least one of those advisers, Paul VI, lived to see the apostolic strength of his Church sapped by those who were spontaneous in their adoption of such false doctrine.

For such men—the Liberation Theologians above all, among the Modernists of Paul VI's day and our own—the Church, the "real" Church, "the people of God," is not merely in the world; it *is* the world.

This Church's viewpoint is not "vertical"—looking toward eternity. Instead, its viewpoint is horizontal, out across the face of man's Earth. This Church does not exist for herself or for an otherworldly goal. She exists to serve the world on its own material and materialist terms. She must not have any so-called Catholic institutions, only human ones. She must be dominated and directed not by Christ's Vicar, the Pope, with his bishops, but by the "community," which must nominate and choose its own "ministers of the Word."

Indeed, priests consecrated in the "old" manner are no longer needed to celebrate the Eucharist, for example, or to forgive sins, or to decide what is morally permissible in peace and in war, in business and in sexuality. All members of the Church, men and women of the "community," will be the true priests. No longer are bishops needed to govern dioceses, or Popes to lay down the law for the Church Universal. The community consensus decides all that.

Above all, the primary task of this "people of God," according to the Modernist, is to promote the social and political aspirations of our increasingly collectivist world in which the archenemy is capitalism, and the ready allies are Marxists, as we move inexorably toward the New Humanity and the total liberation of the human in us all.

And so it is that a convert to Modernism such as Eugene Kennedy can confidently predict that "the essential changes of the coming decade will not come from agreements or documents signed and sealed by Church officials but from the already well-established attitudes and behavior of the believing community. . . . We are being called out of bondage to see the world and each other more clearly. . . ." This "is the promise of the power of the post-immigrant Church in the interstellar age."[4]

Eugene Cardinal Tisserant, a one-time sympathizer and supporter of Montini, came with his acerbic, merciless Gallic wit, to compare the surprise of Pope Paul VI at the onslaught of change in the Church with the hurt surprise of the elite Parisian art world at the rough, rude, caricatural quality of Jean Dubuffet's first exhibition of *l'art brut* ("art in the raw") in 1944. To the shocked question "Is this art?" most people responded with an equally shocked, "No!" Those who had expected a reborn School of Paris were as distressed as Paul VI was; distressed for the same reasons, and as helplessly, as Paul was. They could not impede Dubuffet's success. Nor could Paul VI impede the progress of the shambles in the wake of his own permissive direction of the Second Vatican Council.

Tisserant's comparison was apt in more ways than the mere parallel between the distress of the aspiring School of Paris advocates at Dubuffet's art and Paul VI's distress at "the spirit of Vatican II."

Dubuffet's was a vigorous, propulsive, irregular style and rhythm of composition, an esthetic of continual change. He regarded the past as "both debilitating and injurious," and he prized forgetfulness as "a liberating force." He wanted, he said, a new candor, a new truthfulness, and an utterly new terrain to travel. "Unless one says good-bye to what one loves," he wrote, "and unless one travels to completely new territories, one can expect merely a long wearing-away of oneself, and an eventual extinction." To travel over that new terrain, he brought his own restless, irascible vitality allied with an insuppressible impertinence and insubordination to bear on his contemporaries. He ended up completely accepted as a leader in the field of art.

Like Dubuffet, the progressivist leaders and thinkers of the Society of Jesus were among the first pioneers to travel over their new "territories"; and like Dubuffet, they brought their own restless, irascible vitality allied with an insuppressible impertinence and insubordination to bear on their contemporaries. Deliberate forgetfulness of the Ignatian ideal liberated them from the traditional obligations of Jesuitism. And, like Dubuffet in the world of art, the new Jesuits ended up as the accepted leaders of their own world—the religious world inhabited by the Society of Jesus and the Church.

The enormous difference, of course, is that a school of art is not in the same dynamic as a religious organization, and the papacy cannot be compared to any artistic elite. For Jesuits to adopt change as the order of the day and to accept forgetfulness of their Ignatian responsibilities to Pope and Church as a mental attitude meant cutting their ties to the ideal of classical Jesuitism. And for Jesuits, the insistence on "new terrain to travel," and a fear that the repetitious grind of the same old style and rhythm would wear them away to eventual extinction, meant they faced contention with papal wishes and objections, and accepted that contention as a permanent fact of life. This acceptance could lead only to open war with the one man who has the power of life or death over their Society, and who could claim their allegiance on the strength of solemn oaths they had once freely taken.

It is an irony that would have hurt Pope John XXIII very deeply, and would have revolted the heart and soul of Ignatius of Loyola, if those men had been alive at the end of the Second Vatican Council. They would have seen clearly that the Council's final documents were already being used by the Jesuits in order to complete their plans for a complete turnabout in Jesuitism, for a conversion of the Society of Jesus into something Ignatius had never intended and John XXIII would have abhorred.

For, on the basis of the liberal-progressive interpretation of Vatican II, the Jesuits were about to take off for "new territories" definitely not included in the Ignatian plan, and were determined to relegate the papacy John XXIII held in sacred honor to a very secondary place in their plans and considerations.

As in most things, the Jesuits were the first, the pioneers, in this "renewal" of Catholicism, beckoning everyone else to say goodbye to what John XXIII had loved and Ignatius of Loyola had honored. That being so, it was just a matter of how to get the job done.

TROJAN HORSE

PART IV

17 | THE SECOND BASQUE

B y October 5, 1964, when Jesuit Father General Jean-
Baptiste Janssens died, the stage was set for the new face
of Jesuitism to make its entrance—the face that bared its
teeth in such an ugly and humiliating grimace at the papacy of
John Paul II not twenty years later.

The backdrop for the drama had been a long time in the making
in the workshops of the Liberators. The spirit of the times—a
contagious and highly romantic euphoria—had primed a huge cast
for the historic roles to be played. Vatican Council II, which had
convened the first of four sessions in 1962, had already been ig-
nited by the sparks of that euphoria. In turn, these sparks were
seen around the world as pyrotechnic announcements that new
and great events were in the offing. But it is unlikely that any
Jesuit then alive could have foreseen the dramatic developments
that would in a few short years transform Ignatian Jesuitism. The
one thing lacking for the drama was a detailed script. That would
be written only after Vatican Council II was over, in the eighty-
four Decrees issued by the 31st General Congregation (GC31) of
the Order.

In a mere eighteen months, between May 1965 and November
1966—the official lifespan of that General Congregation—226
Delegates managed to clothe an array of profoundly important
statements and picayune matters alike in more or less traditional

language and concepts. But when the script was finished, it was the announcement of a new mission and a new spirit.

Neither mission nor spirit was derived from Rome. They came with the Delegates from the Provinces of the Society all over the world. Everything and anything that had come down to them from the 420-year history of the Society had to be subjected to a severe triage, a vigorous sieving and sifting, in view of that new mission. No matter what the traditional mission and character of the Society, no matter what papal authority indicated as its will, no matter how long or hard the labor, the call now was for a fundamental transformation of Jesuitism. As its General Congregations go, so goes the whole Society.

It was unfortunate from the point of view of the papacy that GC31 coincided with the all-important Second Vatican Council, the bellwether event of the Catholic Church in the second half of the twentieth century. When Vicar-General John Swain, temporarily in charge of the Jesuit Order after Janssens's death, approached Pope Paul VI for permission to convoke GC31, the Pontiff's attention was distracted, to say the least.

From its start on September 14, 1964, until its closing day, November 21, Session III of Vatican II was scarred by new and bitter crises between the progressivist body of bishops and the traditionalists. It was during one of these crises that Father General Janssens was stricken. Paul VI did find time to visit the dying man, and to make sure his office sent the usual expressions of papal sorrow and condolence after his death.

Almost ritually and mechanically, Pope Paul gave Vicar-General Swain his permission to convoke GC31; the Jesuits had to elect a new Father General. Paul had little time to notice subsequent Jesuit events for the remainder of the year. He was racked with problems. His energies, always limited by his inborn timidity, were stretched thin and divided unevenly by the jam-packed schedule of Vatican II and the realization that the Council was going out of his control. At the very least, its debates and discussions, both in public and in private, opened up for consideration subjects of extreme delicacy and importance. Atheism was only one thorny question; issues ranged from the nature of the Church and the relationship of bishops to Pope when exercising power in the Church, to marriage and birth control and the attitude of the Church to Jews.

Paul was still preoccupied with a plethora of problems in the New Year 1965, when Vicar-General Swain's letter of January 13 informed Jesuits worldwide that the opening day of GC31 would be the following May 6. Each of the Jesuit Provinces held a Provincial Congregation at which they chose their Province Delegates for GC31. Each one then began the work of assembling its chosen *postulata,* the subjects it wished GC31 to discuss.

Swain's letter was received in the provinces as a trumpet blast, mustering the Society to its new mission. Already abroad in the Order there existed among a sizeable number of Jesuits a lack of enthusiasm or understanding for the old character of their Society. They no longer saw themselves as an ecclesiastical Rapid Deployment Force at the beck and call of their Pope. On the contrary, they ardently wished for the "democratization" of Catholicism and of the Society. Away with the idea of Pope and hierarchy, and of a special fidelity to one man, the Pope, occupying a hierarchic position in one place, Rome!

By spring, Vicar-General Swain and his staff in Rome had already received an enormous number of *postulata.* They would reach some 1900 in all, the highest number ever sent in by the Provinces. For GC30 in 1957, by way of comparison, there had been about 450 *postulata,* and that was considered high at the time.

As the avalanche poured in, it quickly became clear that the GC31 *postulata* concerned everything in the Society—its governing structure, its mission, its ministries, the formation and training of its young men, its relations with the papacy, its life of piety and religion, the imbalance of influence between young and old in the Society. Changes in the *Institute* itself—the very definition of Jesuitism drawn up by Ignatius and incorporated by Pope Paul III in his Bull of 1540 creating the Society of Jesus—were even suggested by some.

Whatever the particulars, it was clear above all that the majority of the *postulata* pointed in an entirely new direction. They clamored for "renewal." *Renewal,* as Swain knew, was the code word current in Vatican Council II for radical change. It had triggered a fever that had raced through all the sessions of the Second Vatican Council, and had spread easily, by way of the many Jesuit advisers, to the bishops in the Council, to the Society itself.

Among the Jesuit Superiors in Rome, sentiments were divided. There were strict traditionalists, to be sure, but there were also progressivist, "antipapalist" spirits. All of them, however, traditionalists and progressivists alike, were amazed by the progressivist, even revolutionary tenor of the *postulata.* All agreed that the time to air this "renewal" in the Society had not yet arrived. Even the most progressivist of Superiors were aware that the timing had to be correct.

The prudent thing for an acting Jesuit General to do in such a situation would have been to warn the Pope, and to say to the Holy Father, in effect: Look, we have a problem. The *postulata* take for granted that the whole idea of fidelity to the Pope is outmoded. For many of our Jesuits out there, Vatican Council II has shown the way. And for those Jesuits, the significance of Vatican II lies chiefly in the fact that ordinary bishops and theologians of the Church have met Vatican officials head-on in debate, have talked back to them, have refuted them, have outmaneuvered them, have outvoted them, have bloodied them, and have forced "democratization" of the Church. For those Jesuits, the Roman lion has been bearded in its den. The Vatican and its Curia have been stripped of their sacrosanct aura; no longer does their word seem to be final. GC31 promises to be more of the same.

Vicar-General Swain did not do that. He did not go into detail either with Pope Paul VI or with other Vatican officials even about the wilder strain perceptible in a goodly number of the *postulata* —anti-Roman, antipapal, antihierarchical, antitraditional voices; voices clamoring for a changeover in the Society to a sociopolitical rather than a papal allegiance; voices attacking the West and capitalism in the same breath with "Romanism."

Nor did Swain share with higher authorities the one fact that had been most surprising to the Jesuit Superiors in Rome: For the first time in living memory of the Order, the conservative and the traditionalist voices taken together amounted to a minority. For most, in fact, GC31 was coming none too soon. The docility and submissiveness that had characterized the Generalate of Janssens was over.

Had Swain raised any alarm at all, it would not have fallen on deaf ears in Paul VI. Only the year before, in 1963, a remarkable number of complaints about the Society had prompted the Pope to request his representatives in various countries to assemble a body of information about the Order and its activities. The famous dossier that later came into the hands of John Paul I and John Paul II was already becoming fat with reports of Jesuits abroad who were severely deficient not only in matters of biblical teaching, in matters of liturgical experimentation, and in basic doctrines such as the divinity of Jesus; some were also deficient in belief about two subjects in which the Roman Catholic Church differed markedly and specifically from all other churches: the nature of the Church, and the prerogatives of the papacy.

The dossier itself did not alarm Paul unduly at the time, the early spring of 1964. He realized as well as or better than any man that his church was in ferment. To his mind, and despite the frigid ending of Session III of Vatican II, it was still a good ferment. In his timid-hearted if stubborn liberalism, Paul could be patient with experimentation, with wrong-headed enthusiasm, even with doctrinal vagaries.

But once the papacy was touched, or once the nature of the Church as he conceived it was touched, Paul was of a totally different mind. Had Swain put him on his guard concerning the large number of *postulata* that clamored for "renewal" in Jesuit relations with and fidelity to the papacy, Paul would have become very chary in his oversight of the preparations for GC31, and of the Congregation itself.

Whatever fears may have been raised in Paul by some of the reports in his dossier, however, they were largely calmed by Vicar-General Swain. The mind of the Jesuits as expressed in the *postulata* was one with Swain's own intent.

Other Jesuits, too, assured Paul that all was in order. These were able and trusted men such as Augustin Cardinal Bea, the powerful and widely revered German Jesuit whom Paul had known since the twenties, and who had been confessor to Pius XII before he had become Pope John's own point man for worldwide ecumenical affairs; and Paolo Dezza, who was Paul's own confessor, and whose Lombardian calm even in times of high tension was enough to shave the peaks off other men's emotion.

With such advice from Swain seconded by his own closest Jesuit advisers, Paul was so confident that, in meetings with Swain that spring, he lifted all restrictions on matters to be discussed, and gave his permission for the forthcoming GC31 to be free to air opinions and proposals about anything pertaining to the life of the Society.

"Let them be free," Paul said. It was a decision he was to regret.

The 226 Delegates who arrived in Rome on May 6, 1964, for the opening of GC31 came, then, with a mind-set radically different from the typically Roman mind, the classical Jesuit mind, and the traditional Catholic mind. How they acquired that mind-set is another question. But the fact is not in dispute.

It was not simply that they were ready, as the *postulata* that had preceded them showed, to dump ancient baggage. It was that in their minds, they had already replaced that "baggage" with something else. Instead of a world and a cosmos arrayed hierarchically, where pre-set forms held a sacrosanct position, the new mind-set required that all forms of human life be relative; in other words, in religious, social, political, devotional, and doctrinal life the new Jesuit cry was for "democratization."

Instead of the traditionally codified formulas and fixed definitions of doctrine and morality, the new mind-set emphasized experience—individual and social experience—as the measure for setting temporary, *ad hoc* formulas and definitions.

That meant, among other things, that there were no longer to be any fixed dogmas and immutable rules. Faith itself no longer provided a basis for rational assent to the reasoned and logically coherent formulas of Catholic belief and practice.

Rather, what mattered in the revolutionary mind-set of the Delegates to GC31 were individual feelings and individual needs for personal growth.

Perhaps the most revolutionary change of all in the new mind-set was its rejection of the Catholic conviction that men and women move within an enclosed historical paradigm, the traditional framework of Christianity: Creation; Original Sin; Redemption by Christ and the founding of the One, True, Holy, Roman, Catholic Church; the long wait for the Second Coming of Christ during which each individual is engaged personally in the spiritual warfare that rages between Christ and Lucifer; and all to be capped in the Final Judgment of the Living and the Dead by a returning Christ, and then by God's eternity—never-ending ecstasy for the Blessed; never-ending, infernal punishment for the Damned.

In the mind of the new Jesuit intellectuals, each building block in that closed history had been systematically honed, modified, rubbed, worn down, chipped, shredded, and finally dismantled by the logic of history and the iron hand of worldly events.

Now, that new mind-set said, human life and human history were not only open-ended, but were at that precise moment opening up to a new age. The only way to prepare Ignatius's Society for that opening was to set about a substantial transformation of the Society in its goals, its preparation for action, and its actual operation.

The only elements that must remain—for how long was another matter—were the traditional language and concepts always used by Jesuits in their documents. Now, however, they would be used with meanings far different from the meanings that they had ever conveyed. Traditional language would, in short, become the most effective camouflage by which these new Soldiers of Christ could get their guns in place to blow the old Order, ancient baggage and all, out of the water.

Paul VI did not guess at one one-hundredth part of this mind-set for change, any more than did the wide world at large. It was unimaginable—as it still seems to be for many—that anyone could change the fundamental character of the Jesuits as papal men, and as very strictly Roman Catholic. Paul did, however, take some precautions. When the Delegates to GC31 gathered together in the Vatican on May 7 for the ritual address Popes always make at the opening of a General Congregation, the Pontiff gave an expected performance.

He described succinctly what the Society of Jesus was for the papacy and the Holy See: "The pledged protector of the Apostolic See, the militia trained in the practice of virtue . . . to serve God alone and the Church, His Spouse, under the Roman Pontiff, the Vicar of Christ on earth . . . the legion ever faithful to the task of protecting Catholic faith and the Apostolic See . . ."

Of course, added Paul, there were "discordant voices" among them; but Jesuits had a harmony, and "most of you partake of this fitting unanimity." The new Father General would see to it that those discordant voices did not disrupt that harmony, Paul added.

Paul was not playing soothsayer; he was telling the Delegates what sort of man must be elected as their new Father General.

The Pope then gave the Jesuits a solemn task of grave importance: "We give you the charge of making a stout, united stand against atheism . . . Research . . . gather information . . . publish . . . hold discussions . . . prepare specialists . . . be shining examples of holiness. . . ."

Inspirational changes such as this had always fueled the Jesuits' greatest achievements. Other such papal calls to action had, in fact, produced some of the greatest luminaries and saints of the Order—the Robert Bellarmines, the Peter Clavers, the Edmund Campions, the Isaac Jogueses.

Just to make sure that his mind was crystal-clear to the Delegates, Paul ended his address by quoting word for word that description of the Jesuit written by Ignatius in 1539:

All who make the profession in this Society should understand at the time, and furthermore keep in mind as long as they live, that this entire Society and the individual members who make their profession in it are campaigning for God under faithful obedience to His Holiness Pope Paul III and his successors in the Roman pontificate. The Gospel does indeed teach us, and we know from the orthodox faith and firmly hold, that all of Christ's faithful are subject to the Roman Pontiff as their head and as the Vicar of Jesus Christ. But we have judged nevertheless that the following procedure will be supremely profitable to each of us and to any others who will pronounce the same profession in the future, for the sake of our greater devotion in obedience to the Apostolic See, of greater abnegation of our own wills, and of surer direction from the Holy Spirit. In addition to that ordinary bond of the three vows, we are to be obliged by a special vow to carry out whatever the present and future Roman Pontiffs may order which pertains to the progress of souls and the propagation of the faith; and to go without subterfuge or excuse, as far as in us lies, to whatsoever provinces they may choose to send us.

You must not regard this, the Pope concluded, as a nice thought, a spiritual benefit merely, just an abstract privilege. It must be practical, "must also shine forth through actions, and become known to all." In other words: Be Pope's men not only in name but in fact. Let it be clearly seen in your actions that you are Pope's men.

Brave words! The words of Christ's standard-bearer sending his elite troops to prepare for a new battle against Christ's enemies. But in those words there was a manifest if unspoken fear of the change operating ever more deeply throughout the Church. Paul, already bloodied by the hurricanes of change, and profoundly disturbed by the strange euphoria abroad in his Church, knew exactly what he needed and must demand from the Society of Jesus. That is why the central and most remarkable trait of Pope Paul's address was his insistence that Jesuits be faithful to the papacy.

At the time, it seemed to many a needless insistence, on a par with a speaker before the American Medical Association insisting that doctors cure patients of their ills. But Paul desperately needed the Society of Jesus in its classical form to bear the brunt of his personal battle. Too much of a Roman, too dedicated to *romanità*, Paul chose to make of his speech a veiled warning.

Veiled or not, the Pontiff's point was not missed by the Roman Superiors of the Society. Among the Delegates, however, if a warning was heard, it was of a completely different kind. The majority reaction was a negative one. It reminded them of the address given by Pius XII to GC30 nine years before. On that occasion, Pius's carping criticisms and warnings of a stand-off between the Pope and the Society had deflated the Delegates' spirit; nothing of any consequence had been accomplished by that Congregation.

This time, the general sentiment ran, the situation would be different. Perhaps the Delegates to GC30 had left the presence of Pius XII dejected, rebuffed, silenced. Not so for the Delegates to GC31 in the crossroads year of 1965; they left Paul VI's presence determined to press ahead according to their original determination. The Delegates had not come to Rome to rubber-stamp papal claims and sentiments, or to further enhance the centralizing authority and authoritarianism of the papacy. They had come for one reason, and one reason only: to refurbish the *Constitutions* of the Society so that Jesuits too could enter the mainstream of the "renewal," march with the "new men and women," and assist manfully at the birth of "the Church" out there among "the people of God" in the very "spirit of Vatican II."

The main purpose for which GC31 had been convoked was to elect a new Father General. But because the majority of Delegates wanted a change in the General's function and power—a change in favor of democratization and away from absolute authority—that purpose was relegated to second place. It would not do to elect a man and then find that he would react to papal pressure, as Father General Janssens had to Pope Pius XII. That would be to halt the Society's renewal before it could be forged.

No; the first order of business had to be to change the very nature of the Generalate itself, before a man was elected not only to lead the Society, but to lead this very Congregation without wavering in the sweeping work that lay before it.

According to the *Constitutions*, the Generalate was a life-long job. That no longer pleased the Delegates; it smacked remotely of totalitarianism. There should be some approved mechanism by which the Father General could retire from the post—or, if it came to that, be retired. There should also be a greater on-going representation of the worldwide provinces in the central Roman administration of the Society. These two changes would lessen the danger of any new General imposing his views, or the Pope's, on the Society as a whole.

The common consensus was quickly reached that "active" or "passive" resignation of the General should be decreed into law by the Society.

Increased Provincial representation was more difficult to achieve, but not long delayed, for all that. Up to 1964, the Father General had been aided in Rome by twelve Regional Assistants, each one entrusted with the middle-level of Jesuit government, groupings of provinces called Assistancies. The Delegates to GC31 decided that in addition to those twelve Regional Assistants, the General from now on would not only be aided, but seconded, in the democratic sense of the word, by four General Assistants. These were entirely new posts in the Society. Each post would be entrusted with some general or universal task of its own—education, social apostolate, publications, and such. But each occupant would also be entrusted with something more: They would form a special group of advisers to the Father General. Not only would they advise him; they would consent to (or dissent from) what he proposed; they would suggest his course of action. He would need them in order to govern the Society as Father General. They would, in other words, be balance-givers and democratizers. Watchdogs? Yes, that too.

So important in the Delegates' thinking was the need for democratization, and so great the fear that a new Father General might from the outset betray the intent of the Congregation, that the election of the four men to fill the new posts of Assistants General preceded the balloting for the election of the new Father General. The first four chosen to fill the new posts were Vincent O'Keefe of the United States; Hungary's Andrew Varga, an expatriate stationed in New York; Canada's John Swain, who, as Vicar-General, had succeeded Janssens in the temporary running of the Order and had prepared so well for GC31; and Italy's Paolo Dezza, an old Roman hand and trusted by everyone.

With so much settled and their minds more at ease, the Delegates proceeded at last to the election of a new Father General in accordance with time-honored procedure.

The ritual four days for the gathering of information about possible candidates began formally on May 18, eleven days after the start of GC31. In truth, the process had already started in private conversations. If Father X's name is mentioned in connection with the desired traits of the next Father General, while Father Y's name comes up more or less disconnected from those particular traits, the conclusion is obvious.

The Delegates knew more or less exactly what they wanted in the new General: A man who "recognized humanity's deep restlessness," as one Delegate commented; a man who was discerning and enlightened, committed to overcome class struggles and national rivalries; a man ready to deal with the uncertainties of the transition from old forms and the old order of things to fresh models and the new order.

Nowhere in the speeches, the minutes, or the other records of GC31 is there any mention of the Ignatian model as the guide to be used by these Delegates in their choice of General. There is no mention of the candidate's being an obedient son of the Church, a submissive servant of the Holy See, the Pope's special man, the companion of Jesus, the contemplative in action, the devoted servant of the Sacred Heart of Jesus. Rather, candidates of "Generalate timber" were to be measured only by analysis of the Society's concrete situation in the here and now, and needed to be acceptable only to the Jesuits themselves.

During those four days of information-gathering and discussion, the Superiors and the recognized "establishment" members of each Assistancy first of all agree as to whether, among their own number, there are one or more men of Generalate timber. Rapidly, representatives of one Assistancy confer with those of another Assistancy, comparing analyses as well as possible candidates. The process continues quickly until the field is narrowed down to two principal candidates, with a third possibility to hold in reserve in case of deadlock.

There were after all still two chief factions at the Congregation: the renewalists, whose whole emphasis was laid on the "renewal" proclaimed in the name of the Second Vatican Council, and the traditionalists, who insisted that the real renewal that was badly needed was the renewal of the classical form of Jesuitism and the Ignatian ideal in the Society itself. The traditionalist group, though by far the smaller coming into GC31, was vocal and persuasive. A deadlock could not be ruled out.

By May 22, the day set aside for balloting, the Congregation had its candidates. One, the choice of the renewalists, reflected the innovative spirit in its extreme form: The program was change, immediate change, from top to bottom in the Society, in accordance with the winds of change that had blown away fidelity to Rome's teaching authority and the papacy's privileged place from the minds of many bishops, theologians, priests, and lay folk. The other, the candidate of the traditionalists, had a moderate stance: Change, yes, but very gradual and in strict accord with the papal vow Jesuits had taken.

If neither candidate garnered sufficient votes, the compromise candidate was there. He stood for compromise only in one sense. He was all for change, and for change soon. But for change with adequate preparation, not an overnight revolution.

In accordance with custom, all of the Delegates attended a special election-day Mass in the Church of the Gesù. In his choice of

the preacher for that Mass, Vicar-General Swain showed his renewalist leanings even more clearly than he had in his failure to
warn Paul VI of the Jesuit mood. He chose Father Maurice Giuliani
of the Paris Province, for whom, as this worthy renewalist made
clear, "the Society's most important task [was] to embrace freely
and uphold strongly this renewal of the Church."

Giuliani summed up in one neat phrase the type of candidate
most desirable for the position of Jesuit General: The new man, he
stated blandly, must keep the Society "united to the world." In
that single phrase, Giuliani swept aside classical Jesuitism in
which, according to Ignatius's own definition after the words of
the Apostle Paul, a Jesuit was to be one "who is crucified to the
world and to whom the world is crucified."

Having turned that far from Ignatius, it was an easy matter for
Giuliani to echo Teilhard de Chardin instead. Jesuits, Giuliani
said, expected their new Father General "to assist the whole Society and each of her children to enter deeply into the mystery of
death which brings fulfillment, so that we will be able in the
difficult circumstances of today to bring a salvation to the world."
The only thing visible through this muddy thought is the vague
Teilhardian notion of absorption of all humans in the onward
evolution toward the Omega Point. Gone is any mention of the
death of Jesus on the Cross or the death of sin in the human soul.

Giuliani was not, in other words, talking about the salvation
already achieved by Jesus through his sufferings, death, and resurrection, and offered now and for the rest of time through the Sacraments of His Church. The salvation Giuliani was placing in the
hands of the new Father General had to do purely and simply with
the sociopolitical liberation—or evolution—of men and women.

Still, no matter; one good turnabout deserved another. Giuliani
went on to say that the new General must guide the Society in
approaching the dawning age so as "boldly to penetrate these new
movements, to evaluate their widespread hopes . . ." Having
turned aside from Ignatius's ideal, and from supernatural salvation
as mission, Giuliani had come to the crux of his sermon: We of
the new Society are here to serve men and women as they set out
on a new conquest. Let us elect a man as General who will lead us
along this path.

In his entire sermon, Giuliani did not give even polite mention,
let alone an exhortation, about following Jesus, the Leader, into
battle against the Evil One; or about the primary fidelity and ultimate loyalty of all Jesuits to Christ's Vicar and to the Roman
Catholic Church.

All in all, it did not augur well for the success of Paul VI's call for Jesuits to be Pope's men in name and in action; it didn't even bode well for the opinion of Jesuit Superiors that "renewal" of the papalist element of the Order was to be approached with some delicacy—with respect for timing, if not for the Pope.

The Mass ended, Father George Bottereau as "Inclusor," or "locker-up," an anciently established role at Society elections, locked all 226 Delegates into the auditorium at the Gesù so that the balloting could begin.

In the ancient practice of elections in the Society, each elector would stand in turn, stretch his arms out in the form of a cross, and repeat his special vow of obedience to the Pope. Then he would write the name of the candidate of his choice on a ballot paper, drop the ballot in a receptacle, and return to his place. When each man had done this, the scrutiny of the ballots was performed then and there, and out loud.

Provision was made in the rules for as many as five unsuccessful, or issueless, ballotings. After each count, the ballots were destroyed. After five unsuccessful tries, recourse could be had to an elected commission of eleven Delegates, selected for geographical representation of the Society at large. This commission would then choose a Father General who was accepted by the whole Congregation.

At GC31, by the end of the second balloting on May 22, it was obvious that neither the prime candidate of the traditionalists nor that of the renewalists could command the majority vote. On the third ballot, the compromise candidate, fifty-eight-year-old Pedro Arrupe, rallied the majority and became the twenty-seventh Father General of the Society of Jesus, and the first Basque to attain the post since Ignatius himself.[1]

*   *   *

Up to that day and hour, there had been only one moment of public limelight in Pedro Arrupe's life of organizational anonymity.

He had been born at Bilbao in the Basque country of Spain in 1906, the only boy in a family of five children. His father was a wealthy architect who had also founded a newspaper, *Gaceta del Nord.*

Like Ignatius, Arrupe did not set out at first to be a priest. His first love was medicine, which he studied at Madrid University. But, again like Ignatius, he experienced a profound conversion. In 1927, on a visit to the Marian Shrine of Lourdes in France, he saw with his own eyes three miracle healings—a Belgian man was cured of cancer, a twenty-one-year-old Frenchman was cured of the then dreaded infantile paralysis, and a nun was cured of spinal paralysis caused by tuberculosis. Arrupe immediately felt called to be a priest. He joined the Jesuit Order, and was ordained a priest in Holland in 1936. He spent an additional two years of in-house training in the United States.

Apparently he wanted to do further studies in psychology, but his Superiors decided otherwise. In 1938, he was posted to Japan, specifically to a missionary post in the city of Yamaguchi in western Honshu. Arrupe's gentle nickname, "the Shinto-priest," dates from this time. He became a Japanophile. As he recounted later, he tried his hand at everything Japanese "except Samurai archery." He prayed sitting on a cushion in a Zen position; he wrote haiku; he practiced Japanese calligraphy and performed the tea ceremony.

Arrupe's principle in all of this was sound, and it was in the Jesuit tradition: Try to enter into the very mind and soul of the people you are sent to convert. Of course, a certain caution had to be exercised; carried too far, this "inculturation" could result in the conversion of the would-be converter to the outlook and even the religion of those he originally set out to convert.

It was at Yamaguchi that Arrupe's character became known in the Society. He had an extraordinary stamina for work, and he went about it in what colleagues described as "a whirlwind manner." In the mornings, winter and summer, he doused himself with cold water, went off for a fast jog, and returned in a boiling state of steam and sweat—"ablaze like a log on fire," his contemporaries said.

He organized a museum to commemorate the sixteenth-century martyrs of Nagasaki. He once gave a concert—billed as "a great concert"—at which he was the tenor solo, accompanied on the cello by his superior, Jesuit Father Lassalle, and by another Jesuit as violinist. "Arrupe was an optimist by definition," one of his colleagues remarked of him, and there seemed no limit either to his energy or his enthusiasm.

When World War II broke out, Arrupe was arrested by the infamous Japanese police, the KEMPEI-TAI. They were suspicious of this *Keto*, this "color-haired one," as the current term was for foreigners. Arrupe spent thirty-five days in prison, and underwent thirty-seven hours of continuous interrogation—in itself a subtle form of torture—at the hands of a military tribunal. He gained the admiration of the commander when, at the end of his ordeal, Arrupe thanked him for "my greatest sufferings in life," telling him, "You were . . . the cause of this suffering."

After his release, Arrupe's Superior, the same cello-playing Father Lassalle, decided that this "Shinto-priest" needed obscurity, so he sent him to the solitude of the Jesuit residence at Nagatsuka, a suburb just four miles north of the heart of lovely Hiroshima, at the foot of the green-clad hills that cradled the city by the Inland Sea. Fatefully and ironically, it was not obscurity that Pedro Arrupe was to find in this place, but his first experience with the broad public limelight that comes with great events.

In 1942, Arrupe was appointed Superior and Novice Master at Nagatsuka. His worked remained largely intramural, training the young Jesuit novices and governing his sixteen-man Jesuit community. With characteristic diligence, he had already added Japanese to the roster of other languages he could speak—Spanish, Dutch, German, and English, besides his native Basque. Eventually, he published eight books in Japanese. He developed a new apostolate in Nagatsuka, and concerned himself with piety and devotional practices among Hiroshima's few Catholics. Bit by bit, he made the acquaintance of other, non-Christian Japanese, and gradually he became known and accepted.

As a member of the Jesuit community, meanwhile, Arrupe became invaluable, a kind of gravity center for his colleagues at Nagatsuka. Simply put, people liked Pedro Arrupe. He was slightly below medium height, with a ring of hair surrounding his balding pate. His quick and radiant smile revealed slightly prominent front teeth and crinkled what had once been dimples into creases. Though his face was owlish—a strong, curved nose beneath a high, broad forehead and light brown eyes—what it conveyed was a charisma that appealed to Jesuits and non-Jesuits, to Christians and non-Christians.

For his part, Arrupe took to the Japanese profoundly; and he liked Hiroshima as a place. Even though the seaport was on a complete war footing—all primary school children had been evacuated; all high-school students had been mobilized to work in war factories; the city was headquarters for one of the four Imperial Armies preparing for the expected American invasion; and some 90,000 officers and men were quartered there—still, for Arrupe, none of all that diminished the charm of this city built on the delta formed by the seven tributaries. Its cobbled streets, the azaleas and cherry blossoms of Hijayama Park, the dozens of bridges, the ancient Mori Castle, all were lovely for him. Even the coastline—though he knew it sequestered 4000 boats packed with explosives against the day when the American landing would come —lost none of its beauty and appeal in Arrupe's eyes.

Until August 6, 1945. At 8:15 A.M. on that day, bombardier Tom Ferebee on board the U.S. Air Force B-29 *Enola Gay* opened the bomb doors at 31,000 feet and watched "Little Boy," the first uranium bomb in history, tumble broadside out of its bay and then nose-dive for its target—the southwestern seaport of Hiroshima.

Forty-three seconds later, at 1890 feet above ground zero, "Little Boy" exploded in a searing fireball brighter than a thousand suns.

From that moment, Hiroshima became something new for Pedro Arrupe. It became a bloody example of what a godless society could wreak; it became a living tableau, etched in pain and suffering, of what Western corruption could accomplish; it became a pathetic commentary on Western misunderstanding of the Japanese mind that was so utterly alien to it.

At 8:15½ that August morning, every window in Arrupe's resident at Nagatsuka was shattered by a roaring shockwave, and the sky was filled with a light he later described as "overwhelming and baleful." By the time he and his community of Jesuits ventured out some thirty minutes later, a firestorm driven by a scorching 40 mph wind had enveloped Hiroshima. As he dispatched his first rescue team into the suburbs—his was the first medical team, rudimentary though it was, to start up in the stricken city—a muddy, sticky, radioactive rain began to fall, turning the heat of the air into an eerie chill.

That evening, one of the first survivors to reach his house in Nagatsuka was a theological student sent by a fellow Jesuit, Father Wilhelm Kleinsorge, who had somehow survived the blast in the middle of Hiroshima. From him, Arrupe got his first eyewitness accounts. But he saw it all for himself during the subsequent weeks as he and his community moved through the devastation like ministering angels.

Tom Ferebee had aimed the bomb at the T-shaped Aioi Bridge spanning the Honkawa and Motoyasu Rivers. But "Little Boy" had found the hub of its nuclear death wheel not on that bridge, but in the courtyard of Shimii Hospital, 150 yards south of the Torii gateway of the Gokoku Shrine, right next to the parade grounds of the Churgoku Regional Army Headquarters.

Nearly 80,000 people died in the 6000-degree heat of the blast. Another 120,000 were dying. Out of 90,000 buildings, 62,000 were leveled. Sixty of Hiroshima's 150 doctors lay dead; most of the rest were injured and dying. Of its 1780 nurses, 1654 were dead or irremediably injured. Hospital facilities had been destroyed. Hiroshima's resources had been destroyed. And the central Japanese government effectively stayed away for the first sixty hours.

Arrupe saw all the mutilation of human bodies and the destruction of buildings. During the subsequent weeks of toil, as he talked with the *hibakusha*, the "explosion-affected" survivors, he heard unbelievable things from their lips, and saw in their persons the handprint of what the terrified Japanese populace called *genshi bakudan*, "the original child bomb."

Perhaps surprisingly, Arrupe's very first reaction to the ghastly sights all about him—the sight of skin dripping away from arms and legs like wax, or coming off the torso like irregular patches and sheets of rotten fabric; the faceless heads; the burns; the peculiar keloid scars appearing under the skin; the dead; the smell of putrefaction—was not a rush of hatred for war. Horror at human suffering, of course, he did feel, and recalled later many times. But he felt no less horror when he was one of the few Westerners who witnessed the clubbing to death of an American flyer at Hiroshima the morning after "Little Boy" was dropped. The American, a survivor from a B-29 called *Lonesome Lady*, was described by one onlooker as "the handsomest boy I ever saw," with "blond hair, green eyes, white waxlike skin, a big body, and very strong-looking like a lion." The Japanese tied him to a pole on Aioi Bridge with a note pinned on him. It said, "Beat this American Soldier Before You Pass." In their humiliation and suffering and defeat, the Hiroshimans passing by clubbed and stoned the boy to a screaming death.

Far more potent in Arrupe's nostrils than the awful putrefaction of the dead and dying was the "electric smell" of ionization given off by the bomb's blast. And infinitely more foreboding for him than rotting flesh or a stoning, was the new power that so easily, in a matter of mere seconds, had turned the asphalt streets into mushy surfaces, had baked potatoes still growing in the earth, had roasted pumpkins still hanging on their vines—had reduced a beautiful city into a debris-strewn graveyard.

Twenty-five years later, as he groped for an adjective to describe the power of Christ, he would call it "superatomic." With the appearance of "Little Boy," he saw "a new era emerging in the creation of a new technological humanism" emanating from the godless circles and power centers of the West. And he saw "the appearance of a new type of man." To the end of his life, Pedro Arrupe would never lose that sense of wonder at this new birth. "Hiroshima," he used to say, "does not relate to time. It pertains to eternity."

In all that catastrophe, he also saw something else. He could see what the Japanese were worth. He could see their stamina, their

indomitable courage, their hardy culture. Bombs could shatter
their cities, true enough; but he could see that the Western minds
that had devised such bombs could not reach in to touch or profoundly change the mold of the Japanese mind—the disposition of
soul that Arrupe had come to recognize as specifically Japanese. It
was, above all, this opaqueness, this "unreachability"—irreden-
tism is the classical word for it—that impressed him.

For their part, the Japanese never forgot Pedro Arrupe's untiring
help in stricken Hiroshima. They never needed to be reminded
that his had been the first rescue team to start up, before so much
as an hour had passed after "Little Boy's" explosion of the world,
as it had seemed.

In a curious twist of fate, his service in the city where he had
been sent to find greater obscurity brought him his first taste of
worldly limelight. He and his Religious Order received public
thanks from the Japanese. Without any doubt, their efforts at aid-
ing the stricken were instrumental in the postwar success of the
Jesuits in Japan.

During the twenty years Pedro Arrupe spent in Japan after 1945
—during his career as Vice-Provincial of all Jesuits in postwar
Japan—he remained a celebrity of sorts. And he still kept up the
same back-breaking pace of work—administering the Province,
fund-raising,[2] preaching, traveling.

But it was in that brief time in Hiroshima that he learned a
fundamental lesson; and it had to do basically with that opaque
unreachability of the Japanese. Surely, it was Arrupe's keen sense
of observation and his feeling for the other person that helped him
learn this lesson. But just as surely, his Basque origins came into
play here, too. In any case, he felt he understood why the Japanese
were so opaque for Westerners. For over 2000 years they had developed in complete isolation from the highly specified and deeply
personalized cultures and civilizations of the Western world. Who
could better understand the meaning of such a history than a man
of the Basques, the prime "separatists" of Europe throughout their
tumultuous history—"our guest aliens in the household of Europe," as Jean-Jacques Rousseau once called them. Living in Spain,
they had never become Spanish; surrounded by Europeans, they
resolutely resisted becoming typically European. Even their language was an Asian anomaly, vibrantly alive in the midst of a
babel of Indo-European languages. Neither Romans nor Visigoths
nor Franks nor Normans nor Moors had succeeded in subduing
them. General Franco never tamed them. They had the dubious
but indubitable distinction of being the first people who cut to

pieces the reputedly invincible army of the first great "European," Charlemagne; it was at Roncesvalles in Basque country that Roland, the quintessential Western knight, died sadly "far from France and the Golden Charles," as the *Chanson de Roland* sang.

Arrupe's own Basque heritage and his experience working with the Japanese in peace and war taught him that Western Christians would have to do more than just be themselves—just live and act and speak as Westerners—if their aim was to reach the minds of these unreachable people.

And the same lesson would hold true for any dealings Westerners had with people of any significantly different culture—Hindu, Muslim, African, Chinese, Polynesian, for example—especially, Arrupe would insist, with Westerners who had a totally non-Christian outlook and culture. In this regard, Arrupe had in mind a very specific type of Westerner—the atheist.

He was convinced that Western atheism had over a long time produced a mind, a culture, and a way of life as opaque and unreachable as the minds and souls of his beloved Japanese, and as "separatist" as his beloved Basques. To reach that non-Christian Western mind, Arrupe became convinced that "inculturation" was needed, as surely as it was needed in Japan or India or China. Indeed, Arrupe would eventually codify that "inculturation" process in half a dozen formulas.[3]

By May 22, 1964, when destiny took Arrupe's hand one more time, to place him on a pinnacle of power where literally the whole world of human society was his proper field of activity, his past in Japan and his experience with "Little Boy" in Hiroshima had cast an aura of seer or prophet around him for his fellow Jesuits. He came to the Generalate trailing a certain mystique. "Arrupe has seen the Apocalypse," they said of him. Short of dying a martyr's death, he had the accomplishments of the classical Jesuit: imprisonment, torture, multiple languages, administrative ability, courage, endurance. In a sense, he had it all.

Well, perhaps not quite. Not yet. For all the mystique Arrupe might have trailed, his choice as General was a compromise, and it was severely rational. Before he could really learn to lead the Society of Jesus into new paths, he would have to undergo some "education" in the big new realities of Jesuit life. And he would certainly have to undergo a change in perspective about what Jesuits should be doing.

*   *   *

Immediately after Pedro Arrupe's election as head of the most highly organized and best educated Order of Roman Catholic Religious men—36,000 of them at that time, in every nook and cranny of the world—that had ever entered the long, chequered history of the Church, notification of his election was sent to Pope Paul VI. The papal blessing and approval arrived almost immediately.

For the foreseeable future, these were the two men—Giovanni Battista Montini as Pope Paul VI, and Pedro de Arrupe y Gondra as General of the Society of Jesus—who would be center stage as chief protagonists in the unfolding drama of the Pope's men versus the Popes. Never—or at least rarely—had human circumstances pitted two churchmen, one against the other, so profoundly different one from the other and yet so inescapably bound between Roman papacy and Jesuit Generalate.

Neither man had been forced into this relationship by an iron fate. Montini had consented to be Pope in June of 1963, believing it to be his destiny and the due crowning of his forty-three years of service as a Vatican secundo. Arrupe willingly agreed to be General in May of 1965, fully persuaded that as a Basque, as a Westerner successfully inculturated with a non-Western mind, and as a Jesuit with a geopolitical perspective acquired in the evil glare of the Apocalypse at Hiroshima, he was best fitted to lead his Society of Jesus in precisely the way that Iñigo, the first Basque, would have done if he had been elected General by the 226 Delegates at GC31 on May 22, 1965, rather than by the unanimous vote of his eleven Companions on April 8, 1541.

Willingly, each of these men had personally striven to reach his pinnacle beyond the reach of petty powerbrokers, one in the Vatican, the other in the Society of Jesus. But, now, from their individual summits they had to deal with each other willy-nilly.

Both Montini and Arrupe were sincere in their belief that their roles were messianic, or at least were forged by high destiny. That God's hand was with them personally, each man was sure; indeed, cocksure. And so both of them freely and enthusiastically assumed positions that placed them not merely in close proximity to each other, but in an iron-bound, legally forged, long-established relationship of dependence, one upon the other. As Jesus's Vicar and Jesus's Companion. As Pontiff and Catholic believer. As creator and creature. As sworn master and oath-bound servant. As ultimate Superior and complete subject. As supreme teacher and privileged assistant. As White Pope and Black Pope.

At the time of their conjunction in the Roman orbit, one as Pope, one as General, neither could reliably have predicted their irreconcilable clash. The sixty-eight-year-old Paul and the fifty-eight-year-old Arrupe were of the same generation, each born into the class-structured society of the late nineteenth century and reared by loving parents well before that society fell apart and "the lights went out all over Europe" in 1914. They even had physical similarities: below medium height, severely balding dome-shaped heads, high foreheads, large ears, wide heavy-lidded luminous eyes, hook-shaped noses, thin-line mouths, creased cheeks, obstinate chins, narrow necks, expressive hands with spatular fingers, fragile bone structures, owlish expressions on their faces, a presence that imposed itself on you when you came within their ken.

Each one had a benign, paternal manner in any private, one-on-one conversation. Each of them, in front of an audience, carried himself like "the One Who Has Been Sent," the emissary bearing fateful burdens. Each of them without remonstration insisted on his dignity—Paul the dignity of hush, Arrupe the dignity of clamor. Both men were obstinate in their pieties; each highly personalized in his style of administration. Neither of them finally could be described as a simple man or as a saintly man, as far as common human perception went. For, in his own way, each one was obviously too preoccupied with himself and his performance to be totally absorbed in God Whom he was elected to serve. "The great," Saint Ambrose of Milan remarked in the fourth century, "often put off being humble until death humbles them. It's their way to God."

When you have said that much, however, you have exhausted all the common traits between these two men. The rest is a diptych of dissonance and disagreement, of antipathy, of incompatibility, of oppositon, and ultimately of failure. For the Pope failed to command, while the General failed to obey. All the rest in their relationship constitutes merely the mortal debris of their lives.

In terms of absolute failure, Arrupe's was to be the greater. Paul, being in absolute command, failed in his effort to command benignly. Arrupe, under the vow of absolute obedience, failed in everything essential, by his effort to be cleverly disobedient.

Yet, Pope and Jesuit General, each was acting in function of the education and the influences that had gone into forming the warp and woof of his mentality. What successes each achieved and what mistakes each made were specific to that education and those influences.

Italian upper-middle-class Montini's character was etched in the singular quest for power in order to do good in God's service. He was of the northern, not the southern, tradition. Nothing of Italy's south—its noise, its heat, the gregariousness of its people and their shouting, gesticulating manner—ever sat well with him. The hush of dignity was his native air.

Montini received the best education provided for the faithful Catholic bourgeoisie who resented the remoteness of the aristocracy and believed in the goodness of the common man. That education can be summed up in two words: French formalism. It was framed on French models—their Gallic logic, their challenging precision, their balance and finish. It was elegant form that mattered. But, as imported by Italians for Italians, the model omitted the French substance—the rigorous intellectualism, the detailed scholarship of the French tradition. Substituted instead was an element more congenial to the Italian mind—a gentle romanticism. This was half colored by the roseate humanism of the Italian *quattrocento* Renaissance without the paganism, and half-colored by the triumphalism of the nineteenth-century Italian *risorgimento* without its revolutionary strain.

The result was like language itself. Italian was beautiful and pliant. A little French spoken as in Paul's case with a heavy accent lent charm.

Out of all this came the kindly intellectualism of Pope Paul VI, who could not understand the fanatic, but entrusted his hopes for success to the forms and molds of reasonable discourse. It was form that mattered. Formalism without content and triumphalism without rebelliousness were parents of his liberal mentality.

Part and parcel of that mentality was a feeling of guilt for being better off than those beneath him, but with no intent of renouncing his status; a presumption of decency and decent motives in those who observed the due forms; a reliance on the proper concepts, the exact words, to be used in every situation; and a perpetual hopefulness that middle class virtues would triumph over both the elitism of aristocracy and the rebelliousness of the lower classes.

The contradictions lying in wait for the gentle liberal ambushed Paul more than once. He could plead passionately with dictator Franco of Spain for the life of a condemned and truly guilty Spanish terrorist who had murdered in cold blood.[4] He could send a proud Cardinal von Fürstenberg to participate in the sinfully gorgeous 1971 celebrations of the Shah of Iran, who fancied himself the successor of emperor Cyrus the Great who had died over 2000 years before. Von Fürstenberg, not conceded a pavilion of his own amid the other glittering personages, raised Cain for "this slight to the dignity of His Holiness"; Paul was in full agreement with the cardinal. Some months before his death in 1978, Paul composed and had read for him over public radio in Italy a passionate plea to the Red Brigades that they free Premier Aldo Moro whom they had kidnapped, free him in the name of decency and humanity and peace.

Taken as a whole, in other words, Paul's performance frequently appeared contradictory. But it was not. It was all typical of his life-long, gentle, romantic, dignified liberalism.

Middle-class Arrupe, meanwhile, came to his Spanish education with a mentality utterly opaque to the parochial regionalism of Hispanidad. The mood of the educated in the Spain of his youth could be summed up in a phrase: "God made Spain—and then there was the rest of the world." Basques had little in common with the sophisticated calm of Paul VI's northern Italy; they had much more to share with the more raucous southern peoples of Tuscany, Calabria, and Sicily.

Swimming in their Spanish ambient, Basques took from it what they needed, but remained always Basques—stolidly independent, fiercely personal, oriented to the collectivity and to Basque country, the *Vascongadas*, but never assimilated into Spain as Spain.

Opposition, in fact, was a central nerve in the Basque make-up —opposition to being Spanish, opposition to Hispanidad, opposition to the phalanx of landed interests, to traditional scholarship and learning, to the clerical establishment of the Catholic Church, and to the economic coalitions of agribusiness and industry that marched in step with all that was alien to the Basque.

This already tough metal of character was, in Arrupe's case, fired and refined in the planned rigors of the old Jesuit training— ascetic, humanistic, philosophic, theological. It was a systematic dialectic that had already produced a thoroughly well-educated corps of men. Their mental and physical powers were studied, pummeled, tested, developed by their Superiors, and then oriented to the work they had to perform as Jesuits, not in Spain merely, but across the wide expanse of the world.

Cultivation of the intellect, however, was not the secret of the success of Jesuitism. The intellect was merely a tool, could shift its ground, could take up and abandon successive positions with ease, could pick up languages and make for polyglots—as Arrupe was. It was the will that was the Jesuit key. The will was honed and polished to its sharpest point, then locked into an ever-forward thrust at the wide world.

When it came time for these two, Pope Paul VI and Jesuit General Arrupe, to communicate, it should at least in hindsight not be surprising that no real communication was possible between them. It was Paul's kindly, slightly vague intellect versus Arrupe's sharply trained, simple-minded, and separatist will. It was formalist versus fanatic. Diplomat versus crusader. Bureaucrat versus activist. Monoglot versus polyglot. The ever hopeful liberal versus the calculating revolutionary. The man reared to singularity versus the man of the collectivity. A slowly burning Roman candle shedding a wavering golden light, versus a Basque firetorch singeing the fingers, darting at the eyes.

If any fire was alive in Paul, it was hidden deep in a chamber of his heart as the tiny flame of piety. A fire did burn in Arrupe—the blaze of passion—but it exploded in his brain.

Not that both did not aim at a Utopia. They did. But what a difference! Paul, faithful to his French formalism, had opted early on for the Utopia of his favorite French philosopher, Jacques Maritain: The Church had only to cease its stridency of effort and its aristocratic stance, need only present itself nakedly and simply to men and women, without the imperialism of absolute authority, without the threat of punishment. The liberal in him knew, but knew with certainty, that immediately all men and women of good will—weren't ninety-nine percent of them like that?—would accept such a Church as the only means of integrating human values and divine revelation. Integral humanism!

The difficulty that Paul seemed unable to see before the fact was that his own formalism joined to Maritain's humanism allowed no room for Original Sin and for the dreadful malice of the Fallen Archangel vis-à-vis the inherent weakness of each individual human.

Arrupe, carried by his will, and with no intellectual roots anywhere in the West, saw in his prophetic vision an end to all classes —in human society, in the Society of Jesus, and in the Church. He saw an end to domination of the stronger over the weaker, of superior over inferior, of hierarch over subjects, of capitalist over worker, of entrepreneur over laborer, of possessor over possessed, of every greater over every lesser.

In only one aspect of their Utopias were Paul and Arrupe similar. Unconsciously perhaps, and certainly for different reasons, but nevertheless in actual fact, they acted under the same urges. They shared the same vague longing for equality; the same emphasis on the humanitarian view of life; the same sentimental formulas; the same tendency to disassociate the concept of evil from the individual man and woman and to place it instead within a societal framework.

In this one similarity, both Pope and General, again perhaps unconsciously, joined hands with the most potent cynic of the eighteenth century, Jean Jacques Rousseau, and his belief in man's innate goodness. It was, Rousseau had said, organized society— Church and State—that had corrupted "the noble savage" man originally had been.

That a Pope of Rome and a General of the Jesuits should finally act out Rousseau's principles would surely have provoked a sneer of contempt from that atheist who did more to undermine religion than anyone in Europe of the last four centuries.

Paul's inbred formalism saved him, at least to some degree, when push inevitably came to shove. Arrupe's burning will undid him. Light can enter an empty mind quicker than grace can unbend a stubborn will. In the days of his decaying success, Paul would be able to abandon the substanceless forms and molds; the lighthearted Italian romanticism had already fled him—had been dispelled by the murder and mayhem on Italian streets, as well as the betrayal by churchmen he had trusted. Paul could and would revert to that tiny flame burning in the secret recesses of his Catholic heart. In his last months, he would mumble the prayers he had learned at his mother's knee and weep continually. He would be able to hope for cleansing and salvation, even if he was leaving his Church in heresy and schism. For Paul, Christ had indeed died for him personally on the cross.

Arrupe, however, appeared to have no recourse but to his continual dedication to the Utopia. He collapsed in full harness, in full passionate gallop. His intellect no longer dictated a fixed position; and whatever formal words and concepts he had inherited from ancient Jesuitism, had been emptied somewhere along his path of their Ignatian meaning. He had made the Jesuit Order over to his own likeness. From that mere collectivity of men, there came no enlightenment.

In the beginning of their individual reigns, there was a certain magnificence about both Paul and Arrupe. Each of them was led sometimes to mistakes, sometimes to impatience, always to greater efforts. But there was in those early times a great charm about both of them. Both were tender, exquisitely perceptive, jauntily confident, calm in storms, hopeful in difficulties, undaunted. Both had a devoted coterie. Both earned steadfast enemies and critics—the greatest proof of their impact.

Gradually, Arrupe appears to have graduated in the school of self-will. He grew stern with any opposition from the traditional-minded; permissive of any serious departure from established norms; willfully deceptive when cornered; impetuous and even capricious when pressured. Eventually, Arrupe became unreachable and untouchable by the most sacred element in him as Jesuit —his solemn vow of obedience to the Roman Pontiff.

This particular Roman Pontiff, Paul VI, gradually declined; but according as his worldliness and weak-kneed reliance on humanism was stripped of its muscle, he became humbler, if weaker; and he became resigned to his fate as the one Pope who could best have halted the destructive hurricanes of change, but failed to do so. Paul's kindness of heart never deserted him. He was thrashed by the demons of hopelessness, spiritual languor, darkness of mind, oppression in his heart. He was deserted by the calm grandeur of great purpose with which he had started his pontificate.

By summer of 1978, his life had taken on a curious thinness and unreality. When Dr. Fontana, Paul's physician, rushed to get an oxygen tank out to Castel Gandolfo on the night of August 5, 1978, it was a mere gesture. The end was inevitable. Paul murmured again and again the words of the Credo: "I believe in One, Holy, Roman, Catholic Church . . . I believe in One . . . I believe . . ." His high fever due to urinary infection, his rising blood-pressure and other complications were only symptoms of the real cause of his death. According to Fontana, it was Paul's heart that had broken. He returned to his God on August 6. By then, for Paul, it was good to die.

Arrupe's fate was different. His suffering, when it came, would not end soon or easily. We will not know on this side of eternity what revisions of his life and achievements he had been able to make. But we do know what can make anyone acceptable to the Lord of life and death: a humble and a contrite heart.

In 1965, however, the intertwined but far different fates of Paul and Arrupe, the two great Roman adversaries, lay shrouded in the mists of future years. In 1965, the same mood reigned over both men, and it was good to be alive. In 1965, it was time for this second Basque General to settle in to the severe, palazzo-like Jesuit headquarters, the Gesù as it is known, at Number 5 Borgo Santo Spirito.

Unlike the little stone house in which Iñigo lived and died, the Gesù has five stories, and one section rises to a sixth floor. Like Iñigo, Arrupe would have three rooms at his disposal behind the Gesù's gray Florentine Renaissance facade—study, bedroom, and chapel.

At the back of the Gesù, a lovely terraced garden rises up on the slopes of the Janiculum hill, decorated with olive, orange, and lemon trees, boxwood, and grapevines. The street, Borgo Santo

Spiritu, curves like a hockey stick at the front of the house. Emerging from the Gesù's main door, Arrupe could look through the Bernini colonnade onto St. Peter's Square and the Apostolic Palace where Paul VI lived. From the roof terrace of the Gesù, he could see the dome of St. Peter's Basilica. Any triumph, any success, any failure he was about to encounter would depend on how he treated the man in that Apostolic Palace; and on what he did relative to the ancient faith enclosed by that dome, as by its proper earthly tabernacle.

18 | OUTWORN CLOTHES

O nce his election as Father General was completed, the heavy work that lay before GC31 was Pedro Arrupe's meat, the accustomed fare of his life, the perfect nourishment for his prodigious energies and his fabled enthusiasm.

Obviously, the first thing needed was machinery adequate to deal with the enormous number of *postulata* that had been received. And cumbersome it was, that machinery.

The new Father General was seconded by a Secretary with two assistants. He presided personally or through a representative at the main sessions. The full body of 226 Delegates was divided into commissions. To the eleven deputies of one of those commissions was assigned the task of screening all the *postulata* that had been received, and of dividing them into general subjects—Studies, Formation, Ministries, and so on.

Six further commissions, composed of anywhere from twenty-four to fifty-nine members each, began to organize and deal with all of the *postulata* about each given subject. Each of those six commissions was subdivided again, into a number of subcommissions of from three to seven members; and even the subcommissions were split futher into committees.

In addition to those complex structures, still a further number of other subgroups was needed to deal with the mountain of *postulata* to be considered. Canonists, procedural experts, text writers, stylistic editors, revisers of official formulas—these were but some of the specialists whose talents were pressed into heavy service.

It was an interesting side note that under Arrupe, with his extraordinary linguistic abilities and his conviction of the need to penetrate deeply into alien cultures, GC31 was the first Jesuit Congregation to experiment with simultaneous translations of speeches at the plenary Delegate sessions.

The specific aims of this intricate machinery were to supply the initial texts for discussion by all the Delegates in their plenary sessions, to revise each text after the discussions so as to bring all of them into line with the will of the Congregation, and eventually to produce a final text under each heading that would be acceptable in the eyes of all the Delegates-in-Session.

The bare bones of the parliamentary process are enough to give some indication of the grinding work to which the Delegates subjected themselves once the work of the Congregation started in earnest. The progress of merely one text through the wheels within wheels gives a pale notion of the intense activity.

The process would begin when a commission—call it Commission I—was asked to supply a Draft Text on a particular subject. Commission I would then confide all of the *postulata* concerning that subject to one of its several subcommissions. The designated subcommission would proceed to study the relevant *postulata*, and to produce Draft Text A. That Draft A would then go up the ladder again to Commission I for comments, and be returned down the ladder to the subcommission for revision. At that stage, and indeed anywhere along the line of preparation, parts of Draft Text A might also be confided to specialist committees of the subcommission for scrutiny under some specialized heading. When the revision—Draft Text B—was prepared, it would be sent to the chairmen of all the subcommissions for their approval. Once Draft B passed muster at that level, back it would go to Commission I, one of whose members would present Draft B to another plenary session of the Delegates.

The Delegates, in turn, would have three or four days in which to give their comments, and then back Draft B would go to Commission I and its subcommissions for review in the light of the Delegates' comments. The process would continue for as long as necessary, until the text—Draft C or D or even E, perhaps—was at last judged ready for acceptance by the Delegates at a plenary session.

Complex as all this may seem, it doesn't begin to take into

account the intermediate phases of discussion and consideration, the consultation among experts, the typing, the reproduction, and all the rest of the support work necessary to the labor of GC31.

There was another matter—aside from setting up the machinery —that had to be addressed from the outset of GC31 if it was to achieve even a fraction of the "renewal" suggested in those *postulata* that were being so minutely studied and scrutinized, and for which many Delegates now clamored in person. In a word, the matter was secrecy. Everyone was aware that, in spite of the strict code of silence imposed by the *Constitutions* of the Society concerning the internal affairs of a General Congregation, leaks were inevitable. And Rome feeds on rumors. One Pope who was asked whether there were leaks in the system replied with stolid realism, "No. Not leaks. We just have an open sewer."

It was to be expected, for example, that traditionalists in GC31, who might be frightened or alarmed at some of the proposals freely aired by the Delegates, would take themselves over to one or another papal office in order to convey their fears to higher authorities. From there, it was a short distance to the newspaper stringers and correspondents who were always eager for hot Vatican headlines. Rank-and-file Jesuits in the Provinces might be given a wrong impression, might become alarmed or dismayed by unfortunately broadcast fragments of news. The Holy See itself could be alerted to the point that it might be forced out of its lethargy and self-confidence.

The whole thing boiled down to a vital question of strategy: How to innovate the "renewal" projects that were to be the stuff of this Congregation without setting off alarm bells in the Vatican, throughout the Jesuit Provinces, and—through the media—to the wide world. Headlines screaming about "palace revolution" or "modernization" or "revolt against papal control" or "change of ancient Jesuit *Constitutions*" were the last things needed just now, what with a questioning Pope, an inimical Curia, and a fascinated public looking on.

What was needed, the Delegates decided rather early on, was an Information Office through which official versions of Congregation affairs could be transmitted to the Society as a whole by means of a newsletter, and to the world at large—including the Vatican bureaucracy—by means of press releases and even press interviews.

The *Constitutions'* rule of absolute secrecy was therefore effectively laid aside, and the Information Office was established under the direction of a trusted member of the Order. Now, in answer to any rumors, or to offset any untimely revelations, the Society could reply: "We have an official source of information, which is authorized and capable, to give accurate statements about the General Congregation."

The value of the Information Office was not entirely defensive, however. One practical lesson learned during the first three sessions of the Second Vatican Ecumenical Council concerned the importance and power of modern media. Indeed, it had been the skillful use of the media that had contributed in no small way to the discomfiture of the Roman Curia, the awakening of a spirit of independence among the bishops, and the creation, among ordinary people outside the Council, of an expectation that Vatican II would initiate great changes. All of that had helped the progressivists finally to capture the center of the Council. It was a lesson not lost on the Delegates to GC31.

The Information Office, like everything under the energetic aegis of Father General Arrupe, functioned well in its role. Its rank-and-file staff was composed of Jesuits—non-Delegates, all of them—who now were given access to the Sessions and meetings, and who worked in close cooperation with the Superiors in charge of the Congregation. The staff was given guidelines and norms, and by dint of close contact with those in authority quickly acquired its own instinct for what should and should not be revealed, and for the acceptably innocuous way in which news about the Congregation was to be given.

While the Delegates were organizing themselves and getting accustomed to the hard daily grind of work, conversations about the real issues of GC31 were already being carried on at an intense level. And even though the Roman Superiors had for some time been aware of the tone and tenor of the *postulata*, this must have been the first time they truly appreciated the extreme that had been reached in the desire for "renewal" and revamping of the entire Society of Jesus. "Renewal," they came now to understand, did not mean mere adaptation of old ideals to new molds, or development of new instruments and innovative means to encompass the classical, traditional goals of the Society.

On the contrary, even the very essence of Ignatius's *Formula of the Institute*, quoted at such length by Paul VI in his May 7 address, was called into severe question. Wasn't the whole idea of special obedience to the Pope an anachronism now? some asked. Especially in the light of the Second Vatican Council, and of the

Document already approved by Vatican II about how the bishops of the Catholic Church shared and exercised power with the Pope over the Church Universal?

If there was any voice raised in these free-wheeling discussions to remind the Delegates that Jesuits were not bishops, that bishops were an institution of God and the Jesuits were an institution of the Pope, or even that the Vatican II Document they invoked stated plainly that the bishops could not act independently of the Pope, such a voice quickly became a cry in the euphoric wilderness of "renewal."

Rather, the whole idea of a special vow of obedience to the Pope —the famous Fourth Vow of the solemnly Professed members in the Society—was questioned and attacked as elitist, as the product of a dead age, an age when the papacy was, temporally as well as spiritually, an absolutist monarchy. Surely such a notion was as absurdly medieval as Church structure itself. It was certainly no longer compatible with the egalitarianism, the democratization, and the servant-complex of the Church announced and blessed by Vatican II—the Church as "the People of God."

"The distinction [between Professed Fathers with a special vow to the Pope and Spiritual Coadjutors without that special vow] smacks of aristocracy," one Delegate remarked, "and has become entirely useless."

If even the heart of Ignatius's *Formula* was to be put up for grabs, then it was clear that nothing would be spared critique. It was clear, in other words, that GC31 hadn't a prayer of resolving itself into an ordinary General Congregation, refurbishing this sector of Jesuit activity, curbing that tendency or the other movement in some of its more headstrong members, legislating changes forced on it by outside circumstances, approving expansion here and advising retrenchment there. All such issues became as child's play compared to what was dominant in the minds of the majority of the Delegates at GC31. They were here to define what the Society was to be in the new age. And to hammer out the true meaning of "renewal" for the Order. Was it merely a question of retooling the dynamo already installed? Or should the Delegates contemplate a wholly new installation? If it came to the latter, these Jesuits would not shy away. Far from it.

"We had to come to Rome and talk together," as one Delegate summed up the mood and the mind of the discussions, "in order to realize that the Society was wearing outworn clothes." One Indian Delegate posed the matter a bit differently, in a way that simply assumed, as many did, that the Society was done and finished with its past: "What now is to be the fabric of the Society?"

These themes and images were taken up by Father General Arrupe in his own subsequent remarks to GC31. Despite the tatterdemalion condition of the Society, he said to the Delegates, they would provide new unbroken threads in order to make a new fabric for the Society. He recognized that in the mind of the progressivist or renewalist majority, everything in the Society needed to be opened up; nothing must be closed off, as in the past, by the use of untouchable formulas or the setting of intransgressible limits.

Was it the will of the Congregation to take the very structure of the Society off the shelf of the sacrosanct, the untouchable, the permanent? If so, then that meant all the fixed formulas for the Society's work in education, in missiology (the organized work of its missions throughout the world), in its social apostolate, its spiritual life, its community life, its system of Professed members in charge of the rest of the Jesuits, and its system of access to positions of power, which depended on a man's age and seniority and scholarship—all had to be submitted to severe handling in view of "renewal."

So be it, then. But Arrupe also recognized that there were still many Jesuits who liked the "outworn clothes." There were some, indeed, who saw them as the very badge of the Society. To make such vast changes in the core and essence of the Order intelligible and palatable all around, time would be needed. The rank and file of the Jesuits out in the Province were not quite ready for changes this huge, this sweeping.

Furthermore, issues that were so vital had to be thought out deeply. When fundamental revolution was the matter for action, it could not be handled in voting sessions, no matter how well prepared, over a few weeks or months.

Nor was Arrupe's voice the only one to be raised for caution; his voice was still a bit new, in fact, to carry the necessary weight just yet. There was the restraining force exercised by the old Roman hands among the Jesuits—men like Paolo Dezza, the confidante of Popes and Jesuit Generals for thirty years; John Swain, former Vicar-General; Pedro M. Abellan, Procurator General of the Society; Augustin Bea, whose position as cardinal took him from the active ranks of the Society, but who still wielded considerable and understandable influence. If change there must be in the Society—and there must—then the attitude of these men was, "*Festina lente.* Hasten slowly." Already the present Holy Father was both sensitive and suspicious. What the Provincial Jesuits had to understand was that in Rome, everything takes quadruple the normal time to accomplish.

What the Roman Superiors had to understand, however, was that such delays were among the things that most infuriated the Jesuit Provinces. So perhaps the weightiest argument that delay would be a greater ally than impatience, was the fruit—or the lack of it—of the mighty labors of GC31. The actual voting on definitive Congregation texts—the final Decrees discussed and approved —included very little other than the arrangement concerning the secrecy of GC31 (which included the decision about the Information Office, though this was also meant to ensure secrecy); and the innovation of the four new General Assistants to ensure that the Generalate would be colored with a certain democratic diffusion of power and authority.

It is not that those two changes were in any way insignificant. Far from it. It is merely that, aside from those Decrees, and the all-important discussions, disputes, and conversations about both substance and strategy, the period between May 22 and July 1 was barren. Despite all the grinding work of all the commissions and subcommissions and committees, it became clear not only to Arrupe, but to the vast majority of laboring Delegates, that there was no reasonable hope or prudent expectation that a total revamping —that ardently desired "renewal"—could be achieved in one summer session of GC31.

Even such an apparently sobering realization, however, far from discouraging the intent or enthusiasm of this remarkable General Congregation, led it to make a decision unprecedented in the history of the Society. It decided it would vote itself into recess.[1]

The vote, taken on July 6, allowed the Delegates to return to their home Provinces for roughly a year, and assured as well that these same Delegates would be the ones to return when GC31 convened for a second session, on September 8, 1966. Overall supervision of the preparation for the second session was put in the hands of Father Vincent O'Keefe as one of Arrupe's General Assistants. There would be interim meetings in Rome, in Paris, and in the United States, where lists of work to be done and texts to be improved could be gone over and better prepared. And the Delegates would all have time for further reflection and study of the matters discussed at this first session.

Some commentators—participants and nonparticipants in GC31—have alleged in hindsight, though not very ingenuously, that the decision to recess was a reaction to the enormity of the task of "renewal," combined with the excessive heat of the Roman summer and the extraordinary number of Delegates. True, Roman heat in June is predictably excessive—enough to drive even the proverbial mad dogs and Englishmen out of the noonday sun with everyone else. But General Congregations had been held in summertime before this —seven out of the preceeding thirty General Congregations[2]—and had finished their work in good order.

True also, the 226 Delegates at GC31 constituted a record attendance.[3] That number did mean more mouths to talk, more minds to think, more objections to answer than ever before. No doubt the heat, the number of Delegates, and the extent of the work to be done were all factors. And so was the admonition of the old Roman hands to make haste slowly, and their own lack of progress. Nevertheless, it would seem more accurate to say that there were other reasons that impelled these Delegates, so restless for change, to vote for a recess.

There was first of all the new Father General, Pedro Arrupe. He was enlightened and modern-minded and enthusiastic, no doubt about that. But he did not yet understand how a successful Roman official achieves his goals in Rome. It would be a sorry thing to refurbish the Society only to have their most public official blunder it all away after the Congregation ended.

And there was also his outlook on the world to consider, and his idea of how the energies of the Society could best be channeled to succor and serve that world. He needed time to absorb the depth and breadth of the persuasion among the Delegates concerning the absolute need to weave a wholly new fabric for the Society.

True, he had already picked up some of the Congregation's more prominent general ideas, had even spoken to them about the new unbroken threads that GC31 would provide to make a new fabric for the Society. And indeed, that showed promise. In Japan, he had already proved himself to be the perfect Provincial. With a little more molding to their will, he could become the perfect General for them.

Another reason in favor of delay, and an important one, was the unfinished character of the Second Vatican Council. At this stage the Council was both an encouragement and a caution. On the cautionary side, Vatican II had not yet, for instance, produced any definitive statements about the renewal of spirit among Religious. The Jesuits were Religious. The Council had debated a basic document about the subject on November 11 and 12, 1964. The clash between progressivist bishops and traditionalists had been sharp enough. The issue would only be decided in the coming fall, in the fourth and last session of the Council.

On the encouraging side, the signs were good that the progressivist point of view would win out. Would it not be better to await that? It wasn't a huge gamble. If things in the Council went as expected, there would be a Conciliar basis for changes in the Society of Jesus. If not, they would in any case not likely be in a weakened position compared to the present moment.

On a still broader plane, something even more revolutionary and liberating could be expected from that fourth session. After all, the progressivist bishops had grown to a majority and seemed more or less in control of the Council now. On famous "Black Thursday" in November of 1961, when Cardinal Tisserant announced there would be no vote on the Conciliar document about Religious Liberty, there had been a near riot in St. Peter's—waves of vocal protests, grumblings, and commotion, bishops swarming out of their seats into the aisles. Speakers at the podium had been unable to make themselves heard, the din was so great. The Pope and his officials had certainly been made to feel the brunt of the bishops' anger then, as well as later in thorny meetings and by written protests.

For the renewalists at GC31, all of this—especially the steady swing of the Council toward the progressivists—augured a new age of independence from the papal Curia and Vatican control. No one could see the trend being reversed. Rather, it should and probably would grow much stronger still.

Altogether, the tide against papal control and curial interference would mean greater liberty for the 31st General Congregation to establish its lines of "renewal" when it reconvened the following year. There was solid hope that all the Vatican II documents would be published and promulgated by then.

After seventy days of the first session of GC31, then, on July 15, the Delegates to GC31 departed for a time. By that date they had managed to pass an additional five decrees—on studies, atheism, the office and length of term of the General, poverty, and the final year of a Jesuit's formation, called his tertianship. The Delegates could hold their heads high enough as they headed home for a year of further preparation.

After the Delegates had departed, on July 15, Father General Arrupe and the four new General Assistants who, so to say, surrounded the Father General now, asked—as was only expected of them—for an audience with the Holy Father in order to explain matters to him. During GC31's first session from May to July, as the Congregation had expected when it decided to form a special Information Office, more than one attending Delegate had stepped across St. Peter's Square to inform Paul's own staff or some other papal office about the main trends in the ongoing Congregation. Paul certainly guessed that his Jesuit visitors were aware of that fact; it was, after all, the way of things in Rome.

Still, Arrupe was not yet a Roman, a fact the Congregation had also understood; and Paul's accurate reading of the mind of GC31 was disturbing for him. The Pontiff did not mitigate his language. Still as gracious as ever, but firm and pointed, Paul underlined the importance of the papalist element in Jesuitism. "We expect obedience from you," the Holy Father said, "even when the reason for the command is not supplied you. For your obedience is to be, as your Father Ignatius said, like that of a dead body. *Perinde ac cadaver*. The fact that We demand this obedience should tell you how much We esteem and trust you."

He understood, the Pontiff said, the reasons for the one-year recess, and, as it were, admonished the Jesuits to make sure of three things: that the Society be faithful to itself; that it face up to the need of some adaptation to meet new circumstances; but that, above all else, the Society remain truly faithful to the Papacy and the Church.

There was an uncomfortable feeling among all five Jesuits as they left the papal presence. The fact that the Pope had told them in no uncertain terms to be faithful to the Society could only mean that there was a possibility that Paul realized that many wished to change the nature of the Society; that he might know of the proposals to change the very "substantials" of the Society, and even to move away from the traditional and specific devotion to the Pope that formed the reason for the Society's existence.

It was not the deviations of GC31 from these Jesuit norms that disturbed Father General Arrupe and the four Assistants. It was Paul's accurate reading—the fact that it was *so* accurate—that was disturbing. Had they but seen the continually growing critical dossier Paul possessed, they would have been more disturbed than they were.

Arrupe's response to the papal exhortations was dutiful. He composed a letter to the whole Society. The letter was dated July 31, the feast day of St. Ignatius. In that letter he repeated some of the Holy Father's words, and exhorted his men to prepare well for the second session of GC31 that would convene in September 1966.

On the same day, July 31, the new General availed himself of Jesuit control over Vatican Radio to address his Jesuits all over the world. His message, because it was also available to the wider public—including the Vatican—was one of traditional exhortation and encouragement.

The following September 27, Arrupe was given a truly extraordinary opportunity to prove his mettle, and his loyalty to the Pope. The fourth and final session of the Second Vatican Council had convened. Arrupe addressed the plenary session of the 2500 bishops who had, in the previous sessions, caused so much anguish and difficulty for Paul VI. This time, Arrupe had not stepped into any ordinary limelight—the sort he had become accustomed to in Japan, for example. Now, his voice and his views would be heard by the most international audience that followed every move of Vatican II with such euphoric and potentially explosive expectation.

Looked at casually, one of the Council Fathers recalled later, the face of the new Jesuit Father General seemed smooth, for all his fifty-nine years. It seemed, as one journalist wrote, adorned "with the tenderness of a nun." But to those seated close up to Arrupe, it appeared seamed and sutured with a thousand tendencies. It is not unfair to surmise that at least two of those tendencies—his loyalty to the Society of Jesus, and his vowed loyalty to his Pope—were at war within him at some level. In any case, the familiars of this hook-nosed, diminutive Basque, "who had the courage of a prophet," said of him that it would be unwise to take him as a clerical simpleton, a religious pushover. Within him, there was human dynamite at the end of a long fuse.

The Father General's performance before the bishops was vintage Arrupe—Arrupe as he had been when he first arrived from Japan. And what he told the bishops produced a sensation in the international media. In his own mind, he was laying a cornerstone for the future anti-atheism edifice he would create in response to the "solemn task" entrusted to him and his Society by Pope Paul VI.

The Church, Arrupe said, had not adopted suitable means of getting its message across to the world around it. The mentality and cultural environment of that world was atheistic. Professionally atheistic. Moreover, this godless society was following what he called "a perfectly mapped-out strategy." He amplified his point in some detail. "It [the godless society] holds almost complete sway in international organizations, in financial circles, in the field of mass communications."

The remedy? Catholics had to sit down and devise a counter-strategy that would enable them to penetrate all the structures of that society according to their own carefully drawn up and orchestrated plans, and in absolute obedience to the Holy Father—a genuine process of inculturation. Once inside, they would infuse their morality and belief into those structures, change and enrich them with Christian value, and so convert that godless society to Christ.

Arrupe's 2000-word speech might have been given by a twentieth-century Ignatius, so true was it to Ignatius's outlook and mission, and yet tailored to the very different needs of the mid-twentieth-century world on the threshold of huge and unavoidable changes. It was the sort of call and spirit, but updated, that Loyola had woven into the fabric of the Society of Jesus with such stunning results in the mid-sixteenth century.

This maiden speech of Arrupe's before the bishops of Vatican II was not his only one. He spoke to the assembled bishops again, less than a month later, on October 7, and lambasted the whole approach of Western missionaries to the peoples of Asia and Africa. Drawing on those ever-vivid, never-fading memories of Hiroshima, his language was scathing—"myopia," "mendacity," "infantile attitudes" were but some of the terms he used. "Roman Catholic missionary work," he told the bishops point-blank, "is conducted on a level for children and illiterates."

Some bishops termed Arrupe's words in that speech as arrogant, patronizing, and schoolmarmish. But as far as his fellow-Jesuits were concerned, it was that maiden speech of his that was the important tip-off. It proved how accurate the Delegates to GC31 had been in assessing his lack of experience in dealing with Rome and the world on Roman terms. If he had not said so outright, he had at least implied to a full international audience that there existed a real, down-to-earth, universal atheistic organization. This alone was apparently offensive enough to assure him several uncomfortable moments during some of the press interviews he went on to give—and in which he denied ever having an idea of such an organization, much less of having announced so in public.

The truth or falsehood of those or any other statements, however, was not what bothered Arrupe's Jesuit colleagues. What they objected to—and fiercely—was what they called the harshness of his language, so opposed to "the spirit of Vatican II." The Council was trying to address itself "to all mankind," and to attract all mankind by its mildness and its positive approach. And here was their new Father General proposing a negative campaign—an assault—couched in almost military terminology. It would not do.

The Father Provincial of the Dutch Jesuits responded by issuing his own public statement deploring his Father General's maladroit and unnecessarily harsh language. Other colleagues disapproved publicly and in private of Arrupe's attribution of prominence to the Pope in any vast undertaking of the Society. It was not in keeping with the spirit of GC31.

Under the barrage of criticism, Arrupe began to backpedal. He did so by engaging in a practice he would use deftly and skillfully for all of his fifteen years in the Generalate—the press conference. It was a good performance from a technical point of view. The new General answered questions in more than one language. There was the right balance of humor and gravity. No question or theme was allowed to become thorny or tense. Questioned about the Pope's commission to the Society to combat atheism, Arrupe pooh-poohed the idea of actual combat—of any sort of oppositive or "anti" campaign. No; what the Jesuits would do, he said, was engage in fruitful "dialogue" with atheists.

When one of the press corps—actually a member of the Humanist Society—suggested that this would be fruitless, Arrupe replied with that quick, engaging smile of his that they could dialogue, then, about the unfruitfulness of their dialogue.

And Marxists? They were professional atheists. Was the Society going to combat Marxism? That was always good for a headline, either way.

No, was Arrupe's reply. Marxists and Marxism were not the targets. The targets for the Jesuits were "social justice" (lacking to the masses) and the "unbridled luxury" of the privileged few. And after all, didn't all good Christians and all good Marxists oppose those two blights? Arrupe doubtless devised that answer with one eye on the invisible but ever present "nonaggression" pact the Vatican had entered into with Moscow; and with a keen memory of what he had heard from the Latin American Delegates to GC31 about the de facto alliance already established in that part of the world between Marxist activists and Jesuits, among other Religious.

Questioned about Teilhard de Chardin and his theories that had been labeled by the Church as leading inevitably to agnosticism and atheism, Arrupe answered confidently that the "positive elements" in Teilhard's teachings—the spirit of inquiry and the love of God's world, for example—were much more important in Teilhard's philosophy than any negative elements.

When this, the first brouhaha of Arrupe's Generalate, was over, he had made some mistakes. His statements about Marxism and about Teilhard would return to haunt him at a later moment. But, taken from start to finish—from his reaction to Paul's tough admonitions at the papal audience on July 15, through his September and October speeches to the bishops in Council, to his press conference performance—Arrupe's actions were a tribute to the accuracy with which his colleagues at GC31 had read him.

There had always been in Arrupe a conviction that he best understood what had to be done in given circumstances. It was precisely to balance such a trait that GC31 had decided on the four general Assistants to surround the General.

On the other hand, Arrupe also had a limitless confidence in the charisma of the Society as an instrument of God; and he nourished a blind obedience to the voice of its General Congregations as the voice of the Society.

By the time the initial press conference was over, a few observers already remarked that Paul VI's original and specific commission to the Jesuits to fight against atheism had now—in a matter of weeks—been transformed into the sociopolitical struggle of the masses. The entire spiritual and supernatural element had been neatly amputated. The voice of GC31 rang authentically in the press conference transcripts, copies of which—heavily scored in red—soon made their way to the Holy Office and to the study table of Pope Paul VI.

Given sufficient time, it seemed safe to say, and with the right kind of encouragement, that blind obedience of Pedro Arrupe's to the Society would take preference even over the blind obedience he had sworn to the Pope, whoever he might be. In that light alone, GC31 had acted wisely from its own point of view in calling for a year of recess, work, and reflection. For, to achieve the sweeping "renewal" that was its aim, General Congregation 31, and probably the ones that would follow, would have to enjoy an infallibility that could rival the dogmatically defined infallibility of Popes.

19 | NEW UNBROKEN THREADS

The gamble the Delegates to GC31 took in deciding to await the outcome of the Second Vatican Council paid off beyond their wildest hopes. The Council became the authentic floodgate for "renewal," and a justification for the thousand and one innovations and experiments that quickly raced through the sluice gates opened by the "spirit of Vatican II."

In the words of Dom Butler, Abbot of Downside, England, who became an important voice among the Vatican Council members and a valued commentator, the Council "was not going to be a superficial adjustment but a radical one. It meant a fundamental reappraisal of Catholicism. . . . This was not only the view of a progressive minority; but it had captured the center of the Council."

If anything, Butler's words were pale beside the reality of Vatican II's "radical adjustment" of Catholicism. The Council had, for one thing, approved the *Document on Religious Liberty*, as the GC31 Delegates had expected it would. Not only that, however; the bishops of the Vatican Council had allowed the wording of that Document to be so vague that it could be read as a Catholic way of saying: No matter what you believe, provided you do it with a good conscience, it is religiously good and your right. The bishops seemed to accord everyone some "natural right" to choose their religion without any regard to error. Inevitably, from this arises the idea that all religions are on an equal footing—something that Catholicism cannot admit. The thinking of the *Document* is truncated and sloppy.

In hindsight, there have been wildly heated arguments about what the bishops in Council intended to do. In effect, however, those arguments make little practical difference, because what the bishops actually seemed to do was to strike the ancient banner of their Church that proclaimed its truth as exclusive. In its place they raised a new banner, proclaiming that they would be members in what amounted to nothing more than a human fraternity. Their work now would be to reach common human goals. The path so long sought out by so many to rid the Catholic Church of its exclusive claim on religious truth had now been mapped, laid down, and paved with smooth stones by the Vatican Council in its *Document on Religious Liberty.*[1]

This document did not stand alone as some sort of aberrant product of the Second Vatican Council. Other Council statements, equally vague in their language, could and would be used to set the Church adrift on a sea of merely worldly choices, and to cut the mooring lines of many in the Church loose from anything inconveniently supernatural. Social apostolates could, by the language of the Council, and would in fact, aim at purely material improvements in the human condition.[2] Liturgy could and would be made over into humanly pleasing and acceptable forms. Priesthood, episcopacy, cardinalate, and papacy alike could and, in many people's minds, would be transformed into social service posts to bolster and encourage mankind's earthly efforts, whatever they might be. Sexuality need no longer be a means of fulfilling human obligations in God's created world, but a means of pleasure to which everyone had a right. Indeed, Godhead itself—just as Teilhard had conceived it—could and, as it proved out, would for many be reduced to the apotheosis of human development.

As if to give the final twist to the wheels that opened all of those floodgates, and as if as well to douse any hope of holding the line for the authority of his papacy, much less for strengthening it, Paul VI chose to conclude the final session of the Second Vatican Council in a fiercely stimulating way. The Pope's address on December 7, 1965—in effect the closing speech of the Council—was made to a full assembly of bishops and theologians, Catholic observers, visiting dignitaries, and media representatives. It was Paul's final *tour de force* as the obedient disciple of integral humanism.

"What," the Pontiff asked as he sat upon his throne in the Basilica of St. Peter, "is the religious value of this Council?" He then
proceeded to make his mind clear about its value.

The Council did not, he said, concern itself with divine truths
as such; it was "deeply committed to the study of the modern
world." It was concerned "with man—in man as he really is today:
living man, man all wrapped up in himself, man who makes himself not only the center of his every interest but dares to claim that
he is the principle and explanation of all reality."

We in the Church, Paul emphasized, have "our own type of
humanism: we, too, in fact, we more than any others, honor mankind. . . . The modern world's values were not only respected [in
the Council] but honored, its efforts approved, its aspirations purified and blessed." In fact, the Pontiff went on, "everything in this
Council has been referred to human usefulness."

Still not content, and as though unaware he was digging a trench
too deep for himself to climb out of, Paul proceeded to shovel out
statements so ambiguous that, no matter how good his intentions,
his language would have been envied by the most rabid Modernists
of the nineteenth century, and would quickly be digested holus-
bolus, in one great gulp, by the Modernists of the late twentieth
century.

Catholic religion and human life, Paul said, reaffirm their alliance with one another; the fact is that they converge in one single
reality: "The Catholic religion is for mankind. . . . Our humanism
becomes Christianity . . . a knowledge of man is a prerequisite for
a knowledge of God. . . ." The Holy Father's hope, Paul concluded,
was that the message of this Council would be "a simple, new and
solemn teaching to love man in order to love God."

It was the simplistic dream of the ever-hopeful liberal, the idea
that if you are nice to people, even if you abandon the most basic
underpinnings of your life, people will be nice to you in return.

Taken together, the work of Vatican Council II and the closing
speech of Pope Paul VI that capped it provided a Magna Carta for
the Delegates preparing the second session of the 31st General
Congregation of the Society of Jesus. As far as they could see, the
mind of the progressivist majority of the Congregation had been
amply expressed by Pope Paul VI himself. They admitted that Paul
had added a cautionary proviso here and there. But never once had
there been on Paul's lips any word about the apostolic hierarchy;
there was not one hint of his own ineffable privilege as unique
Vicar of Christ, nor about firm Christian belief in the triumph of
a crucified and resurrected God-man. Nor, for that matter, had

there been a single word about the One, Holy, Catholic, and Apostolic Church, centered in Rome and in his public persona as Pope.

Small wonder, then, that for minds already leavened by Modernism, already won over by the winsome doctrine, and already chafing and bucking in the harness of Ignatius's call to be in the world of man but not to belong to it, Paul's speech was not merely a permission but an invitation to kick over the traces.

As the preparations for the second session of GC31 rolled into the New Year ably coordinated around the world by Roman Superiors of the Society, Father General Pedro Arrupe showed no signs of wearying, no further signs of backpedaling. Practically speaking, Paul's speech had removed any need to worry about allegiance to the papacy versus allegiance to the Society.

Arrupe's first big undertaking, in April 1966, was a two-week, whirlwind, coast-to-coast tour of the United States Provinces of the Society of Jesus. It was no mean enterprise. Almost one-quarter of all 36,038 Jesuits in the world were in the United States; the Society there boasted twenty-eight universities catering to 140,000 students, and fifty-six high schools with 35,000 pupils.

In the presence of the largest gathering of Jesuits ever on the North American continent, Arrupe celebrated his first "folk Mass" at Fordham University, in New York City. There, too, he gave a speech in which he first publicly proclaimed the manifesto of the "new Society." And, both in the Mass and his speech, he struck the most relevant notes for the "new" age.

The Mass itself was innovative for its time, and distinctly post–Vatican II. It was mostly in English, and featured a guitarist who accompanied himself as he chanted Black spirituals, while the congregation took up the refrains. Later, in the afternoon, Arrupe spoke on campus to an audience of some 2500 or so. He lauded the "American democratic experiment." He observed that now, after the Second Vatican Council, "the noble task of building the earth —a better world for man to live in . . ." was no longer "a merely secular ideal." It was Christian, he told his audience. He assured them that such theories as evolution and religious liberty were now acceptable to the Church. Indeed, he demanded complete academic freedom for the university, even to the point of welcoming "teachings and practices contrary to Catholicism," for ". . . otherwise invaluable sectors of human experience are inevitably cut away . . ."

Openness, complete freedom, emphasis on human experience— these were his themes, as they had been the themes of Paul's closing speech to Vatican II. But above all that, Arrupe called for new solutions to the religious problems of the day; without those new solutions, whatever they might be, Arrupe said, "I am afraid we may repeat yesterday's answer to tomorrow's problems." Arrupe did not say precisely that the business of a Catholic University was no longer to foment Catholicism, but that was his meaning. Father Joseph Tinnelly of St. John's University, also in New York, found it necessary to say the next day that his university "seeks to foster the Catholic religion. . . . Otherwise we do not believe we would be a Catholic University." Father Tinnelly was one of the few to remark that Arrupe had proposed that Jesuits should return to secular ideals, away from specific and exclusively religious goals. But Tinnelly's voice was not heard by Jesuit educators. The euphoria of the moment allowed no caviling.

Indeed, Arrupe's American trip—particularly the innovative Mass at Fordham, and his speech there with its promise of liberation from restrictions—began to bring Arrupe into the limelight in a new fashion that endeared him to his American Jesuit colleagues. His reputation from his days in Japan began to make the rounds; captivating little facts, such as his installing a Pepsi-Cola machine at Jesuit headquarters in Rome, seemed tailor-made for the Americans, and were frequently repeated to them. His winsome ways overcame the somewhat patronizing strain that was still a part of his manner. All in all, for American Jesuits bucking to be let loose at the task of changing things in the Society and the Church, he seemed the perfect fit as General.

The Americans were not long in setting about the task, either. In July of 1966, less than three months after Arrupe's invigorating visit, Brother James M. Kenny was appointed to the post of vice-president in charge of planning at Fordham University. This was part of the new democratization. Kenny, a Lay Brother, now occupied a position hitherto reserved for priests.

All in all, the recess paid off for GC31 in more ways than one, and in more countries than America. While Vatican Council II was popping the seeds of its "spirit" and wafting them outward from Rome to the wide world, the General Congregation's Delegates in recess had spaded their own patch of ground to cultivate those seeds.

In Rome that August, Pedro Arrupe fell ill. With just about a month to go before GC31 would gather for its second session, General Assistant Vincent O'Keefe, who had been directing the worldwide preparations—consultations, meetings, trial texts, and so on—for the congregation, took over the helm of the Society while the Father General recovered. If all went well, according to Arrupe's mind, O'Keefe would one day succeed him as General.

From the start of GC31's second session on September 8, 1966, the atmosphere according to some was a little like the aftermath of the French Revolution. Equal rights, democracy, fraternity—and isolation of the papacy—were the themes and the goals for the Congregation now, and anyone who didn't call everyone else "citizen" was likely to be guillotined.

The Americans were not the only Delegates yearning to go. Already in the first session, the majority in favor of "total renewal now" had put the finger on three matters of primary consequence, matters that would affect everything else in the Society.[3] Now, a year later, the enthusiasm was high and widespread to head straight into the main bout; this time, there would be no tiptoeing around the issues with warm-ups or test votes; nor would they bother much with minor issues whose outcome would neither help nor hinder the "renewal." In everything from full sessions to subcommittee meetings to private conversations among individuals, the serious talk focused on those three central matters.

The first and most important was the "pontifical" character of the Society; that is, its specially vowed allegiance as an Order to the Pope—the very issue that Paul VI had several times warned them could not be touched. The second matter of central importance—the privileged status of the Professed Fathers in the Society—was closely related to the first, precisely because of the special and personal vow of obedience to the Popes sworn individually by every Professed member. Not surprisingly, given the democratic dimension that was mandated for "renewal," the third major issue too was linked to the pontifical issue. It had to do with the eligibility of Jesuits for participation in Provincial Congregations, the smaller, regional ("Provincial," therefore) versions of the General Congregations such as GC31.

The nettle that vexed the Delegates here was that as Jesuit rules dictated, those Provincial Congregations were not open to any Jesuit who was not a Professed Father, or was not of a certain age, or both. By definition, then, other Jesuits—Spiritual Coadjutors, say, who had no special vow to the Pope and were barred from being Major Superiors; and certainly lowly Lay Brothers, who weren't even priests—were denied both a voice in the Society and an early foothold on the path to power in the Order.

All three practices were denounced in round terms as repugnant to the modern mind, as counter to the goals of democratization and fraternalism demanded now in religious matters, and—the worst offense of all—to "the spirit of Vatican II."

Objections to such deep revolutionary demands were raised by the more traditionalist-minded Delegates on the grounds that these "substantials" of the Society were being attacked, and harshly, on purely sociopolitical grounds. Jesuits, insisted these traditionalists, were not a sociopolitical club; they were not the Knights of Columbus, say.

The objection was useless, though. These traditionalists did not yet have the proper "citizen's" mentality. It was, after all, merely an issue of fairness and justice. The equal rights of individuals and the democratization of religion were part and parcel of "renewal." Otherwise, "renewal" could not be either religiously genuine or genuinely religious.

Tautologies and question-begging aside, traditionalists and re-newalists alike among the Delegates understood what was at stake here. Taken together with the changes already made in the post of Father General, alteration of these three major "substantials" by the official Decrees of GC31 would change the structure of the Society of Jesus radically, compared to the Society Ignatius had built. But that wasn't the half of it. There was much more on the minds of some Delegates. Not only was the "monarchic character" of the Society under attack; some Delegates and quite a number of the *postulata* proposed changing even the priestly character of the Society. Why not have married lay people as Jesuits? (Perhaps the Knights of Columbus weren't so bad after all?) Indeed, why not look forward to the day when priests would be allowed to marry? Why not, in plain terms, envisage married men as functioning Jesuits?

The same realism that had led the Delegates to recess the year before dictated that such trends were too extreme for the moment. Voices became carefully muted, and the priestly issues were put off for a more propitious time. Not so, however, with the determination to change the "monarchic" system of the Society.

As early as September 19, a plenary session of GC31 approved the final text of Decree #4, which said unequivocally that "the 31st General Congregation . . . has determined that the entire government of the Society must be adapted to modern necessities and ways of living; that our whole training in spirituality and studies must be changed; that religious and apostolic life itself is to be renewed . . . and that the very spiritual heritage of our Institute, containing both new and old elements, is to be purified and enriched anew according to the necessities of our times."

Inevitably, and quite early on in the process, the push of GC31 toward doing away with the monarchic system of the Society became known "across the way" in the papal office. All those complaints still pouring in from Pope Paul's Apostolic Nuncios and Delegates and Legates all over the world of Catholicism to swell his dossier on the Society's failings were being borne out as true by GC31. The Society as a whole was being leavened by a spirit of disobedience; the monarchic way had largely been deserted by Jesuits in their actual practice. Decree #4 would provide the stamp of approval, the official license that would transform what was now disobedience into approved chaos with no control possible.

Paul VI summoned Father General Arrupe into his presence, and in that audience the Pontiff made no bones about his suspicions and his fears about the way the Congregation was going. The image of the Society that the Holy Father drew for Arrupe was not a flattering one. He cited the Society's doctrinal deviations; its frequently un-Catholic interpretations of moral law; its sometimes acrid and always negative critiques both of the Holy See in general and of Pope Paul himself in particular; the nonobservance by Jesuits everywhere of the Society's own laws concerning poverty, community life, obedience, traveling, politicking, the formation of Jesuit trainees. The Pontiff's words painted a vivid portrait of a Religious Order in revolt against papal control and in great divergence from the ancient *veritas catholica*, the Catholic Truth.

Did the Society wish, Paul VI wanted to know, or did it not wish to preserve its pontifical status? Did the Society want to be reckoned as in special service to the Pope and the Holy See, or did it not? Did GC31 really mean what it said, that "the very spiritual heritage of our Institute . . . is to be purified and enriched anew?" Did that mean abolishing the special vow of obedience to the Pope? Abandoning the monarchic structure of the Society?

The sting in the Pope's rebuke was still to come, and it went deep. If things continued in the fashion they were going now, if the Society unilaterally and arbitrarily redefined its religious status vis-à-vis the papacy and Church authorities, then the papacy and Church authorities would have no recourse but to redefine *their* relationship with the Society of Jesus. "We want no other Society of Jesus," Paul emphasized, "but the Society Ignatius of Loyola constructed and left behind him." If GC31 were wise, it would consider the distinction of grades in the Society—the hier-

archic division of Professed Fathers, Coadjutors, and Lay Brothers
—as a closed issue.

The implications were as clear for Pedro Arrupe as they were for
the Delegates of GC31 when he reported back to them after his
session with Paul. The wisdom of what many of the older hands
in the Society had been saying to the impatient renewalists now
became clear. Yes, the Society's traditional clothes may have become outworn; but, unless they wanted to provoke a much sharper
and even destructive retort by a stubborn-minded and already incensed Pope, the Delegates to GC31 had better content themselves
with providing the "new unbroken threads" Pedro Arrupe had
talked of the year before. Such threads, carried over into the next
General Congregation—for GC32 now became a gleam in the Society's eye—could be woven into a new set of clothes for the Society. And only God knew: Perhaps the Church would have a more
"renewal"-minded Pope by then. *Cunctando regitur mundus.* If
you can wait long enough . . .

It is a measure of the recalcitrance of GC31, and of its determination to continue spinning those new threads, that even after
Pope Paul's stern rebuke, the Delegates voted, in Decree #5, to set
up a permanent commission that would last beyond the life of
GC31, and whose purpose would be to study "the whole matter of
suppressing the grade of Spiritual Coadjutor" or "granting solemn
Profession also to the Temporal Coadjutors" (Lay Brothers). In
other words, in spite of Pope Paul VI's prohibition, the Society was
not going to close the question of grades or, for that matter, of the
"monarchic" character of the Society. Either all the peons would
be declared aristocrats, or all the aristocrats would join the peons.
Either way, the Society would be classless.

Recalcitrant and determined though they were, the Delegates
had learned more than a few lessons from Vatican II. Just as the
extraordinarily valuable idea of setting up their own Information
Office had come from the experiences of the Vatican Ecumenical
Council, so did the lesson on how to word even revolutionary
Decrees: The vaguest language had to be used. Phrases must be so
loose that a renewalist coach-and-four could later be driven
through the traditionalist-sounding language of the provisions.
And all of it must be wrapped in the silky cocoons of *romanità*'s
accepted forms and formulas.

Did the Pope object to Decree #4 and its call for renewal of
religious apostolic life? Did His Holiness also object to the purification of the Jesuits' spiritual heritage? Well and good. It was a
simple matter to add to Decree #4 the declaration that the *For-*

mula of the Institute—Ignatius's text on which the pontifical status of the Society is founded—"has obtained in a special way that status of pontifical law. . . . For the *Formula* exhibits the fundamental structure of the Society. . . ."

Paul VI had won that skirmish; but the battle wasn't over.

Even *romanità* could not thoroughly cover the revolutionary bent of the Decrees of GC31, however; it broke through the cocoons of *romanità* again and again. In one text, for example, the "mission of the Society of Jesus today" was declared to be to work under the Roman Pontiff; but, since "we find ourselves in a new age," GC31 "finds the conditions of human history profoundly changed." The conditions that affect religious life have therefore changed. Behind tantalizing fans made up of feathery language about the estrangement from the world that the teaching and the life of a Christian impose on him, and about the sociopolitical misery of millions, there danced half-naked declarations that GC31 "offers itself completely to the Church," and has striven in its Decrees "so to promote a renewal that those things may be removed from our body which could constrict its life and hinder it from fully attaining its end."

Because of Pope Paul's "solemn commission" to the Society that it "combat atheism . . . with united forces," GC31's document on atheism (Decree #3) was one of its most important. It therefore came in for some especially deft handling that has since been acidly labeled "typically Jesuitical."

The Decree itself quotes the essence of Paul's fighting words:

> The most terrible form of atheism is that which is wickedly aggressive not only in denying the existence of God in theory and practice, but in deliberately using its weapons to destroy at the roots all sense of religion and all that is holy and pious. . . . It is the special task of the Society of Jesus to defend religion and holy Church in the most tragic times. We entrust to it the charge of opposing atheism with its total, concentrated effort, under the protection of Saint Michael, the prince of the heavenly hosts.

Then, in a display of turnabout that is both verbal and mental, Decree #3 takes all the fight out of Paul's words by exhorting Jesuits to "give more attention to atheists," and to "be cautious in passing judgment" on them. Some atheists are "gifted with a greatness of spirit," after all. Atheists, in fact, are to be comforted by letting them see "our lives and actions, our ways of living."

In a few well-turned phrases, Decree #3 implies that much of atheism is due to unjust and demeaning social conditions, to the injustice perpetrated on the poor and the disenfranchised. Further, Jesuits should, "in good time, have some personal contacts with atheists" in order to understand them. In general, closer contact with atheists, careful and charitable evaluation of their minds, and a kindly approach to them are proposed.

The Decree justifies its own waffling by providing that while all this contacting and understanding and charitable evaluation was going on, the Father General was to ask Pope Paul what exactly he had in mind with this solemn task of combatting atheism.

Into the making of this Decree went also a new-fangled version of a very old idea. Jesuits in the past had striven to adapt themselves and their Catholic message to the alien minds of Asia and Africa. *Adaptation* was a watchword in traditional Jesuit missiology. The new word was *inculturation.* The idea was to adapt so severely to the culture of the alien that the missionary would acquire the mind of that culture, and would revamp both doctrine and moral practice to fit that alien culture.

Inculturation now threw its shadow over the Decree, as did Arrupe's own conviction that atheism was to be treated like any other alien culture. What was new, dangerous, and un-Jesuit about this inculturation was the use of these ideas to mask purely sociopolitical objectives and an exclusively this-worldly ideal.

All of that, plus the use of mush as the language of a major decree, together with recourse to "misunderstandings" and requests for clarification, certainly provided a model at the highest levels for Father Fernando Cardenal and others in their fight some fifteen years later against Pope John Paul II. But it did more than that. It provided the opening through which the Society would drive a very special and important coach-and-four. It would be argued in the coming years that atheism, like everything else, has a purely social cause; that atheism comes from disillusionment with the failures of the Church. Because Romanism had failed the poor, atheism was the fault of the Roman-based Church. To rid the world of atheism, Jesuits must make "a preferential option for the poor." That, in turn, would mean they must combat all who were not poor, as well as the system that enables some not to be poor, while it leaves the poor even poorer. That system was the capitalism of the West.

Therefore—so the reasoning would go—the papal call to combat atheism is a call to combat capitalism.

The full line of reasoning would not be drawn out and elaborated for another few years yet. But the new sociopolitical outlook of the Society in the seventies and beyond would be fashioned in just this way, and on the basis of just such "new unbroken threads" that would be drawn from the spindles of GC31's artfully ambiguous Decrees.

Quite a number of spindles were wound with these new threads before GC31 was over. Certain structural changes were worked out, for example, that would inevitably lead to the blurring of any practical distinction between those hated grades of Jesuit rank. Arrupe insisted that youth must be impressed with a "new image" of the Society. "A most serious business," he called it, "to distill all the good contained in the numerous proposals and requests of our young men, and to properly channel that force and dynamism . . . is an absolute necessity. We are dealing with a biological law or social law which is irresistible. We should not try to resist it, unless we wish to bring complete upheaval."

In that spirit, the Delegates decided that the smaller regional, or Provincial, Congregations would no longer be restricted to Professed Fathers and other Jesuits with seniority of service. Participants in such Congregations would now be elected by full Provincial memberships; furthermore, Lay Brothers and Spiritual Coadjutors would be as eligible for election as Professed Fathers. No seniority rules were to apply any longer.

Another assault—one that would have equally wide consequences in the Society—was made on the "privileged" class of Professed Fathers, despite the fact that it meant tampering yet again with the *Constitutions*. The matter this time concerned the vow each Professed Father made never to change the Society's rules about poverty except to make them stricter. Ignatius himself had written this vow into the *Constitutions*, wishing that houses of Professed Fathers should have no fixed income or endowment.

Decree #18 of GC31 in effect overruled Ignatius, and declared that "gain from or remuneration for work done according to the *Institute* is a legitimate source of material goods which are necessary for the life and apostolate of Jesuits."

Of course, that matter, like the changes in eligibility for membership in the Provincial Congregation, belonged to the "substantials" of the Society. Nevertheless, the Delegates were not yet content. They spun another of those new threads to be carried forward and woven into the "new fabric of the Society." They decreed that the Father General and four other officials were to prepare a revision of the entire legislation about the observance of the vow of Poverty.

By the time GC31 completed its work on November 17, 1966,

it had changed, or provided the "new unbroken threads" to change, every facet of spirituality and action in Jesuit life. The language of its Decrees by and large makes ample use of Roman and traditional Jesuit forms and formulas. But the same open-ended ambiguity breathes through GC31's Decrees as through those of the Second Vatican Council. Indeed, given the heady fumes of the euphoria and the still vaguely defined "renewal" that were the very essence of "the spirit of Vatican II," it is perhaps not surprising that the Delegates rampaged through the Jesuit wardrobe of "outworn clothes" like teenagers trashing a high school cloakroom. Encouraged by the unbounded enthusiasm and verve of Father General Arrupe, and bolstered by the direction of the new element of leadership they themselves had installed in Rome—the four General Assistants—the Delegates addressed themselves to just about every nook and cranny of Jesuit life: education and scholarly activity, the priestly apostolate of Jesuits, pastoral institutions, missiology and its missions to non-Christians, ecumenism, the arts— all were infused with the spirit of "renewal."

In decreeing changes in the formation and training of Jesuits, for example, GC31 did away with many of the structured systems that had seemed so mysterious and yet were so envied for their effectiveness by so many. In place of those systems, GC31 provided some broad and suitably vague principles, insisting primarily on experimentation. The old Jesuit rules of asceticism and self-discipline were laced with new exhortations about self-acceptance, freedom of movement, emotional balance, and training by psychologists.

Superiors were earnestly urged to trust rather than to train their juniors. Obedience was to be modified according to a new principle of "consultation." Practically speaking, the effect of this principle did away with the systematic obedience of Jesuits to any Superior, Provincial or otherwise. Each Jesuit would now be "consulted" as to whether, in the light of his personal growth, his emotional balance, his right to freedom of movement, and his needs in general, he wished to comply with a command or an instruction. He might just as easily say "no" as "yes," in the light of this new principle of "obedience."

More than that, however, this new declaration of independence issued by the General Congregation as the "highest Superior" of the Society meant that each community of Jesuits would have a say as to what its Superiors could command. In this new rule as in others was enshrined the desire to be democratic, and to leave each individual alone so that he could achieve "integration" in the manner that best suited him.

Along with the old language and practice of poverty and obedience, the traditional language of the Society concerning devotion and the interior life of the spirit was also abandoned. No one in the Society was to be bound any longer to any form of prayer or any specific time-length for prayer. Devotion to the Sacred Heart, one of the most popular and widespread devotions in the Church Universal and one that had been fostered and championed by Jesuits since the seventeenth century, was to be studied (GC31 did not say "practiced") in order to find out why so many Jesuits found it useless if not repugnant.

Nor would they maintain any longer the age-old and devotionally effective habit of having someone read a suitable text to the community while at meals. Among the statutory materials to be read had been the Jesuit Rules and other fundamental documents of the Society. With one blow, it was ensured that the younger generation of Jesuits would grow up ignorant of the Society's basic documents.

Having provided the basis from which to demolish Jesuit obedience to the Society's Superiors and eliminate large swaths of Jesuit training and piety, GC31 proceeded to provide a whole new setting for the experimentation that was its preference for the "new Society." That setting was in the bowels and entrails of the world. GC31 disapproved of the traditional concept of having Jesuit houses of formation, and particularly the novitiate, separate from the crowded, urban areas. Neither novices nor those Scholastics in ongoing training were any longer to be kept apart from ordinary people or from the secular world. Furthermore, the entire question of what ministries Jesuits were to engage in—what work they were to do specifically as Jesuits, in other words—was no longer to be decided by Superiors and Professed Fathers, but was to be thrown open to democratic examination. Each Province was to set up its own special commission to study how greater flexibility in tasks and assignments could be achieved. Thus was opened the door to individualism and communal decisions, doing away with the command of the Superior who formerly decided, on the basis of the overall picture, where to concentrate his men.

One could devote pages to such changes. Indeed, the Decrees of GC31 fill many pages. But when the postmortem is done, when all of the *romanità* is sliced away and the bare bones are extricated from the layers of soft, fleshy ambiguity and the camouflage of traditional-sounding phrases, what stares back at you from the examination table is a headless creature destined for calamity. The Decrees of GC31 were destined to lead the Society of Jesus into tumultuous chaos. Jesuits were not only largely free now, but urged to turn their hands to the most diverse tasks, assignments, and experiments, many of which could have little or no bearing on the salvation of souls. The way was open for converting Jesuits into social workers, political activists, and ideological campaigners.

The same open-ended ambiguity, the same "spirit of Vatican II," and the same enthusiasm for "renewal" and verve for equality that marked the Decrees of GC31 would become the hallmarks and the justification for such Jesuits as Fernando Cardenal and Robert Drinan as they laid waste to all former ideas of religious obedience. And it would become the touchstone for such non-Jesuit Religious as those who wrote the manifesto of Liberation Theology, which transformed the Vicar of Christ from being leader of the Church Universal to an unwelcome alien in the lands where the faceless "People of God" reigned in his place.

More immediately, however, in the early storms that would follow GC31, the Congregation's voice in those Decrees would prove a sturdy shelter for Father General Arrupe. The General Congregation, the highest Superior in the Society, had spoken. He was merely its servant.

The first of those storms, though by far not the greatest, broke over the Society just as the Congregation was preparing to close.

Paul invited all the Delegates to assemble with him in the Sistine Chapel of the Vatican. There he would concelebrate Mass with five of the Delegates (including Arrupe), and then address the entire body of GC31. Paul's act of inviting them all was a paternal gesture both of affection and appeal. It said: You are all my sons, in spite of any hard things I have said or shall say to you. Let us do all things under the papal roof and as a family.

His papal presence, his papal blessing, the unifying action of concelebrating Mass together, all spoke of Paul's hope that the aberrations of the past could be just that—aberrations and past. His papal speech that followed the Mass, meanwhile, gave the Delegates a peek at the other side of the coin. Many of the Delegates, perhaps lulled by the papal invitation into thinking things weren't so bad after all, were surprised that such "hard things" as came from Paul's lips in his speech could be wrapped in so mild a mood of welcome. Despite their own recalcitrance, they apparently did not anticipate some of the things he had to tell them.

Although Paul was already undergoing severe afflictions in his health, he did not blench in his address that day from a thorough-going realism. GC31, the Pontiff said, had a particular historical significance. It was an occasion for Pope and Society to define their mutual relationship. As candidly as *romanità* allowed him, Paul went on to ask the same questions of the full Congregation that he had asked Pedro Arrupe in the early weeks of GC31's second session, when he had painted so dismal a picture of what the Society was becoming.

We have two questions to ask you, the Pontiff said. Do you Jesuits wish to be Jesuits as Ignatius conceived Jesuits to be, and as Jesuits have always been up until now? It was jarring that he seemed to assume a negative response to the question. "Strange and sinister ideas that would change the nature of your *Institute*," Paul said, "are at the root of your refusal. There are among you members who no longer believe in the Catholic Truth or in the personal charisma of the Pope." A false activism and a deceptive worldliness had replaced that Truth and that charisma for some.

Paul's first question and his own dour answer to it were followed by two more questions. Like the first, the Pope had asked them of Arrupe in that earlier private interview. And like the first, they were acute and accusatory:

What was the relationship of the Society to the Church and the Papacy?

Did the Church and the Papacy today still think the Society was "their special and most faithful militia"—the militia that had specifically set out "to defend and promote the Catholic Church and the Apostolic See"?

Again, to ask such fundamental questions at all was already to answer them in the negative. Paul went on, however, to give a conditional answer for Papacy and Church. In that answer, he touched on the points about which the Society had already erred grievously, according to reports in the papal dossier.

"As long as your Society will be intent on striving for excellence in sound doctrine and in holiness of religious life, and will offer itself as a most effective instrument for the defense and spread of the Catholic Faith, this Apostolic See and, with it, certainly the whole Church, will hold it most dear."

Mercifully, Paul did not draw the other side of the condition: If your Society does not strive for excellence in sound doctrine, We will not hesitate to abolish and suppress the Society of Jesus. To say so much would have been counter to *romanità*, which exacts penalties from those who show their hands before they are ready to play them, and which in any case frowns upon the use of bloody-minded language.

Instead of the stick, therefore, Paul used the carrot. You can be great again, he told the Jesuits gathered with him in the Sistine. Go, practice real devotion to the Sacred Heart of Jesus. Work hard at Catholic education of youth, and at converting non-Christians in the mission fields.

Yet not all the rest of the Pontiff's speech was bright-eyed liberalism and paternal hope. There was another good dollop of informed foreboding as well; and this time it was not of the expected or ordinary kind.

Let Us remind you, the Pontiff said in effect, that in spite of all the roseate things said during your deliberations about the beckoning world and the new age and all that, there are in this world whose newness and modernity fascinate you, two classes of people, or, rather, two worlds meshed into one. There is "the world of the Compact," into which have entered all those who turn from light and grace. And there is the world of "the vast human family for which the Father sent His Son, and for which the Son sacrificed Himself." Make sure, Paul said to the gathered Jesuits, that you belong to and work exclusively for the second world of the family saved by Christ, and not for "the world of the Compact."

Paul, as several of his listeners knew only too well, was putting his finger on the fact that several Jesuits had not only behaved and talked as if Christ was not a saving God, but they themselves had joined more than one organization which was either religiously neutral or religiously inimical to Catholicism.

Actually, the parallel between this address of Paul VI and Pedro Arrupe's maiden speech at the Second Vatican Council the year before is striking—a fact not lost, perhaps, on the Delegates in the Sistine. Had Paul said in blunt terms—as Arrupe had very nearly done—that there was a universal plot against the Church manned by people who had compacted themselves into a specific organization dedicated to promoting Lucifer and Lucifer's cause, he could not have produced a more skeptical raising of eyebrows, more scathing aftercomment, or a more resounding rejection of his plea. Actually, Paul had gone further; he had implied that some Jesuits had entered the Compact.

"This is just overkill," one prominent member of Jesuit headquarters in Rome said later in dismissing the entire papal speech. No amount of papal threat or impassioned pleading—and Paul's speech ran the gamut from one to the other—could alter the resolve of GC31 and its leaders.

Indeed, by that November day of 1966, a full year after Arrupe had made such a similar plea to the fourth session of the Vatican Council, the Father General had obviously altered his own perspective. On November 24, Arrupe held a press conference to talk about the accomplishments of GC31. Under close questioning about Paul's words in that November 16 speech concerning the new type of obedience embraced by the Jesuits, Arrupe became both arrogant and untruthful.

"I don't know," Arrupe said, "what His Holiness meant when he spoke of our members entertaining strange and sinister ideas of changing the character of the Society of Jesus." He went on: "There is a risk that the situation might transform Obedience into collective government. But, if examined closely, it is really nothing more than the community and the Superiors uniting their efforts." In other words, the new situation was not collective government because on closer examination it was collective government. Arrupe was becoming a master of political double-talk.

He was also becoming a master of the art of selective forgetfulness. Seemingly gone from his mind were the times during GC31 when he had personally been called on the papal carpet to account for those "strange and sinister ideas" about which he now seemed so mystified; ideas about "democratizing" the Society, about "consultation" in place of religious obedience, about all the proposed aberrations from classical Jesuitism that went even so far as to contemplate abolition of the Society's priestly character. "I don't understand what the Holy Father meant," he said blandly, "when His Holiness spoke of strange and sinister ideas."

Arrupe was asked at the press conference if there had been any clashes between the Holy See and the Society during GC31. Of course not, Arrupe pooh-poohed such a ridiculous thought. "I do not want to defend any mistakes the Jesuits might have made; but the greatest mistake would be to stand in such fear of making an error that we would simply stop acting." But, he went on, there was harmony between His Holiness and himself as General of the Society.

20 | SEARCH FOR THE PRIMITIVE CHARISM

"Look to the very near future!" one Italian reporter summed up the minds of the Delegates interviewed after GC31. "By trial and experiment, discover what the Society should become, what it should be doing in this world of men today. Then return to Rome soon for the next and definitive Congregation."

Father General Pedro Arrupe put the case in more traditional sounding terms. The work of the Society of Jesus now would be to prepare for GC32; specifically, to develop and make increasing use of the "new unbroken threads" spun by GC31 so as to make Jesuits "capable of giving new expression to the primitive charism of the Society."

Arrupe and his collaborators were persuaded they knew exactly what they meant by those words. Almost certainly they had in mind a goal resembling the quasi-miraculous success of the ancient Society as it had suddenly sprung to life and to power in the new world aborning in the 1500s. The Jesuits of those days had dazzled the eyes of all with their mastery and their shining gifts in every field of endeavor. They had filled men's ears with the song of a new and thoroughly Christian humanism, and their minds with a fresh intellectualism. They had given hope and light. They had been conduits of grace and divine comeliness. With all their faults, in that first 150 years of their existence, the Jesuits had succeeded in their grand enterprise; they had succeeded beyond the wildest hopes of their papal masters, and certainly beyond the limits assigned to them by the virulent hate and opposition of their enemies.

Almost certainly, too, Arrupe and his colleagues understood that those ancient Jesuits had succeeded because they had been able literally to invent a new way for Roman Catholicism—for Popes and bishops, priests and nuns, theologians and philosophers and laity—to walk "in the way of the Lord Jesus" in accordance with Catholic doctrine, and so to cope with the new world that broke over men's heads in the sixteenth century.

All of that surely was in Arrupe's mind and his plans when he spoke of "giving new expression to the primitive charism of the Society."

It is somewhat more questionable whether he and the other Jesuit leaders of the twentieth century any longer understood charism—primitive or otherwise—as charism had always been understood before: as a totally gratuitous gift of God.

God might give that gift—as he did to Ignatius—at the end of a long, intense period of hidden prayer, scrupulous self-examination, rigid penance, humble and humbling activity, all performed in the absence of any self-seeking or personal aggrandizement. As with any supernatural gift, in other words, charism would certainly not be discernible or attainable at the hands of a vast bureaucratic effort looking not to God but to sociological surveys, managerial studies, discussion forums, doctrinal experiments, situation morality, and actuarial tables.

Computer experts of a later day have become fond of saying, "Quality in, quality out; garbage in, garbage out." Jesuits in the aftermath of GC31 might have coined a similar if less catchy cautionary slogan: Spiritual preparation in, charism out, if God so wills; social and political preparation in, arrogant and self-serving social gospels out.

In any case, in the history of human organizations, surely a record was set by the Society of Jesus between the years 1966 and 1974 in the maximum use and disposal of its material resources to the end that GC32, when it should assemble in Rome, would somehow breathe that "original and primitive charism" into its Decrees, and so catapult the Society into the forefront of the "new age in which the human race finds itself."[1] In essence, the Society of Jesus came to resemble a worldwide array of cogs and wheels, spools and spindles, dynamos and engines, all regulated by a huge central flywheel in the inexhaustible person of Pedro Arrupe.

Jesuit communities talked and studied and discussed among themselves; they coordinated their talk and study and discussion with the talk and study and discussion in other communities of their Province. Provinces, in turn, coordinated with communities of other Provinces in the same Assistancy. Communities and Provinces in one Assistancy coordinated with those in another Assistancy. And all the Assistancies belched forth whatever might be produced by such massive coordination toward Jesuit headquarters in Rome.

In a fairly short time, inexhaustible lines of print in six languages filled mountains of paper. The end purpose of all this meticulous research was to be the establishment of adequate and proper conditions among Jesuits everywhere, so that they could send new Delegates to Rome filled with the euphoria of discovery and a new confidence in the Society—the Delegates to the "definitive" 32nd General Congregation.

As things worked out, GC32 was not to take place as soon as some had so hopefully foreseen. The work to be done beforehand would take eight years. Still, considering the enormous effects their labors would produce, eight years was a remarkably short time.

The first Society-wide task of this corporate mechanism began soon enough. In the late autumn of 1966, a massive three-year "Sociological Survey" of the entire Order was begun, in accordance with GC31's conviction that only by knowing themselves could Jesuits discover their proper roles in this new age.

Every known method of assessment was used to discover the state of the Society in every Province around the world. Management consultants, survey research units, and entire academic departments produced everything from individual psychological profiles to the broadest and yet most detailed actuarial tables.

From the United States alone came a five-volume report containing 140 research studies about the American Provinces. After all their efforts, the two Jesuit editors of that study had to conclude somewhat lugubriously, "Only a profound, concerned and continued rethinking of . . . our beliefs and rationales (for our assumptions) can provide a basis for the unity and consensus required for survival."[2]

Perhaps those editors saw more than they realized. In any case, what they had come up with was certainly not the euphoria of discovery and the new confidence that was to animate GC32. They seemed more concerned with the very survival of the Society than with recapturing Arrupe's "primitive charism."

In the light of such a mood among rank-and-file Jesuits, a project begun as early as 1967 is particularly noteworthy. In that year, a group of top-flight and already highly placed Jesuits met at the University of Santa Clara in California. These leaders were charged by their Superiors with nothing less than choosing "the future directions" the Society would take. It was their aim to form a concept and system of "total Jesuit development." Despite the enormity of such a task, their report would be ready in 1969, a mere two years hence. And it would be stunning.

As for Father General Pedro Arrupe, meanwhile, he was in his element. His energies seemed to feed on the frenzy of work that was set in motion. In fact, he probably set some sort of personal record for untiring zeal. He gave of his best. His output, as he literally crisscrossed the globe time and again, seems almost dizzying. Everywhere Arrupe went he tried to meet not only with his Jesuits, but with civil leaders of every stripe and description as well—with U Thant of the United Nations; with President Marcos of the Philippines; with Whitney Young, president of the Urban League in the United States; with Indian Government planners. To one and all, whatever the subject of talk, his essential message was identical with the one he gave U Thant: "We [Jesuits] are pledged to work with right-minded men of all creeds and races for a more truly human society . . . justice and peace, a sense of family and of joint effort among the nations. . . ." Surely a magnificent expression of secular humanism.

His life became a continuous round of plane trips from Rome to Manila to Dublin to Duala in the Federal Republic of Cameroon to Bombay and Goa to New York to Madrid to Genoa and back again to Rome, only to start again on another round. Everywhere he went, he would talk about the most diverse subjects, delivering his ideas on ecumenism, the liturgy, social justice, peace, religious vocations, commitment, education, communication, Ignatius Loyola's *Spiritual Exercises*, missiology, episcopacy, priesthood, the virtue of poverty, the Sacraments, social problems, dialogue, generosity, theology, the Saints, the cause of peace, political involvement.

He poured out streams of words and reams of ideas to Jesuits, Jesuit alumni, non-Jesuits, bishops, Religious, layfolk. His writings to the Society and to others multiplied apace. All in all, it was never-ceasing, ever-sustained, never-less-than-vintage Arrupe. And he thrived on it. His ebullience had never shone more visibly.

"His face lights up when he's on the road," one aide remarked. As always, his enthusiasm was contagious—and that was the point of the exercise.

Arrupe's primary purpose in all of this travel and talk and correspondence was to know his Jesuits—and for them to know him and, through him, to catch the same fever for "renewal," his enthusiasm for finding and rekindling that precious "ancient charism," and for moving the Society forward as its huge study mechanisms slowly gathered the momentum that would culminate in GC32, "the next and definitive Congregation."

At the same time, his willingness to see and talk with just about everyone who came across his path by chance or choice—his or theirs—was not without its own aim. For his purpose also was to put the Society "on the map" in the minds of public authorities everywhere, and to grasp at that subtle but nonetheless real power that clothes someone who becomes an international personality.

In the midst of all this activity, the commissions established by GC31 also set to work, each concentrating on a specific aspect of current Jesuitism. The distinction of grades or "classes" in the Society, for example, which had become such a thorn in the side of Paul VI, was the subject of study for one commission. Standards of poverty among Jesuits were taken up by another commission. Several others were quietly working on educational and disciplinary questions.

The enormous and intricate machinery that would leave nothing of the Society untouched was just about getting the kinks out and pumping up some real momentum in 1968, when the first big test came of Arrupe's frequent protestations of Jesuit loyalty to the Pope. It was also the first clear indication of the paths along which the feverish search for "primitive charism" were going.

In that year, Pope Paul promulgated the most famous encyclical letter of his entire reign, *Humanae Vitae*, "Human Life." In it, Paul reconfirmed the Church's ban on all forms of artificial contraception, and he did so without nuance, distinction, or exception. He reiterated the traditional doctrine: Contraception was unacceptable; there was no way a Catholic could lawfully practice it. The Pope's position was as absolute as that of any Pope before or since his day.

If traditional doctrine was completely on the side of Paul VI in *Humanae Vitae*, practice among Catholics was another matter; for birth control had spread far and wide among them in Europe and the Americas, with the connivance of both priests and bishops. Jesuits, meanwhile, whether in Europe, the United States, or

the Third World, had made no secret of their approval of the Pill
that had revolutionized popular thinking about contraception. Nor
had Arrupe, who had been in the post of General by now for just
over three years, done anything to bring them in line.

In the feverish aftermath of Vatican II, Paul's totally traditional
encyclical was seen by many—though not by all—as papal med-
dling in a matter that intimately concerned virtually every Catholic in the world; it was like an off-key trumpet blast interrupting
an otherwise pleasant symphony. What followed that trumpet
blast was an international parliament of howling protest, of painful reproaches, of open repudiation, and of ridicule.

Whole national bodies of bishops—the Indonesians, the Dutch,
the Germans, the Austrians, to name but some—openly declared
that while of course they supported the Holy Father, contraception
was a matter of individual conscience.

Among Jesuit intellectuals, there was not even such transparent
attempts to appear obedient or supportive. The United States Jesuit publication *America Magazine*, under a new editor, Donald
Campion, S.J., published two articles criticizing and attacking *Humanae Vitae*. Almost as quickly, Germany's theological heavyweight, the widely revered Karl Rahner, S.J., who had helped the
German bishops write their two-faced answer to Paul's encyclical,
came out under his own name with a forceful and unequivocal
attack that was nothing less than a challenge to papal infallibility
in matters of faith and morals. All the Pope's arguments, puffed
Rahner, are "actually, materially and substantially false."

A cluster of Jesuits—almost the entire faculty, in fact—at the
Jesuit School of Theology at Berkeley, California (JSTB), published
a joint manifesto, again in *America Magazine*, denouncing *Humanae Vitae*. The Berkeley manifesto actually produced a brouhaha of its own, for it was answered by another cluster of Jesuits
loyal to Paul VI, who claimed that all should be obedient to the
Pope. They in turn were answered by JSTB president Richard Hill,
S.J. As father of his flock, Hill wrote to the Archbishop of San
Francisco insisting that the dissent of his Jesuit faculty members
was necessary because they shared "the anguish" of so many Catholics. (When one official of the San Francisco Chancery read about
"the anguish" of Hill's staff, he couldn't resist a wry crack of his
own: "What have these Jebbies been up to on their weekends off?")

To his credit, at one level California Provincial Patrick A. Don-
ahue reprimanded the JSTB dissenters. On a more important level,
however, he did not penalize them for attacking the moral teaching of the Pope. Yet precisely that—attacking the Pope on moral

grounds—had always been the unthinkable crime, the transgression *par excellence* in the Society against its own mission and purpose.

Such wholesale disobedience and disarray in the Society rested finally on Pedro Arrupe's shoulders. He did not himself agree that contraception was always morally wrong or that, even if it were, the encyclical should be obeyed. After all of his travels to date, he knew quite well the attitudes of many of his men. He knew, too, that in certain areas they promoted contraception and even received grants from the Planned Parenthood Federation of America.[3]

Of course, *romanità* required that Arrupe write a letter to the whole Society supporting the Pope in this matter. In fact, he sent three circular letters to his Jesuits. The first two must be taken together as a marvel of creative imagination.

The first letter was a reminder to his men that they were Jesuits, that the Pope was Pope, and that he was General. This encyclical of the Pope's needed "unswerving and decisive loyalty," accompanied as always by "creative thought which," he acknowledged, "is by no means easy or convenient."

In his second letter, Arrupe analyzed what he meant by "creative thought." Do not just read the bare words of the encyclical, he told his Jesuits, but show "a willingness to embark on an intensive course of study in order to discover its meaning and intent, both for oneself and for others." In his further advice, it became clear that Arrupe was either unaware or uncaring that he was speaking to Jesuits about a traditional, hard-and-fast rule of ordinary Catholicism; that, in bald terms, both his basic theology and his basic Jesuitism were innately weak. "The views [of *Humanae Vitae*] may not at first be compatible with one's own," he wrote, "but it is only by transcending one's own individual perspective that their correctness will be revealed."

It was not the weakness of his theology or his Jesuitism that brought a small deluge of protest down on Arrupe's head, however, but his weak-kneed waffling, his possible willingness to accommodate the Pope's "backward step" in this matter of sexuality.

The Provincial Superiors of both Jesuit Provinces in Germany, Father Krauss in Munich and Father Ostermann in Cologne, repudiated the Father General's two letters, and contested Paul VI's teaching about contraception. Over a hundred Jesuits assembled in Frankfurt's St. George High School, where they drafted a stolidly worded letter to Arrupe: "The Society of Jesus cannot accept the position which you have made it your duty to adopt in both your letters." In other words, what you tell us to think and to do, you don't believe in yourself. You don't accept Paul VI's letter, so why should we? On this point, at least, the German Jesuits were accurate.

Though the critical assault on Arrupe was nothing compared to the tidal wave that was engulfing Paul VI, Arrupe's response made of him the living example of an unflattering old proverb: "Choose a Jesuit as confessor, because he will always put pillows under your elbows." Arrupe wrote a third letter. His other two letters, Arrupe said, had been misunderstood. He had not intended to halt "scientific and objective discussion" about the subject. Jesuits should continue their "researches and thinking" on the matter.

It was the green light. From that moment, all pressure on Jesuits from their Roman Superiors ceased with respect to *Humanae Vitae*.

Paul, meanwhile, was in desperate need of help of all sorts. His health had been deteriorating. In an operation that took place on the fourth floor of the Apostolic Palace in November of 1967, the Pontiff's prostate gland was removed. Contrary to rumors, there had been no metastasis. More miseries of the mortal kind came from the extremely arthritic condition of Paul's legs, and from his cervical arthritis. That last condition forced him to wear a stiff collar beneath his robes in order to lessen the pain—a circumstance that saved his life during his visit to Manila. The kris wielded by the Bolivian painter and would-be papal assassin Benjamin Amor y Mendoza was sharp enough to have severed Paul's jugular veins as Mendoza slashed twice, once to the right and once to the left side of Paul's neck. Had it not been for that stiff collar and the speed of Paul's private secretary, Monsignore Macchi, who caught Mendoza's arm and slowed its force, Paul would have been killed. As it was, he was wounded slightly on both sides of the neck.

By 1968, in the middle of the storm over *Humanae Vitae*, Paul had not recovered his strength or his nerve. The full blast of rejection, hatred, mockery, and wholesale betrayal by his bishops and clergy brought him so low that, in the aftermath of the encyclical letter's publication, Paul was genuinely near dying from a broken heart. In that sickening almost unto death, the Jesuit reaction played a dominant role.

With any other Pope, physically robust or not, it would have taken little time for a violent reaction to set in against the path the Society of Jesus had now clearly indicated it was following. Paul's stand in the situation was weakened, however, by many of the stands he himself had taken and the causes he had supported in his career as Pope, as cardinal, and as archbishop. His own words could be quoted against him now. He had himself held a liberal torch high for much of his ecclesiastical career. His was the dreamy sort of liberalism whose manifesto envisions that when one is nice to everybody, everybody will be nice in return, even when the chips are down. That manifesto was being torn to shreds before his eyes, not only by his enemies, but by the very cadre— the Society of Jesus—sworn to support him.

Paul was, then, in no fit form for the subtle infighting against him that he now knew Arrupe and his Jesuits were capable of. When the Pope did protest in a series of letters, Arrupe was able to send the Pope a copy of his own letters to the whole Society in which he had advocated support of *Humanae Vitae.*

By April of 1969, an impatient Paul was reduced to making a pitiful appeal to Pedro Arrupe and an assembly of twenty-two Jesuit Provincials gathered in Rome: "Help the Church! Come to the aid of its needs! Show again that the sons of Ignatius know what to do!"

At about the same time, however, Arrupe was caught up in another Jesuit imbroglio; and his handling of it was an all too clear reply to Paul's misguidedly weak plea for help.

In October of 1968 a Dutch Jesuit, Father Josef Vrijburg, left the Society vowing that he would be married in August of 1969, but that he would continue as an active priest. His statements included a mockery of virginity and vitriolic attacks on priestly celibacy. Vrijburg was supported in his action and his views by two Jesuit university chaplains of Amsterdam. Huub Oosterhuis was one; he was a Dutch poet and essayist, and one of the Jesuit collaborators in the writing of *The Dutch Catechism,* published some years before, in which basic Catholic teaching on such matters as the divinity of Jesus, the Assumption of the Virgin, and of course birth control were challenged and denied. The other Jesuit chaplain, Ton Van Der Stap, was less illustrious than Oosterhuis, but just as adamant.

Arrupe demanded that Oosterhuis and Van Der Stap stop defending Vrijburg and his bitter attacks on celibacy. Together with their Provincial, Father Jon Hermans, who acted as their shield, both men traveled to Rome to beard Arrupe in his den at the Gesù. The Father General told Oosterhuis and Ven Der Stap to leave the Society. They refused. Superior Hermans refused to expel them.

As blatant as the case was by any standards, the Dutch were not without support among their Roman Superiors. One of Arrupe's

Rome-based Regional Assistants, Swiss-born Father Marius Schoenenberger, went so far as to borrow a page from the General's book. He called a press conference in the Sala Rosa of the Rome Hilton. Cocktails were served for the newsmen while Schoenenberger announced that he was leaving the Society, and explained clearly that he was doing so because the Society was behind the times in this matter of celibacy.

Whether spurred by Schoenenberger's widely publicized act or not, Arrupe dismissed the two Jesuits from the Society and sent a letter to the Dutch Jesuits justifying his dismissal of Oosterhuis and Van Der Stap. There need be no fear, Arrupe said in essence, that the dismissals had come because of any deviant ideas the two men held on virginity, celibacy, and the priesthood; it was merely a disciplinary requirement. "Please do not fear," he reassured the Dutch Jesuits, "that I will impede your dynamism and your Apostolic creativity."

Arrupe's reassurance was effective; the situation quickly returned to what had become normal—the Jesuits in Holland went on approving of divorce, a married priesthood, masturbation, homosexual marriages, abortion, and contraception.

The dust of the Dutch controversy had not settled when a deviation that was obviously far more threatening and unacceptable to Arrupe, despite its pitifully small dimensions, raised its head in Spain. The context this time was counter-renewalist, and Arrupe's reaction rekindled memories of that absolutist-revolutionary atmosphere that had drowned out all traditionalist sentiment at GC31.

The action centered around a group of some 100 Spanish Jesuits —out of a total of about 3500 in Spain—who petitioned the Vatican that they be allowed to return to the original Jesuitism of the Society. Implicit in such a request, certainly, was the idea that whatever the "primitive charism" Arrupe was searching for might turn out to be, it was not the charism of Ignatius, and whatever road Arrupe was traveling to find that novel charism, it was not the road of authentic Jesuitism.

Now there was heresy! Arrupe and his four General Assistants pointed toward Spain like bloodhounds surrounding a rabbit. What finally sent them in for the kill was a meeting of the Spanish bishops in December of 1969 in which by a slim majority the bishops endorsed the petition of the conservative band to be allowed to separate from Arrupe's Society and return to the "primitive rule."

After a thorough research into the lives and records of each one of the conservative dissidents, Arrupe arrived personally in Spain on May 1, 1970, armed with all the documents he would need to deal with the uprising. By the time he left on May 11, he had cajoled, converted, threatened, or beaten down every last man of the group. There was no question of his "impeding their dynamism" or their "apostolic creativity." He simply quenched it.

All the clangor and din of the public battle over *Humanae Vitae* that erupted in 1968, and Pedro Arrupe's success in sidestepping the demands and pleas of a weak and beleaguered Pope, seemed to pump new juices into many of the Decrees of GC31. One Decree in particular seemed to lead the field in the rapidity of change it spawned in the Society of Jesus.

In its Decree concerning the formation of Jesuit young men, GC31 had opted for locating all the houses of training in urban settings. Novitiates for beginners, as well as philosophates, theologates, and centers for the humanities were to be uprooted. "First-rate theology," as one Jesuit put it, "requires an urban community setting and ecumenical contacts; bucolic surroundings can be an obstacle to relevance." Never mind that these "bucolic" schools had long records of producing relevant theologians; the mood was for a new sort of relevance. "The Society is moving toward a more personal style . . . ," one of the former Delegates to GC31 stressed; "smaller communities, more personal contact."

The American Provinces were leaders in the relocation of their houses of training and in much of what followed as a consequence. What happened in the United States, however, happened as well in European Provinces.[4]

By September of 1968 it had been decided to relocate a number of major Jesuit training centers into city surroundings. The Weston School of Theology was moved to Cambridge, Massachusetts, where it would share facilities with Episcopal Theological College. St. Mary's College of St. Mary's, Kansas, was transferred to St. Louis University, a Jesuit school whose ownership and control were handed over to a board of laymen. In a similar move, the Jesuit University of Detroit would later turn over half the seats on the board to laymen; and the following year, 1969, fabled Fordham University in New York shifted control of the University from Jesuits to a board of laymen.

To follow the change at just one of these relocated Jesuit training centers is in large part to follow the change that took place in all of them.

By 1969, the Woodstock Theologate in Maryland had behind it 104 years of a solid tradition in theological training, philosophical and theological inquiry, scholarly research, and accumulation of resource material. It had produced generations of Jesuits excellently trained in moral theology and Jesuitism. Because its surroundings were bucolic, it afforded thousands the possibility of calmly acquiring knowledge and of training in asceticism. Now that rich tradition was to be smashed to smithereens. The entire institution of Woodstock was moved to Morningside Heights, near Columbia University, in New York City.

The offices of "Woodstock, N.Y.," as the theologate was now called to distinguish it from its original Maryland location and heritage, were located in Manhattan, at 119th Street and Riverside Drive, in the Ecumenical Center of Union Theological Seminary. Residences for the Jesuit "community," meanwhile, were now scattered among a cluster of apartments at five locations ranging along Manhattan's Upper West Side from 95th Street to 125th Street.

The emphasis now was placed on personal freedom of young Jesuits in formation, and on a sense of responsibility. Inevitably, many of the "substantials" of Jesuit life were affected. Poverty, obedience, and chastity all fell quickly by the wayside. Each young Jesuit now received a monthly allowance, opened a checking account, and managed his own budget, for all the world like any up-and-coming New Yorker.

It was perhaps unavoidable that some of these new Jesuit "residences" became nothing more than "crash pads" and beer-and-coffee stops, where the young men came and went as they pleased. They experimented with unorthodox living-room liturgies, went on dates just like "regular guys," and were not accountable in any effective manner to any Superior either for studies or the practice of religious life.

Along with everything else, personal decorum changed. Beards, sideburns, long hair tied at the back in ponytails all sprouted on preening young men anxious to "fit in." Turtleneck sweaters, slacks, jeans, cut-offs, and sneakers all seemed preferable to clerical clothes and round collars.

It was all going according to plan. As Father Walter Burghardt, editor of the *Jesuit Theological Review*, observed, "Experimentation with different life-styles is indispensable for our Jesuit studies, if we are to prepare them [the young men] for a contemporary ministry." Father William J. Bryan, as director of Field Education, obviously agreed: "The new environment favors the development of maturity and resourcefulness."

As to anything reminiscent of community life, the only thing to point to were the dinners, catered by Schrafft's Restaurant, at the residence at 220 West 98th Street. There, thirty-one apartments had been redesigned, refurbished, and amalgamated by Richard P. Hunt, S.J., for the Jesuits' new life-style. Hunt spent several enlightening months buried in the study of curtain fabrics, carpeting, paint, shingles, furniture, and lighting fixtures. Hunt, cheerfully if a little lamely, described his experience as "important as a learning process."

Of course, following the provisions of GC31, there no longer was any reading during meals. The abandonment of this practice alone would amputate from the new Jesuit mind not only all justification for obedience, poverty, and celibacy, but any knowledge of what had gone before them, any specifically Ignatian or characteristically Jesuit mold for their spirituality, their minds, their mission, and their actions. In time, Jesuits would exhibit two notable traits: an ignorance of what religious life—and Jesuit religious life in particular—meant, and a similar ignorance of the Society and the Church.

In that state of ignorance and liberation, it is little wonder that the men who stayed were, like their Superiors, fully in favor of "Woodstock, N.Y." Always present was the note of rebellion and independence. In the words of Gerald Huyett, S.J., a young American Jesuit in training, the strength of the Society "has always been that it operated on the fringes of the Church and didn't follow the party line. It's true we're in flux; but that's good because so is the rest of the world."

It was just as the process of relocation and reformation of Jesuit houses of studies was in its greatest period of ferment that the conference of top-flight and highly placed Jesuit leaders who had first gathered in 1967 at the University of Santa Clara in California to begin the task of forming a concept and system of "total Jesuit development," issued its final report.

In any context that report, written as it was by important and influential men of the Society, would have been explosive. In the context and climate that had taken hold by 1969, it was nothing short of a stunning blueprint for the rebellious lines that Jesuits would follow in their war with the papacy and the traditional Church in the seventies and eighties. The rebellious hue and cry against *Humanae Vitae* would pale beside the rebellion legitimized if not spawned by the report of this Jesuit Conference. To read that report is in effect to read a document drawn completely in the spirit of secular humanism and un-Catholic sentiments.

Gone was the former idea of a Jesuit—one who fitted into a

specifically Jesuit mold. Rather, the education and formation of young Jesuits was now to be organized and directed according to standards drawn from contemporary trends in science and humanism. The Society should be adapted to suit the individual in "personal self-discovery, integration and growth."

Obedience was to be replaced permanently by "consultation" and "dialogue" between all in the community, including (magnanimously enough) the Superior. Chastity was held to be impossible without "the capacity to love which is developed by the experience of human love, and this is not always exhausted by one man's love for another. A man's love for a woman and her response can add dimensions of sensitivity that might not otherwise be attained." The conference admitted that there were dangers here, but held that they had to be risked. While *fornication* was not a word used in the Conference report, the conferees thought that instead of marriage or celibate chastity, a third way should be open to Jesuits: intimate relationships with women that would not involve marriage, formal or common-law.

In other matters that had always been deemed equally vital in the original Jesuitism of the Society, the same totally new spirit of secular humanism was manifest. Devotion to the historical Jesus was discouraged: Jesuits should not direct their attention to "an imaginative creation of the Jesus of 2,000 years ago" but to "the living Christ, now present in his people."

The most sacred form of Catholic prayer—the celebration of the Mass—was to be opened up to adaptation and experimentation, notwithstanding what either bishops or Pope might command. Indeed, instead of obligatory daily attendance at Mass—definitely "counterproductive," the Conference said—there could and should be "professionally directed sensitivity lessons" for young Jesuits.

In its totality, the conference report left no aspect of Jesuitism —either its "substantials" or its normal support system—untouched.

When it was complete, the report was read by American and foreign Jesuits, and received plaudits not only from the American Jesuits but especially from the Dutch, the Germans, the French, and the Latin Americans. Father General Arrupe praised the overall diligence of the conferees. He did not allude, much less object, to the underlying lack of any traditional Jesuit or Catholic principles. He did point out that some of the conference's proposals— the one on "celibate chastity," for example—would provoke too much objection from Church officials.

Such petty objections aside, however, it was clear that the report did accurately express the mind of the movers and shakers of the Society in many of the Provinces of the world, and in Rome as well.

No doubt about it, the prodigious machinery set throughout the worldwide Society for investigation and analysis of itself was developing into a vast network of interchanges and exchanges. Each year, that network increased in its effectiveness, as sector after sector, community after community, and all the Provinces and Assistancies accumulated results, formed conclusions, and began to partake of the officially nourished persuasion that an epoch-making General Congregation of the Society of Jesus was in the offing. As early as 1970, in fact—barely four years after GC31 had ended—Pedro Arrupe took the first quasi-official sounding to test whether the time was ripe to decide on convoking GC32. Every three years, a Congregation of Jesuit Procurators, composed of one delegate from each Province, meets in Rome. Procurators in the Society are men appointed to represent some concrete interest of a particular Province. In consultation with the 1970 Congregation of Procurators, Arrupe decided that the Society at large was not yet ready for the "definitive" GC32. Jesuit law requires a General Congregation to take place within a specified time after it has been officially convoked; if Arrupe were to announce GC32 in October of 1970, then he would have to convene it by April of 1972 at the latest. Considering that the whole Society would have to be ready in advance for the "deep, realistic and open considerations" of GC32, which was to serve "as the center of convergence for [the] vast network of interchanges" still in process, the plain fact of the matter was that more time would be needed.

Nevertheless, progress was swift enough so that by April 1971, Arrupe felt it was at least time to set up a six-man Remote Preparatory Commission under the direction of his four General Assistants. The responsibility of this Remote Preparatory Commission was to organize still more conferences, assemblies, meetings, and forums throughout the world, at which yet again every aspect of Jesuit life would be even further discussed and dissected—but now it would all be done in the light of more than four years' work, and the fruits of diligently directed research and experimentation; and it would all focus in a concerted way on the crowning event that the 32nd General Congregation would surely be.

That Arrupe could barely contain his own anticipation of that great event seemed evident in his Christmas message that year to the whole Society. Entitled "Communal Spiritual Discernment," it insisted almost to the point of tediousness on the way each community as a whole could arrive at intentions and realizations about its own mission. Just as in Ignatian spirituality the individual should monitor the various spirits that buffet his soul and discern which was the good spirit and which the bad, so now— according to Arrupe—a whole community should monitor itself in a like manner. Needless to say, Ignatius never thought of a Jesuit community as Arrupe was now considering it. Arrupe drew his inspiration for this signal departure not from Ignatius, but from modern psychology. It was a very daring but not quite successful attempt to take one of Ignatius's ascetic principles about the individual and adapt it to a social (and sociological) context.

By Christmas of 1971, such "intentions and realizations" were already almost as numerous as the communities themselves, and continued over the next few years to become as varied as the customs and social whims of the countries in which Jesuit houses were located. Signs of "vigor" were everywhere, if one only had the eyes to see. Some Jesuits were still leading endangered lives; they were to be found at the very forefront of the struggle for social justice everywhere. In the Sudan, for example, from which Jesuit missionaries had been airlifted in 1964 in order to save their lives, by 1972 some Indian Jesuits had repenetrated the Malakal district in that country's southern region. In the Philippines, three Jesuits who had been arrested in Mindanao for championing workers' rights were released in October of 1972.

Arrupe himself met with Jesuits from Soviet satellite countries and learned from them that "our members enjoy considerable freedom. . . . We can preach the Gospel, teach doctrine, even criticize the government objectively and in a moderate tone. . . ." Everywhere, Jesuits were fighting back against political oppression, poverty, ignorance; and some were doing so at enormous personal risk. In Rhodesia, Father Clemence Freyer and other Jesuits were captured by Robert Mugabe's murderous guerrillas in July of 1973. Throughout Latin America, but especially in Nicaragua, El Salvador, Guatemala, Chile, and Peru, Jesuits were laboring to spread the new Theology of Liberation, coaching high school and college students in Marxist tactics, fomenting Base Communities of la iglesia popular, joining guerrilla bands as fighters.

And it was all done for the soundest sociopolitical reasons. "We Filipinos must no longer wait for miracles," one young Jesuit Superior put the case for his community in the area of Negros Occidental, where he was engaged in the mission of teaching the sugar workers how to unionize. "We must act now to bring social justice to the people."

It was not only in the mission fields that such stunning success cheered Pedro Arrupe and many of his colleagues in the Society's leadership. The evisceration of the theological tradition of Jesuit training was racing forward to the point that it would no longer even be a shadow play of formation for religious life.

By 1971, New York–based William V. Dych, S.J., could peacefully and truthfully observe, "It is difficult to say what the three vows [of poverty, chastity, and obedience] now mean." And indeed, the younger as well as the older men of the Society had come to be highly suspicious of any arrangement that would subordinate or sacrifice their individual gifts to the needs of the institution. "I'm not going to give up having a son just in order to prefect a study hall," went a fairly typical if rather vivid expression of the new attitude.[5] "Any married teacher can do that. If the Superior doesn't have anything better in mind for me, and if he just sits on his ass and convinces me that this is his Society, I'm getting out. It's not the game I signed up for."

So much for obedience, not to mention chastity, and a devotion of priestly life to others for the love of Jesus and for the sake of salvation—one's own as well as that of others. But not to fear; for in the place of those virtues there was now a thrilling sense of adventure. At least, that was the way American Jesuit Gerald Huyett saw things: "It is helpful," he fairly cooed, "to study theology in an environment where everyone else isn't a believer" because "you can go out . . . and ask yourself whether it [theology] makes sense and whether anybody really cares."

As it happened, apparently fewer and fewer people did care any longer—at least about the Jesuit call for a new "primitive charism." The number of Jesuits in training at Woodstock, for example, in 1969—the year it became "Woodstock, N.Y."—was 158. By 1972, it was down to 102, a drop of 35 percent. One year later, in 1973, it was all the way down to 70 men—66 percent off from the time "renewal" of Jesuit training had begun a bare five years earlier.

Reason did pop its head in the scholastic door for a moment, like an old alumnus on a brief visit home. Doubts were raised about the wisdom of "Woodstock, N.Y." But the young men who were left by that time complained that the suggestion to terminate "Woodstock, N.Y." was "a loss of nerve," as one of them was quick to say. Another objected, "To pull out of New York City, and say we can't make it here means we are asking a lot from these

Christians who do live and work in the city." Theological studies had apparently been reduced to a game of "I Double-Dare You."

The fall-off in Jesuit recruitment was not only evidenced in "Woodstock, N.Y." In the entire United States, where 350 recruits used to enter the Society each year, the number was down over two-thirds by 1972, to 100. And the recruitment picture was the same in all Western countries.

With an invincibly blind optimism and an absolute self-confidence, Arrupe justified his nearly crazed quest for "the primitive charism" by looking instead at the picture in India where, out of a total Jesuit membership of 3100, 2600 were native Indians; and where the Society ran a medical network of 400 hospitals, 600 dispensaries, and India's only Social Science Institute. It was a special consolation to Pedro Arrupe, given his unusual concept of mission work, that the Jesuits in India were adapting, being "inculturated" into their Hindu ambient. Ceremonial practices from the worship of Kali and Shiva were integrated into the celebration of the Mass. Jesuits joined the ranks of the *sanyasi*, the holy men. Swami Animananda ("Taking Joy in the Immaculate"), S.J., and Swami Amalananda, S.J., both traveled, dressed, and lived like *sanyasi*, complete with robes, staff, begging bowl, and all the other accoutrements. Swami Animananda built a chapel at Deshunar in the style of a Hindu *mandir*, or temple. He also started a savings bank and a seed bank for the local farmers.

In all his enthusiasm for "inculturation" and the adaptation of the Christian message to Indian subcultures, Arrupe seems never to have perceived how the Hinduization of the Catholic Mass was eviscerating that ceremony of its essential meaning. Evidently Arrupe, claimant expert on "inculturation," did not see any harm in the wholesale adoption of Indian serving dishes, Indian gestures, Indian language, and Indian postures, even though for the Hindu mind all of those things had specific religious meanings that were irreconcilable with the Catholic meaning of the Mass. For instance, in the "Indian rite" used by Catholics in Poona, genuflection before the Eucharist has been abolished in favor of *"anjali haste,"* the profound bow Hindus concede to minor gods. Prostration (*shastangam* or *ashtangam*) is reserved for the Great God, but not given to Jesus Christ. Hinduizing priests of this day do not give even the *"anjali haste,"* but only a cursory nod, to the Eucharist. In spite of a specific veto from the Vatican on the subject, the mantra OM is used in the "Indian rite."[6] OM in Hindu theology is the Hindu god Krishna. Its use in Hindu ears means worship of Krishna.[7]

Arrupe, however, is not on record for any perceptive treatment of this abusive Hinduization of Catholicism.[8]

Another sure consolation for the Father General was the success of GC31's Decree about the arts. Concrete expression of the Decree was to be found in the Jesuit Institute for the Arts, founded in 1969.[9] It had its own permanent staff, and drew its members from an international set that crossed all lines of religion, color, race, and ideology. Though it was certainly not as shatteringly important as "inculturation" in India and elsewhere, the Institute represented a quiet breakthrough for an idea close to Arrupe's heart: Jesuits needed to "penetrate" modern arts and thus be thoroughly modern men.

There was a lot to be said for Pedro Arrupe's invincible optimism and his absolute self-confidence. By Easter of 1972, the Father General and his advisers judged that the entire Society would finally be ready for GC32 sometime in 1974–1975. As it was the time-honored custom to do, Arrupe informed Pope Paul VI of his intention to convoke the General Congregation, "For the greater perfection of the Society as an instrument in the hands of God, and for the propagation of the faith."

It is to be doubted that, at Easter of 1972, Paul knew exactly what to do about Arrupe and his Jesuits. Over the years since 1965, he had been in regular, though not exactly frequent, contact with the Jesuit General by letter and face-to-face. Most often, it was about some Jesuit in some part of the world who was guilty of some especially gross violation of Church doctrine or practice.

With Arrupe, however, it always seemed to be a case of unmanageable contradiction. Each time the Holy Father complained, the Jesuit General explained. Scores of times he explained, on bended knee, so to speak. In Arrupe's mouth, it always seemed to be a matter of justice, of fairness, of waiting. In time, each individual case went away. But always another one or two or three would pop up. They never seemed to stop. Under Arrupe, nothing ever seemed to be resolved. Accordingly, Paul's dossier concerning Jesuit transgressions and excesses worldwide kept swelling.

Much nearer home, meanwhile, private reports reached Paul from his informants "across the way" in Jesuit headquarters, the Gesù. The main thrust of those reports was discouraging. In the preparation for the next General Congregation, it appeared that everything sacrosanct in the Society of Jesus might be put up for change or abolition. Paul had harped against such changes continually with Arrupe; and Arrupe had just as continually assured Paul that all was well.

In conjunction with his advisers, Paul decided it would be better to assemble Jesuit leaders all together in Rome. The hope was that these leaders could then be educated about what abuses there were and what they should properly be doing, and what precisely was the will of their Pope. Notwithstanding the subtle war that Jesuits seemed to be waging against his papacy, the gentle and ever-hopeful liberal in Paul told him that the unthinkable—a genuine, all-out revolt by the Jesuits—was impossible.

For these and perhaps other reasons as well, Paul "acknowledged" Arrupe's notification of his intent to convoke GC32. That is to say, he did not disapprove. But the Pontiff did send Arrupe a letter in which he stressed that GC32 must not be used to change the character of the Society. And yet again Paul stressed fidelity, and orthodoxy of doctrine.

Perhaps, therefore, Arrupe didn't have a green light from Paul, but he didn't have a red light either. The Remote Preparatory Commission, set up only a year before, now called on all Jesuits to make a special effort of spiritual preparation for the coming Congregation; "spiritual preparation" meant that in every community of Jesuits, there were to be studies and discussions about the vocation and mission of the Society, about what apostolic service meant today after six years of "renewal" and search, and about Jesuit religious and community life.

While the communities were so engaged, Arrupe completed the so-called remote phase of preparation for GC32. Between October 1972 and October 1973, the Father General met personally with all Jesuit Provincial Superiors. Those Superiors were divided into five groups based on languages and geography. A series of five meetings took place—one each in Goa, Nice, and Mexico City, and two in Rome—in which the General and his Superiors from around the world thrashed out with each other all major issues that had boiled to the top of the cauldron during the Society's unremitting study and examination that had been mandated by GC31. It was in this fashion that the general lines for the 32nd General Congregation were drawn up.

Arrupe came away from those high-level meetings convinced at last that the moment was almost within his grasp, and that GC32 would be the Congregation of "definitive" change—that it would indeed give "a new expression to the primitive charism."

At this point in his career as Jesuit Father General, Pedro Arrupe reached perhaps the acme of his perception about the role of Jesuits, the role of the Catholic Church, and the role of religion in the everyday material world. He had now spent almost seven feverish years building toward an ideal. At his fingertips, destiny had placed a first-class organization with an institution second to none, filled with educated minds and gifted intelligences from all over the world. Into him, as the ultimate receptacle, had been poured the ideas, the ideals, the characteristics, and the qualities of black, white, yellow, and brown men—the off-givings of their aspirations, the juice of their cultures, the frills of their imaginations. Perhaps no man alive in that year 1973 could match Arrupe's experience, could speak with such firsthand knowledge about the world and human society as a whole. It would truly have been difficult to find his equal in detailed knowledge of different cultures, races, causes, social conditions, political environments; difficult because few—probably no one—had had his exposure.

And, let it be said, no one with such an enormous global exposure to the human condition had been driven by the ideology that had formed Pedro Arrupe. When he spoke to the President of the Philippines, the Secretary-General of the United Nations, the Prime Minister of Japan, the Minister for Energy in Venezuela, the Pope in Rome—to whomever—he was speaking to men confined by their very professions. By contrast, he, Arrupe, could see all around them, beyond them, and through them. He would, in a human sense, be the bigger man in any such twosome.

It all came together for him that spring and summer of 1973—his path, the path of the Society, the path of his Church, the path of human society. He no longer had any doubts. He was not any longer confined by a Roman chair, no longer hemmed in by a nationalism, an ideology, a tradition. No particularism could be detected in him. Nor would he be browbeaten or cowed or made apprehensive by the red robes of a cardinal, the Fisherman's Ring of the Pope, the crown on a prince's head, or the assured power of political dignitaries. He was at his height. He feared no man. He did not fear at all; the word was not in his vocabulary, and the emotion had never been his.

In Arrupe's increasingly wide-angle social optic, the beloved particularities of Jesuitism disappeared like so many inconsequential relicts and shavings. It was the big picture that counted. His Jesuitism and his Catholicism changed accordingly. Jesuitism ceased for him to be a specific brand of Catholic asceticism, a fixed and sacred tradition governed by the very thoughts, the very words, the very rules drawn up by the first Basque who had founded the Society of Jesus. The Society now for Arrupe was an organization that drew its meaning and value and scope from the world around it, from the society of men and women.

What was specifically Catholic—papacy and Pope, Rome of the Vatican, exclusive and exclusivist teaching authority, bishop and priest, saving Sacrifice of the God-Man and cleansing Sacrament of Penance, superiority of virginity and contemplation, childlike devotion to Mary and the saints—all of it was placed within Arrupe's wide-angle optic and reduced to minimal significance, to the status of symbols or memorials. The big picture . . .

Arrupe took pains to enunciate the world view he now had from the peak on which he had arrived. On July 31, 1973, he addressed the Jesuit European Alumni at their 10th Annual International Congress in Valencia, Spain. The speech, like his maiden speech at the Second Vatican Council, made international headlines. One basic theme from that maiden speech came up again: the "network of domination, oppression and abuses . . . which keep the greater part of humanity from sharing . . . in the enjoyment of a more just and more fraternal world." But in Valencia, his main theme was a strikingly different one.

"We must be men-for-others. We must train men who are men-for-others. What they must do and we must train them to do is to humanize this world of ours." Arrupe was expounding to those laymen at Valencia the core idea and the driving motive of his new Jesuitism.

Liberation of the economically poor and the politically oppressed was to be a constituent part of preaching the Gospel. It was a "social asceticism." To do this, Jesuits must use modern "technologies and ideologies," for "the Christian ethos cannot possibly construct a new world without their assistance." And it was, Arrupe said, a question of constructing a new world. For this, Jesuits need to be "converted." To what? To opposition against the consumer society; against those who profit from unjust sources. And then? To be agents of change.

This, Arrupe concluded, was the extension into the modern world of the Jesuit humanist tradition derived from the *Spiritual Exercises* of Ignatius.

Of Christ and his salvation, of the Church and her divinely appointed role, of Jesuits and their supposedly supernatural mission, of the Sacraments, of personal holiness, of their personal relationship with Christ, there was not a word. Of Heaven and Hell, of sin in the supernatural sense, there was no word. Nor could there be, given the secularization of Jesuit Arrupe; and given the this-worldly ideal which now, in its shimmering grandeur, had entered his being and exploded in his brain.

It was this Arrupe—no longer the companion of Jesus, but very

much a man who was a man-for-others—who had organized
preparation for, and who would carefully oversee, the revamping
of Ignatian Jesuitism in the forthcoming General Congregation.

So certain was Arrupe of success that in September 1973, a
month before his meetings with the Regional Superiors were quite
finished, he took what he later called the biggest decision of his
Generalate. He officially convoked the long-awaited, much-
prepared 32nd General Congregation of the Society of Jesus for
December 2, 1974, fifteen months hence.[10]

On September 8, 1973, one week after Arrupe's announcement
of the convocation of GC32, a letter arrived from Pope Paul which
was intended for the whole Society.

In its original form as prepared by Cardinal Secretary of State
Jean Villot, the Pope's letter expressed Paul's doubts, reservations,
and misgivings about the many deviations that had manifested
themselves in the Society since the last General Congregation in
1966. In particular, Paul warned Arrupe and his colleagues that on
no account and under no pretext should the hierarchic system of
governance in the Society even be discussed, much less tampered
with. Paul was merely reiterating what he had said in at least six
letters since 1966.

The papal letter also sounded a threatening note: The Holy See
wanted the Society of Jesus as it was. Any effort to force a change
in its "substantials"—the system of grades, or government by obedience, for example—could only draw down a sharp response.
Overall, there had been distinct signs that the spirit of religion and
orthodoxy was failing badly. It was to this problem, Paul insisted,
that the forthcoming GC32 should pay most attention.

Arrupe simply could not send this letter as it stood to his
Jesuits. Not after the last seven years of "renewalist" fervor
and the vast bureaucratic effort in which all the traditional
formats of Jesuitism and a new Society of Jesus adapted to a new
age.

There followed between Jesuit General and Pope protracted negotiations masked by the comings and goings typical of Vatican
politics. Arrupe's plea—ultimately accepted—was that he needed
a much more "paternal" and "benign" format for the papal letter.
Surely he had, as the Vatican well knew, a cageful of lions to deal
with. To get them to Rome in anything resembling a conciliatory
mood, he needed a different letter from the Holy Father. One
stressing the positive; encouraging, warning—yes, of course, in
general terms; but, for the love of God, at least welcoming. Revolt,
Arrupe pointed out, was just beneath the surface of Jesuit life in

many provinces. In fact, he would rather recall the convocation and put off the General Congregation *sine die,* than send out the letter as he had received it.

For Paul VI, there was no real alternative. If Arrupe were to call off GC32 now, after it had been announced, still more damage would be done. He had to consent to a milder format, the format of the letter dispatched by Arrupe on October 4. In it, Paul said he was writing to the Jesuits "to encourage you and send Our best wishes for a happy outcome to the Congregation." Paul expressed his happiness over the "Society's great effort . . . to adapt its life and apostolate to the needs of today." Of course, he said in passing, there had been certain noticeable tendencies of "an intellectual and disciplinary nature" during the past few years which could "lead to serious and possibly irresponsible changes in the essential structure itself of your Society." That was now as far as the papal admonition went. As to papal warning, there was none.

Once the official announcement of GC32 was made, the time of remote preparation quickly gave way to the more familiar activities and routines of official preparation. In each Province, Congregations were held to elect the Delegates to GC32; the *postulata,* or subjects each Province wanted discussed at GC32, were determined; individual Jesuits began sending their own *postulata* to Rome. In time, the 1020 *postulata* received in the Gesù filled 500 pages of typescript.

The final bureaucratic touches were put to all this complex preparation in the summer and autumn of 1974, when three Preliminary Committees assembled in Rome. On the basis of the meetings Arrupe had held with the Provincial Superiors, and a preliminary study of the *postulata,* those Committees prepared the all-important list of preeminent topics to be discussed by GC32. They also decided that there would again be an Office of Information organized for the duration of GC32—an international press office, in effect—from which regular bulletins about GC32 were to be published in English, French, and Spanish, and where press conferences would be held.

If, as the eve of GC32 approached, Pedro Arrupe and his collaborators were concerned in any way with the steady and seemingly inexorable decline in Jesuit vocations—the Society as a whole had now dropped from over 36,000 in 1965 to under 30,000—there was no sign of it. Rather, the mark of the Jesuit leadership was its unflappable and almost eccentric self-confidence. And in a certain sense, those leaders had earned the right to such self-confidence. For close to eight years they had presided over a sea-change of

Jesuit attitudes and behavior, and had successfully walked through the minefields of Vatican objections and papal disgust.

Not that Paul VI was quiescent, exactly, or unaware of what some viewed as the increasing tide of fatuities and stupidities of individual Jesuits over the eight-year search for "the primitive charism." What roused the Pope's ire, however, even as he gave his grudging permission for GC32 to convene, were the significant lapses in Arrupe's administration. Paul could not understand, for example, how Arrupe could allow Robert Drinan, S.J., to function for years in the United States Congress as a leading pro-choice champion. In Paul's eyes, that was a fundamental betrayal of morality not only by Drinan, but by Drinan's Superiors—and ultimately by the Father General who traditionally was the leader of those Superiors.

Nor could Paul justify such a case as that of John W. O'Malley, S.J. In 1971, O'Malley published an article in the American *Jesuit Theological Studies* that was a model of unblushing Modernism. In effect, O'Malley propounded the idea that the Second Vatican Council had liberated the Catholic Church from its former iron-clad, close-minded, outmoded, and unsuitable viewpoint on the truth about God and salvation. Because the modern era had so deeply changed human affairs, O'Malley's argument ran, and even the very soul of modern man, the Catholic Church had to renounce any exclusive claim to the truth—absolute or even relative truth. The whole bent of man today, O'Malley insisted, was search. The only absolute was flux in culture, in historical events —and in any claim to truth. Truth and any claim to have it was just a part of the search. Nothing more.

In Paul's eyes, and in those of many in and out of the Vatican, O'Malley had deserted traditional and official Roman Catholic doctrine. What was incredible about the affair, however, was that Arrupe did not demand from O'Malley or from the editors of *Theological Studies* a repudiation of an article that constituted a violation of Jesuit oaths, and that gave currency to the strong tide of Modernism in the thinking of thousands of Jesuits.

Paul was painfully aware that the cases of Robert Drinan and John O'Malley did not occur in a limpid vacuum. The reports that continued to come in and his own Jesuit contacts kept him amply informed of the manner in which Jesuit seminaries were being run, on the deviant teaching of some Jesuit professors who had departed from traditional doctrine, about the free-wheeling life-styles of Jesuits in Europe and the Americas, and about the nature of the new proposals being readied for GC32.

Those proposals, in fact, were a source of enormous concern to Paul. They called for abolition of the Jesuits' Fourth Vow of special obedience to the Pope. They called for all-out support of socialist politics and for fomenting revolution in Third World countries. They called for shortening the training period for young Jesuits; for the formal affiliation of married couples to the Society; the diminution of the priestly character of the Society; still further modifications in the matter of Jesuit obedience—or what was left of it; open support for homosexual marriages, for divorce and abortion, for premarital sex and masturbation, for still more experimentation in Religious discipline of every kind; for Hinduization of Catholic Theology. There seemed no end to the number of such reports about the Jesuits that reached the papal office, and no limit to the portrait of excess they painted in the Society's search for their renewed "primitive charism."

Nor did Paul need to rely entirely on those secondhand reports. The Pope himself listened to Arrupe as he fervently addressed the world Synod of Bishops in Rome on three occasions, on such subjects as the relationship of bishops and clergy to Religious Orders and the true evangelical apostolate. The Pontiff heard Arrupe admonish the bishops "to abandon paternalism and authoritarian attitudes." He heard Arrupe warn the bishops that "the public image of the Holy Father has suffered great damage in relation to priesthood and social justice." Paul wondered—so he told his private secretary—if Arrupe knew whom he was dealing with.

In all his self-confidence, it seemed clear that Arrupe knew well whom he was dealing with, had long since taken Paul VI's measure. In one letter, for example, that Arrupe wrote to the whole Society, he tartly admonished all Jesuits to "foster love and respect for the person of the Holy Father." Arrupe complained that his men had unjustly criticized Paul for *Humanae Vitae*, for his conservatism, for his indecision, and for his lack of personal warmth.

So great was the note of Arrupe's personal condescension in that letter that many came to share the opinion of Jean Danielou, S.J. —an intimate of Paul's who later became a cardinal—that the letter was not an admonition to the Jesuits, but Arrupe's not very subtle way of telling Paul what was wrong with him in the eyes of the Jesuits.

If Arrupe was aware of Danielou's interpretation of the letter, it surely gave him no more worry than Danielou's denouncement, in 1972, of the "renewal" of Jesuit training and religious life as creating a shambles of the Order. Danielou received a sharp and acid reply from Arrupe: Religious life was never better in the Society than now. And indeed, "religious life" could be construed as having nothing any longer to do with independent spiritual values or with salvation. If "religious life," in other words, meant placing Holy Orders at the disposal of purely secular ideology, social programs, and political movements, then Arrupe's reply to Danielou was accurate; a long litany of examples made that much clear.

As early as 1968, Theophane Matthias, director of the Jesuit Educational Association of India, had declared that "saving souls from eternal damnation is no longer a valid theology for the worldwide church's missionary effort." Carl Ambruster, S.J., in a 1971 report commissioned by the American bishops, demolished all foundation for the Catholic priesthood. Ambruster then left the priesthood.

In that same year, 1971, Peter Brugnoli, S.J., became the founder of a new movement of priests and laymen in Rome to oppose the conservative structures and politics of Paul VI. "The November 17, 1971 Movement," as it was called for the day of its founding—the day after the closing of the Synod of Bishops in Rome—included about 400 priests, ex-priests, dissident theologians, and radical left-wing laymen. They insisted they must set up rebel churches throughout Italy, expose the Holy See's political ties, and end the 1929 Concordat between the Holy See and the Italian State, among other things.

The year 1971, in fact, had produced a bumper crop of examples of this newly defined "religious life." The winter and spring of that year saw Gerald L. McLaughlin, S.J., participating in the leftist government of Jamaica; the defense by Bishop Antonio Parilla-Bonella, S.J., of Puerto Rican terrorists as "heroes"; the culmination of the antiwar activities of Daniel Berrigan, S.J., in the allegations that his brother Philip and some of his associates were involved in a bizarre plot to kidnap Secretary of State Henry Kissinger and to bomb federal installations in Washington. By 1972, "religious life" had been "renewed" to the extent that Jesuit Provincial Superiors concelebrated Mass without the prescribed vestments—something that would have called sharp judgment down upon their heads at one time; now it was accepted with remarkable ease.

When 1973 rolled around, Jesuit theologian Daniel Toolan laid out what seemed by then to be the single trail of the Society's search for "the primitive charism": "If any of this generation decide to take seriously the spiritual journey, they are virtually forced to renounce the Church of Christ."

An argument could be made that the closest detailed expression of the aims and the mission of the "renewed" Society of Jesus was attained in a document put out in 1972 by a group in the United States known as the "Christian Maoist" Jesuits. The document, entitled "National Planning and the Need for a Revolutionary Social Strategy," was regarded in some quarters as an oddity, and its authors as oddballs. But the fact that Jesuits calling themselves "Christian Maoists" could publish a document on national planning and revolutionary social strategy in a Jesuit publication at all argues differently. And that no rebuke or disciplinary action was taken against them by Arrupe or any American Superiors is more significant still.

The document put the "need" of its title in the form of a challenge: "If the Society of Jesus seeks an active role in overcoming alien, congealed objectivity of the external world . . . the Society must purge itself of its bourgeois social consciousness and identify itself with the proletariat. . . . The proletariat simultaneously knows and constitutes society." In a quasi-blasphemous somersault that landed on its head somewhere between traditional language and the call of Teilhard de Chardin, the document then observed that, "It is at this point that we are very close to understanding the mystery of Jesus' own proletarian background."

That much established to the satisfaction of the "Christian Maoists," the document proceeded to attack the "reformist strategy" pursued hitherto by the Society of Jesus as bringing Band-Aids to bind the wounds of the proletariat. This strategy had failed "on the international level." The new "national and international social strategy of the Society of Jesus in the U.S. must be founded upon the recognition that the development of backward countries is incompatible with the total development of the capitalist world." There was now, the document insisted, "an irremediable gap between the philosophy of peaceful co-existence and the program of revolutionary vanguards of the Third World."

What to do about all that? The document gave the answer in its outline of what sort of planning the Society of Jesus must adopt in order to adapt to and cooperate with the proletariat in its irresistible march toward nothing less than the purification of the entire human population.

If Mao had his vociferous disciples among the Jesuits of the early seventies as the Society raced toward its "definitive" Congregation, Marx was certainly not be be outdone. A close friend of Pedro Arrupe, Father José María Diez-Alegría, had for years been a well-known professor of sociology at the Jesuit-run Gregorian University of Rome. Arrupe knew, as everyone did, that Diez-Alegría stayed in contact with extremist groups in Spain, Italy, West Germany, and elsewhere. That was hardly worth noticing, in fact. In 1973, Diez-Alegría published a book which, on the evidence of its title, was intended as a new credo: *I Believe in Hope,* the book was called; *Yo Creo en la Esperanza.* The book created a sensation, not because of Diez-Alegría's ideas—he had after all been lecturing at the Gregorian for years about those ideas, and had published articles about them as well. What made the book a bestseller in Europe was that to gather together his ideas at this particular moment, and to set them up as a countercredo to that of the Church, was to blast Pope Paul VI full across the face.

"Marx," Diez-Alegría confessed, "has guided me to rediscover Jesus and the meaning of his message. . . . Acceptance of Marxist analysis of history with its elements regarding the historical meaning of the class struggle and the necessary overthrow of private ownership of the means of production, is not in any way opposed to faith and the Gospels." The conclusion was obvious for Diez-Alegría. "We must make common cause with all those who commit themselves to the revolutionary cause of socialism. . . ."

Concerning the Roman Catholic Church, the judgment was final: "As it has existed in history, it contains little that is Christian"; the Church displayed a "visceral anti-socialism." In fact, "the Church and its apparatus is anti-Christian in a bourgeois way."

Diez-Alegría was apparently at least as disturbed by the Church's concern for chastity among priests, Religious, and laity in accordance with their stations in life, as he was with the Church's sociopolitical sins. Celibacy should be abolished, Diez-Alegría said, because it was a "factory for madmen." As for anyone trapped in celibacy, Diez-Alegría said, "I advise him to get out as soon as possible." Nor did he find anything objectionable about masturbation; presumably anything was superior to celibacy.

Though what Diez-Alegría had to say about the papacy and about Paul VI in particular were of a piece with the rest of his views, they probably contributed a great deal to the temporary problems Diez-Alegría faced. The Pope's primacy and infallibility, he said, were "mere extrapolations of the New Testament," but nothing more. The Pope would do better to give away a large part of his "unpleasant and disquieting wealth."

Unlike the case of the "Christian Maoist" Jesuits who had published their plan for revolutionary strategy only the year before, it was commonly said by those around Arrupe in Rome that the Father General and his General Assistants knew of the book's contents beforehand, and knew of the plans to publish it. In that view, the Diez-Alegría credo—his "I believe" for extreme renewalists—could serve as a trial balloon. As long as it did not have the official imprimatur of the Society, it could do no harm; if necessary—if its publication caused too much heat for comfort—the Superiors could always jump on the author later.

As it turned out, the heat wasn't too bad after all. Arrupe thought it best merely to ask Diez-Alegría to absent himself from Rome temporarily, and to suspend him from all activity for two years—not for the blasphemy of his proposed credo, but for not having submitted his book to the Society's censors before its publication.

The contrast with Arrupe's quenching of the "uprising" of the hundred or so Spanish conservatives in 1971 forces itself to the fore about now; for there was never an official repudiation of any of Diez-Alegría's views, nor was he required by the Father General to retract even his bitter attack on the papacy. Rather, he was allowed to live and work within the folds of the Society, and to return to fight another day—a day in 1980 when he would call a public press conference along with two other Jesuits to denounce John Paul II's opposition to the divorce bill then being prepared in the Italian Parliament for a national vote.

The Diez-Alegría affair was still hot in 1973 when another verbally active Jesuit brought the fight into the papal arena in a more personal way. Peter Hebblethwaite, S.J., who in his own right was editor of the English Jesuit magazine *The Month*, published in the May 15 edition of the *London Observer* a highly critical and even abusive attack on Monsignore (later Cardinal of Florence) Giovanni Benelli, Paul VI's closest aide and his second-in-command at the Vatican Secretariat of State.

Benelli, variously nicknamed by his contemporaries as "the Gauleiter" and "the Berlin Wall," among other epithets, because of his brusque—not to say rough—manner of dealing with people, was no friend of Pedro Arrupe and his Jesuits. In fact, wrote Hebblethwaite in the *Observer* piece, Benelli was a "universal hatchet man," had "an opaque and impenetrable style of operation, is authoritative and alarmist, sees enemies under every bed and is more concerned with prestige when many of us are trying to make the Church a simpler and a more fraternal place to live in."

As with the Diez-Alegría case, rumor again had it that the Hebblethwaite article was published with the awareness of Jesuit Superiors in Rome; indeed, the rumors this time went considerably farther, suggesting that the article had been written by Hebble-

thwaite at the direct suggestion of his Roman Superiors in order
to light a fire under Benelli. If so, of course, it made Hebblethwaite
a hatchet man in his own right; and even if not, the Jesuit proved
himself at least a match in the roughness of his manner.

Unlike the Diez-Alegría case, this time Arrupe did apologize to
Monsignore Benelli as the offended party. But when Hebblethwaite proceeded to publish a second article on the same subject
and in the same vein, the Father General did not apologize. He left
the matter, he said, in the hands of Hebblethwaite's English Superiors. They did nothing, however. In the eyes of Arrupe and other
Jesuits, Benelli was the enemy.

And Benelli was.

Whatever view one may hold about the correctness of the Jesuit
tide toward purely secular activity or their doctrinal aberrations,
or any of the rest of it, and whatever love or hatred or mere indifference one might have for the Church, for the papacy, and for
Paul VI as Pope, the single greatest wonder in this entire, complicated march toward war between Jesuits and papacy is that Paul
allowed GC32 to take place at all. But Paul VI had made up his
mind on two points. It was better to assemble Jesuit leaders in
Rome where he could get to them directly; and, whatever drastic
action he might be forced to take, he would make sure nobody
could say the Jesuits had not been warned against allowing matters
to go too far in the course of the forthcoming 32nd General Congregation.

In October of 1973, Paul sent Father General Arrupe yet another
papal letter of complaint and warning. There were, Paul wrote in
that letter, "intellectual and disciplinary tendencies among Jesuits
which, if they were to receive support, would introduce very grave
and perhaps irreparable changes in the very structure of the Order.
. . . If you adopt decision-making methods that dilute obedience,
the Society's character will change. . . . You must shun innovations that would lead the Society astray. . . . You must end permis-
siveness. . . . You must lead an austere life that makes it possible
to resist a spirit that is devoid of concern for sacred things, a slave
to fashion. . . . Obedience and discipline are the sources of Jesuit
charism."

Even that much of Paul's letter made it abundantly plain that
the Pontiff had continued to be well-briefed on the means and
directions of the Jesuit search for "the primitive charism," and
that he did not approve of any of it—the sociological surveys, the
psychological profiles, the personal exposés, the outlines for per-

SEARCH FOR THE PRIMITIVE CHARISM

sonal integration, or most of the rest of the paraphernalia used to prepare for GC32.

Paul's letter also made clear that he saw where Arrupe and the Jesuit establishment wished to take the Society—and wanted none of it. That warning was both implicit and explicit in Paul's letter. A fundamental change in the Society's structure by GC32 would be no more acceptable than it had been in GC31 eight years before. If such a change were attempted, then "the Holy See would have to examine its relationship with the Society all over again." That, as Arrupe knew, was *romanità* at least for his own removal as Father General, and possibly even for suppression of the Society.

"We once again express our desire," Paul concluded his letter of warning, "that Jesuits remain a religious, apostolic, priestly Order linked to the Roman Pontiff by a special bond of love and justice.

"Communicate this, please, to all Jesuits."

Arrupe did communicate the papal letter to the full Society; and, although he omitted certain elements which properly concerned only Higher Superiors—that is to say, the possibilities that he would be forced to resign or that the Society might be suppressed—Rome was immediately abuzz with rumors that the sixty-five-year-old Jesuit General was about to resign or be "resigned."

The worldwide reaction from Jesuits to the papal letter was predictable. Anger at Paul's "bullying" of "Pedro"—as Arrupe was and still is affectionately known in the Society—was as pronounced as the stern determination to push ahead in the search for "the primitive charism" of the Society. Only from a small, vocal minority was there any support for Paul.

It was much too late—or perhaps much too early—for a return to such traditional modes of Religious life and Jesuit activity as Pope Paul was calling for. The floodtide of expectations for huge changes, for a new and refurbished Society of Jesus, was far too great to accommodate any ripple tending in the direction of recall and tradition. Even the possibility of Arrupe's "resignation" provoked no hesitation or second thoughts.

Indeed, as the day of GC32 approached at long last, the changes already installed as matters of daily practice had made a new thing of the Society of Jesus. The experimentations in the "new lifestyles," the continual rain of permitted and sanctioned dissent from Catholic orthodoxy, the sustained deviations from Catholic morality—and, perhaps above all else, the unremitting criticisms

and attacks on the person of Pope Paul VI coupled with the dilution of religious obedience into an agreement that each Jesuit community should plough ahead independently as each decided—all
of this sprang from something alien to anything known before in
the Society of Jesus.

True, wonted phrases and consecrated words were used—"the
good of the Church," "the salvation of souls," "respect for the
Holy Father," "the apostolate of the Society," "the service of
the Holy See," "our filial devotion to the papal Throne." But the
vast bulk of facts—words, actions, proposals—belied the spiritual
values that had always been conveyed by such protestations and
phrasings.

The unique effectiveness of the original Jesuitism of Ignatius
had rested on its deliberate and scientific analysis and regulation
of an individual's activity, of his motives, of his source of inspiration, of his foresight, his resources, his purposefulness, his fallback
positions, and finally of the scope of his view and the length of his
aim. All of this, Ignatius had outlined in his *Spiritual Exercises.*
All Jesuitism rested on those brilliantly traced circles of ascension
to the immaterial, to the divine Eternal One; and on the descent
again into the human, the re-immersion into the cosmos of matter
and of human concern for eternal life with God. Both ascent and
descent were to be accomplished, according to Ignatius, not
through sociological poll-taking, but through the humanity and
divinity of Christ—through the attainment of the divine by means
of personal holiness within the human cosmos, and this to a degree of perfection as great as divine grace, one's own willing consent, and one's foreordained destiny allowed one. Within those
parameters, the apostolates of Jesuits would take each individual
as far as the independent heart of Godhead decided in the mystery
of Godhead's eternity. This was Ignatian doctrine about Jesuits
and Jesuitism—a doctrine, in Paul VI's words, that had never been
"a slave of fashion," but was supernatural from beginning to end.

The search for "the primitive charism," on the other hand, as
far as one can judge, was based on principles and aims that were
untranslatable into, and therefore irreconcilable with, the Ignatian
mold. More than that, however, Jesuitism in Arrupe's Society had
not only lost the character of the Society, but had begun to lose
even the character of a Religious Order.

Since Saint Dominic founded the Order of Preachers in the
1200s, nearly 300 years before Iñigo's time, it has been the Religious Order itself, and not the isolated house or community, that
was the basic unit in any Religious Order. And in any Religious

Order, all members are subject to one superior general, and all regulations bear the unmistakable mark of the founder. This also is—or had been—the tradition in the Jesuit Order.

Wherever the Society of Jesus was headed in December of 1974 as it convened for its "definitive" General Congregation, it was not in any direction ever associated before with Religious Orders, or with the primitive charism of Ignatius of Loyola.

21 | THE NEW FABRIC

Euphoria and invincible self-confidence—that was the mood of the 236 Delegates[1] as they gathered at long last, on December 2, 1974, for the opening of the 32nd and "definitive" General Congregation of the Society of Jesus.

And why not? Never in Jesuit history had any General Congregation been so thoroughly prepared in advance; never had the expectations of Delegates and non-Delegates alike been raised to such a fever pitch of expectation. And now, the time had finally arrived to draw all the "new unbroken threads," provided eight years before by GC31, into "the new fabric of the Society"—to declare and define in the official Decrees of the Order the new substance and the modern meaning of "the primitive charism." Nothing less than the subsequent history of the Society—its structure, its inspiration, and its mission—would be molded in the coming weeks.

Euphoria and confidence weren't the whole of it, though. Not any longer. There was another dimension to these Delegates by now—they were case-hardened. After nearly a decade of preparation and testing, of astonishing success at sidestepping the pressure and authority of the Vatican, and of nearly constant defiance of the papal will by individual Jesuits, by entire Provinces, and by the Father General himself, the Delegates who gathered in Rome would not be easily turned aside now. Understandably, then, December 2 was a day shot through with deeply felt emotions.

The official day began bright and early, when the Delegates gathered in the auditorium of the Gesù to hear Father General Pedro Arrupe give his opening address. One Delegate to GC32 later surmised that neither Arrupe nor those who collaborated with him in preparing his address had any idea of what they were really about to accomplish. Given the fact that Arrupe and his advisers had edited reams of material and had held endless discussions precisely to distill the spirit and direction of GC32 into a single speech, it is hard to know what to make of such an assessment, other than a desire to remove blame from Arrupe's shoulders by cloaking him instead with an intellectual and spiritual blindness.

In any case, whatever his understanding, Arrupe's mood was as euphoric and as confident as that of the Delegates who heard him. His speech expressed both his enthusiasm and his expectation of great things ahead for the Society.

Of the troubles and dissensions of the past eight years, Arrupe said nothing consequential or striking. He did not in any way address the continuing and ever mounting dissatisfaction of Pope Paul VI, or the open rebellion of Jesuits against papal direction, or the increasing tendency of the Society to regard itself as *sui juris* and independent of papal authority—as capable of and justified in proceeding on its own way even in the gravest of Church problems.

Rather, the Father General reviewed the eight-year work of preparation for this Congregation. He described the mentality of his Jesuits as he had learned it from his travels, from the sociological and psychological studies, from the planning reports, and from the *postulata* that had come in to Rome from the Provinces and from individual Jesuits. He outlined the preeminent topics on the basis of which the Society must now decide its future—topics such as structures and grades, formation and training, and overall mission. He pointed out that they could all approach their work in serene trust in the Lord. And, as if Paul VI had never made any objection, Arrupe defined the goal of that work to be "the radical transformation of the world."

Arrupe made clear that by "transformation" he did not mean instilling prayer habits in people, or evangelization by preaching Christ crucified, or promoting devotion for the Sacraments, for the Sacred Heart of Jesus, for the Holy Father as Christ's Vicar, or for the Church. He was speaking of what he called "Ignatian radical-ism," which he defined as a total Jesuit dedication to "social and political justice as a sign of the credibility of the Society's Chris-tian faith."

That need to effect the "radical transformation of the world," in other words, was basic to the determination by GC32 of what kind of service the Society should offer to the Church at the present time. And so it was that in his "keynote address," so to say, Arrupe claimed for his Society a place under the sun in competition with socialists, conservatives, liberals, capitalists, social-gospelers, and all those engaged in building the City of Man.

The ebullient mood of the Delegates and their Roman Superiors found visible expression when they all attended a communal Mass that same evening, along with some five hundred or so other Jesu-its who were in Rome either as residents or for training or other work. The setting for this moment of glory was the large and resplendent Church of the Gesù, built on the very site of the ear-lier chapel—Santa Maria della Strada, it was called—where Igna-tius had celebrated Mass during his years as the first Father General.

The Church of the Gesù was built only after Ignatius had died. It was begun by Giacomo da Vignola, and was completed by Gia-como della Porta, to be a mirror of the very reason and purpose of the Society itself: a showcase for the triumph of the name of Jesus. Everything in the interior of that structure was designed as one more element in the expression of the faith and joy, the unalloyed happiness and supernal satisfaction of the Romanist spirit that animated Ignatius and his companions, and those who had come after. Its sumptuous baroque style was so distinctive that it was adopted by many of the Society's churches and became known as the Jesuit style.

The gracious interior is everywhere decorated with Baciccio frescoes and Raggi stuccoes, with colored marbles and bronzes, with sculptures and gilding. The walls of the upper story are flanked by spirals and scrolls and volutes. In the transept to the left of the main altar, beneath a huge globe of lapis lazuli symbolic of the earth, and surrounded by columns also fashioned of precious lapis, stands the altar-tomb of Ignatius of Loyola. Beneath the altar, Iñigo's remains are contained in a gilded bronze urn. Above the altar stands a silver-plated statue of Ignatius, its eyes seeming to gaze in imitation of the arrow-straight purity with which Loyola had always followed his objective. The massive, solid silver origi-nal on which the present statue is modeled was ordered melted

down by Pope Pius VI to pay the indemnities levied on the papacy
by Napoleon in 1797.

In the transept to the right of the main altar, is the altar of St.
Francis Xavier, companion of Ignatius in the Church of the Gesù,
as he had been in life to the Jesuit founder.

Vaulting high overhead, above the main altar and the sanctuary,
the glory of the arched ceiling surpasses all of the other glories of
the Church of the Gesù. For there the vast Baciccio fresco *Triumph
of the Name of Jesus* bathes everything beneath it in the sensuous
shade and light of its faces and its gestures, the bravura of exulta-
tion and ecstasy engulfing its figures. This is the fresco in which
Keats said he could hear the sound of "otherworld music."

On that December evening of 1974, it was not "otherworld
music" that filled the Church of the Gesù, but the sounds of a
meeting hall, a celebration in a properly democratic amalgam of
languages and styles. Nor was it the arrow-straight purity of Ignatian purpose that Pedro Arrupe celebrated in his enthusiastic homily. The Father General did of course invoke the authenticity of
the Jesuit mission as Ignatius of Loyola had conceived it and Francis Xavier, "Apostle of the Indies," had implemented it. But the
vision now was to be the vision of the renovated Society.

The moment was one of genuine feeling for all, and perhaps no
better setting could have been chosen for the irony pictured at this
particular crossroads in the long, chequered career of Iñigo de Loyola's Company. It was not that the blue jeans worn by the Italian
Jesuit novices present seemed inappropriate to the rich surroundings; the Gesù has certainly seen its share of patched and threadbare cassocks. It was more that the jeans were not a modern
equivalent of such cassocks—not a sign of holy poverty—but the
social badge of conformity to a new generation in the world at
large. And it was not that the mentality of many Jesuits present
was repelled by the sumptuousness and the religious sensuality of
the Church. It was rather that those Delegates, as a body of men,
were already miles apart from the faith that had made joy and
satisfaction in this baroque creation possible.

That evening, the new Society already conceived and cradled in
the minds and intentions of the Delegates was brought the nearest
it would come to the old Society as expressed in the art of the
Gesù, and in the *Triumph of the Name of Jesus,* the visible symbols of the overall goal of Ignatius. That goal was the reason the
Company bore its name. By that night, however, those gathered
beneath Baciccio's fresco had long since translated the Jesuit goal
into terms far removed from Loyola's.

There were not men from whose lips would come impassioned pleas for the Society of Jesus to seek the triumph of that name. These were men whose passion—whose anger, indignation, pleading, and insistence—had been aroused for goals already denounced by papal authority as irreconcilable with true Jesuitism.

In retrospect, that evening was the high point of Pedro Arrupe's Generalate. And it was perhaps the last time when an unalloyed enthusiasm for their whole Jesuit enterprise would animate the Society's members. When the brilliant lights went out in that ancient Church of the Gesù, when the perfume of the blue incense smoke had been dissipated and the sacred music was stilled, the focus turned to the nearby auditorium, and to the real work of GC32.

That Paul VI was aware of the state of mind of Arrupe and his colleagues is certain. Between 1966 and 1974 he had made his mind very plain to the Jesuit General. He was aware of the "groundswell," as the Jesuits called it, for autonomy and for joining with the "people of God" who were already hard at work building the "new world."

The Pontiff was convinced he knew where that "groundswell" was heading. Paul could see what path the Society would follow if the grades system were changed so that the monarchic and priestly character of the Order were no longer salient or essential. And he could see what its mission would become if the Society, stripped of its priestly essence, turned to what was being called sociopolitical justice. Not too far down that road, there might be at least as many nonpriests as priests in the Society; certainly the Order would no longer be professionally bound to devote itself to spiritual and religious objectives. That was what Paul had warned against as early as 1966, when he had referred so startlingly to "sinister and distorted ideas"—a phrase Arrupe professed to newsmen he could not understand. Now, the Pope had only to look at the way Jesuits everywhere—in Europe, the Americas, and the Third World—were behaving, to be convinced that his analysis was justified.

The Pontiff's consistent thinking about the Society was no secret. His letters to Arrupe of March 26, 1970, February 15, 1973, and September 13, 1973, had been made public; but they were only three out of a much more voluminous correspondence between the Pope and the Jesuit General. Arrupe and his close collaborators knew well how near to disaster they had come at Paul's hands.

Paul VI chose to make his mind clear once again, and this time to the full gathering of all the Delegates. Indeed, one of the reasons he had allowed GC32 to convene at all was precisely so that he could make his mind plain to the worldwide Jesuit leadership.

The occasion was the customary papal address at the beginning of GC32. The date was December 3, the second day of the Congregation. In spite of the complexity of formal papal language and of Paul's inability to call a spade a spade, the Pope was remarkably clear.

This was an hour of destiny for the Society, Paul said; a time of special seriousness. He as Pope was the highest Superior of the Society. He had already indicated clearly by written word what he found wrong or dangerous in the tendencies of the Society: the desire to tamper with the grades system, doctrinal deviations, disciplinary infractions.

There was no mystery, Paul observed, about where the Jesuits had come from. They had been molded by the hand of Ignatius and the will of the papacy as a special militia at the disposal of every Pope on the Throne of Peter. Similarly, everyone knew who the Jesuits were: "Members of an Order that is religious, apostolic, priestly, and united with the Roman Pontiff by a special bond of love and service in the manner described in the *Formula of the Institute.*"

Having reminded them in so many words of their origins and purpose, Paul went on to recognize that the Jesuits nevertheless were affected by a crisis of identity. How faithful were they, he asked, to the teaching authority of the Church? What sort of fidelity did they exercise in the spiritual life? Where were they going as they now were? They must modernize, he acknowledged; but had they forgotten the Ignatian vow to work under the Roman Pontiff?

As if to remind these democratic-minded Delegates that there were Jesuits who did not agree with the way the leadership was taking the Society, Paul drew their attention to the continual complaints he received about the Society. He spoke of his obligation to watch over the Society in its General Congregation. He must not listen, Paul said, merely to some (who desire radical changes) and neglect others of the Society who were distraught and worried that in the name of apostolic necessity the very essence of the Ignatian Institute was being abandoned. "One must not call apostolic necessity what would be nothing else but spiritual decadence."

That heaviest of papal reproaches was followed by Paul's recommendation to the Delegates: "Study and restate the essentials of the Jesuit vocation in such a way that *all* your confreres will be able to recognize themselves, to strengthen their commitment, to rediscover their identity. . . ."

Paul concluded by sending the Delegates to their labors at the Congregation with his blessing; and with his assurance that he would be watching intently every step they took.

The Delegates' reaction to Paul's address, and perhaps even their priorities for GC32, might have been somewhat mitigated had Arrupe advised his Jesuits worldwide in anything like a timely manner of Paul's clear message, so often repeated during the years from 1966 to 1974, that the Society must not in any way touch the Ignatian system of grades. Arrupe had not done so, however; nor had he enjoined them under obedience anywhere along the road to GC32 to keep hands off the grades system. One result was that by the time the Delegates sat and listened to Paul's exhortations on December 3, fifty-four out of their eighty-five Provincial Congregations had already sent in no fewer than sixty-five separate *postulata* dealing precisely with that forbidden topic—and forty-five actually favored abolition of grades altogether.

To say the least, the Delegates' reaction to Paul's speech could only be negative. And so it was. In their view, the Pope's call to redefine their Order once more along religious and apostolic lines linked as closely as ever to the Roman Pontiff was "orthodox," "traditional," and "conservative." Their description of themselves, meanwhile, was "unorthodox," "new," and "challenging."

What makes Father Arrupe's behavior particularly blatant in this matter of his failure to communicate the expressed will of the Holy Father to his Society, is that Arrupe went to great lengths in his attempt to continue the subterfuge into the life of GC32. On December 3, the same day that Paul addressed the Delegates in person, he also sent a letter by his Cardinal Secretary of State, Jean Villot, in which he repeated yet again that no proposed change in the grades system would be acceptable to the Holy See. This was an admonition and warning of the highest order. Arrupe decided not to share even that letter with the General Congregation for fully two weeks. By the time he did so, it was already December 16, discussions among the Delegates were well underway on the subject, and Arrupe no longer had to be concerned about arresting the "groundswell."

Based on Arrupe's own long silence with the Jesuits on this subject of grades, and on his handling of Paul's December 3 letter, and based, too, on an examination of the documents relevant to GC32 and the continual friction between Paul VI and Arrupe from 1964 onward, there can be little doubt that the first of the two great and radical priorities set by Father General Arrupe for this Congregation was precisely to transform the hierarchical structure of the Society. Paul's address had been accurate in every detail. For it was not just transformation Arrupe was after, but the removal of the system of grades designed by Ignatius and approved by Popes, and its replacement by a democratic—and, if at all possible, a less priestly—system.

Unless that first major priority could be achieved, Arrupe's fear and that of his close colleagues was that the second priority—the concentration of the full energies of the Society on its new mission of collaboration in the "liberation" of peoples from sociopolitical injustice and oppression—might also go aglimmering. In fact, everything else to be discussed and decided at GC32 would be conditioned by what could be achieved in the fight with the papacy over grades and classes—over hierarchy and authority in the Society.

The "groundswell" feeling among the Delegates had become stronger than ever that the division of Jesuits into some priests who took the special Fourth Vow of Obedience, and some priests who did not do so, and some who were still Scholastics—young men in training—was a system incompatible with modern feelings about equality and democracy. It was downright uncomfortable. Ignatius had been an aristocrat, after all; and his age was the age of kings and princes and all that hierarchic inequality. The Second Vatican Council had quite rightly emphasized a feeling that had been underground among Jesuits and others for a long time anyway, a feeling that somehow priesthood wasn't all that was claimed for it. Every Christian, it was argued, was priestly—had a share in the priesthood of Christ. If that sort of reasoning meant a 180-degree turn in the Catholic doctrine of priesthood, then so be it; many had taken that turn without difficulty.

Once reasoning got that far into heresy, it was only a short hop to the conclusion that priesthood had no meaning specific to itself at all. And if that was so, why single some people out as "priests" and leave others aside on a lower grade, as it were, in this matter of a special vow?

As with every heresy, the subject did not end with itself. The question of grades and hierarchy obviously had to involve Religious Obedience. The idea of one Superior commanding the rank and file, for all the world like a king commanding his subjects, was simply embarrassing; it was no longer in vogue. Hadn't the Jesuits themselves already shown what could be achieved out in the Provinces by community dialogue? And never mind the Provinces;

hadn't GC31 already set a powerful precedent when it provided even the Father General himself with a "Council" of four elected Assistants whose advice and consent was needed for command decisions? No doubt about it, autonomy was out, and Obedience with it.

Now, it only remained to convince Pope Paul VI on the matter.

The first attempt to deal with the papal prohibition—once GC32 was finally told about it—was discreet. On December 17, a day after the most recent papal letter was revealed, Father General Arrupe and two Delegates asked for a confidential and unofficial meeting with Cardinal Secretary of State Jean Villot, through whom the Pope's December 3 letter had been sent them.

Once in the cardinal's office, Villot's unofficial visitors unofficially told him that, Pope or no Pope, the Delegates in the Congregation over at the Gesù were going to discuss the grades. They couldn't be stopped. Now, would it not be perfectly feasible for the Congregation simply to apprise the Pope later of those discussions? Of course, the Congregation would obey the Pope absolutely. But was it wise to forbid discussion of the subject as the Pope had done? The Pope did not know what the Congregation thought on the subject; shouldn't he, in all wisdom? Besides, forbidding discussion was really to nullify the Congregation right from the start. That might provoke more trouble than the Pope had had up to now with the Jesuits. Wouldn't it be better, then, for the Congregation to move ahead on the proposition of granting the Fourth Vow to all Jesuits, and then give the Pope its reasons?

All in all, there was not one argument or threat that was neglected in that carrot and stick approach to Villot. But the fact was that the Cardinal Secretary himself did not care one way or the other about the matter at hand. He did have his own rear to guard, however; and he had no fear of Arrupe.

Yes, Villot answered as *romanità* required, he would unofficially and confidentially report this unofficial, confidential visit to the Pope. As the Jesuit Superiors had asked, neither their Congregation itself nor the outside world would know anything about it. But, Villot said as well, the Holy Father's mind was well made up and clear.

Some days before Christmas, Arrupe received a call from Villot asking him to come across St. Peter's Square to the cardinal's office, or to send someone as his spokesman.

Arrupe sent someone.

The interview between the Jesuit spokesman and the Secretary of State was bizarre. There was a note waiting on the cardinal's desk when the spokesman entered Villot's office. The Jesuit was asked to read it. It said that the Holy Father wished no change in the matter of grades. The Jesuit asked if the Congregation could discuss changing the Society's legislation about grades. Apparently there was a fine difference in his mind between allowing the Delegates to discuss changes in legislation with a view to making those changes, and allowing the Delegates actually to change the legislation. Perhaps, like teenagers on Daddy's sofa, it was all a matter of self-control.

If the Pope had made up his mind—and he had—Villot, speaking unofficially, could not agree that the Jesuit's fine line of difference mattered a whit. Officially, he refused to comment at all about the note lying on his desk like a radioactive hot potato. It was agreed again between Villot and the Jesuit spokesman—at the spokesman's request—to keep this second meeting confidential.

If this had been any world except Rome, or if the Father General had been any man except Pedro Arrupe, the jig might have been considered up. But Arrupe seemed to feel he had maneuvered rather well—had even gained a fraction of an inch, perhaps. The Pope had been put on notice that the powerful "groundswell" in the General Congregation was bucking the papal prohibition, and also that, if the prohibition was maintained absolutely, there could be trouble that would be hard to contain. Also, Arrupe could say that one way or another he had kept the Pope informed. He was, after all, only the servant of the highest ranking Superior in the Society, which for Arrupe (Ignatius's rules and Paul's speech of December 3 aside) was not the Pope but the General Congregation. That the Congregation's mission was obedience to the Holy Father was extraneous to the defense. The point was that Arrupe had successfully conveyed the idea that he was sitting on a boiling cauldron and doing his best to keep the lid on.

That feeling of urgency was conveyed as much by the hush-hush, let's-keep-it-confidential tone of those two meetings with Villot as by anything that was said on either side. Judging from what some Delegates said after GC32 was over, however, it would seem that both of those conversations were an open secret for many of the Delegates. Arrupe was not so much sitting on the cauldron as swimming in it.

Having gained a fraction or two of an inch, Arrupe was not a man to retreat. The next step in dealing with the bothersome papal prohibition on Jesuit priority number one was to decide that the papal prohibition was not very clear. Not clear at all, in fact, on a closer look. Was the Holy Father talking about a mere *discussion*

of the grades, or about the actual *extension* to all Jesuits of the
special Fourth Vow? Did he mean to rule out all discussion? Or
just discussions of theory with a view to change? What discussions
of theory?

Well, clarification of difficult problems had always been the
meat of the Society, had it not? Hastily, therefore, and in yet another blatant breach of Paul VI's manifest will, a special commission of the Congregation was set up, which just as hastily
proceeded to draw up a fifty-four-page report outlining every possible change in the system of grades and hierarchy, thereby "clarifying" what the Pope might possibly have meant to prohibit.

While the Delegates were busy absorbing the report, the commission was already preparing the final version, a digest of the
fifty-four pages. Open debate took place in a plenary session on
January 21 and 22 of 1975.

Case-hardened as they were, the Delegates seemed untroubled
about carrying on all this feverish activity over a subject already
decided by the Pope. Quietly determined to wear down papal resistance, the Congregation justified itself by saying that the matter
was merely being *discussed*, not *decided*; and therefore not
changed. Literally, therefore, they were obeying the Holy Father's
order to change nothing.

Of course, it wouldn't hurt anything to take a series of straw
votes on the matter of grades. A regular vote would have violated
the Pope's prohibition, but straw votes would merely be unofficial
"indications" of sentiment—and they would have the effect of
heightening the sense of urgency still more.

That much they certainly did. With ten abstentions, the straw
votes indicated by a two-thirds majority that the Congregation felt
it should deal with the question of grades, that the Fourth Vow
should be extended to all Jesuits, that the Society should take this
course despite Paul VI's prohibition, and that a delegation should
be sent by the General Congregation to the Holy Father to inform
His Holiness of the Delegates' *decisions*. According to almost
three-quarters of the Delegates, the charade of extending the
Fourth Vow to all Jesuits should itself be abandoned, and the Society's grades should simply be abolished altogether.

The end of the unofficial voting on January 22 brought with it a
renewed feeling of euphoria; straw vote or no, and in the teeth of
endlessly repeated papal wishes and commands, the mind and decisions of the Congregation were put on record as official. GC32
was getting places at last.

The final step in this remarkable process was one of notable simplicity or unconquerable arrogance, depending on one's reading. In any case, the Congregation sent all this material to Pope Paul on that very same day, January 22.

On January 23, Paul's answer came back like a boomerang. There could be no doubt at all, the Pope said, about what he wanted. He had made it abundantly clear in writing and by word of mouth, directly and indirectly, personally and through third parties, recently and in past times, in Latin, in French, and in Italian: There was to be no change in the grades system. Arrupe's duty, in which he had failed, had been to stop the Congregation from ever undertaking consideration of the grades system. Why had the Pope's wishes been violated?

The full-floor discussion of Pope Paul's reply to the Congregation was one of the hottest and most frank of all the many debates of GC32. And it demonstrated amply that Arrupe could, when it suited him, lash his Jesuits into line. The Delegates blamed the Pope for "not making his intent clear"; they blamed him as well for "the confidentiality of meetings that concerned the Congregation intimately." They blamed him in fact for everything.

Unwilling to see the "groundswell" dissipate itself into ineffective handwringing over who was to blame for their current crisis with Pope Paul, Father General Arrupe weighed in with his own tongue-lashings. But this time he wasn't after the Pontiff; instead, he berated the "lack of fidelity" in certain Jesuits who "reserve to themselves the right to accept or reject what the Society . . . has decided to decree. . . ." That wasn't the half of it, Arrupe insisted. "It will be impossible to allow happen again what happened in recent years. . . . Some [Jesuits] regarded GC31 as something of a deviation from the spirit of St. Ignatius . . . publicly . . . and in anonymous letters. . . . [If this were to happen] this would render the government of the Society impossible. . . ."

It is to be noted that, as heated as these exchanges were, neither Arrupe nor any Delegate pointed out in clear terms that the primary fault lay with Arrupe and his Assistants and the managers of the General Congregation for their violations of the Pope's clear will—violations by obfuscation, by artificial confidentiality, by evasiveness and equivocation, by delaying tactics—in sum, by every means that seemed useful.

At the end of all the acrimony, Arrupe was satisfied that it had all been worth the trouble. At the close of a tense session of the Congregation, he explained gently and cleverly to the Delegates that they now had a very nearly legitimate excuse for exposing to the Holy Father their reasons for desiring a change in the grades system! The Holy Father had asked why his wish had been violated. They would answer another question—why they wanted to alter the grades system—as though that had been the question the Pope had asked.

If there were some who smiled at that little triumph of classic "Jesuitry," their mirth was short-lived.

About a week later, GC32 sent Paul VI a full account of its debates about the grades system. Within two weeks, Paul's answer came back that there could be no change in the grades system. Furthermore, once GC32 was over and its Decrees and other documents were completed, the Holy Father wanted all such papers for examination before they were made official and promulgated to the Society.

Paul seemed to be tightening the screws; for by ordering GC32 to submit its documents for papal review and approval, the Pope had rescinded an ancient privilege of the Society; for a very long time, no Jesuit Congregation had been required to have its documents pass Vatican muster.

Participants in GC32 reported that the Delegates were "reeling" in consternation and were "crestfallen" at the contents of Paul's latest letter. Not so Arrupe. Never meek, he decided to take his boldest step to date. Confident that in a person-to-person encounter he could either best Paul or win him over, or at least mitigate the Pope's anger and win back that precious exemption from scrutiny, Arrupe asked for an interview with the Holy Father.

That the interview took place at all is not widely known. That it was in the nature of a personal rehearsal by Pope and General for the open warfare that was shaping up as unavoidable between the papacy and the "new" Society of Jesus has become clear in hindsight.

Arrupe arrived for the papal interview in the company of his most trusted General Assistant, Vincent O'Keefe. O'Keefe, however, was left at the door of the meeting place.

Inside, Arrupe found not only the Pope, but Paul's own trusted aide, the Society's nemesis in the Vatican, Monsignore Giovanni Benelli. Without a doubt, Benelli still smarted from the disrespectful and downright insulting attacks that had been aired against him in 1973 by Peter Hebblethwaite, S.J., in the London Observer, and by Arrupe's pointed refusal to do anything effective to blunt even the most personal epithets Hebblethwaite had hurled at him.

In Paul's mind and in Benelli's, the point by now was stark in its very simplicity. Pedro Arrupe would have to go; he would have to step down from the Generalate of the Society. Ill health—or whatever—could be alleged. Furthermore, GC32 would have to be recessed, and its recall put off *sine die.*

This discussion rapidly became acerbic. Benelli's was the only loud voice—but that was his usual manner when on his mettle. Nevertheless, the interview centered quickly on two things: Paul's request and Benelli's insistence that Arrupe clear out for the sake of the Jesuits and for the good of the Church, and Arrupe's impassioned but quick-witted resistance. It was Arrupe's most arduous hour since his tortuous interrogation thirty years before by Japan's notorious KEMPEI-TAI.

The Pope's reasons were laid out in painful detail: Arrupe's gross mismanagement and ill-governing of the Society of Jesus; his blatant disobedience in regard to the manifest and repeated orders of His Holiness that GC32 was not to touch the question of grades in the Society; his sustained tolerance—at the very least, tolerance —of heresy, antipapal sentiment, and morally wrong as well as morally unsound doctrine in the Society at large.

The storm against Arrupe did not come solely from Paul VI. The General's leadership since 1965 had been scored by many, even as his leadership of GC32 now was harshly criticized by some of the Delegates themselves.

Paul could not understand Arrupe's blatant disobedience except as disobedience. There was no way Arrupe could find a way to justify himself except to plead guilty by reason of his piety toward the Society as embodied in the General Congregation.

But Benelli was having no more of such double-talk. Arrupe had to go.

Arrupe's answer: He was appointed constitutionally and juridically by the General Congregation. The Congregation was the only one, constitutionally speaking, that should remove him. For just cause.

Benelli's argument: There was ample and just cause—Jesuit abandonment under Arrupe of the papal position on contraception, as demonstrated in the Society's nearly wholesale attack on the officially promulgated *Humanae Vitae;* abandonment, too, of the papal position on the heresy of Modernism. Need Benelli go on?

Arrupe's counter: He could produce a sheaf—even a whole file —of his personal letters to all Jesuits, endorsing and vindicating these Catholic and papal positions.

Benelli's conclusion: The Holy Father still felt that for the good of the Church and the well-being of the Society, his Reverence Father Arrupe had to go.

There are those who are of the opinion that Arrupe was at last reaching the point of caving in; that in his mounting desperation he simply flung out every argument, no matter how contemptible. If go he must, Arrupe said, then he would; Jesuits would always be the first to obey. But he should still, properly speaking, be told to go by the General Congregation, if everything was to be legal and above board. All Jesuits entered the Society in full knowledge of the Ignatian *Constitutions*. If he was dismissed here and now, and in a way incompatible with the *Constitutions*, how could His Excellency Monsignore Benelli know what Jesuits would say? His Excellency talked of the good of the Church and the well-being of the Society. How would His Excellency like to see a Karl Rahner, S.J., or a Henri de Lubac, S.J.—among other prestigious men whose names carried enormous weight—repudiate Arrupe's firing by the Holy Father, and their own allegiance to the Society? Wouldn't such men conclude that if the Holy See—the ultimate guarantee of all due order and constitutional right—acted in a way incompatible with the *Constitutions*, then Jesuits could do the very same? If the *Constitutions* did not matter to the Holy See, why should they matter to the Society? And how would that serve the good of the Church or the good of the Order?

During the course of what obviously if needlessly became a ragtag argument, there was an unforeseen interruption; the Pope's attention was urgently required in another matter. Arrupe was asked to wait outside.

When the General joined his Assistant for the brief reprieve, his weariness was evident. What he needed was a good jolt of courage and reinforcement. And that is precisely what his General Assistant provided: How could Arrupe forget the seven long years of preparation they had all put in for GC32? How could he forget the enthusiasm of the two sessions of GC31? How could he abandon his Jesuit brethren by caving in to the animosity of Giovanni Benelli, or of Jean Villot, whose hand was probably somewhere in all this? What would become of the multiple programs already begun by Arrupe and his men so that the Church might be helped to turn the corner and start walking earnestly in pace with modern man?

Besides all that, Arrupe was reminded, this very question of the *Constitutions* was paramount. Did Paul and Benelli realize even in a dim way what effect Arrupe's dismissal and the delay or cancellation of GC32 would have on other major Religious Orders? On Dominicans, Franciscans, Carmelites, Benedictines? Like the Society itself, all of them were in crisis, all were following in the same path as the Jesuits, all were facing into Church "renewal" in the same way. Since 1965, over 7500 men had abandoned the priesthood. Did Paul and Benelli realize that three times that number would up-and-out if the Pope persisted? Why, the hullabaloo over *Humanae Vitae* would seem like a chorus of sparrows compared to the howling cacophony that would fall on the Holy See if the Pope removed Arrupe.

If all of that was not enough to galvanize Pedro Arrupe, there was, finally, the ultimate Jesuit argument. Ignatius had promised his men persecution and misunderstanding from enemies and friends. Hadn't the Society been correct in its various stances in the past? And yet was it not condemned by the Holy See? And had the Holy See not—after it was too late—acknowledged its mistake? Father Ricci himself, the last General of the old Society, had said as much as he lay dying in the papal prison of Castel Sant' Angelo.

Realistically, and speaking of death, Pope Paul himself had not all that amount of mortal time left to him. Arrupe had to hold on; that was what this was all about. All the signs were that the next Pope would correspond more faithfully to the new trend of the Church.

By the time the Holy Father called Arrupe in for the second session of the interview, the General was restored to his strength. His purpose could no longer be to sidestep papal review of GC32's documents; he was fighting for his survival. But that he did very well.

Humbly, Arrupe proposed a compromise. Absolutely speaking, His Holiness could remove Arrupe from office, thus suspending the *Constitutions* temporarily. Arrupe would not fight this solution; he would obey with Jesuit alacrity. Presumably, the next Jesuit General would be elected juridically according to the *Constitutions*. But Arrupe could not violate his conscience as Jesuit and as Father General. In other words, Arrupe would not obey; he would not resign.

Paul and Benelli saw the traps Arrupe was setting at their feet; he was gambling that they would not want to step into them. Both of these men had themselves gone far down the road in fomenting the idea of the Church as "the People of God." Benelli had spoken arrogantly to traditional-minded Catholics about their "old" idea of the Church compared to the "new" idea of the Church. "We have a new ecclesiology," he had told them. Paul himself had gone down the same road with more or less the same jaunty fecklessness: "Ah!" he had remarked when a conservative bishop died in 1967, "he never understood our new way for the Church."

For Paul now to act by absolute fiat—for him to act as a monarch, to put it plainly—would raise just the storm Arrupe's Assistant had described in the waiting room moments before. Religious Orders, bishops, diocesan priests, already "liberated" nuns, and laity would all be caught up in a new and ferocious fire storm of reproach and revolt against Paul and the papacy.

Even if Arrupe could suppose—he could not, but his analysis was surely thorough in so capital a gamble—that Paul would take the chance of provoking a storm in the Church by removing him as Father General, what then? If Paul allowed the Jesuits to assemble in General Congregation, as the *Constitutions* laid down, to elect a new General, was there any surety they would not come up with someone from Arrupe's "leadership group"? Somebody even more unacceptable? Or even with Arrupe himself, elected once again in triumph by a recalcitrant Congregation?

Arrupe may or may not have been aware that Paul had his own choice for General waiting in the wings. But Paul knew well enough that one word as to that candidate's identity and, as things stood, the man would not get one vote, and would probably end his days living out of a suitcase on a permanently roving mission to the Bushmen of the Kalahari Desert.

Arrupe won his desperate, end-game gamble. Paul and Benelli backed off from those traps. The rehearsal for open warfare moved toward a temporary compromise. Arrupe would see to it, the awkward agreement stated, that His Holiness's will was carried out. As to the dissatisfaction in the Society with his leadership, Arrupe would, by way of test, take the unprecedented step of asking GC32 to adjudicate his leadership.

When Arrupe returned to the bosom of the General Congregation, he did explain to the Delegates some of what had happened across the way in the Apostolic Palace; he made certain they understood how much the Holy Father loved them all and depended on them, and how desirous the Pontiff was to see their Father General any time he wanted or needed to consult the Holy Father. And GC32 did in fact become the first General Congregation to confirm a Father General in his post.

And so GC32's huge effort to change that all-important "substantial" of the Society—the Ignatian grades system with all its implications for priesthood, for obedience, and for the hierarchic Church—was finally broken on the obstinate will of Pope Paul VI.

Incredibly enough, however, even after all the travail and pain, there was still more than a whimper of insubordination left in GC32 on the subject of grades in the Society. Decree #18 took its own place in the official Acts of the Congregation; and though it was puny by comparison with the original intent of Arrupe and the Delegates, the hope was that GC32 could yet attain its aim by "peaceful" and "legal" means, by changing the question of grades from a hot issue to a meaningless one. Accordingly, Decree #18 stressed "the unity of vocations" in the Society. "Unity of vocations" was a sort of coded language; it meant that grades did not matter all that much: To create something like a general "Jesuit vocation," would be to place all Jesuits on an equal footing. Indeed, the Decree asked Jesuits to ensure that the grades "not be a source of division." This, in spite of the fact that Ignatius had intended divisions to exist, and that he also admonished his followers not to make the divisions between classes into a source of divisiveness. GC32 somehow seemed to get that message of Loyola backward. To avoid "divisions," the non-Professed—those Jesuits without the Fourth Vow—should be helped to participate in "the life and apostolic activity of the Society"; and the norms according to which priests were admitted to Profession of the Fourth Vow (norms already "better adapted" by GC31, it was stated) should "be put into practice."

In plain language, the norms for attaining the coveted Profession of the Fourth Vow would be lowered so that over time all priests in the Society would, it was hoped, become eligible for the Fourth Vow. If the Decree were actually applied, the Ignatian distinction of grades would become increasingly diluted. Eventually, a similarly "peaceful" and "legal" way might be found to bring Scholastics and Lay Brothers to the same level in the Society with priests. Decree #18 put grades at least on a footpath, if not the desired highway, toward oblivion.

As engulfing and strife-torn as the priority issue of grades was for GC32, it did not take up all of the Delegates' attention. And it did not deflect the Congregation's purpose concerning the companion priority issue to grades: the question of the mission of the Society of Jesus in the modern world. In a certain sense, in fact, one can argue that the brouhaha over the grades question enabled GC32 to get by unscathed with its new definition and understanding of the Society.

"Mission," in this sense, was used to express the fundamental reason for the society's existence, much as it is said the mission of the U.S. Marine Corps, for example, is to fight, or that of the U.S. Supreme Court is to judge.

Real innovation was at work here, the more so as nothing less than the definition of the new "primitive charism" of the Society now rested fully on GC32's successful handling of the question of the Jesuit mission in the modern world. And unlike grades, this matter of mission was handled skillfully from the outset.

Obviously—as Paul VI had emphasized in his December 3 address to the Delegates—the Society was supposed to be an "apostolic" body; that is, it was to be composed of latter-day apostles of the Church engaged in ministries befitting such apostles.

Near the start of GC32, a task force of Delegates picked out eight general topics—all priorities of some rank—to be considered by the Congregation. Two of these priority topics were at the core of the overall priority of the Society's new mission:

What criteria should be used in choosing suitably apostolic ministries?

How to promote sociopolitical justice among men today?

It was not hard to see that these priority questions should be linked, and that the answer to the second could essentially become the criterion for the first. Justice would become the criterion for deciding which ministries were suitably apostolic. If, for a particular locale, baptizing newborn babies or hearing confessions did not help found a labor union or overthrow an unjust government, then you shouldn't baptize or hear confessions. For justice meant social justice; it meant political liberation; and it meant economic independence. There was no flavor here of Biblical "justice"—of being justified by God's grace and in God's eyes, of helping people by the Sacraments and by preaching to obtain such inner divine grace.

The official linkage of these two priorities was accomplished in a plenary session of the Delegates, where Arrupe and the Congregation's Council insisted on the creation of a Priority of Priorities, comprised precisely of those two questions: the criteria for apostolic ministries, and the promotion of justice. To satisfy Paul VI's commission to the Jesuits that they combat atheism, this task was woven into the Priority of Priorities. The proposal passed immediately.

The task then became one of the definition and outline of this new Priority of Priorities; and no fewer than four Decrees were devoted to the exhaustive treatment of the matter.

Together, under the general title *The Society's Response to the Challenges of Our Age,* those four decrees make up the whole first section of the final and official Decrees of GC32. These are the keystone Decrees, then, and upon them rest the valid interpretation of all the others. Indeed, the remaining twelve Decrees of the Congregation were tailored to suit the Priority of Priorities—the new concept of the Jesuits' "primitive charism."

There was little question of Ignatian leadership or inspiration at work in these four key Decrees, much less any question of what the Church, in the authority of its papacy, demanded. True to the overall title of this first part of GC32's official Decrees, the Congregation sought to redefine the Society of Jesus in terms of what it thought the age demanded. It is accurate to describe the Delegates as beside themselves in the matter of "promoting justice." Indeed, it is difficult in mere words to convey the almost messianic and "inspired" attitude of the Delegates in regard to this new focus.

The basic premise for the most important thrust of the Decrees is tucked neatly into a single phrase in the opening paragraphs.

"What is it to be a Jesuit?" the text asks; and then quickly supplies the answer: "It is to engage under the standard of the Cross, in the crucial struggle of our time: the struggle for faith and that struggle for justice which it [faith] includes."

That last phrase, that gratuitous and illogical addition, is the necessary link with the desired conclusion: The Society "chooses participation in this struggle as the focus that identifies in our time what Jesuits are and do."

Of the four Decrees that follow, the capital one—the one that finally and fully gives voice to the new "primitive charism"—is Decree #4, entitled "Our Mission Today: The Service of Faith and the Promotion of Justice." In the eighty-one paragraphs of Decree #4, the authors stitched together two distinct elements for a very definite purpose.

The first element is the Congregation's determination to decree into living vigor both a corporate and an individual Jesuit obligation to work for the restructuring of the sociopolitical systems of our modern world.

The second element is the attempt to include some indication of the traditional spirituality and religious ideology of Jesuits. Normally, it is this basic, theological element that would be the dominant one; no Decree of any Congregation can pass muster unless it displays the true marks of the Society's classic spirituality and ideology. Now, however, this traditional dimension is pro forma; it is tacked to the first as an academic requirement, as an exercise in protocol—as a "safe-pass," in essence, to guarantee the acceptance of the whole document.

When these two elements are disentangled from one another, the picture that emerges in Decree #4 is geometrically clear. The Society commits itself to a corporate and personal solidarity with the victims of "social injustice" and "political enslavement"—

terms which are given a technical meaning within the language of
the Decree.

The Decree recognizes that social injustice and political enslavement are all around us. "Millions suffer from poverty and
hunger, from the unjust distribution of wealth and resources, and
from the consequences of racial, social and political discrimina-
tion." The difficulty for Jesuits up to this time had been, as the
Decree goes on, that "the framework in which we have preached
the Gospel is now perceived as being inextricably linked to an
unacceptable social order, and for that reason is being called into
question."

Now, however, "it is . . . within human power to make the
world more just. . . . We can no longer pretend that the inequalities
and injustices of our world must be borne as part of the inevitable
order of things."

So much for the "pretentions" of the old, Ignatian charism. A
new plan was needed. The first part of that plan was "a firm commitment to make our world other than it is, to make it the visible
sign of another world, the sign 'of a new Heaven and a new
Earth.'" That much of a bow to traditional language accomplished, the nature of the Jesuit makeover of modern society is
clarified: " . . . in a world where the power of economic, social, and
political structures is now appreciated, and the mechanism and
laws governing them are now understood, service according to the
Gospel cannot dispense with a carefully planned effort to exert
influence on those structures."

Because these structures of society—the political systems, the
banking systems, the hospital systems, the transport systems, the
construction industries, the military-industrial complexes, the educational systems—"are among the principal formative influences
of our world," Jesuits must make their own in a personal as well
as a corporate manner "the struggle to transform these structures
in the interest of the spiritual and material liberation of fellow
human beings. . . ."

No allusion is made to the fact that Jesuits had recently abdi-
cated their "formative influence" in many of the educational systems and that the result had been chaos. On the contrary, the new
mission is embraced in glowing terms: Jesuits will "enter into
solidarity with the voiceless and the powerless."

To be certain that all Jesuits would understand the importance
of the Decree, it was emphasized that the promotion of justice was
"not one more apostolic area" among others; not merely "the so-

cial apostolate." It should be the concern of "our whole life and a dimension of all our apostolic endeavors." Jesuits must, then, be committed to building a new material society and, along the way, to combating "institutionalized injustice," which is "built into economic, social and political structures that dominate the life of nations and the international community."

To give the authors of this text their due, it is clear that they struggled manfully to link the "promotion of justice" with the priestly calling—a particular necessity, because GC32's failure in the issue of grades meant that Jesuits would still have to be ordained as priests. The links are rickety, however, and fail to cover large and unseemly gaps in logic.

Having asserted, for example, that the promotion of sociopolitical justice—the transformation of the very structures of society —is the new focus of the Society of Jesus, the text is casual and even presumptuous in its leap to spiritual justification: "We do not acquire this attitude of mind by our own efforts alone. It is the fruit of the Holy Spirit. . . ." Ignored is the classic requirement for a sound argument that must underlie any such assertion. Logically at this stage of presentation, it would be required to demonstrate from theology, from Scripture, from the teaching of the Church Fathers, and from theological reason that the promotion of sociopolitical justice had anything to do directly with apostolic ministries and with the ministries proper to the Society. But this essential step is omitted.

Instead, like a major-leaguer who decides all by himself that he doesn't have to touch third base before he can score, the authors of Decree #4 prance blithely over the theological gap to clutch at their prize: "It is by this [the fruit of the Holy Spirit] that we know that the promotion of justice is an integral part of the priestly service of faith." The manifest satisfaction in this illogicality and obfuscation is overwhelming. But the demand on the Holy Spirit's indulgence is unique in Jesuit Congregations.

This then is the new "primitive charism" of the Society of Jesus for which Arrupe and his Jesuits had quested so relentlessly and for so long. When it is finally summarized in one paragraph of the Decree, it stands as a pitiable model of false doctrine in which sound theological underpinning is replaced by sociopolitical aims conveniently stitched together with the trill-notes of spiritual-sounding mush: The grace "that enables us to seek the salvation of souls—might be called in contemporary terms, the total and integral liberation of man—leading to participation in the life of

God himself—is the same grace by which we are enabled and impelled to seek our own salvation and perfection." The abyss over which this leap takes place is ignored and quickly left behind.

In the remainder of its Decrees, GC32 was true to the animating spirit of this novel "primitive charism," the new focus for the Society of Jesus. In their ninety-six days of work, the Delegates took part in eighty-three plenary sessions, in uncounted meetings of commissions and subcommissions, of committees and task forces. They cast 1300 ballots on Decrees; for the Decree on Poverty alone, they cast 153 ballots on specific amendments over a period of four hours in order to get final approval for the whole Decree. They displayed an enthusiasm, a patience, and a perseverance that were remarkable. And in the end, they succeeded in producing a tacit—and at times not so tacit—condemnation of capitalist society.

In that same Decree on Poverty, for example, that took 153 ballots to get just right, poverty is not one of the classic virtues and professional badges of the Religious man, the Jesuit who by his vow of poverty identifies with a spiritual dimension of soul of the historical Jesus. Poverty as vow and virtue was now undergoing "socialization": It was now a professional badge of integration and identification with the economically deprived and the sociopolitically oppressed.

The only reference in the final Decrees of GC32 to the nearly disastrous confrontation between Pedro Arrupe and Paul VI over the attempted breakthrough in the matter of grades and authority, is a bland reference in the historical preface to the Decrees. There it is recorded that the Congregation had carefully examined the grades system and presented the matter to the Holy See for its decision. There had been some "misunderstanding," the text more or less admits, and then the Congregation had "accepted the decision of His Holiness obediently, and faithfully." Sincerity and frankness as well as humility would have been better served had such self-serving obfuscation been totally omitted or had the actual events been recounted.

When at last it came on March 7, 1975, the ending of GC32 of necessity bore no resemblance to the ending of GC31 nine years before.

Back on that distant November morning of 1966, the Pontiff had personally received all 226 black-robed Delegates in the solemn and privileged atmosphere of the Sistine Chapel. There he had concelebrated Mass with Pedro Arrupe and five of the Delegates. He had given an affectionate, encouraging farewell address.

True, he had expressed some misgivings; but in those closing hours of GC31, the tensions and the tugs-of-war were laid aside. The mood had been one of rambunctious and rebellious sons who had tested their father's authority. And way back then, even the most cynical-minded among those sons must have felt something special. Whatever flame of faith burned in each one; whatever gleam of love for Christ as the Supreme Leader, of desire to serve, of self-sacrifice, of hope in God's eternity; whatever seed of attachment to the Church remained—all of it must have been fanned and brightened, burnished and enlivened on that November day long gone. Those Jesuits, and all the others represented by them, had been received as trusted, valued members of the Holy Father's household, to share the sacred intimacy of the Sacrifice of Christ with the man their faith told them was Christ's personal representative on earth. They were favored with his Apostolic Blessing, personally given. It had all seemed so good, so promising. Many of those Delegates remembered that day long after as the springtime moment of their plans and hopes. They recalled their mood as smiling, happy, talkative. "Cozy and comfortable," was how one American described it.

But those seemed ancient days by March 7, 1975. GC32 had been a series of skirmishes and battles, some lost, some won, but all of them portending a longer, wider war. There would be no gathering of Delegates, no Mass in the Sistine Chapel, no communal celebration between a father and his obstreperous sons. There was to be no peace any longer between Pope and Jesuits.

Instead, there was a final confrontation.

The General Congregation was still at work on its last official day when Pedro Arrupe left the Delegates behind in the auditorium of the Gesù and made his way across St. Peter's Square, surrounded this time not by any happy throng of colleagues but by his four General Assistants, Vincent O'Keefe, Yves Calvez, Horacio de la Costa, and Parmananda Divarkar. Their destination was not the Sistine Chapel, but a place of daily papal business in the Apostolic Palace. They would be meeting with Paul VI less perhaps as Christ's Vicar than as Lord of the Keys, their ultimate Superior on this earth.

In that meeting, Paul VI's performance was, for this once at least, exceptional. He was indeed the Supreme Pastor and Roman Pontiff. There were no harsh words from him, no strident tones. He made brilliant use of *romanità* in word, in indirect but telling action, and in symbolism.

The very ordinariness of the place the Pontiff chose in which to address the Jesuits, in fact, was part of the symbolism. In that place the Father General and his Assistants sat as emissaries between two embattled camps in an undeclared war, and listened to the measured words of their chief adversary.

At once the Holy Father put Arrupe and the others on notice: He knew, he said in the cadences of *romanità*, where the Jesuits wished to go with their Society; he disapproved. He said exactly what path they should follow.

Paul said: We are glad to have another opportunity to show Our solicitude for your Society, in addition to the last opportunity during the Congregation when We went out of Our way to make sure you realized We meant what We said when We told you there was to be no change in the system of grades.

Paul said: Some of you thought you couldn't transform your Society with a new vigor unless you introduced substantially new elements into it. We did not and will not allow that. Deformation is not transformation. Only loyalty to Ignatius will give you the Jesuitism of Ignatius.

Paul said finally: Not by natural means, but only by God's grace, can you succeed. And your success or failure as Religious will be watched by many other Religious Orders. You were once the standard-bearer of what good Religious should be. What you do is important.

When Paul had finished his address, Arrupe was given a typewritten copy by a papal aide; he was to return with it to the Gesù and share it with the Delegates of GC32.

The symbolism of *romanità* then became prominent in the subdued ceremonies. Paul gave the Jesuit emissaries a parting gift: a large seventeeth-century crucifix that had been the personal possession of one of the greatest of Jesuit saints, Robert Bellarmine. The symbolism was clear. Bellarmine had been two things mainly: the world-famous defender of the Pope's prerogatives, and the great defender of orthodox doctrine against the heretics of his day.

Once back in the auditorium of the Gesù, Father Arrupe read the Pope's solemn and pointed address to the Delegates. It was received in the silence that greets significant and unexpected obstacles. When Arrupe then displayed Bellarmine's crucifix for the Delegates' inspection, its symbolism of loyalty to the papacy and to papal doctrine was inescapable.

Some seemed to recall, however, that Bellarmine had also opposed at least one Pope. And hadn't he in his doctrines mitigated the extent of papal power? Perhaps that too was part of Paul's symbolism. In any case, for men bent on plying their own will in contravention of any papal norm, there could be no frank and simple acceptance either of Paul's direct words or of his equally direct symbolism.

The Delegates went back to the final hours of their work. Late in the afternoon, when all the voting was completed, Arrupe made one final speech of encouragement, of confidence in the decisions taken during their deliberations, and of exhortation that the Decrees should be observed and obeyed as the bastions for future success in the veritable revolution taking place. From those bastions, they and others would for years to come fire as many damaging salvos as they could; most of them would be aimed at the papacy and at the authority of the universal, apostolic authority of the Roman Church.

After dinner on that March 7, once all the hard work was done, the Delegates entertained themselves at the Gesù with an impromptu concert of songs from their native lands. Father Arrupe joined in with his pleasant tenor voice.

Did Arrupe know that his subsequent relationship with Paul VI would remain strung out along the wires of the dark but now accepted tensions between them until Paul's death? Probably. In any event, for the remaining three years of the Pope's life, no interference or intervention by Paul VI ever deflected Arrupe and his generation from their arrow-straight pursuit of what they called "renewal" and "the primitive charism" of the Society. And certainly they appeared untroubled on that last evening together in Rome.

Folk songs weren't the same as High Mass with the Pontiff in the Sistine, perhaps; but it was amusing and delightful. The mood was "family."

The final notes of GC32 were sounded when the Jesuit-run Vatican Radio publicly announced the Congregation's closing. This Congregation, the tongue-in-cheek statement observed, "will go down in history on account of the pastoral interest and authoritative directions with which the Holy Father followed its preparation, its performance, and its conclusion." The Holy Father would, Vatican Radio's commentator added, "intervene again whenever the good of the Society and of the Church requires it."

A departing Delegate mirrored another less papalist point of view. "Pope Paul is afraid that the Order will disappear by becoming too secular. But there's a danger he may annihilate it by taking it over and turning us into dusty little papal valets."

22 | PUBLIC STANDING

T he Roman spring of 1975 was a breath or two away. The preamble to war between the Society of Jesus and its creator, the papacy, was ten years old. It had been a decade since the Delegates at the first session of GC31 had initially, if perhaps rather vaguely at first, conceived of spinning new threads from which to weave the new Jesuit identity and mission in the modern world. After all their skirmishes with Pope Paul VI and the Holy See, the Society's leadership had at last, in the ninety-six days of GC32, succeeded in hammering out Decrees that would allow the Order to change in the most fundamental ways while at the same time maintaining, on the basis of its new "primitive charism," that Jesuits remained the same loyal cadre they had always been, the leaders and standard-bearers of the true faith and loyalty, in the Ignatian tradition.

The difficulty for Pedro Arrupe and the Jesuits in the aftermath of GC32, however, was that, General Congregation or no, they had lost the upper hand. The Decrees of GC32 were in Paul VI's possession for careful scrutiny by the papal office. Rumors were making their way around Roman corridors and offices like quicksilver eels. The Holy Father's conservative advisers, one rumor said, were recommending wholesale rejection of the Decrees. No, another rumor went, the Holy Father would not return the Decrees at all, but would keep them *sine die*, leaving GC32 in a state of suspended animation and the entire Society of Jesus in a canonical limbo. Perhaps, still another rumor said, a section of the Society would be allowed to break away from the main body and stick to the pre-GC31 and pre-GC32 Jesuit framework. According to yet another rumor, there was going to be wholesale revision of GC32's Decrees.

Whatever the rumors, the brute fact of life was that, for the first time in hundreds of years, a Pope had not automatically accepted the resolutions of a General Congregation. That fact spelled trouble. Anything could happen.

Any of these rumors might have been a true reflection of reality in those weeks after the end of GC32, had Paul VI been in any sort of a robust physical and psychological condition. But, at this crucial moment in Church history, Paul was anything but robust. For years the poor circulation in his legs had worried his doctors; it only grew worse in the seventies. His arthritic condition, which at first yielded to some remission, gradually made serious inroads, making his every movement a matter of delicate calculation— how best to reach, to sit down, to shake his head, to turn around, to perform the most ordinary actions, and still avoid the needle stabs of intimate pain.

Though his physical problems were several and serious, Paul's personal physician insisted that during those last four very hard years, from 1975 to 1978, it was Paul's pain in mind and soul that was causing the deterioration so evident by then in the Pontiff's physical powers. None of His Holiness's physical ailments, the doctor maintained, could account for Paul's slippage toward the grave.

Among those with whom the Pope discussed the Decrees of GC32 that he now held, some later reported their impression that Paul's entire experience with the Jesuits had an eye-opening effect on him. From the first clashes with Arrupe over the behavior of GC31, down to the emergence of the Decrees of GC32 despite his specific prohibitions, Paul could see the papacy's most valuable Religious Order galloping toward a precipice.

Worse than that was Paul's realization that, as the ultimate authority in the Church, he himself was largely to blame for what he now regarded as an ongoing disaster. He was increasingly haunted by his early bright-eyed idealism; his too-ready willingness to see ancient modes of worship jettisoned; his early compromises with ecclesiastical rebels and sociopolitical activists; above all, his now clearly seen acquiescence in the Second Vatican Council's single-minded will to help man build his material world here

below. All his mistakes—his short-sightedness, his patent betrayal of loyal churchmen who refused to go along with his "new"
ecclesiology—forced Paul willy-nilly to draw near that precipice
where he was convinced that Jesuits were headed, forced him to
look down into the chasm.

Paul's will now was to pull his Church back from that brink.
The most direct and present means to begin to do that would, he
determined, be to brake his Jesuits' gallop. Evidently, he saw the
Decrees of GC32 as taking the papacy's elite troops over the edge
and into the chasm; and he judged, as other Popes had before him,
that many, in imitation, would follow them.

To bring himself to a realistic analysis of the danger was one
thing—and painful to be sure. To find a way around that danger
was another matter. What was he to do, realistically? Retain the
Decrees indefinitely and make the conclusion of GC32 *sine die?*
In his condition, this was impossible. Too many friends and sympathizers of Arrupe and the Society pressed around the Pope for a
resolution of the situation. Reject the Decrees? Demand wholesale
revision of the Decrees? Paul no longer had any stomach for the
case-hardened, argumentative resistance of the Jesuits. Neither
physically nor emotionally could he undergo another session like
GC32. If the Jesuits had meant to wear the Pontiff down, they had
done a good job of work.

Of all the dymanic elements at play for the Society of Jesus,
meanwhile, in the troubled aftermath of GC32, perhaps the most
surprising was the very surprise of the Jesuits themselves at the
sudden freezing of relations between the Society's headquarters at
the Gesù and Pope Paul VI's Vatican. Yet, from their own point of
view, the majority could not understand either the freeze in the
relationship or the delay in Pope Paul's approval of the Decrees. If
there did seem to be a tug-of-war—or perhaps even the beginning
of a true war between Society and papacy—this was not felt to be
the most important factor to consider. After all, neither the Delegates to GC32 nor their Roman Superiors had acted out of any ill
will in their refusal to conform to the papal commands, directives,
and exhortations. There was, sure enough, acrid criticism and
much anger among Delegates on the subject of the Pope. But none
of that was felt to be an expression of perversity.

Rather, it was a felt emotion, noble in its own limited way; an
emotion made up partly of anger at the injustice that kept millions
in daily pain and hopelessness, partly of an intellectual confidence
colored with arrogance and pride: None of the majority doubted
for a moment that they knew better than the Pope; nor had they

hesitated to assert as much, both in their stubborn intransigence or their public statements against the will of Paul VI. There was also an unadmitted element of weakness visible in their behavior; their desire to be with the "new world" in its making inevitably included a certain vanity in the tinsel of notoriety and a surrender to the lure of material achievements that would be visible to the eyes of their contemporaries.

Ignatius would have shunned that emotion and all of its parts; and after manful efforts to transform that emotion, he would— with sadness perhaps, but with neither hesitation nor qualms— have dismissed any Jesuit who displayed its symptoms as a man duped by Lucifer, the Enemy.

A virtuous emotion—compassion, or a justifiable wrath at human injustice—tested in the difficult crucible of fidelity and obedience to the papacy and adhesion to Roman orthodoxy, certainly has led scores of saints to achieve spiritual and supernatural wonders whose effects have been felt in the daily, worldly lives of ordinary men and women. Some great figures spring to mind: Ignatius himself; Francis of Assisi; Vincent de Paul; in our own time, Mother Teresa of Calcutta. None of them sought inspiration in the world around them. None of them adopted the solutions proffered by the world. In other words, none of them was transformed by the world; they transformed their world instead.

By contrast, the Society of Jesus in the seventies consented to be transformed by its world. Fidelity, obedience, and orthodoxy had been marinated in the new spirit that had captivated GC32 and run amok among Jesuits. The latent and silently professed Modernism of many Jesuits had made them vulnerable to the brilliance of technology and science. Deficiency in faith was mirrored in a too easily adopted contempt for papal teaching authority. The dazzling hurly-burly of new nations clamoring for more bread, more freedoms, more modern satisfactions, more trade, more dignity, more equality, was matched among Jesuits by the cry that this was a new age, a fresh age, a stupendous era which they intended to catch at its first sea-swell, before the wave could crest and rush onward, leaving them behind in its backwaters.

It was not ill will, then, that had motivated GC32, but the desire for immersion in that hurly-burly; the desire to take up the cry of the dawning age; to be new—newer than the newest; to be in the vanguard of those determined to put themselves and all they possessed at the disposal of those building the new order in human society. It was a common spiritual and intellectual disease in the Roman Church by then.

What marked GC32 as of capital importance was the simple if lamentable fact that this General Congregation of the Society of Jesus made this spiritual and intellectual disease the living breathing spirit of its discussions. Its Delegates formalized the symptoms of that disease into a new creation—the new Jesuitism—built stick-and-board in the shadow of the Palace of the Popes. They sheathed their new construction with the trappings of classic faith and apostolic mission. And when it was all polished and done, what they had built and wheeled into place in the City of the Popes, at the very heart of Catholicism, was an ecclesiastical Trojan horse.

Still engulfed as they were in the emotional "groundswell" for democratization and the autonomy of the Order that had propelled GC32 forward, many Jesuits could only be puzzled by the Pope's attack on their new creation. Paul VI's actions seemed designed only to deflect and blunt their efforts. They could not understand, for example, why Paul's closing address to Pedro Arrupe and his General Assistants on March 7 was so critical. Roman Superiors and the actual architects of this latter-day Trojan horse saw quite clearly why Paul wanted none of their new format. But the rank and file did not, for they had gone beyond the point of any self-doubt. They could not, for example, accept the clear symbolism of the Bellarmine crucifix, nor understand why their beloved "Pedro" was given such rough treatment by Paul and his Secretary of State. But above all, they chafed at having to wait for a seemingly endless time once they had sent GC32's Decrees across St. Peter's Square for papal examination and approval. The more irreverent and rebellious among them saw this as a diminution of the Society's ancient privilege of immunity from close supervision. Not for a couple of centuries had the Society been under the papal gun like this. It spelled papal distrust.

That last factor was particularly worrying for the Jesuit Superiors in Rome. Indeed, in the light of Paul's address to Arrupe and the others on the Congregation's final day, that worry seemed more than justified. In the very last paragraph of that address, Paul had said: "You should be aware of the fact that not only the eyes of contemporary men in general, but also and especially those of so many members of other Religious Orders and Congregations and even those of the Church, are turned towards you. . . ."

Paul's meaning in its bare essentials was clear: We can no longer rely on you Jesuits to be the papal front line. Others, many others, depend on the Society of Jesus to set an example. Other Religious

Orders and Congregations are thinking along the same lines of "modernization" as you have been doing in GC32—to Our papal displeasure. If you get away with what We condemn, what do you think other Orders and Congregations are going to conclude? Moreover, the world at large—the ordinary faithful as well as secular governments—have heard of your attempted revolt against Our papal control. What you do now will influence their view of the papacy and of you. "You should be aware of the fact. . . ."

Arrupe was aware. He knew as well as the Pontiff that in this very matter of "renewal," Jesuits were seen, as they always were, as standard-bearers. Arrupe and his colleagues were deeply convinced that GC32 had made a positive contribution—*the* contribution—toward bringing the "new mission" of a "renewed Catholicism" into a "new world." GC32 pointed the way for Catholic Religious Orders and Congregations to bring the Roman Church out of its nineteenth-century ghetto, past its twentieth-century morass, and into the glorious perspectives of the dawning twenty-first century of men and women on earth.

If that was not true—if what GC32 had decided was not the path—then GC32 with all its pomps and works was a dead-end alley, and the Society of Jesus had stumbled and failed at last.

How, then, could Arrupe and his colleagues be anything but deeply worried about Paul's examination of GC32's Decrees? All those negative rumors about what the Holy Father might do with those Decrees were not ignored at the Gesù. News of any such papal reactions would not be good for the Society, or for its public standing.

To make matters more tense, already before they had left Rome —and more so once they were safely back in their native airs— many Delegates were outspoken in their condemnation of the papal handling of the Decrees as "highhanded," as "undemocratic," as "infringing" on the constitutional rights of the General Congregation, as being "a leftover" from the old hierarchic and authoritarian Church, which many already viewed as discarded. Such public comment from Jesuit lips could be no help to the Society's cause in the Vatican.

On top of such outspokenness, moreover, there had been leaks during the course of GC32 itself. In spite of the best intentions and efforts of Jesuit authorities, wisps of intelligence concerning the rough passage of arms between the Society and the Pope had made their way to the outside world. While there were not large numbers of the Delegates who were in total disagreement with the "groundswell" of new Jesuitism, there were just a few too many to allow the inner disputes of the Congregation to remain confidential.

In the papal offices, too, it had suited some to make sure the media got wind now and again of what was going on—a bitter dispute about Arrupe's leadership, perhaps, or a clash between Arrupe and Paul VI, or whatever seemed newsworthy.

The Information Office of GC32 with its twenty full-time Jesuit workers had done all it could—had done a good job in fact. But historically, both Rome and the Society of Jesus have been international whispering galleries. In the circumstances, it was not possible to block all the leaks.

Eventually headlines, screaming and snickering by turns, about GC32 did appear in Italy, in Europe, in the United States, and in India. In more ordinary times, it would have been a simple matter to dismiss the media as rumor-mongering, and to brush away their stories as one might pluck so much fluff from one's sleeve.

These, however, were not ordinary times. Paul VI had not yet finished with GC32. Everything still hung in the balance. The danger had to be faced that the reaction, both among other Religious Orders and in the media, might be negative to the bad press being generated against the Pontiff by outspoken Jesuits; might produce doubts about Jesuit preeminence in the Church, and diminution of prestige, therefore, at the least. That would be bad enough in itself. But it might also help to stiffen Paul's stubborn opposition to the thrust of GC32.

Worry, however, particularly in Pedro Arrupe, had never meant fear, had never brought on paralysis of action. Quite the contrary. A way simply had to be found to answer such papal criticism of GC32 as had already become public, to vindicate the path chosen by the General Congregation, and if possible even to force the Holy Father to renounce his opposition to GC32 and give his approval to the Decrees and his permission for their implementation.

A plan was formed. In the opinion of Father General Arrupe and the Jesuit Superiors in Rome, they found themselves in a situation that needed what the Americans called "public relations." That meant taking yet one more step that no General Congregation of Jesuits had ever dreamed of doing: It meant giving a public and quasi-official explanation of the Decrees of GC32; and it meant doing so in Rome, not in some outlying Province of the Society.

If it could be done well—in the proper forum, with all the required authority of voice and the impressive trappings of the Society at its best—it could be the perfect solution to all the worry.

It could be the means to offset any negative reactions to GC32 either among other Religious Orders or in the general media, for it would appeal to the existing tendency in many to approve of any change proposed for the sake of "renewal" in "the spirit of Vatican II." It could provide the platform from which to answer innocently the papal criticism. Authoritative interpretations of GC32 would be on public record. Exaggerations could be corrected. The Society's answer to many papal criticisms that were not yet even known abroad could be published, as it were, by the way. Most importantly, it would vindicate the path chosen for the Jesuits by GC32.

There would be certain side benefits, as well. How better in this twentieth century to get back at a superior—be he Pope or president or chairman of the board or leader of the party—than by public relations? The Jesuits had a desire not only to make sure that the other Religious Orders and Congregations knew their point of view—to protect the Jesuit pride of place among Religious, in other words—but to be sure also that the papal enclave of conservative critics and traditionalist enemies huddled around an embattled Paul VI be answered; that they hear what Arrupe and his General Assistants would like to have said in response to Paul's disturbing exhortation to them at the close of GC32 on March 7.

The plan drawn up by the Jesuit Superiors was for a series of lectures to be given in Rome by some very weighty voices. The topics to be covered were the cardinal points of GC32's main Decrees, the so-called priority topics: the grades system, Jesuit identity today, poverty, community life, inculturation, formation of Jesuits, and the promotion of justice.

Accordingly, seven public lectures were planned for the end of May 1975, not quite three months after the closing of GC32's final session. The lectures would all be delivered at Jesuit headquarters in the Gesù, and each would be given by one of seven speakers. Those speakers in turn would be carefully chosen to form an international team of men with established reputations, men of Jesuit authoritativeness, men with records of heavy involvement in the toils and labors of GC32, men closely associated with Pedro Arrupe's Generalate in Rome.

The team chosen was formidable indeed. Jean-Yves Calvez, a Frenchman, had received doctorates in sociology, political science, and international studies. He had been Provincial of All France before heading the Jesuit center for social studies in Paris. Cecil McGarry, an Irishman, held a doctorate in theology and had been a Provincial Superior. Both men were now General Assistants in

Arrupe's Jesuit Curia in Rome. Edward F. Sheridan of Canada and Ignacio Iglesias of Spain had also been Provincials in their own countries, and both were now Regional Assistants to Arrupe in the Gesù. Sheridan had a doctorate in theology. Iglesias was the only one without a doctoral qualification. Vincent O'Keefe of the United States was not only yet another of Arrupe's General Assistants in Rome; he was Arrupe's personal choice to succeed him as Father General of the Order. Francisco Ivern of India functioned in the Gesù as Arrupe's counselor for social and development problems. No one had the facts and figures about the Vatican's most important Asian mission field—the subcontinent of India—as Ivern had. Carlo G. Martini of Italy was rector of the powerful Pontifical Biblical Institute in Rome, enjoyed a just prestige for orthodoxy, and was earmarked as a future cardinal.

An eighth man, chosen to set the tone of lectures in a welcoming speech and to issue the formal invitations to all seven "guest" speakers, was Luis Gonzalez, S.J., Director of the Ignatian Center of Spirituality located in the Gesù.

The most immediate audience for the lectures was to be other Religious—priests, lay brothers, and nuns. The central importance of such groups in the Jesuit mind was underlined in the published version of the lectures, where the editors noted in the cover matter that: "Members of other Religious Institutes of men and women, too, will probably find much that is interesting and helpful in these descriptions of developments within General Congregation XXXII of the Society of Jesus."

While the press was not formally invited to the lectures, it was certainly not kept in the dark that the Society was about to give an unprecedented and public explanation of the excellence of GC32's Decrees; nor was the press kept away.

The nicely engineered public ballyhoo that preceded the lectures did force the papal hand. One doubts if the papal office would have been so rapid in its dealings with the bothersome Decrees if it hadn't been for the dispersal of invitations to a wide potential audience to come and hear a top-flight team of Jesuits speak about the Decrees. In the parlance of *romanità*, to do this in Rome under the eyes of the Vatican meant either that you had Vatican approval, or that you were stronger than anyone in the Vatican, including the Pope, and could thumb your nose at one and all.

The announcement of the lectures literally created a crucial moment, both for the papacy and for the Society. It was the last moment when Paul VI could have done something effective to arrest the onward rush of the Jesuits toward that brink from which he himself had shrunk back.

The major advantages all appeared to be on Paul's side. He was Pope, with all the authority in his hands and all of papal power at his disposal for the taking. Furthermore, the fact that he still held the unapproved Decrees of GC32 meant that technically speaking, those Decrees did not legally exist; nor would they, until he permitted their promulgation. Above all, Arrupe and his colleagues were in blatant if technical violation of the law. They had set up a series of lectures on the Decrees of GC32, for all the world as if those Decrees were acceptable as the official mind of the Society. In Roman law, however, they could not be held as acceptable until the moment the Pope declared them acceptable. And Paul had not yet done that.

Into the fabric of the entire Jesuit plan for a public relations coup against the Pope was woven that self-same arrogance Paul had met so many times over the ten years of the Arrupe administration. The Jesuit Superiors were acting as if they, not Paul, were the Pope. Once again, a Jesuit gesture said: We are going ahead with or without papal approval. If it was a calculated risk for the Jesuits, it was only one more among the many they had already taken with such success.

As for the Holy Father in this crucial moment, he was literally drained. Always gentle, always intelligent, until lately romantically liberal and humanistic, the one thing Paul had perhaps never been was tough and strong enough to be Pope in such times as these. One word from him and Arrupe would have had to cancel the lectures. It was the obvious thing to do. Yes, Paul was advised officially, he could do that. But then nothing could prevent Arrupe from holding "private" lectures for the same audience in the same place. On the other hand, if Paul did nothing, then once more the Jesuits would have learned that it paid to face down this Pope.

There was a tension-packed interval while Paul's ultimate decision was in the making. Despite the outward serenity of Arrupe and his colleagues, they knew the odds: The Roman sky might fall on top of their heads. All could be lost. But it was now or never. It was all or nothing. Pope and Jesuit General reproduced a Roman version of the two gunfighters in storybook westerns, each glaring at the other, each man waiting to see if the other would blink first.

Paul blinked. His solution, born of weakness and nourished by his deep feeling of helplessness, was no solution. He sent back the Decrees through the office of his Cardinal Secretary of State, Jean

Villot, thus implicitly conceding they could be promulgated as official. By that act, he broke the tension and lost the battle. The Jesuits had their precious Decrees back. The road mapped out by GC32 spread open in front of them. Nothing else mattered.

Paul VI did instruct Villot to send a letter along with the Decrees, and he personally went over the points of that letter in detail. Though it came on the official stationery of the Secretariat of State and bore the Cardinal Secretary's signature, in other words, that letter was in reality Paul's. It was dated May 22, five days before the first scheduled lecture; it was five pages long. Its tone was as testy, peremptory, and patronizing as possible within the bounds of *romanità*. And, translated into ordinary language, the message Villot delivered was plain and practical.

Circumstances quite well known to everybody, the cardinal observed icily, had obviously prevented GC32 from obeying Paul VI's recommendations. To that extent, those decrees were unsatisfactory. Villot's reference to Arrupe's maneuvering and to the Delegates' recalcitrance was clear. However, Villot's letter went on, I am sending your decrees back to you, hoping you will be genuinely faithful to the charism of St. Ignatius and the recommendations of His Holiness. Not all is clear in your Decrees. Some of them, being ambiguous, can be wrongly interpreted. In any doubt whatever, you are to practice Jesuit obedience, and follow the norms already laid down by His Holiness on various occasions.

Villot cited some of the significant dangers most evident in the Decrees. In your "promotion of justice," he told them, do not substitute human development and social progress for apostolic ministries. You profess loyalty to the Holy See in matters of doctrine; but you proceed to dilute your expression of that sentiment by saying at the same time that "freedom should be intelligently encouraged" in the case of your theologians. That way, loyalty can be abandoned for the sake of freedom "intelligently" encouraged. Especially so, as you also neglected to place the study of St. Thomas Aquinas's theology as a prime necessity for orthodoxy.

We have also noticed, Villot continued in essence, the attempt to democratize the Society by conceding a greater and greater say in Jesuit government to those who are not permitted to take the special vow of the Professed. This tendency violates the norms laid down by the Holy Father. It is an attempt to dilute the grades system. Your behavior in this matter will be subject to continuing review.

If Paul VI still nourished a small hope—as Villot's letter seems to show he did—that there remained some lean possibility that a final rupture between the Society and its own heritage of Ignatian Jesuitism could be avoided, or that the Society would finally recoil from its official alienation from the papacy and traditional Roman Catholicism, that hope surely died a quick death once Arrupe received Villot's letter of complaint.

Criticism or no criticism, the Decrees of GC32 could now be officially promulgated to the Society. Short of outright papal rejection of the Decrees, no letter would matter; certainly, one more litany of papal exortations would not be enough to recall the Jesuits to order.

Nor did the Jesuits have to fear any longer that the Society's public standing would be affected in any significant way by the sharply critical papal response to GC32's Decrees. The simple fact was that, as such things are normally done in Rome, Villot's letter was not meant for the world at large; it was not to be published.

Not so the lectures. With the Decrees safely back in hand to be prepared for promulgation, the public Jesuit performance in the Gesù that May paid off as a plan of public relations genius. Indeed, one must admire the skilled moderation, if not the candor, of those lectures on the revolutionary changes introduced into the Jesuit *Institute* by GC32. They were listened to in person by hundreds. They were published abroad in Europe, the United States, and the Far East; and even before publication, tape recordings and transcripts made their way to Jesuit houses all over the world.

As planned, Luis Gonzalez, S.J., set the tone of the lectures nicely in his "Words of Welcome" that preceded the first lecture by Jean-Yves Calvez on May 27. Gonzalez offered the lectures to those "who with us form a part of a pilgrim Church and who live in a period of history charged with development, vitality and hopes of a world which, though shaken, is looking for profound renovation."

In his general summary of the lectures that would follow, and of the meaning of the Decrees themselves, Gonzalez's explanations might as easily have been given by a Hottentot or an atheist as by a priest. There was nothing specifically Roman Catholic in his words, nor any specifically Jesuit note to his remarks. They were well molded to that pleasing vagueness, noted by Villot in his letter, that is so characteristic of "the winsome doctrine."

In the lecture by Calvez that followed, and in the ones given on the ensuing dates, the effort of each speaker was to establish a line of legitimate development between classical Ignatian Jesuitism and the new Jesuit program legislated in the Decrees of GC32. That effort may in fact be the clearest admission that the reality of what the Congregation had done constituted a displacement, both in spirit and in concrete policy, of the vital "substantials" of Ignatian Jesuitism.

The effort becomes an admission, because the effort failed. In no lecture did any speaker, for example, succeed any better than GC32's Delegates had in working out the new meaning of the Society's special bond with the papacy. Instead, the whole concept of the Church comes out as of a crowd of pilgrims, all on an equal footing, all going the same way, all making the same mistakes, none of them—whether Pope or bishops—privileged in any way. Indeed, one must ask after going through the lectures, why in the new Jesuit view should any fellow pilgrim take it upon himself arrogantly to critique other fellow pilgrims who were blazing a new trail?

Nor were the lectures any more successful in working out the Jesus-oriented spirituality of the Society as Ignatius had conceived it. On the contrary, the recurrent references in all of the lectures to "the Society"—"what the Society intends," "has determined to do," "is capable of," "demands of Jesuits"—slowly inculcated the heady and fantastic idea that "the Society" had replaced both Christ and the papacy he instituted; that "the Society" itself was now both the norm-giver and the principal determinant of Jesuit behavior and of the Society's program.

The liberal sprinkling about of classical Ignatian words, phrases, and passages was not enough to paper over the huge leaps that were made by GC32. Nor did repeated assertions of continuity with classical Jesuitism retrieve the lectures from their cliché-ridden, generalist language modeled on the ambiguity of government reports and the generalist style typical of modern bureaucratese.

By contrast with each of these lectures, the language of Ignatius and that used traditionally in the Society until now, had always been almost painfully specific; and it had always been loaded with references to and connotations of personal and corporate spirituality and the Society's apostolate.

For all their efforts and contortions, not one of these seven lecturers successfully demonstrated in sound logic how the apostolic ministry of Jesuit priests was to be maintained, while the corporate energy of the Society was totally consumed with the problems of social abuses and political repression. The continuing apostolic nature of the Society was stated in a hundred ways, but not once was it demonstrated.

Indeed, in all seven lectures, such matters as the grades system,

Jesuit identity, poverty, community life, training, and all the rest of GC32's priorities were dealt with in terms that emphasized the newness of the Congregation's program for the Society. There was no wavering on this point; it was made over and over again, and in each of the different subjects covered by the lectures.

To practice truly evangelical poverty, it was now necessary to live with the poor, to be poor in exactly the way that they are poor. To achieve spiritual formation, it was now necessary to be immersed in urban settings. Evangelization could only take place if the deformed Christianity and Catholicism imported from the West to Asia and Africa were replaced by local expressions, specific to those populations, and different from the expressions chosen nearly two thousand years ago for and by Western Christians.

As with the other topics discussed, the danger of such "inculturation"—as evangelization was now called—was ignored. It seemed not to matter that universality of doctrine and belief was in effect shelved, and that the truth of Christian dogma became the plaything of relative and changing standards popular in any region of the world at any given moment.

It was not even mentioned that such inculturation, once applied, would of necessity wipe away priestly authority and, with it, the Transubstantiation of the Bread and Wine of the Mass, the Mass as the human sacrifice of Jesus to achieve divine forgiveness of sins, penance, and the forgiveness of the specific sins of each individual. All of this, and all else known through the same source, the universal teaching authority of the Church, would have to go.

That none of this was a problem for the Jesuit pantheon of speakers is as evident by what they did not talk about as by what occupied the center of their minds. Absent from the lectures were Catholic and Jesuit references and allusions to Pope and papacy, to Church and to teaching authority, to Jesus, his mother, and the saints. Absent too were the hallmarks of Ignatian thought—the inherent fallibility and weakness of mankind due to Original Sin, the constant warfare waged with the living and malignant Archangel, and personal devotion to Jesus as the burning heart of Jesuit strength and apostolic force.

So great was the desire of these men to legitimize what GC32 had done that they seemed blinded by the splendor of their own plan. They had no inner means any longer of holding that splendor up to the honest, hard scrutiny of Ignatian tradition, or of allowing its light to be fractionated by the pure prism of supernatural faith.

As though they were but so many more ordinary bureaucrats of just one more ordinary secular government, all they seemed able to do was to take refuge in the woolly concepts of "coordination of energies," "total integration," "context theologizing," and "communal discretion."

Perhaps the glaring lack of spiritual dimension and of Ignatian hallmarks was evident enough to Arrupe and his Roman colleagues, for the published version of the lectures carried an added essay by General Assistant Jean-Yves Calvez. The title of his essay was "The Congregation and Closer Contact of Jesuits with Men," and in it, Calvez treated all the themes dealt with in the seven lectures. The evident purpose of this added material was to make one more valiant effort to establish the truly Jesuit character of the changes introduced by GC32. What it provided instead was an instructive insight into the mind and outlook of Major Jesuit Superiors.

After pages in which he detailed the need and desirability of the "closer contact" of the essay's title between Jesuits and men, Calvez suddenly switched tone. He quoted Ignatius's own word picture of Christ the Leader and Lucifer the Enemy. Satisfied with so blatant and unsuitable a patch in his text, he leaped illogically back into his central theme—the Jesuits' need to break out of "our own world" and reach out to men.

This effort at clarification—if that is what the essay was—is as jarring and as confused as the entire series of lectures. And in that, at least—in their confusion and their diffuse and disorderly treatment of the "substantials" of Jesuitism—the lectures themselves are the very mirror they were intended to be of the 32nd General Congregation. Virtuous compassion and justifiable wrath were linked willy-nilly to pride and arrogance. Yes, the new Jesuits said, let us be Christ's men, but by opposing Christ's Vicar. Yes, let us understand doctrine, but by jettisoning the teachers of fifteen hundred years. Yes, let us promote authority, but by undermining and paralyzing the only authority given to the Church by Christ. Yes, cultivate the spirit of inner devotion, but do this by immersing our young Jesuits-in-training in all the razzle-dazzle and distraction of "relevant" urban settings.

Taken as a whole, the lectures and the added chapter of clarification were the final touch to complete construction of the Jesuit Trojan horse. Confusion was presented as clarity; recalcitrance as obedience; worldly relevance as faith; disobedient Jesuits as faithful leaders true to their traditions. Meanwhile, the long, deep shadow of error cast by that Trojan horse continues to this day to block out the supernatural light of Christ that Ignatius had chosen as the only light that should guide his tiny company of men on their path of service and salvation. The Jesuits of GC32, converted into single-minded evangelists of social, political, and psychological progress, had no eyes any longer for the soul's vision, nor ears for the tiny voice of Spirit.

Still, there is no denying that if the lectures were not successful in their attempt to establish a legitimate line of development linking GC32's Decrees to Ignatian Jesuitism, they were supremely successful in their primary purpose. In public—in the very heart of the Rome of the Popes, in fact—the Jesuits had successfully flaunted a novel set of standards for Religious Orders and Congregations. That Company of Jesus, which had been founded by Ignatius and which had now for hundreds of years been the Holy See's own pacesetter for the Church's vast and variegated family of Religious men and women, had achieved what it advertised as "approval" by the Holy See for the virtual abandonment of the regulations that gave the Order the unmistakable mark of Ignatius of Loyola, and that had made of his Company, truly, the Society of Jesus. But that is a sorry achievement; an achievement apart from —and, in a major way, in spite of—the papacy which the Jesuits purported still to serve.

Donald Campion, S.J., who was editor-in-chief of *America Magazine*, and who had been in charge of the Information Office at GC32, gave a press interview after the Congregation closed. There he stated what appeared to be closer to the truth than any of the much publicized lectures at the Gesù. The evidence, Campion said then, was that the center or middle-of-the-road position in the Order was considerably broader than most people, even Jesuits, had thought. The "way-out-left," he explained, and the "hard-core-right" represented a small body of no significance in the Society.

What neither Father Campion nor most of the Jesuit center had noticed was that the gravity point of the Society had shifted dramatically between 1965 and 1975. The "new unbroken threads" that had been spun by GC31 and by the energetic activity of Pedro Arrupe and the Jesuit establishment over the eight years following, had by might and main hauled the middle-of-the-roaders as a bulk to the left. Yet they still saw themselves as centrists. Their perception of themselves had not changed, in other words; it was everyone else who had changed. Somehow, the old traditionalists and conservatives of the Order had become hard-core right. They could even point to a few from the old left wing who had become, as one might say, overliberated and now formed the "way-out-left" of the Society.

But the greatest pity of it all was the failure of perspective that allowed such an analysis at all. For whether they were "right," "center," or "left," all the factions viewed their positions relative only to one another. None measured their distance from the Holy See, or their position in relation to the traditions of Ignatian Jesuitism. In point of fact, the Holy See had ceased to be the standard by which any of the factions determined their orthodoxy. Perennial Ignatian tradition ceased to be the standard for measuring Jesuitism. Each faction claimed to be orthodox and Ignatian. But the absolutes were gone. All was relative.

In the language of St. Paul, a different sort of analysis is justified. The "Angel of Light" had cornered and trapped the good and the virtuous and the chosen of God. The Enemy had infiltrated Christ's special militia, the best and the brightest, the Jesuits. *Corruptio optimi pessima est.* Corruption of the best is the worst.

*   *   *

The victory of Arrupism and its thoroughgoing infection of the Society can be measured by its fulsome perseverance through thick and thin. Even when Arrupe and O'Keefe were removed in October 1981 by direct papal order of John Paul II and even after a fourteen-month "regency" by John Paul's own appointees, Arrupism was never stronger.

John Paul allowed GC33 to meet in 1983. After fifty-four days of meetings, forty-three plenary sessions, and the usual round of consultations, from September 2 to October 17 of the same year, GC33 had elected a new General, Piet-Hans Kolvenbach, and issued twelve Decrees.[1] In those Decrees you will find a reproduction in shorter form and an exact echo of the spirit and outlook of GC32.

Asserting that "in recent years, the Church has summoned us to a greater solidarity with the poor, and to more effective attempts to attack the very causes of mass poverty,"[2] the Congregation stated "we have found it difficult to understand the Church's emphasis on changing the structures of society."[3] But "the promotion of justice" was a matter of growing urgency. Therefore, by concentrating on the issues of human rights, refugees, minorities, exploitation of peasants, workers, women, and the helpless, the Society would be committing itself to "the promotion of a more just world order, greater solidarity of rich countries with poor, and a lasting peace based on human rights and freedom. . . . We must strive for international justice and an end to the arms race . . ."[4] By those "works of justice," Jesuits would be "foreshadowing the new age which is to come."[5] But the "validity of our mission" would depend to a large extent "on our solidarity with the poor."

To underline that new dependency of the Jesuit mission, GC33 made a statement that will surely be questioned theologically by a later and wiser generation: "Only when we come to live out our consecration to the Kingdom in a communion that is for the poor, with the poor, and against all forms of human poverty, material and spiritual, only then will the poor see that the gates of the Kingdom are open to them."[6]

If by "the Kingdom" was meant eternal salvation in God's heaven, the above statement is not merely anomalous theologically, but it contradicts the given experience of millions of poor who lived and died in the last two thousand years; for Christian charity and hope must presume that some at least achieved eternal salvation. And it is to make a supernatural transformation of soul dependent on material abundance.

This and the other statements of GC33 were nevertheless in perfect cohesion with those of GC32. Despite even the most direct intervention by John Paul II, nothing had changed. The salvation of the collectivity, the vision of a new age of peace and plenty for which Jesuits must work, the need to immerse themselves in sociopolitical frameworks of activity—all remained the same.[7] The Delegates of GC33 were fully satisfied that they had weathered "the trouble with the Pope," as it was called, pleased that expectations were exactly as they had been under Arrupe, and confident that in Kolvenbach they had elected a strong Arrupist as General of their Society.

Now they were ready to return to their home Provinces and join in building man's world. And who was left to say no?

ON FIRE
TO BUILD MAN'S WORLD

B efore the turn of this century, the Jesuits decided to open a school in Birmingham, England. They did not ask permission of the local bishop whose diocese included Birmingham. Strictly speaking, they did not need his permission. Some hundreds of years before, at a time when many bishops were, as they are now, refusing to conform to Roman teaching, the papacy had empowered the Jesuits with the privilege of opening a school wherever they saw fit, without nod or say so from any local ecclesiastical authorities. It had remained a recognized and sometimes used privilege.

This time, however, the Bishop of Birmingham decided to contest the Jesuits. He instituted an ecclesiastical suit against them on the grounds that his episcopal authority had been flouted, that the ancient privilege of the Jesuits no longer held, and that, therefore, the Jesuits should obey him and close the school. The case thus addressed the question of Jesuit priority and independence of action, versus the authority of the bishop and his right to be obeyed by all clerics—even Jesuits—operating within his diocese.

The suit wound its seemingly endless way through the local ecclesiastical courts in England until finally it ended up on appeal at the highest Catholic ecclesiastical court, in Rome itself. After one of the many court sessions in Rome, the bishop's Canon lawyer met the Jesuit Canon lawyer outside the courtroom.

"Well, Father," he said, "this time, I think, you Jesuits are beaten."

"Well, Monsignore," the Jesuit replied unhesitatingly, "if the Holy Father commands us to submit to the Bishop, we will be the first to obey."

"The first to obey!" The bishop's lawyer, exasperated after the long-drawn-out struggle against Jesuit priority, could only shake his head. "Must you people *always* be the first?"[1]

In the best of senses, the answer to the question in that legendary tale had always been yes. From their start, preeminence—being the first in whatever they did—was an Ignatian and a Jesuit goal. Neither as hidalgo nor as apostle could Ignatius himself accept second-best. The very motto he chose for his Society—For the greater glory of God; *ad maiorem Dei gloriam*—was in its own way a statement of that goal.

Small wonder then that when, in GC31 and GC32, the Jesuits set about constructing their modern version of the Trojan horse to serve in what became their war against the papacy, they excelled by far the wooden contraption put together by the ancient Greeks.

After ten long years of siege and battle against Troy, the wily Greeks constructed their giant weapon secretly, filled its hollow belly with the forces that would destroy the Trojans once they accepted the horse into the heart of their otherwise invincible city, and then departed in the dead of night, leaving the horse to tantalize the Trojans with curiosity the following morning.

Pedro Arrupe and his generation of Jesuits went those Greek warriors one better on every count. Over a space of ten years, from 1965 to 1975—the first decade of Arrupe's Generalate—the Society's leaders constructed their Trojan horse in broad daylight, under the eaves of the Pope's residence, as it were; and they aimed not at the capture of one paltry city, but at capturing the momentum of the entire Roman Catholic Church, and at changing the sociopolitical structure of our contemporary world.

As the Greeks decked out their Trojan horse with all that would impress the enemy, so the Jesuits clothed theirs in the trappings most likely to impress their contemporaries. Even the name they gave it—"Renewal"—was an element in those trappings. Renewal of the Jesuit mission in the contemporary world, they said, was a necessary adaptation of the religious renewal demanded of all Catholics by the Second Vatican Council.

Even before the whole structure was finished, they made no bones about proclaiming its excellence to all and sundry. As they had done so often in the past, and true to their quest for corporate preeminence, the Jesuits were the first representative Roman Catholic body off the mark and running once "the spirit of Vatican II" began to blow the roof off the Catholic Church. They were the first to analyze the then current situation minutely and meticulously, even before the Second Vatican Council was over; the only ones to draw up detailed plans at such an early stage; and, in the heady years of 1975 to 1980—the final years of Pedro Arrupe's Generalate—they were already perfectly placed as the vanguard and standard-bearers of the way in which Catholics should conduct their lives and think about the world.[2]

It was a simple enough matter by then to wheel their Trojan horse of renewal into the vacuum created by the papal weakness of Paul VI and the winds that were labeled "the spirit of Vatican II." Once in place, further enhancement of the renewed Jesuit mission was achieved by presenting it as a faithful prolongation of the self-same mission Ignatius of Loyola had assigned to his Company of Jesuits.

It is difficult to say whether it was more grave that this renewed Jesuit mission was based on a distortion of what Vatican II demanded by way of religious renewal, or that it was an abandonment, rather than an adaptation, of classical Jesuitism as Ignatius had inaugurated it, and as Jesuits had practiced it for over four hundred years.

Distilled from all of its documents and statements, the intent, the effort, and the message of Vatican II were simple. They formed an attempt on the part of the Roman Catholic Church to present its age-old doctrines and moral outlook in a new way that would be intelligible to the minds of modern men and women. The Church changed no doctrine. It changed no part of its hierarchically structured bishops and Pope. It abandoned not one of its perennial moral laws. It affirmed all.

What it did do was go out of its way to turn to the contemporary world, and to say: Examine—re-examine, please—my Catholic aims. I can help you in your difficulties. I can channel guidance to you in your daily life, hope to you in your mortal days, and eternal life to you when you come to die.

In the renewed Jesuit mission, however, this turning of the Church to the world became the whole message. The Council's attempt at presenting age-old Catholic belief and morality in freshly minted language was translated—one should really say it was transmogrified—into something that never entered the heads of the bishops who spoke to their world through the documents of Vatican II. All should be changed; the new Jesuit mission could have it no other way. What mattered now was the "people of God," "the people's Church"; and it alone had authority from God to teach what was to be believed.

There was nothing for it, then, but to insist that the hierarchic structure of the Roman Church must be "adapted" to this modern view of the modern mind and of modern conditions. The prerogatives of the Pope—his teaching authority and his personal infallibility—as well as the dogmas and moral rules inherited from the recent and remote past of Catholicism—all of it could and must be changed. Abandoned. "Adapted."

The Jesuit distortion went further, of course. For no such presentation of the teaching of the Church or of one of its Councils would have been possible without a fatal distortion of classical Jesuitism, the bedrock and foundation on which the Society rested.

Classical Jesuitism, based on the spiritual teaching of Ignatius, saw the Jesuit mission in very clear outline. There was a perpetual state of war on earth between Christ and Lucifer. Those who fought on Christ's side, the truly choice fighters, served the Roman Pontiff diligently, were at his complete disposal, were "Pope's Men." The "Kingdom" being fought over was the Heaven of God's glory. The enemy, the archenemy, the only enemy, was Lucifer. The weapons Jesuits used were supernatural: the Sacraments, preaching, writing, suffering. The objective was spiritual, supernatural, and otherworldly. It was simply this: that as many individuals as possible would die in a state of supernatural grace and friendship with their Savior so that they would spend eternity with God, their Creator.

The renewed Jesuit mission debased this Ignatian ideal of the Jesuits. The "Kingdom" being fought over was the "Kingdom" everyone fights over and always has: material well-being. The enemy was now economic, political, and social: the secular system called democratic and economic capitalism. The objective was material: to uproot poverty and injustice, which were caused by capitalism, and the betterment of the millions who suffered want and injustice from that capitalism. The weapons to be used now were those of social agitation, labor relations, sociopolitical movements, government offices. If necessary, even armed and violent revolution was sanctioned for Jesuits; as Father General Arrupe once commented, only a Jesuit on the scene could make such a judgment.

Immediately, the most basic elements of Jesuitism were affected. Obedience and service to the papacy were replaced by on-the-spot independent Jesuit judgment based on purely social conditions. Unilaterally, the Jesuits centered their mission within the prime geopolitical struggle of the twentieth-century world; and because they still wore their public mantle as the Pope's men, their leadership at a vital moment went a long way toward dragging the radical papal strategy of the present Pope into deep compromise and jeopardy. While the Pontiff fought to blaze a way out of the injustice caused by capitalism and by Marxism, a far too simplistic and even Manichean dualism was frozen into the new Jesuit vision. The poor who were good, were being trampled by the nonpoor who were evil. The "preferential option for the poor" absolutized revolutionary thought and divinized political action.

It is safe to say that one man can be pointed out as summarily responsible for this complete turnabout of the Society of Jesus—Pedro Arrupe, the twenty-seventh General of the Society. To say that, however, is not to pillory the man for a catalog of his personal failings—his diluted beliefs in basic Catholic doctrines such as papal infallibility, and in basic Catholic moral laws such as those governing sexuality and abortion; his deviousness vis-à-vis the Jesuit vow of fidelity to the Pope; his fecklessness regarding the basic pieties of Jesuitism; his unwarranted partisanship of left-wing religious views. In his prolonged illness with its sufferings, and in whatever Purgatory Christ exacts from him after death, perfect judgment will be passed on Pedro de Arrupe y Gondra.

Rather, it is the errors of Arrupism, which lives on in the Society as its ruling ethos, that clamor for judgment. And, in particular, one principal error of Arrupe's about man and man's destiny on this earth.

The basic error of Arrupism was that it turned the mighty energies of Ignatius's Society to achieve the ideal of the New Man in a terrestrial setting, leaving the supernatural ideal presumably to be taken care of at a later stage, once the here-and-now was established in ideal conditions. All of Arrupe's other mistakes—his neglect of papal warnings, his disobedience to the wishes of three Popes, his sanctioning of excesses in his Jesuits that violated the laws of God and the traditional rules for religious behavior—flowed from this one error.

The historical rationale for his pursuit of this erroneous ideal was what has been called "Arrupe's apocalypse." To be sure, he was a privileged witness and survivor of the devastating explosion of "Little Boy" over Hiroshima on August 6, 1945. And to be sure, he regarded that event in an apocalyptic light. The only difficulty is that the atomic explosion was not apocalyptic, was not even remotely like what Catholic faith teaches about the real Apocalypse at the end of this mortal globe's existence. "Little Boy" was the biggest, dirtiest military weapon ever used. There are now bigger and dirtier in daily preparedness; yet, in turn, their horrible devastation would not be apocalyptic. And there remains no hard evidence that the world is rushing to an atomic incineration. Every year, the danger of that recedes. The dominant reality of our human cosmos today augurs quite a different future.

Nevertheless, Arrupe took that atomic explosion as nothing less than a cleavage of history, an event that literally, in his eyes, cut him, his Society, the Church, and all of us off from everything that had gone before. A new era had dawned of whose horrors and devastation the Hiroshima explosion was only a foretaste.

Just as the institutions of the various national states and of the Church had not been able to save the people from the decentralizing devastation of "Little Boy," so in this new era neither the Church as an institution, nor any of the secular states and governments of the world, would suffice. If that was true, then it followed that the Society would be of no use either, if it continued in its old traditional tracks. The Society's energies had to be redirected, totally overhauled; they had to concentrate on the material conditions of the people. With effort, the New Man for the new era could be fashioned, in spite of the "apocalypse."

So the Society, through the Decrees of GC31 and GC32, was made over to serve in a new mission, sociopolitical in character, antipapal and antihierarchic Church in its bent, and beyond control of the papacy. Within the Society, the traditional mode of Jesuitism was wrecked. Arrupe and his Jesuits were now on fire with a passion to help the New Man build his new world.

It never seemed to strike Arrupe or his generation of Jesuits that he and they had become Modernists; that Arrupism was merely the latest shape taken by the undercurrent of Modernism that had been flowing steadily through the arteries of the Church and the Society for over a hundred years. Arrupe and his generation of Jesuits were merely accepting that current as their guide and model in the "new" Jesuit way of thinking. Their corporate destiny became meager survival: to be alive after "the spirit of Vatican II" blew the roof off traditional Roman Catholicism, and the "spirit of renewal" was proclaimed with its double principle, the rejection of the old and the adoption of whatever was new.

The wide non-Catholic world might well shake its head at all this as just one more sorry tale of intra-Catholic decadence if it were not for the fact that Arrupism—the new Jesuitism—throws the considerable weight of the Society of Jesus into the scales in favor of those who regard both democratic capitalism and economic capitalism as the great evils to be scourged from human society. For the new Jesuit passion to build man's world did not burn in some never-never land of make-believe. From the beginning, it was a hands-on exercise in the worldliest of worldly affairs. Arrupe knew his Jesuits in Central America were training Marxist cadres; were themselves active Communist guerrillas; were cabinet members of a Marxist government; were fomenters of revolution; were participants in bloody and sometimes sacrilegious events. How could he have accepted all that in the teeth of papal pleas, objections, and complaints, and still remain a Jesuit in the classical sense?

His treatment of the Soviets makes one think further. On his way to Sri Lanka and Indonesia for meetings with Jesuit Superiors of those regions in July 1977, Arrupe stopped off in Moscow where he welcomed every effort to make him feel that he was on the right track. The Soviet authorities allowed him to preach at a Russian Orthodox service in the Church of the Dormition in Novodevichy Monastery. The permission came through Metropolitan Juvenali, head of the External Affairs Department of the Orthodox Church. Arrupe was honored there by a visit from the infamous Metropolitan Nikodim, second-highest ranking prelate in the Soviet Union. And he was so feted and welcomed by these two colonels of the KGB that, after his return to Rome, he spoke glowingly of the "growing religious vitality" in the Soviet Union and, he said, the obviously greater interest in religion demonstrated by the detailed way the Tass News Agency had covered his trip.

This was the madness of Arrupe's position, of course; he attracted the Soviets the way mayflies attract trout. But it was a madness reflected faithfully in the Society he led. It became part and parcel of Arrupism that in the continually seesawing struggle between the two superpowers—between capitalism and socialism—the weight of Arrupe's Society was thrown against capitalism. And so it remains today.

It was inevitable that Pope John Paul II would do what Paul VI was never strong enough to do: remove Pedro Arrupe from the Generalate of the Society and Arrupe's chosen successor, Vincent O'Keefe, from any possibility of becoming General. John Paul's papal strategy of reasserting the prerogatives of the papacy and establishing an alternative to capitalism and Marxism had no chance of succeeding as long as the power and influence of the Society was directed by Arrupism. That much was clear.

When, on October 5, 1981, John Paul forthrightly and by papal
fiat intervened in the highest affairs of the Society by removing
from its helm the two men he saw as primarily responsible for
what he regarded as the shambles of the Order and replaced them
with men of his own choosing—Paolo Dezza and Giuseppe Pittau
—the Pope dropped the flag on the start of fourteen critical
months. It was a time when powerful leaders both in and out of
the Church held their breath and waited. If this Pope could take so
bold and unprecedented an action, who could tell what he might
do next?

Within the Society of Jesus, the renewalists and liberal-progres-
sivists—which by 1981, six years after GC32 had enshrined Arrupism, meant all Major Superiors in Rome and throughout the
Provinces, as well as most of the leading Jesuit theologians, writers, and social activists—read the handwriting on the wall. Unlike
Paul VI, this Pope was capable of taking the law into his own
hands. He couldn't any longer be counted on to follow the rules of
the Roman game that Jesuits and others had assiduously learned
to play to their advantage. And, unlike Paul VI, this Pope was
capable of the unthinkable—at least, it had been unthinkable until
that October day of 1981; he was prepared to reverse Arrupism. He
had put in his own superiors; he might go further still. He might
reduce the canonical status of the Society from that of a major and
privileged Religious Order to that of a local congregation; or force
pre–Vatican II Jesuitism on those very Jesuits who had formulated
the new vision in the Decrees of GC32; or effect wholesale expulsion of Jesuit dissidents; or foment the traditionalist membership
of the Society. A Pope who had shown himself to be so unreason-
able as this Pope had might do anything; the colorful variations in
the fears and indignations and angers of Jesuits were as impressive
as they were imaginative.

The Jesuits had ample company in their fear of John Paul. Other
Roman Catholic Religious Orders of men and women had followed an equally liberating "Renewal"; they therefore expected
similar judgment.

Beyond Religious Orders and Congregations, the entire ladder of
Vatican officialdom saw this Pope as capable of acting on his own
initiative in matters of finance, foreign policy, missions, clergy,
doctrine, bishops' appointments, the Sacraments, marriage. After
all, when he put a rough hand straight into the heart of governance
in the Society of Jesus, he hadn't so much as alerted Cardinal
Eduardo Pironio, whose specific job it was to deal with Religious
Orders on behalf of the Pope. *Romanità* did not look kindly on

such brusqueness. Was Vatican administration in for a strong-arm papacy by a non-Roman, non-Italian, non-Western Pope—a man who knew no better than to ride roughshod over the delicate network of carefully constructed rules? Why, such a man might even upset the fragile balance of Vatican-Moscow relations based on that twenty-year-old pact between a previous Pope and the Soviet politburo; or interfere in the delicate subtleties of the financial section of the Vatican.

For everyone, the wait for the outcome of the Jesuit affair was excruciating.

Though all heads were turned toward him, the outcome for John Paul II could only be problematic. Unfortunately, he had removed Arrupe and O'Keefe before he had devised any plan or goal beyond removing two major irritants. What was more lethal for his general papal strategy was that he had acted without a full knowledge of all the widespread interests—in Rome, in the Church Universal, and in the secular world—that were vested in the continued autonomy of Arrupism; in the Society of Jesus, in other words, as a spearhead of a new antipapal, anti-Roman and anticapitalist movement among Catholic bishops, clergy, nuns, and laypeople. "Know thine enemy" was not an adage that came readily to John Paul's lips when he spoke of the Jesuits, simply because he did not yet fully realize they were his enemies, and that their friends and imitators would therefore be his enemies.

For all the worry, then, no one, including John Paul himself, knew how the totally new dilemma of the Jesuit Order was to be solved. By its very nature, structure, and size, the Society held much of the Church in a stranglehold. In a crisis situation, which demands speed and thoroughness of action, John Paul could do nothing sweeping without causing more chaos than he might be able to endure.

Almost as abruptly as he had removed Arrupe, therefore, John Paul allowed his personally appointed Superior General, Paolo Dezza, to announce that the Pope would allow a General Congregation of the Society of Jesus to meet in Rome. GC33 would convene in September of 1983 in order to elect a new Father General in the time-honored manner, and "to treat of those matters which are to be reviewed in accord with the will of the Holy See." The tension was broken. The collective sigh of relief was almost audible. The governance of the Society was back in its own hands.

Still, when Piet-Hans Kolvenbach was elected as the twenty-eighth Jesuit General by the Delegates of GC33 in September 1983, many observers hoped, and some surmised, that behind his

appearance of strength and somewhat Olympian detachment there
might be a spirit that could impose a turnaround in events—that
in his quiet and almost sing-song manner of speech, he might
pronounce the first words of real intention to cease the Jesuit war
against the papacy.

Any such hope of a turnaround surely died with the words Kolvenbach addressed to the Delegates of GC33, who elected him in
a single ballot: We will serve Pope and Church, the new Father
General said in a clear affirmation of Arrupism, if to do that is to
serve man. To serve man in his preoccupation with political injustice and material want would remain as well the primary preoccupation of Jesuits.

The mortal remains of hope for a change were buried in a continuing landslide of Jesuit dedication to Liberation Theology and
its redefinition of the Church and its teachings; of Jesuit magazines plugging away without pause at the erosion of papal and
Church authority over morality and doctrine; and of ever bolder
attacks, in Jesuit writings and sermons, on the person and the
papacy of John Paul II and the basic dogmas of the Church he
heads.

For many, the single most organized and sweeping affirmation
of Arrupism by Father General Kolvenbach has come in India. For
Pedro Arrupe, that area with all of its religious deviations and
excesses that can only be described as the sanctioned Hinduization
of Catholicism, was the mission field he and his new Society could
point to with the greatest pride and satisfaction. In Michael Amaladoss, S.J., who was appointed by Kolvenbach as one of his own
General Assistants, the policy of Arrupe in India has found a new
and energetic champion.

Amaladoss has made it clear that he considers all religions—
Hinduism no less than Catholicism—as "faith commitments
leading to the same goal." No one religion can claim priority.
Indeed, as George Tyrrell once spoke, so speaks Amaladoss today:
"The Church may be called on to die . . . this is true of all religions." Any "claims of fullness on behalf of the Church can hardly
be maintained."

In other words, though he claims the labels of Catholic and
Jesuit as his own, Amaladoss does not think or speak as a Catholic,
or as a Christian. Like so many others, he appears delighted that
the Jesuit Trojan horse has landed him in a position from which
he can labor to change the very essence of the Church whose
beliefs and dogmas are patently unacceptable to him.

None of this is to say that the Society of Jesus has lost its drive or its ability for preeminence. Neither Kolvenbach nor the post-Arrupe leadership as represented by the Father General's Roman staff—the General Assistants and Regional Assistants—are to be taken as starry-eyed idealists. They are hard-nosed realists who have not forgotten John Paul's first striking attempt to rein in the Society, and who know it will not be his last. Before most Church-men have even seen it, they have watched a new cloud gathering on the horizon, and they have understood that one day soon in the continuing pontificate of this stubborn Pope, that cloud may en-velop their whole sky and threaten the existence of the new Jesuit-ism they have espoused.

That cloud is John Paul's growing conviction, shared by many in his papal entourage, that the prime necessity in the Roman Catholic Church of the eighties is the authoritative interpretation of the documents of the Second Vatican Council. So taken aback were John Paul and many others by the Jesuit championing of Liberation Theology and by Jesuit deviations from orthodoxy, that it has taken quite a time for them to focus on the fact that all the deviations and all the excesses—not only among Jesuits, but throughout the Church—are ultimately to be traced to and justi-fied by the liberal-progressivist interpretations of the vaguely framed documents of Vatican II. By that door, as they are now convinced, has Modernism seeped into the Church and made its way through the hierarchy, the Religious Orders and Congrega-tions, and the laity.

Father General Kolvenbach's early assessment of John Paul in this regard has been amply confirmed by concrete events. In 1984, Joseph Cardinal Ratzinger issued an official *Instruction* for all Catholics concerning Liberation Theology. Ratzinger heads the Congregation for the Doctrine of the Faith (CDF) and is the official directly responsible to John Paul for maintaining the doctrine of the Catholic faith in its purity. When he speaks, it is normally as the mouthpiece of the Pope. In his *Instruction*, Ratzinger made one overall point: No political and economic liberation of people —however needed and justifiable—can be confused with the only liberation the Catholic Church promises, which is liberation from sin and sin's effects.

Kolvenbach immediately and with Arrupe-like arrogance issued a public commentary on Ratzinger's *Instruction*—that meant a commentary on John Paul. He was disappointed, Kolvenbach said with an air of patient regret, by the "negative aspects" of the Rat-zinger *Instruction*. And, he went on, certainly the social activism and political involvement of Liberation Theology was quite justified. And it would continue. There would, Kolvenbach promised somewhat mysteriously, be another and better document about Liberation Theology.

Hardly had the dust settled on that skirmish when John Paul convened a special synod of selected bishops to meet at the Vatican between November 25 and December 8, 1985, in order to discuss matters connected with the Second Vatican Council. All his cardinals, 151 of them, would meet with John Paul between November 21 and 23. Clearly, John Paul was beginning to focus in on the heart of all his trouble—the false interpretation of Vatican II —and on the central plank of the new Jesuitism of the Arrupist generation.

The signs became more ominous for the Modernists—Jesuits and non-Jesuits—when Ratzinger gave a long interview to an Italian journalist-writer, and then published the interview as a book.[3] Ratzinger's point: Since Vatican II, and because of a false interpretation of its documents, there is not one area of Church belief and morality that has not been corrupted.

A simpleton could read the handwriting on the wall; and neither Kolvenbach nor any of his advisers are simpletons. Kolvenbach and his aides within the Society do not need a house to fall on them to understand that someone has burrowed beneath them and torn away the foundations. They realize that John Paul II has found another way to try forcefully to reassert papal prerogatives. If that special synod of bishops were to declare that the current interpretation of Vatican II was Modernist and was false, this would put the new Jesuitism in extreme jeopardy.

It is not that Father General Kolvenbach disagrees with John Paul's analysis of the situation. On the contrary, he is as aware as anyone that the twist from classical Jesuitism to Arrupism depends vitally on the maintenance and preservation and further fomentation of the Modernist interpretation of Vatican II. Together with Churchmen who favor the ordination of women; who would sanction abortion, contraception, and homosexuality; who abandon belief in the supernatural character of the Sacraments; who ardently embrace, in place of the Sacraments, left-wing politics and activism; who want ever greater autonomy from the papacy; Kolvenbach, too, understands that any change in their interpretation of Vatican II would spell death within the Church to all they now stand for. The victory of their twentieth-century Modernism would be turned into sharp defeat.

Under Kolvenbach's direction, therefore, the Jesuit war against the papacy has focused on mounting the theological equivalent of a preemptive strike on John Paul's new offensive on the current Modernist view of the Church. He had promised another and better instruction than Ratzinger's 1984 *Instruction* on Liberation Theology.

The Jesuit point man in this new phase of the war, the author of several books, is often referred to endearingly by his supporters as "the Karl Rahner of Liberation Theology." Juan Luis Segundo is his name. Though he was born in Uruguay and has done most of his work in Latin America, Segundo holed up in Regis College, a bastion of liberal-progressive Catholicism in Toronto, Canada, and there composed the Jesuit reply to John Paul II. That reply is a 1985 book entitled *Theology and the Church.* Although it purports to be an answer to Ratzinger, from its manner it appears to be really a warning to John Paul II.

That a man of Segundo's rank should write a public reply at all to the highest official in doctrinal matters of the Church Universal, and should issue a warning to the Church to beware of what that official teaches, is already an enormity of arrogance. If Segundo or anyone of his stature has genuine difficulties with an official *Instruction* of Ratzinger's office, he has an easy recourse: He can communicate directly and personally with the cardinal. Or, if he finds that disagreeable or impossible, he can communicate indirectly through Jesuit headquarters, which stand within a stone's throw of Ratzinger's personal office in Rome.

But Segundo's purpose is not to solve his own difficulties; he has none. His purpose seems to be to put John Paul II on notice that if he as Pope accepts and blesses Ratzinger's *Instruction* on the Theology of Liberation, then he as Pope will have trouble, much trouble.

Segundo's arrogant warning to the Holy Father is not subtle. It is, in fact, emblazoned in the subtitle to his book: *A Response to Cardinal Ratzinger and a Warning to the Church.*

Segundo, in his book, gets quickly enough to the heart of the papal threat. This Pope, he says in effect, has criticized us, the Liberation Theologians, but his criticism is ignorant and unjust. The Pope doesn't understand either Liberation Theology or the Marxism of which we stand accused. But do not be distracted by this feud over Liberation Theology, Segundo continues. The real aim of this Pope is to change the whole of Vatican II theology. Here, says Segundo, is the Pope's hidden agenda, his real and underhanded purpose: to set the Church back into pre–Vatican II molds, and thus to betray the true teaching of Christ's Church as Vatican II taught it to us.

The meat of Segundo's argument is straight out of the Modernist book. Until Vatican II, Rome or the Vatican or the hierarchic Church—for Segundo the terms are interchangeable—taught Catholicism on the basis of a "two worlds" theory: the spiritual world and the material world. As Segundo sees it, the Church encouraged religious fervor and practice for the spiritual world, but decried any immersion in the material world. The result was that the Church did nothing to help men and women in their material problems. It concentrated on personal sins and personal salvation, never on social sins and social salvation. Anyone who engaged in that sort of activity was said to have become "secularized"—a very dirty word, as Segundo sees it, in the pre–Vatican II Church.

Unfortunately for John Paul II, Segundo's argument is not only well-thought-out, witted, knowledgeable, and appealingly democratic; it is also based in part, and however erroneously, on the explicit words of Paul VI. For it was, says Segundo, under Paul VI that Vatican II changed that prior so-called "spiritual" outlook of the Church. And it was Paul VI who said that the Council had abandoned the "two worlds" theory; that the Church now looked instead on man as one integrated being, needing material as well as spiritual salvation and liberation.

The Church, says Segundo, offered itself to the world as a participant and co-worker in achieving that integrated liberation; and he quotes the speech with which Paul VI closed Vatican II on December 7, 1965, and which was such an inspiration for the Jesuits of GC31 and beyond: "Will it not be said that the thought of the Church in the Council has deviated towards the anthropocentric positions of modern culture?" And Paul gave the answer: "Deviated—no! Turned—Yes!" Religion, Paul explained, is completely at the service of man's good. Because the Church wants man's spiritual good, it will labor equally for his material good— for his liberation from poverty and economic slavery and political domination.

The point, for Segundo, is that the popular church or "the people's Church," as distinct from the hierarchic Church of Rome, has arisen out of modern culture precisely on the basis of this unitary view of man. This, he declares, is now basic Church doctrine, accepted Catholic theology. It is in this "people's Church" that the true "teaching authority" of Christ now arises and is found and is to be consulted.

Let the "people's Church" beware, Segundo's warning rings loud and clear, that this Pope is endeavoring now to change the theology of Vatican II in order to suit his personal and partisan outlook. And let Cardinal Ratzinger and Pope John Paul II beware, Segundo is saying further, not to sin against the voice of this new, true "teaching authority" of the Church of Christ.

Despite Segundo's criticism of Ratzinger's treatment of Liberation Theology and the occasional venomous vigor Segundo uses to decry the Cardinal's personal motives (at the least, such comments as that Ratzinger must have had "a certain measure of malevolence" to write as he did, should have been removed by Jesuit censors), his clear target throughout is Pope John Paul II. In attacking Liberation Theology, Segundo is saying, the Pope is attacking the true "teaching authority" of the Church; he is out to reassert the old dualistic mentality of stiff-necked Roman clerics, and to destroy this "teaching authority."

To give Segundo his due, the Jesuits could not have chosen a better man to fire the first salvo in the Society's latest campaign against the traditional papacy. No Jesuit theologian has explained in such detail and so cogently the theological basis for the Society's departure from classical Jesuitism. His book is the clearest admission and the best justification so far of the new Jesuitism that the Society has produced.

Segundo's defense of the new theology is neither more nor less than a defense of the new mission fashioned and adopted by the Society of Jesus in GC31 and GC32, and ratified once more in GC33. As such, it is a defense of every Jesuit priest who shoulders a carbine and joins the jungle guerrillas. It makes clear why Jesuits can be ministers with portfolio in Marxist governments; why Jesuits can attack John Paul II acridly for his teaching on sexual morality; why Jesuits spend their days and their lives solving union problems, organizing sugar-cane workers, running factories, constructing low-cost housing, helping the Planned Parenthood Federation of America spread the use of contraceptives; run nationwide hospital and dispensary networks; organize political demonstrations for this and against that, according as the issues of the day are presented by the "teaching authority" of the "people's Church." These are the actions of the new faith, true to the new theology according to which the material needs of men must be the prior object of the Church's efforts.

Indeed, so far-ranging and thorough is Segundo's "warning" that there is room not only to defend all the activities dear to Liberation Theologians, but to push the "preferential option for the poor," to add fuel to the attack on "transnational capitalism" as found in the United States, and to bolster the intent to change the sociopolitical structure of nations.

Whether by intent or not, Segundo's is the ultimate answer of Father General Kolvenbach and his Jesuits to the continued and continual dissatisfaction of Popes with the new Society. That the Jesuit General and his Roman staff sanction such a book makes it in essence their answer to John Paul, and to anyone else who would alter the course of the Jesuit Order as set during the two decades since GC31 and the emergence of Pedro Arrupe. With its publication fades whatever slim shadow of hope might have remained in some optimistic mind that this twenty-eighth Father General might, of his own accord, do anything to arrest the war between papacy and Jesuits. Hope fades that this Society of Jesus might, at this crucial hour in the decaying history of the visible structure of the Roman Catholic Church, come forward with a solution as apt to catapult it out of its difficulties and into the new age as Iñigo de Loyola's solution did when Rome faced the enormous difficulties in the mid-sixteenth century.

In the minds of thousands who know the value of Ignatian Jesuitism, and who pridefully expected the Society of Jesus in the sixties to repeat their brilliant sixteenth-century triumph, there is regret tinged with almost infinite pathos. Like John Paul II when he was a Bishop in the Second Vatican Council, they thought butterflies would emerge from the cocoons they had spun.

What emerged instead was liberal-minded partisanship that quickly solidified into a totalitarianism of thought, an approach so dogmatic that what at the beginning seemed a refreshing clarity of vision, quickly became a trap of self-righteous, self-justifying moralism. All who disagreed were considered to be immoral. Conservatism or traditionalism was not tolerated. Those who were guilty of either suffered. Some were silenced. Some were eased out of the Society. Some left of their own accord. Some remained Jesuits, but took refuge among more tolerant clerical colleagues in parish work and elsewhere.[4]

No matter how heroic some Jesuits are today—and the Order still includes at least hundreds of heroes who labor and suffer and hold on in the most trying circumstances, humanly speaking—the mass of the Society has been leavened by Arrupism. The Church of Rome has lost to others the invaluable support and services of the one body of men that, in its pristine form, could have halted the destruction wrought by those hurricanes of change that began in the sixties to force everything to rotate around a new center.

The Jesuits could once more have made the difference between a Church in shambles, as it is now, and a Church acting vigorously to take control of a situation that, in actual fact, renders Pope and bishops and churchly institutions helpless. But the Jesuits will not be the ones to save the day now for the Roman Catholic Church.

*   *   *

When, at a later and more peaceful time in the history of the Roman Church, historians assess the factors that brought about the decay of twentieth-century Roman Catholic institutions, surely some, with the wisdom of hindsight, will spell out what the Society of Jesus—the Religious Order *par excellence*—could have done when the Roman Church began its paroxysm of "renewal" in the sixties of this century.

They will underline the unwisdom of the ways in which Paul VI directed the attention of Vatican II to what he called "the world of man." Mankind did not need to be "honored," and it knew that. It no longer had "values" to be "respected and honored." It had only two values: money and power. All men knew those values could neither be honored nor purified. The last thing the world wanted or needed was for some religion to "approve its efforts," for those efforts had been and daily were evidently in vain.

At the very moment Paul VI spoke, the realization of modern men and women was that they were caught helplessly in a trap of their own making. They were trapped with John Kennedy and Nikita Khrushchev, the two most powerful men in the world (as they admitted coldly to each other one day in the back seat of a shiny limousine); neither of them could break the horrible deadlock that held the superpowers fast. Modern men were trapped in the wholesale desertion of Catholic morality and its destructive influence on marriage, family life, and private as well as public morals.

Modern men and women were trapped on every side, in fact. They were trapped in Vietnam, entering its agony; in sub-Saharan Africa with its dying millions; in the endless bloodletting of Ireland and Angola and Afghanistan and East Timor and the Middle East. They were trapped in the perpetual talks and stalemates on disarmaments that always led to further armaments; in the endemic misery of Latin America; in the gradual dissolution of the American nation into a mere common citizenship that they feared would become a hollow, uncompelling, ghostly legal fiction, and nothing more.

Anyplace on the human scene where the normal and reasonably informed believer or nonbeliever looked, it was obvious that the last person likely to have a solution was the "modern man" whose praises and honor were sung by Paul VI in his speech, and by his Council in its documents.

With reason could hard-headed realists ask: How are you going to purify and bless rigid capitalism? Or dialectical Marxism? Or secular humanism? Yet that is what Paul seemed to imply his Church had done. A latter-day seer like Malcolm Muggeridge—still pawing his way back to the truth—could see the blind alley into which had arrived the "mankind" Paul and the Council discussed as their norm, the "people" Arrupe and his Jesuits set out to cultivate. Muggeridge could see the tattered parade of "humanity" dispassionately and verbalize its condition sadly but accurately. "There is not," he wrote, "the faintest expectation that, in earthly terms, anything could be salvaged; that any earthly battle could be won, or earthly solution found. It has all just been sleepwalking to the end of the night."

Mankind knew that it was past midnight for human integrity; that all the energies of the world had ended in stalemate and weariness. Not so Paul VI, or the busy interpreters of Vatican II, or the Jesuit Delegates to GC31 and GC32. They chose to come at the heel of the human parade, and to speak in an un-Catholic manner about an issue that was not the one facing the Church and the Society.

In truth, it was the authentic voice of Catholicism that was lacking both in those speeches of Paul VI and in Arrupism. It was lacking because neither Paul nor Arrupe nor the Jesuit generation of GC31 through GC33 had made a Catholic religious analysis of the Church's situation and the condition of man's world at mid-century. Their effort was not to transform the world around them in the light of their faith; their will was that they themselves be transformed—and therefore accepted—by that world.

There is nothing specifically Catholic, Christian, or even religious about the needs, real as they are, for low-cost housing; steady employment; unpolluted air; civil rights; political liberties; unionization of workers; the manufacture, development, and use of offensive and defensive weapons; national economic planning and international trade policies; agribusiness; nationalization of industries. All of these are areas of human activity that call for the exercise of practical judgment. Certainly that judgment will benefit from sound religious and moral underpinnings; but by no stretch of the imagination can you analyze the religious condition of humanity in those terms with any hope of producing a blueprint for the spiritual betterment of the men and women who work for low-cost housing, steady employment, unpolluted air, and all the rest.

If you try, you will find youself caught with everyone else in the clashing gears of material wants, material gains, material desires, material ambitions.

The Jesuits tried. You can read all the Decrees of GC31 and GC32; you can study all that Pedro Arrupe spoke and preached to and about Jesuits, and about their work, and about their world; you can pore over Paul VI's words that so inspired the Jesuits on the subject of the Church and the world around it at the time of the Second Vatican Council. Nowhere will you find a religious and supernatural analysis of any aspect of the human situation.

Both Paul and Arrupe sensed that something had changed. But, because they both became immersed in the myriad details of complex modern life spinning out in ever newer and more dazzling mechanizations, in ever more departments of human life—because, in other words, they accepted purely human instead of rigorously religious analyses—they never understood the stupendous change that had actually taken place. Consequently, neither ever faced the dominant reality of our time.

Instead, like everyone else, the Jesuits were trapped into an activism about material things unbefitting the apostles of a supernatural God; and they decided that their first allegiance was not to the occupant of Peter's Throne, but to "the people."

Meanwhile, Paul VI found his authority and primacy overwhelmed in a stormy sea of merely human ambitions encouraged by the compromises he had accepted in order, as he thought, to have access to the world.

* * *

For the eyes of Iñigo de Loyola, both the enormous change that had taken place and the dominant reality of our time would have been crystal-clear. He might have begun with, but would not have gone on with, the gentle pessimism of a Malcolm Muggeridge. And he would certainly not have settled, as Arrupism has done, for mere survival masquerading as leadership.

Back in the sixteenth century, Iñigo analyzed the world exclusively from the point of view of the Lord and Savior he wished to serve. He recognized and defined the problem then clearly: The See of Peter was at that time in gross danger from intellectual error and theological heresy. Its greatest lack in resisting that danger was its medieval structure. That was the Church's vulnerability: Faced with men immersed in the modernity of the 1500s, the Church had thrown up defenses that had been useful two centuries before in an entirely different world. Iñigo designed and set his Company in motion in order to erase that vulnerability. Hence, the special vow of obedience to the Pope; the mobility of his men; the versatility, the enterprise, and the worldwide educational thrust by an utterly homogeneous and rigorously trained group whose sole intent was to leaven the completely new human scene with the perduring and never changing reality of Spirit as revealed in Christ and through the Church.

Similarly today, for Iñigo it would be a question of isolating and clearly defining the huge change that has taken place in our world; and of analyzing the reality and the problems faced by mankind and by the Church.

The first step for Iñigo, then, would be to define the basic element at stake. Paul VI and the Jesuits called it globally "mankind," the "world of man." They did this because they had already accepted the collectivist, egalitarian view of humanity that rates all men and women anthropologically.

But sacred history, the story of God's dealings with man, says otherwise. Neither Catholicism nor the religious history of Christianity allows all of humanity to be lumped together under the generic title of the human species, as *Homo sapiens.* It admits, accepts, and insists instead that while all men and women have the same human nature, this is no more than one aspect of our real identity—and not the most important, at that. This, Christianity says, is not the whole human story; and if you confine your analysis of human potential, human needs, human dangers, and the future of humanity to that dimension, you are already in big trouble.

The other aspect of the human identity—by far the most important—concerns a cornerstone event in the story of that human race that changed irrevocably and forever all human nature in every single individual man and woman who has ever lived, does live now, or will ever live and breathe. This is the redemption of each man and woman by the sufferings and death and resurrection of Jesus. In other words, the human race is not essentially a collection of intelligent animals grouped together as *Homo sapiens.* It is, above all, a race of men and women whose human frame and nature from their beginnings have been changed by the fact that they were redeemed by Christ and given the possibility of seeing the face of the all-powerful, majestic God forever.

The second step in Iñigo's analysis would be to see this redeemed human race in its actual condition today. He would divide it into two main parts.

One part, which would be the object of his greatest concern, would consist of the people of those lands where the good news of Christ's redemption had been preached for a long time, and not only preached but largely accepted. Today, these would be the lands of Europe and the Americas where Christianity, totally accepted once upon a time, had entered the warp and woof of ordinary human life. It colored and influenced and frequently made possible the laws, the languages, the customs, the ambitions, the sociopolitical framework, the sexuality, the learning, the amusements, the very fibers of thinking and feeling and acting. For a modern-day Iñigo, these lands and people would comprise the Heartland of Christianity.

The second part of the world in such an analysis would be composed of all the other lands; lands into which the preaching and the practice of Christianity have so far penetrated only very partially; lands whose culture and way of life were never saturated for any appreciable length of time with the good news of Christ's redemption; lands mainly to be found in Africa and Asia. This, for Iñigo, would be the Outland.

With modifications and exceptions, this would be Iñigo's basic definition of the "world of man." Within that world, he would understand Islam as a Christian heresy of the Outland; classify Buddhism, Hinduism, and Shintoism as pagan aberrations in the Outland; see Marxist-Leninism as a cancer of the Christian Heartland; and Judaism as a mysterious and mystical component in the sacred history of mankind as a whole, a component that we have not yet been allowed by God's revelation to understand—that we will not understand until the existence of our cosmos is ended.

The third step in his analysis would be crucial: to determine the condition of Christianity, and of Catholicism in particular, throughout the Heartland. What, he would ask, is the dominant, the preponderant reality about the existence of Christianity there?

As harsh as the answer is, he would not shrink from it today, any more than he did four centuries ago. That dominant reality is the nearly fully achieved *abolition* of what made Europe and the Americas possible: Christian faith.

Increasingly and extensively—and soon totally—all over those heartland areas, the life of entire populations is lived in the conviction that nothing of Christ's salvation and nothing of Christianity's teaching about that salvation, matters to human life in any way. Politically, socially, educationally, culturally, sexually, intellectually, life is in essence and in practical terms already barren of any Christian influence. As a way of life—even as mere fond sentimentalities or harmless pieties—Christianity has been abolished.

It is not a question of the agnostic's protest, "I don't know if God exists," or of the formal atheist's assertion, "I don't believe God exists." Both protest and assertion imply God, imply that there is now a vacuum that was once filled by belief.

The new condition of human society in the Heartland areas is that people see no vacuum at all. They have no need to protest that they don't know if God exists, or to assert that they can't believe he exists. There is no longer any felt need to protest or deny. The situation seems to them to be self-evident and absolute: There is nothing but what we see and feel and smell and touch and hear; if you can't see it, you can't believe it. All over the Heartland, the basic conviction now is that there is nothing real behind faith, behind doctrine; that "good" and "right" and "true" are merely synonymous with one's own advantage; and that only success in money, in status, and in pleasure is of any importance.[5]

The most difficult problem to be solved in the classic Ignatian analysis of our modern condition concerns the minds of these millions who live and think and act within a world from which Christianity has been abolished. For they would be the first to deny it. In fact, they would deny the fundamental fact that Christianity had made them possible, made their language, their civil law, their culture, their literature—even their dress and everyday manners—possible; made possible the entire human order of things out of which they came. They have no memory of that.

Nevertheless, so ingrained still is that order within the very being of those millions, and so true is it that they, like all humans from the beginning of the race, live in a world redeemed by Christ, that they do not—cannot—know what it would be like to live in a world unredeemed by Christ. The fact that their condition now is that they cannot even contemplate such a reality only heightens the pathos and the problem. By way of analogy, if a man once civilized falls into complete barbarity, he will not then know he has become barbaric. If he were capable of knowing that, he would not have become barbaric.

How, the Ignatian analysis must ask, do you even begin to explain to those who live within the Heartland from which Christianity has been abolished that they are human because of Christianity—because of Christ's redemption? By what symbols? What logic? What words? What gestures? What way of life?

Whole generations of millions of people are now conceived, born, reared, and educated with no reference or relation to Christ.

Theirs indeed is the *abolition* mentality: They work, suffer, love, politick, marry, grow old, sicken, and die; but, in their minds, Christ and his salvation have nothing to do with them. Whole continents go from year to year; the everyday business of nations, regions, and localities is carried on; people and governments prosper, or they don't; they have wars and wants; but all takes place outside of Christianity. All the nations and all the people deal with each other on the same basis of Christianity's abolition.

At the tail end of this third and disheartening step in his relentless analysis, Iñigo would note that the Heartland is slowly pulling the Outland into its orbit. Technologically and in terms of political and military power, the prosperity and plenty of the Heartland promise to solve the fundamental economic and industrial needs of the Outland. Witness only the financing of the Outland by the Heartland to the annual tune of some $800 billion; and note the increasing tendency of the nations and peoples of the Outland to acquire and adopt the clothes, food, pleasures, and way of life of the Heartland. Borne on the high winds of importation and imitation, comes as well the *abolition* mentality of the Heartland.

Through the first three steps of analysis, it is already clear that a rigorous examination of the sort Iñigo brought to bear in the sixteenth century, comes up with far different views when compared to those of Arrupism. The Jesuits of GC31 and GC32 made no fresh and certainly no spiritual analysis of their Church or their world. They simply accepted and used the views the world handed to them about human identity, the condition of the human race, and the condition of Christian and Catholic belief in the world.

Arrupism did face the fact that Christianity was rapidly being abolished from the life and the minds of a rapidly growing number of people. However, as Arrupism had skipped the first three steps of Ignatian analysis, accepting instead the humanist view, it was inevitable that here, at the fourth step of analysis—the determination and definition of the *causes* of the abolition mentality—the new Jesuitism would enter the situation as secularist apostles within Christ's Church. GC31 and GC32 framed the only definitions the Society had: Christianity had been abolished because of poverty; or because justice had failed in South Africa, in Chile, in the Soviet Union, or elsewhere; or because there were still hungry people in the United States; or because there was an arms race and a danger of nuclear catastrophe; or because a mass of people wanted sexual pleasure without parental responsibility; or because pornography, white slavery, drugs, crime, and a thousand evils besides plagued our lives.

For the first time in its history, the Society of Jesus made the egregious mistake of missing the forest for the trees. It turned its entire well-organized might to the fight against mere material conditions and symptoms.

Now, while the problem glared out at the world in those symptoms, and while the symptons were and remain terrible, none of that alters the hard fact that if you throw all of your energies into a struggle to better the symptoms, to change nothing more basic or more causal than those symptoms, the general deterioration will continue. In fact, more and still more symptoms will arise to harass you and the people for whom you intended to be an apostle.

Moreover, while you continue to expend all your energies on material symptoms, even with the purest intentions in the world, you will probably cease to be an apostle at all; almost necessarily, you will become what you are doing. If the material symptom that inflamed you with a desire to help is social degradation, you will become a sociologist. If poor housing becomes your mission field, you will become a building contractor or a lawyer. Political oppression will make a guerrilla or a politician of you. But none of it will make you an apostle; or a Jesuit; or a Catholic; or a Christian.

Ignatian analysis would approach this fourth analytical step with the understanding that the abolition of Christianity from the Heartland, with all its awful and heartbreaking symptoms, was effected by spiritual causes.

In analyzing what those causes are, a modern Iñigo, like his model, must keep clearly in mind that causes are not the same as stages. The Modernism of the nineteenth century was a stage of Christian decadence, not a cause of that decadence. The Marxization of mind noticeable in many Catholics and Christians today is not a cause, but a stage of Christian decadence. The widespread use of abortion, contraception, and divorce by Catholics is not a cause, but a stage in Catholicism's deterioration. Determination and definition of causes still cries out for an Ignatian analysis.

The fifth step, when you work your way to it, will be to begin to define fundamental courses of action. The question must be posed as to how far the abolition of Christianity has gone. In other words, is it still reversible? Or has it gone so far that the wise thing to do is to lay out a program for survival?

Survival in this Ignatian context means how best to carry intact through this night of Christianity all the essentials of Christ's redemption as taught by his Church. It does not mean, as it meant in Arrupism, jettisoning everything or almost everything, and grasping at whatever driftwood floats to hand from the world around us.

One can imagine what would have happened if the vast organizational energies, mental acumen, and executive skills of Arrupe's 36,000 Jesuits had been let loose on this analysis back in the mid-sixties, and on its follow-up plan of action. But that, unfortunately, must remain one of the most tantalizing might-have-beens of history.

Paul VI once thought the Jesuits of the twentieth century would turn around, would perform that difficult analysis of their world and of themselves, and then formulate an adequate response—an Ignatian response. Back in the late sixties, when Arrupism was still in its formative stages, and when the Pope was under severe and distressing attack for his encyclical letter *Humanae Vitae*, in the paroxysm of his helplessness and pain he made an impassioned plea to Arrupe and the Jesuit leaders gathered in the Vatican. "Help the Church!" he cried out. "Defend the Holy Father! Show once more that the sons of St. Ignatius know what to do in this hour."

From his superb vantage point as Pope, Paul could see clearly what was needed by the Church. He expected the brilliantly endowed and intelligent Society of Jesus to meet that need: To fashion and produce Catholic answers—not answers borrowed or filched from contemporary anthropology, psychology, or politics —to contraception, to abortion, to homosexuality, to divorce, to premarital sex. To elaborate a Catholic alternative to rigid capitalism and to atheistic Communism, which would safeguard the liberty and inventiveness and regard for human rights of the one, and to include the concern for the poor and the oppressed that atheistic Communists make as their exclusive claim. To reinterpret the current animus of so many Catholics—clerical and lay—against the papacy and the hierarchic Church; and to eliminate all irritants, while preserving the dogmatic belief in papal infallibility and papal primacy. To study anew the problem of ecumenism; and, while not renouncing for a moment one whit of Roman Catholicism's claim to be exclusively the One, Holy, Catholic, and Apostolic Church founded by Jesus, to evolve a new way whereby the grace of Jesus could descend on all warring Christians, clearing the scales from their eyes and leading them into "one fold with one shepherd" in the name of the one Savior of all.

Concrete solutions, concrete Catholic solutions, were and are needed to those problems. There are still others—problems whose solutions will frame the quality of existence as we pass over the threshold of a vastly different time; problems posed by the new genetics, atomic warfare, space exploration, to name a few of the most obvious.

It would have caused no great surprise either in Paul VI or John Paul II if the Jesuit Delegates to one of the last three General Congregations had sent a straightforward message to their Pope, saying in effect: "We have concluded, after much prayer, reflection, and communal discussion, that the present and foreseeably future circumstances of the papacy and the Church are and will increasingly be such that our Society cannot and will not be able to fulfill our role vis-à-vis the papacy and will not be able corporately and individually to find concrete solutions for the multiple problems assailing Catholicism, unless there is a total and fundamental rethinking—and, if necessary, reformulation—of the *Constitutions* Father Ignatius composed for us and the Holy See has consistently approved and blessed.

"In fact, there are only a limited number of items in our *Constitutions* that, in our opinion, should stand as Father Ignatius drew them up. The whole, we submit, needs revision. We therefore petition the Holy See to sanction this step of total revision.

"At the same time, as Delegates for the whole Society, we hasten to assure the Holy See and His Holiness in particular that the sacrosanct nature of our Jesuit vocation remains and will remain intact. We see this nature of our vocation as Father Ignatius saw it: to be professionally a Roman Catholic corps of Religious completely adhering to the prerogatives and teachings and policies of the Roman Pontiff; and to have any and every sector of human activity as worthy of our devoted attention provided the Roman Pontiff desires it while, as Christ's personal representative on earth, he governs and directs the forces of Catholicism in the perpetual warfare between God and Lucifer."

Such an attitude and such a determination by Arrupe and the Jesuits of his generation to preserve the Ignatian mold throughout all change would surely have altered the history of the Catholic Church in the sixties and seventies; and the Church of the eighties would not be the stumbling shambles of schism and heresy and defection it is today. The historical responsibility of Pedro Arrupe and his colleagues is heavy and frought with the frightening prospect that they, each one of them, will have to answer personally to Christ not only for what they did not do, but also for what they did do to the Society and, consequently, to Christ's Church which he loves.

For the concrete answer given by Arrupe and the new Jesuits to the pathetic Paul was Arrupe's fevered and pathetic search for "the primitive charism," and all the betrayals of GC32 that such a search imposed on the Society. One wonders if that terrible and anguished cry of Paul VI still rings in Arrupe's memory as he lies in the Gesù immobilized in body, perhaps darkened in mind, by his illness.

Given that internal failure of the modern Jesuits, a last painful question arises: What is to become of the Society of Jesus?

There are two ultimate and outside possibilities.

The Holy See may finally find it necessary to suppress the Order, as it once did in the eighteenth century. Then, the action, extreme though it was, was taken for purely *ad hoc* reasons that we now know in no way reflected on the sterling service of the old Society. In those far different circumstances, it was little wonder that, given half a chance, the Holy See resurrected the Society some forty years later.

If the Holy See were to suppress the Society now, however, it would be because this time no other way could be found to end the war between Jesuits and papacy; no other way to limit the damage Jesuits do to the cause of the Church; no other way to protect the papacy.

The second ultimate possibility is that soon, quite soon as human times goes, the Superiors and the rank and file may accept a genuine but very different reform of the Society, ending their war with the papacy, eviscerating the new Jesuitism, reviving the Jesuitism that was the hallmark of Iñigo de Loyola's original Company. In that event, a totally new scenario would open up for the Society of Jesus.

Miracles apart, it must be said that there is very little probability that the Society can now turn around and accept reform—even though reform and not Arrupism is what it needs if it is to survive.

On the other hand, outright suppression by John Paul II's Holy See is not probable either. For whatever reason—the shock of the assassination attempt against him, the repercussions such an action would have, the chaos that would ensue in the short run—John Paul no longer has either the strength of will or the ruthlessness of mind required. Nor does he seem able to muster the ecclesiastical support from his bishops, his Vatican Curia, and other Religious Orders that would be necessary in order to take such a step.

The sad fact is, however, that after nearly eight years on the Throne of Peter, John Paul II is in precisely the position of Pope Paul IV when he put into the hands of Iñigo de Loyola the document that brought the Company of Jesus into existence. John Paul reigns but does not govern. His churchly institution is split by schism and heresy, and seems to be out of his control. He must accept vilification in public by Dutch Catholics, and agonize over the desecration of his person and his sacred functions as Pope in Nicaragua. He reads Ernesto Cardenal's latest poem lauding the Sandinista regime because now, under Sandinista rule, the rabbits breed more abundantly, the lizards bask peacefully in the sunshine, the fresh-water storks have returned to the land, and the shrikes are nesting there again. Where Cardenal can spout his paean to the Sierra Club, John Paul could not preach a sermon on Christ's redemption of all men.

John Paul began his pontificate with the boldest and most innovative strategy that could have been devised for the situation around him. For a moment, he gave the world a glimpse of another salvation, a third way out of the superpower dilemma that is strangling the world and leaves half its population in the darkness of oppression and the agony of hunger.

But now John Paul must content himself with being a clear sign that much of the Church has indeed been split away from him. To this end, he will keep on reiterating the doctrine of Catholicism, the *veritas catholica*, and the news that his post as Vicar of Christ on earth is indestructible. This role will perhaps suffice for John Paul. And indeed, to keep on doing just that requires giant faith and supernatural strength.

If, as seems likely, neither of the ultimate possibilities are brought to bear on the Society, then it faces a twilight of gradual decay and ossification, as its numbers continue to diminish, and its operational importance for the Holy See is gradually reduced. Perhaps it will be replaced in the affections of the papacy by some more pliant, more genuinely Roman Catholic organization—some religious organization similar to the Prelature of the Holy Cross and *Opus Dei* (commonly called *Opus Dei*). Or perhaps the decline of the Jesuit Order may well herald a new situation in the Church, a new time when Religious Orders must vacate the primacy of position they have held for so long. Perhaps their day is done in the churchly institution of Catholicism. All is in flux.

In its twilight time, the Society may indeed undergo traumata. Internal schisms may force parts to break away from the main body. Legal action on the part of the Holy See may strip the Society of its privileged position as the Pope's special militia, and its Father General of his pride of place as the Black Pope, and thus limit the damage the Society can do to the Church.

Whatever form those traumata may take, and however dire may be the Society's ultimate fate, they must pale in comparison with the fatal mistake its leaders made in their decision to make war on the papacy. For when the memory of what Jesuits and their Society once were has become as dim as the onetime glory and prestige and power of the Cluniac Order of the tenth–thirteenth centuries,[6] the papacy will still exist in the person and the office of the Bishop of Rome. For only that individual, whoever and wherever he may be, has Christ's inviolable promise of perpetuity; whereas the Society of Jesus was never more than one more and merely human instrument raised by God's providence to serve God's purpose, but with no lease on immortality. Mortgaged to a passing day's service, it is bound for the compost heap of failure and death.

But even so, what is true now will still be true then: the Society of Jesus in its pristine form—in the fullness and freshness and genius of its genuine "primitive charism"—was and is irreplaceable. No organization in the Church's history ever came as brilliantly and efficiently equipped. Theirs was an enviable list of dazzling gifts: internal cohesion and discipline; sure grasp of Catholic piety and devotion; intense intellectual development; professonal obedience and rocklike fidelity; developed methodology of operation and terrier-like refusal to let go; complete flexibility in the use of means; doctrinal soundness and reliability; versatility of gifts, marvelous camaraderie in a grand and holy enterprise, and a deep sense of cosmic destiny.

Once in its history, when its enemies pressured Pope Clement XIII to change the unique and distinctive *Constitutions* of the Society and to make of it an Order like any other Religious Order, the Pope's answer was confined to six pregnant monosyllabic Latin words that defy an equally short translation: "*Sint ut sunt, vel non sint.* They will stay as they are, or they will cease to be."

It was, if you wish, the classical equivalent of "Take it or leave it." I will not change them. Either I leave them as they are, or I will abolish them.

In the paradigm of human time measured over against eternity, that very expression can be seen as the response of the omnipotent God to the endeavor of Arrupism:

You refuse to leave the Society as I raised it up? Very well, it will cease to exist. For as it was, the Society was as near perfect a formula for success as can be achieved with fallible men and in mortal affairs. It was a gift of the Holy Spirit's wisdom, a blessing from the Father's love, an extension of Christ's own redemptive power. He would not concede to it anybody else's whims or ideas, above all not to the Enemy. It bore His name, after all. It was His Society.

NOTES

THE WAR

1. "The titles of Servant of God, Venerable, and Blessed are given to those whose causes are still in progress, whereas the title of Saint indicates that the process [of canonization] has come to its completion." See J. N. Tylenda, S.J., *Jesuits, Saints & Martyrs* (Chicago: Loyola University Press, 1983), p. xxiii.

1. PAPAL OBJECTIONS

1. Mindszenty had stayed bottled up in the U.S. Legation in Budapest for fifteen years, untouchable by the Communists, a symbolic thorn in their side. Promised by Paul VI that no successor would be appointed in his place as Primate of Hungary during his lifetime, he consented to go into exile in 1971. Three years later, in violation of his solemn promise, Paul VI appointed a successor, Laszlo Lekai. The appointment was published simultaneously in the Vatican and Budapest on February 5, 1974. "The dismissal of Josef Mindszenty," the President of the State Office for Ecclesiastical Affairs in Budapest wrote, "has been greeted with understanding by the thinking, progressive public, both inside and outside ecclesiastical circles."

3. WHITE POPE, BLACK POPE

1. There is also a Roman official who is called "the Red Pope"—the cardinal who heads the all-powerful Congregation for Propagating the Faith, now known as the Congregation for the Evangelization of Peoples, a Congregation that has enormous expenditures and eats up a goodly part of the yearly Vatican budget. There are some who hint that red in this case refers to red ink. In fact, however, the title is a doff of the Roman hat to the reality that money always betokens power of some sort.

2. Actually, the new Code would be promulgated by John Paul on January 25, 1983. No change in the status of the Society of Jesus was legislated.

3. Some close observers of the scene say that a majority of Jesuits under management level (parish priests, simple professors and teachers, etc.) would support John Paul's action.

5. SUMMARY DISOBEDIENCE

1. The public repudiation by twenty-four Catholic nuns of the Church's doctrine about abortion in October 1984 and the public violence, scurrilous treatment, sacrilegious actions, and gross irreverence shown John Paul during his 1985 trip to Holland, which finds few parallels in recent papal history, are but two of many examples.

2. Pena's bishops stood by him loyally. In August of 1985, Pena was sent to Rome for a two-year course in Canon Law. This marks him as a potential candidate for bishop in Nicaragua later. Another loyal priest, Father Bismark

Carballo, similarly besmirched by the Sandinistas, became official spokesman for Cardinal Obando y Bravo.

3. The phrase "African Conference" was used by the Franciscans to refer to a new structure of the Church they were trying out experimentally: Small groups of Franciscans were to live independently of the local parishes and carry on their apostolic ministry independently of the parishes. The basic purpose was to detach their flocks fom the spiritual jurisdiction of the legitimate parish priests and bishops. This Franciscan version of the *iglesia popular*, developed in Latin America, was in clear violation of Church Canon Law.

6. IÑIGO DE LOYOLA

1. Historians call this draft *text a*. From it, Iñigo made another version that is called *Text A*, and is the first complete Spanish draft of the Society's *Constitutions*.

2. This version is called *Text B*, an autograph in Spanish, provided with corrections and marginal insertions by Iñigo. From this *Text B* a new Spanish text was produced, called *Text C*. In the meantime, Iñigo's secretary, Juan de Polanco, S.J., made a Latin translation. In 1558, a meeting of Jesuits in Rome approved the Spanish *Text C* and Polanco's Latin version as authoritative. The Latin version was chosen as the official text, but *Text C* has always been used for interpreting the Latin text. There was still another Spanish Text (D) produced in 1594. Today, it is the 1936 edition of the Spanish and Latin text that is most in use.

9. THE CHARACTER OF THE SOCIETY

1. The curriculum was known in history as the *Ratio Institutioque Studiorum*, or more simply, the *Ratio Studiorum*. It went through three editions (1586, 1591, 1599) before reaching its final form.

2. Their multiple enemies, of course, saw other roles supposedly played by the Jesuits: the Jesuit Plotter, the Jesuit Revolutionary, the Jesuit Rationalist, etc.

3. "Minister" was one name for the Jesuit Superior in a house who was charged with public discipline, money, and living conditions. One penance imposed on those who had violated some public rule of behavior was to eat while kneeling at a low table in the presence of the community who sat at normal tables.

4. Gerard Manley Hopkins, *Fragments*, #113 in the Robert Bridges' edition of 1948 (Third English Edition), Oxford University Press.

5. Hopkins, *The Wreck of the Deutschland*, #5.

6. It has been incidentally remarked that both Margaret Mary Alacoque and Claude La Colombière had two very ordinary names, both based on the names of birds.

7. Literally scores of Popes have propounded this devotion since then. In 1872, Jesuit Father General Peter Beckx consecrated the Society itself to the Sacred Heart of Jesus; and no Jesuit was surprised that the membership of the Society more than doubled, from 5000 to 12,000, during Beckx's thirty-four years as Father General.

8. On the same day, September 22, 1774, the then ex-Father General, Lorenzo Ricci, and his immediate Jesuit colleagues were imprisoned in the papal dungeons of Castel Sant'Angelo in Rome.

10. THE HIGHEST RANKING SUPERIOR

1. GC is used hereafter as an abbreviation for General Congregation. Thus, GC1, GC2, etc. The first General Congregation was held in 1558, two years after Ignatius had died; the last to date (GC33) was held in 1983. There were also five Interim Congregations (IC) during the forty-one years (1773–1814) when the Society had been suppressed by the papacy everywhere except in Prussia and Russia, and a minuscule group of Jesuits survived in those two territories.

2. The tone and decisions taken in GC31–33 differ generically from those of all preceding General Congregations.

3. Pius had a Jesuit confessor, two Jesuit day-to-day collaborators, at least two Jesuits whom he used as special emissaries to various governments on delicate missions, and about half a dozen other Jesuits he relied upon for expert advice in various technical and professional fields. Pius also sent more than one Jesuit on clandestine visits to the USSR.

4. Already during World War II, Pius was disturbed by the doctrinal deviations of some Jesuits. Some commentators date Pius's disillusionment with the Society to the midforties, and specifically to the bitter opposition thrown by some Jesuits at a new institute, the *Fathers of the Holy Cross and Opus Dei*, founded by a Spanish priest, Jose-Maria Escriva y Balaguer. Reportedly, a wave of calumny and slander flooded Vatican corridors from Spain just after the end of World War II, the target being *Opus Dei*. A written report finally made its way to Pius's desk. His immediate aides heard Pius scream out loud with indignation once he read the scurrilous report: *"Chi ha mai pensato una tale infamia!"* (Whoever could have thought up such a disgusting story!) The vilification campaign ceased almost immediately. What galled Pius, as he remarked to Augustin Bea, S.J., was that it was precisely such vile calumnies that the first enemies of the Society had used way back in the sixteenth century. That the Jesuits, or some Jesuits, would now use the same underhanded tactic against another infant Church organization in the twentieth century revolted Pius. *Opus Dei*, it must be admitted, was then, and forty years later is more than ever, the real rival of the Society for pride of place near the heart of the papacy.

11. HURRICANES IN THE CITY

1. To be mentioned here especially as enjoying a new season of prosperity and diffusion are the publishing houses of Orbis Books (specializing in Liberation Theology publications), Paulist Press (publisher of *Human Sexuality*), and Crossroads.

2. Some commentators have already remarked that the abuse, disappearance, exile, or silencing of Jesuit moral theologians of the stature of John Ford, John Lynch, Joseph Farraher; of editorial staffers of *America* such as Thurston Davis, Robert Hartnett, Francis Canavan; the harassment of Cornelius Buckley and others, together with the forced exclusion of orthodox-minded novices, all constitutes a whole story in itself that would be well worth documenting and telling.

3. Organizations such as the Association of Chicago Priests, the National Federation of Priests Councils, and the National Coalition of American Nuns, are now constituent elements of the Catholic scene in the United States.

4. In this encyclical letter, entitled *Mediator Dei*, Pius condemned in detail many of the "adaptations" that became bedrock doctrine to the renewalists twenty years later in the wake of Vatican II.

12. THE WINSOME DOCTRINE

1. James Turner, *Without God, Without Creed* (Johns Hopkins, 1985), p. 262.

2. *Ibid.*, p. XV.

3. *Ibid.*, p. 267.

4. Vivekananda was born Narendranath Datta on January 12, 1863, in Calcutta. A disciple of Ramakrishna from an early age, he decided to heal the materialism of the West with Hindu spirituality. He died on January 4, 1902, at the age of thirty-nine, near Calcutta.

5. A few careful scholars tucked away in their ivory towers poured over the ancient Indian literature, the *Upanishads* section of the *Vedas*, the works of Goudapada and Shankarayarya, and realized what the Swami had put across on the public was Vedantism, or the Vedanta.

6. Under the impulse of the Swami's mind-set, there finally arose a Humanist organization in the United States—the Humanist Foundation, and the American Humanist Association, and the Humanist Society. A first Humanist Manifesto was issued in 1933, calling for a "socialized and cooperative economic order," "autonomous and situational ethics," "many varieties of sexual exploration," and "the development of a system of world law and order based on a transnational federal government." Humanist Manifesto II of 1979 omits all explicit endorsement of "socialized and cooperative economic order," but advocates the same sexual ethics, while roundly rejecting all belief in any reality beyond the visible, tangible world. Not all secular humanists subscribe to the Humanist Manifesto.

7. The catalyst and unifying force behind the brotherhood in its first phase from the 1880s to 1910 was certainly the exotic figure of Baron Friedrich von Hügel, naturalized Englishman, theologian, philosopher, mystic. He provided the living link between many covert and some overt Modernists of that time: George Tyrrell and Edmund Bishop in England; Alfred Loisy, Abbé Henri Brémond, Laberthonnière, Hébert, Leroy, Duchesne, Mignot of France; Antonio Fogazzaro, Minocchi, Buonaiuti, Semaria in Italy. The Baron successfully evaded condemnation from Rome by openly attacking Modernist theses.

8. See Pierre Leroy, S.J., *Letters from My Friend Teilhard de Chardin*, translated by Mary Lukas (Ramsey, N.J.: Paulist Press, 1976), pp. 70 ff.

14. PIERRE TEILHARD DE CHARDIN, S.J.

1. *"Eppur se muove"* was actually coined some 130 years after Galileo's death by French Jesuit Abbé Traith.

2. A marvelous example of the Teilhardian style is to be found in a commentary Teilhard wrote to a friend about "the steady state" theory of astronomer Fred

Hoyle. "According to Hoyle, the corpuscular Quantum of Matter forming the Universe is not constant. He holds that there is a current of continuous intensity in which we are caught up, as by the jet of a fountain. The perspective interests me because, if the Universe were formed this way, then Spirit, too, would be formed by continuous generation. But how to reconcile this with the existence of a 'Divine Foyer' of Cosmic Centration?—Instead of a 'Foyer,' would we not have a 'Line'?—I think I see vaguely that if, in such a universe, consciousness is to be saved biologically all the way, we will have to establish in the system a new curve of another kind (that of the continuous generation of Matter) which would create itself in some kind of 'spiral' *around* the Cosmic Foyer of Psychic Reflection, and instead of stretching out in a line, would appear as a continually deepening Center." (Letter of June 5, 1952, to Jesuit Father Pierre Leroy.)

3. *Present* is put in quotes to underline the word used by Teilhard in order to avoid any idea of creation by God. Consciousness suddenly was "present." The term *consciousness* itself, on Teilhard's lips, was also technical; a two-cell organism was "conscious," he said. Anything that was not completely unitary was conscious.

4. He saw plenty of war at its rawest while serving as a stretcher-bearer during the battles of Verdun, Ypres, Chemin des Dames, and the Marne—the classical slaughter houses of World War I. Teilhard was a corporal, but refused to become a chaplain with the rank of captain.

5. See *Letters from My Friend Teilhard de Chardin*, by Pierre Leroy, S.J., translated by Mary Lukas (Ramsey, N.J.: Paulist Press, 1976).

6. Teilhard de Chardin, *The Divine Milieu*.

7. "La Vie Cosmique," collected in *Écrits du Temps de Guerre*, Editions du Seuil, Paris, p. 22.

8. Teilhard commented on Hinduism rather negatively. Yet Vedantic and Tantric thought weaves crazily throughout his entire "poetry of evolution."

15. LIBERATION THEOLOGY

1. This much is clear even from the names cited by Gutierrez in his book as progenitors of this thought: Alfaro, Bouyer, Chenu, Congar, de Lubac, Dumont, Duquoc, Haering, Kasper, Metz, Moltmann, Rahner, Schillebeeckx, and Spicq, among others. One European author on whom Gutierrez and the few Latin American Liberation Theologians (Mariatequi, Pironio, Sanchez, Vasquez) lean heavily is, of course, Karl Marx. Present-day prominent Liberation Theologians (Juan Luis Segundo, Jon Sobrino, and others) are Europeans who have become naturalized citizens of Latin American nations.

2. For example, Pope Pius XII blessed the efforts of Don Luigi Sturzo (1871–1959), who organized and promoted the Demochristian Party in Italy. The situation of the Church with Mussolini was *in extremis*—as it is today in Poland.

3. *Instruction on Certain Aspects of the "Theology of Liberation,"* August 6, 1984, and *Instruction on Christian Freedom and Liberation*, March 22, 1986. The 1984 *Instruction* has been harshly attacked, notably by Juan Luis Segundo, as presenting merely the beliefs of Joseph Cardinal Ratzinger, Prefect

of the Vatican Congregation for the Doctrine of the Faith (CDF). Most Liberation Theologians who have so far commented on the 1986 *Instruction* have declared it to be a formal approval of their Liberation Theology. But the Cardinal Prefect's language is unequivocally clear in separating a genuine "theology of liberation" from Liberation Theology. Much confusion could have been avoided by the author of the 1986 *Instruction* if he had stayed with the traditional Roman Catholic term *salvation. Liberation* has been jealously appropriated by those who would use the Cardinal's *Instruction* to show that the Church supports them in a doctrine already condemned in the 1984 *Instruction.*

16. THE SECOND VATICAN COUNCIL

1. All in all, the Council documents contain 103,014 words. The Latin originals are the authoritative texts and must be referred to in textual matters of interpretation. The longest of the documents (*Pastoral Constitution of the Church in the Modern World*) has 23,335 words. The shortest (*Declaration about Relationships between the Church and Non-Christians*) has 1117 words.

2. See Schreck's *Catholic and Christian,* and the quotation from it in the charismatic publication *New Covenant,* May 1984, p. 16. Another Franciscan, somewhat more "gumshoe" than Schreck, John Quigley, has disseminated a cassette as of March 1980, on which he states that "the Church of Christ is much bigger than the Catholic community. . . . We believe that the Church is much larger than the Catholic Church. OK?" That "OK" is pathetic. The entire question about the *subsists in* phrase has been notably dealt with by James T. O'Connor in *Homiletic and Pastoral Review,* January 1984.

3. The quotation is worth reading: " . . . a wave of serenity and optimism has spread through the Church and the world from the Council; a consoling and positive Christianity acceptable and amiable, friendly to life, to men, even to earthly values, to our society, to our history. We might almost see in the Council the intention to make Christianity acceptable and amiable, an indulgent, open Christianity, free from all medieval rigorism and from any pessimistic interpretation regarding men, their customs. . . . This is true."

4. Eugene Kennedy, *The Now and Future Church* (Garden City, N.Y.: Doubleday, 1984), pp. 172, 179, 191.

17. THE SECOND BASQUE

1. More Italians (eleven) have been elected to be Father General than any other nationality. There have been four Spaniards, four Germans, eight Belgians, two Basques, and one each from Holland, Poland, and Switzerland.

2. He is credited with raising $10 million for the University of St. Sophia in Tokyo. When he arrived in Japan, the University had 1500 students. By 1973, with Arrupe as Provincial and then as General, there were 8200 students.

3. Two of his letters, one to the whole Society and dated May 14, 1978, the other to Indian Jesuits and dated June 24, 1978, give his thoughts on "inculturation" extensively.

4. The case was that of a nineteen-year old Basque, Ignacio Sarasqueta. The international clamor that arose from left-wing organizations, the liberal

media, and Soviet satellite countries to spare him was deafening. To this Paul
—and, of course, Arrupe—joined their voices.

18. OUTWORN CLOTHES

1. Except for GC8 in 1646, which lasted 114 days, and GC27 in 1923, which ran
for 105 days, the average span of previous General Congregations covered
anything between fifty to eighty-five days.

2. GCs 1, 2, 12, 13, 17, 21, 22. Seven others were held in springtime (GCs 3, 4, 6,
11, 19, 26, 28), ten in the autumn months (GCs 5, 7, 8, 20, 23, 24, 25, 27, 29,
30), six during winter (GCs 9, 10, 14, 15, 16, 18).

3. Up to GC31, the number of Delegates attending General Congregations had
varied all the way from 20 (GC1) to 185 (GC30), but it usually hovered around
65 to 85 members.

19. NEW UNBROKEN THREADS

1. The fact that another Council document, *Lumen Gentium*, made exclusive
claims for the Church's possession of truth, and still another, *Dei Verbum*,
gave the Church exclusive authority over Scriptures, has not helped. Those
documents, on these points, are neglected.

2. Paul VI's *Evangelii Nuntiandi* (1975) aimed at correcting this error; but by
then the error had been translated into concrete systems of corporate work
and individual life-styles.

3. Much that was mentioned in GC31's decrees could be classed as incidental,
in one sense. Decrees of GC31, for instance, that concern Interprovincial Cooperation (#48), the Arts (#30), Election Rites (#50), Reading at Table (#20),
Visitors (#45), a Catalog of Censures and Precepts (#53), the Vatican Radio
Service (#36), the norms for access to Final Vows (#11), and such are to be
classed as incidental. In the final analysis, however, the major Decrees were
of such a sweeping nature that everything was "renewed," so to speak, in their
wake. For example, Decree #20 ("Reading at Table"), concerning what was
read to Jesuit communities while at their meals, accepts the fact that overall
the ancient practice of reading a summary of the Jesuit *Constitutions* had
simply been abandoned. The General is advised to do something about this,
so that Jesuits still remain acquainted with their *Constitutions*. That issue of
table reading is not in the same class with the question concerning Poverty or
Obedience or eligibility for positions of power in the Society; but that and
other issues, major and minor, could not help but be affected by an opening
up of the "substantials" of the Order.

20. SEARCH FOR THE PRIMITIVE CHARISM

1. GC31, Decree #1-1.

2. B. R. Biever and T. M. Gannon, *General Survey of the Society of Jesus in the
North American Assistancy*, vol. 3.

3. The situation among the Jesuits in the Philippines, for example, which only
came to light in 1971, was such that Father J. B. Reuter, Superior of the
Jesuits engaged in social communications in East Asia, accepted grants from
Family Planning International, a division of PPFA, on condition that the
Jesuits submit "a report on the amount of contraceptives by type and quan-

tity used and on hand at the end of each quarter and grant year." Reuter, in commenting on his apostolate, said that in it "emphasis will be to legitimize the involvement of Catholics in family planning programs." All of this goes down on record as a neat piece of double-talk on an absolutely vital subject.

4. The changes recommended by GC31 reached even the Pontifical Gregorian University in Rome. The "Gregorian," as it is called familiarly, has spawned eight saints of the Church, fifteen Popes, hundreds of cardinals, tens of thousands of priests. Since GC31, it has gone co-ed; on a typical day, at least half the students (nuns and priests) are in civilian clothes. The "Gregorian" has also lost its reputation as a center of orthodoxy.

5. Quoted by George Riemer in *The New Jesuits*. Illustrated. Little, Brown. 1971.

6. In the Bhagavad-Gita, Krishna is quoted as saying: "I am the mystic OM. Bow and worship me."

7: The depiction of Brahma, Vishnu, and Shiva in Church windows, the use of *arati* (a lighted lamp waved before the face of the celebrant at Mass), and the placing of a pot on top of the Church instead of a crucifix (the pot contains the god whose church it is) are but some of the many other Hinduizing practices.

8. The subcontinent of India, in the eyes of Vatican planners, has a primordial importance as the one country in Asia where the Church could make huge headway. The Roman Catholic Church has poured vast resources into India. Religious orders run 115 colleges with 135,000 students, 1200 high schools with over 500,000 pupils, 242 technical schools with over 400,000 students. It is estimated that 60 percent of all students in India attend Roman Catholic schools and colleges. In those seats of learning, 50 percent of the teachers are non-Christian. Jesuits are involved on the local, state, and national level. The Hinduization of Catholicism can thus be seen as a hazardous experiment in a vitally important area.

9. The Institute was founded by Fathers Thomas Culley and Clement McNaspy of the United States. Institute members in 1972 included French painter André Bouler, Cuban painter-sculptor Oscar Magnon, Buffalo Symphony Orchestra violinist Cyril Schommer, and the husband-and-wife concert team of Ivan and Susanna Waldbauer. That summer's session was held in Villa Mondragone at Frascati, southwest of Rome, and consisted of classes, intramural concerts, exhibitions, dramatic presentations, excursions, and good meals washed down with the excellent wine from Jesuit cellars.

10. Generals of the Society can call for a General Congregation for more than one reason. Twenty-five of the thirty-three General Congregations to date were called to elect a new Father General. One General Congregation was called by a Congregation of Jesuit Procurators in 1608. Three Congregations were summoned by Popes for their own reasons. Three more were called by Generals who wanted the help of a Vicar-General because they themselves were sick. One, in 1923, was called by Father General Ledóchowski in order to adapt the Jesuit *Constitutions* to the new Church Code of Canon Law. The 32nd General Congregation called by Arrupe was, however, an exception to every rule and precedent. He was in perfect health; the Pope had not called

for it; there was no question of electing a new Father General. GC32 was extraordinary by such measures.

21. THE NEW FABRIC

1. Eighty-eight were there ex-officio (the General, his Assistants, Provincial Superiors, and other Roman officials of the Society). 148 had been elected "democratically" in their home provinces: They came from Western Europe, the U.S.A., Latin America, Canada, England, Ireland, Australia, India, the Philippines, Japan. There were seven Poles and three Yugoslavs present. East Germany, Czechoslovakia, and Hungary were represented by expatriate Jesuits. By March 7, 1975, the number of Delegates had dwindled to 205.

22. PUBLIC STANDING

1. Significantly, Eduardo Cardinal Pironio, prefect of the Vatican *Congregation for Religious*, visited the General Congregation of the Jesuits on October 17. It will be recalled that John Paul had not informed Pironio when removing Arrupe and O'Keefe in October 1981. There was no closing visit by John Paul II, or any general audience of the 215 Jesuit Delegates with the Pope. The symbolism of John Paul's act in allowing Pironio to make the end visit was important in Rome, where symbolism is used extensively to convey meaning: The Pope was allowing the Society to slip back into its normal place in the machinery of the Vatican.

2. Decrees of GC33, Part I, paragraph 26.

3. Decrees, Part II, paragraph 32.

4. Decrees, Part II, paragraph 46.

5. Decrees, Part II, paragraph 42.

6. Decrees, Part II, paragraph 48.

7. There are subtle but nonetheless clear indications that the dream of doing away with the grades system was by no means dead in GC33. See Decrees, Part I, Paragraph 16. But the theme is muted. Doubtless, it will be maintained and fomented in the years to come, when a more favorable moment arises.

ON FIRE TO BUILD MAN'S WORLD

1. This story is told in Jesuit folklore with many variations as to the exact city and the length of the court case.

2. Jesuit participation in the revolt of Religious Women's Orders Against Roman authority has yet to be documented.

3. *The Ratzinger Report*, 1985.

4. Vincent Miceli is one of the most egregious American examples in recent years of someone eased out of the Society because his traditional writings on theology and his blunt criticism of Jesuit deviations were unacceptable to Superiors and colleagues. The most outstanding example of a silencing is that of Cornelius Buckley, S.J., historian at the University of San Francisco and valued columnist. When Buckley openly criticized the serious, semiblasphemous liturgical practices at the Jesuit School of Theology at Berkeley, JSTB's

president, Richard A. Hill, S.J., demanded Buckley's silencing. Four years after it took place in 1980, Buckley's silencing is still strictly enforced.

5. Friedrich Nietzsche was the first to invent a term to express this abolition. He called it nihilism.

6. At one stage in Church history, you could go nowhere in ecclesiastical preferment without the patronage of Cluny. The Cluniac Order gave at least three Popes to Rome; and it influenced papal policy for nearly two hundred years.

SOURCES AND MATERIALS

For the recent history of the Society of Jesus in Europe, the Americas, and Asia, the main sources were the printed media, religious and secular, from those areas, in addition to special documents and government reports. For the history of Ignatius and his Society over the past 440 years, standard works were used, as well as the writings and letters of Ignatius himself. For individual Jesuits such as George Tyrrell and Pierre Teilhard de Chardin, their own published works were used; in Teilhard's case, *Letters from My Friend Teilhard de Chardin* by Pierre Leroy, S.J., was of particular interest. Some papal documents relevant to the Society and coming from Pope Pius XII, Pope John XXIII, Pope Paul VI, and Pope John Paul II are to be found in the monumental *Acta Apostolicae Sedis;* others are only in the *Acta Romana Societatis Jesu.* Also available were the monographs published by the *Institute of Jesuit Sources* and the *American Assistancy Seminar on Jesuit Spirituality,* as were documents and studies and publications from individual Provinces of the Society. Certain confidential sources of materials within the Society and the Roman Curia provided both information and commentary throughout.

INDEX

ABOUT THE AUTHOR

Malachi Martin, eminent theologian, expert on the Catholic Church, former Jesuit and professor at the Vatican's Pontifical Biblical Institute, is author of the national best-sellers *Vatican, The Final Conclave,* and *Hostage to the Devil.* He was trained in theology at Louvain. There he received his doctorates in Semitic Languages, Archeology and Oriental History. He subsequently studied at Oxford and at the Hebrew University. From 1958 to 1964 he served in Rome, where he was a close associate of the renowned Jesuit Cardinal, Augustin Bea, and Pope John XXIII. He now lives in New York City.